Linking Smallholder Producers to Modern Agri-Food Chains: Case Studies from South Asia, Southeast Asia and China

Linking Smallholder Producers to Modern Agri-Food Chains: Case Studies from South Asia, Southeast Asia and China

Editors

Vijay Paul Sharma, Bill Vorley, Jikun Huang, Abid Qaiyum Suleri, Larry Digal and Thomas A. Reardon

ALLIED PUBLISHERS PRIVATE LIMITED

New Delhi • Mumbai • Kolkata • Chennai • Nagpur
Ahmedabad • Bangalore • Hyderabad • Lucknow

ALLIED PUBLISHERS PRIVATE LIMITED

1/13-14 Asaf Ali Road, **New Delhi**–110002
Ph.: 011-23239001 • E-mail: delhi.books@alliedpublishers.com

47/9 Prag Narain Road, Near Kalyan Bhawan, **Lucknow**–226001
Ph.: 0522-2209942 • E-mail: lko.books@alliedpublishers.com

17 Chittaranjan Avenue, **Kolkata**–700072
Ph.: 033-22129618 • E-mail: cal.books@alliedpublishers.com

15 J.N. Heredia Marg, Ballard Estate, **Mumbai**–400001
Ph.: 022-42126969 • E-mail: mumbai.books@alliedpublishers.com

60 Shiv Sunder Apartments (Ground Floor), Central Bazar Road,
Bajaj Nagar, **Nagpur**–440010
Ph.: 0712-2234210 • E-mail: ngp.books@alliedpublishers.com

F-1 Sun House (First Floor), C.G. Road, Navrangpura,
Ellisbridge P.O., **Ahmedabad**–380006
Ph.: 079-26465916 • E-mail: ahmbd.books@alliedpublishers.com

751 Anna Salai, **Chennai**–600002
Ph.: 044-28523938 • E-mail: chennai.books@alliedpublishers.com

5th Main Road, Gandhinagar, **Bangalore**–560009
Ph.: 080-22262081 • E-mail: bngl.books@alliedpublishers.com

3-2-844/6 & 7 Kachiguda Station Road, **Hyderabad**–500027
Ph.: 040-24619079 • E-mail: hyd.books@alliedpublishers.com

Website: www.alliedpublishers.com

ISBN : 978-81-8424-824-1

Published by Sunil Sachdev and printed by Ravi Sachdev at Allied Publishers Pvt. Ltd., Printing Division, A-104 Mayapuri Phase II, New Delhi -110064

Preface

This publication examines the processes and impact of market restructuring through comparative in-depth empirical case studies in selected Asian countries, namely, China, India, Indonesia, Philippines, Sri Lanka and Thailand. These countries represent both a broad geographic coverage and a range of stages of market concentration in the region. The country papers address important questions such as what determines the participation of producers in different channels, what is the impact of farmer participation on incomes and what institutional, technological, economic and other reforms are necessary to enhance their effective participation in the emerging and restructuring markets.

Small producers have many competitive advantages in their interface with modern markets but there are difficulties in integrating smallholders with modern markets like large volumes required by these markets, food safety and quality requirements or high transaction costs for the companies dealing with large number of smallholders. In some of these countries small-scale farmers have connected successfully to dynamic markets, doing business with processors and supermarkets and in some cases smallholders have been excluded from markets as supply chains evolve in complexity. The case studies attempt to identify major factors that affect smallholder producers' access to output markets, input markets, e.g. seeds, fertilizers, agrochemicals, technology and services such as credit, extension, insurance. Each case study has tried to analyse one specific innovation and these innovations are specific arrangements built on public policies, business initiatives, collective/group action by small-scale producers, etc. that appear to have played a positive role in supporting greater inclusion. The studies aim to derive models, strategies and policy principles to guide public and private sector players in promoting greater participation of small-scale producers in dynamic markets.

We hope that the book will be extremely useful for policy planners, researchers, developmental organizations and agribusinesses community with a keen interest in improving market access of smallholder farmers, thereby supporting smallholder production system.

Editors

Preface

Acknowledgements

Several individuals and institutions have helped us during this study. Acknowledging all individually would be impossible but we would like to mention a few without whose support it would have been difficult to complete the publication. First and Foremost, we would like to express our sincere thanks to the authors of country case studies and the coordinators of case studies, especially, Julio Berdegué, RIMISP- Latin American Centre for Rural Development, Chile, Lucian Peppelenbos, Royal Tropical Institute (KIT), Netherlands and Estelle Biénabe, Centre de Coopération Internationale en Recherche Agronomique pour le Développement (CIRAD), France.

We are grateful to the UK Department for International Development (DFID), International Development Research Centre (IDRC), Ottawa, Canada, ICCO, Netherlands, Cordaid, Netherlands, Canadian International Development Agency (CIDA) and US Agency for International Development (USAID) for providing funding support for this work.

The preparation of this book would not have been possible without the support of Indian Institute of Management, Ahmedabad, International Institute for Environment and Development (IIED), London and collective endeavours of the Regoverning Markets consortium and we would like to extend our sincere thanks to them.

Needless to mention while we owe debt to the numerous persons who have helped us during the study, the responsibility of data and views in this report and any omissions or errors that remain in the text are ours alone.

Editors

Acknowledgements

About the Contributors

1. India

Sudha Narayanan is Research Associate at the Cornell International Institute for Food and Agriculture Development (CIIFAD), Cornell University, USA.

Deepthi Kolady is a Visiting Fellow at the International Programs in the College of Agriculture and Life Sciences at Cornell University, USA. Deepthi holds a Ph.D. in Applied Economics from Cornell University.

Sujana Krishnamoorthy has an MPhil from the Jawaharlal Nehru University, New Delhi, India. She has researched and worked across India on issues of labour rights, governance and livelihoods.

Ghayur Alam is Director, Centre for Sustainable Development, Dehradun, India.

Deepti Verma is with the Centre for Sustainable Development, Dehradun, India.

2. Sri Lanka

Parakrama Samaratunga is currently a Research Fellow and the Head of the Agricultural Economics unit of the Institute of Policy Studies (IPS) of Sri Lanka. Before joining the IPS he was the Director, Economics and Planning in the Sri Lanka Department of Agriculture at Peradeniya.

3. Thailand

Songsak Sriboonchitta is Associate Professor in the Faculty of Economics, Chiang Mai University, Thailand.

Aree Wiboonpongse is a Professor in the Department of Agricultural Economics, Faculty of Agriculture, Chiang Mai University, Thailand.

Puttawan Khuntonthong is with the Faculty of Economics, Chiang Mai University, Thailand.

4. Indonesia

Ronnie S. Natawidjaja is Director, Center for Agrifood Policy and Agribusiness Studies (CAPAS), Padjadjaran University, Bandung, Indonesia.

Yosini Deliana is a Researcher with Center for Agrifood Policy and Agribusiness Studies (CAPAS), Padjadjaran University, Bandung, Indonesia.

Tomy Perdana is a Researcher with the Center for Agrifood Policy and Agribusiness Studies (CAPAS), Padjadjaran University, Bandung, Indonesia.

Hanny Sulistyoningrum is with the Center for Agrifood Policy and Agribusiness Studies (CAPAS), Padjadjaran University, Bandung, Indonesia.

Yovie M. Rahayu is with the Center for Agrifood Policy and Agribusiness Studies (CAPAS), Padjadjaran University, Bandung, Indonesia.

Wayan Rusastra is with the Centre for Alleviation of Poverty through Secondary Crops' Development in Asia and the Pacific (CAPSA), United Nations Economic and Social Commission for Asia and the Pacific (UNESCAP), Bogor, Indonesia.

Togar A. Napitupulu is with the Centre for Alleviation of Poverty through Secondary Crops' Development in Asia and the Pacific (CAPSA), United Nations Economic and Social Commission for Asia and the Pacific (UNESCAP), Bogor, Indonesia.

5. Philippines

Sylvia B. Concepcion is Dean, School of Management, University of the Philippines, Mindanao, Davao City, Philippines.

Joan C. Uy is Vice President, Northern Mindanao Vegetable Producers Association Inc., Philippines.

Luis Hualda is with School of Management, University of the Philippines, Mindanao, Davao City, Philippines.

Rene A. Guarin is with Upland Marketing Foundation, Inc., Santolan, Pasig City, Philippines.

6. China

Dinghuan Hu is Professor at the Institute of Agricultural Economics, Chinese Academy of Agricultural Sciences, Beijing, China.

Qiao Liang received his doctorate from Zhejiang University, China in March, 2011 and is post-doctoral fellow in School of Economics, Zhejiang University. His research interests focus on farmer cooperatives, agricultural supply chain and other farmer organizations.

Xia Dandan is with Institute of Agricultural Economics and Development, Chinese Academy of Agricultural Sciences, Beijing.

Naiquan Sang is with School of Economics, Nanjing University of Finance and Economics, Nanjing, China.

Huang Zuhui is a Professor and Director, Center for Agricultural and Rural Development (CARD), Zhejiang University, China.

Liang Qiao is a student at the Center for Agricultural and Rural Development (CARD), Zhejiang University, China.

Song Yu is a student at the Center for Agricultural and Rural Development (CARD), Zhejiang University, China.

Zhurong Huang is with the Centre for Chinese Agricultural Policy, Chinese Academy of Sciences, Beijing, China.

Xianfang Niu is with the Centre for Chinese Agricultural Policy, Chinese Academy of Sciences, Beijing, China.

Huayuan Zhi is with the Centre for Chinese Agricultural Policy, Chinese Academy of Sciences, Beijing, China.

Suxia Wang is with the Institute of Agricultural Economics and Development, Chinese Academy of Agricultural Sciences.

About the Editors

Vijay Paul Sharma is a Professor in Centre for Management in Agriculture, Indian Institute of Management, Ahmedabad (IIMA). He has been Chairman PGP-Agribusiness Management from 2002 to 2004 and Chair, Centre for Management in Agriculture from 2005 to 2008 and 2010-2012 at IIMA. He has wide ranging research, teaching and consulting interests in the areas of agri-food policy, commodity markets, international trade and development including the WTO, subsidy issues, food retailing, agribusiness competitiveness, food safety and quality issues. He teaches courses on Agricultural and Food Policy, Agriculture Futures and Options, International Agricultural Trade and Policy. He has been a member and chairman of several committees including Mid-Term Review of Five Year Plan, Empowered Committee on Agri-Infrastructure Development, Five Year Plan Working Groups, Advisory Group on Agriculture and Food Processing, Long-term Fertiliser Sector Policy and Expert Committees constituted by Govt. of India. Currently he is a member of Task Force on Performance Measurement and Evaluation of Govt. of India Ministries and departments constituted by Performance Division of Cabinet Secretariat, Govt. of India. He has been a consultant to various national and international organizations. He has worked as Advisor to the USAID's Economic Reforms Project in the Central Asian Countries. He has published extensively in national and international professional journals. Because of his outstanding contribution, he has received several recognitions. His recent publications include books on "Economic Policy Reforms and Indian Fertilizer Industry", "Glimpses of Indian Agriculture: Macro- and Micro Perspectives" and "Edible Oils and Oilseeds Economy of India".

Bill Vorley has a background in ecology, and trained in the farm fields of southern England and SE Asia. After eight years working in agribusiness, he continued his research interest in the 'greening' of industry, spending three years at the Leopold Centre for Sustainable Agriculture in Iowa, after which he joined the Institute for Agriculture Trade and Policy in Minneapolis, Minnesota as director of the Environment and Agriculture Programme. He moved to London in 1999 to join the International Institute for Environment and Development, with a focus on policy and market research for sustainable agriculture and rural development. He has coordinated the Regoverning Markets programme since 2003.

Jikun Huang has been the Director of the Center for Chinese Agricultural Policy (CCAP) at the Chinese Academy of Sciences in Beijing since October 2000, where he is also a Professor. He is a visiting professor of economics at Zhejiang University in Hangzhou and Nanjing Agricultural University and vice president of the Chinese Association of Agro-Technology Economics. His research interests are in the areas of agricultural and rural development, R&D policy, consumption, price and marketing, policy, applied econometrics and statistics, agricultural resource and environmental economics. He is member of several policy decision making committees. He has received several national and international awards.

Abid Qaiyum Suleri has a Ph.D. in food security from University of Greenwich. He is heading Pakistan's premier policy think-tank Sustainable Development Policy Institute (SDPI). Prior to joining SDPI he served as Head of OXFAM GB Pakistan Programs. He has conducted intensive research on Food Insecurity, Regional Trade, and Globalization and Rural Livelihoods. His other research interests include regional integration, institutional reforms, disaster management, poverty-environment nexus and sustainable natural resources governance. He represents the civil society in various working groups, steering committee, and technical committees formed by Planning Commission, Ministry of Commerce, Ministry of Food, Agriculture and Livestock, Ministry of Environment (MOE), and Pakistan Agriculture Research Council. He also represented the Pakistani civil society at the Doha and Cancun Ministerial Conferences of WTO as well as World Food Summit (FYL).

Larry Digal is an Associate Professor in the School of Management of the University of the Philippines and teaches managerial economics, agricultural price and policy analysis, strategic management and quantitative economics. He served as Dean of the School of Management. Dr. Digal finished his Ph.D. and MS in agricultural economics at the University of Sydney Australia and Purdue University West Lafayette Indiana USA respectively. He finished his undergraduate in the same field at the University of the Philippines Los Banos. His research interests include agribusiness value chain, market power, policy and contractual arrangements and he has published various articles in these areas. Prior to joining the academe, Dr. Digal has worked in both the private and public sectors.

Thomas A. Reardon is Professor in the Department of Agricultural, Food and Resource Economics at Michigan State University, USA, where he has researched and taught since January 1992. From 1986 through 1991, he was Senior Research Fellow at the International Food Policy Research Institute (IFPRI), in Washington DC. From 1984 to 1986 he was Rockefeller Foundation Post-Doctoral Fellow attached to IFPRI and also working with ICRISAT in West Africa. Tom finished his Ph.D. in Agricultural and Resource Economics at University of California at Berkeley in 1984. Tom is widely recognized as the leading global expert in links between the "supermarket revolution" and development of agrifood value chains and farms in developing regions, as well as links between agrifood industry transformation and food security. He has also worked extensively on rural nonfarm employment and food security. He is on the World Economic Forum (Davos) Global Alliance Council for Food Security, and has been a food security advisor to the Chicago Council for Global Affairs and an invitee to Davos. He is listed in "Who's Who in Economics," and received a Distinguish Faculty Award from MSU. Tom's research work is mainly in India, China, Indonesia and Nicaragua, including studies of the rise of supermarkets, the transformation of value chains in horticulture, shrimp, dairy, and rice, and the emergence of rural business hubs and other linkages between farmers and the modern food industry.

Contents

Part 4: Countries in Transition from State Controls: China Case studies

Part 5: Conclusions

List of Tables

List of Figures

1

Changing Structure of Agri-Food Chains in Asia: Opportunities and Threats for Small-Scale Producers

Vijay Paul Sharma, Bill Vorley, Jikun Huang, Abid Qaiyum Suleri, Larry Digal and Thomas A. Reardon

Agriculture plays an important role in economic growth and development of a large number of developing countries. It accounts for a large share of Gross Domestic Product (GDP), employs a large portion of the labour force, and represents an important source of foreign exchange (Table 1.1). It generates 10.7 per cent of the GDP in Thailand while its contribution in Pakistan's national GDP is 21.6 per cent. Agriculture employed about 67 per cent of the labour force in India in the mid-1990s. The share of agriculture in exports range from about 4 per cent in China to nearly 25 per cent in Sri Lanka. In addition to being a source of growth for the national economy, agriculture also provides investment opportunities for the private sector, and is a prime driver of agri-business industries and the rural non-farm economy.

Table 1.1: Macroeconomic Indicators in Selected Countries: 2007

	India	*China*	*Pakistan*	*Sri Lanka*	*Indonesia*	*Philippines*	*Thailand*
Population (million) (2005)	1134.40	1313.00	158.10	19.10	226.10	84.60	63.00
Share of agriculture GDP in national GDP (%) (2006)	19.60	12.80	21.60	14.60	13.70	14.20	10.70
Employment in agriculture (%) (1996)	67.00	44.00	42.00	34.00	44.00	37.00	43.00
Share of agricultural products in exports (%) (2006)	11.70	3.40	13.10	24.60	17.70	6.50	16.50
Share of agricultural products in imports (%) (2006)	4.20	6.50	13.90	13.00	9.30	7.20	5.70
Population below poverty line (%)	28.60	4.60	32.90	22.00	27.10	36.80	4.60

Source: World Development Indicators 2007 (CD-ROM); Washington, D.C.; ESCAP Statistical Yearbook for Asia and the Pacific 2007; http://www.unescap.org/stat/data/syb2007/

Although agriculture is no longer a major contributor to national GDP, poverty levels are still high in these countries (ranging from 4.6 per cent in Thailand to 36.8 per cent in the Philippines). It is well established that agriculture plays a major role in poverty reduction. But this requires improvement in skills and asset position of agricultural producers (mainly smallholder producers) and linking them to dynamic agri-food markets.

Rapid changes are taking place in developing countries and emerging economies, with implications for the ability of agriculture to contribute to economic growth, poverty reduction, and sustainable rural development. Small-scale agriculture, which supports the livelihood of most of the rural poor, is perhaps ill-equipped for these changes. Tensions run especially high in Asia where agrifood systems have been undergoing modernization and restructuring.

Drivers of Change

A number of global and national factors are influenced by agri-food markets. In order to understand the dynamics of the agrifood sector, there is a need to understand both global and domestic drivers of change. It is also important to understand implications of these trends for different stakeholders in value-chain in general and for small-scale producers' inclusion in particular. Although there are common drivers influencing markets worldwide, factors at the domestic level can also have a significant influence. Consequently the nature and pace of change varies between different countries, or even different continents (Reardon and Berdegué, 2008). Important demand-driven factors influencing agri-food markets include rising per capita income growth, urbanization, population growth, changes in consumer requirements including increased concerns for food safety and quality, and policy on foreign direct investment (Table 1.2). Supply-side factors include growth of supermarkets, changing procurement systems, domestic economic and trade policies, and improvements in logistics and infrastructure.

Reardon and Timmer (2007) note that developing countries' food industries, including all three of their components—wholesale, processing, and retail—have undergone transformations very rapidly from the early 1980s. From the first stage of traditional food systems, developing countries in general went to a second stage of food system development with a period of public-sector induced or governed food system transformation mainly in the 1960s to the early 1980s. In this stage, governments invested heavily in modernizing the fragmented/traditional wholesale sector by building wholesale markets. Also, as part of import substitution industrialization, there was substantial government, domestic private sector, and foreign investment in the processing sector, leading to its growth and incipient consolidation. The third is the market liberalization and globalization stage, initiated in most countries in the 1980s or the early 1990s. In this stage, while developing country governments continued to build wholesale markets, the main developments were in further development and consolidation of processing, and the rise of supermarkets, with progressive consolidation and multinationalization in that sector. At the same time world food trade doubled, within which trade in fresh produce and livestock products quadrupled. Agri-food systems in developing and transitional countries are experiencing unprecedented restructuring, partly as a result of the process of

Table 1.2: Factors Influencing Agri-Food Markets in Selected Asian Countries

	India	*China*	*Pakistan*	*Sri Lanka*	*Indonesia*	*Philippines*	*Thailand*
Urban population share (%) (2005)	29	41	35	15	48	63	32
GP/capita (PPP US $)	3452	6757	2370	4595	3843	5137	8677
GDP/capita (USD) (2005)	736	1713	711	1196	1302	1192	2750
Average annual GDP growth rate (2000–05)	6.90	9.50	5.80	4.00	4.70	4.70	5.10
GDP per capita annual growth rate (%) (1990–2005)	4.20	8.80	1.30	3.70	2.10	1.60	2.70
Consumer spending/ capita (USD)	577	908	743	1,183	1,145	1,129	2,185
Retail sales, net (USD mn)	447,501	885,975	77,831	14,277	163,163	62,129	83,431
Grocery retail sales, net (USD mn)	298,500	559,752	50,030	8,516	101,133	37,898	48,283
Grocery retail sales as % of retail sales	66.70	63.18	64.28	59.65	61.98	61.00	57.87
Foodservice sales, net (USD mn)	35,762	147,626	6,300	1,370	15,886	5,761	7,543
Total food spending, net (USD mn)	334,262	707,378	56,331	9,886	117,019	43,659	55,826
Modern grocery distribution, total sales (USD mn)	114,619	661,697	13,064	3,125	46,265	15,212	36,848
Modern grocery distribution, grocery sales (USD mn)	100,732	578,216	11,201	2,610	40,186	13,832	30,424

Source: Planet Retail, World Bank (2007b). World Development Indicators 2007. (CD-ROM); ESCAP Statistical Yearbook for Asia and the Pacific 2007; http://www.unescap.org/stat/data/syb2007/.

development and/or transition in which they are vigorously engaged and partly in response to the rising importance of supermarkets in the food retail sector.

In recognition of these challenges, an intensive programme of collaborative research and policy support—the regoverning markets programme—was undertaken between 2005 and 2008. The aim of the programme has been to provide strategic advice and guidance to the public sector, agri-food chain actors, civil society organizations, and development agencies on approaches that can anticipate and manage the impact of the dynamic changes in local and regional markets. The specific objectives have been to understand the keys to inclusion of small-scale producers into agri-food systems under different degrees of restructuring, to deepen the research on implications and opportunities for small-scale producers, to understand what is the best practice in connecting small-scale producers with dynamic markets, and to bring these findings into the wider policy arena.

This introductory chapter describes the design of the programme and presents some of the emerging findings on the state of market restructuring, drawing in particular form outcomes from intensive case studies in China, South, and South-East Asian countries.

Markets are Restructuring and Modernizing

According to the World Development Report 2008 (World Bank, 2007) of the world's 1.9 billion rural poor, around 280 million live in agriculture-based countries, mostly in Sub-Saharan Africa, where agriculture still contributes significantly to growth, and where the key policy challenge is to help agriculture to play its role as an engine of growth and poverty reduction.

But the majority of the rural poor—1.5 billion—live in transforming countries, where agriculture contributes less to growth, yet poverty remains overwhelmingly rural. The Asian economies dominate this group.

The Report paints a picture of rising urban-rural income gap in transforming countries, accompanied by unfulfilled expectations which create political tensions, concluding that "Growth in agriculture and the rural non-farm economy is needed to reduce rural poverty and narrow the urban-rural divide".

It is in transforming countries, too, where domestic markets are undergoing rapid but uneven modernization, with large supermarket retail chains and branded processed food product manufacturers growing alongside informal and traditional markets. Modernization of agri-food markets has been accompanied by intense policy debate, especially in India, where local traders—but also farmers—sense a threat to their livelihoods from the growth of modern organized retail. Market liberalization, a reduced role of the state, a shift into market-driven policy, changes in consumer preferences and purchasing power, and modernization of food processing and retailing are primary drivers. It can take developing and emerging market economies as little as ten years to reach the levels of agri-food market restructuring that took five or more decades in Western Europe or North America (Reardon and Gulati, 2008). The food industry is assessing its "realm of responsibility" in the supply chain; producer organizations are debating appropriate responses and strategies; governments are devising new forms of market governance to promote private sector investment while ensuring social inclusion; public and private sector organizations are joining forces in novel alliances; and donors are revisiting their support to agriculture in the context of the Millennium Development Goals (MDGs).

Market modernization offers increased economic opportunities for small-scale producers and small- and medium-scale enterprises (SMEs), consumers, and other actors in the food chain. New buyers in the countryside are competing for farmers' produce.[1] But there are also risks of domestic businesses being bypassed, and of costly market entry requirements which favour the better-resourced. If the Millennium Development Goals (MDGs) are to even be partially met by 2015, agriculture and SMEs in transforming as well as agriculture-based countries must contribute to the delivery of equitable growth. Market modernization and restructuring challenge the expectation of a growth and equity 'win-win' derived from agricultural development.

The World Development Report 2008 calls for action in response to the modernization of procurement systems in integrated, modern supply chains, whereby small-scale producers can share in these growth opportunities. Disproportionate attention has been paid to export markets, despite the far greater importance of domestic markets for the majority of small-scale farmers. The impact of transformation of the processing sector on farmers has also been well studied including contract farming where one could link a clear change (rise of big processors) with a clear participant group. The least researched area has been the impact of modern grocery retail on farmers.

The following key research questions are of immediate interest to governments, producers, and the private sector:

- Can the new food giants, including supermarkets and food companies, be partners in the economic growth of rural areas?
- Can small-scale farmers meet the high expectations for quantity and food quality and safety?
- Can public policy provide successful market linkages between business and small-scale farming and can anticipatory policy make any difference?

Regoverning Markets Programme

The Regoverning Markets Programme set out to address these questions through empirical case studies and practical experience in policy dialogue and outreach. The programme has stressed the importance of basing policy response to the challenge on evidence rather than anecdotes.

The Regoverning Markets Programme (2005–2008) represents a global consortium of 15 institutions worldwide, coordinated by the International Institute for Environment and Development (IIED). The consortium carried out state of the art empirical research, commissioned case studies of innovative practices, and conducted policy consultation processes. Around 40 case studies with global coverage have been documented on connecting small-scale producers with modern markets. Together

[1] Modern retail offers wide choice, farmers want to exercise it all. LiveMint.com/Wall Street Journal 12 Feb 08.

they address areas for innovation respectively for business, policy makers, farmers, and multi-stakeholder chain-wide learning.

Empirical Studies

Country-based research studies undertaken by national institutions have examined the processes and impact of restructuring through a comparative in-depth empirical analysis in China, Indonesia, South Africa, Turkey, India, Poland, Mexico, and Zambia. They have addressed the following questions:

1. What restructuring is occurring? What distinct market channels do farmers face and how do they differ? How have they changed over time?
2. What determines the participation of farmers in different channels (e.g. farm size, non-land assets, policies).
3. What is the impact of farmer participation on technology and incomes?
4. What are the policy implications?

How are Markets Restructured?

There are large differences in observed market restructuring among developing and emerging market economy countries. For example, relatively more food market restructuring has taken place in Latin America (Mexico), followed by Eastern Europe transitional economies (Turkey and Poland), South Africa, Southeast Asia (Indonesia), East Asia (China), and South Asia (India). It is less developed in Sub-Saharan African countries (Zambia). There are also large differences in observed market restructuring among commodities. Generally, market restructuring has been more rapid in dairy and livestock sectors (e.g. poultry and meat) than in fruit and vegetables.

The combination of retail restructuring policies and rising urbanization and incomes (in most of the countries) led to the rapid rise of modern food retailing during the 1990s at 3–5 times faster than the growth of GDP per capita. In urban Mexico supermarkets and hypermarkets had a 52 per cent share of overall food retail in 2006, up from around 5 per cent in 1990; the share of supermarkets in fresh produce was 25 per cent by 2006, up from near zero in 1990. In China, from one supermarket in 1990, the number grew to 53,000 by the mid 2000s. In Indonesia, the market share of supermarkets has grown from around 5 per cent to 30 per cent of food retail between 1995 and 2005, and is spreading to middle class, lower-middle, and working-poor areas. The penetration by supermarkets in fresh produce retail significantly lags behind that of overall penetration; for example, in Mexico, supermarkets have 55 per cent share of overall food, but only 25 per cent share of fresh produce; in Indonesia, 30 per cent and 10 per cent; in Turkey, 35 per cent and 20 per cent respectively.

In most of study countries, the food processing sector started to restructure before the retail sector, though there is evidence that there has been mutual benefit between the large processing sector and the supermarket sector. There has been rapid consolidation in the processing sector, in particular in second-stage processing.

The wholesale sector itself has not been public sector controlled, apart from the market premises in most countries though there are some exceptions, with India and Turkey both instituting state control (via licensing) of wholesalers in public wholesale markets. In both cases, this was motivated by the idea that it would avoid speculation and dominance of middlemen in the wholesale sector that would possibly endanger food security and farmer incomes. In both countries state control over the whole-sale sector is undergoing a change; in India, retailers can buy direct from farmers rather than operate through government-controlled Agricultural Produce Marketing Committee (APMC) markets.

Many of the case studies show consolidation emerging in wholesale markets. For instance in West Java in the mid 1990s, the wholesale sector was dominated by small brokers. By the mid 2000s larger wholesalers were preponderant and smaller brokers were in the minority, and mainly operating in the more hinterland areas. There is evidence that wholesalers are buying directly from farmers and the role of small local brokers is declining. Other types of restructuring are also emerging in the wholesale sector, the most prominent being specialized/dedicated wholesalers who sell to supermarkets and food service, and have preferred suppliers.

What Impact on Procurement?

Supermarkets tend to source from larger second-stage processors for reasons of food safety and quality and reduced transactions costs. Small-scale processors tend to be the main sources for traditional retailers, except where the processing sector is already consolidated.

In all the study countries, all supermarket chains source fresh vegetables (mainly tomato), from wholesale markets, with the exception of the leading South African chains, which source tomatoes mainly from large commercial farmers via preferred supplier relationships. The shift by South African supermarkets to using preferred suppliers was greatly facilitated by the sharply dualistic farm sector structure. The major supermarket chains were found to source tomatoes from large commercial farmers, and revert to small-scale farmers only to meet gaps in supply from their main suppliers. Only a small share comes from commercializing small-scale farmers and, with a few exceptions among retailers, very little from the "emerging predominantly black farmers". This compares with China, where small-scale farmers dominate, and where no evidence was found of such farmers being excluded from vegetable production and markets.

Large processors sometimes work in preferred supplier relationships with small-scale farmers on a semi-contract farming basis. In these relationships, sometimes credit, seed, inputs, and technical assistance are offered, and the product is collected at or near farm-gate. In other cases the relationship is merely that of the spot market. The studies note only a relatively low degree of procurement restructuring among wholesalers—regardless of whether they are large on-market wholesalers or off-market specialized wholesalers.

Traditional Retail

It is often assumed that traditional retail is static. However, large public markets such as bazaars, wet markets, and street markets are themselves restructuring and upgrading, focusing on higher quality to compete with supermarkets on quality and service and to reduce the gap in market infrastructure and hygiene. This means wholesalers and farmers will increasingly have to contend with both forms of retail segments (modern and traditional-now-modernizing) that demand quality and reduced transaction costs.

Traditional markets are resilient and can coexist for significant periods of time with restructured markets. In fact, the restructuring process often includes interactions and spillover effects between 'old' and 'new' markets. There are instances of "partially restructured" markets, with faster and deeper changes downstream and continuity of traditional patterns upstream. Small-scale farmers usually operate in multiple market channels, new and traditional, displaying diversified marketing strategies in order to meet different economic needs (e.g. access to credit or improved cash flow, controlled risk levels) or social needs (e.g. inclusion in social networks that are interlinked with marketing networks).

What is Happening at the Farm Level?

In all the countries where the case studies were done, at least for the study products, there was a complete or near-complete dominance of small farms on the production side. Large farms existed in some countries, but usually in enclave sectors and often focused on exports.

The observed market restructuring at the upstream level has been much less than the observed market restructurings at downstream. Penetration from downstream changes or the modern retail revolution to other segments of the food marketing chain has often been stopped at midstream by wholesale operations, processing firms, and other intermediaries. The China study concluded this as an indication of a very competitive wholesale market, efficient small wholesalers in linking down stream and upstream, and high transaction costs of modern retailers and exporters with millions of small producers. Supermarkets were found to procure a third of vegetable supplies from large specialized/dedicated wholesalers or directly in the production zones, and a small proportion from their own or contracted land. For all of these except own-production, buying is done in spot relations from farmers, so that brokers or wholesalers who interact with farmers are indistinguishable from the viewpoint of the farmer.

There is evidence of penetration from downstream to midstream (e.g. processors and wholesalers) and there is also rising evidence of the responses of midstream to the changes in downstream. The typical pattern is for supermarket chains to source via specialized/dedicated wholesalers.

When restructuring does reach as far as the farm-driven by business needs for traceability, for example–and farm income from modern markets increases, exclusion of smaller, less well capitalized producers becomes a reality. Exclusion of whole regions that are not endowed with the characteristics demanded by downstream agents in the chain can also arise. Restructuring and modernization comes with requirements for quality, quantity, consistency, and traceability, with a large fixed cost element that favours farmers with assets and capacities to access the necessary finance, information and technology. This requires some threshold investments by producers.

Reardon and Huang (2008) report a mixed record of producer organizations providing members with economic benefits such as access to dynamic markets. Membership of producer organizations was correlated with participation in modern markets in some countries; elsewhere, the correlation was either not significant or negative. This is indicative of the very mixed role of producer organizations.

Generally, better road and marketing infrastructure facilitates farmers' participating in modern market channels though the impact is not statistically significant in some countries. There are various market structure and regulatory constraints that buffer small-scale farmers from substantial restructuring downstream. The responses from intermediates to retail market restructuring have softened the shocks of retail changes on farms. The extent to which this reduces the capacity of the small-scale farming community to build up resilience within demanding agri-food markets is, however, open to question.

Innovation and Good Practice: What makes for Successful Linkages between Small-Scale Farmers and Modern Markets?

Over 40 case studies with global coverage have been documented in the Regoverning Markets programme on connecting small-scale producers with modern markets. Thirty of these case studies focused on innovations by chain actors that support greater small-scale producers' inclusion at domestic or regional levels. 'Innovation' refers to the actions and policies of private companies, public institutions, farmer organizations or non-governmental organizations that resulted in enhanced market participation of small-scale producers. The case studies that form the basis of this book were selected through two rounds of global competition, one in 2005 and another in 2006. From 131 case studies submitted to the competition, 35 were selected and this book includes 12 case studies from China, India, Indonesia, Philippines,

Sri Lanka, and Thailand. In these countries small-scale farmers and businesses have connected successfully to dynamic markets, doing business with agri-processors and supermarkets. These countries represent both a broad geographic coverage and a range of stages of market concentration (Figure 1.1). The studies aimed to derive models, strategies, and policy principles to guide public and private sector actors in promoting greater participation of small-scale producers in dynamic markets. The analytical framework of the case studies is described in Box 1.

Each case study analysed one specific innovation. These innovations are specific arrangements built on public policies, business initiative, collective action by small-scale farmers, and support from development agencies that appear to have played a positive role in supporting greater inclusion. We term these 'innovations' because they countervail the tendency that small-scale farmers become excluded from markets as supply chains evolve in complexity.

Fragmented Markets	**Emerging Markets**	**Maturing Markets**	**Consolidated Markets**
e.g. Pakistan, India, Sub-Saharan Africa	e.g. China, Vietnam, Indonesia, Philippines	e.g. Thailand, South Africa, Mexico, Korea	e.g. USA, Western Europe, Brazil
Key features:	*Key features:*	*Key features:*	*Key features:*
Large traditional wholesale and retail markets; many small independent retail shops/outlets; low technology	Large traditional wholesale and retail markets; many small independent retail shops/outlets; low technology; emergence of dedicated suppliers	Regional, national and global retailers; some sourcing from traditional wholesale; growth of dedicated service providers; preferred suppliers; mixed levels of technology application	Full vertical integration of market chains including dedicated logistics and preferred suppliers; high technology; global sourcing; reduced or changed role of traditional wholesale markets; growth of small specialty stores
Market concentration: < 5%	Market concentration: < 20%	Market concentration: > 45%	Market concentration: < 65%

Fig. 1.1: Different Stages of Market Concentration

Source: Vermeulen *et al.* (2008)

'Inclusion' or 'exclusion' is not defined in terms of the farmers' situation at a single point in time, but rather in terms of the capacity of small-scale producers to sustain their participation in a given supply chain as it evolves and becomes ever more challenging and competitive. Hence, it is necessary to analyse the problem from an evolutionary or 'innovation history' perspective. In addition, 'inclusion' or 'exclusion' does not indicate *per se* any difference in welfare outcomes: It is not automatic that a group of small-scale producers who are 'included' will be better-off than those who are 'excluded', in terms of net income or net assets, exposure to risk, or autonomy in decision-making. That inclusion leads to significant welfare gains is a hypothesis to be critically examined by the case studies.

Each case study sought to generate the following insights:

1. *The drivers of inclusion:* What factors explain that the small-scale producers in the case study are included in dynamic markets and others are not?
2. *The elements of inclusion:* What technical, organizational, managerial and financial changes did small-scale producers have to implement to be included in dynamic markets?
3. *The costs and benefits of inclusion:* What financial and non-financial costs and benefits do small-scale producers obtain from their inclusion in dynamic markets?
4. *The sustainability of inclusion:* What type and level of direct/indirect subsidies have contributed to the innovation? What implications do these have on the sustainability?
5. *Upscaling and replication:* What public and private policies contribute to the up-scaling of the innovation? What lessons can be derived for public and private policies to promote market inclusion of small-scale producers elsewhere?

Box 1: Analytical Framework

- Strategies of agri-processors and food retailers operating in restructured markets result in new procurement chains characterized by specialization of wholesalers, centralization of distribution, consolidation of preferred suppliers, and more stringent grades and standards, and in certain cases internationalization of procurement.
- The emergence and continuous restructuring of these markets provides incentives to suppliers, including small-scale farmers, to undertake successive and never-ending changes in the areas of technology, management, and inter-firm organization, all of which have significant financial implications.
- The capacity of small-scale farmers to keep pace with this continuous stream of changes defines their inclusion or exclusion in the evolving supply chain and, thus, the restructured market.
- Public policy, private business models, collective action by smallholders and/or intervention by development agencies can change the set of incentives facing the small-scale farmers and/or strengthen the farmers' capacities in facing these incentives.
- Inclusion can take different forms, from mere participation as individual suppliers of raw material to collective action with other suppliers to meet basic demands for volume and consistency of supply, to becoming a specialized supplier on the basis of value-adding activities, to becoming co-owner of a supply chain or one of its segments.

Source: Berdegué *et al.* (2006)

Studies were also carried out on specific policies and/or institutional changes that have contributed to inclusive market development. These were drawn from developing country experiences and included codes of practice on supplier-retailer trading relations, functioning of agricultural broker associations, and the legal framework that supports the functioning of producer groups.

Drawing on these cases, key success factors include the bringing together of the three key actors: farmers who are trained, organized, empowered to deliver quantity and quality in a consistent and cost efficient way; a public sector with a conducive business environment including infrastructure, contract enforcement mechanisms, financial intermediation; and a receptive business sector (Figure 1.2). For working with these different actors there is a need for some type of partnership facilitation or brokerage. This does not always have to be a third party; it can be a "chain champion" but there needs to be somebody in or outside the value chain who facilitates and bridges the worlds of farmers and business. This may not be in the form different organizations—any of the actors could champion a process and work in any configuration. All these elements need to be present. If some are missing then the business case will hit an early growth limit, and the sustainability of the market linkage may be jeopardized.

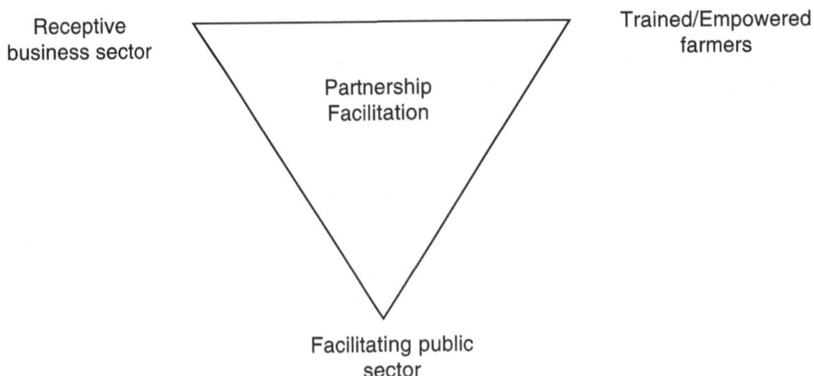

Fig. 1.2: Keys to Inclusion of Smallholder Farmers in Dynamic Markets

The main challenge for these networks of actors is the organization of supply, which is central to overcoming the dispersion of producers, diseconomies of scale, poor access to information, technology and finance, inconsistent volume and quality, lack of traceability, and management of risk. Supply may be organized by producers themselves seeking a market; large farmers seeking extra supply volumes; processors, exporters, and retailers seeking to assure supply; traders and other traditional market actors; NGOs and other support agencies; or national and local governments seeking regional development such as the Dragon Head companies in China.

Both producer and buyer ends of value chains usually want to "cut out the middle man" and shift from a dependency on traditional wholesale markets in pursuit of value, improved quality, and product assurance. Direct procurement is often presented as a win-win-win situation for customers, business, and producers. Improved information flow among the supply chain segments reduced the marketing risk faced by the company and farmers. Another reason for businesses to organize their own supply base is when there is a lack of collective producer action, often because of suspicion of cooperatives or laws that insulate producers from the market.

But organizing direct procurement can have high transaction costs for private players. Buyer-organized direct sourcing can also be highly paternalistic and create dependence rather than empowerment among producers in the chain. Producers will accept paternalism when it is compensated for by the certainty of sales, rapid and guaranteed payment, and technical and financial support. But processors or retailers can encourage their suppliers to organize into more autonomous groups, and thus construct a partnership rather than an exclusive buyer-driven supply network.

Chain intermediaries often are vital in linking small-scale producers with dynamic markets and are of particular importance to small-scale producers and to those located further away from the markets and main roads. The existence of these intermediaries often makes the difference between successful and sustainable small-scale farmer inclusion and failure. Their legitimate and useful roles in the value chain need to be acknowledged and supported in order to streamline the value chain. When the market is dominated by smaller traders, there is also a great challenge in meeting demands for food safety.

Business has to work with the new generation of intermediaries who understand both ends of the value chain (small-scale farmer production and modern retail marketing) to ensure traceability and due diligence. In fact, some of the successful specialized intermediaries which are both business-oriented and development-motivated are fully private-sector-driven and are independent from any support from government or NGOs, such as the Bimandiri Company in Indonesia. Other models of modern intermediaries began with donor support and have now become independent from them such as the Normin Group in the Philippines. New platforms for multiple service provision of input and output sides of the farm-to-consumer value chain are being developed with particular focus on poorer households. India is leading in such innovation in the agri-food sector through contract farming. The potential of the private sector in promoting economic growth in rural areas is significant. Agribusiness can be effective in linking small-scale producers with dynamic markets. However, this potential of the private sector as a partner in development is largely underutilized.

The world of financial services and that of market access and value chain development are still largely separated. It is important to bridge that gap and develop innovative financial products that cater for the needs of SMEs including producer organizations in value chain development.

Collective action remains an important strategy for increased small-scale producer participation in dynamic markets. The case studies show that in view of lower transaction costs and more effective capacity transfer, private companies often prefer to work with organized farmers rather than individuals despite the increased bargaining power that groups enjoy.

Conclusion

The challenge of connecting small-scale producers with dynamic agri-food markets is still a relatively new field with few proven and replicable models and methodologies. Evidence of limited penetration so far of downstream restructuring into upstream primary production means that producers, policy makers, support agencies, and business have time to work together to develop new and innovative means to better secure small-scale producers' and entrepreneurs' market inclusion over the longer term. The empirical research has demonstrated that participation of small-scale farmers in supply networks is quite resilient, even as modernization advances downstream. In dualistic economies, the modern and small-scale were never connected, so is less a case of exclusion and more a case of parallel evolution. Modernization appears to be more an accelerator of rural differentiation rather than a primary driver. But the introduction of food safety regulations—either private or public sector—can greatly speed up the rate of rural change.

Successful and durable inclusion is built on foundations of—supportive public policies; organized producers; and a receptive business sector; combined with a facilitation 'space'. Governments and businesses have significant room for introducing pro-poor policies, interventions, and investments even within an overall framework of free trade and competitive markets.

There is a need to identify and communicate successful and good practices from around the world, based on experiences of different policy initiatives, and for each country and region to identify the most appropriate best practice for their situation. There is an identified need to build a platform to maintain debate and promote knowledge across countries, building on the knowledge base of Regoverning Markets research, innovation and outreach. There is a need for the studies of the Regoverning Markets programme to be widely disseminated and fed back to country level for further debate, including how the evidence and the issue is perceived by local stakeholders: farmers, agribusiness, and government. This book is a small step in disseminating that knowledge in Asia.

References

Berdegue, Julio A., Peppelenbos, and Biénabe, Estelle (2006), "A Method for the Analysis of Innovative Practices in Connecting Smallholder Producers with Dynamic Supply Chains," *Resource Paper for Component 2, Regoverning Markets Programmes,* (IIED London: International Institute for Environment and Development).

Reardon, T. and Gulati, A. (2008), "The Rise of Supermarkets and their Development Implications: International Experience Relevant for India," *IFPRI Discussion Paper* 00752. Washington, D.C.: International Food Policy Research Institute.

Vermeulen, S., Woodhill, J., Procter, F.J. and Delnoye, R. (2008). Chain-Wide Learning for Inclusive Agri-food Market Development: A Guide to Multi-Stakeholder Processes for Linking Small-Scale Producers with Modern Markets. London: International Institute for Environment and Development, and Wageningen: Wageningen University and Resource Centre.

World Bank (2007), *World Development Report 2008: Agriculture for Development*. Washington, D.C: World Bank.

2

India's Agrarian Crisis and Smallholder Producers' Participation in New Farm Supply Chain Initiatives: A Study of Contract Farming

Vijay Paul Sharma

The direct contribution of the agricultural sector to the economy is reflected in its share in total Gross Domestic Product (GDP), foreign exchange earnings, and supplying savings and labour to other sectors. Agriculture and allied sectors such as forestry and fishing accounted for 18.5 per cent of GDP in 2005–06 (at 1999–2000 constant prices) and employed about 58 per cent of the country's workforce (CSO, 2007). It accounted for 10.95 per cent of India's exports in 2005–06 (GoI, 2007). About 46 per cent of India's geographical area is used for agricultural activity.

There has been a structural transformation in the Indian economy during the past few decades. The composition of GDP at 1993–94 constant prices reveals that the share of agriculture, including forestry and fishing, has declined as growth in industrial and services sectors far outpaced that in the agricultural sector (Figure 2.1).

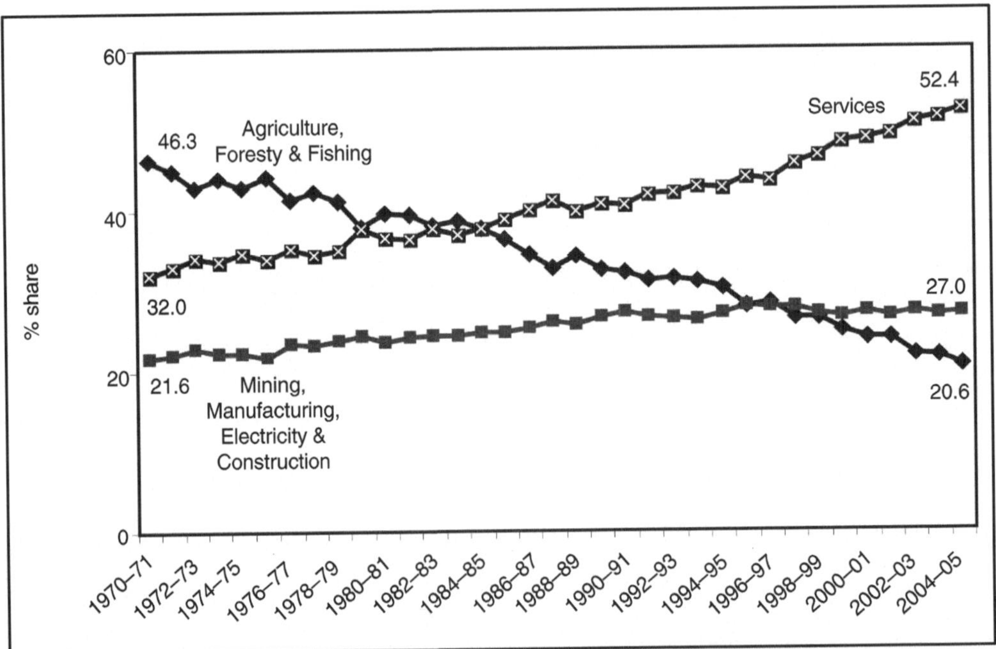

Fig. 2.1: Share of Agriculture, Manufacturing and Services Sector in GDP

Source: CSO, 2007

The share of mining, manufacturing, electricity, and construction sectors increased from 21.6 per cent in 1970–71 to 27 per cent in 2004–05, and the share of the services sector increased significantly from 32 per cent to 52.4 per cent during the same period. Despite a steady decline of its share in the GDP, agriculture plays a significant role in the socio-economic development of the country. Therefore, fostering rapid, sustained, and broad-based growth in agriculture remains a key priority for the government.

Consistent with the trends of economic development at national level, the role of the agricultural sector in state economies is also changing. In some states such as Bihar, Punjab, Uttar Pradesh, Haryana, Rajasthan, and Orissa, the sector today contributes more than one quarter of the Gross State Domestic Product (GSDP), while in others such as Gujarat, Kerala, Karnataka, Tamil Nadu and Maharashtra, the sector contributes less than 20 per cent to GSDP (Figure 2.2).

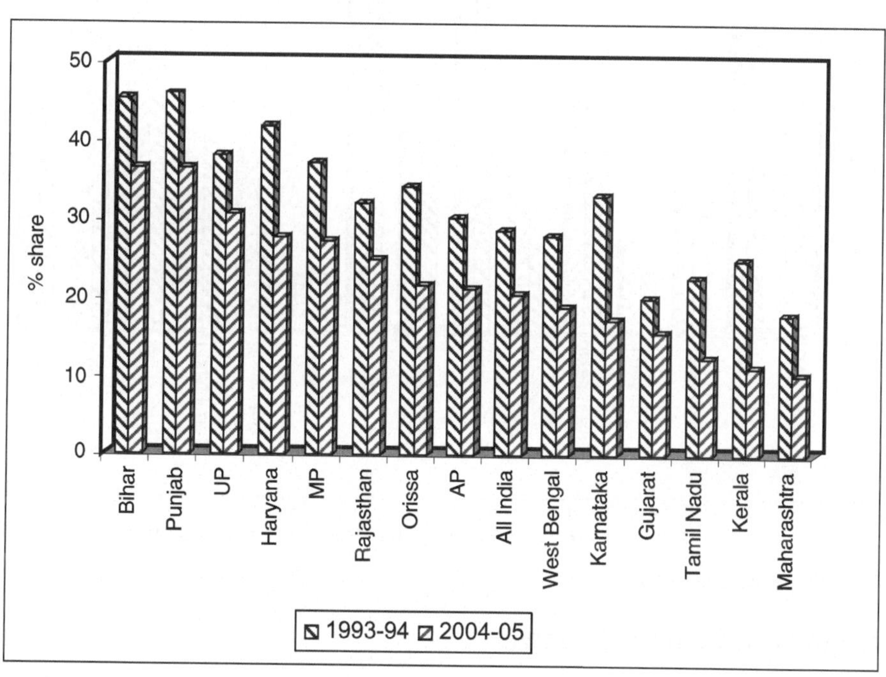

Fig. 2.2: Share of Agriculture and Allied Sectors in GSDP

Source: CSO, 2007

However, the contribution of agriculture to GSDP declined in almost all states between 1993–94 and 2004–05. The decline was the highest in Karnataka (16 per cent), followed by Haryana (14.2 per cent), and Kerala (13.7 per cent). In Karnataka, the decline was mainly because of a significant increase in the share of the service sector (from 37.9 per cent in 1993–94 to 54.7 per cent in 2004–05), mainly driven by the Information Technology (IT) industry. In Haryana the decline is again because of the faster development of the services sector in cities around the national capital, New Delhi.

Despite the declining share of agriculture, the majority of the workforce continues to depend on the agricultural sector for employment; in rural areas dependence on agriculture is more, with about 75 per cent of the rural population employed in the sector. However, employment is disguised because of limited opportunities for rural non-farm employment. Disguised employment leads to lower labour and resources productivity in the sector relative to other sectors. Low labour productivity leads to higher rates of poverty in rural areas (Figure 2.3).

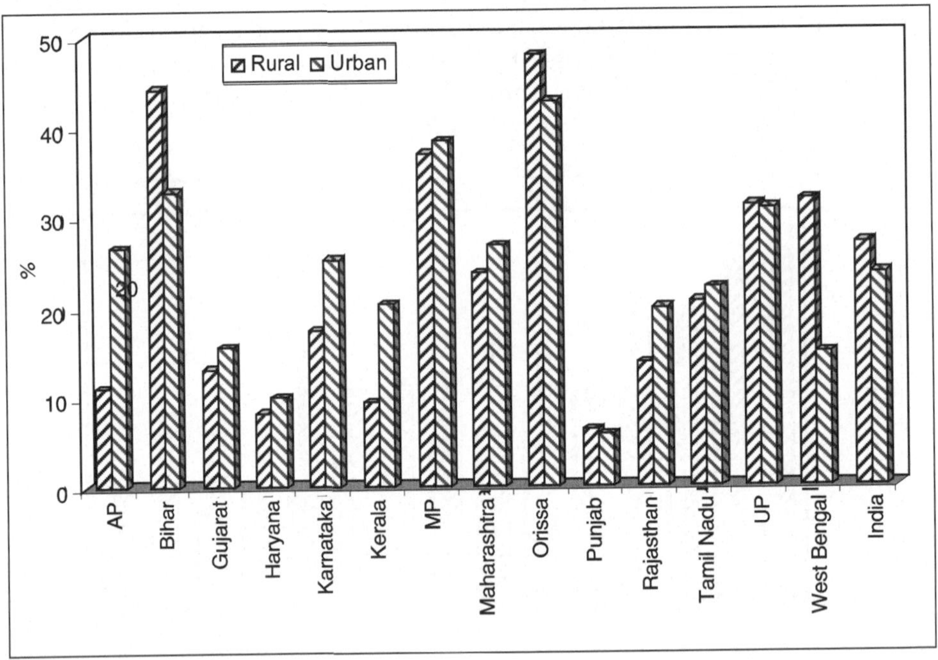

Fig. 2.3: Estimates of Rural and Urban Poverty Ratios, (1999)

Source: Planning Commission, 2002

Deceleration in Agricultural Growth

India's GDP grew at an annual rate of 5.8 per cent from 1995–96 to 2004–05 at 1993–94 constant prices, but agricultural growth declined to about 2 per cent, owing to stagnation or decline in productivity during the last decade. Plan-wise trends of growth of total GDP and GDP from agriculture are presented in Figure 2.4. The agricultural sector has grown more than the targeted growth rate during the sixth, seventh and eighth Five Year Plans, but fell short of the targeted growth during the ninth and tenth plans (Figure 2.4).

During the tenth plan, agricultural GDP grew at an annual rate of only 2.1 per cent against the targeted growth of 4 per cent. With about 70 per cent of the population living in rural areas and about 58 per cent of the country's workforce engaged in agriculture, the country needs positive change in its agricultural sector. Therefore, in the eleventh Five Year Plan, the National Development Council has adopted a 14–point resolution dividing responsibilities equally between the central and state governments, with an aim of achieving 4 per cent agricultural growth by the end of the eleventh plan. The agricultural sector has been allocated an additional ₹ 250,000 million from the central government in the next four years.

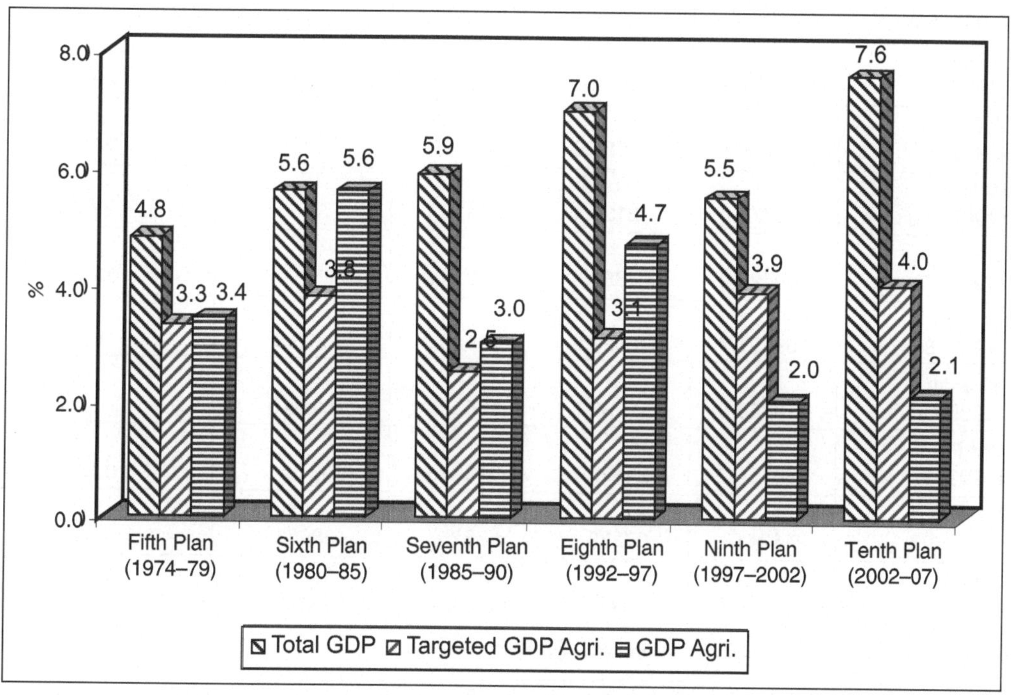

Fig. 2.4: Plan-wise Trend of Growth of Total GDP and Agriculture GDP (including Allied Sectors) at 1993–94 Constant Prices

Source: CSO 2007

Declining Public Investment and Rising Subsidies

One of the important reasons for the deceleration has been declining investment in agriculture and allied sectors, and in irrigation (Table 2.1). As Figure 2.5 illustrates, the share of agriculture and irrigation in total plan expenditure has declined from 37.3 per cent in the first Five Year Plan to 10.6 per cent in the tenth Five Year Plan.

In the sixth plan, an additional head of rural development was introduced whose share increased from 6.4 per cent in the sixth plan to 9.5 per cent in the ninth plan, and slightly declining to nearly 8 per cent in the tenth plan.

The share of the public sector in gross capital formation in agriculture has declined from 30.9 per cent in 1995–96 to 25.6 per cent in 2003–04, while the share of the private sector has increased from 69.1 per cent to 74.4 per cent during the same period (Figure 2.6).

Table 2.1: Plan Expenditure on Agriculture and Allied Sectors, Irrigation and Rural Development

(₹ crore)

	Total Plan Expenditure	*Agri. & Allied Sectors*	*Irrigation*	*Rural Development*	*Share of Agri. & Irrigation in Total Plan Expenditure*
I Plan (1951–56)	1960	289.9	441.8	–	37.3
II Plan (1956–61)	4671.8	549	541.6	–	23.3
III Plan (1961–66)	8576.5	1088.9	1019.1	–	24.6
IV Plan (1969–74)	15778.8	2120.4	2415.7	–	28.7
V Plan (1974–78)	39426.2	4864.9	3925.8	–	22.3
VI Plan (1980–85)	109291.7	6623.5	10929.9	6996.8	16.1
VII Plan (1985–90)	218729.6	12792.6	16589.9	15246.5	13.4
VIII Plan (1992–97)	485457.2	24895.7	31398.9	40372.1	11.6
IX Plan (1997–02)	941041	37239	67875	88965	11.2
X Plan (2002–07)	1525639	58933	103315	121928	10.6

Source: Planning Commission, 2001; Tenth Five Year Plan

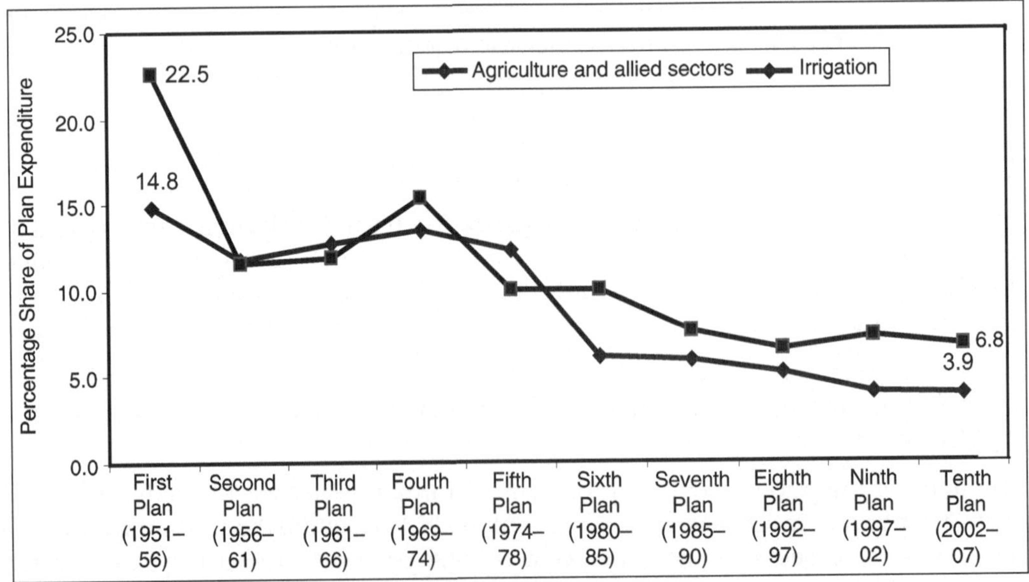

Fig. 2.5: Share of Agriculture and Allied Sectors and Irrigation in Plan Expenditure

Source: Planning Commission, 2001; Tenth Five Year Plan

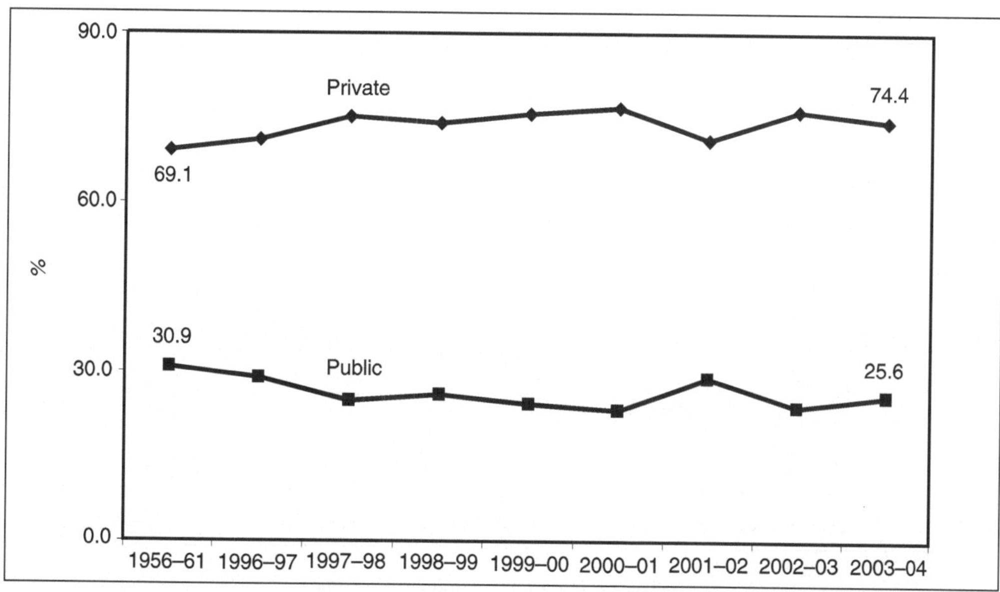

Fig. 2.6: Share of Public and Private Sectors in Investment in Agriculture (at 1993–94 prices)

Source: GOI, 2007a

However, because of the high degree of complementarity between public and private investment in agriculture, there is a need to increase public investment. The share of the agricultural sector's capital formation in GDP has declined from 1.9 per cent in the early 1990s to about 1.2 per cent in the early 2000s, which is a cause for concern. However, there is an indication of reversal of this trend of late, with public sector investment in agriculture reaching ₹ 52,490 million in 2003–04 at 1993–94 prices the highest level since the early 1990s (GoI, 2007a). This has helped in improving the share of the agricultural sector's capital formation in GDP from 1.28 per cent in 2001–02 to 1.31 per cent in 2003–04. A key reason for declining public investment in agriculture has been ever-increasing agricultural subsidies for fertilizers, power, irrigation, food, etc. Total agricultural subsidies have increased at an annual compound rate of about 12 per cent between 1993–94 and 2002–03 (from ₹ 140,690 million to about ₹ 365,140 million). The share of fertilizer subsidies in total agricultural subsidies is about 36 per cent (GoI, 2007b). Trends in food and fertilizer subsidies during the 1990s and 2000s are presented in Figure 2.7.

The subsidy on fertilizers has increased from ₹ 43,890 million in 1990–91 to about ₹ 224,520 million in 2006–07 (at an annual compound growth rate of 10.6 per cent). Food subsidies have witnessed a significant increase during the 1990s and 2000s, up from ₹ 24,500 million in 1990–91 to ₹ 251,810 million in 2003–04, and marginally declining to ₹ 242,000 million in 2006–07. Food and agricultural subsidies are greater than public investment in agriculture and allied sectors, irrigation, and rural development combined. In addition, there has been a deterioration of institutions/organizations providing inputs and services such as credit, seeds, technology, and extension to the agricultural sector.

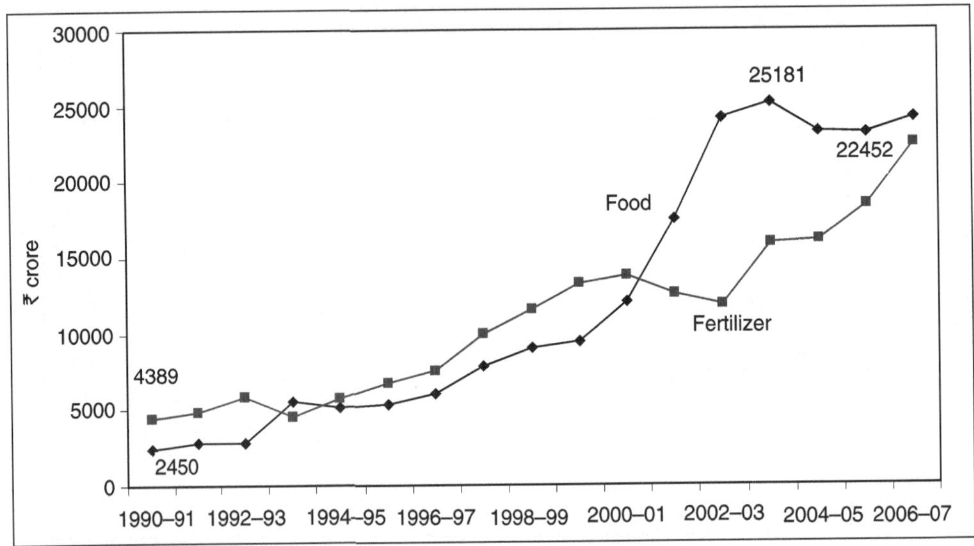

Fig. 2.7: Food and Fertilizer Subsidies

Source: GOI, 2007 b

Land Fragmentation

The agrarian structure in India has undergone significant changes since the 1970s. Recent data show that the share of marginal and small farmers (farmers owning land from 0.1 ha to less than 2 ha) increased from 69.7 per cent in 1970–71 to approximately 82 per cent in 2000–01 (Table 2.2).

The share of small and marginal farmers in total areas operated also has increased, from about 21 per cent in 1970–71 to about 39 per cent in 2000–01. The average farm size has declined from 2.3 ha in 1970–71 to 1.41 ha in 1995–96 and 1.32 ha in 2000–01. The size of land holdings in India is very small and is subject to fragmentation, because of reasons such as land ceiling laws, population increase, inheritance laws which have stipulated an equal division of property among sons, lack of off-farm occupations, etc. Small holdings are often overmanned, resulting in disguised unemployment and low labour productivity. Moreover, there are several tenancy restrictions in many states ranging from a complete ban in leasing some states to complete freedom in others. There is a growing consensus about the need to have a review of current tenancy legislations, which sometimes restrict participation of the private sector in agriculture. However, under the Indian constitution, land administration falls under the state governments, hence the large variation across states.

Cropping Pattern Shifts and Stagnant Productivity

Foodgrains continue to occupy an important place in Indian agriculture, and commercial crops such as fruits and vegetables, fibres, condiments and spices, etc.

Table 2.2: Distribution of Operational Holdings in India 1970–71–2000–01

Category	*1970–71*	*1980–81*	*1985–86*	*1990–91*	*1995–96*	*2000–01*
Number ('000)						
Marginal (< 1ha)	35,682 (50.6%)	50,122 (56.4%)	56,147 (57.8%)	63,389 (59.4%)	71,179 (61.6%)	76,122 (63.0%)
Small (1.0–2.0 ha)	13,432 (19.1%)	16,072 (18.1%)	17,922 (18.4%)	20,092 (18.8%)	21,643 (18.7%)	22,814 (18.9%)
Semi-medium (2.0–4.0 ha)	10,681 (15.2%)	12,455 (14.0%)	13,252 (13.6%)	13,923 (13.1%)	14,261 (12.3%)	14,087 (11.7%)
Medium (4.0–10.0 ha)	7,932 (11.3%)	8,068 (9.1%)	7,916 (8.1%)	7,580 (7.1%)	7,092 (6.1%)	6,568 (5.4%)
Large (>10 ha)	2,766 (3.9%)	2,166 (2.4%)	1,918 (2.0%)	1,654 (1.6%)	1,404 (1.2%)	1,230 (1.0%)
Total	70,493 (100%)	88,883 (100%)	97,155 (100%)	10,6637 (100%)	115,580 (100%)	120,822 (100%)
Area ('000 ha)						
Marginal (< 1ha)	14,545 (9.0%)	19,735 (12. 0%)	22,042 (13.4%)	24,894 (15.0%)	28,121 (17.2%)	30,088 (18.82%)
Small (1.0–2.0 ha)	19,282 (11.9%)	23,169 (14.1%)	25,708 (15.6%)	28,827 (17.4%)	30,722 (18.8%)	32,260 (20.18%)
Semi-medium (2.0–4.0 ha)	29,999 (18.5%)	34,645 (21.2%)	36,666 (22.3%)	38,375 (23.2%)	38,953 (23.8%)	38,305 (23.96%)
Medium (4.0–10.0 ha)	48,234 (29.8%)	48,543 (29.6%)	47,144 (28.6%)	44,752 (27.0%)	44,752 (25.3%)	38,125 (23.84%)
Large (>10 ha)	50,064 (30.9%)	37,705 (23.0%)	37,705 (20.1%)	28,659 (17.3%)	24,163 (14.8%)	21,124 (13.21%)
Total	162,124 (100%)	163,797 (100%)	164,562 (100%)	165,507 (100%)	163,357 (100%)	159,903 (100%)
Average size of operational holding (ha)						
Marginal (< 1ha)	0.41	0.39	0.39	0.39	0.40	0.40
Small (1.0–2.0 ha)	1.44	1.44	1.43	1.43	1.42	1.41
Semi-medium (2.0–4.0 ha)	2.81	2.78	2.77	2.76	2.73	2.72
Medium (4.0–10.0 ha)	6.08	6.02	5.96	5.09	5.84	5.80
Large (> 10 ha)	18.1	17.41	17.21	17.33	17.21	17.18
Total	2.3	1.84	1.69	1.57	1.41	1.32

Source: GOI, 2007a

have gained a significant share during the last decade. The share of foodgrains in total cropped area has declined from about 77 per cent in the triennium 1970–72 to about 65.6 per cent in TE 2000–02 (Figure 2.8).

Area under rice has remained almost constant, about 23 per cent of the cropped area, while area under wheat has increased from 11.5 per cent to 14 per cent. However, area under coarse cereals has declined significantly, from about 27 per cent to 16 per cent. Area under pulses has also declined, from 13.3 per cent to nearly 12 per cent. Area under other crops, mainly fruits and vegetables, fibres, and condiments and spices has increased during the last decade.

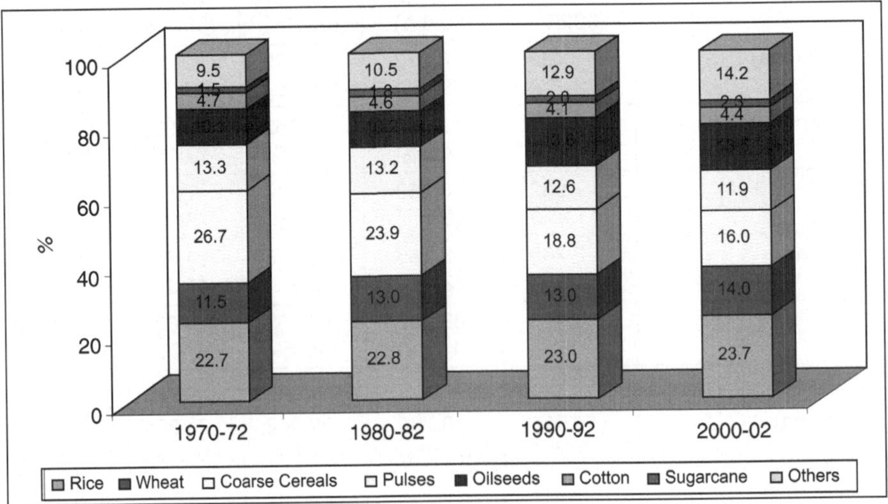

Fig. 2.8: Shifts in Cropping Patterns

Source: Agricultural Statistics at a Glance, Various issues.

Agriculture growth rate has become stagnant, as is productivity growth. Trends in growth rates of production and yield of principal crops during the post-Green Revolution period (1966–67 to 2004–05) are presented in Figures 2.9 and 2.10.

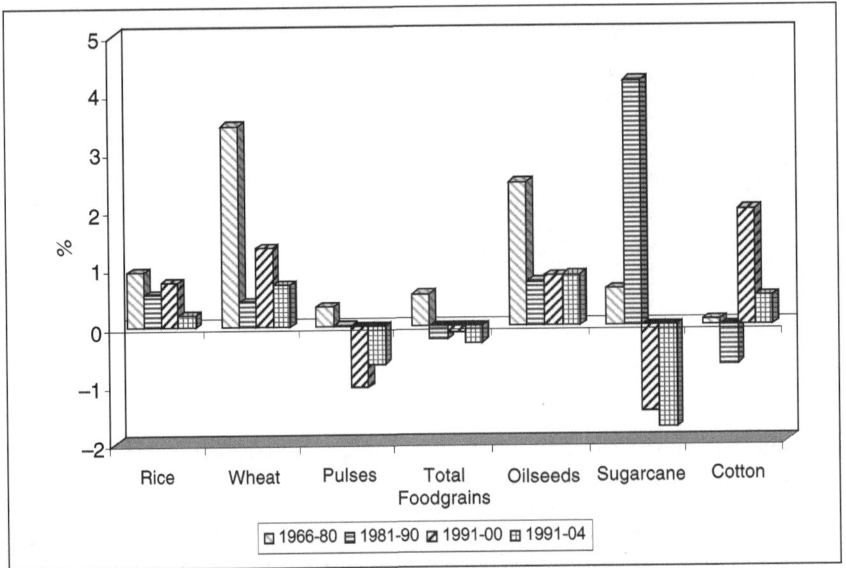

Fig. 2.9: Growth Rates of Production of Principal Crops

Source: Agricultural Statistics at a Glance, Various issues.

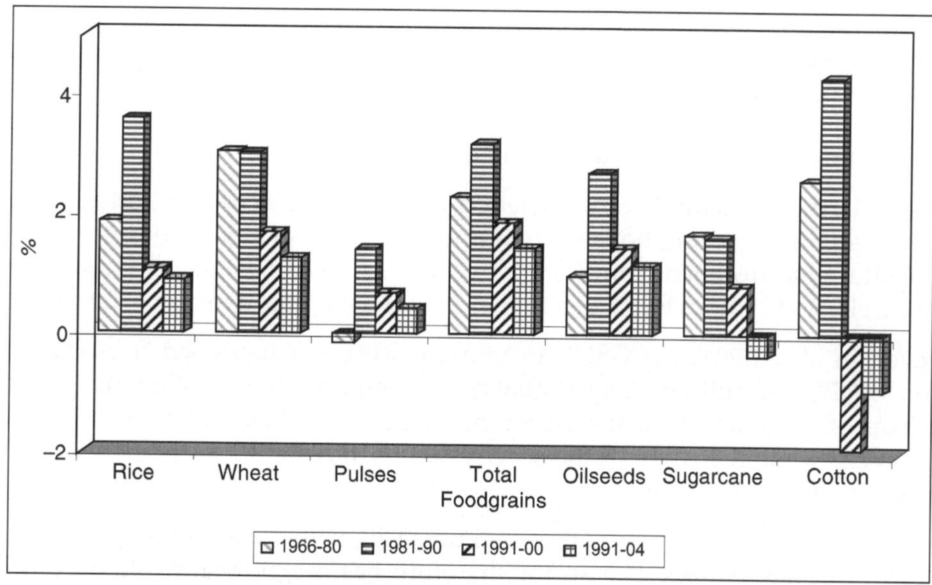

Fig. 2.10: Growth Rates of Productivity of Principal Crops

Source: Agricultural Statistics at a Glance, Various issues

Pulse production has declined considerably owing to declines in crop area and productivity. There was a significant shift from pulses to superior cereals (such as

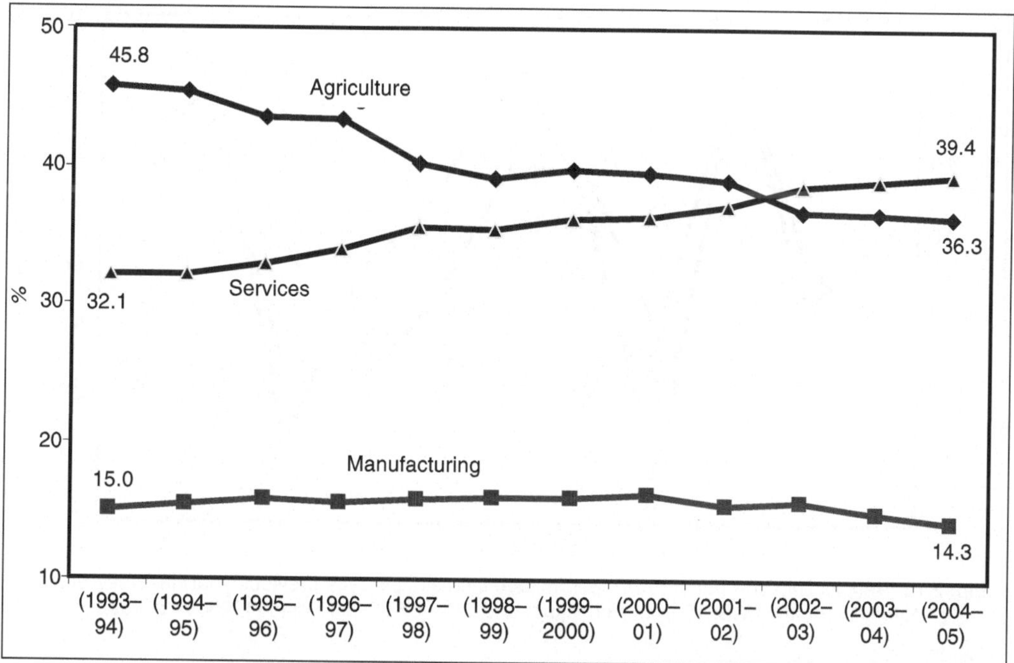

Fig. 2.11: Share of Agriculture in Punjab's GDP (1993–94 prices)

Source: CSO, 2007.

wheat and rice) and non-foodgrain crops (mainly fruits and vegetables). Growth rates of production for most crops were significantly lower during the 90s owing to lower growth in productivity.

Agrarian and Ecological Crisis in Punjab

There has been a structural transformation in the Punjab economy in recent times, with the agricultural sector, however, continuing to play an important role. The share of agriculture has declined from 45.8 per cent in 1993–94 to 36.3 per cent in 2004–05 (Figure 2.11), which though is much higher than the national average of 20.5 per cent.

However, in absolute terms GSDP from agriculture has increased from ₹ 13,853.6 million to ₹ 19,145.7 million at an annual compound growth rate of nearly 2 per cent. The share of the manufacturing sector has marginally fallen from 15 per cent to 14.3 per cent while the share of the services sector has significantly increased, from 32.1 per cent to 36.3 per cent.

Nearly two-thirds of the population in Punjab lives in rural areas and is mainly dependent on agriculture. The sector therefore has a significant influence on the growth of the state economy. In six out of 11 years (1994–95 to 2004–05), agricultural GSDP witnessed a lower growth compared with the previous year, and this lower growth pushed the overall economic growth to the lower side. Figure 2.12 shows the relationship between growth in agricultural GSDP and total GSDP.

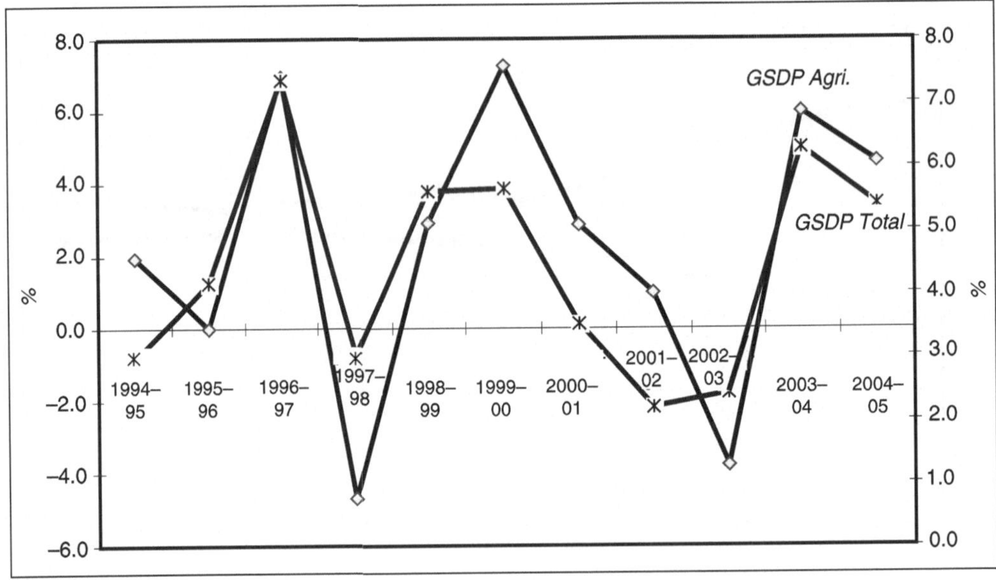

Fig. 2.12: Relationship between Growth (percentage increase over the previous year) in Gross State Domestic Product (GSDP) from Agriculture and Total GSDP in Punjab (1993–94 prices)

Source: CSO, 2007.

The Slow Growth in Agriculture

The slow rate of agricultural growth at the national and state level is worrying policy makers. The sector grew at an average annual rate of 2.1 per cent from 1993–94 to 2004–05. This is in contrast to the industry and services sectors, which grew at 5.04 and 6.45 per cent respectively (Figure 2.13). Punjab's agricultural growth, one of the highest in the 1970s and 1980s, has been below the national average during the 1990s and 2000s. Since agriculture still constitutes about 36 per cent of Punjab's GSDP (as against 20 per cent at the all-India level), slow agricultural growth has resulted in overall economic decline. Punjab's GSDP growth rate was the third lowest, above only that of Uttar Pradesh and Madhya Pradesh (Figure 2.14). The agriculture growth rate was below the national average as well as below that of states such as West Bengal, Andhra Pradesh, and Uttar Pradesh.

States which are heavily dependent on agriculture have recorded witnessed a lower growth in agriculture. Weak agricultural performance, especially among the poorest states such as Orissa, Bihar, and Rajasthan, makes it difficult to reduce income disparities. Similarly, poor performance in states such as Punjab and Haryana amplifies the challenge of achieving overall economic development. Table 2.3 illustrates the wide disparity in performance of both agricultural and allied sectors and overall GDP growth in major states.

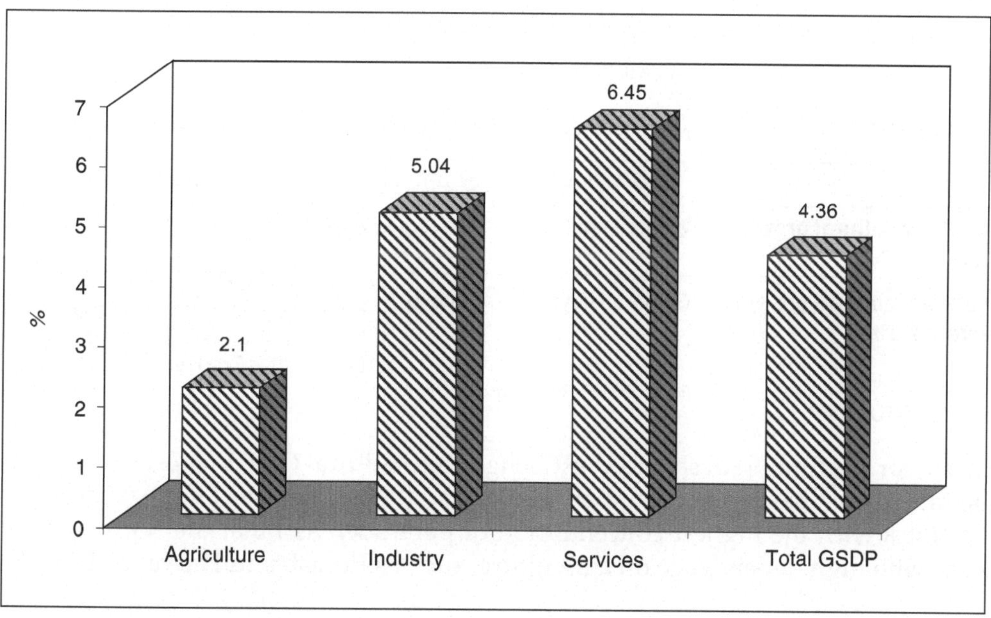

Fig. 2.13: Growth Rates in Agriculture, Industry, Services and Total GSDP (1993–94 constant prices)

Source: CSO, National Accounts Statistics, Various issues.

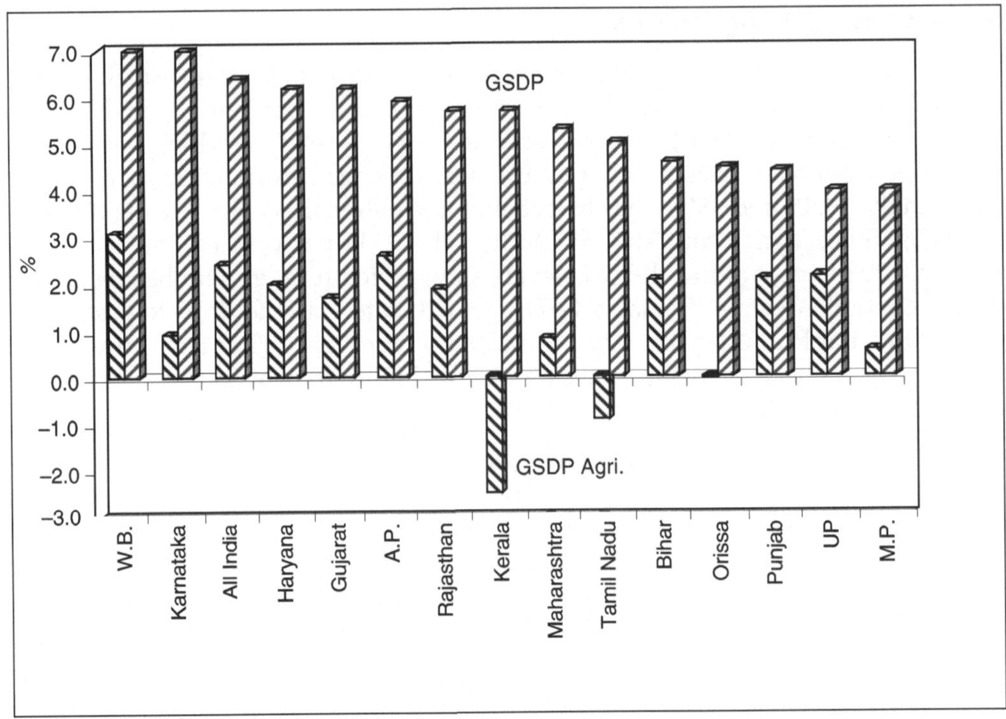

Fig. 2.14: Growth Rate in GSDP and GSDP from Agriculture in Selected States (1993–94 Prices)

Source: CSO, National Accounts Statistics, Various issues.

Table 2.3: Classification by Agricultural and Allied Sectors' GDP and Total GDP Growth Rates

	GDP Growth Rate ≥ 6%	*GDP Growth Rate < 6%*
GDP agricultural growth rate ≥ 2.4%	West Bengal	Andhra Pradesh
GDP agricultural growth rate ≤ 2.4%	Gujarat, Haryana, Karnataka	Bihar, Kerala, Orissa, Maharashtra, Madhya Pradesh, Rajasthan, Tamil Nadu, Uttar Pradesh

Source: CSO, 2007.

Except for Andhra Pradesh and West Bengal, agricultural GDP in most states grew at the rate of less than 2.5 per cent per year during the last decade. Of great concern are the states with the highest concentration of poor such as Bihar and Orissa, as well those with high dependence on agriculture, such as Punjab and Haryana (Table 2.4).

Dominance of the Rice-Wheat Cropping System

Cropped area in Punjab has increased from 5.678 million hectares in 1970–71 to 7.941 million hectares in 2000–01. Whole the cropped area has remained almost constant,

Table 2.4: Association between Share of Agriculture in GDP and Average Annual Growth Rate in GDP from Agriculture and Allied Sectors (1993–94 prices)

	High Dependence on Agriculture (> 20% Share in GDP)	*Low Dependence on Agriculture (< 20% Share in GDP)*
High growth in agriculture (≥ 2.5%)	Andhra Pradesh (2.6%), West Bengal (3.1%)	Kerala (–2.5%)
Low growth in agriculture (< 2.5%)	Punjab (2.1%), Bihar (2.1%) Haryana (2.0%), Orissa (–0.02%), Madhya Pradesh (0.6%), Rajasthan (1.9%), Uttar Pradesh (2.2%)	Gujarat (1.7%), Karnataka (0.9%), Maharashtra (0.8%), Kerala (–2.5%), Tamil Nadu (–0.9%)

Source: CSO, 2007.

while the net sown area has declined from about 4.25 million hectares in 2001–02 to 4.20 million hectares in 2004–05, owing to the diversion of productive land to non-agricultural uses. The cropping intensity in Punjab has increased from 140 per cent in 1970–71 to about 189 per cent in 2004–05, as against the national average of about 133 per cent. The share of foodgrains in the cropped area has increased from about 73 per cent in 1980–81 to 79.6 per cent in 2003–04 (Figure 2.15) while at the all-India level the share of foodgrains in the cropped area has declined from 74 per cent to 65.5 per cent (Figure 2.16). Rice and wheat account for more than three quarters of the cropped area. Pulses account for less than 1 per cent of acreage. In 1980–81, the share of rice in the cropped area was 17.5 per cent, wheat accounted for 41.6 per cent, and coarse cereals accounted for 7.7 per cent. A significant increase in area under rice has taken place at the expense of coarse cereals, pulses, and oilseeds. Area under rice increased to 33.1 per cent and that under wheat to 43.6 per cent in 2003–04, while the share of coarse cereals declined to 2.3 per cent and pulses to less than 1 per cent.

The reasons for the increase in area under rice and wheat in Punjab are the steady increase in Minimum Support Prices (MSP) of wheat and rice, especially during the 1990s, and assured procurement by the government. MSP of wheat has increased from ₹ 280 per 100 kg in 1991–92 to ₹ 750 per 100 kg in 2007–08. In the case of rice (common variety), MSP increased from ₹ 230 to ₹ 580 per 100 kg (Figure 2.17).

Punjab has become the breadbasket of India, contributing about 35 per cent of rice and 57.4 per cent of wheat procured by the Food Corporation of India (FCI) (Figure 2.18).

Rice production in Punjab has increased fifteen-fold from 688,000 tonnes in 1970–71 to 10,437,000 tonnes in 2004–05. Wheat production increased almost three-fold from 5,145,000 tonnes to 14,695,000 tonnes. However, continuous cultivation under the rice-wheat cropping system has created many agro-ecological crises in the state. These are discussed below.

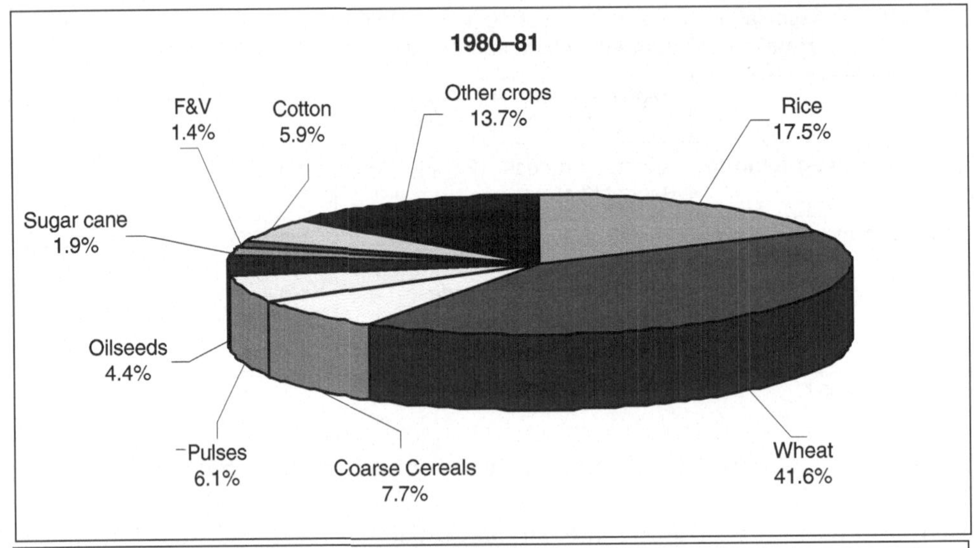

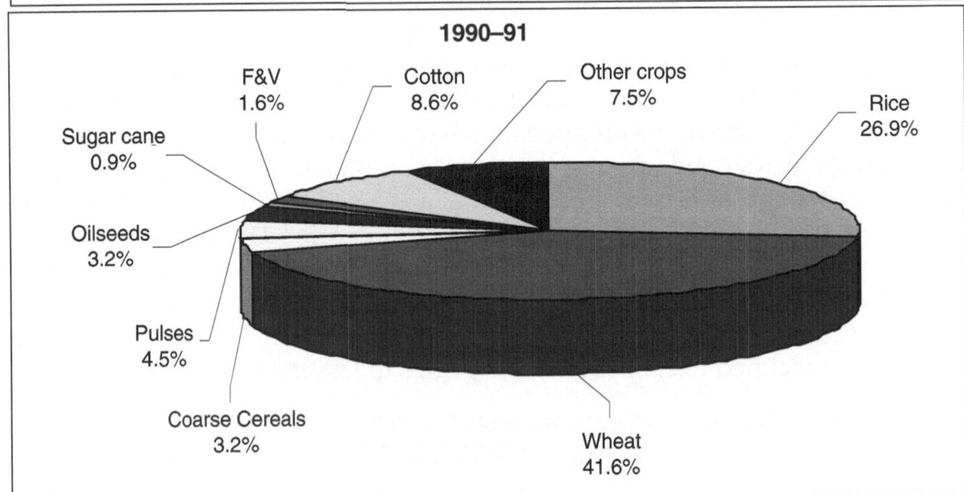

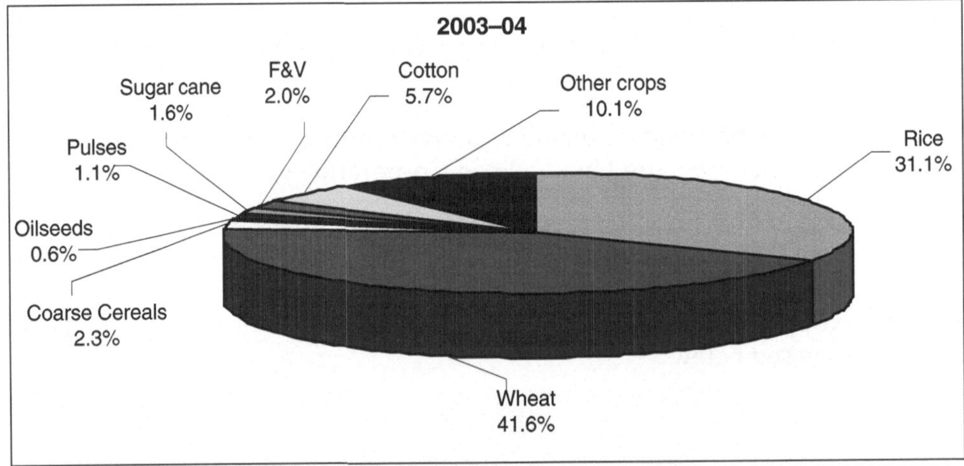

Fig. 2.15: Cropping Pattern Changes in Punjab

Source: Agricultural Statistics at a Glance, Various issues.

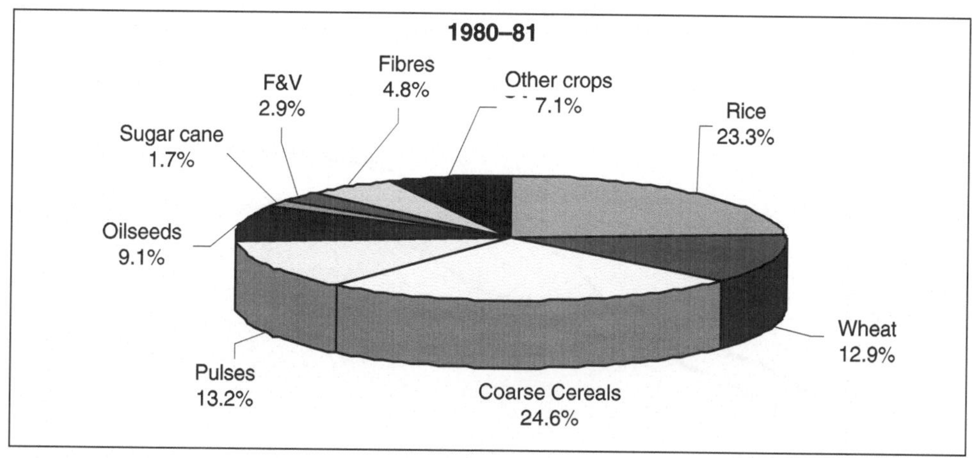

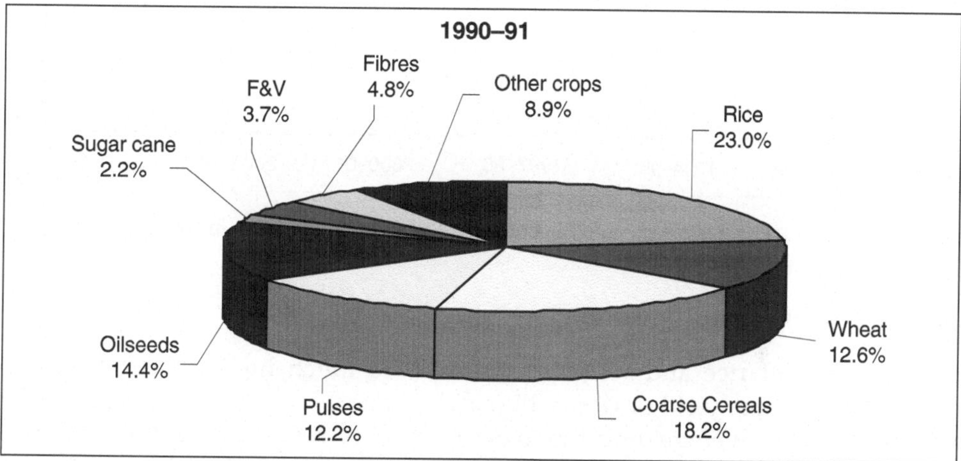

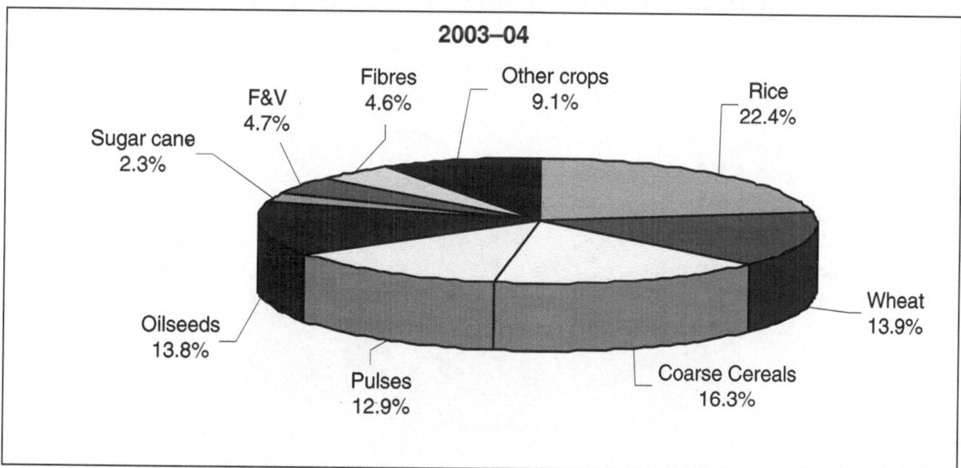

Fig. 2.16: Cropping Pattern Changes in India

Source: Agricultural Statistics at a Glance, Various issues.

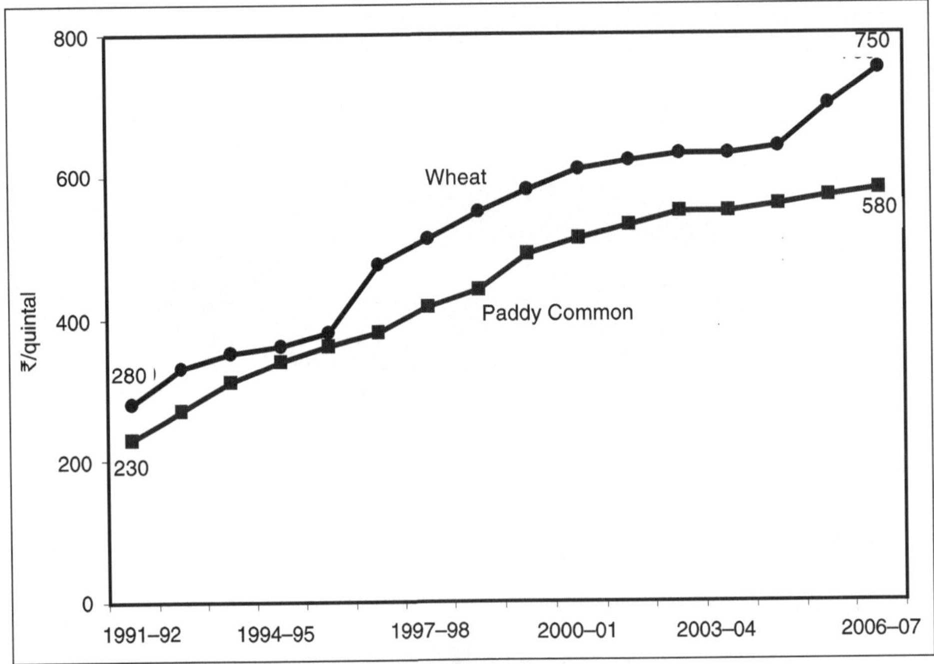

Fig. 2.17: Minimum Support Prices of Wheat and Rice in India

Source: GoI, 2007b.

Stagnant and Declining Crop Yields

Average yields of rice and wheat in Punjab are much higher than the all-India average. The average yield of rice in Punjab is around 3.9 tonnes per hectare, almost twice the national average, and the average yield of wheat is about 4.2 tonnes per hectare, compared with the national average of about 2.6 tonnes per hectare.

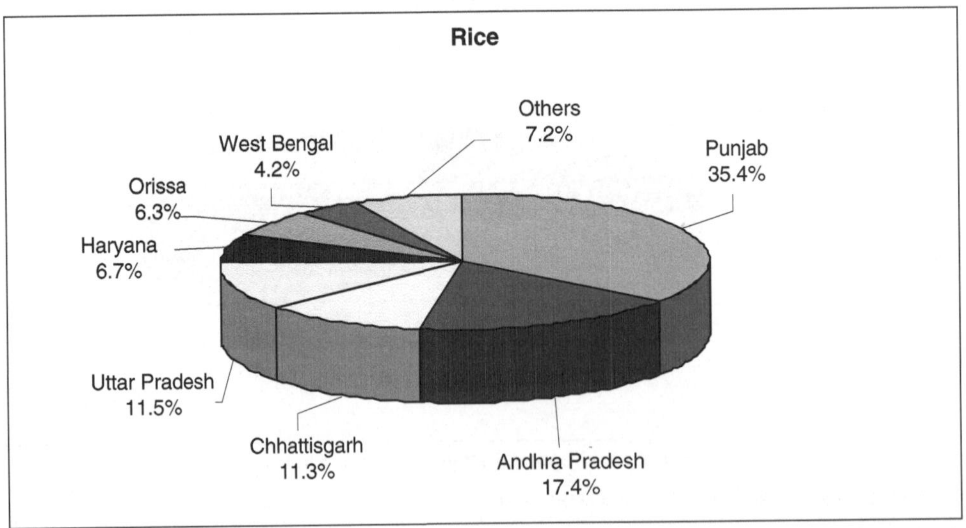

Fig. 2.18 continued

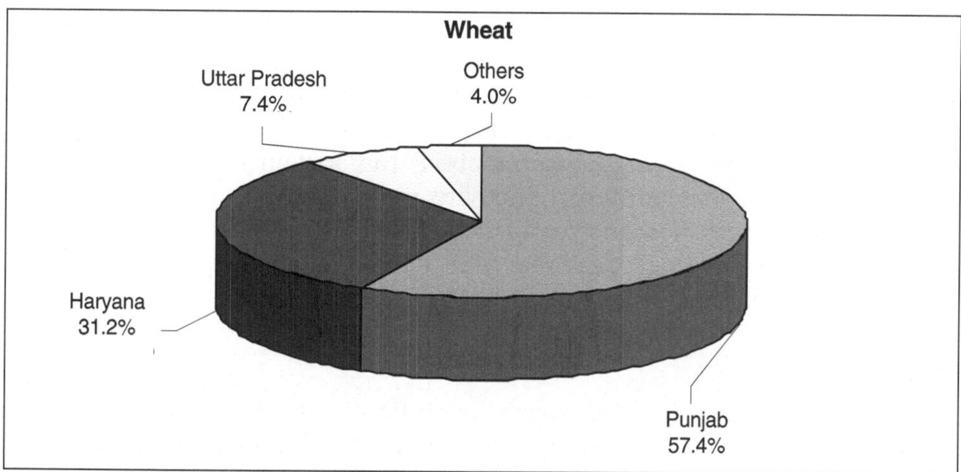

Fig. 2.18: Share in Procurement of Rice and Wheat in Major Rice and Wheat-Producing States

Source: GoI, 2007 b.

Increases in crop productivity in the state have come from the intensification of agricultural production and the adoption of yield-enhancing technologies, especially modern high-yielding varieties and fertilisers in late 1960s. However, there are indications that the per-hectare yield of wheat has been falling in Punjab for the past few years. In 1999–2000, the per-hectare average yield of wheat was about 4.7 tonnes, declining to about 4.2 tonnes/ha in 2005–06 (Figure 2.19).

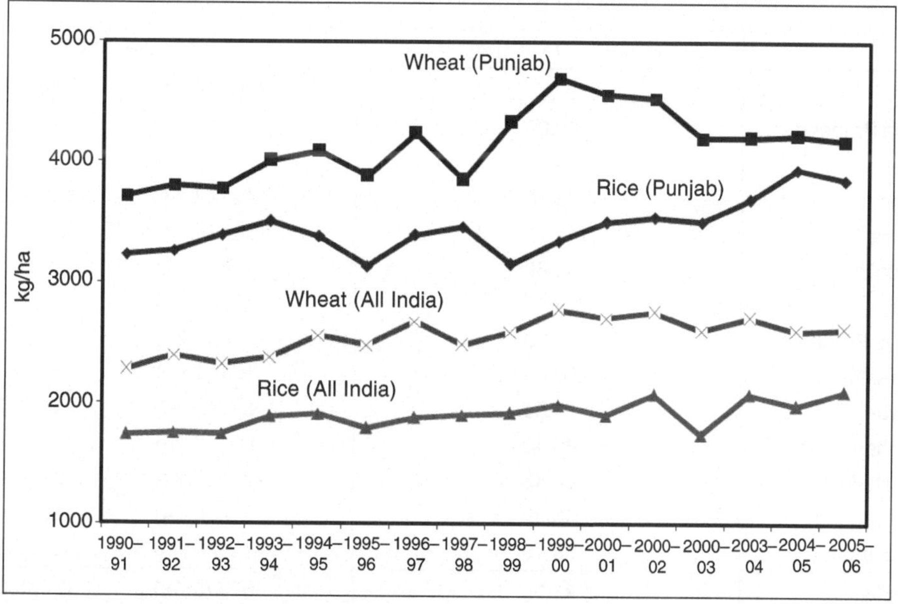

Fig. 2.19: Trends in Yields of Rice and Wheat in Punjab and India

Source: GOI, 2007a.

In the case of rice, yield has stagnated at about 3.1–3.3t/ha during the 1990s but marginally improved during the 2000s. Yields of wheat and rice have also reached a plateau at the all-India level. Stagnating productivity and production of rice and wheat in Punjab and indications that yields are declining or becoming stagnant in a rice-wheat rotation are raising concerns about the sustainability of this cropping system. Declining or stagnating productivity trends can be directly linked to the ecological consequences of intensive monoculture systems, including the build-up of soil salinity, water logging, declining soil fertility, increased soil toxicity, and increased pest populations, particularly soil pests.

Ecological Crises

For a state that spearheaded the Green Revolution in the 1960s and 1970s, Punjab today is facing a major crisis on the agricultural front. With the introduction of High-Yielding Varieties (HYVs) during the Green Revolution period and an assured market and price for marketable surplus, rice-wheat crop rotation became dominant in Punjab. The HYVs require an assured supply of irrigation water, large amounts of chemical fertilizers, and pesticides; the long-term ecological consequence of this combination are being felt now.

Groundwater Overexploitation

With rice and wheat being heavily water-dependant, farmers have every reason to over-exploit groundwater. The inevitability of groundwater extraction has also been

Table 2.5: Groundwater Resources Development in Selected States

	Groundwater Development (%)	*Number of Blocks*	
		Overexploited	*Dark/Critical*
Andhra Pradesh	25.86	118 (10.20)	79 (6.83)
Bihar	46.33	6 (1.52)	14 (3.55)
Gujarat	55.16	41 (22.78)	19 (10.56)
Haryana	112.18	30 (27.03)	13 (11.71)
Karnataka	34.60	7 (4.00)	9 (5.14)
Kerala	22.17	3 (1.99)	6 (3.97)
Madhya Pradesh	27.09	2 (0.64)	1 (0.32)
Maharashtra	37.04	154 (6.65)	72 (3.11)
Punjab	***97.66***	***81 (58.70)***	***12 (8.70)***
Rajasthan	86.42	86 (36.29)	80 (33.76)
Tamil Nadu	64.43	138 (35.84)	37 (9.61)
Uttar Pradesh	46.89	2 (0.24)	20 (2.44)
West Bengal	38.19	0	61 (22.18)
All India	**41.57**	**673 (8.49)**	**425 (5.36)**

Source: Ministry of Water Resources, http://wrmin.nic.in/

politically exploited; successive governments have even given free electricity to farmers. Water tables have fallen at alarming rates in many places. Providing free electricity for agriculture and very low rates for canal water has encouraged inefficient use of water. Intensive use of tubewell irrigation has led to depletion of water resources in Punjab. About 98 per cent of groundwater resources in the state have already been exploited (Table 2.5). Nearly 59 per cent of blocks in the state, the highest in the country, have overexploited groundwater resources, and another 12 per cent are in the dark/critical zone. On the other hand, injudicious use of canal-irrigation water without regard to soil conditions and inadequate attention to drainage has led to water logging and salinity in many areas.

High Use of Fertilizers

There has been a substantial increase in fertilizer consumption in the last three decades. Total NPK (N, P_2O_5 and K_2O) consumption has increased more than seven-fold (from 213,000 tonnes to 1,687,000 tonnes) between 1970–71 and 2005–06 (Figure 2.20). Per-hectare fertilizer consumption increased from about 37 kg to 221.7 kg in the same period. Fertiliser consumption in Punjab is the highest in India (Figure 2.21).

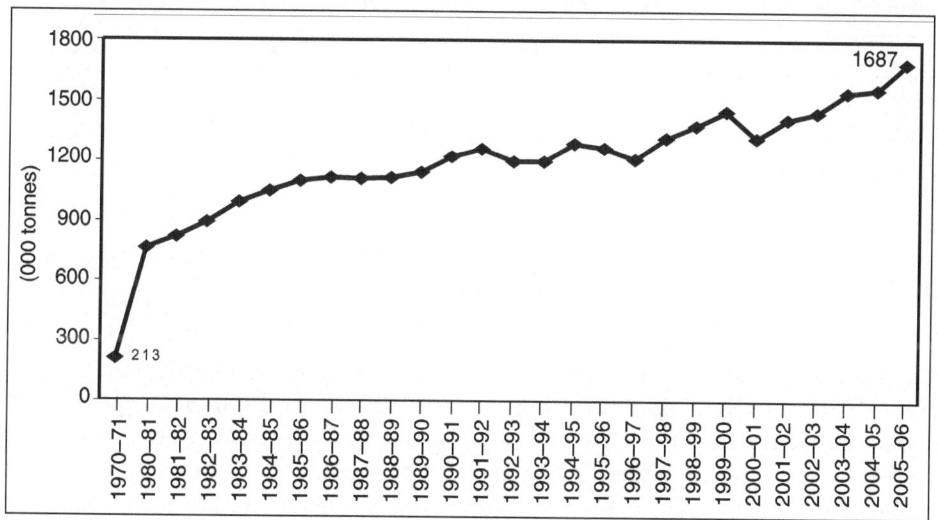

Fig. 2.20: Consumption of Chemical Fertilizers in Punjab

Source: FAI, 2006.

In addition, overuse of nitrogenous fertilizers thanks to higher subsidies on urea has led to an imbalanced use of fertilizers in the state. The N : P_2O_5 : K_2O ratio at 27.8 : 7.3 : 1.0 is one of the most distorted, as against the generally recommended ratio 4 : 2 : 1 (Table 2.6).

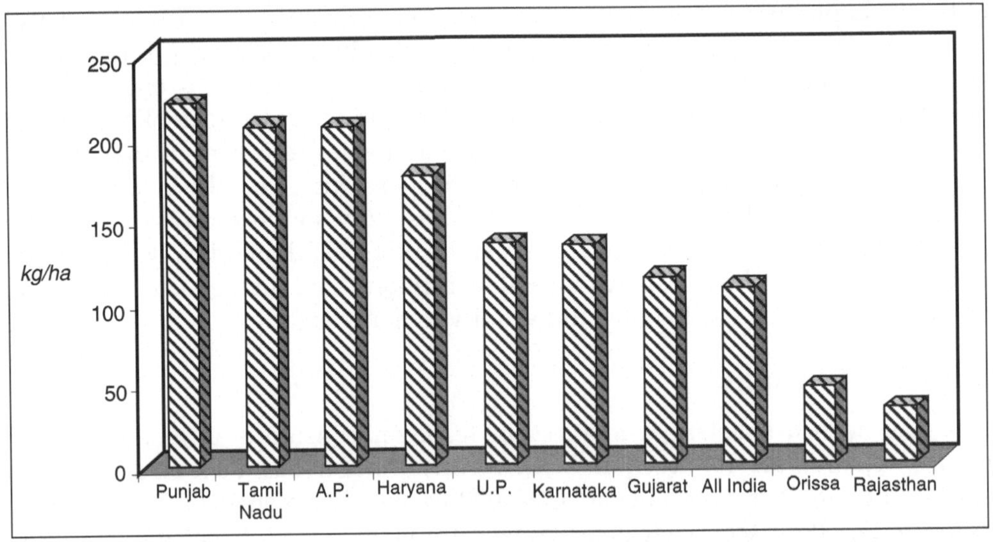

Fig. 2.21: Per hectare Use of Fertilizers in Selected States in India: 2006–07

Table 2.6: Consumption Ratio of N and P_2O_5 in Relation to K_2O in Punjab and India: 2005–06

	N	P_2O_5	K_2O
Punjab	27.8	7.3	1.0
All-India	5.3	2.2	1.0
Recommended	4.0	2.0	1.0

Source: FAI, 2006

Diversification through Contract Farming

Concerns about the sustainability of intensive cultivation of rice and wheat in Punjab were expressed as early as the mid-1980s. The government constituted a committee with Dr. S.S. Johl as Chairman in 1984–85 to look into the problem. It suggested a need to diversify agriculture in the state and shifting of at least 20 per cent of the area under rice and wheat crops in general, but rice in particular, to other competitive and profitable crops such as fruits and vegetables. However, no action was taken on this report. In the late 1990s and 2000s when the impacts of agrarian and ecological crises (declining productivity, depleting groundwater table, deteriorating soil quality, soil and water pollution/degradation, etc.) in the state became clearly visible, the government set up another committee headed by Dr. S.S. Johl to recommend remedial measures. The committee recommended that one million hectares under rice and wheat be shifted to other crops such as oilseeds and pulses which have a lower water requirement and are ecology and soil-friendly, and those farmers who diversify should be compensated with ₹ 12,500 per hectare.

An ambitious programme to encourage diversification through contract farming became the cornerstone of the government's strategy. A multi-crop, multi-year contract farming scheme was launched by the state government to promote diversification, and Punjab Agro Foodgrains Corporation (PAFC) was designated as the nodal agency for promoting and coordinating contract farming and diversification of agriculture. The objective of contract farming was not to increase yields but to preserve natural resources such as land and water. Contract farming was first initiated in spring 2002, covering about 22000 acres with 9000 farmers (PAFC, 2007).

Several restrictions existed on the participation of the private/corporate sector in agriculture and all related activities. For example, the Essential Commodities Act (ECA) of 1955 restricted trade in food products to licensed traders. Food processing was reserved for the small-scale sector. Most importantly, the Agricultural Produce Marketing Committee (APMC) Act required that farm produce be sold only at designated government markets through registered intermediaries. Under the Act, the private sector/processing industry could not buy directly from farmers. Farmers were also restricted from entering into direct contract with any buyer because the produce was required to be channelled through regulated markets. These restrictions acted as a disincentive to farmers, trade, and industries. Amending the restrictive APMC Act became a priority. The central government drafted a model APMC Act (since agriculture falls under the jurisdiction of state governments) in 2002, which allowed private players to set up markets not regulated by APMCs. Under the new Act, it was not necessary to bring agricultural produce covered under contract farming to APMC/private markets; it could be sold directly from farmers' fields to contract farming sponsors. Several state governments have already initiated steps to allow farmers to sell their produce in open markets, and this has given a boost to contract farming. Punjab was one of the first states to allow private players, including national and multi-national agribusiness firms, to engage in contract farming directly with farmers.

Contract Farming in Punjab

In the late 1980s, the central government allowed Pepsi to enter the Indian market on the condition of establishing an agro-processing facility in Punjab, as part of a strategy to create employment opportunities in the state. Pepsi built a very large tomato processing plant with a capacity to process 650 tonnes of tomatoes a day. Pepsi faced problems in procuring tomatoes as tomato production in Punjab was small compared with the plant capacity. To ensure availability of tomatoes, Pepsi entered into a contract with farmers for tomato production and in turn provided better quality seed, extension services, and a package of practices. Studies in the 1990s showed that contract farming improved farmers' income, although the beneficiaries were large farmers. Pepsi sold the processing plant to Hindustan Lever once the government's condition was no longer binding, and the plant was again sold in 2000.

Besides PAFC, many national as well as international agribusiness companies are engaged in contract farming in Punjab. Pepsi procures basmati rice from farmers under contract farming. Frito-Lay, a subsidiary of Pepsi manufacturing potato chips, procures potatoes from farmers directly. Hindustan Lever has entered into contracts with farmers to procure basmati rice for export. United Breweries, the world's second largest brewer and the largest in India, in collaboration with PAFC, is growing malting barley on about 4,614 ha. The company is planning to increase the barley acreage under contract farming to 10,117 ha by 2007–08.

Agri-inputs industries in the business of seed, fertilizers, and agrochemicals, namely Escorts, Tata Chemicals, DCM Shriram Consolidated, Mahindra Shubhlabh, and ITC, have signed agreements with farmers to provide extension services and assured buyback with PAFC support. However, none of the companies involved in contract farming in the state provide all required inputs, such as pesticides, fertilisers, and more importantly credit to farmers. Most farmers are still dependent on middlemen, traders, or moneylenders for production and consumption finance. Most provide seed and extension services to contract farmers. There are certain concerns about the quality of extension services provided by almost all companies, except for a couple that have hired professional agricultural graduates for providing these services.

The Role of State Government in Contract Farming

To boost the diversification of agriculture, the Punjab government launched a comprehensive programme of contract farming in October 2002. PAFC, the nodal agency for implementing contract farming, provides or arranges high yielding varieties of seeds, technical supervision, and follow-up on agronomic practices to farmers, as well as assured buyback at MSP or agreed or market price, depending upon the crop. PAFC has adopted a model involving various stakeholders: farmers, private agribusiness firms, and government/PAFC (Figure 2.22).

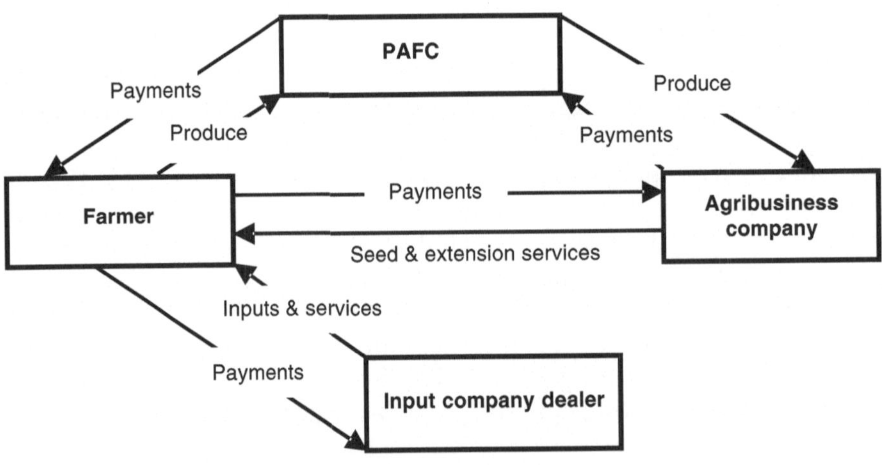

Fig. 2.22: Link between Farmers, Input Suppliers and PAFC

PAFC acts as a facilitator between farmers and agribusiness companies. PAFC entered into an agreement with agribusiness companies on behalf of farmers. Farmers sell their produce to PAFC, which in turn sells it to agribusiness companies. Payments are made to farmers through PAFC at the contract price. Once trust between farmers and company is built, PAFC withdraws and there was direct contract between farmer and agribusiness company.

In one year market prices of basmati rice crashed because of excess production, and the buyer started rejecting the produce on quality considerations. PAFC procured basmati rice at the contracted price to build confidence among farmers. Based on this experience, contracts have been made more flexible and farmers are allowed to sell outside the contract if the market price is higher than the contracted price. Even in the case of contracted prices, prices are fixed for grades, based on quality parameters. While most farmers are committed to the contract price, some farmers do take advantage of market conditions and sell the contracted quantity in the open market if the price is higher.

Private firms include a number of players such as input suppliers, extension service providers, agro-processing companies, and exporters. Because of the long and strong association of farmers with government agencies through procurement operations and supplies of inputs and services, farmers have great confidence in them. Farmers are not comfortable with private companies since they feel that they are more concerned about their own welfare than that of farmers. Moreover, farmer's entire wheat and rice marketable surplus is procured, regardless of quality, by government agencies at government-announced MSP. It was therefore extremely difficult for the private sector to get into contract farming in the initial period. With committed political leadership and dedicated bureaucracy, contract farming has shown very good results (Figure 2.23).

PAFC first started the programme in spring 2002, covering an area of about 9,000 hectares with 9,100 farmers. In 2006–07 an area of more than 280,000 hectares, involving more than 1,00,000 farmers, has been covered under a crop diversification programme through contract farming (PAFC, 2007).

As the main objective of contract farming was to shift areas from rice-wheat to less water-intensive crops, emphasis was given to crops such as basmati rice, hyola, sunflower, durum wheat, pulses, and maize (Figure 2.24).

State Interventions and Incentives

The state government has given several incentives to agribusiness companies involved in contract farming. For example, the Punjab State Agriculture Marketing Board, which was established on May 26, 1961, to control and supervise the marketing network of sale, purchase, storage, and processing of processed or unprocessed agricultural produce and establishment of markets for agricultural produce in the state, levied 2 per cent market fee on purchase or sale of all agricultural produce. In addition to this, the state government also levied 2 per cent tax for rural development fund on purchase or sale of agricultural produce. These levies acted as a disincentive for private companies to operate in agricultural markets. The state government has reduced levies to 0.25 per cent each (except for wheat and rice), leading to an aggregate saving of 3.5 per cent, which makes procurement of agricultural produce competitive. All processing units have been allowed to purchase agricultural produce directly from farmers by amending the Punjab APMC Act.

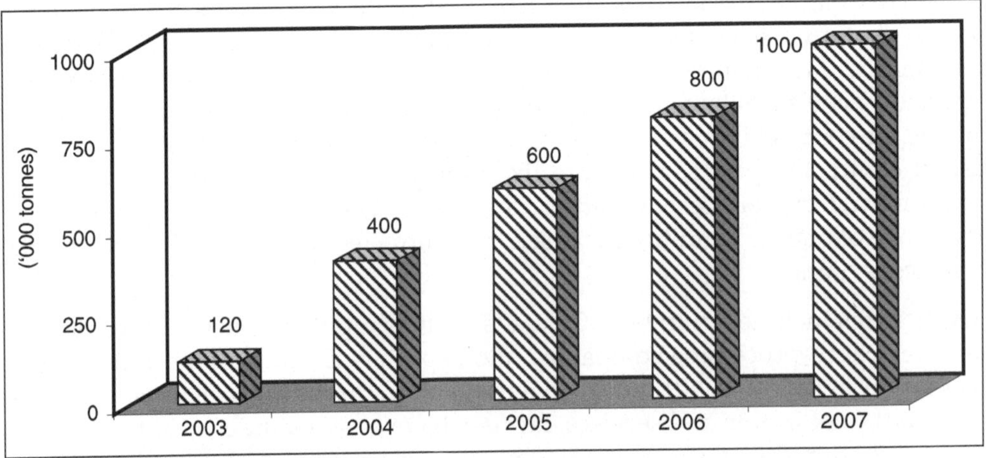

Fig. 2.23: PAFC's Five Year Plan for Contract Farming

Source: PAFC, 2007.

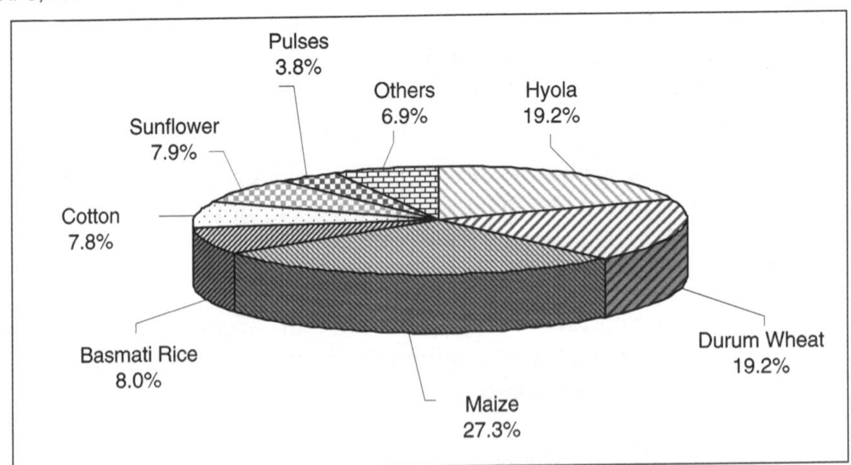

Fig. 2.24: Share of Major Crops under Contract Farming

Source: PAFC, 2007.

Similarly, companies were supposed to charge farmers for extension services which farmers were not willing to pay. PAFC paid about ₹ 200 per hectare for all contracted crops (₹ 250 per hectare for maize) to companies providing extension services for first three years. Thereafter, companies were expected to absorb these costs.

In order to promote mechanization, PAFC bought some new equipment such as a sub-soiler (soil chiseler), maize planter, dehusker-cum-thresher, sunflower combine harvester, maize-ear dehusker, rice disc puddler, etc. for use by farmers, either on a custom-hiring basis or free. In addition, it also provided financial/infrastructural support to agribusiness companies engaged in contract farming for awareness programmes.

Restrictions on stocking and movement of foodgrains, sugar, and edible oils have been also removed.

Smallholder Producers' Participation in Contract Farming

Table 2.7 shows the distribution of operational holdings and area operated by major size groups in Punjab from 1970/71 to 2000/1. There are fewer than one million operational holdings in the state. About 29.7 per cent of operational holdings in the state are small and marginal (compared to the all-India figure of 81.9 per cent), operating 7.9 per cent of the operational area (compared to 39 per cent for all-India). Land holdings in the marginal and small groups declined in the state, while medium to large group holdings have increased, which is the opposite of all-India trends. Farmers cultivating less than four hectares (marginal, small, and semi-medium farmers) form the majority in Punjab (62.5 per cent in 2000/1), cultivating about 29.7 per cent of the area. The number of operational holdings in Punjab declined from 1,375,000 in 1970/71 to 997,000 in 2000/01 (a 27.5 per cent decline), but this is increasing at the national level. The decline shows that reverse tenancy is common in Punjab. The average size of an operational holding in Punjab is more than three times of that in the country (4.03 ha compared to 1.32 ha in 2000/1), but is still small by private-sector standards.

Small and marginal farmers are generally excluded from contract farming since as companies prefer large farmers, perhaps in order to avoid problems of dealing with a large number of small and marginal farmers and high transaction costs. Studies by Rangi and Sidhu (2000), Singh (2002), Singh and Asokan (2005), and Kumar (2006) support smallholder exclusion. A recent study has shown that only 15 per cent of contract farmers in Punjab are small and marginal; the rest are medium and large farmers. Sometimes, small and marginal farmers find it profitable to lease out land, since the rent on land is higher than net returns. In addition, off-farm employment opportunities are available in the state.

Basmati Rice Contract Farming: Case Study

India is the largest producer and exporter of basmati rice. Annual production is around 1.5–2.0 million tonnes a year, of which around two-thirds is exported. The Himalayan foothills are said to produce the best basmati. Basmati rice is grown exclusively in Punjab, Haryana, and western Uttar Pradesh. Punjab is the fourth largest producer of rice, contributing over 11 per cent of rice production in the country. In 2005–06, Punjab produced 10.2 million tonnes of rice (GoI, 2007a).

Table 2.7: Operational Holdings in Punjab

Category	*1970–71*	*1980–81*	*1985–86*	*1990–91*	*1995–96*	*2000–01*
Number ('000)						
Marginal (< 1 ha)	518 (37.6%)	197 (19.2%)	256 (23.5%)	296 (26.5%)	204 (18.7%)	123 (12.3 %)
Small (1.0–2.0 ha)	260 (18.9%)	199 (19.4%)	208 (19.1%)	204 (18.3%)	183 (16.7%)	173 (17.4%)
Semi-medium (2.0–4.0 ha)	281 (20.4%)	287 (28.0%)	291 (26.7%)	289 (25.9%)	320 (29.3%)	328 (32.9%)
Medium (4.0–10.0 ha)	248 (18.0%)	269 (26.2%)	260 (23.9%)	261 (23.4%)	306 (28.0%)	301 (30.2%)
Large (> 10 ha)	69 (5.0%)	74 (7.2%)	74 (6.8%)	67 (6.0%)	80 (7.3%)	72 (7.2%)
Total	1,375 (100%)	1,027 (100%)	1,088 (100%)	1,117 (100%)	1,093 (100%)	997 (100%)
Area ('000 ha)						
Marginal (< 1ha)	–		139 (3.4%)	164 (4.1%)	122 (2.9%)	78 (1.9%)
Small (1.0–2.0 ha)	–	399 (10.3%)	311 (7.6%)	328 (8.1%)	240 (5.8%)	242 (6.0%)
Semi-medium (2.0–4.0 ha)	–	791 (20.3%)	840 (20.5%)	842 (20.9%)	833 (20.1%)	876 (21.8%)
Medium (4.0–10.0 ha)	–	1566 (40.3%)	1589 (38.7%)	1622 (40.2%)	1754 (42.3%)	1731 (43.0%)
Large (> 10 ha)	–	1135 (29.2%)	1225 (29.7%)	1077 (26.7%)	1198 (28.9%)	1096 (27.3%)
Total	–	3,890 (100%)	4,104 (100%)	4,033 (100%)	4,147 (100%)	4,022 (100%)
Average size of operational holding						
Marginal (< 1ha)	–		0.54	0.55	0.60	0.63
Small (1.0–2.0 ha)	–	1.01	1.50	1.61	1.31	1.40
Semi-medium (2.0–4.0 ha)	–	2.76	2.89	2.91	2.60	2.67
Medium (4.0–10.0 ha)	–	5.82	6.11	6.21	5.73	5.75
Large (> 10 ha)	–	15.34	16.55	16.07	14.97	15.14
Total	–	3.79	3.77	3.61	3.79	4.03

Source: Government of Punjab, 2006.

Basmati rice accounts for less than 10 per cent of the 29 million tonnes of rice traded annually in the world market (FAO, 2007). However, it generates three times more returns than non-basmati rice in both international and domestic markets. From a small beginning in the late 1970s when India exported a few thousand tonnes, there has been an upward trend, and the highest volume (1.16 million tonnes) of basmati rice exports took place in 2005-6 with record foreign exchange earnings of

₹ 30,431 million (Figure 2.25). In fact, basmati rice has been one of the fastest and consistently growing export items in recent years.

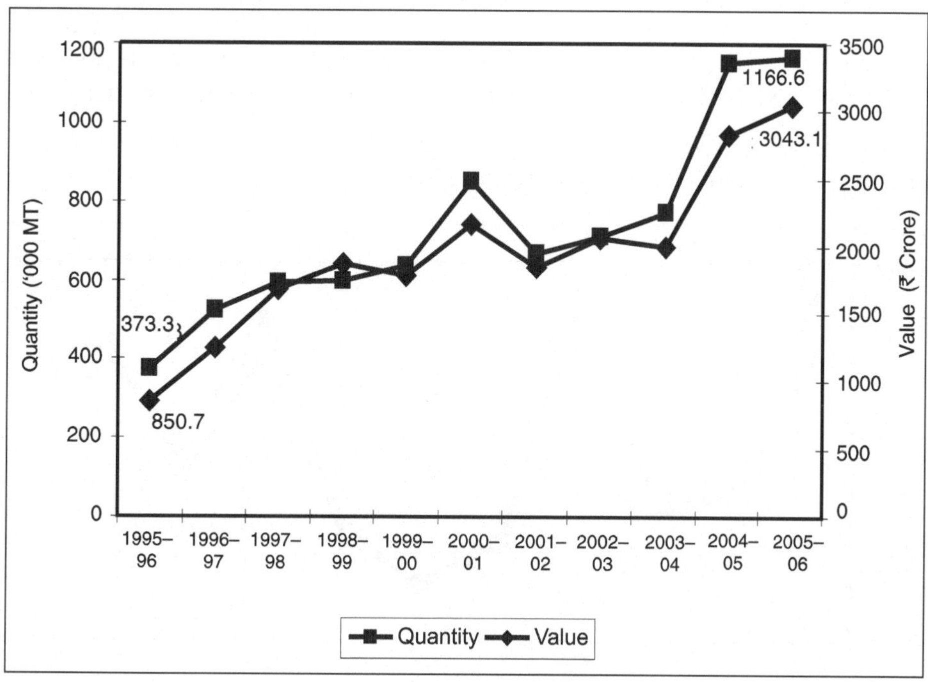

Fig. 2.25: Export of Basmati Rice

Source: APEDA 2007.

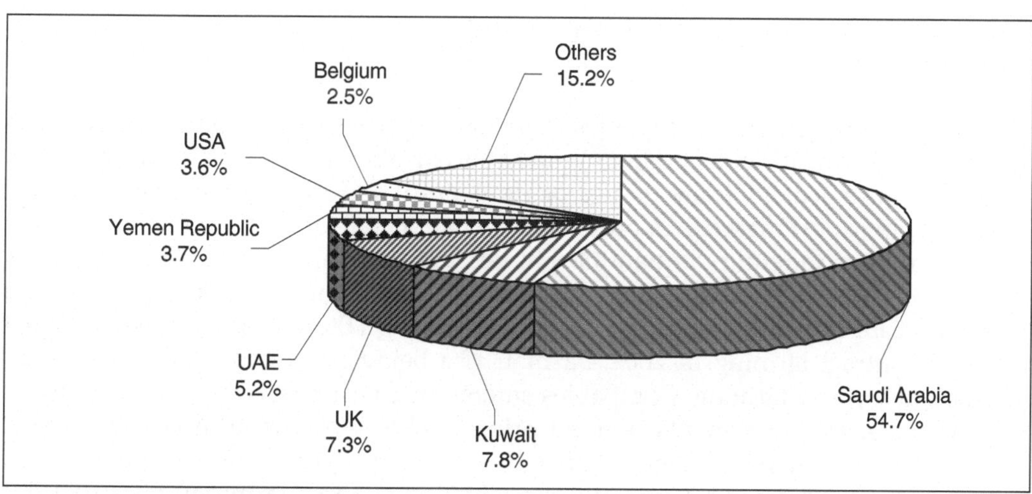

Fig. 2.26: Share of Major Importers of Indian Basmati Rice (2005–06)

Source: APEDA 2007.

India's markets for basmati rice exports are Saudi Arabia, Kuwait, United Arab Emirates, and Yemen Republic. Other importers include UK, USA, Belgium, Italy, Netherlands, and Canada. Saudi Arabia has traditionally been the largest importer of Indian basmati rice, with a share of more than 50 per cent; this is followed by Kuwait (7.8 per cent), UK (7.3 per cent) and United Arab Emirates (5.2 per cent) (Figure 2.26). Pakistan is the sole competitor in the international market for basmati rice.

Non-basmati rice is also a major item of export but exports have been fluctuating because of government intervention (Figure 2.27).

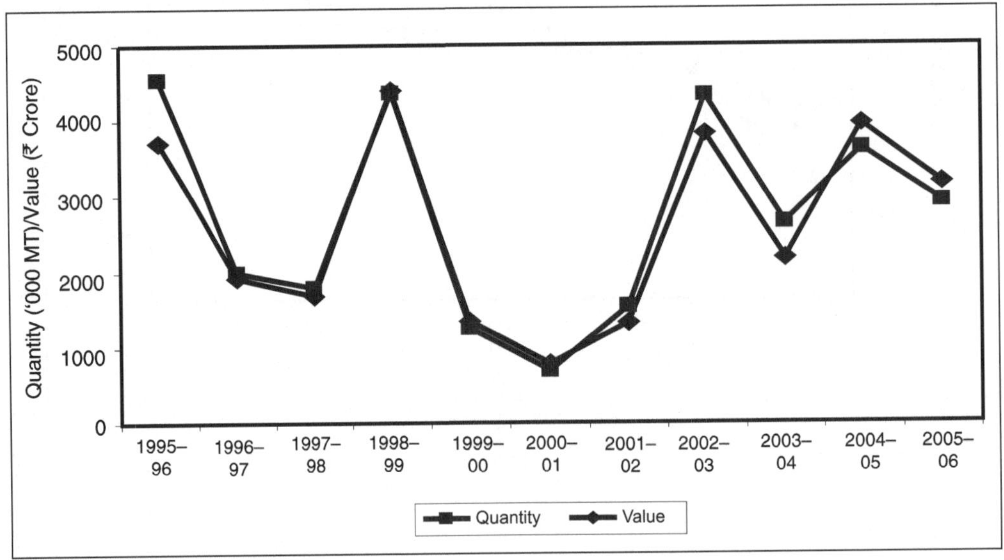

Fig. 2.27: Exports of Non-Basmati Rice

Source: APEDA, 2007.

Previously, most private companies purchased basmati rice from market yards (mandies) in Punjab and Haryana and exported after processing it according to clients' requirements. Of late, issues of traceability and quality have become very important in export markets. In order to have better control over the procurement of quality produce in required quantities, in the late 1990s and early 2000s companies started investing in backward linkages and introduced contract framing of basmati rice in Punjab. The initiative received a large boost from the state government when it allowed contract farming in 2002, basmati rice being one of the commodities for promoting contract farming. Companies entered into written as well as oral contracts with farmers. The agreements covered price; quality in terms of moisture content, admixture, broken percentage, etc.; delivery points; purchase agreement; crop management practices; etc. Companies involved in contract farming of basmati rice include Pepsi Foods, Tata Chemicals, Chambal Agritech, Naranjan Rice Exports, and Hindustan Lever.

Methodology

The study team had detailed discussions with PAFC and some companies involved in contract farming in the state about selection of crops and districts to examine the impact of corporate-led agricultural growth and recent experiments with contract farming in foodgrains. The study was restricted to basmati rice since there was no contract farming in wheat and non-basmati rice in the state. Keeping in view the time and resource constraints, the study was confined to two districts, namely Ludhiana and Jalandhar, covering about 50 farmers. However, a final sample of 29 contract farmers and 10 non-contract farmers growing basmati rice was used for the study because the rest grew other crops such as hyola and maize.

Socio-Economic Profile of Sample Households

Table 2.8 shows the demographic characteristics of sample households. Almost all households in the sample were male-headed, with an average size of six per household under contract farming and ten in non-contract households. The average age of household heads of contract farmers was lower (39 years) than that of non-contract farmers (43 years), which indicates that younger farmers have a strong preference for contract farming. Most of the sample households (for both contract and non-contract) were literate, but it is worth noting that in the case of contract farm households, household heads attained higher formal education levels than non-contract household heads, indicating that educated farmers are more keen on contract farming. The average number of years in school of the household heads in the contract farmer sample was ten; for the non-contract farmers it was seven. Crop farming is the main occupation for almost all contract and non-contract farming households. Dairy farming is a subsidiary occupation for more than 80 per cent of households. These figures reinforce the observation that most households have a mixed-crop farming system.

Table 2.8: Demographic Characteristics of Sample Households

	Contract Farmers	*Non-Contract Farmers*
Age (years)	39	43
Education (years of schooling)	10	7
Family size	6	10
Male	2	3
Female	2	3
Male children	1	2
Female children	1	2
Main occupation (%)		
Agriculture	96.5	100
Subsidiary occupation (%)		
Dairy	86.2	80.0
Others	13.8	20.0

Source: Field Survey.

Land Ownership

The land ownership pattern of sample households is shown in Table 2.9.

Table 2.9: Land Ownership Pattern in Sample Households (ha)

	Contract Farmers		*Non-Contract Farmers*	
	2007	*2002*	*2007*	*2002*
Owned land	5.5	5.5	1.6	1.6
Leased-in	5.0	3.0	3.2	1.5
Leased-out	0.1	0.0	0.0	0.0
Operational holding	10.5	8.4	4.8	3.1
Terms of lease				
Fixed rent (%)	100	92.3	100	100
Share cropping (%)	0	6.7	0	0
Average lease (Rs/ha)	25,755	20,910	23,887	20,591

Source: Field Survey.

The average size of operational holdings was larger (10.5 ha) in the case of contract farmers than for non-contract farmers (4.8 ha). In the case of contract farmers, the majority of households (41 per cent) have an average operation holding of more than 10 ha, followed by 28 per cent of households having 4–10 ha, while the proportion of small and marginal farmers (~2 ha) was only 7 per cent. In contrast, the proportion of farmers with an operational holding of less than 4 ha (the average farm size of the state) was nearly 60 per cent. These results show clearly that medium and large farmers are major beneficiaries of contract farming in the state.

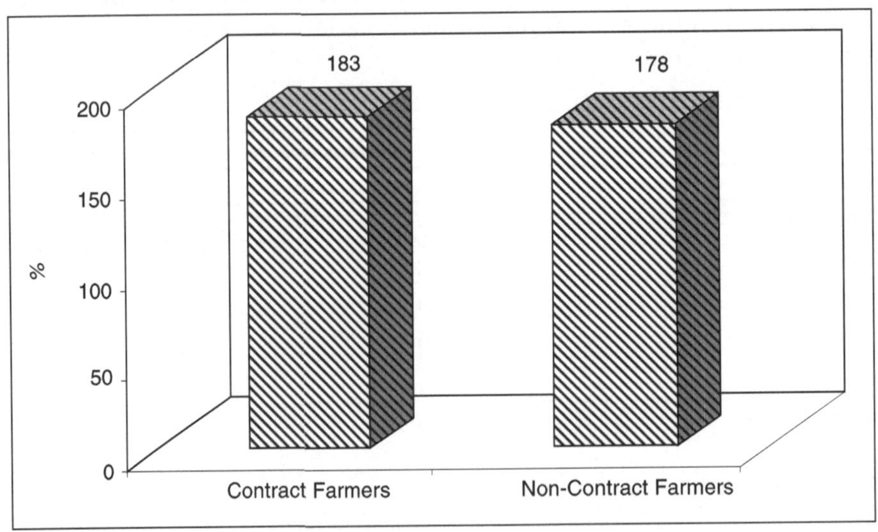

Fig. 2.28: Cropping Intensity in Sample Households

Source: Field Survey.

Tenancy is allowed in the state, and leasing of land is quite common. The average area under lease is higher (5 ha) in the case of contract farmers than non-contract farmers (3.2 ha). Area under lease increased from 3 ha in 2002 to 5 ha in 2007 in the case of contract farmers; the corresponding figures for non-contract farmers are 1.5 ha and 3 ha. The data show that mainly medium and large farmers are leasing in land to increase their operational holdings in order to enter into contract farming, which most companies prefer. Fixed rent and payment in cash are the dominant practices, and rent is fixed per hectare. The average rent per hectare per year in the study area was higher (₹ 25,755) in the case of contract farmers than for non-contract farmers (₹ 23,887). The average cropping intensity is marginally higher (183 per cent) in the case of contract farmers than for non-contract farmers (Figure 2.28).

Cropping Pattern

Farmers in the study area grow a variety of crops (Figure 2.29). In contract households, rice (basmati and non-basmati) is the main crop, occupying 41 per cent of

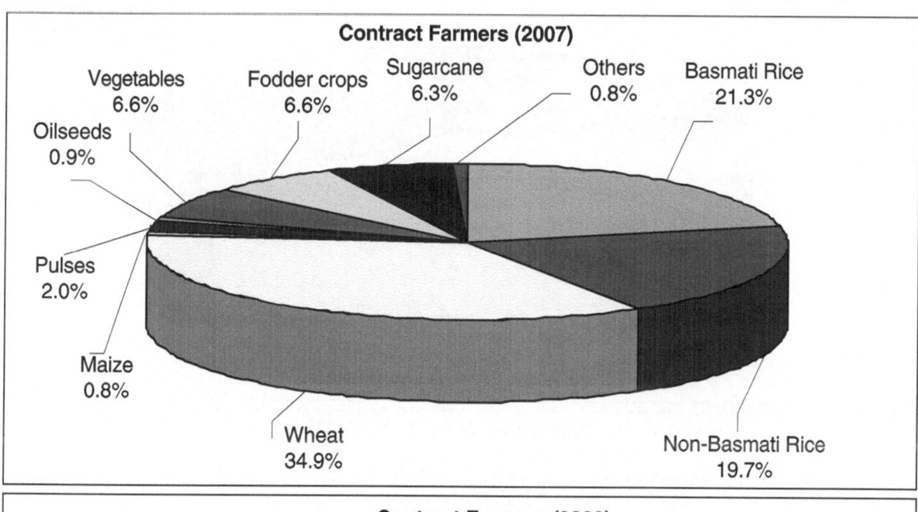

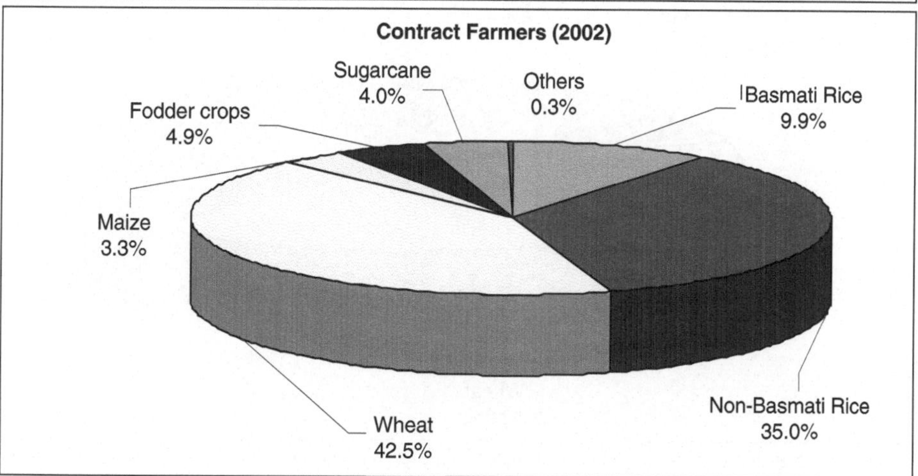

Fig. 2.29: Cropping Pattern Shifts in Sample Contract Farmer Households

the gross cropped area during kharif (autumn). Wheat occupies 34.9 per cent in rabi (spring); the two crops account for over three-quarters of the cropped area. Vegetables and sugarcane are other important crops, occupying about 13 per cent of the gross cropped area. The average area allocated to fodder crops is about 6 per cent. Area under basmati rice increased between 2002 and 2007, whereas that under non-basmati rice declined.

The cropping pattern on non-contract farms is also dominated by rice (37 per cent) in kharif and wheat (37.1 per cent) in rabi, accounting for nearly three-quarters of the gross cropped area (Figure 2.30). Sugarcane accounted for over 7 per cent of the acreage, followed by oilseeds (6.2 per cent), and fodder crops (6.2 per cent). Area

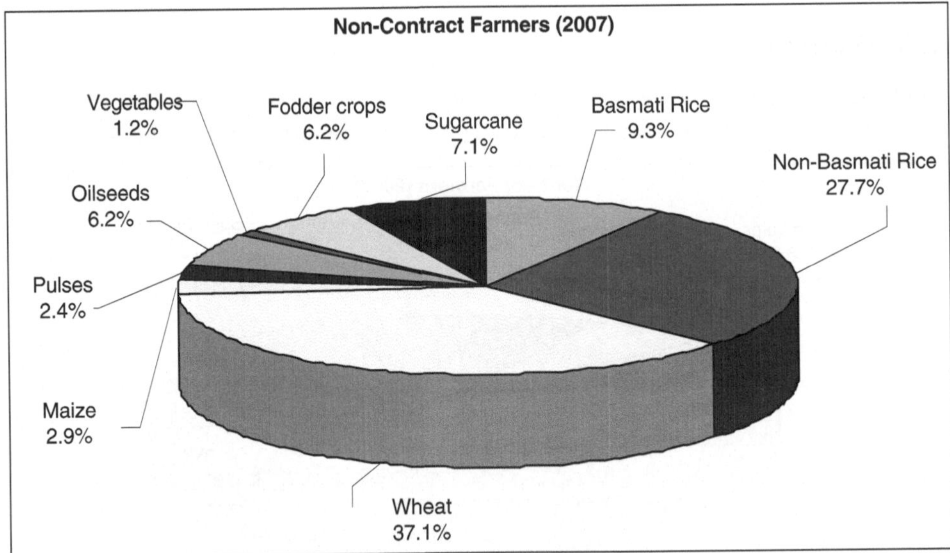

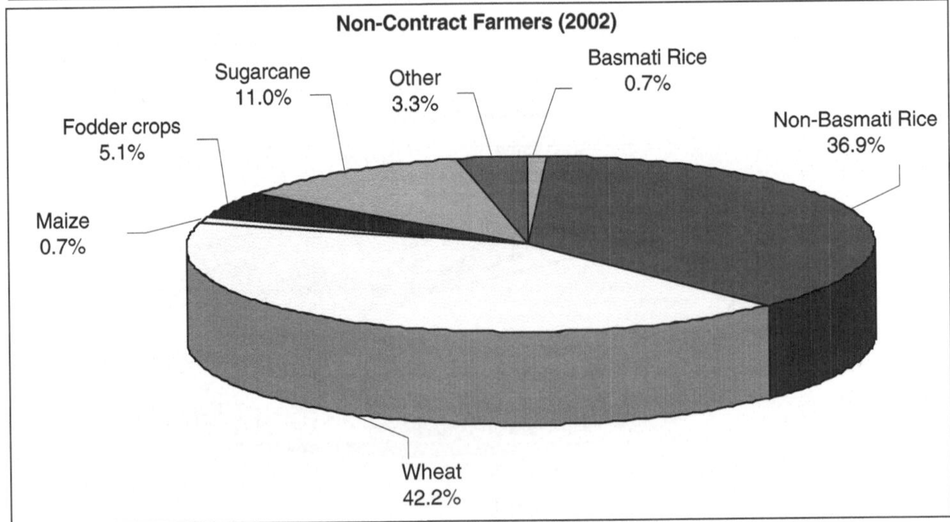

Fig. 2.30: Cropping Pattern Shifts in Sample Non-Contract Farmer Households

under basmati rice increased between 2002 and 2007 that under non-basmati rice declined (Figure 2.30).

It is interesting to note that area under basmati rice is significantly higher (21.3 per cent) in the case of contract farmers than non-contract farmers (9.3 per cent). In contrast, area under non-basmati rice is higher (27.7 per cent) in the case of non-contract farmers (19.7 per cent). There has been a shift from water-intensive non-basmati rice to basmati rice in the case of both contract and non-contract farmers after contract farming was introduced in the state. However, this shift is more pronounced for contract farmers than non-contract farmers. These results show clearly the impact of government efforts to shift areas from water-intensive non-basmati rice to less water-intensive basmati rice.

Impact of Contract Farming

Contract farming has been used to promote new high-value crops, which are more input intensive, risky, and market dependent for profitability; to lower costs, either by yield improvement or by cutting input costs through better extension services; and to raise returns by adding value to primary produce. In order to examine the impact of contract farming in yields, we compared productivity levels of major crops such as rice (basmati and non-basmati) and wheat between 2002 and 2007 on contract farms as well as between contract and non-contract households in 2007. The results are presented in Figures 2.31 and 2.32.

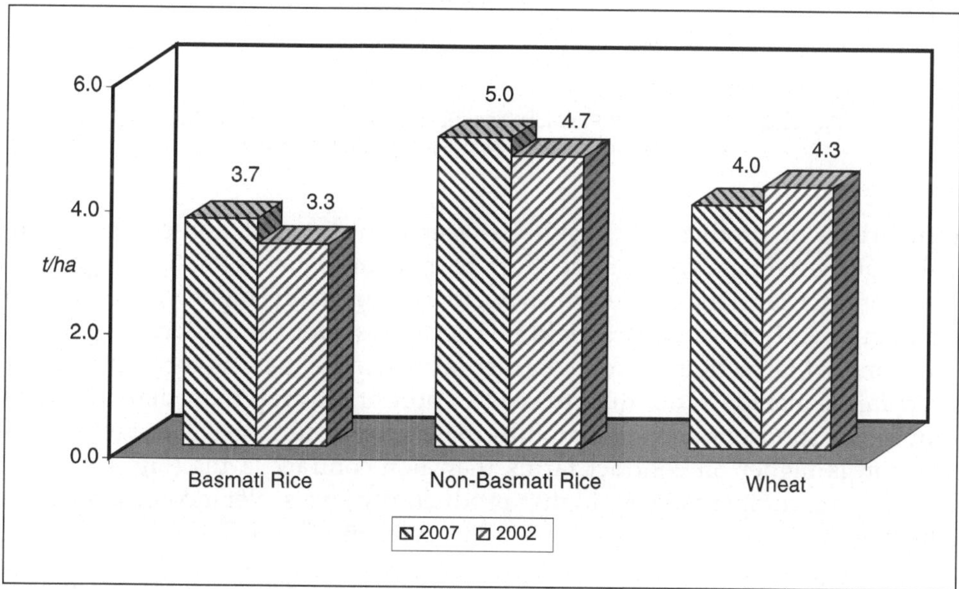

Fig. 2.31: Trends in per-hectare Productivity of Rice and Wheat on Contract Farms

Source: Field Survey.

Per hectare productivity of basmati rice under contract farming showed an increase of about 12 per cent (3.7 tonnes in 2007 compared with 3.3 tonnes in 2002), followed by non-basmati rice (a 6.4 per cent increase). Wheat productivity witnessed a declining trend: yield declined from 4.3t/ha in 2002 to 4t/ha in 2007, which is consistent with state level productivity trends (Figure 2.31). Because of an increase in crop productivity, area under basmati rice has also increased. Many farmers believe that better quality seeds supplied by the companies along with better extension services have been responsible for increased crop yields.

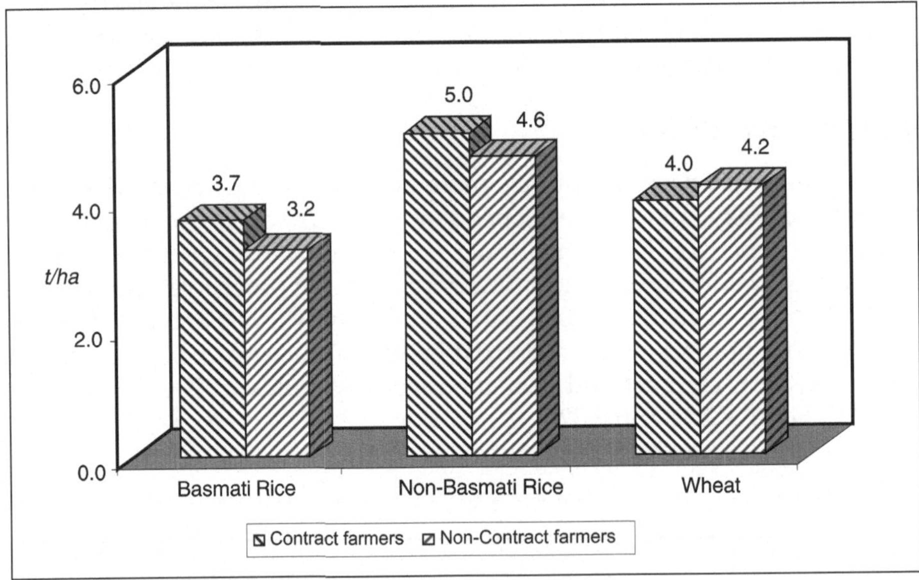

Fig. 2.32: Comparison of Productivity of Basmati and Non-Basmati Rice and Wheat on Contract and Non-Contract Farms (2007)

Source: Field Survey.

A comparison of productivity levels between contract and non-contract farmers reveals that the average yield of rice (both basmati and non-basmati) is higher in the case of contract farmers, while wheat yield is marginally higher on non-contract farms (Figure 2.32). Basmati rice yield per hectare is about 16 per cent higher in the case of contract farmers than non-contract farmers. The reasons for higher yield on contract farms include better quality seeds, appropriate crop management practices introduced by sponsors, and close monitoring of crop at all stages. The average cost of production is higher on contract farms than non-contract farms (Figure 2.33), but higher costs are compensated by higher productivity levels. Net income per hectare is also higher on contract farms than non-contract farms (Figure 2.34).

Perceived Benefits of Contract Farming

In order to understand the perceived benefits of and constraints on adoption of contract farming, selected households were asked to list the reasons for adopting contract farming. Assured market price is the most important reason for adopting contract farming (Table 2.10). Assured price ranks second (52 per cent of respondents), followed by better extension services (45 per cent of respondents).

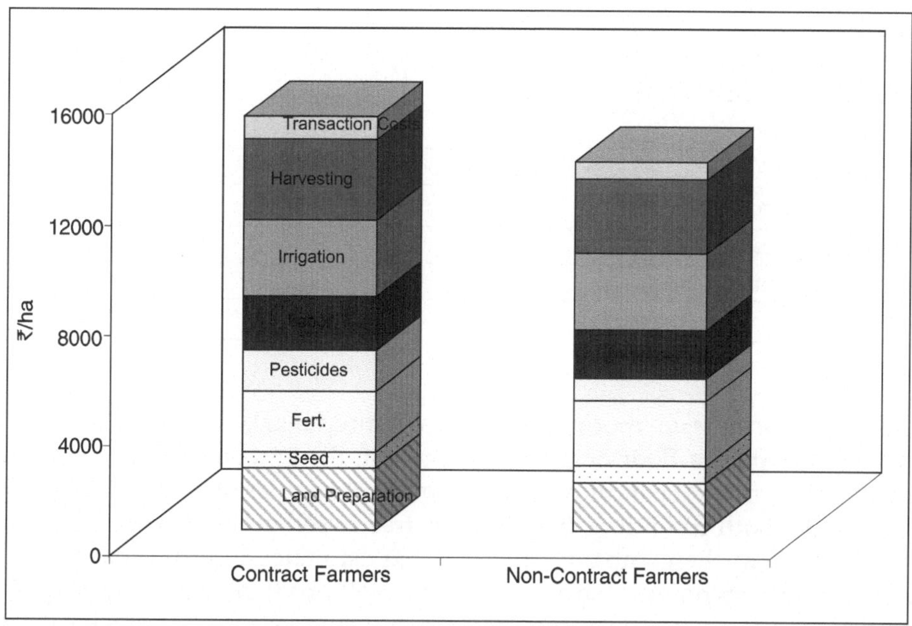

Fig. 2.33: Comparison of Cost of Production of Basmati Rice on Contract and Non-Contract Farms (2007)

Source: Field Survey.

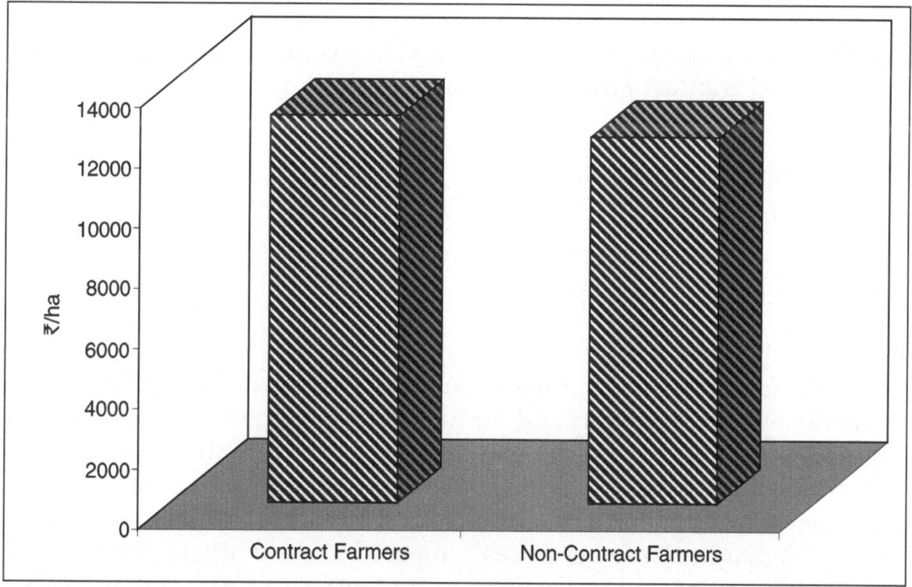

Fig. 2.34: Comparison of Net Income from Basmati Rice on Contract and Non-Contract Farms (2007)

Source: Field Survey.

Table 2.10: Reasons for Adopting Contract Farming

Reasons	*Percentage*
Assured market for produce	83
Assured price	52
Minimum floor price	38
Better price than alternative marketing channels	24
Good extension services	45
Less water requirement compared with competing crops	28
Higher returns than competing crops	14
Less incidence of diseases	7
Inspired by other contract farmers	4
Personal relations	4

Source: Field Survey.

This shows that farmers are more in need of an assured market than an assured price. Some companies offer a floor or minimum price in the agreement and final price is decided based on market conditions, while some companies announce a fixed price. However, under both conditions the farmer is free to sell in the market if the market price is higher than the company's price. Some estimates indicate that more than 60 per cent of farmers honour the agreement and sell produce to the company. Other reasons given for adopting contract farming include higher returns from basmati rice than competing crops, lower water requirement of basmati rice, inspiration from fellow farmers who have adopted contract farming, and personal relations with the company.

It is also important to understand the downside of contract farming. Some farmers have discontinued contract farming or changed company. Reasons for doing so are presented below:

- Unable to meet quality standards
- High rejection rates
- Lower price compared with market price
- Distance of sales/delivery point
- Delay in payments.

Majority of the farmers could not meet the quality standards set by the companies. Quality checks by private traders and/or the Food Corporation of India are not very stringent. However, most of the companies engaged in contract farming are export oriented and therefore have stringent standards on quality. The rejection rate is quite high in some cases, and is a reason for discontinuing contract farming. Some companies paid marginally lower prices compared to the market price, because they provided better extension services, seeds and other inputs that improve farm productivity, thereby giving farmers a higher net income. However, some of the farmers were not able to appreciate the increase in net income and were driven by price (which is not a good indicator).

Non-contracting farmers were asked to give their reasons for not adopting contract farming. These are given below:

- Companies not keen because of smallholding
- High market price compared with companies involved in contract farming
- Can get extension services provided by the company from fellow farmers (public good and market failure problem)
- Reluctant to share information about land with private company
- Not sure about policies of the company.

Size of holdings has prevented small and marginal farmers from entering into contract farming.

In some cases, market prices were marginally higher or on par with contract prices, so farmers did not find it beneficial to enter into contracts.

Conclusion

Agriculture is and will remain the mainstay for a large proportion of India's rural population, many of whom are poor. Promoting more rapid and broad based agricultural growth will be extremely important for alleviating poverty in rural areas. The current crisis in Indian agriculture will only exacerbate prompt remedial action is initiated by the government. One way to increase agricultural growth and farm incomes is to shift from a traditional cereal-based cropping system to high value agriculture, and link producers to markets. High value agriculture gives higher returns but is also risky. Majority of farmers are small and marginal, and have poor links with markets and low risk-bearing capacity, which restricts their participation in fast changing markets.

Corporate agriculture, especially through contract farming, is being promoted by central and state governments to solve some of these problems. Contract farming is expected to enable farmer's access better quality inputs and credit. Contract farming also has the potential to eliminate and/or reduce the market and price risks that farmers face. However, success is dependent on the nature of contracts, legislation for regulation of contract farming, enforcement, dispute resolution mechanisms, etc.

The present models of contract farming are not completely integrated, since companies provide only seeds and sometimes extension services. None supply other inputs such as pesticides and fertilizers and, more importantly, credit. For credit farmers are still dependent on informal sources. One finding from the study is the exclusion of small farmers from contracting companies have a preference for medium and large farmers, in order to reduce their transaction costs and ensure quality standards. Success of contract farming will largely depend on integrating small and marginal farmers in the contract farming system.

How can contract farming can be developed further? Firstly, it is important to provide an integrated set of services, including credit, and not just extension services and seed. Secondly, partnerships between public- and private-sector companies or organizations are needed in order to provide integrated services. Thirdly, there is need to improve the bargaining power of smallholder producers while also reducing the transaction costs for companies through promotion of producers' groups, associations, or cooperatives. Small farmers will be able effectively to participate in the changing markets and establish links with new market chains (supermarkets, agribusiness companies, processors, exporters, etc.) only if they have access to basic infrastructure, inputs, and services, and are organized.

References

APEDA (2007), 'Export Statistics for Agro & Food Products 2003–04 to 2005–06.' Agricultural and Processed Food Products Export Development Authority, New Delhi.

CSO (2007), 'National Accounts Statistics 2007 and Back Issues.' Central Statistical Organisation, Ministry of Statistics and Programme Implementation, Government of India, New Delhi.

FAI (2006), 'Fertiliser Statistics 2005–06'. The Fertiliser Association of India, New Delhi.

FAO (2007), *Rice Market Monitor 2006–07*, Volume X, Issue No.1, Commodity Markets, Policy Analysis and Projections Service. Trade and Markets Division, Food and Agriculture Organization of the United Nations.

GoI (2001), 'Indian Planning Experience—A Statistical Profile'. Planning Commission, Government of India, New Delhi, January.

GoI (2002), '10th Five Year Plan (2002–2007)'. Planning Commission, Government of India, New Delhi.

GoI (2006), 'Towards Faster and More Inclusive Growth: An Approach to the 11th Five Year Plan (2007–2012)'. Planning Commission, Government of India, December.

GoI (2007a), 'Agricultural Statistics at a Glance 2006' various issues. Directorate of Economics and Statistics, Ministry of Agriculture, Government of India, New Delhi.

GoI (2007b), 'Economic Survey 2006–07 and back issues.' Economic Division, Ministry of Finance, Government of India, New Delhi.

Government of Punjab (2006), 'Statistical Abstract of Punjab 2005'. Economic and Statistical Organisation, Government of Punjab, Chandigarh.

Kumar, Pramod (2006), 'Contract Farming through Agribusiness Firms and State Corporation: A Case Study in Punjab.' *Economic and Political Weekly*, Dec 30, 2006, 5367–75.

Ministry of Water Resources (2007), Government of India, http://wrmin.nic.in/

PAFC (2007), http://www.punjabagro.com/cf.htm

Rangi, PS and MS Sidhu (2000), 'A Study on Contract Farming of Tomato in Punjab'. Agricultural Marketing, 42(4): 15–23.

Singh, Gurdev and SR Asokan (2005), *Contract Farming in India: Text and Cases*. Oxford and IBH Publishing Co. Pvt. Ltd., New Delhi.

Singh, Sukhpal (2002), 'Contracting Out Solutions: Political Economy of Contract Farming in the Indian Punjab.' *World Development*, **30**(9): 1621–38.

3

Marketing Cooperatives in a New Retail Context: A Study of HOPCOMS

Deepthi Kolady, Sujana Krishnamoorthy and Sudha Narayanan

Across the developing world, transformations in the retail sector are spearheading a change in local food systems. Until recently, less than 5 per cent of retail food sales in India took place in the organized sector. This is changing, and the retail revolution in the agri-food sector is well underway. Organized retail now encompasses 74 cities, up from 18 a year ago, and is growing at the rate of 30–40 per cent every year (Gulati and Reardon, 2007). A large number of domestic players such as Big Bazaar, Spencer's, Reliance, Bharti, and Choupal Fresh have drawn up ambitious plans for expansion and foreign players are devising ways to enter the market.

At this juncture, the relative position of the small farmer comes into prominence. The new retailers have focused on disintermediation in the supply chain to benefit farmers and consumers. Notwithstanding the income gains, how much of this retail transformation is benefitting small farmers? Small farmers face several constraints in making investments for meeting quality. Even when retail transformation is inclusive, will eventual retail consolidation pose particular problems for small-holders, weakening their bargaining power? And what would happen to those who fail to be part of the supply channel? This is a critical question for India, which is a nation of small farmers,[1] many of whom are becoming smaller.

In this context, documenting institutions that attempt to link small producers with markets is vital. We look at one such venture, a state-managed farmer cooperative—the Horticulture Producers Cooperative Marketing and Processing Society Limited (HOPCOMS), in Karnataka.[2]

Background

In some ways, HOPCOMS (founded in 1959 and established in its current form in 1987), with its focus on vertical coordination and disintermediation predates the 'new' retail philosophy by decades. We hope to demonstrate, through the HOPCOMS case, that these institutions can perform an innovative role in the new retail

[1] Households with 1 hectare or less land accounted for 66 per cent of all farmer households in India (NSSO, 2005). Situation Assessment Survey of Farmers, NSS 59th Round, NSSO, May 2005, Report no. 498.

[2] Karnataka is the third largest producer of fruits and stands fifth in area and production of vegetable crops.

landscape. Indeed it is our belief that such institutions might be increasingly relevant in the new context. On the one hand, small and poor farmers may be excluded from the network of large private sector retailers, unless they get technological and organizational assistance, while large farmers may prefer to tie up with large-scale private retailers. In such cases, alternative institutions need to be nurtured to redress the problems faced by small farmers. These institutions, by being viable alternatives to large scale retailers, empower small farmers by expanding their choice set of marketing channels. The case of HOPCOMS, despite its many failings and problems, raises the possibility of an 'other', alternative revolution paralleling the private sector-driven retail revolution. Rather than letting cooperatives such as HOPCOMS be undermined, there might be considerable value in scaling up and replicating successful models.

This paper seeks to generate five essential insights into small farmer participation in dynamic markets (Berdegue *et al.*, 2006):

- What are the drivers of inclusion?
- What financial and non-financial costs and benefits do the small-scale producers obtain from their inclusion in dynamic markets?
- What amounts of direct and indirect subsidies have contributed to the innovation? What implications does this have on the sustainability of the innovation?
- What public and private policies will contribute to the up-scaling of the innovation?
- What lessons can be derived for public and private policies to promote market inclusion of small scale producers elsewhere?

This paper compares two independent HOPCOMS entities—a profit making in Bangalore and a loss making one in Mysore—to ascertain what distinguishes the performance of the two, and what might be the constituents of successful intervention. Extensive field visits and a survey of 186 farmers spread across six districts around Bangalore and Mysore provided the data.

Agricultural Marketing in India

The agricultural market in India is dominated by rural primary markets that meet local demand, secondary markets that serve distant demands, and wholesalers who gather produce from different sources for retail in the country. The objective of regulated markets established by the government was to regulate trade practices, increase marketing efficiency through reduction in marketing charges, eliminate intermediaries, and protect the interest of producer-seller. Though regulated markets helped in reducing multiple charges on producer-seller, it failed in checking trade malpractices, making it highly restrictive and inefficient and dominated by traders.

To overcome the defects of regulated markets and to increase productivity a direct marketing system parallel to the existing system was sought to be put in place. These would be outside the purview of the Agricultural Produce Marketing Committee (APMC) acts and hence ensure transparency, efficiency, quality control, and fair play. Direct marketing by farmers was experimented with *Apni Mandis* in Punjab and Haryana. A modified concept was introduced in *Rythu Bazars* (AP) and *Uzahvar Santhaigal* (TN). In the meantime, private players such as Cargill India, Mahindra, ITC-e Choupal, Bharti etc. have emerged with sophisticated supply chain management systems and vertical coordination.

Agrarian Context of Karnataka

In spite of being almost synonymous with the booming software and service sectors, Karnataka is still primarily an agrarian state. Sixty-six per cent of the population in Karnataka resides in rural areas, and is engaged in agriculture and allied activities.[3] Growth rates in agriculture have been low, between two and three per cent per annum during the last three decades, a period marked by droughts and natural calamities.

Rainfed agriculture is still the order of the day as only 26.5 per cent of the gross cultivated area is irrigated. Most of the areas in Karnataka lie in the low rainfall region. Small (1–2 ha) and marginal (less than 1 hectare) farmers dominate Karnataka's agricultural scenario accounting for 72.9 per cent of holdings; 1.74 hectares is the average size of an operational holding.[4]

With its ten agro-climatic zones and nine distinct soil types, Karnataka is ideally suited to grow various kinds of horticultural crops.[5] The Karnataka Agricultural Policy (2006) aims at moving away from traditional grain-based agriculture towards crop diversification, promoting horticulture, poultry, and live stock. As horticulture provides higher unit productivity, requires less labour and is more remunerative with greater scope for value addition, it is being favourably viewed by farmers and is spreading throughout the state. Horticultural crops are grown on 13 per cent of the net cultivated area (16.30 lakh hectares) and annual production is about 95.81 lakh tons. Income generated from the sector accounts for over 40 per cent of the income derived from the combined agriculture sector and 17 per cent of SGDP.

Micro-Context: Bangalore and Mysore

Smallholder agriculture in southern Karnataka is best understood in the context of the trajectory of Bangalore's spectacular growth. Since the 1990s, Bangalore, once known as the pensioner's paradise, has been growing at an estimated 30 per cent in size thanks largely to a booming information technology industry. The spatiality of the city has been changing rapidly especially in the past decade (Nair, 2005). As software

[3] Agriculture contributes 21 per cent to the SGDP while the secondary sector contributes 25 per cent and the tertiary sector 52 per cent (Karnataka Agricultural Policy, 2006).

[4] Agricultural Census, 2000–01.

[5] For details see : http://horticulture.kar.nic.in/horticulture_development_scenari.htm

companies and real estates drive land prices up, agriculture is shifting farther into the hinterland.

Urban water demands have rendered peri-urban agriculture extraordinarily difficult in recent times.[6] Faced with increasing costs of production, eroding resource base, and escalating land prices, farmers have been tempted to sell out. For others farther out into the countryside where the real estate windfall has not struck (as yet) these difficulties have prompted them to switch to occupations like silk rearing, which are relatively less resource intensive and for which the government offers price support.

Thus, on the one hand the growing demand for horticultural crops provides a great incentive for commercial cash crop cultivation in areas around Bangalore.[7] On the other hand, rising land prices and eroding natural resource base presents a countervailing force to give up the land for alternative uses. How these competing demands on land will play itself out is open to question. The answer depends, not to a small extent, on whether there are enough incentives and appropriate institutions to enable smallholders to tap into large markets.

While this is especially true for Bangalore, Mysore, which is much smaller, is not far behind.[8] Mysore is now regarded as the alternate destination for investment by the IT sector and is being developed as a satellite city to Bangalore. Mysore is poised for growth, pretty much the way Bangalore was a decade ago.

Data and Methods

We use a unique dataset of around 186 farmers spread across six districts around Bangalore and Mysore. The districts are Mysore, Chamarajanagar, Mandya, Banga-

Table 3.1: Timeline of Significant Occurrences at HOPCOMS

Year	*Significant Occurrences*
1959	Founded as Bangalore Grape Growers Cooperative Marketing & Processing Society Ltd.
1965	Operation extended to cover all vegetables in the state
1983	Renamed as Bangalore Horticultural Producers Cooperative Marketing and Processing Society Ltd.
1987	Renamed as HOPCOMS
1997	District level HOPCOMS were spun off as independent units
2006	Redefinition of administrative area: Bangalore HOPCOMS having three districts (Bangalore Urban, Bangalore Rural and Kolar) as its area of operation and handing over its branches in the remaining districts to the respective Horticultural Societies as per government order.

6 This was apparent throughout the course of the survey. As a farmer emphasized, until five years ago, the water table was at 75 feet, at the time of survey, that farmer was considered lucky who hit water at 1000 feet.

7 The growing middle class in India is more health conscious and prefers diversified diet comprises meat, fruits, and vegetables, a change from the earlier generations which preferred low value large grain food.

8 Based on 2001 census, population size in Bangalore Urban and Mysore districts are 6.5 million and 2.6 million respectively.

lore (Rural), Bangalore (Urban), and Kolar. The first three are under the jurisdiction of HOPCOMS (Mysore) and the latter three of HOPCOMS (Bangalore) (Table 3.1).

Farmers were selected using choice-based sampling, simultaneous selection of farmers who visited the wholesale *mandi* and the HOPCOMS collection centre. Days and dates for sampling farmers were selected so as to cover different time periods during the day as well as different days of the week. Data were collected on various aspects of marketing of horticultural produce including transactions costs associated with alternative channels. While the survey is the base we also draw on insights from conversations with a wide range of supply chain actors.

We define a HOPCOMS farmer as one who has used HOPCOMS to sell a crop on the day of sampling. A non-HOPCOMS farmer is one who has used a channel other than HOPCOMS to sell a crop on the day of sampling. Thus, either the farmer or someone else on his/her behalf was present in the market to sell the crop. The notions of inclusion and exclusion are derived from this characterization. We deem the HOPCOMS farmer to be included and the non-HOPCOMS farmer to be excluded. Our choice of use of HOPCOMS as the basis for inclusion, rather than membership, is justified because even non-members can use HOPCOMS.

We first map the socio-demographic and economic characteristics of HOPCOMS farmers in order to ascertain who transacts with HOPCOMS. We perform simple statistical tests of comparison between HOPCOMS users and non-HOPCOMS farmers to see if there are specific characteristics that distinguish these two groups in a substantive way.

Then, we map out the attributes of the different marketing channels to see how these relate to farmers' decisions. Through this we hope to get some sense of the correlates of 'inclusion' and 'exclusion', to see if the aspects of the institutional design of HOPCOMS that were hypothesized to promote smallholder participation really do.

Thereafter, we attempt to measure the benefits and costs to the farmer from inclusion (or exclusion) in a manner to be elaborated later.

Horticultural Marketing Channels

Like elsewhere in developing countries, most farmers depend on relation-based transactions rather than rule-based arrangements. Most horticultural producers market their produce through commission agents and intermediaries which reduce the producers' share in the market price of the produce, while increase the marketing cost and retail price for consumers. Because of the perishable nature of the produce, poor marketing facilities, and lack of education, poor and small farmers are exploited by the middlemen. The traditional and predominant supply chain is long with as many as five to six intermediaries before the produce reaches the consumer.

The traditional channel involves markets regulated by state agencies, although the regulation is often only in name (Figure 3.1). Most of the vegetables and fruits in larger cities and towns are traded in the central market area, usually a municipal market. The wholesale trade of fruits and vegetables is carried out by commission agents and the trade is through small auction sales or negotiated sales.

A) Farmer → Agent who brings to the *Mandi* (Buying Agent) → *Mandi* Agent who auctions or sells in larger lots → Retailer (vendor) → Consumer

B) Farmer → Pre-harvest contractor *(dallal)* → *Mandi* Agent who auctions or sells in larger lots → Vendor → Final Consumer

For some crops like sugarcane and paddy, traditional channels mean selling to the mill. In horticulture, this is not relevant.

Fig. 3.1: Traditional Channels

Recent changes have brought about a greater diversity of marketing channels in Karnataka (Figures 3.2 and 3.3). In particular, horticulture marketing has been the focus of special efforts. An apex federal body, the Karnataka State Horticultural Co-operative Federation (KHF), performs the activities similar to that of the Karnataka Milk Federation. Direct marketing initiatives through farmer markets or *Raithara Santhe* have also been taken by the Karnataka State Agricultural Marketing Board. The board has created infrastructure for marketing fruits and vegetables directly from growers to consumers without any middlemen or commission agent. Safal fruit and vegetable auction market, a project implemented by the National Dairy Development Board, is developing cash and carry stores in prime localities of cities as are other private sector players.

A) Farmer → Consumer in the local area Local *sales for perishables and small quantities*

B) Farmer → Consumer in the city *Through state-initiated farmer-markets*

Fig. 3.2: Direct Sales

A) Farmer → Consolidators → Supermarkets → Final Consumer

B) Farmer → Export processing firms/Supermarkets through contracts → Final Consumer

Fig. 3.3: Modern Channels

HOPCOMS as an Innovation

Marketing of highly perishable fruits and vegetables is fraught with many problems. Farmers had little bargaining power, middlemen collected commissions from producers, there were frequent delays in payments, and produce was sold on the basis of volume, prices determined to the advantage of retailers and not farmers.

In order to tackle these issues HOPCOMS was founded in 1959 (established in its current form in 1987) as a cooperative under the Indian Cooperative Societies Act.[9] It has a membership base comprising farmers, state financial organizations, and the state government. It is managed by officials appointed by the state, drawn from the Department of Horticulture and the Department of Cooperation. As of 2007, there are 17 HOPCOMS in the state each working independently, with demarcated districts of operation. Over the years, the society had undergone major structural changes and the timeline of significant such events is reported in Table 3.2.

The aims and objectives of the society are:

- To ensure remunerative prices to producers of horticultural crops
- To free both producers and consumers from the clutches of middlemen
- To ensure quality supply of fruits and vegetables at reasonable prices
- To expand marketing and cold storage facilities progressively for the benefit of farmers
- To promote horticultural development on scientific lines by providing inputs and technical advice.

Table 3.2: Scope of Survey

	Districts Covered	*HOPCOMS Centres*	*Mandis*
Mysore	Mysore, Mandya, Chamarajnagar	Mysore (Mysore)	RMC Market & Devaraj Urs (Mysore) Gundlupet (Chamarajnagar) K.R.Pet (Mandya)
Bangalore	Bangalore (Rural) Bangalore (Urban) Kolar	Chennapatna (only for banana) (Bangalore Rural) Sarjapura (Bangalore Rural) Hoskote (Bangalore, Rural) Lalbagh (Bangalore, Urban)	Chinthamani (Kolar) Yeshwanthpur K. R. Market Ramanagara

Growth of HOPCOMS

The society started with 507 farmer members and share capital of ₹ 1269 in 1959 (nominal terms) this has grown to 15000 members in 2005 (as of March 31, 2005) ₹ 258.59 as share capital. The share of the state government in the share capital steadily increased from 35 per cent in 1970–71 to 96 per cent in 1996–97 (Rao, 1997). By March 2007, it stood at ₹ 228 lakh (88 per cent of total share capital).[10]

By 1997, HOPCOMS had developed a network of procurement centres, godowns, retail outlets and input supply centers in eight districts with Bangalore being the

[9] For more details on HOPCOMS, see Rao (1987).

[10] HOPCOMS, Brief Note on HOPCOMS (collected in March 2007).

largest and most important. At that time, the district level HOPCOM which were functioning as an integrated entity were spun off as independent units. In 2006 the organizational structure underwent a change with Bangalore HOPCOMS having three districts (Bangalore Urban, Bangalore Rural, and Kolar) as its area of operation and handing over its branches in remaining districts to respective horticultural societies.

Supply Chain of HOPCOMS

A HOPCOMS unit procures horticultural produce directly from farmers against an indent (an informal preference is given to members) through a network of decentralized collection centers.[11,12] The procurement centres also supply inputs like manure, fertilizers, hybrid seeds, fungicides, etc . The price is announced for the day, and is typically a mark-up on the price at relevant *mandis* where price for the region is set.[13,14] Through low cost means and frugal infrastructure, it consolidates the procured produce at its central headquarters, channeling it into a network of its own retail outlets managed by employees.[15]

As part of its marketing strategy HOPCOMS (both in Bangalore and Mysore) has sought to situate its outlets next to milk booths to enable consumers to pick up daily necessities at one go. HOPCOMS outlets selling fruits at railway stations, bus stands, and other prominent locations are another aspect of the marketing strategy. The retail outlets work between 10.30 am and 8 pm with a break in the afternoon and are staffed by two persons, one of whom is a permanent employee of HOPCOMS and the other an assistant on temporary roll.

The retail price is a fixed mark-up on the procurement price, and is same across the outlets. HOPCOMS is therefore the only intermediary between farmer and consumer (Figure 3.4). Theoretically, because the farmer is also a member of HOPCOMS, rather than being a pure intermediary HOPCOMS is more of a front-end aggregator and distributor for the farmer. According to the society, it pays 80 per cent of the price paid by consumers to farmers.[16] Apart from retailing, HOPCOMS bottles fresh fruit juice. Essentially then, HOPCOMS attempts to combine the efficiency of vertical coordination with empowerment through horizontal coordination.

---

11 The preference seems to vary across procurement centres. Also, it seems to kick in when supply of a commodity outstrips 'demand'.

12 In the case of Bangalore HOPCOMS, Lalbagh is the biggest procurement centre and accepts quantities ranging from 30–40 kg to amounts as large as 750–900 kg. Other procurement centres procure on average 1–1.5 tonnes a day with the accepted amounts varying from 20–30 kg to 150-200 kg.

13 There is no formula or declared mark-up. Officials meet every morning in Bangalore and arrive at a price based on the prevailing prices each morning at 4–5 reference *mandis*. While this is likely to be higher, this is not a given.

14 Amounts are paid immediately, and when the amount exceeds ₹ 5,000 payments are made through cheques.

15 According to Rao (1997) most of the outlets are owned by HOPCOMS and cost around ₹ 1.25 lakh per unit to construct.

16 Personal communication with Manager, Procurement, HOPCOMS Bangalore.

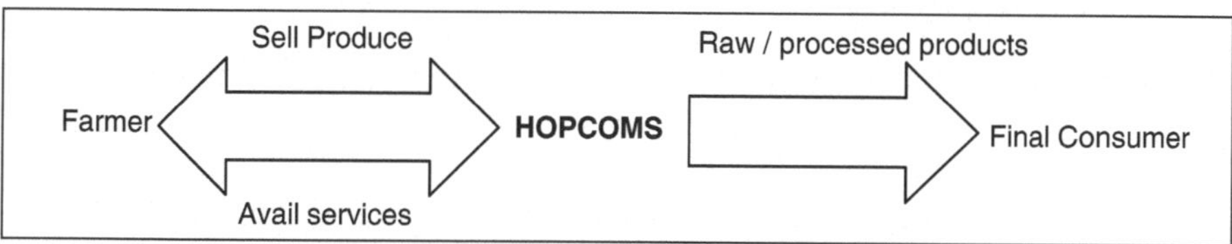

Fig. 3.4: The 'Other' Channel

Theoretical Foundation of HOPCOMS

To place HOPCOMS in right perspective, we assess the sense in which it can be considered an innovation in the new retail context.

Recent discussions of farmer organizations are invariably set within the context of vertical coordination. Horizontal coordination is proposed as a way for farmers who are up the supply chain corner a larger share of the efficiency gains from vertical coordination in modern marketing channels. Also, farmers' associations tend to be necessary but not sufficient: they are necessary because they reduce transactions costs, the single most important factor that constrains participation of smallholders. On the other hand, investments in management, institutions, and infrastructure to comply with supermarket standards are essential to ensure continued participation in retail supply chains. However, vertical and horizontal coordinations are usually regarded as militating against each other. Over-focusing on horizontal goals could undermine the benefits of vertical integration and leave fewer surpluses for sharing among producers (Treville, 1986).

An institution like HOPCOMS seeks to achieve a harmonious combination of vertical and horizontal coordination, akin to a state-cum-farmer-owned company.[17] It is in this sense that HOPCOMS can be characterized as an innovation. It differs from simple marketing cooperatives in that it is itself the ultimate seller—the retailer. It differs from other forms of disintermediation in the private sector by including farmers and bringing them together as owners of institutions rather than mere participants. It is not an innovation embedded in a new supply chain, rather it is an alternate competing supply chain by itself. This is the distinguishing feature of HOPCOMS as an innovation. To what degree it has been successful in achieving the difficult combination of horizontal and vertical coordination is question that we attempt to answer.

HOPCOMS in Practice

HOPCOMS as an innovation can now be assessed along three issues—as a vehicle for small farmers, as a vertical coordinator, and as a cooperative.

---

[17] Unlike Amul, however, where there are many farmer organizations—one at each village—that elect representatives within a hierarchical structure, HOPCOMS functions like a farmer-owned company without decentralized farmer associations.

As a Vehicle for Small Farmers

The findings from the survey suggest that HOPCOMS is inclusive of small farmers in more ways than one. First, the proportion of small farmers participating in HOPCOMS in the sample was somewhat larger than their corresponding proportion in southern Karnataka (Table 3.3). Data show that 77 per cent of those who transact with HOPCOMS are marginal and small farmers. This favours comparably with region's figure of 69 per cent. So small farmers are definitely included in HOPCOMS and are over-represented. HOPCOMS farmers also trade significantly smaller quantities than their *mandi* counterparts.

Table 3.3: Small Farmers in Southern Karnataka, HOPCOMS, and the *Mandi*

	In Southern Karnataka %	*HOPCOMS Users in the Survey*	*Non HOPCOMS Users in the Survey*
Marginal farmers (below 1 ha)	41.9	32.18	37.4
Small (1–2 ha)	27.3	44.83	34.34
Semi medium & medium (3–10 ha)	28.9	21.84	22.22
Large (> 10 ha)	1.7	1.15	1.01
TOTAL	100%	100%	100%

Source: Authors' Survey; Indiastat (2006).

Second, the flexibility of HOPCOMS is being incorporative of small farmers provides an additional alternative marketing channel and hence expands the choice set. The fact that the landholding class profile is similar among users of the *mandi* and HOPCOMS sets up *mandis* and HOPCOMS as complements. In districts, where there are no HOPCOMS procurement centres, farmers have no choice but to choose the *mandi*. In this manner, too, HOPCOMS provides a marketing channel to farmers at large and to the small farmer especially. One of the aspects that becomes apparent from the data on both HOPCOMS users and non-users is that the marketing channels available to small farmers are either the *mandi* or the HOPCOMS procurement centres. We speculate that large farmers with big landholding or transacting large quantities of produce are those who may have opted or been selected to be part of the modern supply chains.

What are the Drivers of Inclusion?

In principle, HOPCOMS is designed to be inclusive, even empowering of small and marginal farmers, although this is not an explicitly stated objective of the cooperative. We hypothesize that the following elements of the institutional design of HOPCOMS promote small farmers participation:

1. Decentralized procurement—this reduces transaction costs for farmers by reaching out to farmers. HOPCOMS then acts as consolidator helping scale up the transactional size of small farmers.

2. An indent system that puts ceilings on quantities procured. This often provides a disincentive to large farmers or those who transact large volumes at a time, who choose to opt out of the system.
3. Fixed pre-announced price, typically a weighted average or mark up of reference market prices. This has the potential to empower small farmers by obviating the need to negotiate a price. In particular, those small farmers who, consequent to poor bargaining power, face the lower end of the market price distribution, might find this beneficial.
4. Membership that offers a channel for representation—redresses power imbalance in the marketing channel. In fact, HOPCOMS even reserves 5 per cent of farmer-memberships exclusively for women.
5. Sale of inputs such as seeds, fertilizers and pesticides. It serves as a one-stop shop for different needs. This improves small farmer's access to inputs while reducing input costs for the farmer through disintermediation at the input end as well. Mark-ups can be anywhere between 15 and 30 per cent when intermediaries are present.
6. Finally, HOPCOMS is not a club 'good'—it is *non-exclusionary*, in the sense that it also accepts produce from non-members and tenant-cultivators. The role of latter in particular is significant. Although HOPCOMS restricts membership to land-owners on the basis of documented evidence of ownership, tenant cultivators can also use it as a marketing channel.[18]

Together, these elements work on both the "set of incentives" facing the small farmer and their "capacities to respond to these incentives" (Berdegue *et al.*, 2006).

Decentralized procurement has the effect of reducing travel costs. This is apparent in the fact that HOPCOMS users travel a much smaller distance to sell their produce. This is a valuable saving for small farmers (Table 3.4). While participation is an important aspect, the intensity of participation is equally instructive. Intensity of participation in this case is defined as the volume of crop sold to HOPCOMS (or *mandi*). This latter is difficult to capture since the farmers sell as many as 26 different crops. We use the percentage excess/shortfall over the average commodity-group average as a measure of trading volumes. Of all the farmers who sell less than the average for the particular commodity, more sell to HOPCOMS than at the *mandi*. This is suggestive that those trading smaller quantities participate in HOPCOMS.[19] Similarly, as much as 72 per cent of all HOPCOMS farmers sell less than average quantities while the figure for non-HOPCOMS farmers is 56 per cent. Across districts, non-HOPCOMS farmers sell greater quantities, than their HOPCOMS counterparts and this difference is statistically significant. Part of this could be the result of the

[18] Membership gives voting rights and preferential allocation of indents, although the latter is dealt with as an informal rule.

[19] To the extent that larger quantities correspond to larger farmers, these results can be seen as a comment on smallholder participation. This may not be true, if large farmers harvest small quantities at any given time, relative to small farmers. There is no reason to believe that the latter may be the case.

indent system that limits quantities sold by a farmer to HOPCOMS whereas there exists no such limits in the *mandis*. These indent systems may however be providing strong disincentives to larger farmers to transact with HOPCOMS, and the latter may be opting out.

Apart from these, there are no statistically significant socio-demographic differences between HOPCOMS and non-HOPCOMS farmers (Table 3.4).

Table 3.4: Profile of HOPCOMS and Non-HOPCOMS Farmers

	HOPCOMS Users	*HOPCOMS Non-Users*	*T-test for Equality of Means (Assuming equal variance) or Z for Equality of Proportions*
Average contribution of farm income to total income	86%	90%	1.09
Proportion who report that farming is NOT their only occupation	25.3%	23.2%	0.33
Proportion of women farmers in the sample	1.15	1.01	–
Average age	40	38.6	–0.86
Average experience (Years)	18.9	19.9	0.595
Proportion who have completed school	26.3%	14.1%	–
Proportion who have NOT studied beyond primary school	27.6%	38.4%	–
Acreage of Land Cultivated	4.5	4.8	0.46
Average Diversity (No. of crops per acre cultivated)	1.16	0.98	–0.88
• The lowest diversity being	0.14	0.1	
• The highest diversity being	13.3	9.4	
Proportion who are tenant cultivators	1.15	5.05	
Average distance to the market	27.19 kms.	43.12 kms.	2.18**

*significant at 10% ** significant at 5% *** significant at 1%

Costs and Benefits of Inclusion: Pecuniary and Non-Pecuniary

Econometric studies attempting to gauge the impact of participation on incomes tend to focus more on the question of *whether* participation increases incomes rather than by *how much* participation increases income. Further, the qualitative dimensions of costs and benefits often take a backseat. On the other hand, case studies tend to highlight non-pecuniary benefits choosing and do not measure pecuniary benefits rigorously.

The assessment of costs and benefit of participation in innovations is rendered difficult by the challenge of constructing an appropriate counterfactual. And this is even more complicated in the context of HOPCOMS's flexibility in inclusion and exclusion. Because farmers can flow in and out of the system by choice, the revealed preference approach would suggest that both users and non-users of HOPCOMS would record positive benefits associated with their choices. To assess the extent of pecuniary costs and benefits, we compute the difference in revenue of a farmer from sale that day in HOPCOMS (*mandi*) and the revenue he/she would have obtained had they opted for the other i.e., *mandi* (HOPCOMS). We are able to do this for a subset of 50 farmers who were able to provide us detailed marketing costs and prices in the alternative channel that they had not chosen.[20] Thus while the results may not be robust, they are illustrative (Table 3.5).

Table 3.5: Pecuniary Benefits and Cost Associated with Farmers' Choices

	Mean Additional Income from using HOPCOMS	*Mean Ratio of Transaction time in HOPCOMS and Mandi*	*Mean Ratio of Travel Time to HOPCOMS and Mandi*
Those non-HOPCOMS farmers who would gain by switching to HOPCOMS (n = 14)	37.7%	0.66	0.91
Those non-HOPCOMS farmers who would lose by switching to HOPCOMS (n = 12)	–33.03%	0.42	1.06
Those HOPCOMS farmers who have lost by choosing HOPCOMS (n = 5)	–33.2%	0.43	0.14
Those HOPCOMS farmers who have gained from their choice of HOPCOMS (n = 29)	42.61%	0.42	0.45

Source: Authors' Survey

Results reveal that over half of non-HOPCOMS farmers would have benefited monetarily had they chosen to use HOPCOMS. The mean percentage by which their income would have increased is 37 per cent. Only for less than half of them would such a switch have reduced their revenue from sales by around 33 per cent.

For HOPCOMS farmers, more than four-fifths of those who responded would have lost 43 per cent of their revenue on average had they gone to the *mandi* rather than HOPCOMS. Only the remaining one-fifth might have gained on average about 33 per cent of their income by going to the *mandi* rather than HOPCOMS. One of the important benefits of inclusion was that the transaction costs were lower in HOPCOMS. The ratio of transaction cost to revenue is 0.45 for HOPCOMS users and 0.72 for non-HOPCOMS users (Table 3.6).

About 65 per cent of non-HOPCOMS users were aware of the price in that particular market before making a decision to sell in it. In comparison, only 35.6 per cent of

[20] The costs that are included are travel costs to market, packing, loading, unloading, packing material, market fees, and payment for procuring market information. The transactions cost does not include commission which is around 8–15 per cent in the mandi and 0 in HOPCOMS. So these benefits are a conservative estimate.

Table 3.6: Some Benefits and Costs for HOPCOMS and Non-HOPCOMS Farmers

Details	*HOPCOMS Users*	*HOPCOMS Non-Users*	*Test of Equality of Mean or Proportion*
Proportion who felt that the price they got was "Fair"	92%	78%	–2.6***
Average transaction cost per unit of cultivated land[@]	₹ 319.8	₹ 596.1	1.55**
Average commission reported	0	9.4% (65% say 10%)	–
Ratio of Transactions Cost to Revenue from this sale	0.45	0.72	2.58***
Proportion who reported making profit on the chosen crop this season	60.92%	49.49%	–1.56**
Average profit per acre earned this season	(+) ₹ 1308	(+) ₹ 1071	–0.55
Average loss per acre for those who suffered losses	(–) ₹ 1525	(–) ₹ 2760	–0.6
Proportion who reported being in debt this season	50.6%	66.7%	2.22**
Average amount of debt per acre cultivated for those who report debts	₹ 10722	₹ 5718	–1.275

@These have not been computed per unit of commodity sold, since there are many commodities.
1 US $ = ₹ 40.9 (August, 2007)
*significant at 10% ** significant at 5% *** significant at 1%.
Source: Authors' Survey.

HOPCOMS' users were aware of the price (Table 3.7). This probably stems from the fact that, quantity and quality of produce permitting, HOPCOMS was always the first choice as they were assured of price equal to if not more than what the market offered to them. This conveys a sense of security that comes along with inclusion, which is a rare and precious commodity in agricultural marketing, especially in the Indian context.

There are other indicators that suggest that HOPCOMS benefits those who are included. When compared with non-HOPCOMS farmers, a significantly higher proportion of HOPCOMS farmers reported making profits and thought price was fair. They had significantly lower transactions cost per acre of land cultivated and significantly lower transaction cost-revenue (from this sale) ratio.

The question remains as to why farmers who stood to gain did not take advantage of it? This is relevant since the farmers themselves report these potential gains. For HOPCOMS farmers who might have gained monetarily by switching, it is interesting that the travel time to the HOPCOMS collection centre is just 14 per cent of the travel time to the *mandi*. The transaction time in the HOPCOMS collection centre is less as well. So the non-pecuniary benefits might overcompensate for the pecuniary gains from switching. For non-HOPCOMS farmers who do not switch, despite non-pecuniary advantages of transacting with HOPCOMS, the answers lie elsewhere (see Tables 3.5, 3.6, 3.7, 3.8 and 3.9). Again, here field interviews suggest that there are two

Table 3.7: On the Nature of Transactions

Details	*HOPCOMS Users*	*HOPCOMS Non-Users*	*Z-stat/t-test*
Proportion who are aware of the price in the market before they sell	35.60%	64.40%	2.30**
Proportion who felt that weighing was unfair on that day	8.00%	4.00%	1.1535
Proportion who think weighing, in general, is unfair ("sometimes unfair" or "always unfair")	34.50%	43.40%	1.7*
Proportion who felt that grading was unfair on that day[21]	10.34%	6.06%	1.0
Proportion who think quality grading is unfair (sometimes unfair or always unfair)	45.98%	54.50%	1.92*
Average time spent on travel to market, and preparing for sale	320 minutes	597 minutes	4.9***
– the above excluding travel time	188 minutes	322 minutes	3.8***
Average transaction time· • Maximum • Minimum	2 hours 4 hours 10 minutes	3 hours 20 minutes 1 day (8 hours) 30 minutes	2.34**

*means significant at 10% ** significant at 5% *** significant at 1%.
Source: Authors' Survey.

Table 3.8: Transactions in HOPCOMS

Details	*Value*
Proportion who use HOPCOMS only as a marketing channel	48%
Proportion who use other services of HOPCOMS	
– Use Yard to Sell	26%
– Buy Seeds	24%
– Buy Fertilizer/Manure	22%
– Buy Pesticide/Insecticide	23%
Proportion who had sold against an indent that day	50.57%
– Proportion of these who sold *more* than the indent	13.80%
Proportion who feel that the process of allocation of indents in generally unfair ("Sometimes unfair" or "always unfair")	25.27%
Proportion of the produce that was rejected that day	4.39%
– minimum	0
– maximum	66
What is typically done with it?	
– Sell it elsewhere at a lower rate	77.14%
– Leave it behind or throw it	11.43%
– HOPCOMS discards it	11.43%

Source: Authors' Survey.

21 Unfair is distinct from malpractice.

Table 3.9: Perception of HOPCOMS by Users

Details	*Value*
Proportion of HOPCOMS Users who say HOPCOMS has NO disadvantages	50%
Proportion who are "Satisfied" or "Very Satisfied" with HOPCOMS	72.41%
Proportion who are "Dissatisfied" or "Very Dissatisfied"	6.9%
The top 5 primary disadvantages of HOPCOMS (as proportion of those who report disadvantages)	
• Proportion that cite Quantity Limits as the main disadvantage	17.5%
• Proportion that cite Quality Standards as the main disadvantage	11.25%
• Cite Weighing and no electronic weighing machine as a problem	6.25%
• "Not all crops are accepted" and "Bigger Farmers treated better"	2.5%
MEMBERSHIP AND OWNERSHIP	
Proportion of HOPCOMS users who are members	50.57%
Proportion of non-member users who would like to be members	72.09%
Proportion of the members who have ever voted	87.23%
• The year of the most recent election mentioned by a farmer in the sample	2004–05
Proportion who have ever held any elected position	0
Proportion who feel they have participated in decision making	46%
• The proportion of these who said they did this by attending meetings	49%
The most important reason farmers don't participate in decision making	No time to attend meetings

Source: Authors' Survey.

major hurdles at HOPCOMS. The first is the indent system that restricts quantities and the second is the quality controls. HOPCOMS accepts only better quality produce and, although the assessment of quality is by visual inspection, this poses a big problem for smaller farmers who feel they have no control over the quality on-farm.

As a Vertical Coordinator

The institutional design of HOPCOMS could bring in efficiency of vertical coordination by starting early in the supply chain by providing crop advice to farmers at no cost and selling inputs at lower than market price (disintermediation). Results in Table 3.8 show that many farmers avail technical services when available. Many farmers who participated in the survey mentioned that they wanted advice on crop choice and agronomic practices. In the Indian context where public agricultural extension services are not very efficient, HOPCOMS can serve as an alternative channel for providing extension services with special focus on horticulture. Besides, by starting fruit juice plants it plans to bring in value addition which benefits both producers and consumers. The turnaround of Mysore HOPCOMS from a loss making entity to a profit making one happened partly because of revenue from sale of fresh juice.

However, in practice HOPCOMS has failed to utilize its potential efficiently. Its half-hearted entry into processing and discontinuation of crop advice services in many centres indicates inefficiency in day-to-day operations. At this time of change, HOPCOMS can capitalize on its backward and forward linkages and can be more attractive to farmers without much investment on market promotion. A strong management with a clear vision about its future can bring in efficiency and success.

As a Cooperative

While theoretically, cooperatives or horizontal farmer arrangements are empowering of smallholder-members, they have some problems of their own. The most important drawback of HOPCOMS is that it is not a cooperative in the sense that decision-making is not bottom up (Table 3.9). While a reasonably high percentage of HOPCOMS users were members who said that they participated in decision making this was restricted to voting at elections. At its best, the ownership gives farmers, especially small farmers, a feeling that they get "good respect". This is valuable in itself, but not enough. There is hence little incentive to be a member. Of the sampled HOPCOMS farmers, only over half were members.

One of the reasons is that rather than decentralized farmer organizations, HOPCOMS functions like a farmer-owned company where farmers are minor shareholders. This is in contrast to Amul. The core of Amul's ethos is decentralized bottom up decision making with promoting the sense that farmers are the real owners of the cooperative. This has contributed to Amul's resounding success.

As has been pointed out earlier (Rao, 1997), awareness among members and their contribution to issues like expanding area of operation of the society, improving the sales network, computerization, and product diversification among other things are absent. Users view the organization more as a government department. Training programmes on meaning of co-operation and capacity building of the members to assume leadership are lacking. From the point of sustainability of the society and its scaling up, this needs to be taken up now.

Then there is the issue of power within the cooperative. Where there is inequality among members, wealthier farmers may enjoy disproportionate power or expropriate the surplus-inverse relationship between heterogeneity and efficiency (Hart and Moore, 1998). In HOPCOMS, this is not conspicuous. Yet, many farmers complained of differential treatment, saying bigger farmers tended to be treated better. It is also a well-known fact that many prominent politicians with farming backgrounds were members of HOPCOMS. So while the connection between political power and HOPCOMS membership is not clear, a link is a definite possibility.

Implications for Sustainability, Scaling-Up and Replication

Sustainability: In any public policy intervention, the issue of sustainability is a big question. How dependent is it on subsidies doled out by the state? In the case of HOPCOMS, the subsidies have so far been on investments in infrastructure and its upgradation and not for its day-to-day operations. For example, HOPCOMS received grants worth ₹ 2.2 crore from the Department of Horticulture, National Horticulture Board, APMC, NCDC, Zilla Parishads of Bangalore, Mysore and Kolar, and the Bangalore City Corporation. However, there is implicit support for HOPCOMS in that it is assured of demand from larger public sector institutional buyers and from the health conscious emerging middle class who prefer high value foods such as fruits and vegetables. The third source of subsidy has to do with the premises which is given free by the state, for procurement centers and retail kiosks.[22]

The sustainability of small farmer inclusion would not be under threat. With its frugal supply chain infrastructure (supported by the government) and decentralized procurement functions, incorporating small farmers makes economic sense. HOPCOMS is a profit-making entity. However, its objective is clearly not to push the topline, it is more of a social welfare maximizer. The backward and forward linkages enable it to share the profits among its users, mainly by increasing farmers' share in the retail price.[23]

Its sustainability as a profit making entity is however not assured in the context of retail competition. There are three ways it could go.

First, HOPCOMS could invest in retail formats and build a new parallel supply chain. This might be first-best from the point of view of small farmer inclusion. But this would also demand significant changes in the organization and mode of functioning of an essentially government-centric entity. It would also require financial capital to develop competitive supply chain management infrastructure.[24] This would be the "other" revolution and, like Safal, it could combine the efficiency gains from horizontal and vertical coordination. Given the current situation, this seems farfetched, although not inconceivable.

Second, HOPCOMS could pursue aggressive marketing strategies through methods like supplying fruits and vegetables to supermarket chains, franchisee arrangements, etc. HOPCOMS would then have bargaining power because of its size and be able to increase fruits and vegetables sold without having to invest in its own retail formats. This is more in line with the role popularly envisaged for farmer organizations in the new retail context. However, this needs intensive negotiations and a trustworthy partner to prevent problems such as unexpected lowering of prices by supermarket chains to push HOPCOMS out of supply chain, which may leave smallholders in a more vulnerable position than before. This also raises the question of implicitly subsidizing private supermarkets with public money, an issue opposed by many farmer members and politicians in the country.

---

22 It is difficult to get precise estimates for these, since the documents are not publicly available.

23 Fruit stalls and juice centers sell products at market rates; however, it attracts consumers because of quality products. This gives it more leverage, passing on benefits to farmers.

24 In fact, this was talked about in the early years of the current decade, but plans have not materialized.

The third option—a status-quo—might work, given the robust demand and stable clientele, but this would have limited welfare implications for the small farmer.

Scaling Up: With agri-food retailing set to increase by leaps and bounds in the coming years, the issue of scaling up is an interesting question. Observers suggest that the story of scaling up is one of missed opportunity. HOPCOMS, according to them, could have become a "monopoly" in horticultural retailing in the state had there been vision and action.[25]

What has been holding it back? According to officials connected with HOPCOMS (in both Bangalore and Mysore), increasing the procurement creates problems of selling it. So HOPCOMS procures only what can be sold through its retail outlets and through institutional sales. HOPCOMS has not made active efforts to expand the space that it operates in. It appears that HOPCOMS, being cautious about a funneling effect in its supply chain, has refrained from expanding the supply pipeline itself. Since HOPCOMS is not interested in pushing the topline, it has financial constraints to open more procurement centres and retail outlets.

One of the issues that is debated is the decision in 1997 to spin-off district-level HOPCOMS units into independent entities. At a time when HOPCOMS could have attained scale through spatial integration, decentralization had the effect of confining the operations of individual units to particular geographic regions. This has also had implications of supply-demand management. Whereas it was easy within an integrated unit, now it is rendered more inflexible, since it now takes the form of inter-HOPCOMS trade.

Some other constraints to scaling up arise from legal issues.[26] However institutional issues also play a large role in this. Some of these relate to the fact that government being the largest contributor to its share capital, it is run as an appendage of the government and as a 'government cooperative'. This manifests itself in the organizational structure where the top brass are on deputation from the Departments of Cooperation or Horticulture for short tenures. What this means for HOPCOMS is that a long term vision and strategy for it is missing.[27] In fact, the tragedy, as some see it, of HOPCOMS is that, at any point of time, it is only as good as the person who leads it.

Replicability: The HOPCOMS model provides exciting opportunities for replication. In particular, it offers an example of an institution that attempts to provide marketing

---

[25] HOPCOMS accounts for around 6-10 per cent of horticulture trade in Bangalore. It has therefore had a "disciplining role" but never "control" over the market, according to an official. It has maintained this share steadily over the 1990s and 2000s.

[26] The huge HOPCOMS procurement yard in Bangalore is in the midst of ownership litigation so upgrading of infrastructure at its largest centre is not possible.

[27] There were cases where bureaucrats even in a short tenure at HOPCOMS were able to impart vision. Mr. Dodda Kende Gowda, Managing Director at Mysore HOPCOMS, in early 2007 is one. He has achieved a turnaround, generating profits for the first time in many years because of aggressive marketing. Mr. Chennapa Gowda, seen as the architect of HOPCOMS success story with a long tenure, is another bureaucrat who set up systems in HOPCOMS.

support to small farmers through a combination of horizontal and vertical coordination. HOPCOMS's case for replicability derives from the fact that the contextual preconditions are minimal and not peculiar or unique to the region it operates in. Clearly, agro-climatic conditions to grow horticultural crops, the existence of demand for horticultural produce, and government support for initial investments such as building procurement centres, retail outlets, and cold storages, and supportive government policies are preconditions. In fact, a strong state would be an asset and critical for effective replication, without which an instituition such as HOPCOMS might languish, unless there is initiative and a culture of cooperation amongst farmers. Beyond these, there is little asset-specificity and no particular investment that farmers need to make. In fact, recognizing the potential of HOPCOMS-like institutions, variants of the HOPCOMS model have been initiated in neighbouring states like Kerala and Tamil Nadu.[28]

It is also possible to contrast the performance of HOPCOMS (Mysore) and HOPCOMS (Bangalore) as a test of replicability. The former was a loss-making entity and the latter made profits. Our attempt to identify the underlying causes for differential performance led us to contextual constraints. When Mysore HOPCOMS was spun off from Bangalore HOPCOMS, it inherited liabilities that have been difficult to meet. The turnaround has also been challenging because of a large permanent staff relative to its requirements. Also, Mysore's scale of operation is about one-tenth that of Bangalore. For example, Bangalore has four procurement centers and 318 retail outlets compared to Mysore's one procurement centre and 40 retail outlets. The general opinion is that, with scaling up, Mysore HOPCOMS could well replicate the success of Bangalore, and indeed it has begun to do just that.

Conclusion

As an institutional innovation, HOPCOMS that combines horizontal and vertical coordination holds great promise in providing a platform for small farmers to connect to dynamic markets. Yet, in its practice, it does well in some aspects and not at all in others.

Its main strength is in vertical coordination. Through low cost means, HOPCOMS is able to procure produce from farmers and get it to consumers through a network of decentralized procurement centres and scattered retail outlets.

The role of HOPCOMS *vis-a-vis* the small farmer has to expand. It might be useful for HOPCOMS to provide crop advisory services, marketing inputs, market intelligence to farmers. Though this objective did figure in the initial objectives of HOPCOMS, this has got diluted over time and today, it figures nowhere in the scheme of things. One of the aspects we noticed during our study was that HOPCOMS has made very little effort to study the profile of those who use its services. There is lack of data on even

---

28 The degree of success that it has achieved is something that we have not explored. Hence we are in no position to comment on it.

such basic issues as to what percentage of small farmers are using these services. In this context, meetings with members may be a good forum to assess their needs and stock inputs accordingly.

HOPCOMS procurement centres have an almost daily presence of farmers in large numbers. This seems to be an ideal platform to provide agricultural inputs and extension services by agricultural universities. Though some procurement centres (notably Chennapatna, Lalbagh, and Hoskote) have facilities for sale of fertilizers and inputs, the offtake is very limited. The ideal situation would be for HOPCOMS to be a one-stop shop for all the requirements of the farmer. Given the rather high level of indebtedness among the sample studied, a tie up with some financial institution by at least providing its premises for setting up banking operations would work to the benefit of farmers.[29] Improvements in vertical linkages such as provision for credit, inputs, crop planning advisories, and inclusion of bottom-up approach in its operations combined with horizontal coordination would unleash a new potential for HOPCOMS to be the innovation it truly ought to be.

For this, however, there is universal agreement that professional management with long term vision for the organization is required. It would have to be guided by the principle that government only manages the collective with real owners being farmers. HOPCOMS, on the other hand, is run like an extension of any government department, as a static organization which does not function as a change agent should. If it continues at this rate, it could well be assigned into oblivion by the currently aggressive marketing practices of retailers. And the losers would be small farmers.

References

Berdegué, A., Peppelenbos, L., and Biénabe, E., "A Method for the Analysis of Innovative Practice in Connecting Smallholder Producers with Dynamic Supply Chains." *Resource Paper for Component 2, Regoverning Markets*, October, 2006. Available at

http://www.regoverningmarkets.org/en/resources/global/component_2_resource_paper

Gulati, A. and Reardon, T., "For a less painful path towards retail revolution," *The Economic Times*, Friday, June 22, 2007.

Hart, O. and Moore, J., "Cooperatives *vs.* Outside Ownership." *NBER* Working Paper No. 6421. 1998. Available at http://users.nber.org/papers/w6421

Nair, J., *The Promise of a Metroplis*, Oxford University Press, New Delhi, 2005.

Rao, V.M., "Integration of Production, Procurement, Processing, and Marketing through Co-operatives: A Study of HOPCOMS (Karnataka)," *Indian Journal of Agricultural Economics*, 1997, 52(3).

Treville, D., *Contract Farming, the Private Sector and the State: An Annotated and Comprehensive Bibliography with Particular Reference to Africa*. Binghamton, NY: Institute for Development Anthropology, 1986.

---

[29] In his survey of HOPCOMS farmers Rao (1997) points out the need for timely credit expressed by farmers who were in favour of linking credit with marketing.

4

Connecting Small Farmers with Dynamic Markets: A Successful Supply Chain in Uttarakhand, India

Ghayur Alam and Deepti Verma

Food markets in developing countries are undergoing quick and major changes. In the past retailing, particularly in the food sector, consisted of a large number of small outlets. This is now changing. Large players, including corporates, are becoming increasingly involved with food retailing activities in developing countries. These changes are accompanied by the adoption of new institutional and organizational innovations. They also involve the use of new technology (especially information technology and food processing). These changes are expected to have a profound effect on the functioning of food markets and on small farmers who are particularly vulnerable to market changes.

As in other developing countries, India's retail food sector is undergoing major changes. Although their implications are widely debated, very little empirical information is available to assess the impact of these changes. This study is aimed at filling some of this gap; it examines a vegetable supply chain in the Indian state of Uttarakhand in order to understand the functioning of food markets involving small farmers and a large retailer.

One of the newly created states, Uttarakhand is located in the Central Himalayas. Agriculture plays a crucial role in the state as about 80 per cent of its working population depends on it. A large majority of farmers are smallholders and produce mainly to meet their own needs. Commercial crops are unimportant in most districts; the proportion of area under commercial crops is less than 5 per cent.

The supply chain being studied here involves the supply of tomatoes by farmers from a number of villages situated in the Naugaon block of Uttarakashi district in Uttarakhand to Mother Dairy, a large retailer in Delhi. These villages are about 400 km from Delhi and 100 km from Dehradun, the state capital. The nearest wholesale grain and vegetable markets are in Dehradun. As in other areas of Uttarakhand, 98 per cent of the population in Naugaon is engaged in agricultural activities. The most distinguishing characteristic of these villages is the importance of cash crops in their livelihood activities. A large number of farmers have started cultivating cash crops (mainly vegetables) to replace traditional food crops.

The study focuses on farmers belonging to two areas in Naugaon block: Naugaon and Dhari-Kafnaul. The Naugaon villages are located on or near roads and are comparatively well connected with markets in both Naugaon town and bigger cities.

Farmers in these villages were the first to adopt tomatoes as cash crops. Beginning in the middle of the 1980s, tomato cultivation had become an important agricultural activity by 2000. Almost 90 per cent of the farmers in our sample had adopted tomato production before 2004.

The Dhari-Kafnaul villages, on the other hand, suffer from poor access to roads and, therefore, markets. Adoption of tomatoes and other vegetables as cash crops began late in these villages. In fact, almost 75 per cent of the farmers in our sample had started tomato cultivation in or after 2004.

Methodology

The study is based on data collected from both secondary and primary sources. Secondary sources include newspaper reports, articles in research journals, and reports of companies and NGOs working in the area. Primary data have been collected from a large number of farmers through a detailed questionnaire. The sample consisted of 273 farmers. In this sample, 174 farmers supply vegetables to Mother Dairy. In addition to these farmers, the sample includes 94 vegetable producers who sell to private dealers alone. This was done in order to identify the drivers of inclusion in the supply chain involving a large retailer and compare the economic benefits to farmers supplying to a large retailer with those supplying to private wholesalers. Additional information was collected through detailed discussions with 48 farmers by the lead researcher to understand various issues in greater depth.

Farmers who are part of this supply chain are organized into four federations. These are: Rawain, Purola, Kamal Ghati, and Dewrana federations. Our study focuses on farmers belonging to two Rawain and Dewrana federations. These federations include farmers from villages in Naugaon and Dhari-Kafnaul areas respectively. They were selected as they represented farmers living in very different geographical areas, with important differences in their linkages with markets.

Farmers were randomly selected in consultation with the federations. The criterion for inclusion was the size of the landholding; the sample consists of groups of farmers representing small, medium, and large landholdings. As shown in Table 4.1, the sample covers 22 per cent of farmers belonging to the federations selected for the study.

Table 4.1: Sample of Farmers

Number of Members (Rawain and Dewrana Federations)	*Number of Farmers Included in the Study*	*Proportion of Total Members [%]*
787	174	22

India's Retail Sector

India's retail sector is large—it is estimated to be worth ₹ 14000 billion (US $350 billion) and is growing rapidly. A very large proportion of it consists of small and tiny shops. Organized retail accounts for only ₹ 320 billion (US $8 billion), which is 3 per cent of the total. This situation, however, is beginning to change. There is a structural shift from small, family-run shops to larger, organized retail outlets. The presence of the organized sector has seen a sharp increase in recent years. It is growing at 30 per cent annually and its share is likely to reach 8–10 per cent in the next five years. The corporate sector is planning to invest about ₹ 16500 billion (about US $ 412 billion) during the period 2006–2011. These include proposed investments by Reliance Retail and the Aditya Birla Group of ₹ 250 billion (about US $ 6.25 billion) and ₹ 150 billion (about US $ 3.75 billion) respectively. As large Indian companies move into the retail sector, there is pressure from foreign companies to be allowed entry. It is expected that foreign companies will also play an increased role in the near future.

Situation in Naugaon before Innovation

In the past, farmers in the area practiced subsistence agriculture; cultivating traditional crops such as wheat, rice, pulses, and millets. Although some farmers grew vegetables for personal consumption, markets played little role in their agricultural activities.

The situation began to change in the mid 1980s when farmers began to cultivate tomatoes and other vegetables. The drive towards commercialization of agriculture was helped by a Dehradun based NGO, called Himalayan Action Research Centre (HARC).[1] An important element of HARC's work in the area has been to promote agricultural diversification through cultivation of vegetables, including tomatoes. It facilitated farmers' training in cultivation and pest/disease control techniques and introduced new seed varieties and other agricultural inputs. This led to a sharp rise in tomato production during the early 2000s.

This large increase in production created its own problems. These included—the small size of local markets which were unable to absorb large quantities of tomatoes; lack of linkages with larger wholesale markets, such as in Delhi; the inability of small farmers to transport their produce to large wholesale markets; shortage and high cost of wooden crates, which were needed to transport tomatoes to distant markets.

HARC and the farmers were not prepared to manage such a large increase in production. In the absence of a market, farmers suffered large losses and dealers and commission agents took advantage of the situation. In fact, during the peak period, a large proportion of the production had to be destroyed because of lack of market.

The challenge before HARC and the farmers was how to find a market to absorb this increasing production. It was in this situation that the innovation described below played a crucial role.

---

1 The main objectives of HARC are to empower small farmers through building and strengthening local institutions and increase farmers' income through improved productivity, greater market access, and enhanced technical capabilities. Its interventions are also aimed at making small farmers more market-oriented and overcome major supply chain challenges that are specific to small farmers.

Nature of the Innovation and the Supply Chain

The innovation consists of the building of a successful supply chain, begun in 2001, linking small farmers producing tomatoes and other vegetables with Mother Dairy, a large retailer.[2] Farmers are organized into federations, which supply off-season vegetables (mainly tomatoes) to Mother Dairy through a purchasing agreement. HARC has played a critical role in setting up the supply chain, ensuring that farmers' capabilities are enhanced so that they can receive maximum benefit from the chain. The federations organize the collection of produce, receive and distribute payment, organize farmers' training, and increasingly, provide farmers with market information.

Farmers see in this arrangement as an opportunity to receive higher prices and a secure market. Mother Dairy benefits as the arrangement enables it to source vegetables from hill areas during the summer season when they cannot be grown in the plains.

A number of factors were responsible for Mother Dairy's interest in procuring tomatoes from the Naugaon area. These include the following:

Mother Dairy relies on mountain areas for its supply of vegetables during summer months, when production in the plains is not possible. Tomato is one of the most important vegetables Mother Dairy requires from the mountains during this time. Until year 2000, it used to meet all its off-season (summer) requirement of vegetables from an area called Solan in Himachal Pradesh (another mountainous area, neighbouring Uttarakhand). As farmers in Solan grew in confidence, and their federations developed links with private dealers in large wholesale markets, they began to demand an increase in price. Mother Dairy decided to counter this by developing alternative sources. Around 2001 when tomato producers in Naugaon were experiencing difficulties owing to lack of market, Mother Dairy was looking for a large group of off-season tomato farmers who could meet its demand.[3]

HARC, under pressure from farmers, approached a senior state government official responsible for rural development to help Naugaon tomato farmers to find suitable markets. This official had previously worked with the cooperative sector and was aware of Mother Dairy's need to procure large volumes of off-season vegetables from the mountains. He invited HARC and Mother Dairy to a meeting to explore the possibility of Mother Dairy purchasing tomatoes from farmers in Naugaon.

---

2 With a turnover of ₹ 17000 million (about US $ 350 million in 2005, Mother Dairy is among the leading cooperatives in India. Formed in 1988, it is one of the largest players in the dairy and vegetable retail market. It markets fresh and frozen fruit and vegetable products under the brand name Safal through a chain of more than 350 owned fruit and vegetable shops and more than 20,000 retail outlets in various parts of India.

3 Once the farmers in Solan realized that Mother Dairy has developed a new source of supply, they agreed to supply on the previously agreed terms and conditions. Mother dairy now purchases 70 per cent of its off-season tomatoes from the Naugaon area and 30 per cent from the Solan area. Farmers in Solan have developed strong links with various wholesaler buyers and their dependence on Mother dairy is now small.

Mother Dairy agreed to buy from the Naugaon area as it fitted with its interest in diversifying suppliers of off-season vegetables and reducing its dependence on Solan farmers for tomatoes. It also agreed to provide plastic crates to farmers to reduce losses during transportation and bring down the high cost and difficulties associated with the use of wooden boxes. The use of plastic crates has reduced the cost of packaging by 70 per cent.

As Mother Dairy always works with farmers' organizations, it helped farmers to form two farmers' associations in the area.[4] Later, as farmers' interest increased, four more federations were formed. Both Mother Dairy and HARC have played important roles in the formation of these federations.

When the first federation was formed, many farmers were skeptical and did not join. But soon, when the benefits of becoming part of the supply chain became apparent, federation membership increased rapidly. The federations include more than 1500 farmers belonging to about 80 villages (Table 4.2). There are no specific rules governing the membership; all farmers in the area are eligible to join.

In the formative years, the federations were helped by both Mother Dairy and HARC. As Mother Dairy had previous experience of working with farmers' organization, it provided the basic framework for the federations. In particular it helped in the preparation of the aims and objective of the federations. HARC provided legal and organizational support needed in the early days. It trained members in organizational

Table 4.2: Farmers Federations

Name of the Association	*Number of Villages*	*Year of Formation*	*Number of Self Help Groups*	*Number of Members*
Rawain Valley Fruits and Vegetables Growers Association, Naugaon	36	2001	36	685
Devrana Fruits and Vegetables Growers Association Dhari Kafnol	08	2004	8	102
Kamal Valley Fruits and Vegetables Growers Association	11	2004	6	126
Fruits and Vegetables Growers Association, Purola	13	2001	13	141
Upper Yamuna Organic Growers Association	10	2002	10	376
Rawain Women Multipurpose Autonomous Cooperative Society Ltd.	14	2003	17	211
Raghunath Organic Growers Cooperative Society		NA	11	126

Source: Three Year Impact Analysis Report of the Institutional Project 2003–06, "*Promotion of rural agro enterprise for the betterment of livelihoods by strengthening civil society, economically viable organization and promotion of sustainable agro-ecological management system in Uttaranchal region*", Project No.317/2491–D and HARC Status Report (2003–2005), Himalayan Action Research Centre, Dehradun, Uttarakhand.

[4] Mother Dairy is working with 36 federations in Uttarakhand and about 300 in the whole country.

matters (such as elections of the office bearers) and maintenance of business records. It also provided the federations with opportunities to visits various wholesale markets and developed capability to gather marketing information. Most importantly, HARC's training has made the federation leaders confident in dealing with buyers of vegetables and suppliers of agricultural inputs.

The federations provide following services to their members:

- Prepare an annual production plan and negotiate supply targets with Mother Dairy
- Organize the procurement of vegetables at collection centres
- Monitor the grading of produce before it is packed at the collection centres
- Act as a mediator between farmers and Mother Dairy
- Provide packaging crates on rent
- Sell agro inputs to members
- Receive payment from Mother Dairy and distribute it to farmers
- To arrange farmers' training
- Arrange to sell farmers' surplus vegetable production to private dealers This is very useful when Mother Dairy is unable to purchase farmers' production during the peak season
- Setting up a relief fund which will provide help to farmers in case of losses owing to natural causes such as landslides. The federations charge ₹ 2 for every 10 kg of produce sold through them for the relief fund.

Description of the Supply Chain

The tomato supply chain involving tomato farmers and Mother Dairy consists of the following:

Tomatoes are harvested by farmers according to production plans prepared by the federations and accepted by Mother Dairy. These are brought by farmers to designated collection centres, which are manned by an employee/volunteer of the federation. The farmers are expected to grade tomatoes at the collection centre according to the quality parameters provided by Mother Dairy.[5] In the case of federations with a small number of members, this does not pose serious problems. The federation representative is able to monitor the grading carried out by the farmers. In federations with a large number of members, on the other hand, monitoring of grading is a problem.

After grading, tomatoes are packed in plastic crates provided by either Mother Diary or the federations. These are loaded into trucks and transported to Mother Dairy's

[5] Farmers and the federations have little say in the fixing of quality criteria. These are, in fact, fixed by Mother Dairy according to customer preference.

Central Distribution Facility (CDF) in New Delhi.[6] On arrival at CDF, tomatoes are again checked for quality. Based on the quality of a sample of tomatoes, the whole truck is either accepted or rejected. If accepted, the whole truck is sent to Mother Dairy's retail booths. If rejected, tomatoes are graded again by Mother Dairy employees. Those which meet the quality criteria are sent to the Delhi wholesale market and the rest are rejected and destroyed.

There were serious difficulties in the beginning. These included:

1. *Opposition from established private dealers and their agents:* The dealers and their agents created many problems, rumours, and physical obstructions. They also used violence to frighten the truck drivers. The situation improved after the Uttarakhand government provided police and administrative support to protect Mother Dairy's operation.
2. *Farmers' lack of confidence in Mother Dairy:* Farmers were not ready to trust Mother Dairy as it was new to the area. HARC played an important role in removing farmers' doubts about Mother Dairy. In the first year (2001) it also participated directly in the supply chain by procuring tomatoes on behalf of Mother Dairy and taking responsibility for payment.
3. *Resistance to grading and quality control:* Farmers were unhappy as Mother Dairy fixed quality parameters unilaterally. They were also and continue to be, unhappy that Mother Dairy accepts only the best quality produce. It is difficult for farmers to sell the tomatoes left over after grading in the market.

In spite of these difficulties and an early reluctance to supply to Mother Dairy, the latter was successful in attracting a number of farmers. Apart from the high price paid, support from a section of community leaders also contributed to the initial success. Some local politicians and community leaders were very active in their support to Mother Dairy and the federations. For example, one of the farmers, who was very active in the formation of the federation, stopped plying his truck which used to transport tomatoes to private dealers. He also stopped selling wooden packing boxes used by farmers to send tomatoes to private dealers.

It must be emphasized that, although the federations and Mother Dairy have a legal relationship, the farmers are not contractually obliged to sell to Mother Dairy. In fact, many farmers sell to both Mother Dairy and private buyers. For example, farmers included in our survey sold only about 30 per cent of their tomatoes to Mother Dairy in 2006; the rest were sold to private dealers. Similarly, Mother Dairy is not obliged to buy a fixed quantity of tomatoes from the farmers. The quantity to be purchased is determined every year through negotiations between the federations and Mother Dairy.

---

[6] This is a large facility, spread over an area of 25 acres. It includes large storage facilities, refrigerators, and deep freezes.

Issues Concerning the Supply Chain

Drivers of Inclusion

What determines a farmer's ability to be part of a supply chain involving a large retailer, operating in dynamic markets? We have considered a number of factors as the possible drivers of inclusion.

Size of Landholding: Size of landholding may have an important influence on a farmer's ability to be part of a dynamic market. For example, a large retailer may prefer to deal with a few farmers with large holdings, rather than a large number of small farmers. Again, large farmers may have greater resources needed to meet the requirements of a large retailer. We find that farmers who supply to Mother Dairy have a tendency (albeit small) to have larger landholdings. For example, the average landholdings of Mother Dairy and Non-Mother Dairy farmers are 3.25 acres and 2.8 acres respectively. Again, while 17 per cent of Mother Dairy farmers have more than 5.5 acres, only 5 per cent of non-Mother Dairy farmers have more than 5.5 acres. However, the proportion of farmers with small landholdings (up to 2.25 acres) is similar in both groups (Table 4.3). As the difference in landholdings of the two groups is very small, it is difficult to assess its role as a driver for inclusion.

Table 4.3: Distribution of Farmers According to Landholding

	Size of Landholding		
	Up to 2.5 acres	*2.6.–5.5 acres*	*More than 5.5 acres*
Farmers who supply to Mother Dairy	84 (48)	61 (35)	29 (17)
Farmers who supply to private wholesellers	46 (49)	43 (46)	5 (5)

Figures in parentheses are percentages.
Source: CSD Survey (2007)

Level of Education: A farmer's level of education can affect her/his chances of participating in dynamic markets. For example, it can increase a farmer's ability to meet a large retailer's various requirements by adopting new cultivation and post-harvest management techniques. Also, the retailer could find it more convenient to deal with educated farmers.

We find that almost one-third of the farmers in both groups are illiterate. Furthermore, there is no significant difference in the level of education of farmers

Table 4.4: Level of Education

Group of Farmers	*Level of Education*			
	0	*Up to Class 5*	*Up to Class 12*	*Graduate*
Farmers who supply to Mother Dairy	58 (33)	46 (26)	62 (36)	8 (5)
Farmers who supply to private wholesalers	36 (38)	20 (21)	35 (37)	3 (3)

Figures in parentheses are percentages.
Source: CSD Survey (2007)

supplying to Mother Dairy and those selling to private wholesalers (Table 4.4). This suggests that level of education has not been a driver of inclusion.

Experience of having Worked with an NGO, and Ability to become Organized: This is found to be the most important driver of inclusion in this chain. As we mentioned earlier, Mother Dairy works only with organized farmers. In the Naugaon area it took HARC's help to form farmers' federations. As a number of farmers were already working with HARC, they account for the bulk of federation members. These farmers trusted HARC, and were therefore prepared to trust Mother Dairy. Also, having worked with HARC, they were used to working as part of a farmers' group.

Changes Required for Successful Inclusion

Farmers interested in supplying to Mother Dairy have to fulfill two major requirements. Firstly, they have to belong to a farmers' organization and, secondly, they have to grade their produce according to norms provided by Mother Dairy.

We find that farmers have had no difficulty in forming farmers' federations. As they were already working with the HARC they were familiar with the idea of farmers' groups and were able to form federations. However, the functioning of these federations has not always been smooth, and the sense of collective good is still missing in many members. This is shown most clearly by the difficulties faced in the grading.

Grading is a new condition for farmers, as private dealers do not require them to grade their produce. They accept all the produce, though the price depends on the overall quality of the lot. The success of Mother Dairy's system depends on farmers behaving in a socially responsible manner and grading honestly. We find that this is still a problem and many farmers (especially in the large federations) try to cheat the system by including poor quality tomatoes. As Mother Dairy itself conducts a sample-based quality check at its facility, this sometimes leads to rejection of a whole truckload because of the action of a few farmers. Mother Dairy and the federations have failed to find a workable solution to this problem.

Sustainability of Inclusion

The supply chain was set up without any subsidies from the government or Mother Dairy. However, HARC provided vital support during the formative years of the chain. In particular, it supported the formation and functioning of federations through financial support. It has also facilitated the training of farmers in various aspects of cultivation and marketing. HARC also finances the cost of certification of the farmers in two of the federations, which have become completely organic.[7] The cost of certification, which is about ₹ 300 per hectare, is being born by HARC at the

---

[7] Only one of these, Dewrana Federation, supplies to Mother Dairy.

moment. HARC also finances an internal control system run by five people.[8] HARC has spent about ₹ 2.6 million on supporting the vegetable supply chain in the Naugaon area during 2001–06.

HARC's activities, in turn, are supported by the state government and a Dutch donor (Coraid). In this sense, the supply chain has been supported by public money. The federations are now self-supporting, so HARC's support is less important. However, HARC is still important for providing training to farmers and for organizing and financing the certification of organic farmers.

Table 4.5 shows the nature and extent of support provided by HARC since 2001. It also shows that the role of HARC has declined over the years, suggesting that farmers and their federations have become increasingly more competent and confident in organizing the supply chain.

Table 4.5: Changes in the Nature and Extent of Services Provided by HARC

Period	*Services provided by HARC*		
	Individual Farmers	*Federation*	*Mother Dairy*
Period 1 (Before 2001)	Introduce the idea of crop diversification and importance of cash crops to farmers; Facilitate farmers' training; introduce new varieties of vegetables, particularly tomatoes.		
Period 2 (2001)	Provide farmers with marketing assistance; introduce Mother dairy to the area; continue with training of farmers in improved cultivation techniques.	Facilitate the formation of the first farmers' federation. Provide legal and organizational support.	Help Mother Dairy in setting up the supply chain. Also collected tomatoes and made payments to farmers on Mother Dairy's behalf.
Period 3 (2002–2005)	Continued with farmers' training. Expanded the training area to marketing. Arranged farmers' visits to wholesale markets. Hosts an annual fair to bring together farmers and suppliers of agricultural inputs.	Helped in the formation of other federations. Trained federation members in legal, organizational, and business matters to make them independent.	Helped the federations and Mother Diary by removing various bottle necks in the supply chain.
Period 4 (after 2005)	Reduced emphasis on farmers' training. Greater focus on improving infrastructure, such as collection centers, and ropeways.	Federations have become self-sufficient. They deal with Mother Dairy directly. HARC helps only when a new activity is to taken up such as certification of organic farmers.	Very little involvement with Mother Dairy.

[8] HARC's employees supervise and monitor the documentation done by the farmers. This reduces the work required to be done by the certifying agency. Consequently, the cost of certification is reduced significantly.

The federations have become self-sufficient through a number of income generation activities:

- One-time membership fee of ₹ 250 (about $ 6.0).[9]
- A 1.75 per cent transaction fee charged to Mother Dairy.
- A service fee (5 per cent of transaction) charged to members for bulk purchases of seeds, fertilizers, pesticides, and other inputs from agri-input companies.
- Renting of plastic crates at ₹ 1/crate per day to members during the harvest season. The fee is ₹ 2 for non-members.

The chain has also benefited from various government schemes to help farmers through improved infrastructure. For example, funds from the state government are being used to build covered collection centres. This will enable farmers to collect and pack their produce without suffering damage from rain and sun. The most important addition to the infrastructure is a ropeway built to transport produce from high altitude villages (with no road access) to a metal road. The ropeway has been financed by the central government as a result of HARC's efforts to link farmers with markets.

As public funds do not play an important role in sustaining the chain, its survival does not depend on the availability of subsidies and other financial support from public sources. However, the organic farmers will require HARC's support for some more time.

Costs and Benefits of Inclusion

Selling to a large retailer could involve a number of costs for small farmers. These costs could be financial as well non-financial, including:

- Increased use of chemical inputs such as fertilizers, pesticides and fungicides to meet the quality norms set by the buyer. Apart from increasing the cost of cultivation, this could seriously damage farmers' health and cause deterioration of the quality of water bodies.
- Greater need for credit to purchase costly inputs, leading to perpetual indebtness.
- Obligation to purchase agricultural inputs from the buyer.
- Contractual obligations to sell only to the buyer.

We find that farmers participating in the chain have reported a large increase in the use of pesticides and fungicides to meet the quality requirements imposed by Mother Dairy. While the Naugaon area as a whole has experienced an overall increase in the expenditure incurred on pesticides, the increase has been particularly large in the case of farmers supplying to Mother Dairy. As shown in Table 5, farmers supplying to Mother Dairy spend about ₹ 3780 per acre on the use of pesticides. Compared to this, non-Mother dairy farmers spend about ₹ 2050/acre. Furthermore, in spite of the large

---

9 The federations also take casual members who do not pay any fee. They can send their products only if the permanent members cannot meet the requirement.

number of fertilizer and pesticide applications and high expenditure, the damage caused to tomato from pest and disease is reported to have increased.[10] Farmers face a serious problem of pesticide resistance and are unable to limit damage from pest and disease. There is no incentive to farmers to employ organic methods, or to reduce the use of pesticides, as Mother Dairy does not differentiate between organic and non-organically cultivated products. Organic tomatoes produced by the Dewrana federation members are purchased at the same price as non-organically ones produced by farmers belonging to the Rawain federation.

We do not find any evidence to suggest that the large expenditure on pesticides has led to an increase in indebtedness among farmers supplying to Mother Dairy. Also, farmers do not have any contractual obligation to purchase inputs from, or sell their produce to, Mother Dairy.

The most important and immediate benefit of Mother Dairy's entry into the market was that farmers supplying to it received higher prices. Before Mother Dairy entered the market, farmers could sell only in the Dehradun wholesale market. The price in Dehradun was low; it ranged between ₹ 3 and 6/kg. At the same time, farmers incurred high transportation and packaging costs. For example, the cost of packaging and transporting 12 kg tomatoes (contained in a standard container) to the Dehradun Market was ₹ 32. The selling price of a container of tomatoes varied between ₹ 36 and ₹ 72. From this, farmers paid a commission of 6 per cent. After deducting various costs, farmers received a maximum of ₹ 4/kg. Sometimes, when there was a surplus of tomatoes and the price was very low, farmers could not cover even the costs of packaging and transportation.

Compared to this, during the first year of its operation, Mother Dairy guaranteed to pay a minimum price of ₹ 6/kg. The actual payments were even higher; after deducting the cost of transportation and packaging, farmers received ₹ 8.50/kg.

We carried out a detailed analysis of the economics of cultivation of tomatoes of farmers who are supplying to Mother Dairy and those who are not (Table 4.6).

Table 4.6: Increase in the Expenditure on Pesticides (2000–2006)

	Area under Tomato Cultivation (acre)	*Pesticide Expenditure (₹)*	*Pesticide Expenditure per acre (₹)*
Farmers belonging to Rawain Federation	27	102050	3780
Non-Mother Dairy Farmers	21	45150	2050

Note: Farmers belonging to the Dewrana federation are not included since they practice organic farming.
Source: CSD Survey.

Farmers supplying tomatoes to Mother Dairy are found to get higher profit/acre compared to those who sell to private dealers. While the former earned ₹ 31,999 per

[10] According to our survey, farmers apply an average of five sprays of pesticides on tomato crop during a cropping season, which is considerably more than the recommended dosage.

acre during 2006, the latter group earned only ₹ 20,388/acre. The difference in profitability is not because of a difference in the price given to farmers by Mother Dairy and private dealers; it is primarily because of the lower cost of marketing incurred by farmers supplying to Mother Dairy. Farmers spent only ₹ 0.14 kg in the marketing of tomatoes to Mother Dairy. Compared to this, farmers supplying to private dealers spent ₹ 1.83/kg on marketing. The difference in marketing costs is largely because of high transportation costs and commissions paid by non-Mother Dairy farmers. Farmers supplying to Mother Dairy do not pay commission, and the price given to them is after deducting the cost of transportation.

Table 4.7: Profitability of Tomato Cultivation (Mother Dairy)

	Yields (Kg/acre)	*Cultivation cost (₹/ Kg)*	*Marketing cost (₹/ Kg)*	*Total Cost (₹/ per Kg)*	*Rate/Kg (₹)*	*Profit/Kg (₹)*	*Profit (₹ /acre)*
Farmers who Supply to Mother Dairy	11635	2.82	0.14	2.96	5.71	2.75	31996
Farmers who Supply to Private Dealers	13592	2.59	1.83	4.41	5.91	1.50	20388

Source: CSD Survey.

It must also be pointed out that because of Mother Dairy prices offered by private dealers are much higher now than they were before. This is because private dealers have to match Mother Dairy's rates in order to remain in business. This has increased the options available to farmers. In fact, many farmers now prefer to sell either to both Mother Dairy and private dealers, or just to private dealers.

An important problem faced by tomato growers in the area was the high cost of wooden crates used for packaging and transportation. Mother Dairy introduced plastic crates, which are reusable. Following Mother Dairy, private dealers also now provide farmers with plastic crates. This has improved the economics of tomato cultivation considerably, and reduced the demand for forest wood.

With increased availability of market for cash crops, land utilization has increased. In the past about 30 per cent of the land in this area was not cultivated, as farmers did not have a market for their crops. With greater access to markets, use of improved farming technologies, and proper crop cycle planning, this land is now being cultivated.

Seventy-six per cent of the farmers felt that their tomato cultivation techniques have improved as a result of their association with Mother Dairy and HARC. As seen in Table 4.8, HARC is considered by a large number of farmers to be the most important source of new technology and information. More than 60 per cent of the farmers reported it to be the most important source of technical inputs. HARC was followed by government departments. Mother Dairy was the third important source of technical inputs. Private dealers and sellers of agricultural inputs were considered by most farmers as the least important.

Table 4.8: Sources of Technical Inputs

Source of Technical Inputs	*Number of Farmers Reporting*		
	Most Important	*Important*	*Least Important*
HARC	107 (61.49)	26 (14.94)	37 (21.26)
Government Agencies	52 (29.89)	34 (19.54)	67 (38.51)
Mother Dairy	8 (4.60)	52 (29.89)	87 (50.00)
Private Companies	1 (0.57)	7 (4.02)	111 (63.79)
Others	3 (1.72)	6 (3.45)	121 (69.54)

Source: CSD Survey.

Technical support includes information on new crops and varieties, training in the cultivation of new crops, and information on agro-inputs, especially seeds and plant protection methods. As a result of this support yields of most cash crops have increased in recent years. For example, tomato production has increased from 8000 kg/hectare to 20,000 kg/hectare. It must, however, be pointed out that the level of training and transfer of information activities has decreased in recent years.

Finally, as a result of the above mentioned benefits, farmers' household incomes have increased. For example, a sample survey of 163 families by HARC found in 2005 that 135 farmers (82.82 per cent) reported increased incomes.

Problems Faced by the Supply Chain

Although the entry of Mother Dairy has provided farmers with a number of benefits, the supply chain is faced with a number of problems.

High Rejection Rates: A large proportion of tomatoes supplied are rejected by Mother Dairy. This is perhaps the most common cause of resentment among farmers, and one of the major challenges faced by the chain. The rejection rates are particularly high in the case of tomatoes supplied by the Rawain and Dewrana farmers, the two federations we studied in detail. According to the data provided by Mother Dairy, more than half (by volume) of tomatoes supplied by farmers of these federations failed the quality parameters and were rejected in 2006 (Table 4.9).

Table 4.9: Rejection Rates (2006)

Federations	*Rejection Rate*
Rawain	59%
Dewrana	56%
Kamal Ghati	31%
Purola	13%

Source: CSD Survey.

There are a number of reasons for the high rates of rejection:

- The quality of tomatoes produced by the farmers is poor. This is particularly true during the early and later parts of the season, resulting in the highest rates of rejection during these periods. The reasons for poor quality include high incidence of pest and disease attacks and small size. The effect of pest attack is made more serious by the fact that the pest (borer) is not seen at the time of grading at the collection centre, as it is already inside the tomato. However, it matures very fast during transportation because of high temperature and damages the tomatoes during transportation to Delhi.

- Poor road conditions and the long distance to Delhi (about 300 km), high temperatures in summer, and lack of cold chains result in considerable damage during transportation. As the farmers are paid on the basis of quality checks carried out by Mother Dairy on arrival at CDS, this contributes to high rejection rates. Quality could be improved if a cooling chain was used, but Mother Dairy does not plan to introduce one as it considers it too costly.
- Self-grading by farmers is not always according to the norms laid down by Mother Dairy. The problem is particularly serious in the case of large federations (Rawain and Dewrana Ghati) as a large number of farmers bring their tomatoes to the collection points and supervision of grading is difficult. Dishonest or careless grading by some farmers leads to the rejection of a whole truck.

The federations are expected to ensure that grading is done strictly according to the criteria fixed by Mother Dairy. In practice, the federations are unable to enforce these norms. This is mainly because of lack of social responsibility among members and lack of influence of the federation leadership. The importance of strong leadership is shown by the Purola Federation. The average rejection rate of this federation was only 13 per cent during 2006. This is because the president of the federation, who is highly respected, personally supervises grading and does not tolerate any deviation from the norms.

The issue of grading has also led to disputes among farmers belonging to the same federation. For example, earlier the Kamal Ghati and Purola farmers belonged to the same federation. They had a very high rejection rate in 2005 (96 per cent). This caused a dispute between the farmers of the two areas, leading to the formation of separate federations. The rejection rates of both federations improved in 2006. The failure of the federations to inculcate social responsibility among its members, to practise honest grading for the greater good of all the members, is considered by many farmers to be one of the most important failures of the chain.

There is a widespread feeling among farmers that the quality control procedures of Mother Dairy are arbitrary. It uses lenient norms when it is in need of vegetables. On days when it has sufficient supplies, it employs strict norms and many trucks are rejected.

A simple solution to this problem is that the produce sent by each farmer is identified at the collection centre. Once individual farmers are responsible for the quality of their products, they are likely to produce better quality products and be more careful in grading. But Mother Dairy feels that it cannot deal with each farmer individually as this will increase its administrative costs prohibitively. It prefers to deal with the whole truck as a unit. This system works without problems when procuring from large farmers from the plains. Each of these farmers supplies a complete truckload to Mother Dairy and is responsible for the quality of produce in that truck. The system is not suitable for a situation where the suppliers are small farmers and send their produce collectively. Mother Dairy is simply using the system which was developed for large farmers in the plains. It has failed to evolve a system suitable for small farmers in the mountain areas. Unless this issue is resolved, high rejection rates will continue to cause resentment among farmers.

Weak Organization, Leading to Transportation Bottlenecks: There is a general feeling that the organization of Mother Dairy has deteriorated over the years. This is shown particularly in poor transportation arrangements; 43 per cent of the farmers surveyed by us reported that Mother Dairy's inability to provide transportation and crates in sufficient numbers is one of the most important problems they face. There is a feeling that there is no fixed time for the arrival of Mother Dairy trucks and farmers have to wait. Farmers also feel that Mother Dairy employees took more interest in the area when they were developing the chain. Now that the chain is established, they are beginning to take the farmers for granted.

Favouritism within the Federations: There is a feeling among some farmers (and villages) that the federations are dominated by groups of people who use their control to benefit themselves and their friends/relatives. For example, some feel that federation leaders get Mother Dairy to procure first from their villages. Only when they cannot meet Mother Dairy's demand, trucks are sent to other villages. Many of these villages have now decided to stop sending vegetables to Mother Dairy and have gone back to private dealers. In many of these villages, agents of the dealers have been active and have succeeded in influencing a large number of farmers to move away from Mother Dairy. Mother Dairy's weak organization and the failure of the federations to unite all farmers have played into the hands of private dealers, who have taken full advantage of the situation.

Table 4.10: Satisfied with Mother Dairy?

Satisfied		*Total Number of Farmers*
Yes	No	
79 (45)	95 (55)	174

Note: Figures in parentheses indicate percentages.
Source: CSD Survey.

We find that as a result of these problems, more than half of the farmers are dissatisfied with Mother Dairy (Table 4.10). This is likely to have serious detrimental effects on the long term sustainability of the chain. In fact, these effects are already apparent in a number of villages, where farmers have stopped supplying tomatoes and other vegetables to Mother Dairy since 2005.[11] As a result, the value of tomatoes sent has come down from ₹ 6 million in 2005 to only ₹ 1.3 million in 2006.

At the same time, we would like to mention that many farmers who are unhappy with Mother Dairy will continue to be part of the chain. This is because they realize that Mother Dairy's presence in the market exercises a check on the practices of private dealers. They are afraid that if the supply chain is damaged and Mother Dairy leaves, the dealers will be free to exploit farmers and the situation will become as bad as it was before the entry of Mother Dairy.

Farmers have made a number of suggestions to remove some of the problems they face. The most common suggestions are: Mother Dairy should fix the price in advance (39 per cent); grading norms should be relaxed to reduced rejection rates (35 per cent); and Mother Dairy should purchase all the production (34 per cent).

A variety of options are being tried by farmers, their federations, and HARC to solve some of the problems. These include—organic cultivation; growing exotic vegetables; and contract farming to reduce farmers' risks. The most successful of these efforts are the conversions by a large number of farmers in the area to organic farming. For example, farmers belonging to the Dewrana federation began conversion to organic cultivation two years ago. Today, all the members of this federation are organic farmers. It is hoped that this will help the farmers to find new buyers and reduce their dependence on Mother Dairy. The federation, with the help of HARC, has already found a new buyer who is prepared to buy their vegetables at a small premium.

This shows that farmers and their federations have grown in confidence and competence to find ways to solve some of their problems.

Impact of Structural Changes in Food Retail Sector on the Chain

India's food retail sector is undergoing major structural changes. These include the entry of the corporate sector, which is making large investments. The impact of these changes is likely to be felt by the chain we studied. Now that the Naugaon area has become known as an important source of off-season vegetables, these retailers are expected to procure from there on a large scale. Reliance Fresh, one of the largest emerging companies in the food retailing business in India, is already considering the possibility of procuring tomatoes from the area. What will be the impact of the entry of private retailers on farmers, Mother Dairy, and private wholesale dealers? Some farmers are happy that with the entry of other large retailers competition will increase and they will get a better price. While they would like Mother Dairy to continue to procure from the area (as a check against any exploitative practices of private buyers) they feel that competition will also stop Mother Dairy from becoming complacent.

[11] These include the following villages: Sonara, Manjali, Thali, Kansola, Kutyal, Pletha, and Uroli. In 2005 all the farmers in Sonara sold to Mother Dairy. None did in 2006. In Naini out of 28 households, only 10 sold (part of the production) to Mother Dairy. This year they have not sent production plans to the federation, which suggests that they do not plan to sell to Mother Dairy.

A majority of farmers, however, feel that the entry of large private retailers will not benefit farmers (Table 4.11). These include both farmers who belong to the supply chain (58 per cent) and those who do not (68 per cent). While agreeing that the entry of large private retailers may benefit farmers in the short run, they are concerned about the long term effect.

Table 4.11: Will Entry of Large Private Retailers Benefit Farmers?

	Will Entry of Large Private Retailers Benefit Farmers?		*Number of Farmers*
	Yes	No	
Farmers Belonging to the Supply Chain	73 (41.95)	101 (58.05)	174 (100)
Farmers not Belonging to the Supply Chain	26 (26.65)	68 (72.35)	94 (100)
Total	99 (36.94)	169 (63.06)	268 (100)

Source: CSD Survey.

As Mother Dairy procures less than 10 per cent of the tomatoes produced in the Naugaon area, entry of other large buyers will not have a serious effect on the supply. Private dealers are well entrenched in the area and have shown great resilience in meeting the challenge from Mother Dairy by offering farmers competitive prices and other attractive terms. They are expected to adapt to the entry of other large retailers as in the past by matching the terms of the latter.

While the situation is extremely unpredictable, it is likely that in the short term farmers will benefit from the entry of large private retailers. However, the long term impact of their entry is difficult to asses.

Replication of the Supply Chain in Other Areas

The supply chain we have studied has a number of distinguishing characteristics, which have contributed to its success. Firstly, the large retailer in the chain belongs to the cooperative sector, with a mandate to increase farmers' access to markets. Secondly, an important objective of the NGO working with the farmers (HARC) is to increase farmers' income through crop diversification and increased access to markets. Thirdly, farmers have been able to form federations. Although there are some difficulties, the federations are able to act as farmers' representatives.

Therefore, the most important condition for the replication of this chain is that large retailers should be prepared to work with organized farmers. This would be in the interest of both farmers and retailers. Farmers will be able to negotiate the best possible terms and the transaction costs incurred by the retailer will be reduced. The chain will also be helped by the presence of NGOs whose objectives include building farmers' linkages with the market.

Farmers and their organizations should not enter into exclusive selling contracts with large retailers. In the chain studied by us, farmers are not contractually obliged to sell to Mother Dairy exclusively. Many of them have benefited from this freedom by selling to wholesalers at a higher price. This freedom is an important way of strengthening farmers' bargaining power and will be especially useful when a number of large buyers compete for produce from areas such as Naugaon.

Our study shows that government subsidies are not necessary to build a successful supply chain. Limited public funding may be necessary to support farmers' organizations in their formative years; however, it must be an objective of these organizations to become self-sufficient by providing paid services to farmers and the retailer. Wherever possible, government and donor agencies should consider supporting farmers' organizations in their formative years. Financial support should also be made available to improve the infrastructure, particularly collection and transportation facilities in the area.

Conclusion

The supply chain has functioned successfully for six years. Farmers have become highly organized; six farmers' federations with about 1500 farmers from more than 80 villages have been set up. The federations organize collection of produce and delivery of inputs, training, and information to farmers.

Farmers' links with an NGO (HARC) and experience of working with farmers' groups are found to the most important drivers of inclusion in this supply chain. The study shows that farmers' ability to form farmers' groups can be an important attraction for a company considering building direct links with small farmers. This could significantly reduce the cost of linking them with dynamic markets and thus reduce the need for public funds. Also, the study suggests that strong farmers' organizations (federations in this case) can take control of the supply chain in due time, giving farmers a greater say in the functioning of the chain.

The supply chain was set up without the use of subsidies. Public funds were used to support the federations in the past, but this support is not needed now. The federations are now financially self-supporting. Their income comes from providing services to the buyer and farmers. Withdrawal of public funds will not affect the survival of the supply chain.

Farmers belonging to the supply chain have received a number of benefits. These include: higher profits, technical support, and increased land use. The household income of farmers belonging to the chain has seen a significant increase during the last six years.

High prices offered by Mother Dairy have had an important influence on the behaviour of private commission agents and dealers from wholesale markets. They have been forced to match Mother Dairy's prices and other terms and conditions. Moreover, as farmers have become more confident in working with markets, many of them are no longer content to accept the prices offered by Mother Dairy. Instead, they actively look for best prices and terms.

Many farmers are unhappy with Mother Dairy and the federations as they face a number of problems. These include: high rejection rates—transport difficulties; and favouritism within the federations. These problems may threaten the survival of the chain, as some farmers have already stopped supplying to Mother Dairy. However, many farmers see the presence of Mother Dairy as an important competitive force, putting pressure on private dealers to behave.

Farmers' ability to respond to changing market demands has increased. For example, many farmers are diversifying to cultivating exotic and off-season (high value) vegetables, crops, and fruits. They are also positioning themselves to take advantage of the emerging market for organic products.

The success of the chain has also led to some serious costs to farmers and the environment. During the last six years, use of chemical pesticides and fertilizers has increased manifold, causing serious environmental and health concerns. Efforts should be made to ensure that when such chains are set up, special care is taken to curtail the use of chemical pesticides. All stakeholders especially the retailer, farmers' organizations and NGOs working with farmers-must ensure that farmers are able to meet the required quality without increasing the use of chemical fertilizers and pesticides.

The supply chain can be replicated in other areas if large retailers are prepared to work with organized farmers and farmers are successful in forming efficient organizations. These organizations may require financial support from governments and donor agencies in their formative years but should aim at becoming self-sufficient by providing income generating services. When replicating, the negative aspects of the chain such as increase in the use of pesticides should be avoided.

References

Baptista, P. (Undated), "Connecting Small Farmers to Markets, Case Study on the Himalayan Action Research Center, Uttaranchal, India", South Asia Agriculture and Rural Development Department, World Bank.

Berdegué, J.A., Peppelenbos, L., and Biénabe, E. (2006) "A method for the analysis of innovative practice in connecting smallholder producers with dynamic supply chains", *Resource Paper for Component* 2, October, www.regoverningmarkets.org

EIU (2006), India: Consumer goods and retail forecast, The Economist Intelligence Unit, May 24th.

HARC (2006), Three Year Impact Analysis Report of the Institutional Project 2003–06 "Promotion of rural agro enterprise for the betterment of livelihoods by strengthening civil society, economically viable organization and promotion of sustainable agro Ecological Management System in Uttaranchal region" Project No.317/2491–D.

Reardon, T. and Huang. J. (2005), "Methods for Assessing Determinants, Costs, and Benefits of Small Farmer Inclusion in Restructured Agrifood Chains, *Resource Paper for Component 1,* October, www.regoverningmarkets.org

Saxena K.G., R.K. Maikhuri and K.S. Rao (Undated), "Managing Biodiversity in the Himalayan Farming Systems", http://www.unu.edu/env/plec/cbd/postersabstracts.xls

Singh S.K, "India Report Retail Food Sector 2006", GAIN Report Number: IN6111, US Embassy, New Delhi, December 12, 2006, www.fas.usda.gov/gainfiles/200706/146291412.pdf.

Teli B.L. (Undated), "Pattern of Variations in the Agricultural Development of the Garhwal Himalayas", in J.L. Raina (ed.) Himalayan Environment, Man and the Economic Activities", Pointer Publishers, Jaipur.

5

Integrating Small Farmers into Dynamic Supply Chains: A Case Study of MA'S Tropical Food Company

Parakrama A. Samaratunga

Sri Lanka is known historically for cultivation of spices such as cinnamon, pepper, cloves, cardamoms, nutmeg and mace (Herath, 2002).[1] Seventy per cent spice production comes from farm units of less than 1 ha of land. Spices currently constitute an important sub-sector of the agricultural sector and contribute 0.75 per cent in value to the total gross domestic product. Exports constitute 1.5 per cent of total exports and 8 per cent of agricultural exports. Exports exceed 50 per cent (when tea, rubber, and coconut are excluded) earning ₹ 10,287.7 million in 2005 (Central Bank, 2005).

Sri Lanka exports spices to about 70 countries of which 20 are major importers who provide a stable market. Spices have become main cash earners for farmers in spice growing areas during recent decades (Sappideen, 1987). Foreign exchange earn have shown a four-fold increase between 1996 and 2005,[2] Matale, is with 1,993.3 km^2 land area and about 442,000 population of whom about 92 per cent live in rural areas, is the leading district in spice cultivation.

Over the years spice-based farming is facing a variety of issues and challenges including productivity, market, technology, and institutional constraints, marketing-related constraints have been the most important in this set. This unorganized nature of marketing and the traditional supply chain have generated a mismatch in the quality of spices, leading to frequent price fluctuations. These constraints have led to low value added in the chain, low incentives to farmers, low farmers' income, and sluggish growth of the spice sector, creating unsustainability of the farming system (Lindara *et al.*, 2004).

The impact of modern retailing and allied changes introduced in the last two decades has been profound at restructured markets and small scale spice producers' levels. Rapid and continuous changes in domestic and export procurement systems have created a new demand pattern shifting the focus to continuous supply of high quality, value added products with improved processing, packaging, and labelling. Small scale spice producers have not been able to go along with the new marketing trends.

---

[1] The International Spice Group has defined spices as any of the flavoured or aromatic substances of vegetable origin obtained from tropical or other plants, commonly used as condiments or employed for other purposes on account of their fragrance, preservative, or medicinal qualities (Herath, 2002).

[2] Value of spice exports has increased from ₹ 2469.8 million in 1996 to ₹ 9986.5 million in 2005 (Sri Lanka Customs).

A new innovative practice of working with small holders in improving their ability to face restructured market conditions has emerged by delivering knowledge, assisting in accessing capital, advice on food sanitation, good agricultural practices, and enterprise planning. Innovations have been introduced elsewhere that enable fulfilling these consumer demands while effectively integrating the farmers in the supply chain. Nevertheless, the capacity of small scale farmers and rural small and medium enterprises (SMEs) to sustain their participation in the supply chain and restructured market has still not been studied, analyzed, and understood adequately. This paper is a study of the innovative practices taking MA'S Foods, basically a "business model" with limited "collective action strategies by farmers" as a case.

Methodology

We have adopted the case study approach as it enables us to obtain a holistic view of the research aspects. It has a considerable ability to generate answers to questions such as; "Who?", "What?", "Where?", "Why?" and "How?" and to make comparisons between different situations like before and after (Robson, 1993; Yin, 1994). It permits both making general and specific conclusions and gaining a rich understanding of the process within the given context (Gummesson, 1991; Yin, 1994). Most importantly, a wide range of information gathering techniques are used in case studies, consisting of both qualitative and quantitative methods (Gummesson, 1991; Morris and Wood, 1991; Yin, 1994).

We have explored all aspects of the innovative practices of integrating small scale farmers with dynamic food markets linked to MA'S Foods. We adopted combinations of research activities and instruments with the intention of covering different players in the supply chain from farmers to supermarkets. These included personal interviews, group discussions (PRA), farm records, and archival records.

A well designed, pre-tested, and repeatedly revised semi-structured questionnaire helped in covering all key points. Sample selection was done purposively to include relevant characteristics that would allow addressing the research questions precisely. The sample comprised 25 farmers with 20 farmers supplying spice products to MA'S and 5 farmers not supplying. One satellite farmer was included in the sample of supplying farmers. We did two comparative analyses—before *vs.* after and suppliers *vs.* non-suppliers—to find out whether the innovation led to significant welfare gains to small farmers in particular and the supply chain in general. We examined first the situation prior to the innovation and the current situation with greater emphasis on the process followed by the MA'S Foods in terms of key factors such as productivity, income, cost, technology, assets, employment creation and non-monitory benefits. The second analysis was a direct comparison between suppliers and non-suppliers in the area.

Semi-structured interviews and group discussions were conducted according to prepared guidelines with relevant representatives of the company and local government and non-governmental organizations (Table 5.1). Secondary sources of information included literature, financial records of the company, farm records, and archival records.

Table 5.1: Individuals and Institutions in the Sample

Backward Linkage	*MA'S Company*	*Forward Linkage*	*External*
Small scale farmers[1] Non-supplying farmers Satellite farmers[4] Village collectors	Managing Director Supply Chain Manager Factory Manager Production Manager RAPID Centre Manager Extension Officer Employees	Nestle[2] Unilever[2] Cargills[5] Keels[5]	NAC[3] Govijana Sewa

[1] Small scale farmers with supply relationships with the company including organic farmers.
[2] Local manufacturing companies.
[3] National Agribusiness Council.
[4] Type of collectors who directly deal with collection and transport of the product in bulk.
[5] Supermarket chains.

World Spice Production and Trade

Over 95 per cent of world production of spices takes place in developing countries and is consumed internally. India is the largest producer of spices contributing to 86 per cent of world production (Table 5.2). Ninety per cent of it is consumed within the country. The United States produces 40 per cent of its annual needs.

Table 5.2: World Spice Production: 2003–2004

	Production (MT)	%
India	1,600,000	86
China	66,000	4
Bangladesh	48,000	3
Pakistan	45,300	2
Turkey	33,000	2
Nepal	15,500	1
Other countries	60,900	3
Total	**1,868,700**	**100**

Source: http://en.wikipedia.org/wiki/spice_trade

Supply of spices in the world market is elastic since they can be grown in varying conditions. Many of the major spices such as chilies, ginger, and turmeric are short-term crops. However, the demand is stable and price inelastic in the short term. World market prices for most spices are volatile, reflecting the fluctuations in export availability determined by climatic variations, stock situations, natural tree crop cycles, and the state of economies in exporting countries. High prices could lead to the use of alternatives, especially in the industrial sector (Dias, 1987).

Annual worldwide imports grew at 8.5 per cent a year, indicating that consumption of spices continues to grow (http://www.intracen.org/bsrt/ppspices.pdf). Only a small quantity of spices traded is consumed as they are. Import and export trade in whole spices in the world is around US $ 5 billion a year, with an annual growth rate of over 5 per cent. This figure does not include internal consumption in the producing countries (Task Force Report on the Spices and Allied Products Industry, 2000). There is a growing trend towards consuming organic spices in the world. World consumption of organic spices is growing since 1995 by around 30 per cent annually (Herath, 2002).

Major importers of spices are the United States of America, Mexico, Europe, Asia, and Eastern Europe (Chandrasena, 2002). On both volume and value basis, the United States is the world's largest spice importer and consumer, with both imports and consumption on an uptrend for the past 10 years (http://www.ers.usda.gov/publications/aib709).

Spice Sector in Sri Lanka

Spices play an important role in the Sri Lankan economy. Main spice crops include cinnamon, pepper, cloves, cardamoms, nutmeg, and mace (http://www.srilankaspices.org/). Sri Lanka was known historically for producing exceptionally good spices. Sri Lankan soil and climate is well suited for producing good quality spices. Many exporters and stakeholders believe that Sri Lankan spices are intrinsically superior to those from other countries (Herath, 2002). In the past the spice industry played only a minor role in terms of employment and income, except for cinnamon which was traded as far back as the 14th century. For recent decades, spices have become the main cash earning enterprise of many farmers in the major spice growing areas (Sappideen, 1987). Production of spices has grown from 27,000 mt in 1996 to 37,000 mt in 2005 (Table 5.3, Figure 5.1). Sri Lanka is the largest producer of cinnamon in the world and contributes to over 80 per cent of global production. In the case of pepper, Sri Lanka's share is around 3 per cent. (http://www.srilankaspices.org/report.pdf).

Spices as a group appears to be geographically concentrated around the wet and intermediate zones. More specifically, cinnamon is found around the Low Country

Table 5.3: Estimated Production of Spices (mt)

Year	*Cinnamon*	*Pepper*	*Cardamom*	*Cloves*	*Nutmeg*	*Total*
1996	12,651	8,536	64	1,900	1,744	27,895
1997	13,484	9,831	87	2,400	989	26,791
1998	13,484	9,831	87	2,200	989	26,591
1999	13,466	9,284	74	3,500	1,221	27,545
2000	13,490	10,670	62	1,600	1,100	26,922
2001	13,600	7,650	60	2,500	1,100	24,910
2002	13,600	12,600	60	4,100	1,600	31,960
2003	14,015	12,660	64	2,360	1,740	30,839
2004	14,875	12,020	74	3,575	1,515	32,059
2005	15,890	15,300	80	4,860	1,860	37,990

Source: Export Agricultural Statistics of Sri Lanka, Department of Export Agriculture, 2003, 2006.

Wet Zone concentrated in the districts of Colombo, Kalutara, Ratnapura, Galle, Matara, and Hambantota. Cardamoms are found in the Up Country Wet Zone and Mid- and Up-Country Intermediate Zones in the districts of Kandy, Matale, Nuwara Eliya, Kegalle, and Rathnapura. Pepper, cloves, and nutmeg are found in the Mid Country Wet Zone in Kandy, Matale, and Kegalle. According to the Department of Export Agriculture, there has been an increase in the extent of cultivation of spices with more than 70,000 ha of land, accounting for about 6 per cent of the land under all perennial crops, under spices in 2005. As total volume of production and export value have increased by 64 per cent and 164 per cent respectively in the period 1997 to 2005.

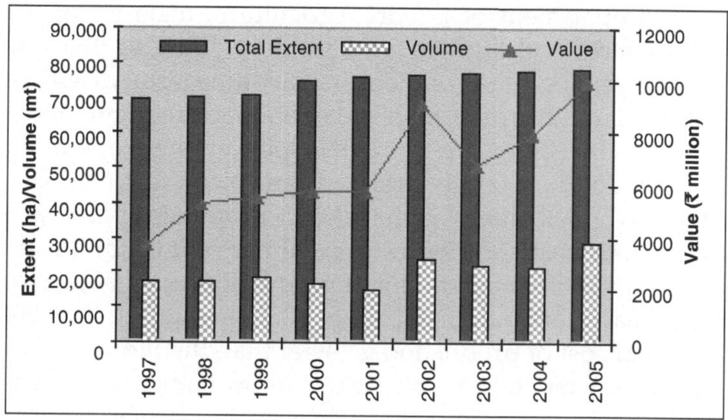

Fig. 5.1: Total Extent, Cultivated Volume and Value (ha, mt and ₹ million)

Sources: Central Bank Annual Reports, 2005 and Export Agricultural Statistics of Sri Lanka, Department of Export Agriculture, 2003, 2006.

Spices are a major source of foreign exchange earnings, contributing 1.5 per cent to total export earnings in 2005 (Table 5.4). Cinnamon is the major earner, adding more than ₹ 5,000 million per year (Central Bank, 2005).

Table 5.4: Contribution of Spices

Year	*Contribution to Agricultural Exports (%)*	*Contribution to Total Exports (%)*
1996	4.66	1.1
1997	6.05	1.4
1998	7.49	1.7
1999	8.35	1.7
2000	7.55	1.4
2001	7.0	1.4
2002	10.1	2.0
2003	7.27	1.4
2004	7.01	1.3
2005	8.27	1.5

Source: Central Bank Annual Report, 2005.

Spices are grown mainly in highly diversified mixed cropping units together with subsistence and other cash crops. Cinnamon and cardamoms are found mainly as pure stands and others are cultivated in mixed gardens up to 2 ha in extent (Sappideen, 1987). Smallholders play an important role in the spice value chain. Spices are grown traditionally by smallholders (Sappideen, 1987). Around 70 per cent of spice production comes from smallholder units that are less than 1 ha. There are approximately 400,000 smallholder farm units cultivating spices and thus the sector has a small farm orientation. Around 50,000 of them depend on spices as main family income (http://www.srilankaspices.org/).

According to the Department of Export Agriculture, majority of spice cultivation owners are subsistence level farmers who are not willing to invest in productivity improvement programmes. Many of them are part-time farmers with other sources of income. Only a small number of farmers have commercial orientation and are willing to improve productivity (Lindara *et al.*, 2004). Spice growers operating about 2 acres get about 30 per cent of their family income from spices. Cultivation and processing are labour intensive and women labour takes a prominent place. In Sri Lanka and other countries, labour cost contributes over 50 per cent of total cost of production (Herath, 2002). In smallholder conditions of production, costs of establishment, use of inputs, and maintenance are minimal if not negligible (Lindara *et al.*, 2004; Sappideen, 1987). Thus, the total cost of production is lower than the farm gate price (Table 5.5). One of the main characteristics of spice crops in Sri Lanka is the absence of clearly defined varieties (Sappideen, 1987). In their absence, farmers generally raise their own seedlings by selecting most vigorous and high yielding mother trees.

Table 5.5: Cost of Production and Cost of Processing with the Farm Gate Prices

Product	*Cost of Production (US $/kg)*	*Cost of Processing at Farm-Gate (US $/kg)*	*Total Cost of Production (US $/kg)*	*Farm-Gate Price (US $/kg)*
Pepper	0.76	0.19	0.95	2.50
Cinnamon	2.00	0.19	2.19	3.13
Cardamom	1.85	0.38	2.23	7.88

Source: Economic Research Unit, Department of Export Agriculture, 2000, in Herath, 2002.

Issues and Challenges in the Spice Sector

There are a number of issues and challenges in cultivation practices, technology, and marketing. Small scale cultivation, high cost of labour, improper quality, lack of research and technology, unorganized market, and impact of world trade agreements have been the most important issues of concern.

Productivity-Based Issues

Since spice is cultivated on small scale, subsistence, and poorly managed land, problems relating to non-commercial agriculture arise. Subsistence nature cultivation has moved growers away from quality consciousness and exploiting marketing advantages (Lindara *et al.*, 2004). Small cultivators lack creditworthiness and have not helped much by government intervention policies. Ignoring the recommended improved practices because of inadequate knowledge, mixed cropping, and lack of financial resources have posed serious threats to the productivity and sustainability of the sector (Herath, 2002). Minimal input use and lack of constant replacement of soil nutrients together with leaching from heavy rains have contributed factors to low fertility. Plant density is below the recommended level and replanting and gap filling have not been given much attention. Adoption of productivity improvement programmes such as land and soil conservation, shade management, and agronomic practices have been hindered by the high labour cost (Lindara *et al.*, 2004).

Lacking of Quality Consciousness

Inferior quality has been a serious issue in the present context of high quality consciousness. A large proportion of spices leave the farm gate with quality that is far below the expected level at the high end of the supply chain. High moisture retention, contamination by microorganisms such as moulds, and presence of exogenous matters like aflotoxin affect the quality of spices. These are mainly attributed to poor weather conditions, low cost processing technology, poor storage facilities, and early harvesting and small scale nature of production. Poor quality leads to a direct loss of potential exports and foreign exchange earnings (Herath, 2002). Many producers do not have processing facilities and are not aware of the quality parameters. Even if farmers produce better quality products, there are no attractive and differentiated farm gate prices. The potential for expanding this sector is high if government and other related institutions pay more attention to these issues (Lindara *et al.*, 2004). Since farm gate quality does not match with accredited standard quality, considerable amount of cleaning and processing is carried out throughout the marketing channel adding to the marketing cost.

World Trade Issues

Market potential for Sri Lankan spice exports mainly depends on the tariff structure and sanitary and phytosanitory requirements dictated by the world trade. The most intractable issue arising from the world trade is quality, quality standards such as ISO 9000 certification and HACCP have established themselves in the food industry. On top of that, international trade agreements such as Agreement on Agriculture (AoA), Technical Barriers to Trade (TBT), Sanitary and Phytosanitary Measures (SPS), etc. have facilitative and inhibitive effects (Herath, 2002). Sri Lankan exporters and producers do not have adequate and timely information about the standards and health and sanitary regulations applicable to spice products in the target markets. The SPS requires the country to establish national enquiry points (NEP) from which information could be obtained on:

- technical regulations and voluntary standards adopted or proposed to be adopted.
- conformity assessment procedures adopted or proposed to be adopted.

- sanitary and phytosanitary regulations adopted or proposed to be adopted.
- control and inspection procedures, production, and quarantine treatment, pesticide tolerance treatment, and food additives approval procedure.
- risk assessment procedures.

The Sri Lanka Standard Institution (SLSI) functions as a focal point for information, but the online linkages of SLSI and international standard setting organizations are very poor. There is no government-managed system to provide compulsory quality certification for spices. The required facilities for quality testing are available at SLSI and a few other laboratories of private organizations but the government does not subsidize the quality certification process. Introduction of Hazard Analysis and Critical Control Points (HACCP), which is required to test the critical points in the production process for standards, is another issue. Setting up testing centres and national enquiry points is costly (Herath, 2002).

The TBT agreement creates the basis for various constraints for the process of organic products. Production constraints, strict quality, certification and accreditation issues, national and regional standards and importing procedures, organic labelling, and stiff competition from other producers are the main obstacles. The products can only be exported if the manufacturer or exporter can obtain a certificate of positive assurance from a recognized institution that the product is in conformity with the standards. Facilities for such processes are still not conveniently available in Sri Lanka and the cost of the process is also not competitively affordable. Technical competence of the available conformity assessment body of Sri Lanka in the eyes of potential importers of value added products is also questionable (Herath, 2002).

Problem of Marketing

An important constraint is the poor relationship between farmers and exporters on information. Middlemen take advantage of this situation by buying the products at lower prices and selling them at higher prices, creating a large gap among the price received by farmers, auction price, and international price (Table 5.6).

Price differences between farm gate and auctions depend on factors such as time lag, product quality, nature of the product (bulkiness in auction sale), demand and supply, etc.

The role of middlemen is perceived to be negative since they are seen as unnecessary agents in the supply chain increasing supply costs and capturing part of the rent accruing to farmers. Thus, the involvement of a large number of non-essential intermediaries who are mainly sales oriented rather than market oriented has ultimately resulted in high wastage, low farm price and high consumer price. These results in low value added in the chain, low incentives to farmers and sluggish growth of the sector.

Table 5.6: Average Prices of Spices (₹ /kg)

Crop	*Location*	2000	2001	2002	2003	2004	2005
Pepper	FG	281.82	188.50	144.24	122.97	138.49	116.89
	AUX	307.22	200.50	167.43	138.26	149.86	129.30
	WM	331.68	n.a.	168.30	163.52	160.52	158.31
Cloves	FG	307.65	658.62	599.34	267.08	390.94	347.94
	AUX	344.21	785.50	675.13	295.02	435.91	372.02
	WM	342.18	472.50	463.40	176.52	299.11	317.95
Cinnamon	FG	290.82	303.76	370.49	345.31	361.50	395.48
	AUX	344.72	361.60	365.08	351.58	356.07	380.98
	WM	639.36	n.a.	n.a.	n.a.	n.a.	n.a.
Nutmeg	FG	266.39	197.76	215.55	238.09	224.61	244.88
	AUX	264.80	218.10	237.80	297.06	238.49	254.20
	WM	612.62	624.70	642.98	636.58	662.72	515.58
Mace	FG	542.29	437.44	558.93	575.66	600.33	688.75
	AUX	593.93	436.10	592.42	617.46	630.69	734.84
	WM	762.55	708.30	675.78	699.05	611.88	863.16
Cardamom	FG	1216.97	1447.73	1252.29	875.89	791.82	744.15
	AUX	1258.46	1530.10	1414.13	1017.34	682.44	828.52
	WM	1317.90	1352.20	1318.38	796.47	813.45	652.02

FG = Farm-Gate Price, AP = Auction Price, WM = World Market Prices.

Source: Export Agricultural Statistics of Sri Lanka, 2003.

Traditional Supply Chain of Spices

The marketing structure of minor export crops in Sri Lanka is characterized by its traditionality at the domestic level and rather high degree of sophistication at the exporter's level. The traditional supply chain is characterized by decentralized purchasing, low quality product purchases and sales, and the presence of a large number of intermediaries without essential function. Those intermediaries include travelling collector, village trader, wholesale buyer, commission agent, and auction broker (Figure 5.2).

The travelling collector is the first and most important link in the traditional marketing channel that purchases spice products from village farmers and sells to traders especially outside the village. Thus, he plays a significant role in remote villages where transport and other facilities are limited. The travelling collector generally operates on a small scale collecting small quantities of produce. He makes direct cash payment to the producer and disposes of the collected produce the same day to the next link in the marketing channel. The village trader is another important first link, operating a small shop in the village. His services are available at always,

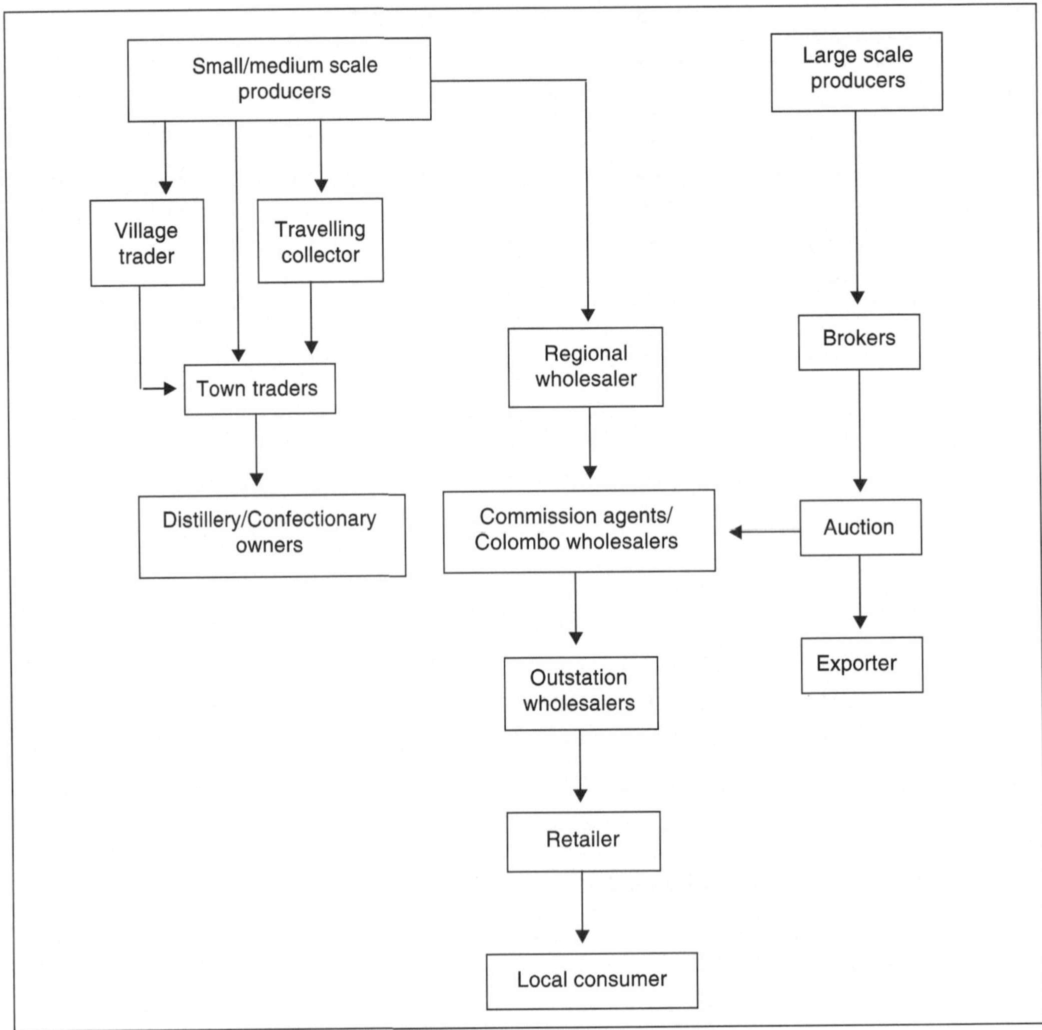

Fig. 5.2: Marketing Channels of Spices

Source: HARTI Agricultural Commodity Review, 2000.

providing the producer an opportunity to sell small quantities of produce at any time (Sappideen, 1987). He pays producers in cash. Producers mostly choose to sell to either travelling collector or village trader since there is no transport cost. The activities of the village trader not being confined only to the spice trade provides the producer the opportunity of combining his sales with purchase of other commodities. Because of the credit-bound relationship between the village trader and producers, producers are compelled to sell their products to the village trader. One significant difference between the travelling collector and the village trader is that while the former goes to the producer in search of produce the latter purchases only what is brought to the shop. The village trader however, does not sell daily like the travelling collector. He prefers to accumulate his stocks until a favourable price is obtained, depending on his liquidity position. Generally, the price received by farmers from the village trader is lower than the price received from the travelling collector. Both village trader and travelling collector sell their produce to wholesale buyers in the town nearest to them (Sappideen, 1987).

Wholesale traders in the spice marketing structure operate at two levels: small town wholesale buyers in the main area of production and big town wholesale buyers in main towns. The primary function of the wholesale trade is to bulk the produce received from producers and dispatch to traders in Colombo. Wholesalers sell small quantities of produce to retailers and sometimes they also do retail sales to consumers directly; the volumes are, however very small. In some locations, there are brokers/ commission agents who link different steps of the marketing channel. Commission agents and auction brokers operate in Colombo and deal with a wide variety of products. Auction brokers conduct auction sales for different products. Commission agents, unlike auction brokers, do not handle any product as such, they only mediate between buyers and sellers. The commission agent and auction broker charge their clients a small fee for their services. The exporter is the final link in the domestic marketing structure. Exporters generally obtain their requirements either through commission agents or auction brokers. Direct purchases from big wholesalers take place rarely where such transactions have been conducted over a period of time and firm personal contacts and confidence established. Most exporters usually buy according to firm orders from foreign clients, preferably on contracts (Sappideen, 1987).

Drivers for the Evolution of Modern Supply Chain

Emergence of supermarkets, urbanization, income increase, high quality retail export markets, high quality bulk procurement, trade agreements with other countries, increased migration of Sri Lankan citizens, and increased women participation of the labour force have created a new demand pattern, shifting the focus towards continuous supply of high quality, value added products with improved processing, packaging, and labelling.

Supermarkets which were traditionally viewed as the "rich man's place to shop" are no longer niche markets for rich consumers in main cities. Supermarkets have succeeded in the food markets of the poor because of their ability to offer competitive prices and better and consistent quality as opposed to the traditional retail markets (Reardon, *et al.* 2003). As in other developing counties, food retail markets in Sri Lanka have gradually evolved from fragmented local markets to centralized wholesale markets and eventually to the emergence of supermarkets. Sri Lanka is currently witnessing a vigorous growth of supermarkets. Supermarkets which previously limited themselves to serving consumers of big cities (i.e. Colombo) are now gradually spreading to urban and suburban areas. The supermarket industry in Sri Lanka consists of supermarket firms with several outlets, with different ownership structures, firms which have persisted in the market for a long period of time, and firms which have emerged recently. There is only one large supermarket chain,

Cargill's Food City began in 1982, which has a comparatively large number of outlets (i.e. 77 supermarket outlets). Apart from this supermarket chain, several supermarkets exist with about two to eight outlets (Keels Super, Sathosa, King's Supermarkets, Family Super, Laugh Sunup, and Arpico) while there are many single outlet supermarkets (Dhanasiri and Royal Mall) all over the country (Weerahewa and Kodithuwakku, 2005).

With the liberalization of the Sri Lankan economy in 1977, there are two evident social strata namely, the new urban middle class and the new working class. Status and individual identity are no longer defined via occupation and heritage but are increasingly defined in terms of lifestyle including the pattern of consumption (Liyanage, 2005). In accordance with these changes, the status determinants of the traditional middle class also shifted from occupation and heritage to the consumption pattern. Compatible with the changing needs of the social segments, the markets have shifted from traditional markets to a new upmarkets in which supermarkets are prime retail outlets.

Monthly household income between 1980/81 and 2002 has increased by 1380 per cent at current prices and by 62 per cent at constant prices (Figure 5.3). Growth in household income will consequently increase the purchasing power of the people giving them the ability to pay for additional services such as convenience, quality of products, etc. This has contributed towards the development of new supply chains over the years.

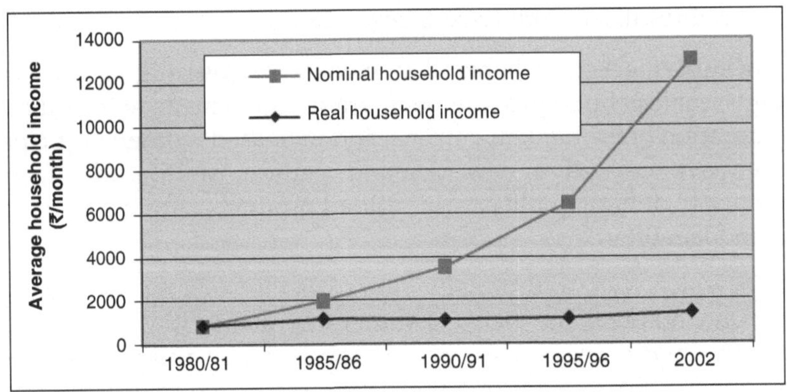

Fig. 5.3: Nominal Income (at Current Price) and Real Income (at 1980/81 Constant Price)

Source: HIES-2002, Department of Census and Statistics.

Urbanization and changes in lifestyle have been the major drivers for the evolution of modern supply chains in Sri Lanka. Rapid urbanization and increase in urban population have broadened the users of new supply chains. Figure 5.4 shows the increase in population in selected major cities.

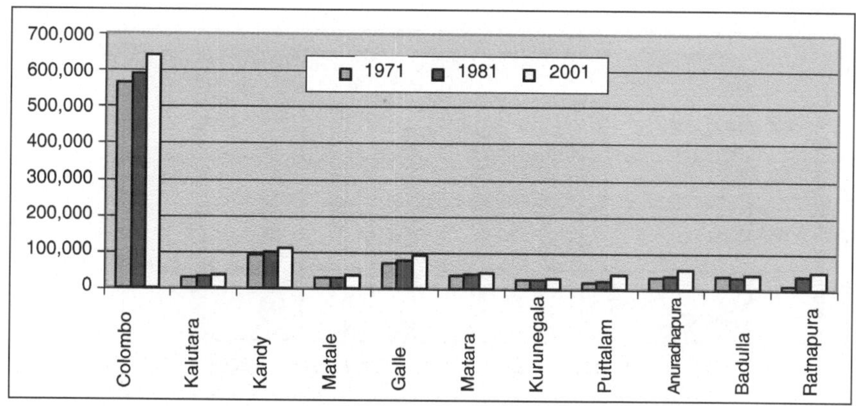

Fig. 5.4: Population Increase in Selected Major Cities

Source: Department of Census and Statistics in Sri Lanka.

Women contribute significantly to household income through farm and non-farm activities as well as by taking employment overseas, most often in the services sector. The number of women in the workforce as well as the female participation rate in the labour force has increased over the past years (Table 5.7). The female participation rate, which was around 20 per cent till the early 1970s, now fluctuates around 32 per cent. The rapid increase in labour force participation in the mid 80s is mainly because of the influx of women into the labour market arising from the open economic framework and because of the structural reforms, which created new job opportunities for women. Women entering the workforce and as a consequence having a higher opportunity cost of time have promoted the evolution of new consumer patterns.

Table 5.7: Female Labour Force Participation Rate and Females in the Labour Force

	Female Labour Force Participation Rate (%)	*Total Number of Females in Labour Force (000')*
1973	20.2	1293
1982	19.4	1439
1993	33.1	2043
1996	31.6	1680
1999	34.1	1975
2003	31.4	2179
2004	31.5	2344

Source: Department of Census and Statistics in Sri Lanka.

With the introduction of open economic policies in 1977, migration of Sri Lankan citizens has increased considerably. As shown in Figure 5.5, the number of Sri Lankans seeking foreign employment has increased by 17 per cent from 182,188 in 2000 to 213,453 in 2004. This has specifically increased the demand for high quality domestic products creating niche markets in these countries.

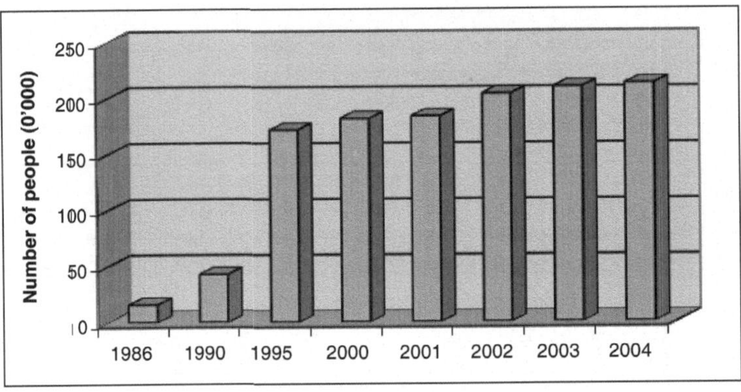

Fig. 5.5: Migration of Sri Lankan Citizens

Source: Department of Census and Statistics in Sri Lanka.

World trade demands a much boarder variety of products, special packaging designs, and high quality standards as a result of international trade agreements such as SPS, TBT, AoA, and ILFTA. The agreement on the application of Sanitary and Phytosanitary (SPS) measures specifies the principles and rules in regulating imported products. The agreement defines SPS measures as those taken to protect human, animal, or plant life or health from risks arising from the entry, establishment, or spread of pests, diseases, disease carrying organisms, or disease-causing organisms; risks arising from additives, contaminants, toxins, or disease-causing organisms in food, beverages, or feedstuffs; and diseases carried by animals, plants, or products thereof (Herath, 2002). The agreement on TBT contains international rules applicable to product standards relating to trade in organic spices and value added products of spices. The aim of the AoA is to establish a fair and equitable market-oriented agriculture trading system by minimizing the use of border measures to control imports and use of export subsidies and other domestic subsidies that governments grant to support the prices of agriculture products and assure a reasonable income to farmers. The essence of this agreement is to reduce and discipline tariff and non-tariff barriers to trade. Spices are included in the reduction structure in many developed and developing countries. These reductions will provide increased market access to developed markets (Herath, 2002). ILFTA in general is a blessing as it provides for India as a preferential trading partner. The direct impact is tariff cuts under the agreement. Reduction of tariff will have short-run benefits such as better prices for the commodities concerned and also long-run benefits such as increased investments, technology transfer, and human capital spillover effects. Since the Indian market is less particular on quality and SPS standards, there is a short-run advantage for Sri Lanka to send more volume of comparatively lower quality spices there. The agreement specifies that products that are not wholly produced or obtained within the participating country should have local content of at least 35 per cent of the FOB value. Under this clause, Sri Lanka can initiate joint ventures to add value to spices and even organic spice mixtures.

MA'S Foods: Profile

MA'S Tropical Food Processing (Pvt.) Limited, established in 1987, is a family-owned spice processing enterprise based in Matale district. It is one of the leading processors of spices and spice-based products such as spices, seasonings, sauces, chutneys, pickles, and ready-to-eat foods. The business has advanced over time beyond the status of a manufacturing unit and has built up the corporate image of a leading food processing company in Sri Lanka. It basically operates in three markets: national food manufacturing companies/restaurants like Nestle, Unilever and Sri Lankan Airlines, supermarket chains like Cargills and Keels, and the export market. Total revenue earned by the company is evenly distributed among the three markets.

Regional Agribusiness and Perennial Initiative and Development (RAPID) established in 2001 is the backward linking arm incorporating small scale farmers to the supply chain, providing them with extension services and ensuring full traceability onto farm level. A large number of farmers have been working closely with the company benefiting from their different programmes. Thirty-nine farmers form the core group of suppliers, supplying products on regular basis. In addition, over 300 farmers comprise the current supplier base scattered in the region. In the beginning, RAPID activities were funded by the Asian Development Bank. Later it received funds from the Regional Economic Advancement Programme (REAP). Now, the company bears RAPID's expenses and provides services free of charge.

MA'S Foods is a national brand leader in the local retail market with a share of around 35 per cent. Nearly 95 per cent of its products are exported in value added form and it is the market leader in the export of processed spices and ethnic foods. Annual sales value (turnover) of the company is around ₹ 123 million in 2004/5 (Table 5.8). MA'S Foods is an internationally certified company of SQF 2000 and HACCP quality standards and supply and processing of organic spices. Moreover, the company has adopted an explicit policy of corporate social responsibility by providing a healthy and safe workplace for its employees.

Table 5.8: Changes in Corporate Income, Assets and Employment

	2000/2001	*2001/2002*	*2002/2003*	*2003/2004*	*2004/2005*
Gross profit (₹)	17,804,560.00	19,063,774.00	29,439,867.00	35,707,169.00	29,770,703.00
Turnover (₹)	74,475,718.00	74,354,086.00	102,676,307.00	113,495,050.00	123,241,211.00
Total assets (₹)	44,011,454.00	45,642,793.00	61,582,446.00	73,279,435.00	99,888,749.00
Fixed assets (₹)	22,615,859.00	22,919,385.00	33,408,171.00	37,881,095.00	51,848,285.00
Employees	104	154	142	144	146

Changes in the Supply Chain

Centralized Procurement

The company has shifted from decentralized to centralized procurement system. Centralized procurement is done by RAPID, which is a subsidiary of MA'S Foods.

Centralized procurement has increased the efficiency through reducing coordination and number of officers required for procurement. This assures a continuous supply of raw materials and eliminates non-essential intermediaries (Figure 5.6). It eventually results in reduced transaction cost and improved information flow among the supply chain segments. Reduction of intermediaries has ensured sharing of profits between farmers and the company. This is clearly evident in higher income of over ₹ 90,000 per acre on average received by the suppliers of the company which is double the income of non-suppliers. Centralized procurement has reduced the marketing risk faced by the company and farmers. Farmers have to transport their produce to the RAPID centre, but sometimes transportation is provided by the company for certain products. This extra movement of produce can lead to increased transaction cost but it ensures timely supply. RAPID is in charge of logistic improvement in the procurement system. It has implemented training programmes on post-harvest and production practices that guarantee a steady supply of products of required quality and improve the efficiency of the procurement system.

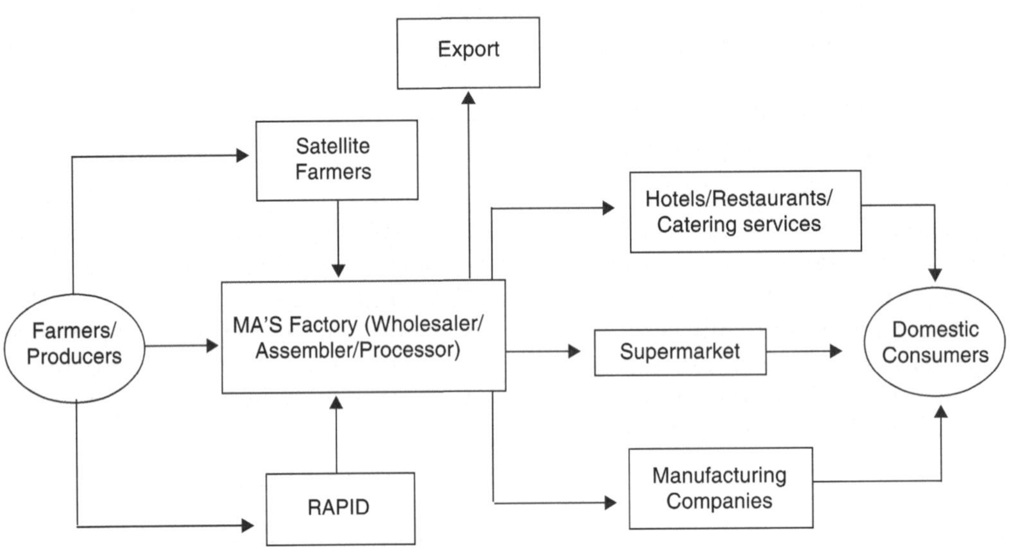

Fig. 5.6: Supply Chain of MA'S Tropical Food Company

Institutional Innovation of Backward Integration

RAPID is responsible for backward integration of the company's activities in the supply chain and for delivering social responsibilities to the region. It offers an integrated set of services to farmers in the region. The services include technical assistance in production and post-harvest practices, training for improved farm management, organic certification in spice production, and supply of high quality planting materials, intermediation of commercial credit from banks, and training on efficient record keeping. Transaction costs of these services are borne by RAPID. Spending on agricultural extension work has shown an increasing trend (Figure 5.7).

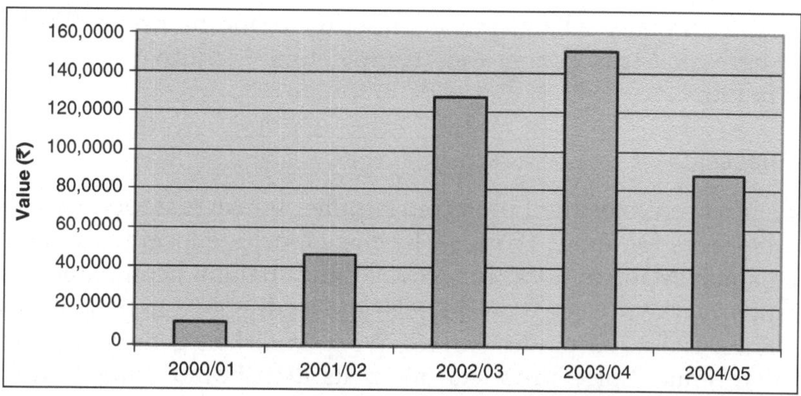

Fig. 5.7: Cost of Agricultural Extension Services

Currently, RAPID has two trained extension officers to disseminate knowledge and technical knowhow. They visit farmers on average once a month and twice a month during the harvesting season. During their visits they inspect fields and provide feedback to farmers about field conditions and advice on improving land productivity. The centre owns two model farms which are used for practical training. RAPID has intermediated bank loans for 14 farmers.

Own Private Standards

The company has set its own standards whole procuring products from its suppliers. This facilitates standardization of products procured from different suppliers. These private standards are used as a tool to differentiate the company's products from others and to discover niche markets. While the company concentrates on the quality of its products, it also focuses on developing a regular and permanent supplier base. Since small scale farmers lack the capacity to cope with rapid changes in the marketing system directly, the company is flexible with the quality requirements initially and offers a considerable adjustment period to bring the produce up to the standards. Farmers who meet those standards are paid premium prices. Normally, the company provides about 20–25 per cent higher price for conventional products and about 50–100 per cent higher price for organic products. For example, producers receive ₹ 1.50 for a nutmeg in the traditional domestic market, but MA'S offers a premium price of ₹ 2.00–2.25 for a nutmeg and ₹ 3.00 for an organic nutmeg.

Logistic Improvements

The company is moving towards logistic improvements in the supply chain. It has introduced new operations to its supply chain such as grading, processing, canning, packaging, labelling, trade marking, and branding. For processing and packaging, it now uses machines. Canning of processed food was introduced two years ago. Those practices have made the company more competitive in local and international markets. Now processing and value addition operations facilitated the introduction of entirely new product lines such as curry mixes and curry pastes, herbs and seasonings. The company sells products under the brand names of "Dad's Garden" (sauces and herbs and seasonings) and "Happy Home" (chutneys and pickles) apart from MA'S brand.

Preferred Supplier

MA'S Foods has been a certified preferred supplier for several food processing companies and hoteliers for about 15 years. Its clients include local food manufacturing companies namely Maliban, local branches of multinational companies (Nestle and Unilever), supermarkets (Cargills and Keels) and leading national institutions like Sri Lankan Airlines. These companies excluding supermarkets generate one-third of the annual total revenue. Spice products under its own brand name and two others supplier to supermarkets in Sri Lanka generate one third of the revenue. Exports constitute the remaining 20 per cent. These take the form of spice products as raw material to food manufacturers and as processed products to ethnic stores in Japan, Netherlands, United States, Germany, Holland, and the European Union.

Specialized Wholesalers

The company is gradually moving towards increased purchasing from specialized wholesalers who can meet its standards. These specialized wholesalers enforce private standards on behalf of the company, reducing the transaction and search cost. Among these wholesalers, satellite farmers who provide spices in bulk are prominent. These farmers are specialized in collecting spices from small farmers in the surrounding area and reprocess into company standards. One satellite farmer has been supplying cultivated and collected spices products to MA'S since 1997 in bulk form. Thus farmer cultivates spices in large scale over 300 acres in which he owns about 170 acres. Fobes and Walkers and Indian Tobacco Company (ITC) also are specialized wholesalers of the company.

Quality Inspection and Assurance

Value chain management has been improved to prevent the risk that products supplied to the restructured markets may not comply with legal and ethical standards and consumer demand. The company has taken several measures to adhere to internationally established basic process standards such as Good Manufacturing Practices (GMP), SQF 2000, and HACCP quality standards. The company itself has been certified for supplying organic products. It guarantees the premium quality, food safety, and superior taste for its products by acquiring the SQF 2000[3] standard in 2003 which is a HACCP quality code. The company is focusing on obtaining British Retail Consortium (BRS) standards to be more competitive in the market.

---

[3] The company has been SQF 2000 certified by SGS Lanka since 2003. Once a year SGS Lanka audits the company.

At each stage of factory operation, there are measures for monitoring the standards. To facilitate monitoring the company has invested on a fully-equipped modern in-house laboratory. It is equipped to perform physical inspection (taste, flavour, appearance, moisture, mould, and infestation) as well as microbiological analysis (yeast, mould, cauliform, total bacterial count, and aflatoxin). Physical inspection and microbiological tests are carried out for both incoming raw materials and final products. Chemical tests (presence of heavy metals and pesticides) and additional microbiological tests are conducted through outsourcing based on the client claims. At each stage of production the company is concerned with product quality as well as employee hygiene. It has introduced hand-wash areas, uniforms, hair nets, slippers, and changing rooms at every stage of factory operations and has provided training on the use of hygienic measures to employees.

Tracking and Traceability Procedures

Raw materials used in the production are fully traceable throughout the production process. Tracking and traceability is assured through a well documented and computerized procedure which is facilitated by Goods Receiving Notes (GRN), stock cards, job cards, and batch numbers (Figure 5.8). For each batch of raw material a GRN that contains information on the supplier, quantity supplied, and quality of the material is issued. After testing for quality, those materials that are consistent with the quality standards are released for food preparation with a stock card. A job card is issued for each item produced in the factory with a batch number. Each and every ingredient used for the production of a particular item is listed in the job card. All these tools are interlinked so that any fault in manufacturing can be identified and corrected without difficulty. There are clear procedures for customer complaint handling which is facilitated by Non-Conformity Identification (NCI).

Corporate Social Responsibility

The company provides a healthy and safe work place for the employees and other stakeholders. An explicit policy of corporate social responsibility has been adopted by the company. Under this policy workers are provided with basic facilities such as meals, lodging, and laundry facilities free of charge. Workers are offered training under diverse issues that enable them to lead a better life. The company has provided employment for the majority of youth in the neighbouring region and for five disabled as a measure of delivering social responsibility to society.

The company has continued to provide extension services to small scale farmers as CSR activity, spending more than 50 per cent of total spending most times. It provides scholarships and financial assistance to students from surrounding communities for study purposes and also provides childcare facilities. It has contributed to the post Tsunami recovery programmes in 2004/05. Contributions towards religious work in the area also constitute a significant share of total spending (Figure 5.9). It has taken steps to minimize negative environmental impacts in all its operations. It is certified by the Central Environmental Authority (CEA) of Sri Lanka for a very good waste management system to dispose of both liquid and solid waste. Thus, corporate social responsibility has in a way become an investment to the company-improving the productivity and attitude of workers, and providing a good image of the company to its clients as well as the society.

Goods Receiving Note (GRN)

For each incoming raw material a GRN is issued giving supplier name, receiving date, and quantity received

↓

Stock Card

For each approved raw material is issued a stock card including supplier name and receiving date

↓

Physical and Microbiological Inspection

Separate raw material inspection file for each supplier

↓

Job Card

Separate job card for each item produced in the factory. Each ingredient used in the production of an item is listed with particular job card number and the batch number given to the item

↓

Batch Number

Separate batch number for each finished product

↓

Non-Conformity Identification

For customer complaint handling

Fig. 5.8: Traceability Flow Chart

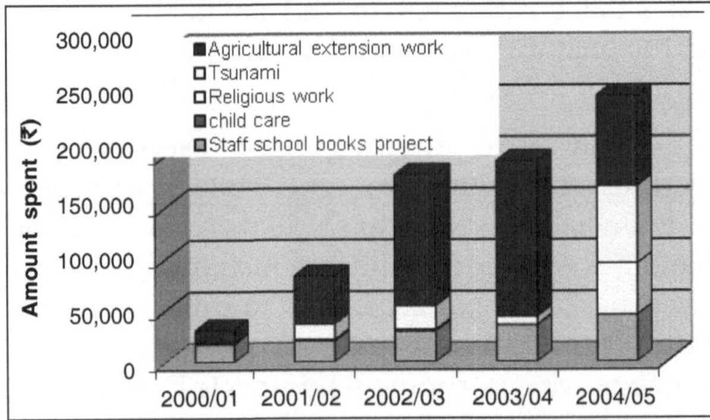

Fig. 5.9: Spending on Corporate Social Responsibility Activities

Note: Spending on meals, lodging, and laundry facilities are not included

Evidence of Inclusion

This innovation has mutually benefited all parties involved in the supply chain. It has resulted in improved corporate income, volume of trade, turnover, farm income, employment creation, non-monetary benefits, and spread of income throughout the year ensuring greater degree of inclusion of small farmers in the new supply chain. The business of the company is backed up by its strong backward linkages with the small holdings sector. Out of 23,000 potential suppliers in the neighbouring region, current supplier number is over 300. Among them 39 farmers who are certified for supplying organic produce belong to the core group of regular suppliers. Another group of 30 farmers has been selected for organic certification (Figure 5.10). They will start supplying to the company this season onwards.

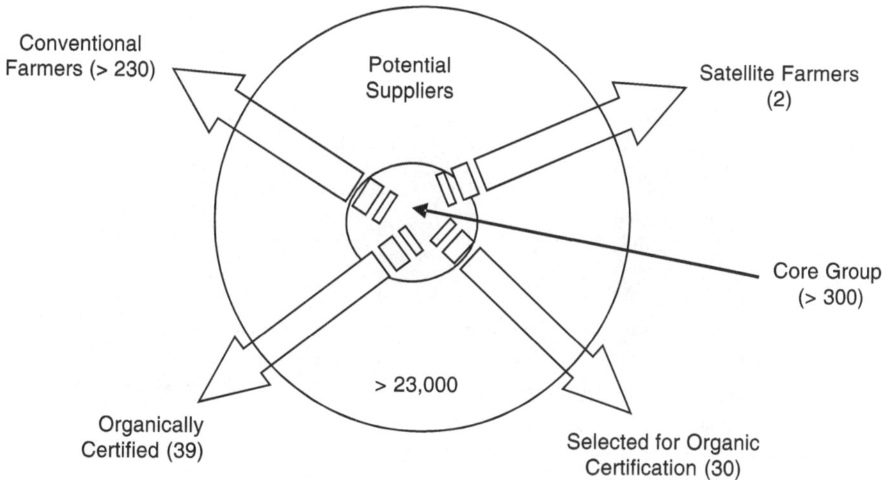

Fig. 5.10: Supply Structure of MA'S Foods

All the farmers are poor subsistent level farmers with lack of productive assets to raise the production to commercial level. Land is the only asset that the majority of them own. Most of them own around 1–3 acres. Only 28 per cent farmers own more than 3 acres. Only 8 per cent of the sample owned land more than 10 acres. Only one farmer who acts as a village trader and collector owns a cinnamon processing machine. Only two farmers in the sample also cultivate rented land. Mixed cropping is the main cropping system except for cinnamon, cardamom, and lemon grass. Nutmeg, pepper, and cloves are cultivated in the same land with other food and timber crops. Cultivating cinnamon stand with pepper is also done. Some farmers solely dependent on income received from spice cultivation whereas some farmers have other sources of income. Either the farmer or a family member has a permanent source of income. 25 per cent farmers in the sample receive retirement payment (pension) as a permanent source of income other than temporary income received from spice cultivation. Rest of the sample are involved mainly in farming and work part time as casual daily wage labourers. Some of the spice farmers are involved in paddy cultivation also. Host farmers do not have technological knowledge of improving land productivity, good understanding of the costs incurred, benefits received, and profitability. They did not have any assurance of the market or good prices before being included in MA'S's supply chain. In the traditional market there was no price differential for quality products.

With inclusion in the supply chain of the company, farmers have received several benefits. The company has taken the responsibility to certify farmers cultivating organic products as organic producers. Primarily farmers were able to gain a premium price for better quality products that fulfilled the company standards (Figure 5.11). They were able to acquire a stable price regardless of the price fluctuation in the market depending on quality. Marketing risk has been minimized by an assured market for their quality products.

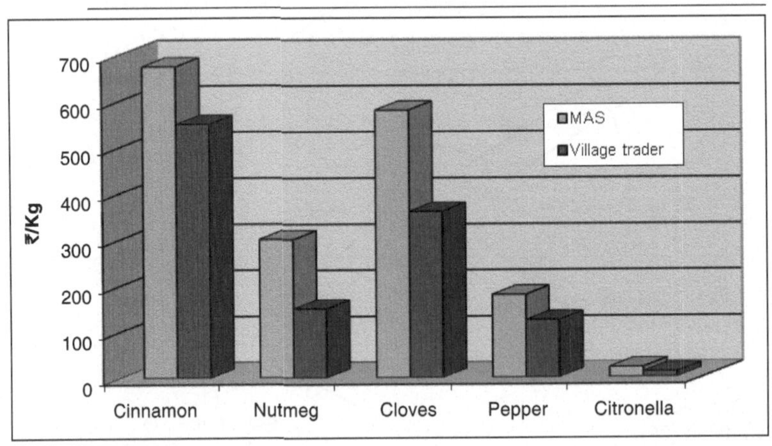

Fig. 5.11: Price Comparison between MA'S and Village Trader

Farmers receive technical knowledge for improving cultivation and post-harvest practices (good agricultural practices) from the extension officers. This has minimized the incidences of pre-mature harvesting enabling year around harvesting with income received by the farmer being spread throughout the year. For example, a nutmeg farmer who cultivates one and a half acres has been able to get two income peaks of around ₹ 32,000 and ₹ 64,000 with some evenly spread lesser income months (Figure 5.12). Continuous supply of produce is guaranteed through this process. It is evident that premium prices and income spread are the major causes for inclusion.

Because the marketing margin of intermediaries is eliminated both farmers and the company get higher profits. At the farmer level, farmers supplying to MA'S receive an income of over ₹ 90,000 an acre annually compared to the income of just over ₹ 40,000 received by non-supplying farmers (Figure 5.13).

After involvement with the company, some farmers (e.g. a group of farmers cultivating cinnamon) have initiated a farmer organization with the support of the company. This facilitates farm activities such as sharing the labour during harvesting

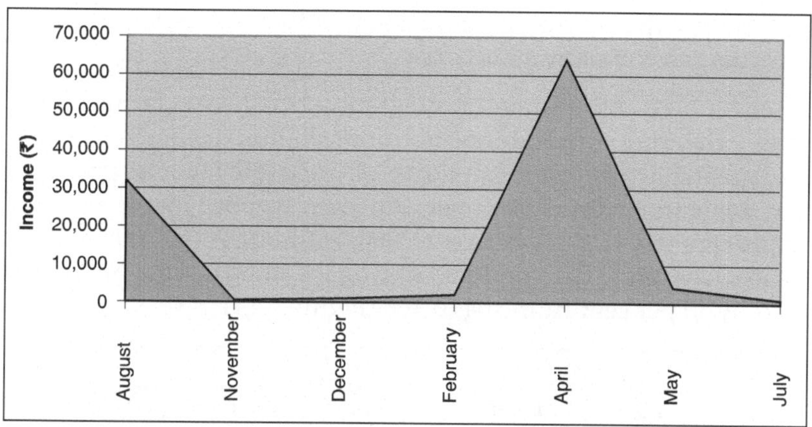

Fig. 5.12: Gross Yearly Income Spread of a Nutmeg Farmer

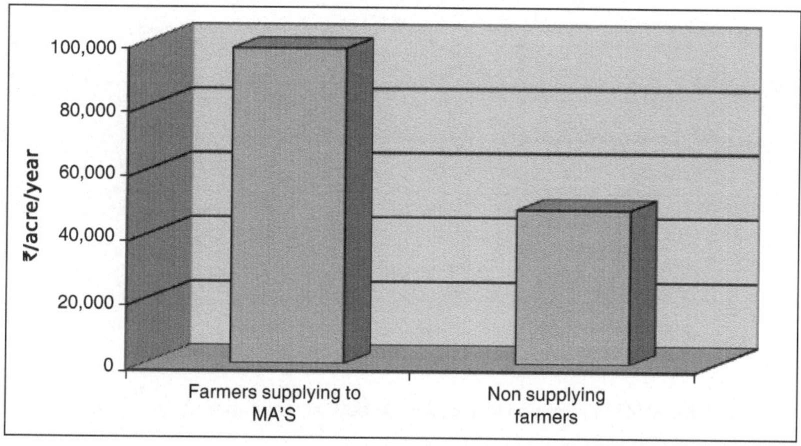

Fig. 5.13: Average Yearly per Acre Income Comparison

periods which eventually reduces the cost of production. Even though the farmer organization is still the nascent stage, it has enhanced the farmers' bargaining power for better quality products. Through the farmer organization, farmers have been able to increase the market price for their products by negotiating with the company. Still the company acts as the backbone of the farmer organization. There should be improvements in the organization to include more farmers and make the organization strong.

Farmers earlier did not have a habit of maintaining records of farming activities. The company has introduced a method of keeping records along with cultivation. Farmers have to enter records on field operations conducted, advice received from extension officers, cost incurred in each operation, yields, prices received, turnover, etc. daily. In addition to this, extension officers also maintain a record book for each farmer. They have to keep records on what they observe in the field and recommendations. By this, farmers can have an understanding of the average costs, yields, and profits and activities that should be implemented to improve land productivity and produce according to company standards.

Even with such a high cost system of integrating small scale farmers with dynamic supply chains delivering corporate social responsibility, the business entity has been able to make greater achievements in terms of corporate income, profits, assets, and employment generation. Total turnover and gross profit have increased by 65 per cent and 67 per cent respectively between 2000/2001 and 2004/2005 while total assets and fixed assets have more than doubled during the same period. Number of workers has increased by 40 per cent from 104 to 146 (Figure 5.14).

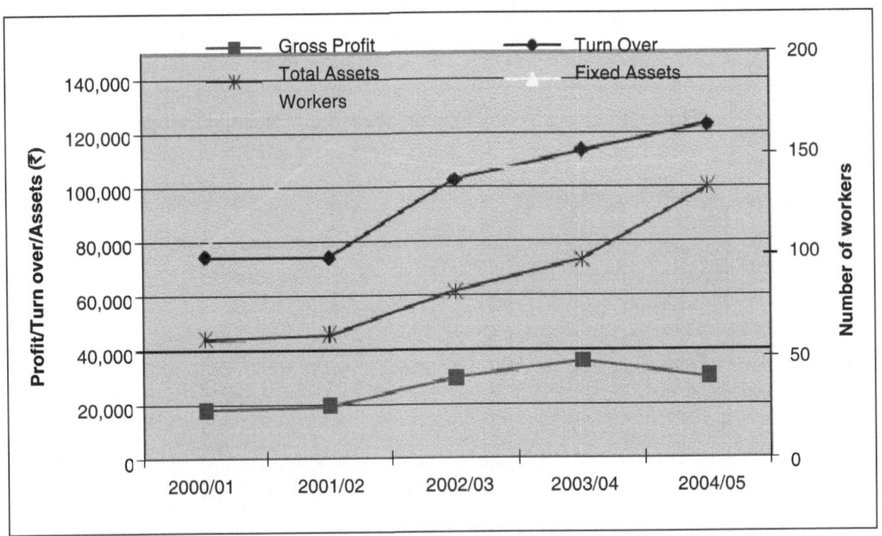

Fig. 5.14: Fluctuation of Income, Assets and Number of Workers

Evidences of Exclusion

There are some evidences of exclusion as well. These are attributed to both organizational weaknesses and lack of capacity of the farmers. Low production capacity of the company is one of the major reasons for exclusion of small scale farmers in the company's supply chain. Even though many farmers are willing to supply their produce to the company while complying with the standards, limited production capacity cannot absorb produce from all surrounding farmers.[4] Higher transport charges are another cause of exclusion. The company does not provide transport facilities to all farmers. For certain farmers, the company provides transport while other farmers have been deprived of this facility. For example, because of high quality considerations extension officers visit nutmeg fields during harvesting and transport the produce with them. Majority of farmers live away from Dambulla where the factory is located and away from urban areas where the infrastructure is poor.

[4] Even though there are over 23,000 potential suppliers, only 300 farmers form the core supply group of the company as shown in Figure 9.

Therefore, it is very difficult for them to find transport and bear the expenses. For each kilogram of cinnamon transported farmers have to pay around 4 per cent of the price they receive as transport charges. This is a heavy burden on poor farmers.

Delayed payments have also induced some farmers to stay out of the system. Farmers had to wait around a month for payment. The company has been able to reduce this lag to around a week. Still this is long for farmers who have to pay wages for hired labour, immediately after harvesting. Because of some farmers are reluctant to sell their produce to the company even if they receive good prices. They feel it is convenient for them to sell their produce to the village trader or town trader since they get payment immediately. In addition to that, the company uses cheque as mode of payment, farmers instead prefer cash.

Credit-bound relationships of the farmers with village traders are very strong especially among those cultivating cinnamon, because of the high labour cost involved in processing. Farmers therefore, sell their produce at whatever price offered by the village trader. Even though farmers have formed an informal farmer organization, lack of coordination and poor structure have excluded a certain strata of farmers from the system.

Conclusions

It is increasingly clear that rapid and continuous changes are occurring in the domestic and export procurement systems. The impact of modern and restructured markets on small scale spice producers who are unable to stay on with the emerging marketing trends is substantial.

MA'S has successfully combined business performance with corporate social responsibility, thereby bringing sustainable benefits to the rural poor in Matale district. Some benefits are:

- At the lowest level, the company works closely with small-scale farmers (community centered) while establishing partnerships with them. This has been achieved by adopting an explicit policy of corporate social responsibility.
- At the highest level, the company operates on a variety of dynamic agro-food markets. It supplies to both supermarkets and processors, both nationally and internationally. It produces a large variety of products, as bulk ingredients and as final consumer items.
- The company is responding to the quality needs of the dynamic market and communicating them effectively to grassroot level farmers.

This innovation has mutually benefited all in the supply chain. This is clearly evident in improved corporate income, volume of trade, turnover, assets and employment creation at the company level and improved farmer income, price premium, market risk reduction, improved cultivation, and better post-harvest practices at farmer level. Besides, strengthening farmer organizations to enhance collective action by farmers, bearing transport and harvesting costs in some cases, and educating farmers about the importance of maintaining quality standards have ensured greater inclusion.

Since this model has been in existence for about a decade, it can be regarded as a sustainable system which can be replicated elsewhere. However, the company has not yet reached its potential capacity and therefore there is some exclusion. Greater inclusion can be attained if the company bears the transport cost or strengthening farmer organizations which are not functioning well owing to institutional and administrative difficulties. Direct cash payments may also result in greater inclusion. Since a limited number of companies like MAS, Lanka Organics, and Bio Foods operate in the area and there are a large number of potential small scale farmers in the region, there are ample opportunities for other companies to follow this model.

At macro level, the government has to play a regulatory role for long-term sustainability of the system. This includes improving private sector participation in the agri-business sector through various incentive schemes (tax holidays), export promotion, trade agreements, and legislative governance.

References

Central Bank of Sri Lanka (2005). *Annual Report*, Central Bank of Sri Lanka: Colombo.

Chandrasena, G.V. (2002). "Export Crop Agriculture Sector other than the Plantation Sector—the Challenges under Globalization." *Economic Review*, May/August 2002: 9–11.

Dias, J.N.S. (1987). "World Market and Marketing of Spices." *Economic Review*, People's Bank, April, Vol. 13, No.1: 16–21.

Export Agricultural Statistics of Sri Lanka. (2003). Department of Export Agriculture, Peradeniya.

Export Agricultural Statistics of Sri Lanka. (2006). Department of Export Agriculture, Peradeniya.

Gummesson, E. (1991). "Qualitative Methods in Management Research as quoted in Perera", Manoshi, Sarath S. Kodithuwakku and Jeevika Weerahewa. (2004). "Analysis of Vegetable Supply Chains of Supermarkets in Sri Lanka". *Sri Lankan Journal of Agricultural Economics*, Vol. 06. No., 01: 79–81.

Henegedara, G.M., Rupasena, L.P., Haturusinghe, Chitra P. and Ravichandran, T. (2000). HARTI Agricultural Commodity Review. HARTI Agricultural Commodity Review Series No. 2. Hector Kobbakaduwa Agrarian Research and Training Institute, Colombo.

Herath, A. (2002). "Cost of Compliance of Sanitary and Phytosanitary Requirements in Beverages and Spices in Sri Lanka." *Economics Research Report No. 15*, Economic Research Unit. Department of Export Agriculture.

Herath, A. (2002). "International Trade Agreements and the Future of the Spice Sector". *Economics Research Report No.* 18, Economic Research Unit. Department of Export Agriculture.

Herath, A. (2002). "Spice Sector of Sri Lanka: Issues, Challenges and Opportunities for the Next Decade." *Economic Review*, May/August 2002: 12– 21.

Household Income and Expenditure Survey, 2002. Department of Census and Statistics, Colombo.

Lindara M.K.J, Fred H. Johnses and Herath M. Gunatilake (2004). "Technical Efficiency in the Spice Based Agroforestry Sector in Matale", Sri Lanka, *Noragric Working Paper No. 34.*

Liyanage, U. (2005). "Profiling the Sri Lankan Consumer—Multiple Portraits and Manifest Patterns." Postgraduate Institute of Management, University of Sri Jayawardanapura.

Morris, T. and S. Wood. (1991). "Testing the Survey Methods: Continuity and Change in British International Relations." *Work Employment and Social Security,* 5: 823–259 as quoted in Perera, Manoshi, Sarath S. Kodithuwakku and Jeevika Weerahewa. (2004). "Analysis of Vegetable Supply Chains of Supermarkets in Sri Lanka." *Sri Lankan Journal of Agricultural Economics,* Vol. 06. No. 01: 79–81.

Reardon, T., Timmer, P. and Berdegue, J. (2003). "The Rapid Rise of Supermarkets in Developing Countries: Induced Organizational, Institutional and Technological Change in Agrifood Systems." *Electronic Journal of Agricultural and Development Economics,* Vol. 01. No. 02: 15–30. Available online at www.fao.org/es/esa/eJADE.

Robson, C. (1993). Real World Research, Oxford, Blackwell as quoted in Perera, Manoshi, Sarath S. Kodithuwakku and Jeevika Weerahewa. (2004). "Analysis of Vegetable Supply Chains of Supermarkets in Sri Lanka." *Sri Lankan Journal of Agricultural Economics,* Vol. 06, No. 01: 79–81.

Sappideen, T.B. (1987). "The Spices Industry in Sri Lanka." *Economic Review,* People's Bank, April, Vol. 13, No.1: 4–15.

Sri Lanka Labour Force Survey, 2004. Department of Census and Statistics, Colombo.

Weerahewa, J. and Kodithuwakku, S.S. (2005). Evolution of Food Retail Chains in Sri Lanka.

Yin, K. (1994). "Case Study Research: Design and Methods" as quoted in Perera, Manoshi, Sarath S. Kodithuwakku and Jeevika Weerahewa. (2004). "Analysis of Vegetable Supply Chains of Supermarkets in Sri Lanka". *Sri Lankan Journal of Agricultural Economics,* Vol. 06. No. 01: 79–81.

http://www.ifpri.org/events/seminars/2005/smallfarms/sfproc/SO2_Reardon.pdf

http://www.intracen.org/bsrt/ppspices.pdf

http://www.srilankaspices.org/

http://www.statistics.gov.lk

http://en.wikipedia.org/wiki/spice-trade

6

Keys to Inclusion of Small Farmers in Dynamic Vegetable Markets: The Case of NorminVeggies in the Philippines

Sylvia D. Concepcion, Larry Digal and Joan C. Uy

This study looks at the case of NorminVeggies, an association of vegetable farmers and stakeholders in Southern Philippines, which saw the need to organize and implement strategies and innovations through its marketing group, Normincorp, to improve its capability to access dynamic markets in the Philippines.

The vegetable farmers work together to build their membership base. They assist each other in the production of quality vegetables, create a group identity, articulate their needs and interests, and access support from various groups. They organize to meet the challenges of a rapidly restructuring market by forming marketing clusters and setting up a marketing corporation. By looking at the factors that help explain their success in these markets, we are able to gain insights into and lessons in linking small farmers to markets.

Traditionally, marketing has not been performed by small farmers and attempts to market farmers' produce collaboratively have failed. These attempts were done with the structure of the cooperative. While Manalili (2000) talks about the high failure rates, she also posits that cooperatives "by virtue of their size, technology requirement, and proximity to and knowledge of the area of production are still the better option to service the marketing needs of rural agricultural producers". The key, however, "is effective management rather than the level of sophistication of the marketing system. Measures should therefore be geared towards enhancing cooperative organizational management and operational efficiencies. Strategies should capitalize on competency-enhancing linkages that enable cooperatives to acquire the capacities of their partners while at the same time 'learning the ropes' of the business."

In a study conducted in Benguet, spot exchange was the most common marketing arrangement used by 58 per cent of producers and traders of the La Trinidad Trading Post and Baguio City market. (Milagrosa and Viane, 2002). The same practices prevail in the rest of the country. While this is highly risky for farmers and even traders, it can sometimes be highly profitable. Frequent transactions occurring in highly uncertain environments heighten the probability of conflict, thus a formal organization is needed. According to Milagrosa and Viane, the type of governance needed is hybrid. The level of uncertainty of spot markets is very high: moderate specificity of assets are involved, where market forces are increasingly unstable and may give false signals to players (at the price levels) making them to respond erroneously. While vertical integration may be an option, this is not at all possible for small farmers because of immense financial and organizational requirements.

In this case, a group of farmers marketed their produce collaboratively and have forward integrated by the last quarter of 2005. They have been surviving and growing for the past six years. The factors that may explain the performance of Normin-Veggies in these dynamic markets are discussed below.

Analytical Framework

Figure 6.1 shows the overall framework of the study adopted from the regoverning markets programme (Berdegue and Peppelenbos, 2005). The study aims to understand the keys to inclusion of small farmers to dynamic markets in the case of producers belonging to NorminVeggies and assisted by Normincorp. Their strategies and innovations are responses to the dynamic external environment where they operate, taking into account their core competencies and constraints faced.

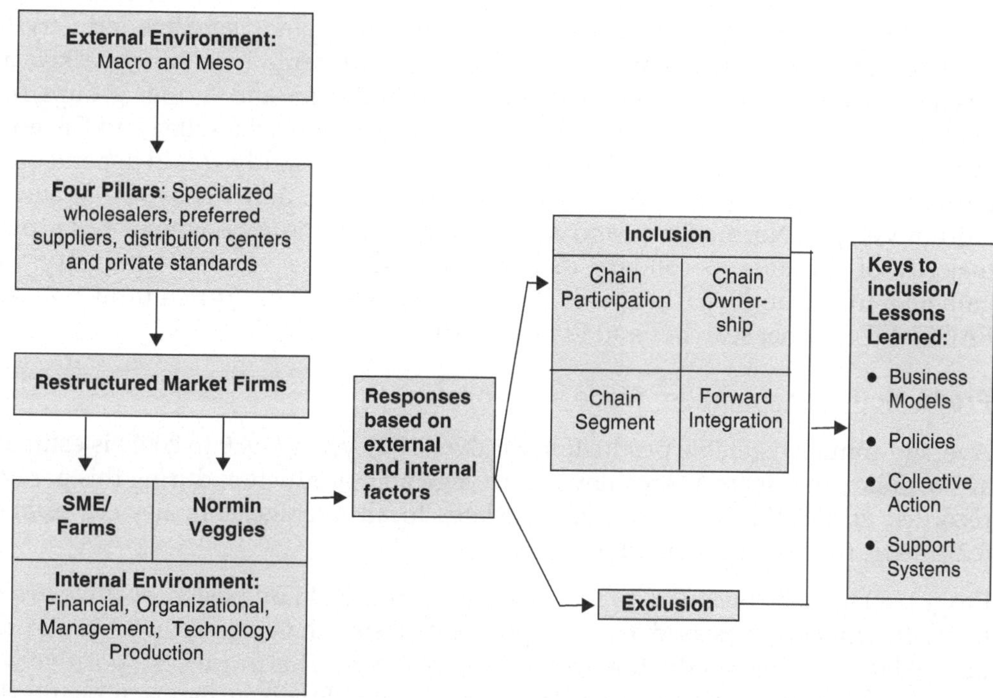

Fig. 6.1: Framework of Analysis: External Environment for Philippine Vegetable Industry

The dynamic external environment comprises the macro and meso environments on two levels. One level is the immediate environment where NorminVeggies operates the Philippine vegetable industry. Here, the restructuring of the downstream firms is critical as it implies changes or adjustments for farmers, particularly the small ones, and small and medium enterprises. The other level is the macro level which refers to agribusiness and macroeconomic factors that affect performance of firms operating in the vegetable industry. The changes in the external environment such as increasing quality and food safety standards require changes for suppliers. These may include upgrading technology, improving organizational setup, or increasing capital. On the other hand, internal factors pertain to resources, competencies, and constraints within NorminVeggies. These include financial, organizational, management and technology.

These external and internal factors form the basis of NorminVeggies' strategies and responses in these dynamic markets, which will result in the inclusion or exclusion of NorminVeggies farmers. It is important to understand key components of this framework and their relationships to expose the underlying factors behind inclusion or exclusion of small farmers.

Following this framework, both primary and secondary data were used. Primary data on NorminVeggies and its marketing group, Normincorp, and the structure of marketing firms in the vegetable industry were gathered using key informant interviews. These included interviews of NorminVeggies and Normincorp (marketing arm of NorminVeggies); stakeholders of the Philippine vegetable industry like vegetable processors, food chain managers, hotel representatives, supermarkets and vegetable consolidators in Metro Manila and Mindanao; and farmer groups from Benguet, Mountain Province, Bukidnon, Cotabato, Compostela Valley and Davao del Sur. It was recognized early on that the success of the case study would depend on the participation of key subject organizations (Douthwaite, and Ashby, 2005) such as NorminVeggies, NorminCorp, and Kaanib Foundation Inc (KFI) who would provide majority of the data. Secondary data on the Philippine vegetable industry were gathered from the Department of Agriculture, Bureau of Agricultural Statistics, FAOSTAT, Internet searches and Planet Retail.

Production, Consumption, Trade and Policies

Average annual vegetable production for the last 25 years (1980 to 2005) is estimated at 3.6 million metric tons. Area devoted to vegetable production during this period is recorded at 438,962 hectares. This translates to an average annual yield of about 8.21 metric tons per hectare (Figure 6.2).

From 1980 to 2005, production, area harvested, and yield all posted positive growth rates. Production increased by 1.34 per cent, faster than the growth in the area devoted to vegetable production which is 1.21 per cent. This produces a positive yield growth of 1.09 per cent per year. These trends are shown in Figure 6.2 with data translated into indices with base year at 1980.

Consumption, on the other hand, is also increasing. Based on the estimate of the Food and Nutrition Research Institute (FNRI) in 1993, a Filipino consumed 39 kilos of vegetables per year. This figure was used to estimate vegetable consumption of the urban and rural population from 1980 to 2003, shown in Figure 6.3. This shows that increase

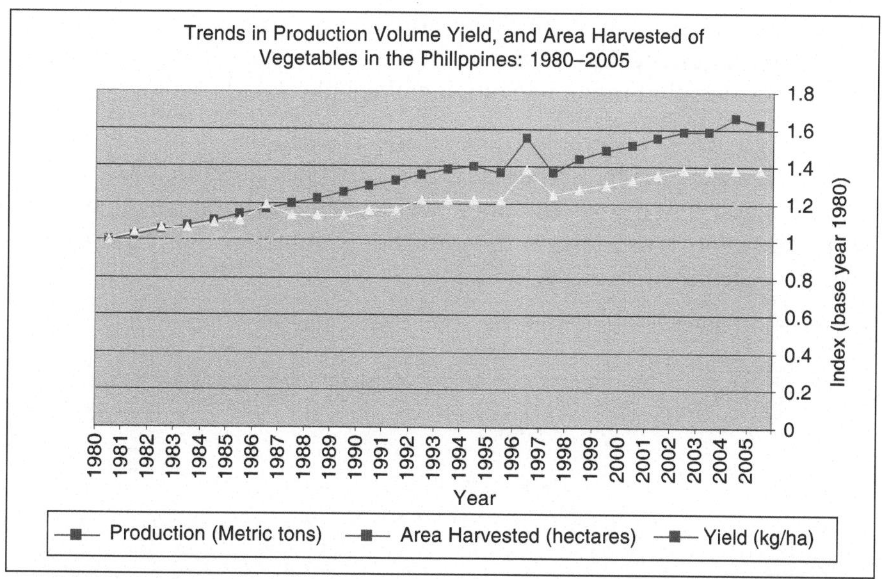

Fig. 6.2: Production, Yield and Area Harvested for Philippine Vegetables, 1980–2005

Source: FAOSTAT 2006

in vegetable consumption is largely because of increase in urban consumers. Urban consumption grew by 4.42 per cent while rural consumption increased by 0.2 per cent. However, based on a survey in Davao, Cagayan de Oro, and General Santos Cities in 2004, vegetable consumption per capita has increased to about 87 kilos in Davao and Cagayan de Oro Cities and to 105 kilos in General Santos City (Concepcion, 2005). Top selling vegetables are squash, eggplant, potato, string beans, cabbage, bitter gourd, okra, tomato, carrots, and native pechay. A recent trend observed by industry players is the increasing demand for high value salad vegetables like lettuce, bell pepper, and tomatoes in the urban Filipino market. As incomes of Filipinos improve, demand for high value vegetables increases. Moreover,

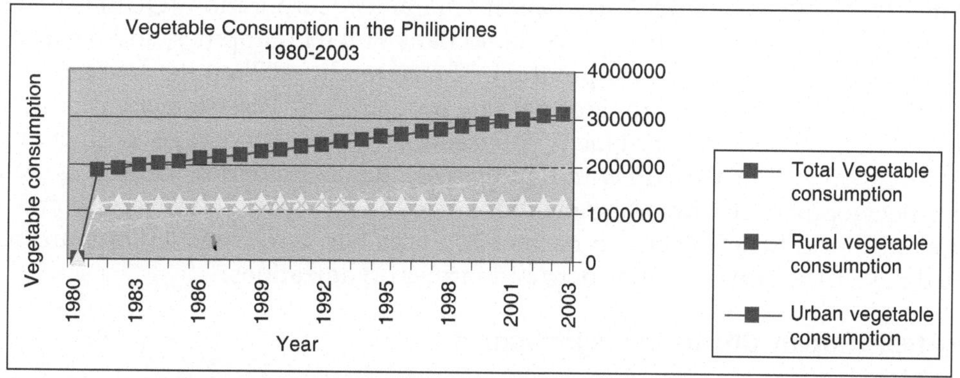

Fig. 6.3: Vegetable Consumption in the Philippines, Urban and Rural

Source: FAOSTAT 2006.

Filipino consumers are getting health conscious, further driving the demand for vegetables. Fastfood outlets, restaurants, and hotels are responding to this opportunity, offering new products that make use of vegetables like salads.

As shown in Figure 6.4, vegetable trade in the Philippines is also expanding. The value of imports increased by 38 per cent per year from 1980 to 2003. Exports even grew faster by 54 per cent during the same period, albeit a drastic decline from 2002 to 2003. Philippines exports asparagus to Japan and US markets and imports lettuce and frozen vegetables from Australia and China.

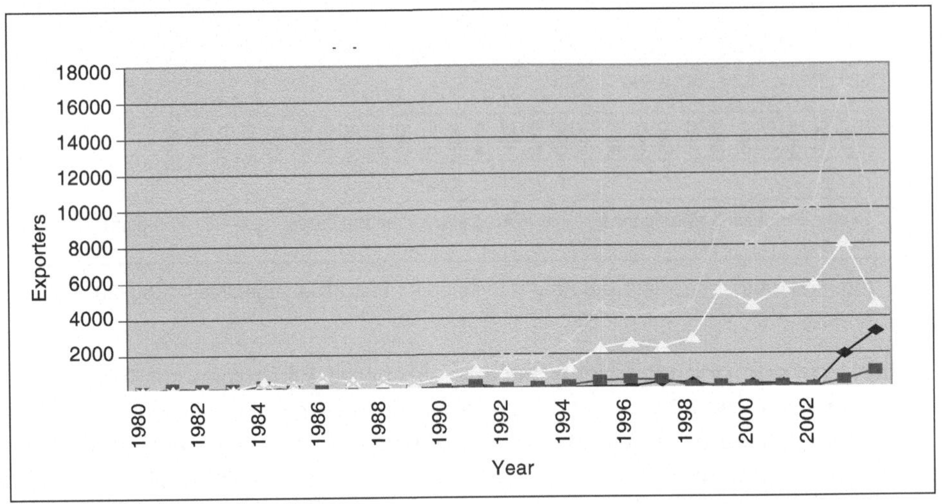

Fig. 6.4: Exports and Imports of Vegetables in the Philippines, 1980–2003

Source: FAOSTAT 2006.

Government, non-governmental organizations, and development agencies are involved in implementing policies and programmes to develop the industry which is largely dominated by small and poor farmers. There are credit programs implemented by the Quedan and Rural Credit Guarantee Corporation (QUEDANCOR), Development Bank of the Philippines, Land Bank of the Philippines, and Small Business Guarantee and Finance Corporation. The Agricultural Training Institute of the Department of Agriculture provides training programmes. These include production, post-harvest, and marketing capacity programmes where the local government units are also involved. The Growth with Equity in Mindanao funded by USAID as well as other development resource organizations like the Catholic Relief Service and the Lutheran World Relief Service in partnership with non-governmental organizations joined the efforts in assisting farmers and farmer organizations.

Vegetable Supply Chains in the Philippines

The changes in demand structure and competition in the Philippine vegetable industry have led to changes in supply chains. In what follows, the typical or "mainstream" supply chain is described followed by a discussion on the changes and emerging supply chains in the Philippine vegetable industry.

Vegetables in the Philippines are grown primarily by small farmers although in recent years, large agribusiness firms with main business in banana and pineapple for exports such as Dole Philippines and Lapanday Foods Corporation have ventured into vegetable production. The latter invested in the industry to produce vegetables primarily for exports but eventually shelved the project.

As shown in Figure 6.5, the vegetable supply chain in the country follows a traditional chain where these farmers sell their produce at the spot market to traders, wholesalers in wet markets, consolidators, and vegetable processors. Wholesalers usually sell vegetables in wet markets while some traders, particularly consolidators and vegetable processors, sell to institutional markets such as supermarkets, fastfood joints, and hotels and restaurants. Very few farmers supply directly to vegetable processors and institutional markets.

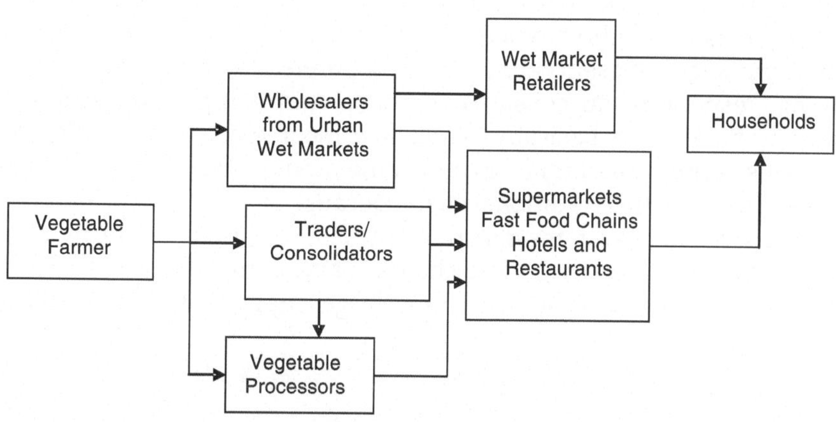

Fig. 6.5: The Philippine Vegetable Supply Chain

The retail market for vegetables is still dominated by wet markets for a number of reasons. Consumers generally buy fresh produce like vegetables in wet markets that offer more variety and assortment of vegetables than supermarkets at lower prices. In Mindanao, 90 per cent of households prefer to buy from wet markets and talipapas[1] in smaller quantities three times a week (Concepcion, 2005). Farmers, on the other hand, rely on traders who sell to these wet markets and consolidators who in turn supply to institutional buyers such as supermarkets, hotels and restaurants.

However, increasing income and changing lifestyles of urban Filipinos have not only contributed to increased consumption of high value vegetables, they have also played a role in the proliferation of fastfood outlets and one-stop shopping malls and

[1] Talipapas are smaller neighbourhood wet markets which source their produce from the central wet market and backyard gardens.

supermarkets. High income markets demand convenience. These have triggered changes in the supply chain of vegetables. Firstly, the number of consumers buying their vegetables from supermarkets has increased, particularly in urban areas (Digal and Concepcion, 2004). This is consistent with the higher growth of vegetable consumption in urban areas presented in Figure 6.3. This is an opportunity now being tapped by supermarkets and fastfood outlets.

An example of this is a large supermarket in Metro Manila which expanded the number of shelves from 2–12 foot long counters in 2001 to 3–12 foot long counters in 2004 (Digal and Concepcion, 2004). Secondly, with increasing display area and assortment, supermarkets have decreased the number of suppliers and prefer to deal with consolidators and concessionaires. Thirdly, as supermarkets deal with high income consumers who are more quality conscious, they impose higher standards.

In the Philippines, the differences between low and high income consumers create a wedge in the supply chain resulting in a dualistic vegetable supply chain: the traditional chain (wet market) and modern chain. This is illustrated in Figure 6.6. Curve A represents the high income segment served by modern downstream firms such as supermarkets and fastfood outlets. Procurement systems in this segment are fast changing, responding to consumer demand and competition. Curve B is the traditional wet market that basically serves low income consumers. Wholesalers in the wet markets supply small retailers and some modern retailers in the Philippines continue to source from this traditional chain. Because of this dualistic nature, the rate of change of procurement systems may not be as fast as in other countries resulting in a flatter curve C. To some extent, these chains A and B are substitutes and therefore they compete and affect one another. One large supermarket in the Philippines

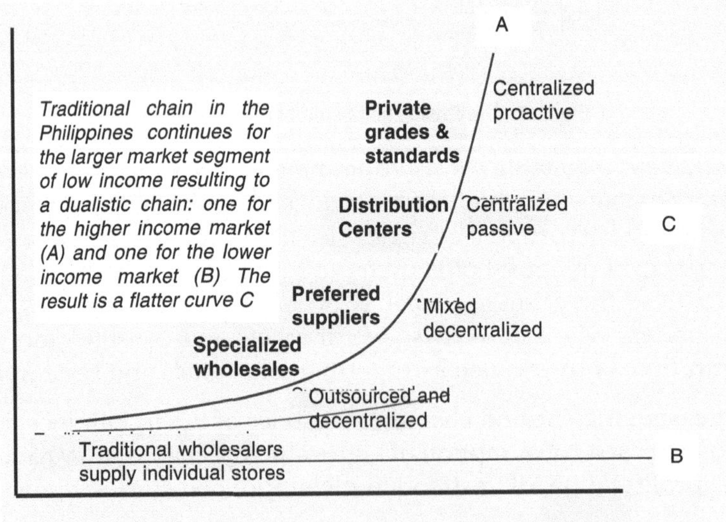

Fig. 6.6: Pillars of Dynamic Supply Chains and Philippine Vegetable Chain

lowers price of vegetables to compete with wet markets. In addition, the Philippine government has launched a programme called "Huwarang Palengke (Model Wet Markets)". This is a competition of wet markets or "palengkes" in the country to encourage these markets to improve services, particularly in the areas of cleanliness, food safety, and good retail practices for consumer welfare. These changes in the procurement systems are reflected in the types of vegetable chain designs discussed below. The traditional vegetable chain in the Philippines continues for the larger market segment of low income resulting in a dualistic chain, one for the higher income market (A) and one for the lower income market (B) The result is a flatter curve C.

Types of Vegetable Supply Chains

Around 75–85 per cent of vegetables in the Philippines are sold through the traditional supply chain, where the wet markets and vegetable traders play major roles. Farmers are generally price takers, accepting what the traders give them at the spot market.

Alternative chain designs have developed in the last three years. Interviews with the different players of the chain from Benguet and the Mountain Province in the northern island of Luzon to Southern Mindanao, the southernmost part of the Philippines, have yielded data which can be typified as alternative chains.

Chain Managed by a Food Processor

The traditional vegetable chain has been the main source of many restaurants and hotels in most parts of the country. In recent years, fastfood chains became drivers for change across the chain. In their need to streamline their own operations and cut costs, fastfood chains no longer wanted to purchase unprocessed vegetables. They, instead, increasingly turned to vegetable processors to supply their needs (Figure 6.7).

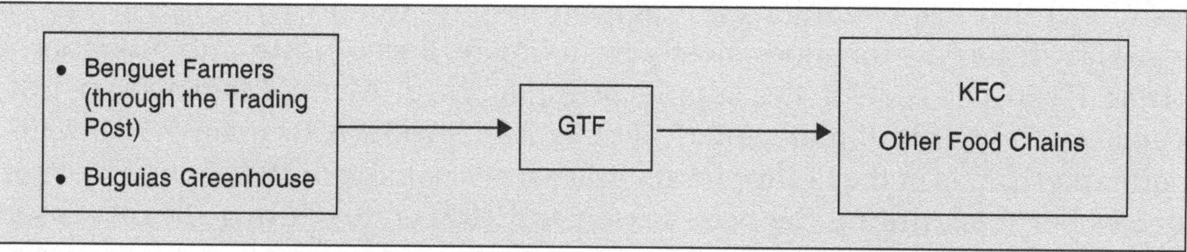

Fig. 6.7: Sample Chain Managed by a Food Processor

They wanted to buy only processed vegetables in the form of washed and cut salad vegetables and processed coleslaw. Their former suppliers who used to be vegetable traders and consolidators were therefore forced to adapt to their demands. Many of these traders went into vegetable processing. Suppliers who could not supply the required processed vegetables had to find processors who would become their new markets. In effect, farmers who used to consolidate and sell to fastfood chains, now find themselves excluded from the fastfood chain market unless they could find a processor who would take their products. Small farmers can be part of this chain if they can supply to a processor or if the trader who buys from them at the spot market sells to a vegetable processor.

An example of such a development is Glorious Taste Foods[2] (GTF), a food processor who supplies coleslaw to Kentucky Fried Chicken (KFC), Kenny Rogers, and other fastfood chains. It sources vegetables from Benguet farmers through the La Trinidad Trading Post and is now closely collaborating with a farmer from Buguias, Benguet, who was able to borrow money to put up greenhouses for the production of different varieties of lettuce for fastfood chains.

Product Specialist Chain

Apart from the traditional supply chain of vegetables which used to be the main source of supply of supermarkets, a specific chain devoted mainly to tomatoes has developed in response to the needs of this market segment (Figure 6.8).

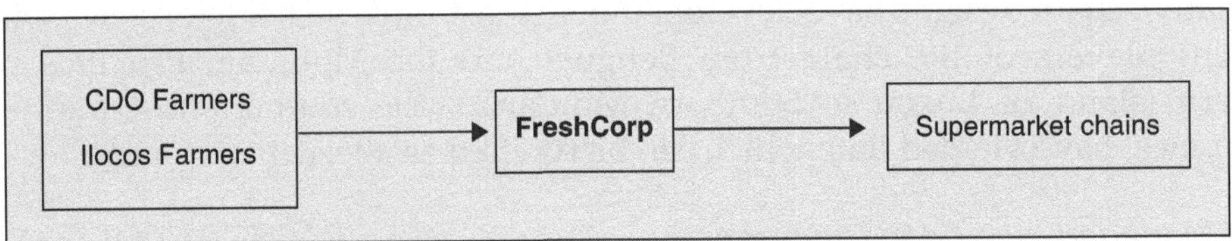

Fig. 6.8: Sample Product Specialist Chain

Tomatoes are grown in most parts of the Philippines, but more predominantly in the cooler regions such as Bukidnon in Mindanao and Baguio in Northern Luzon. Tomato varieties suitable for the lowlands are also grown in lowland areas like Quezon, Ilocos Sur, Nueva Ecija, and Batangas provinces.

One such chain is managed by a large agribusiness corporation, Fresh Corporation (FreshCorp) that has operations in Cagayan de Oro, Cebu City, Quezon City, and Davao City. It sources tomatoes mostly from Cavite, Ilocos Norte, and Bukidnon and controls 15–20 per cent of the supply of tomatoes in Metro Manila from July to December. It brands its tomatoes and all other fresh produce. Its main markets are the supermarket chains in the Philippines. It transacts a volume of 10,000 crates[3] of native tomatoes per week during the peak season and 1000 crates during the off season. It gave tomato farmers agronomic support, production advice, and in a few occasions financing agricultural inputs. FreshCorp purchases from the spot market in Luzon and through marketing contracts with farmers in Mindanao. The seasonality of tomatoes is addressed by tapping farmers from different regional areas. The Luzon farmers supply tomatoes January to June, while the Mindanao farmers supply July to November.

[2] Names in this case are disguised to protect the privacy of the company.

[3] A crate of tomatoes is usually 23–25 kg.

Tomato farmers in Mindanao, who want to supply FreshCorp, sign a marketing contract wherein farmers commit to a specific weekly volume and a price ceiling. Such quantities are determined by the farmer himself. FreshCorp commits to sell for farmers the specified quantity and to a price floor. Deliveries and payments are weekly. Production scheduling is done by farmers so that they are able to comply with the required regularity of delivery.

FreshCorp has around 20 farmers in Mindanao in this kind of contract, each with 2 to 10 hectares of either owned or leased land. The high cost of transport from Mindanao necessitated contracts with farmers from the area. FreshCorp acts as a marketer for the produce and provides farmers with quality specifications of the supermarkets. Farmers pay FreshCorp 22.5 per cent commission for the sale.

Different supermarket chains have different purchasing arrangements with FreshCorp. With one supermarket chain, FreshCorp has a concession and is responsible for filling the shelves with produce, cleaning, wrapping, replacing, coding, and others. The supermarket earns from the rental of the shelves as well as a percentage of sales. With other supermarket chains, FreshCorp has an outright purchase agreement where the buyer orders and pays after 7–15 days.

Because FreshCorp has control of the majority of supply of quality tomatoes, it has the reliability when it comes to this specific product. Even the competitors purchase tomatoes from it in periods of scarcity. FresfCrop is able to maintain the relationship with supermarket chains and supplies them with other items as well. Its ability to specialize in one product opened the doors to other products.

Market Specialist Chain

Another arrangement recently observed in the Philippines is the market specialist chain where supermarket suppliers will focus their strategies on providing supermarket chains anything that they need. In the words of one of the respondents, "we will give them whatever they want". This means that the market specialist provides a wide array of vegetables including, minimally processed, pre-cut and mixed, packed, coded and tagged, and any other combination thereof. They brand their products particularly their packed salads. The company name is visible in the price code of each pack of vegetables. The market specialists are given the assurance by the supermarket chain that they are the preferred supplier and all needs for fruits and vegetables will be sourced through them (Figure 6.9).

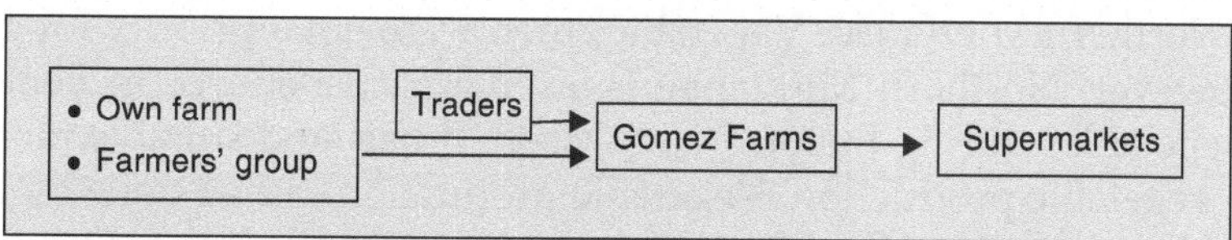

Fig. 6.9: Sample Market Specialist Chain

One of the bigger market specialists, Gomez Farms, has a strong relationship with the biggest supermarket chain in the Philippines and supplies almost all the larger supermarket chains. Major supermarkets have designated Gomez Farms as their preferred supplier and give it priority when purchasing fruits and vegetables, to the extent of protecting it from suppliers who want to have a share of the supermarket business. In this type of relationship, supermarkets benefit because their preferred supplier will get them anything they need at the frequency and quality they require. Gomez Farms gets different produces from its own farms and from multiple sources including other vegetable consolidators, domestic suppliers, and importers in order to satisfy supermarkets. The ability to source whatever product the supermarket needs gives Gomez Farms an edge over competitors.

Implications to Small Vegetable Farmers

The Philippine vegetable industry is restructuring. This is largely driven by demand factors such as increasing population and income and changing lifestyles of urban consumers. These create opportunities for the modern chains to respond, particularly supermarkets and fastfood chains. Their procurement systems also change to respond to these opportunities and remain competitive. Increasing demand for salads prompted fastfood chains to source processed instead of unprocessed vegetables. This requires changes in production protocols for farmers who supply to vegetable processors. Large supermarkets deal with preferred suppliers who also brand their vegetables. As large supermarkets continue to raise standards, the volume of vegetables sold that are branded is expected to increase. This will result in larger consolidators who also venture into vegetable processing, particularly cut vegetables and packed salad vegetables.

This in turn will require changes in production protocols if farmers are to be part of this chain. Small farmers will have difficulty responding to these opportunities in the modern chains as these would mean investments to produce quality vegetables. However, small farmers cannot be eased out as an assortment of vegetables is an integral part of a supermarket's merchandising strategy. In what follows, we examine the case of NorminVeggies to provide an example of how an organization of small and medium farmers respond to opportunities and challenges in the market.

Keys to Inclusion: Case of NorminVeggies

Northern Mindanao Vegetable Producers' Association (NorminVeggies) was organized by small farmers to have a concerted effort in the development of the vegetable industry in Northern Mindanao. Vegetables then were not a priority for government support. However, Northern Mindanao is an alternative source to Benguet/North Luzon for vegetables during Luzon's wet season. It has land suitable for year-round commercial vegetable production. Vegetable production can be done by any farmer, and is a source of nutritious food for the farmer's family (food security).

Specifically, NorminVeggies wanted to:

- have a voice for the thousands of vegetable farmers in Northern Mindanao.
- have a venue where small farmers can interact, share concerns, opportunities, and be more aware about the directions of the industry, with the intention of increasing the income of vegetable farmers.
- be pro-active in developing the vegetable industry.
- relate in an organized way with government and other development support organizations.

Objectives

NorminVeggies aims to be competitive in the vegetable industry producing high quality commodities for domestic and international markets.

Its specific objectives are:

On Production: Increase and sustain production of "safe and healthy" assorted vegetables through sustainable agriculture to meet market demand. Innovative technologies for nurseries, tropical rain shelters, use of mulching and drip irrigation systems are just some of the few adapted technologies used by the farmers of NorminVeggies to move towards sustainable agriculture.

On Food Safety: Use and adopt environment friendly technologies. Farmers of NorminVeggies get training on the use of biological control agents to control pests whenever the technologies are available, vermiculture and composting to reduce dependence on the more expensive inorganic fertilizers, and use of "category 4" crop protection inputs.

On Market: Sustain and expand existing markets and access new markets through a system of market information sharing, promotions through branding, packaging and processing, and establishment of a vegetable consolidation centre.

On Post-Harvest: Practice consistent quality management of produce for all the farms involved in a marketing cluster and ensure that the same good quality is maintained as the produce moves downstream along the supply chain at competitive costs and minimal post-harvest losses.

On Advocacy: Advocate for policies that will reduce the cost of doing business; influence government's decisions on how to maximize limited resources for highest impact on industry development; and actively participate in the Philippine vegetable industry and key networks.

NorminVeggies conducted several activities in fulfillment of these objectives. These were towards the establishment of a presence in Metro Manila, Visayas, and Mindanao markets. It did trials (simulation) of shipping vegetables using reefer van, conducted trial planting, and prioritized the development of key crops where Northern Mindanao would be most competitive in the market.

It then conducted training on production technologies, post-harvest handling, and marketing for its members. Production protocols that were successful were freely shared with members. It printed and distributed booklets on production technologies of selected vegetables. The clustering approach was used to attain volumes to deliver to institutional markets. NorminVeggies through its marketing group, Normincorp, linked farmers to consolidators at the local wholesale vegetable trading centre called Agora as well as to buyers in the neighbouring provinces of Mindanao and in Visayas and Manila markets.

Aside from these activities, NorminVeggies also participated in trade exhibits, hosted several Vegetable Congresses, and convened the Philippines. Vegetable Industry Development Board (PVIDB), and provided valuable inputs to the preparation of the Department of Agriculture's Southern Philippines Vegetables Industry Roadmap.

NorminVeggies also successfully tapped government resources for two reefer trucks, two chillers, one pre-cooling/cold storage facility, and use of reefer van and establishment of a vegetable consolidation centre in the Agora wholesale market in Cagayan de Oro.

Normincorp

There are two organizations closely reinforcing each other. One is NorminVeggies and the other is Normincorp. NorminVeggies is a non-stock, non-profit organization. It is a servicing organization for its current 85 members comprised of various types who commonly share a stake in advancing the vegetable industry: *independent farmers*—those who are small farmers but have a financial base and can independently pursue technologies and markets, *small farmers*—those small farmers needing special development interventions to undertake vegetable production and marketing, *development foundations* assisting small farmers, *corporate farms* which can vertically integrate business operations, *input and service providers*—like seed companies, *local government units,* particularly their departments servicing directly vegetable farmers. NorminVeggies is the organization that accesses support from government and from private resource organizations like Growth with Equity in Mindanao-USAID (GEM-USAID) and the Food Agriculture Organization of the United Nations (FAO), and also works to advocate for pro-vegetable farmer policies and programmes with the government.

Normincorp is the marketing group, a corporation with five incorporators which organizes marketing for a core of independent farmers and lead farmers for various crops. They are: (a) Wilfredo Javier, heading three clusters with his farm, Valley Fresh Farm producing mainly bell pepper, broccoli, cabbage, Chinese pechay, sweet corn, and romaine lettuce, (b) Hector San Juan–Helms Farm producing mainly iceberg lettuce, cabbage, salad tomato and broccoli, (c) Queritess Queja with her farm, TriQ Farm, producing romaine and iceberg lettuce, (d) Juanita Montalvan with her farm, Bukidnon Plateau Gardens, growing mainly strawberry and herbs, (e) Joan Cua Uy, heading the lettuce cluster, with her Green Haven Farm producing mainly iceberg lettuce, broccoli, Chinese pechay, and sweet corn, and backing up farmers' supply for squash. Two independent growers were invited to join Normincorp: (a) Antonio Fernandez with his farm, CountryVeg Farm, and (b) Carol Yu with her farm, Betina Green Farm.

At present, Normincorp services the marketing needs of 23 independent farmers and a core of 60 small farmers being assisted by Kaanib Foundation, Inc. (a NorminVeggies member) in partnership with its development resource organization, Lutheran World Relief Services (LWR) and Catholic Relief Services (CRS). They grow mainly cabbage, carrots, sweet pea, spring onions and tropical vegetables: squash and bitter gourd.

NorminVeggies has increased membership from 15 members in April 1999, to 85 members of good standing as of July 2006 (Table 6.1).

Table 6.1: Members of NorminVeggies, (July 2006)

Farmers		72
Individual Producers	52	
Development Foundations	2	
Corporate Farms	7	
Farmers' Associations	4	
Farmer's Cooperatives	7	
Associate (Inputs/Service Providers)		9
Honorary (Institutional Partners)		4
Total		85

There are actually three types of producers in NorminVeggies: (a) corporate farms (b) independent farmers, and (c) small farmers.

Corporate farms are those that are vertically integrated and do their own marketing. However, in this case, the focus is on independent farmers and small farmers since they are the ones involved in vegetable production clustering and they are considered small and medium farms. Independent farmers have farms with agro-enterprises that can be referred to as SMEs, with the owners having high educational background, entrepreneurial abilities, financial base, having access on their own to technologies and services. Small farmers, on the other hand, are those with limited capital and need external support to improve farm production and access markets. These small farmers are serviced by the NGO member of NorminVeggies which is the Kaanib Foundation, Inc (KFI). Normincorp services regularly 23 independent growers and a core of 90 small farmers supported by Kaanib with assistance from its development partners: Lutheran World Relief Services and Catholic Relief Services. Clustering is being tried out for a core group that is willing to undertake programming of production and market planning. Other NorminVeggies' growers continue to market under spot trading practice (whenever they have harvests) at the wet market. Also, there are many small farmers assisted by Kaanib growing home garden vegetables and they gradually become part of the cluster when they start to transition from home consumption to producing at least one marketable vegetable under programmed production for a targeted market.

Independent farmers have other investments or sources of income other than vegetable farming (owned independently or as a family business). These include corn trading, commercial poultry and piggery production (for integrators), commercial poultry production, restaurant and food catering business, and chicken hatchery. Farm size ranges from 5 to 20 hectares. All share a passion for farming, agree to take up the challenge to advance the vegetable industry, and have accepted that Normincorp is to be opened to assist especially the small farmers.

Small farmers are in the Kaanib project area in the municipality of Impasug-ong, Bukidnon. This geographical focus is to enhance project support and the monitoring process. These farmers are considered marginal but they have an asset base particularly land (ownership or access through rental or use for free in the case of a common family owned farm), draft animal (70 per cent owning), plough (70 per cent), and garden tools (60 per cent). Their farms are family operated so most of the labour requirement is provided by family members. They have some experience in vegetable farming so that they could build on existing production. Tenants are not included because they will not be able to decide independently on their farming and their produce.

The LWR assisted group of 40 farmers is located in highlands (i.e. 1000 meters above sea level areas) so their crops are mainly cabbages and carrots. Their areas are vegetable growing so they are exposed to commercial vegetable farming. Modifications were just made in production-marketing arrangements to make them favorable to farmers under project assistance. On the other hand, the CRS assisted group of 50 farmers is located in lower elevation areas (600 to 900 meters above sea level). This group is composed mostly of rice and corn farmers, and vegetable growing is a diversification. Vegetable products are sweet pea, squash, bitter gourd, and spring onions. It is a new venture for them so the approach towards markets and commercialization is gradual.

Age profile ranges from 24 to 61 years old; about even distribution of those below 40, between 41 and 50, and above 50 years old. Those assisted in the LWR project have experience in commercial vegetable farming under the local trader/financier. Those in the CRS areas have experience in backyard vegetable production. About 70 per cent are from within Impasug-ong while the rest are from families that migrated from other provinces in Mindanao, Visayas, and from Benguet.

The infrastructure constraint is poor roads. Most of these farms are accessed through a dirt road for animal drawn carts because they are not alongside the village roads. At times, when rains are heavy and continuous, farmers have to resort to manual hauling to bring their products to the road accessible by a vehicle. This has implication on their efficiency of product movements at certain times.

Roles in Marketing Cluster

At this stage when small farmers are still being organized into a functional sub-cluster together with the vegetable clusters in marketing, much of the decision making on markets rests on independent farmers. Normincorp continuously seeks good markets and these are presented to Kaanib as options that can be discussed and decided by the farmers themselves. The mechanism of assigning certain products (i.e. cabbage, carrots, squash, bitter gourd, spring onions, and sweet pea) to be grown with small farmers in the cluster provides that decisions will always have to be taken by them because they will be part of the supply source for the vegetables.

The key person is the Kaanib project staff that is the link between Normincorp and the six sub-clusters of farmers. He introduces situations as opportunities for capability building of the farmers as they are initiated into commercial marketing operations.

Production protocols are adjusted from time to time based on the requirements of the markets. These are reviewed in NorminVeggies by a core of growers involved in the production facilitated by the association's vice-president for production. NorminVeggies has a vegetable coordinator who goes around the members to check on their production situation relative to the production protocols recommended. The vegetable coordinator links directly with Kaanib for the farmers.

Normincorp's president decides with the cluster heads and lead growers on the post-harvest arrangements per crop. These are circulated to all growers involved in the form of a post-production guide. Kaanib is part of the group on behalf of the farmers. Independent farmers are assumed to take care of their post-harvest needs. Kaanib organizes the post-harvests operations with farmers with the Municipal Economic Enterprise Development Office of the local government of Impasugong since Kaanib maintains a close collaboration with LGU for the CRS project.

Normincorp's president also decides with the core of 23 independent growers and with Kaanib regarding the markets to be chosen after pricing and terms/conditions are openly discussed. Kaanib consults the farmers and represents the group in the decision making. This is a transition phase. After a capability building period of about a year, farmers who can be trained to be sub-cluster heads can directly represent the farmers in the deliberations.

Independent farmers take care of their own capital or credit requirements. Kaanib facilitates the credit requirements of small farmers. It should be noted that the credit package is designed by Kaanib with the farmers and is part of the development assistance from its partners. In the past six months, Kaanib deposited a leverage fund from the CRS project in the local cooperative (Kauyagan Savers Coop) and the coop with financing from the Land Bank of the Philippines matched this with 75 per cent amount to finance squash farmers under a trial financing scheme.

Normincorp is a corporation operated with staff. Day to day activities are handled by a paid staff (both at the consolidation centre and for outshipment to buyers).

Factors of Inclusion/Exclusion

In the case of independent farmers, inclusion is by invitation of the old cluster members. The important consideration is that the grower can work in a group as observed in his/her participation in NorminVeggies' activities. The grower should be a serious producer with existing vegetable farm interested to go into programmed plantings with the cluster for group marketing. Moreover, the grower should be willing to have his farm visited anytime by other members especially small farmers and ready to teach others as s/he has been taught at the start by other members on the production and postharvest protocols. Emphasis is given on the core value of sharing because this is at the heart of the success of clustering and group marketing.

In the case of small farmers, inclusion is decided initially by the Kaanib project staff with a core of lead growers/farmers in the village. Additional members are also invited by the rest of farmers based on criteria. At this stage, screening and decision making is done with the Kaanib project staff. Criteria applied for screening are as follows:

- It has own farm or has access to land that can be rented or used for free (in the case of family farms)
- It has the basic assets (owned or access to): draft animal, plough, garden tools, etc.
- It has a family operated farm (external labour is only about 25 per cent)
- It has experience in vegetable farming (either commercial or backyard)
- It does not have a big obligation to local traders/financiers (to eliminate tensions)
- It has demonstrated willingness to work in a group (willing to work with scheduled planting to come up with a reliable supply with the rest of farmers)
- It has road access (even if just for animal drawn cart)
- It has potential access to water
- It can work with the group.

Innovation

NorminVeggies in partnership with Normincorp successfully overcame obstacles in tapping dynamic markets. They have become preferred suppliers because of their ability to respond to changes in market requirements and have recently ventured into forward integration by setting up their own wholesale outlet at the Agora vegetable wholesale market in Cagayan de Oro City. The key to this linkage is the organizational setup. Included in the innovation is the involvement of development foundations with the non-governmental organization working together with NorminVeggies for the development intervention targeting the need of the small farmers.

There are now many farmers in the Philippines forming groups to market their products as one. Small farmers are increasingly becoming aware of the need to collaborate their production and marketing efforts in order to maintain their access to markets.

In response to the challenge of accessing more stable markets, farmers from Northern Mindanao collaborated with each other to coordinate their production and marketing efforts. As marketing clusters, they were able to achieve economies of scale in transporting produce, access development assistance from government and NGOs, and share market intelligence, production, and post-harvest technologies. The uniqueness of the innovation is the organizational set-up that the Northern Mindanao farmers adopted. The collective action did not stop at membership but was implemented at different nodes of the supply chain from production, post-harvest, and marketing up to collection.

They also organized a private corporation which acted as a marketing arm and charged a percentage market facilitation fee. This marketing arrangement is very attractive to farmers because they retain ownership of their products up to the end buyer or institutional market. They receive the sale of their products less the facilitation fee for the marketing services they received.

In 1999, Joan Uy, who owns Green Haven Farm, became dissatisfied with the way her lettuce were being sold at the Agora vegetable wholesale market in Cagayan de Oro City. The traders at the Agora market would automatically remove 20–25 per cent from the weight of the lettuce even if the quality of the lettuce was better than those coming from other farms. She started to seek out for other markets.

In January 2000, Joan supplied local fastfood joints and restaurants in Cagayan de Oro. She adjusted to the weekly deliveries by planting weekly. By April, she was supplying 200 kg of lettuce to Cebu weekly. In July, she entered the Metro Manila market by supplying a supermarket supplier. She sent 400 kg of lettuce by plane weekly to Manila. Metro Manila is considered an important domestic market because it is the largest and most densely populated area in the Philippines. It also has the largest concentration of upper and middle income households than any other part of the country.

Production of lettuce was improving and Green Haven started to produce larger heads of iceberg lettuce. Unfortunately, the supermarket supplier did not want larger heads, and the improvement in production made Green Haven lose its supermarket market. By January 2001, Joan stopped supplying the supermarket. Green Haven started to go after the Metro Manila fastfood market which wanted larger iceberg lettuce heads.

By February 2001, one vegetable processor supplying McDonalds fastfood chain responded to Green Haven's offer to supply. After farm visits and negotiations, Blue Dairy Corporation, the McDonalds vegetable processor, placed a weekly order of

400 kg of lettuce to be delivered by plane every Tuesday from Green Haven. Another farm in Bukidnon supplied Blue Dairy with 400 kg every Thursday.

In the six months that followed, Green Haven had to learn to produce the quality required by Blue Dairy. Its manager, Mr. Ped Miguel, extended technical advice and postharvest techniques to Green Haven. By August 2001, Blue Dairy suggested refrigeration to preserve the quality of the produce. At the same time, Blue Dairy was willing to increase the volume of lettuce purchased from Mindanao. The challenge was then to fill a 20–foot refrigerated container van with 3.5 tons of lettuce weekly.

To respond to the challenge, Joan invited five other farmers, who previously expressed interest to grow lettuce, to form a marketing cluster. To facilitate the development of the group, she shared production technologies and market information. About the same time, these farmers started to join Northern Mindanao Vegetable Producers' Association (NorminVeggies) to be able to access assistance from development agencies. They would later join her as incorporators to put up Normincorp. The lettuce cluster shared the experience with the other vegetable farmers and other vegetables clusters were formed: carrot cluster, strawberry cluster, etc.

While the innovation started to be formed outside of a larger farmers' group, it achieved maturity as an idea when the entire farmers' association adopted it as a strategy to assist small farmers gain access to stable markets aside from the spot market transactions of the wet market.

A summary of the history of innovation and responses of NorminVeggies to dynamic changes in the market is presented in Table 6.2.

Table 6.2: History of Innovation and Responses, NorminVeggies

Date	*Supply Chain Event*	*Innovation Event*
Jan 2000	• Difficult traders market	• Trial of Green Haven Farm to find alternative markets like supplying direct to local restaurants and fast food markets.
	• Weekly deliveries were required by the fast food market.	• Trial crop programming.
April 2000	• Encouraging results from the field	• Used Cagayan de Oro contacts to connect to Cebu fast food markets.
	• Distant markets	• Utilized vegetable distributors as a response to distant markets.
	• Strict quality standards of the fast food markets and year round supply needed.	• Supplied the wet markets after the produce was sorted, giving the better quality products to the fast food markets. Farmer planted extra rows of crops as back-up in case of crop failure of some of the farmers. This necessitated programming and production scheduling.

Contd...

Table 6.2 Contd...

Date	*Supply Chain Event*	*Innovation Event*
July 2000	• Recurring typhoons in Luzon where 60% of temperate vegetables are produced. • Fastfood processors resorted to imports. • Strict supplier evaluation procedure, included visits to farms. • Distance from the Manila market complicated the relationship.	• Used its track record to build links with the fast-food processors who supplied international fast-food chains operating in Luzon. • Promoted products as import substitutes. • Weekly plantings on field with post harvest procedures to show that the farmer can respond to the market. • Manila based intermediary was utilized (received goods, turned over for receiving at the processor, got results, communicated to Cagayan De Oro, and then transferred payment based on terms).
April to Sept 2001	• Difficult quality standards • Buyers challenged the farmers by saying that volume will be increased if they can refrigerate.	• Green Haven worked hard in postharvest, quality and supply chain management. • Innovations and adjustments done by trial and error. • Green Haven Farms sought other farmers; started the idea of clustering because the demand was 3 tons of lettuce weekly supplied in refrigerated van. • Cluster requested processor for a period of 6 months to build production.
March 2002	• Government support and GEM–USAID support to build a vegetable farmers' organization — trade fairs — trainings — research.	• Green Haven Farm and other lettuce farmers formed the lettuce cluster. This group became the transition group to the formation of a business entity. • NorminVeggies supported the formation of marketing clusters and became the rallying point for accessing government, private and development agency support.
June 2002	• GEM linked the group with business service providers.	• Refrigerated truck loan. NorminVeggies got to be known. Inquiries were received.
July 2003	• Other buyers (i.e., supermarkets distributors) contacted not just for lettuce but other products as well.	• Opened new markets • Other clusters formed • Produce sent to supermarkets suppliers • Learned of the seasonality of supply in Luzon and adjusted production program.
Mar 2004	• Fast food chain which bought from the processor switched processors. This processor in turn stopped buying from the lettuce cluster.	• Lettuce cluster attempted to follow the fast food chain market by moving to other processors but found it difficult because they were not preferred by the new processor.

Contd...

Table 6.2 Contd...

Date	*Supply Chain Event*	*Innovation Event*
Aug 2004	• Another fast food chain required supply. • Typhoon in Luzon opened a window of opportunity.	• Opened links with the new fast food operator. • Use of the Manila intermediary was stopped and the newly formed Normincorp started to handle the marketing instead. They hired a marketing coordinator.
Jan 2005	• Lettuce demand in the fast-food chain market changed from fresh to processed form. • New product launched (salad greens). • Corporate farms entered the industry. Competition from big, forward integrated companies.	• Transacted with the fast-food processor. • NorminCorp withdrew from the fast-food market in Manila to study options. Retained the fast-food market in Visayas and Mindanao, which were still buying unprocessed vegetables.
Mar 2005	• NorminVeggies has no retail outlet.	• Opened Veggie corner. • Tapped Department of Agriculture (DA) for 2 chillers.
July 2004 to 2005	• Inventories required by new type of buyers. • Government support for cold chain.	• Rented commercial storage space. • Broccoli and strawberry air-freighted 3x a week. • Tapped DA refrigerated van facility at Metromart as storage and contact point. • Rented refrigerated truck in Manila.
July 2005	• Supermarkets supplier gave Normincorp requirements for July to Dec 2005. • Continuous year round requirement in Visayasand neighboring Mindanao provinces.	• Expanded with more vegetables (tomato, sweet pea, carrots, squash). • Partnership with DA and Growth with Equity in Mindanao. • Base of supply built in Agora market through trader contacts.
May 2006 up to present	• A core of buyers from Mindanao, Visayas with regular requirement from Normincorp.	• NorminVeggies opened NorminVeggies Consolidation Center (NVCC) at the Agora Wet Market. • Supply for Luzon buyer during the months of July to December. • Year round supply for supermarket and fast-food distributors as well as other wholesalers/ retailers in Visayas. & Mindanao. (Supply form 18 independent and 60 small farmers) • Distributors tapped in Visayas & Mindanao.

Elements of Organizational Innovation

Normincorp's regular supply is coming from 12 marketing clusters which are product based. These 12 clusters are: lettuce, broccoli, Chinese pechay (wongbok), bell pepper, sweet pepper, cucumber, cabbage, sweet pea, Kentucky beans, bitter gourd, eggplant, and squash. The first half of these clusters comprises only independent growers, while the remaining six clusters are a combination of independent farmers and small farmers assisted by Kaanib. The groups of Kaanib assisted farmers based on the barangays (villages) constitute sub-clusters of the NorminVeggies marketing clusters.

A cluster is an informal group of 5 to 10 small scale farmers who commit to undertake a common marketing plan for a particular product (or set of products) for identified markets. Each product cluster has a designated lead farmer who acts as the coordinator of production of the farms involved in the cluster. The lead is a farmer who is the best for that type of vegetable. S/He is also responsible for teaching other farmers in the cluster of applicable production techniques in order to maintain the quality specified by the market. Usually, the lead farmer is one of the independent farmers, since they are more educated and financially independent. These clusters consist of the core of 18 independent farmers and 60 small farmers. The 60 small farmers are organized into six sub-clusters based in six villages in the municipality of Impasugong, Bukidnon.

A marketing cluster can be formed to take advantage of an opportunity at a certain period of time. For the high demand of tomato from Manila during July to December, a tomato cluster is formed just for the period. The next year, it can be formed again but not necessarily with the same members/farmers. Similarly, servicing the Manila supermarket distributors with a set of vegetables will require the formation of a Manila cluster just for the season of supply. It has been observed though that cluster members tended to be the same in the succeeding years.

The cluster may appear loose but what holds it together is the commitment of supply and the cluster agreements. Important cluster agreements are the volume of supply per farmer, delivery schedule, and compliance to a common quality standard which necessitates agreement on practices in plant/farm management, harvest, and post-harvest management. The cluster, therefore, is not just an ordinary grouping. It is one with a marketing objective and a management system, requiring discipline from each farmer to protect the reputation of the group in the market. Being a small group, it is capable of quick response to buyer feedback and requirements.

Clustering is the strategy for farmers to become a valued supplier in the higher value and growth markets, particularly fast foodchains through their processors, and supermarkets through their consolidators. In the cluster, farmers get to talk about the market and the value addition in the supply chain, and farmers in the cluster decide together on the markets to be served. This empowers farmers and enables them to become a dynamic player in the market, share collective know-how (particularly the best practices in the farm), resources, technologies, and market contacts, otherwise inaccessible or costly to them as individual farmers.

Indeed, the benefits of clustering include: (a) higher economies of scale and ability to handle large product volumes at lower transaction costs, (b) access to good markets, (c) business deals with service providers, and (d) effective linkage with government and private resource organizations.

New Business Model

Normincorp was established in December 2003. Its formation signified a new development in the marketing set-up for small farmers. While established as a stock corporation, it functions more like a cooperative and has a social enterprise character. It was a set up and operated with keen business sense but also with full empathy for small farmers.

An innovation is that Normincorp is not a trading company. Rather, it is a market facilitator linking the farmer through the cluster direct to the buyer. The farmer is given the buyer's price, and s/he is therefore accountable for the product and retains ownership of the product up to the institutional market's end. This encourages the farmer to supply the best quality since the price is given to him/her and all sales are remitted directly to him/her after deducting the market facilitation fee based on accepted vegetables. Conversely, all rejects are individually charged to the concerned farmer. Labelling of products by farm or farmer provides this traceability.

Market facilitation fee is charged by Normincorp based on the value of the product and the kind of vegetables. Table 6.3 shows the rates.

Table 6.3: Normincorp Facilitation Fees

Value/Kg (Php)	*Squash/ Ginger*	*Cabbages (flat, round, wongbok)*	*Other Vegetables & Fruits*	*Table Tomato*
Up to 2.00	0.20	0.20	0.20	
2.05 to 5.00	0.25	0.20	0.20	
5.05 to 10.00	0.50	0.50	0.75	
10.05 to 20.00		0.75	1.00	
20.05 to 50.00			2.00	
> 50.05			3.00	
Up to 300/crate				5.00
> 300/crate				10.00

Note: Same rates apply for storage fees charged by NorminVeggies at NVCC

As market facilitator, Normincorp saw to it that production is programmed by the clusters with their respective cluster leaders according to marketing plans, that quality farm and post-harvest management can be done by each farmer in the cluster, and that coordination can be provided for the sequence of activities that include order taking, outshipment logistics, billing/charging, collection, and remittance to farmers. For these services, Normincorp earns a market facilitation fee based on the value of sale and uses the income to cover the marketing management overhead.

Breakeven operating levels require a significant volume of vegetables channelled through the corporation. To operate in the Visayas market requires an overhead of P50,000 or a sale of P500,000 per month. To include Manila operation is to double this overhead requirement. Normincorp devised a cluster map that specifies, the farmers will produce which crop and at what volumes. This is matched with a planting/ delivery calendar (also called a crop ruler).

The process of developing the cluster map and the harvest/delivery calendar came by trial and error, to respond to the management needs for efficiency and effectiveness. While the market was being developed, farmers were going through the "learning curve" in farm supply management. The incorporators of Normincorp contributed funds other than the facilitation fees paid for vegetables handled to ensure viability of the marketing clusters. At certain times when there were drastic changes in volume (because of weather or to dynamics of market competition), the incorporators shelled out additional funds.

Without this readiness on the part of the incorporators to support the business establishment needs, Normincorp would have folded up during its first year. It helps that the incorporators are farmers who share a common vision to promote solidarity among small scale farmers to make a difference in the industry. They are also financially independent farmers whose farms can be classified as SME farms. At this stage though with the operation of NVCC handling considerable vegetable volumes, Normincorp is financially sustainable from the market facilitation fees earned. NorminVeggies, being the owner of NVCC and provider of storage space with its allied services, also earns from storage fees equivalent in value to Normincorp's market facilitation fee. This way, both organizations are financially sustainable.

Supply Chain Management

NorminVeggies attempted to build a positive brand image by assuring the market of reliability in quality and regularity of supply as well as reasonableness of pricing. Quality management was worked backed on the farm itself. For example, when the market asked that carrot should be deep orange with small inner core, the carrot cluster looked into the seed varieties to be used. When a particular size became a requirement, the cluster checked planting distances and cultural management. No carrot came out for the Visayas supermarket distributor that was not washed and air-dried as this was the quality specification agreed upon. To guide the quality management on field and in post-harvest handling, the cluster came up with a quality assurance plan that guided each farmer.

For the market, i.e. buyers of supermarkets or consolidators for the Visayas, Normincorp related quality to reliability of supply from the farmers through the cluster. It tried to build the image that NorminVeggies growers marketing through Normincorp can be a valued supplier to whom buyers would find the least problems or "headaches" with their buying transactions. This is opposite the prevailing market image of small farmers as unreliable. Normincorp's president is also NorminVeggies vice president for marketing, and this facilitated the integration between these two organizations.

The marketing clusters were prepared to do the extra things which included flexibility in packing requirement, lead time for them to be informed of changes in price, or shortage in supply. This is particularly important for consolidators of supermarkets or fastfood chains, where non-delivery of product or delivery of low quality products can be costly.

Delivery reliability implied that interrelated activities such as production scheduling, post-harvest requirements, logistics (transport, seaport, and airport operations), farmer and buyer communication, invoicing, payment collection, and sale remittances to farmers are attended to.

Normincorp set up an office in Cagayan de Oro as its contact point, and hired a full-time marketing coordinator, a logistics in-charge (that handled the outshipment activities), a full-time cashier, part-time accountant, and in Manila, a marketing representative (paid on commission basis based on accepted vegetables) was tapped to attend to the distribution needs in a distant place.

Whenever a shipment is prepared for the Visayas by boat on the regular schedules of Tuesday and Saturday, all the cluster farmers involved in the diversified product supply harvest simultaneously and bring their vegetables to an agreed consolidation area near the port on the latest at 5:30 pm as the boat leaves at 7:00 p.m. For the small farmers, the truck of the independent farmer nearest them handles the transport to the consolidation point. This was before NVCC was set up by NorminVeggies. Most of the products prior to shipment is gathered in NVCC. Exceptions are products loaded in the container vans that are consolidated direct at the container yards near the port.

There is no time to check the quality of vegetables. It is presumed that the cluster farmer, guided by a quality assurance plan, will comply with the agreed quality standards. In case the buyer has complaints, it is easy to segregate the product and supplier since all boxes carry a farm/farmer label, and each farmer fills up a packing list that is recorded and kept at the Normincorp office.

When NVCC opened for spot market trading, traders from the neighbouring provinces in Mindanao, particularly those servicing supermarkets and fast-food chains, started to procure the high quality vegetables from the centre. From a core of five Normincorp buyers who have been steady buyers from Visayas, new buyers came to NVCC and the number of weekly buyers increased to 10 in just a span of about three months operation. New buyers are coming in expressing interest to procure at the consolidation centre for outshipment areas.

Networking and Linkages

Each farmer continues to operate his/her own small farmholdings but enjoys access through NorminVeggies, competence enhancing linkages with business, government, and private resource organizations. Good relations are maintained with service providers for outshipment and packaging, with government agencies like the Department of Agriculture (DA) and the Department of Trade and Industry (DTI), and with their main private resource organization partner, GEM/USAID.

There is synergy in activities because of collaborative effort. The co-sponsorship of the government and private support in the training, technology, and product/market development has given important breakthroughs for the association. For example, NorminVeggies is able to pursue cold chain development efforts with interest free, five-year loan of DA to the association for the acquisition of a reefer truck and two chillers. During the simulation for cold storage shipment, GEM support allowed the farmers to travel and directly observe results of refrigeration and also to be in consultation with the buyers. While the bulk of resources came from the farmers, these types of assistance fill the gaps that enable the farmers to keep abreast of market demands and have staying power in the market.

Development Interventions

Normin wanted small farmers to be part of the marketing cluster. Several attempts were made by individual small farmers to join but it always ended with non-delivery and poor reliability and sustainability. The hurdles small farmers face in marketing their produce is too complex for other independent farmers to assist. What is needed is the support of development agencies that address the vulnerabilities of small farmers and open the door of opportunity for them to be part of the clustering effort.

The opportunity to work with small farmers as a group came when Kaanib Foundation (a member of NorminVeggies) together with Lutheran World Relief Services requested Normincorp to evaluate their vegetable production assistance to an organized group of vegetable farmers and asked for recommendation about how to make the project take off.

KFI and LWR allowed Normincorp to redesign the development interventions, not just in marketing but in production assistance. A new group of 10 individual farmers who had the experience in vegetable farming was formed. These were those who were not deeply indebted to the locality's trader/financiers, and who were open to working in a group along the concept of clustering. It was important that each farmer in the group understood delivery reliability by agreeing to take turns in planting weekly so that a stable volume could be produced weekly from them. This became the base of the farmer's clustering.

These 10 farmers increased to 25 by the last quarter of 2005, and into 30 farmers in March 2006, with staggered production of cabbage and carrots, and then reduced to its current number of 20. This supply goes into the Visayas markets as part of the multiproduct cluster marketing. In effect, this group of farmers is called the Kitanglad Small Farmers Cluster.

Kaanib made available a production fund that creatively financed the farmers in a way similar to the financier/traders. The fund was not made known as project fund but it was a financing from Kaanib coursed through Green Haven Farm and Normincorp. This way, it was immediately perceived as a business transaction, and not a dole out. The credit support covered material inputs, one sack of rice after planting, a budget for harvest, and post-harvest handling. Together with this credit fund support is the assistance that a vegetable technician could be hired to guide them and that an administrative person could help set the recording and marketing systems in place.

There was no talk of interest payments for the loan. Adopting the 50 : 50 sharing of net proceeds scheme followed by the local traders/financiers, the farmers had to give 30 per cent of the net sale proceeds (i.e. after deducting the farm inputs and other costs borrowed) as cost of money. This 30 per cent is deposited in the local cooperative (Kauyagan Savers Cooperative) which together with the grant fund from LWR for production credit will constitute in the future a loan fund to be managed by the local coop. In January, the farmers agreed to make it a 35 per cent deduction from the net sale proceeds, with 5 per cent as fund source for their cluster.

The Kaanib intervention that is direct to them is the irrigation support for which they pay a rental fee per cropping.

It was quite a challenge assisting the small farmers even if KFI/LWR fund support was available for the limitation is not only in credit availability but in infrastructure weaknesses and in their attitudes. Poor farm to market roads isolated their production areas and made it expensive to transport their inputs and products. There were countless times when the farmers' cabbage and carrots could not be delivered in their required quality and packaging standards as farmers did not have ready access to water just to wash the carrots.

Harvest operations were at times hampered by rains, and the products could not be brought out from the fields that did not have all-weather road access. Every failure of product delivery, or a delivery of poor quality, exerted pressure on the rest of the Visayas cluster farmers since marketing is through the group, and the failure of a farmer is viewed as a failure of the whole group. Expectedly, this brought about tensions and doubts among the independent farmers as to the capability of small farmers to be in the cluster.

Lately, however, KFI/LWR has extended support so that a consolidation area with packing facility can be put up at the location central to the farmers. This way, farmers can harvest a day in advance and bring the products to this consolidation area where they can implement the required quality management procedures. Hopefully, this needed support system will ease up some of the tensions of bringing together in the cluster the better-resourced independent farmers with small farmers.

The other challenge had to do with changing small farmers' values and attitudes. Used to the trader/financier for the "one-time, big-time" plantings where their capital risk is very high, it takes time for them to understand that the secret to viability is planting in small areas with high quality production, and coming up with a crop-mix of at least three vegetables. Convincing them of the "economic module" size of 500 square meter per vegetable for four types of vegetables was difficult. It took the success of a few of them to finally convince the rest that given their limitations, manageable areas with high technical care and adequate inputs ultimately yield higher returns.

Time was also needed to change their discipline in terms of compliance to quality standards. Used to heavy application of agrochemical inputs under financing from the local traders, a small farmer tended to apply the inputs on hand because this way s/he would feel "secure" that his/her crop would not be damaged, and s/he can pay his/her loan to the financier.

A technician was provided as part of the development support to guide small farmers closely on integrated pest management using newer, safer inputs. Given their higher cost, it was necessary for the technician to control the access of chemical inputs so that usage could be kept to the minimum and chemical withdrawal periods were strictly followed. This is important because the small farmers in the cluster have to go with the cluster's definition of quality which is not only freshness but also food safety. The technician also helps diagnose problems as they arise so that farmers do not immediately resort to spraying when it is not necessary.

Technical guidance is very important not only in production but especially in post-harvest. Even when farmers are shown how harvesting and post-harvest handling ought to be done through visits to other farms, they still need to be guided very closely because at times, the problem is not the know-how but the discipline to uphold the standards of performance and quality.

Given time, however, it is hoped that small farmers will grow to appreciate the value of this discipline. With the cost and returns computations given out to them wherein they can see in detail how their product was unloaded, they are taught that sorting pays in terms of the price differentials, and that rejects or trimmings deducted from them affect their earnings considerably.

The added benefit of showing the farmers their costing is that the farmers realized for many years that the trader/financier just wrote the figure of their net income (or loss) on a small piece of paper, they did not really know how their farming turned out. This time, they can be critical about their farm practices in terms of how they translate to cost that reduce or increase their earnings.

After a year, management of the credit fund is now fully under Kaanib with Normincorp just handling the marketing activities. Kaanib has provided this year irrigation support which farmers pay through rentals per cropping for the use of the facility so that there is no break of production during the summer months.

In the third quarter of 2006, Kaanib ventured to expand vegetable production support to include another 20 farmers in two other villages in partnership with another development resource organization, Catholic Relief Services. Learning from its experiences in the LWR-assisted project given the tremendous constraints of small vegetable farmers, Kaanib with CRS extended assistance utilizing a development framework that immediately built partnership with the local government and invested in a lot of participatory processes to prepare the farmers before actual market engagement and build up.

Observations show that it was easier to work with CRS assisted farmers who did not have much interaction with traders with its negative and dependent relationship, and accordingly, were more forward looking. At present, the CRS assisted vegetable farmers number 38 (i.e. 12 in sweet pea and 22 in squash production). They have recently consolidated products for the Manila supermarket consolidator under a year round marketing arrangement with the buyer, and following weekly pricing procedures but within a negotiated fixed bottom/ceiling price range. A different financing scheme was tried out. CRS put in a small production capital fund in the local coop (Kauyagan Savers Coop) which is a time deposit and a leverage fund for the coop to match it with an equal credit fund. This leverage is further increased with the coming in of financing from the Land Bank of the Philippines through the local coop to match both CRS and coop financing. In effect the CRS fund is multiplied four times.

In all, Kaanib extends assistance to 60 farmers grouped into six clusters based in six villages in the municipality of Impasugong. In all the challenges of extending development assistance to small farmers in LWR and CRS assisted projects, it was critical that the incorporators of Normincorp gave all-out support to the farmers. All sorts of innovative practices were tried out to maintain that cabbage, carrots, sweet pea, and squash can continue to be supplied by small farmers. This at times meant that Normincorp would purchase at the Agora wholesale market when there was a supply gap from small farmers in a particular week, instead of allowing an independent farmer to takeover the production of these products earlier allocated for small farmers' participation. Since procuring from the wet market proved disadvantageous because of poor quality, Green Haven with other independent farmers eventually planted these crops as back-up as the farmers were still building up regular production.

Participation of Normin in Chain Management

Before the concept of marketing clusters, the individual farmers marketed their produce to the traditional wet market in Agora. Farmers harvest their produce even without a ready buyer and are compelled to receive the price given by traders. Many times, their produce was sold the following day at very much reduced prices. They were subject to market distortions when buyers wait to transact the next day so the value of the product is very much reduced though it is not yet damaged.

The first marketing cluster was for lettuce. They marketed to a specialized wholesaler serving the fastfood industry, Blue Dairy Corporation. Aside from the fastfood market, they also had contacts with wholesalers in the Visayas.

The farmers decided to market as a group to the Visayas wholesaler and the fastfood industry in order to get a better price for the quality of lettuce produced by the cluster.

Blue Dairy was the main driver for the collaboration which developed with the lettuce cluster. Blue Dairy needed the farmers to use a refrigeration system when shipping the goods in order to preserve the quality and compete with lettuce from Australia.

A three ton weekly supply from NorminVeggies's lettuce cluster was 40 per cent of the supply requirement of Blue Dairy, with the other 60 per cent sourced from farmers of Benguet. The cluster grew to eight farmers, and the weekly supply of refrigerated lettuce to Blue Dairy continued for the next two years until it stopped supplying to McDonalds. The fastfood chain had begun to source from another processor, and NorminVeggies took this to be part of the dynamics in the highly competitive market of fastfood supply.

In August 2004, NorminVeggies lettuce cluster supplied another fastfood chain, Kentucky Fried Chicken (KFC), directly for the first six months, and then through its processor in the succeeding months. By March 2005, the supply to KFC's processor was stopped because the lettuce market demand in fastfoods had changed significantly from raw to processed vegetables and that unless vegetable processing could be done by Normincorp, it would not have the market strength that comes with being able to deal directly with the end-user. At this time, corporate farms supplying the fastfood markets had forward integrated their production with processing to take advantage of the emerging trend in the fastfoods industries to serve salad greens.

In addition, the lettuce requirement had shifted from the iceberg type grown in the open field to the romaine and leafy lettuces that needed greenhouses or rain shelters for production. The technology of rainshelter gives high harvest recovery at lower cost, and yields a highly differentiated product in terms of product safety because less agrochemical inputs are used. In the second quarter of 2005, Normincorp withdrew from the fastfood market to study the options. The fastfood market in Manila ordered only from July to December and treated NorminVeggies supply as an off-season supplier to the Benguet supply.

By the last quarter of 2005, Normincorp had the potential to re-enter the market. Several lettuce farmers had invested in indigenous greenhouses and started to grow the romaine type of lettuce. At this time, NorminVeggies became a beneficiary of support from the Food and Agriculture Organization (FAO) for technology development with the demonstration project on three units of indigenous rain shelters. A feasibility study was done on vegetable processing to look into the economic viability of farmers competing with corporate groups already servicing the high end market for processed salad greens. The risk was found to be very high considering that fastfoods change processors and suppliers depend on competitive price offers, among other considerations.

Normincorp has opted to still go back to supplying the institutional market through the processors. At present, it has a commitment during the rainy season to ship a container van (content of three tons) of refrigerated lettuce mix comprising iceberg lettuce, leaf lettuce, and romaine for a processor servicing fastfood requirements.

Other products are being planned for supply to the processor for the requirements of the fastfood industry and caterers. These are for camote, cabbage, broccoli, and cauliflower. Another processor has also negotiated with Normincorp for the annual contract of supply of sweet pepper.

This is now the most common system of purchasing in the Philippines where preferred suppliers service all the needs of supermarkets. One or two preferred suppliers service one supermarket chain or specific branches of the chain.

Having built a track record of quality and delivery reliability, other buyers in Manila contacted NorminVeggies as early as 2003 not just for lettuce but also for other vegetables. This was the beginning of its expansion. New growers joined NorminVeggies and marketing clusters for broccoli and strawberry were formed.

NorminVeggies farmers developed excellent lettuce, broccoli, and strawberry which are difficult to procure at high quality in Manila. It was the marketing strategy to build a name for quality Bukidnon supply in the institutional markets using them, to change the image of small growers as unreliable suppliers through the clustering strategy, and to assure markets that typhoon-free Mindanao is in the unique position to address their needs when they have to import these products at high cost during the typhoon months of July to November in Luzon. This strategy worked as Normincorp products developed a brand image in the market, and were identified as coming from "Normin" in contrast to those of Benguet.

With lettuce, broccoli, and strawberry, Normincorp was able to open to other types of buyers in July 2004. These are: (a) supermarket distributors; and (b) hotel/restaurant distributors. When necessary, commercial cold storage space was rented to hold at least a ton of lettuce as inventory for ready supply. Broccoli and strawberry ice-packed in styrofoam boxes (the way the Australian supply is packed coming into the country) was airlifted to Manila three times weekly at a consolidated volume of one ton weekly. When the Department of Agriculture (DA) allowed NorminVeggies to use a refrigerated van in its Metromart facility (at Boni Avenue) as storage facility, NorminVeggies ventured to directly supply the high-end restaurants in Ortigas and Makati. It rented a refrigerated truck for this purpose.

The new markets taught Normincorp the marketing dynamics of seasonality for vegetables. While the fastfood market arrangement is year round, it found out that those of Manila based supermarkets, hotels, and restaurants that are priced weekly or monthly are economical to serve during the rainy, typhoon months of July to November when the freight costs to move these products from Bukidnon to Manila could be adequately covered. As a result, it supplies to Manila only for these months. While Normincorp supplies only half of the year, volumes were doubled and included other vegetables, like cooking tomato, sweet pea, and squash.

In 2004, Normincorp supplied the off-season market (July to November) for Manila supermarket distributors. These are the typhoon months in Luzon when the Mindanao supply is more stable. It soon became uneconomical to maintain a storage facility and a permanent management set-up in Manila just for a six-month supply per year, so a marketing coordinator was hired to facilitate the service needs for this seasonal supply. This marketing coordinator became a business partner offering representation for Normincorp in Manila and is now paid on commission basis.

At present, Normincorp maintains a supply relationship with a preferred supplier of a leading supermarket chain in Manila. This preferred supplier handles 200 items and supplies to 18 Manila stores of this supermarket chain. Normincorp moves squash and sweet pea products of CRS assisted small farmers into this market together with other items from the independent farmers. Price is negotiated weekly but to provide a safety net for small farmers, agreement is to set price within a bottom/ceiling price range. The preferred supplier pays the farmers weekly but its credit term with the supermarket chain is 30 days, at times extending up to 45 days. Normincorp also supplies to a vegetable consolidator in Manila with supply for the caterers and canteens of big companies. Also, Normincorp supplies directly a supermarket in Cebu (Visayas) under direct outright purchase arrangement (i.e. not anymore going through a consolidator).

Forward Integration

NorminCorp then decided to build up its Visayas markets (Iloilo, Bohol and Cebu) and in Mindanao that are year-round. As part of the response for the challenge of bulk consolidation with expanded markets in Visayas as well as neighboring Mindanao provinces, NorminVeggies has entered into partnership with DA and GEM-USAID to be able to put up its consolidation Centre (NVCC) in Agora in early 2006. NVCC started operation in May 2006 with NorminVeggies handling storage/warehousing services and Normincorp managing marketing.

Through NVCC, NorminVeggies was able to establish its track record as a supplier to Cebu, Bohols and Iloilo supermarket and fastfood market distributors as well as the Mindanao buyers in other provinces. The growers have maintained consistency of supply and quality. Each cluster has a target volume to deliver every week and the farmers bring their produce to NVCC (before direct to the port) where the produce is consolidated and shipped except for those shipped in container vans that are brought direct to the container yards near the port.

Buyers in the Visayas determine the proportion of acceptable goods and pay the corresponding amount to Normincorp. Normincorp gets a percentage market facilitation fee from the face value of the sale, deducts NorminVeggies storage fee, and the balance is remitted to the grower. An improvement after a month is that Normincorp has used its bargaining power to negotiate better arrangements. Some buyers have started to agree to send their consolidators who pay immediately cash to Normincorp when vegetables are withdrawn from NVCC.

This eliminated the problem of trimmings in transit, and the waiting time for payment. These made the farmers very happy with NVCC services. It has created a big impact on the operations of NorminVeggies. The stall is leased by NorminVeggies and therefore all storage fees go to NorminVeggies. Normincorp moved from the office of Green Haven Farm to hold office at NVCC at the Agora market. Marketing of vegetables is the responsibility of Normincorp which receives the marketing facilitation fee.

Outshipments to the Visayas and the neighbouring Mindanao provinces are regularly done every week. The consolidators of these markets pay for the shipping cost and transact in cash. Normincorp with its reputation for quality and reliability has become their preferred supplier. The advantages offered by Normincorp makes it convenient for the consolidators to move fast in a very narrow window of time in a transaction day to be in time for shipping or for the trucks to move out at a designated time.

Many farmers, whether members of NorminVeggies or not who are not part of any cluster and bring their produce without any prearrangements, are also being serviced by Normincorp. Their produce will be supplied to the markets who want to purchase from the spot market. At the consolidation centre, farmers are also able to get exposure to how the market buys and Normincorp gets them acquainted with the quality desired by the market. These farmers gradually realize that they can get better prices if they have better quality and are part of a cluster. Since NVCC was opened, more farmers have joined the marketing clusters.

In terms of market opportunities, Normincorp currently supplies a network of 15 regular buyers comprising fastfood suppliers, supermarket consolidators, hotel and restaurant suppliers, and wholesalers and retailers. Normincorp is considered as their preferred supplier.

After a year of operation, Normincorp is taking an aggressive market push by targeting to consolidate a weekly volume of 75 tons of assorted vegetables coming from its established 13 marketing clusters and assorted lead growers for special products (herbs, cherry tomato, zucchini, Japanese cucumbers, etc). This scaling up will give NVCC, the only farmer owned consolidation center/outlet among 100 vegetable outlets in Agora wholesale market, the competitive edge. This is drawing from the experience of the lettuce cluster that consistently supplied a ton daily at NVCC, and thus was able to capture 60 per cent of the traded lettuces at the Agora wholesale market. This hold on the market enabled Normincorp to be a price setter in the Agora market (with iceberg lettuce priced at a high level of P40 to P50 per kg all throughout NVCC's operation for one year).

As a strategic move for scale and influence in the market, the experience of lettuce will be repeated for 12 other vegetables available daily at NVCC and to be supplied from the programming production of 12 marketing clusters starting July 2007.

To adapt to realities of having to deal with more product variety and volumes, as well as to become highly organized at this time when NVCC links to many buyers and has to harmonize flow of products between farmers and buyers, NorminVeggies with Normincorp has invested in computerization. This strategic move is being supported by NorminVeggies' partners, namely: GEM-USAID and the Department of Agriculture.

Also, service fees have been reduced to make it cheaper for the farmers given NVCC's bigger scale of business. It is now computed as a percentage of product sales to make it simpler.

The evolution of Normincorp (N) supply chain and its participation in chain management is shown in Figure 6.10.

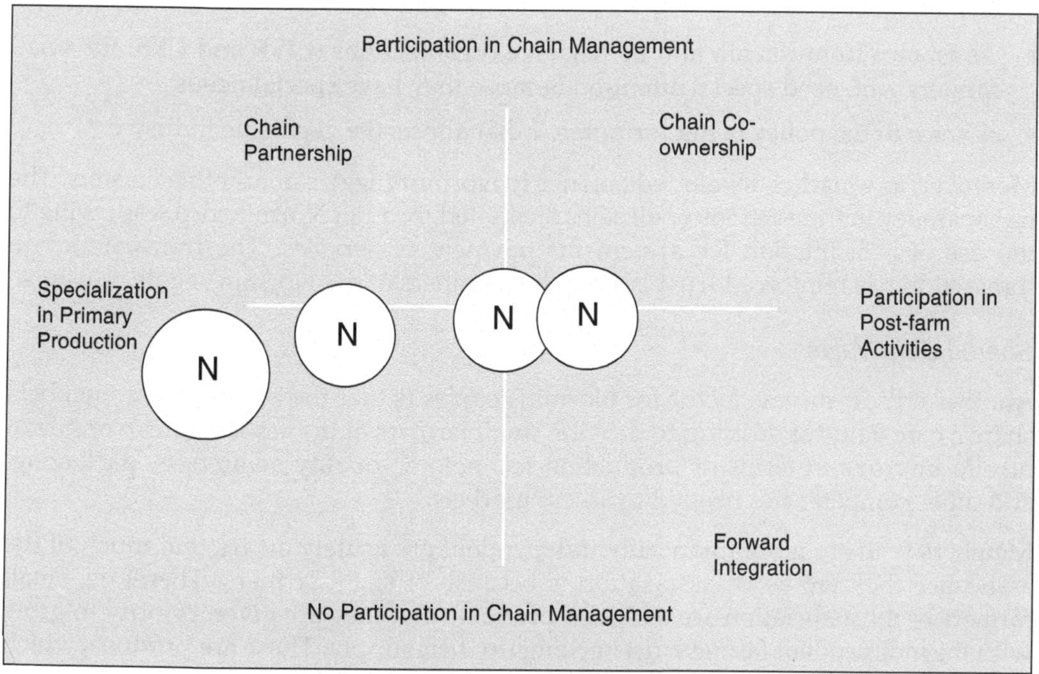

Fig. 6.10: Participation of Normin in Chain Management

Keys to Inclusion

The ability of NorminVeggies to remain competitive in these dynamic markets is because of the strategies or elements of their organizational innovation. However, successful implementation of these strategies is another matter.

Critical Success Factors of Inclusion: NorminVeggies operates as an association which aims to benefit its members. One of the critical success factors of NorminVeggies is that it is able to tap a support system which gives members access to resources available only to groups and not to individual farmers such as training, technical upgrading, and market assistance. Benefits include the following:

- Production protocols are available to members so that they do not have to resort to trial and error; farms are open to each other for sharing of experiences

- Assistance from NGOs and development agencies like FAO which gave them marketing training and techno-demonstration on rain shelters
- Assistance from Growth Equity in Mindanao (GEM) aimed at institutional strengthening. GEM also provides 80 per cent of the funds for administrative staff, and support for events like Vegetable Congress
- Assistance from the Department of Agriculture on technology and production related training, access to a cold chain, a refrigerated truck, and other new technologies
- Assistance from Kaanib and its resource organizations (LWR and CRS) for small farmers who need special attention because they have special needs
- A voice in the policy being formulated that affects the vegetable industry.

Moreover, any market developed belongs to NorminVeggies' marketing clusters. The transparency in transactions of all sales facilitated through Normincorp was owing to the use of a facilitation fee system for payment of services. The transparency in transaction has reinforced trust among the members of the NorminVeggies clusters.

Shared Core Values

Another critical success factor for NorminVeggies is that the organization members share a core value of desiring to provide small farmers of the association an opportunity to improve in terms of production technology, quality awareness, packaging, and other competencies needed to access markets.

Members who are more financially independent are acutely aware that much of the assistance they tap as an association is because of small farmers. Therefore, small farmers of the association are assigned products that they are given priority to grow with the independent farmers just backing up their supply. These are products which are labour intensive, low risk, and have lower costs of production. The more financially independent farmers, on the other hand, provide the back-up system for small farmers in case there is a crop failure. Aside from providing production back-up for small farms, the independent farmers are also open to smaller farmers for observation and sharing of knowledge.

The core value of sharing is being emphasized among all producers including small farmers. It is understood that when a farmer is taken into a cluster, s/he is under strong obligation to work with the group including to protect its name as a producer and a marketer. This emphasis is to tie up support from NorminVeggies clusters to the individual farmer with his/her obligation to help others in the group. This core value is given high importance and failure to meet this expectation from a cluster member can be a reason for a grower to be removed from the cluster. This unity to the group is severely tested when growers are tempted to polevault (i.e. renege on a commitment to supply an agreed buyer in favour of other buyers for short term benefits of pricing).

Learning Organization

A third critical success factor is that these are learning organizations, flexible and adaptive to the changes in the industry. They are able to respond because communication among the members of the board is open and transparent. When the lettuce cluster and other products started to pick up in volume, the board decided that a corporation will have to be formed to deload the volunteer facilitator from the board. It decided that a corporate structure is best and that this corporation must be run like a professional organization because decisions needed to be made swiftly. Thus Normincorp was born.

Marketing activities of the association, including market information, market development, shipping, negotiation and other market related activities, are coursed through Normincorp. Normincorp actively seeks high value markets and constantly analyses the changes in the market. This information is openly provided to Normin-Veggies members who want to avail of marketing services by Normincorp and agree to the clustering practice. Normincorp contributes 10 per cent of its gross revenue from the market facilitation fee to NorminVeggies to support the servicing organization and to add up to NorminVeggies storage fee income.

Leadership and Managerial Competence

A fourth critical success factor is the composition of the core group of the association. It composed of persons who have either been involved in the vegetable industry for a long time, have been business executives of other industries, are graduates of agriculture and its related fields, or have the passion for the industry and small farmers. The group as individuals are responsive to the markets and believe that any market developed belongs to all members of NorminVeggies clusters.

It cannot be denied that the strategies employed by the group such as marketing clusters, forming a marketing group (Normincorp), forward integration, quality and supply chain management, and developing farmers to take on the discipline required in business have been realized because of the presence of people who have managerial, entrepreneurial, and leadership skills as well as a genuine desire to help very small farmers.

Benefits and Costs of Inclusion

The key benefit of farmers who are members of the marketing clusters and selling to Normincorp is increased profit. This increase is because of more stable markets (i.e. vegetable supermarket consolidators or distributors), higher value for quality vegetables, and a premium for reliability in supply. For these reasons, Normincorp can get a price premium of 10 per cent to 20 per cent compared to that offered in the spot wet market dominated by traders in the traditional supply chain.

For example, buyers want to source their carrots from Normincorp because of quality and reliability. This means less cost for buyers and higher recovery. "Value for money" can be the main selling point.

Given all the work put into quality management and delivery reliability, Normincorp can discuss with the supermarket supplier a good pricing that is enough to compensate for the effort. The price for carrots, even if pegged weekly, is always above the Agora wet market price. If the price of carrots at the wet market is P 30 per kg, Normin quotes at P 38, to factor in the high recovery rate for the supermarket supplier. When s/he receives the carrots that are washed, air-dried, sorted, and neatly packed in boxes, s/he saves on handling labour since the vegetables are ready for chiller display. When s/he compares this to the wet market carrots that are unwashed, unsorted, and in sacks, a P 8 per kg additional price is still lower than the costs associated with sorting, washing, and preparing carrots for display, as well as the high reject level for the procured vegetables (estimated at 8 kg for every 60 kg sack). For quality supply, the farmer's additional cost is P 3.50. S/he still enjoys an additional income of P 4.50. This is the case also of lettuce. From Normincorp that has daily supply of lettuce, the price is 10 per cent higher compared to that in the wet market.

Higher income is also coming from sorting of the vegetables. Carrot in the spot market is usually sold "all-in" wherein the price is averaged from big to small sizes. All-in carrots can mean a price difference of P 18 per kg when big sized carrots command a price of P 30. In most cases, farmers resort to all-in trading because carrots in the wet market has six sizes (large, big, medium, standard, small, and super-small) with a price range of P 30 to P 3 for large to super-small size. Traders are arbitrary in their own sorting. Normincorp being the only one in the wet market handling high quality carrots was able to impose just three size categories (big-medium, standard, and small) with a price of P 38, P 30, P 22 per kg respectively. Super-small carrots are no longer sold to the high value market and are instead unloaded to the wet market retailers that slice vegetables as off-size carrots.

Increased sales, and accordingly income, is not only through better quality, sorting, and price, but also through better assortment. The mix of independent farmers who have financial resources and small farmers with limited financial resources becomes a source of competitive edge. Independent farmers produce capital intensive vegetables such as salad vegetables while small farmers produce those that are not capital intensive such as cabbage, carrots, and sweet peas. Wide assortment combined with stable volume and quality achieved through market clustering is important in supplying to supermarkets and restaurants (or their consolidators) which require assortment.

The Visayas vegetable supermarket consolidator or distributor takes in from Normincorp an assortment of 20 products from a single shipment. Independent farmers supply the following: iceberg lettuce, romaine lettuce, salad tomato, cherry tomato, bell pepper, strawberry, cucumber, sweet corn, young corn, herbs, etc. This set is combined from that of small farmers, namely carrots, cabbage, sweet pea, sweet pepper, squash, table tomato, eggplant, and other tropical vegetables. This range of products gives Normincorp the bargaining powers in terms of pricing and sales volume. Handling the transaction with a set of products provides leverage that all products have to be taken in from both independent and small farmers. This means that Normincorp will supply high value, difficult to get strawberry if ordinary squash is also taken in.

Moreover, there are savings on costs. Since production of those farmers involved in the marketing clusters is "programmed", storage fees are minimized. In other words, vegetables are sold even before harvesting. As a group and as members of Normin-Veggies clusters, they access resources that would help reduce their cost such as assistance on production, marketing, institutional strengthening, and benefits derived from advocacy such as increased access to resources. They also save on logistics cost because of volume or economies of scale.

Normincorp before NVCC was set up used to handle about 30 to 40 tons per month of assorted vegetables mainly to the Visayas market. When marketing was coursed through NVCC, the volume increased to 50 tons during the first month (May 2006), then 60 tons/month in the following two months. It peaked at 100 tons in August 2006 then reduced to 60 tons for the remaining months in 2006. It reduced further to 30 tons from January to March 2007 based on expectations that vegetable supply would reduce in the first quarter as experienced in the previous years with the marketing done through the Agora wholesale traders. What was not foreseen was that, with a network of buyers already established by Normincorp in NVCC, this supply requirement would not follow the pattern of reduction in the first quarter. NorminVeggies responded by adjusting production. In May 2007, this volume increased to 50 tons per month. And production is underway for the July 2007 harvest to increase volume dramatically to 200 tons per month.

During the rainy season of July to December, about 20 per cent of consolidated vegetables is for outshipment to the Luzon markets, 30 per cent for the Visayas markets, 40 per cent for the neighboring eight Mindanao provinces, and the remaining 10 per cent for the local spot market.

The benefit of cash payment right after withdrawal from NVCC meant more stable income to farmers. There is no more trimming to factor in after the vegetable distributors get the vegetables because the ones left at the stall are also purchased by local retailers who slice the vegetables for the consumer market.

The increase in price, sorting, and leverage of Normincorp in the negotiation both for higher price and lower transaction cost, together with savings in better management of trimmings/rejects with the NVCC facility is altogether estimated to translate to an increase to profit to individual farmers ranging from 25 per cent to 35 per cent. This has encouraged more growers to join NorminVeggies. Since the opening of NVCC in May 2006, 10 new members joined the association.

The key to these benefits is the organizational innovation which led to inclusion and increased participation of the group in these dynamic markets. The cost involved in organizing appears high for people who invest their time, efforts, and money in meetings and developing and implementing strategic decisions. But by organizing, they are able to gain more benefits to lower their cost of organizing thereby providing incentives to sustain the initiatives. They hire staff to run the organization to minimize their efforts and continue the work of improving quality to get better prices, access resources to reduce cost, and ultimately increase profits.

Normincorp's income from facilitation fees increased by 30 per cent since the opening of NVCC and the better deals with the markets (Table 6.4). Normincorp's revenue can cover all operating costs with net incomes at the level of 20 per cent of the total facilitation fees generated.

Table 6.4: Marketing Clusters' Weekly Production Program (July to December 2007)

Cluster	*Number of Members*	*Weekly Volume (tons)*	*Small Farmer's Weekly Share of Total Volume (tons)*
Iceberg Lettuce	8	8.0	
Cabbage	10	20.0	2.0
Chinese Pechay	10	10.0	
Bell Pepper	5	1.0	
Broccoli	5	0.5	
Sweet Pea	8	0.7	0.2
Kentucky Beans	11	2.5	0.5
Bitter Gourd	7	3.0	0.5
Sweet Pepper	8	3.0	
Cucumber	5	2.0	
Eggplant	7	2.5	0.5
Squash	8	20.0	8.0
Total		73.2	11.7

Note: Small farmers are those assisted by Kaanib; Kaanib represents the farmers in the clusters and is counted as a member. Altogether, farmers contributing above volume add up to 74.

Table 6.5: Adjusted Normincorp Market Facilitation Fees (2007)

Value/Kg (Php)	*Various Vegetables (as percent of sales)*	*Table Tomato (Php/per crate)*
Up to 10.00	5%	
10.01 to 20.00	4%	
20.01 to 50.00	3%	
> 50.00	2%	
Up to 300/crate		2.50
> 300/crate		5.00

Note: Same rates apply for storage fees charged by NorminVeggies at NVCC.

The volume levels in the first three months of NVCC marketing operation is the reference for attaining the breakeven point in the operation.

Table 6.6: Normincorp Income Statement in Pesos (From NVCC Marketing Operations), May to July 2006

Item	*May*	*June*	*July*	*Total*
Income				
Market Facilitation Fees	25,610	30,072	36,614	92,296
Expenses				
Salaries & Wages	12,500	16,000	18,500	47,000
Employee Benefits	1,066	1,066	1,066	3,198
Employees' Meals	1,145	1,335	2,455	4,935
Communication	248	448	477	1,172
Travel & Transportation	516	520	682	1,718
Light & Water	469	351	561	1,381
Accounting Services	1,000	1,000	1,000	3,000
Office Supplies	1,492	2,223	1,735	5,449
Miscellaneous	100	100		200
Total Expenses	18,535	23,042	26,475	68,053
Net Income Before Tax	7,075	7,030	10,138	24,243
Less : Normincorp Contribution to Normin Veggies (Mktg Premium)	2,559	2,988	3,618	9,166
Net Income	4,515	4,042	6,520	15,078

Note: 1$ = 53 pesos

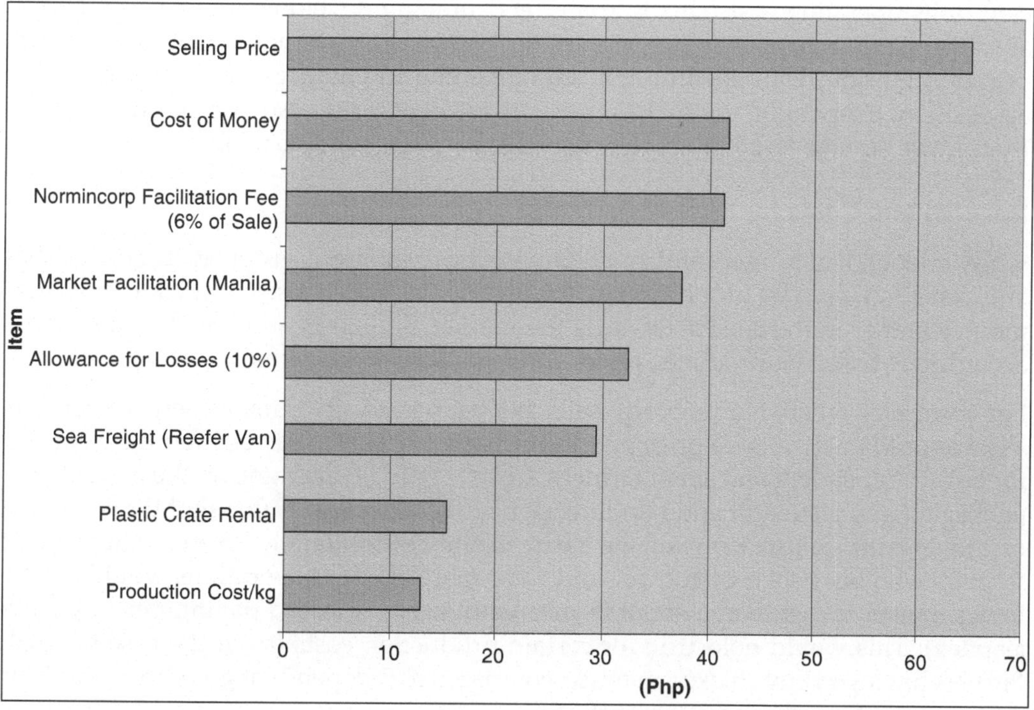

Fig. 6.11: Value Chain for Iceberg Lettuce from Bukidnon, Northern Mindanao, Philippines

Table 6.7: NorminVeggies Consolidation Center Income Statement in Pesos, May to July 2006

Item	*May*	*June*	*July*	*Total*
Income				
Storage Fee Income	25,786	30,248	36,418	92,453
Packaging Income	316	981	1,577	2,873
Marketing Premium	2,559	2,988	3,618	9,166
Total Income	28,661	34,217	41,613	104,491
Expenses				
Salaries	12,075	11,075	11,250	34,400
Benefits (Employer's Contribution)	569	569	569	1,707
Daily Wages (Hired Labor)	1,800	3,050	3,780	8,630
Rent	10,000	10,000	10,000	30,000
Transport Expense	378	122	36	536
Light & Water	1,633	1,033	1,333	4,000
Office Supplies & Miscellaneous	2,392	59	134	2,585
Miscellaneous	127	63	366	556
Pre-Operating Expense	2,266	2,266	2,266	6,799
Total Expenses	31,239	28,237	29,734	89,211
Net Income	–2,578	5,980	11,879	15,280

Note: 1$: 53 pesos

NorminVeggies also earned income from storage fees that enables it to cover 20 per cent of its operating cost. This is a very encouraging development because there is sustainability mechanism now to reduce dependence on external sources like the support of GEM-USAID for institutional strengthening and management of the servicing association. Hopefully, more income will be generated also for NorminVeggies through its storage fees with higher volumes coming in (Table 6.7).

Benefits and Costs by Type of Farmers

Since independent farmers and small farmers have different assigned crops, the costs and benefits would be proportionate for both types. Independent and small farmers move together in the cluster towards the market, and costs and benefits are shared accordingly based on products, price, and costs actually incurred.

For example, when Normincorp sells bellpepper to an outshipment buyer (i.e. Visayas or Manila), it has a price premium above the local market of about P 10 per kg for both independent and small farmers. Costs would be the same on the market end: packaging and airfreight and handling per kg. What would differ slightly is the cost of moving the product out of the farm to the consolidation centre. Independent farmers who have their own truck and have more efficient operations would have a lower transport cost than a small farmer who has to resort to paying per box (on a jeepney). This would hold true for certain production costs (as in the case of small farmers having to buy chicken manure, compared to independent growers using their own manure from their poultry farms).

However, the cost for small farmers is higher when one factors in the capability building work such as training, technology demonstrations, and technical assistance in the form of a full-time technician/organizer working side by side with them to initiate them to clustering procedures and the market.

To show the benefits and costs of inclusion in the case of a small farmer, the case of Henry Hidagan is highlighted below.

It should be noted, however, that independent growers belonging to the lettuce cluster when they were supplying to the vegetable processor in Manila for the fastfood market in 2004 earned higher compared to selling through the Visayas cluster for a supermarket consolidator or through the Normin Veggies Consolidation Center. But financial requirements are high and risk is greater. Recent discussions in the Normincorp reveal that highly increasing vegetable volume in the consolidation centre warrants lowering the market facilitation fee to half from September (see Table 6.4).

Better Chance for a Small Farmer in a Cluster

Henry Hidgan is a small farmer producing carrots for the cluster for the consolidators supplying in the Visayas market (supermarkets). He plants in a 1,000 square meter area in Impagsugong, Bukidnon, in the Northern part of Mindanao. He is assisted by Kaanib Foundation in production as well as in post-harvest aspects to meet cluster requirements. He is also provided financial assistance and a production budget and financial package for a module of 1,000 square meters production area. Actual production and financial performance for the first batch or cycle is compared to the budget as shown below. Note that 30 per cent of the net processed is deducted by KFI to be set aside for the project to sustain its assistance to small farmers.

Cost and Returns (1000 sq. meter production area for carrot)	*Budget*	*Actual*
Expected Production (kg)	2,500	1,396
Expected Price/kg	P12/kg	Various
Gross Sales	30,000	24,828
Less: Marketing Fee (10%)	3,000	2,483
Net Sales	27,000	22,345
Less: Production Cost	10,109	13,740
Net Returns	19,891	11,088
Amount Financed	9,349	12,240
ALLOCATIONS		
Net Cash (Sales Less Amount Financed)	17,651	10,105
70% Share to Farmer	12,356	7,073
30% Share to Project	7,060	3,031

He is encouraged to plant only 1000 sq. m. per batch. After the first batch, he can plant another relay of either carrots or cabbage. The production budget is only a guide.

Kaanib's project staff will assess the situation as to the need of the farmer and adjustments are made. The hurdle to tackle is that the areas of small farmers are not yet conditioned for vegetable farming. Though organic fertilizer (manure) is applied it takes time to build up the organic matter content/fertility of the soil. It is possible the first crop is a loss or yields just a little income, but the next relay plantings will be progressive, except of course if the damage is because of the climate. In the above case, actual production and financial performance is below budget. This is where the clustering is very valuable. Without the cluster's market that is outshipment to the Visayas, his yield would not be able to cover the costs. In this case, price received by the Hidgan is 27 per cent or P 8/kg higher than the wet market. While he incurs additional cost of P 3.5/kg for washing, packing, and sorting and his yield is low, he is better off because his market is better as part of a cluster that supplies to a consolidator sourcing for supermarkets in Central Philippines (Visayas).

For ease of computations using computer software in the consolidation centre, Normincorp plans to do away with the charging of facilitation fees based on type of vegetable and the value by bracket. Instead, it will utilize straight percentage: 3 per cent of sales for bodega fee (NorminVeggies) and 3 per cent of sales for market facilitation (Normincorp); or altogether 6 per cent. Compared to the current system, this is a reduction of fees from about 10 per cent to 6 per cent, or 4 per cent less. With the discussion with KFI, Normincorp shall factor in the development costs by still charging the 4 per cent. That is 10 per cent facilitation is retained but with savings of 4 per cent will be set aside as the sustainability mechanism for the NGO (KFI) support to them.

With this type of arrangement, the cost of accessing the markets is spread out and not borne by one type of grower because the 20 per cent net income of Normincorp is what is used for expenses to open and develop new markets. This is the investment for all growers in the cluster so that each grower does not have to sell out individually an amount to open the market.

But this in reality is a counterpart because the Department of Agriculture and GEM also invest in market development.

However, the difference in the costs and benefits would be significant if one compares farmers who are included in the cluster and those who are just selling locally because they do not have access to a better market. For example: sweet pea in the local market in Impasugong in Bukidnon where the small farmers in the cluster are located or proximate is selling at P 80/kg only when Normincorp was already selling it at P 120/kg. Even if packaging, transport, bodega fee, and marketing fee are deducted, the net price would still be higher than the Impasugong price.

Marketing premium is Normincorp's contribution to NorminVeggies. NorminVeggies is 20 per cent owner of Normincorp. To simplify computations, 10 per cent of Normincorp's facilitation fee at NVCC is NorminVeggies' share. This is recorded as marketing premium. Salaries are paid to the consolidation in-charge and a night guard. Daily wages are the hired labour NVCC maintains in unloading vegetables from the vehicle to the consolidation centre to augment the labour provided by farmers and for general maintenance. Based on policy, the unloading cost is the expense of farmers. Rent covers the rent for the land.

The building valued at P 475,000 was constructed by the Department of Agriculture as support of the government for vegetable industry development through NorminVeggies. The agreement is free use (usufructuary agreement). Even if members contributed, pre-operating costs are computed which will be amortized in a period of five years so initial capital generated is intact.

Sustainability of Benefits for Small Scale Farmers

A key question to ask in assisting small scale producers is whether the cost development assistance can be recovered. That is, whether the cost of assisting these small scale producers can be covered by the benefits or increase in their income because of development assistance. It is recognized that small scale producers need assistance in terms of access to credit and market facilitation through cluster development. But can this sustain the benefits generated?

To answer this question, a survey of 43 vegetable farmers who received technical assistance in cluster development was conducted in October 2007. Vegetables covered included squash, cabbage and carrots (Table 6.8). About 79 per cent of the farmers interviewed were males and the balance females.

Table 6.8: Farmers Surveyed by Crop (October 2007)

Vegetables	*Number of Farmers*	*% to Total*
Squash	14	33
Cabbage	8	19
Carrots	21	49
Total	43	100

Results show that there are various factors that affect profitability of clusters. These include productivity or yield level, price, production, and post-production expenses. Of the three crops, only squash registered a negative profit (Table 6.9). However, if one does not consider family labour or the amount of time the owner or family members spent in producing the crops, all three vegetables yielded positive net income (Table 6.11). Squash production was affected by too much rain and most farmers produced way below the expected yield. Moreover, costs for squash are relatively higher compared to other crops particularly shipping and transportation costs (Table 6.9). When the cost of assisting these farmers is included, squash apparently yielded negative profits (Table 6.10). However, when family labour is accounted for or paid for, squash farmers earned positive profit (Table 6.12).

It is interesting to note, however, that despite the cost of assistance, squash farmers earned positive profit when they supplied to supermarkets (Metro Gaisano). Table 6.13 shows profitability per type of market outlet. Squash was sold to three different market outlets. Two were wholesale markets in Agora (Suping) in Cagayan de Oro City located in the island of Mindanao which is the nearest outlet to the farmers. The other was in Cebu (Ondong) located in Visayas in the central part of the Philippines. The third outlet was the supermarkets (Metro Gaisano) located in Cebu. Of the three outlets, squash farmers earned positive profit only by selling to the supermarkets (Metro Gaisano). For carrots, farmers sold to two types of markets. One outlet was a wholesale market (Agora) and the other one was a consolidator for institutional markets including supermarkets in Cebu. While carrot farmers earned positive profits for both outlets, they earned better profits by selling to consolidators. Cabbage farmers on the other hand, sold to two buyers: a wholesaler and a mixed of buyers both located in Agora wholesale markets. In both outlets, farmers gained positive profits.

Based on the above results, the following conclusions can be derived. Firstly, the cost of assisting farmers can be recovered. Secondly, profitability and hence the ability of

Table 6.9: Percentage of Profit to Sales per Cluster

Commodity	*Cabbage Cluster*		*Carrots*		*Squash*	
	Amount	*% to Sales*	*Amount*	*% to Sales*	*Amount*	*% to Sales*
Yield	1,542.50		969.52		3,232.86	
Price	9.50		19.33		4.82	
Sales	14,538.75	100.00	16,415.71	100.00	15,143.57	100.00
Production Cost	11,461.25	78.83	10,110.00	61.59	10,160.00	67.09
Shipping Fee			1,507.69	9.18	3,328.18	21.98
Facilitation Fee	646.00	4.44	820.79	5.00	1,035.39	6.84
Transpo (Imp-CDO)	1,143.75	7.87	709.52	4.32	1,508.67	9.96
Miscellaneous	183.00	1.26	113.52	0.69	779.55	5.15
Profit	1,508.50	10.38	3,728.55	22.71	(683.82)	(4.52)

Table 6.10: Percentage of Profit to Sales per Cluster Net of Assistance Cost

Commodity	*Cabbage Cluster*		*Carrots*		*Squash*	
	Amount	*% to Sales*	*Amount*	*% to Sales*	*Amount*	*% to Sales*
Yield	1,542.50		969.52		3,232.86	
Price	9.50		19.33		4.82	
Sales	14,538.75	100.00	16,415.71	100.00	15,143.57	100.00
Production Cost	11,461.25	78.83	10,110.00	61.59	10,160.00	67.09
Shipping Fee			1,507.69	9.18		
Facilitation Fee	646.00	4.44	820.79	5.00	3,328.18	21.98
Transpo	1,143.75	7.87	709.52	4.32	1,035.39	6.84
Miscellaneous	183.00	1.26	113.52	0.69	779.54	5.15
Cost of Assistance	500.00	3.44	500.00	3.05	500.00	3.30
Profit	1,008.50	6.94	3,228.55	19.67	(1,183.82)	(7.82)

Table 6.11: Percentage of Profit to Sales per Cluster Using "Cash Cost" (Production Cost Less Family Labour)

Commodity	*Cabbage Cluster*		*Carrots*		*Squash*	
	Amount	*% to Sales*	*Amount*	*% to Sales*	*Amount*	*% to Sales*
Yield	1,542.50		969.52		3,232.86	
Price	9.50		19.33		4.82	
Sales	14,538.75	100.00	16,415.71	100.00	15,143.57	100.00
Cash Cost	9,451.25	65.01	7,850.00	47.82	7,600.00	50.19
Shipping Fee			1,507.69	9.18	3,328.18	21.98
Facilitation Fee	646.00	4.44	820.79	5.00	1,035.39	6.84
Transpo (Imp-CDO)	1,143.75	7.87	709.52	4.32	1,508.67	9.96
Miscellaneous	183.00	1.26	113.52	0.69	779.55	5.15
Profit	3,518.50	24.20	5,988.55	36.48	1,876.18	12.39

Table 6.12: Percentage of Profit to Sales per Cluster Using Cash Cost Net of Assistance Cost

Commodity	*Cabbage Cluster*		*Carrots*		*Squash*	
	Amount	*% to Sales*	*Amount*	*% to Sales*	*Amount*	*% to Sales*
Yield	1,542.50		969.52		3,232.86	
Price	9.50		19.33		4.82	
Sales	14,538.75	100.00	16,415.71	100.00	15,143.57	100.00
Cash Cost	9,451.25	65.01	7,850.00	47.82	7,600.00	50.19
Shipping Fee			1,507.69	9.18	3,328.18	21.98
Facilitation Fee	646.00	4.44	820.79	5.00	1,035.39	6.84
Transpo (Imp-CDO)	1,143.75	7.87	709.52	4.32	1,508.67	9.96
Miscellaneous	183.00	1.26	113.52	0.69	779.55	5.15
Assistance Cost	500.00	3.44	500.00	3.05	500.00	3.30
Profit	3,018.50	20.76	5,488.55	33.43	1,376.18	9.09

farmers to pay for any development assistance depends on a number of factors. Productivity or yield is an important factor especially that small scale farmers do not have rain shelter or greenhouse to control temperature or avoid negative effects of weather (e.g. too much rain). Finally, the type of market also affects the capacity of farmers to recover development assistance. In two cases (squash and carrots) farmers selling to high value markets such as supermarkets have higher chances of earning more profit.

Conclusions

The organizational innovation of NorminVeggies has several elements: product consolidation through the clustering strategy, a new business model through Normincorp, supply chain and marketing management, networking and linkage, and development intervention for greater inclusion of small farmers.

Table 6.13: Percentage of Profit to Sales per Market by Cluster (Net of Assistance Cost)

	Squash Cluster						*Cabbage Cluster*				*Carrots Cluster*			
	Agora Suping	*% to Sales*	*Cebu Metro Gaisano*	*% to Sales*	*Cebu Ondong*	*% to Sales*	*Agora Different buyers*	*% to Sales*	*Agora Wholes aler*	*% to Sales*	*Agora*	*% to Sales*	*Cebu Conso-lidators*	*% to Sales*
Yield	2,883.33		2,733.33		3,551.25		1,562.86		1,400.00		1,392.86		757.86	
Price	3.00		9.50		3.75		9.29		11.00		11.14		23.43	
Sales	8,650.00	100.00	25,966.67	100.00	13,520.00	100.00	14,415.71	100.00	15,400.00	100.00	15,401.43	100.00	16,922.86	100.00
Production Cost	10,160.00	117.46	10,160.00	39.13	10,160.00	75.15	11,461.43	79.51	11,460.00	74.42	10,110.00	65.64	10,110	59.74
Shipping Fee			2,733.33	10.53	3,551.25	26.27							1,400.00	8.27
Facilitation Fee	432.50	5.00	2,596.67	10.00	676.00	5.00	584.00	4.05	770.00	5.00	770.07	5.00	846.14	5.00
Transpo (Imp-CDO)	1,153.33	13.33	1,093.33	4.21	1,420.50	10.51	1,164.29	8.08	1,000.00	6.49	992.86	6.45	50.00	0.30
Miscellaneous	690.00	7.98	18.00	0.07	823.50	6.09	186.29	1.29	160.00	1.04	158.86	1.03	90.86	0.54
Assistance cost	500.00	5.78	500.00	1.93	500.00	3.70	500.00	3.47	500.00	3.25	500.00	3.25	500.00	2.95
Profit	(4,285.83)	(49.55)	8391.33	32.32	(3,611.25)	(26.71)	935.86	10.82	1510	9.81	2,869.64	18.63	3408	20.14

The clustering strategy enables small farmers to be active players in the supply chain, meet the basic demands for volume and quality consistency in supply, and join the dynamic markets like fastfood chains, processors and supermarkets.

It takes time to develop a functioning cluster. It starts with a random group of farmers producing as individuals. Those who can work in the cluster (particularly in the sharing of best practices, commitment to quality and delivery reliability, willingness to pay the costs of management) will join. Those who cannot will leave as willingly as they came in. When growers can understand and experience the benefits of cooperation, only then can there be cohesion in the cluster.

The cluster is not an ordinary grouping. Rather, it is one that has marketing goals and management systems. A business organization taking bold steps as a social enterprise is needed to realize the goals that benefit a wide base of growers that include small farmers. A core group of enterprising and agribusiness oriented farmers is necessary to provide the internal muscle to the organization and pull small farmers along.

Small farmers have the productive potential because of their number and spread. However, infrastructure gaps, low productivity, attitudinal problems, and other constraints mean that they need development interventions from private development resource organizations and government to address these limitations. There is also a slow maturation period required as small farmers gradually are trained, learn new values and skills, and are primed for business-like operations. However, there is some evidence as shown in this study that the cost of development interventions can be recovered given the right approach such as cluster development in assisting small scale farmers.

The key to successful marketing is effective management rather than the level of sophistication of the marketing system. This implies that what counts are organizational management (or how farmers can get their acts together) and operational efficiency (a high level of coordination in a sequence of activities that move products cheaply from farmers to buyers).

Staying power in marketing is a result of how fast farmers can keep up with continuous changes in an evolving supply chain. Competition from vertically integrated suppliers like corporate groups can exclude small farmers from the market. There is a need to constantly invest in technology development, market research, communication and good financial management.

Competence enhancing investments can be within the reach of small farmers through linkage with government that can provide supportive programmes and policies, with the business sector, and with private resource organizations.

For this to work, several critical factors must be in place. The benefits or incentives of organizing are clear. Members should share a core value of helping each other to galvanize the efforts toward strengthening the organization. While incentives exist to organize and access resources, the organization will not be strengthened further if core values are not shared. Considering the volatility and dynamism in modern chains, it is important that the organization should be a learning organization, adaptive to the changes in the market to remain competitive. Another key factor is the presence of managerial and leadership competence. The quality of people making strategic decisions is essential. NorminVeggies and Normincorp are blessed with people who have business experience and genuine desire to help small farmers. If these elements and factors are in place, the degree of inclusion can be improved, replicated, and sustained.

References

Berdegue, J.A. and Peppelenbos, L. (2005). "A method for the analysis of innovative practice in connecting smallholder producers with dynamic supply chains." *Resource Paper for Component* 2, Regoverning Markets Program.

Concepcion, S.B. (2005). "Vegetable purchase and consumption patterns in Mindanao", a paper presented during the Mindanao Vegetable Industry Stakeholders Collaboration: A Stronger Linkage to Markets, August 18–19, 2005, Davao City.

Digal, L.N. and Concepcion, S.B. (2004). "Regoverning markets: Securing small producer participation in restructured national and regional agri-food systems: the case of the Philippines."

Douthwaite, Boru and Jacqueline Ashby (2005). "Innovation histories: A method for learning from experience." *ILAC Brief* 5.

Masajo-Manalili, N. (2000). "The quality assurance challenge: Can village marketing and cooperatives respond?" edited by G.I. Johnson, Le Van To, Nguyen Duy Duc and M.C. Webb, *ACIAR Proceedings 100.*

Milagrosa, A.P. and Ir. J. Viane. (2002). "Marketing of Vegetables in the Cordillera Region: A Transaction Cost Analysis." *BSU Research Journal* 35 & 36, June & October.

http://faostat.fao.org/

http://www.bas.gov.ph

http://www.planetretail.net

7

Keys to Inclusion of Small-Scale Organic Rice Producers in Supermarkets: The Case of Upland Marketing Foundation Inc.

Sylvia Concepcion, Larry Digal, Rene Guarin and Antonio Luis Hualda

In the Philippines, the number of supermarkets has been growing as Filipinos, thanks to rising population and people's purchasing power. However, many small scale producers of agricultural and non-agricultural products find it difficult to access these supermarkets. They are challenged to meet their requirements on quality, volume, reliability and consistency in supply. This study throws light on an innovation linking small scale organic rice producers to supermarkets.

The Upland Marketing Foundation Inc. (UMFI) took the role of a marketing consolidator for small scale producers who had difficulty in accessing supermarkets. Small scale producers are inherently at a disadvantage when supplying to supermarkets. Notwithstanding requirements on quality and price, supermarkets demand volume and consistency of supply of a variety of products. Small scale producers do not have volume but when consolidated especially across products, economies of scale and scope may be achieved. This case shows that it is possible for small scale producers to access high value markets such as supermarkets through the innovation made by UMFI.

Framework of Analysis

It is important to use a framework in understanding the keys to inclusion of small scale producers in dynamic markets. In this study, we use the framework of Berdegue, and Peppelenbos (2005) (Figure 7.1).

Innovations that enable small scale producers to tap modern markets are actually responses or strategies of organizations such as UMFI to the challenges and opportunities in the industry given its competencies and resources available. These challenges and opportunities are rapidly changing in these dynamic markets. Procurement strategies of supermarkets for example change over time. Their standards become stricter, and they streamline suppliers to lower transaction costs and improve efficiency. Thus, preferred suppliers, specialized wholesalers, and distribution centers emerge.

The quality of responses or innovations made by organizations such as UMFI and other players in the chain such as organic rice farmers will determine their ability to compete and sustain access to these modern markets. These responses or innovations must be translated into improving its competitiveness in terms of meeting the changing requirements of the market. Otherwise, these farmers will be excluded.

The components or elements of the framework in Figure 7.1 provide a systematic way of understanding the factors that underlie the exclusion or inclusion of small scale producers in modern markets.

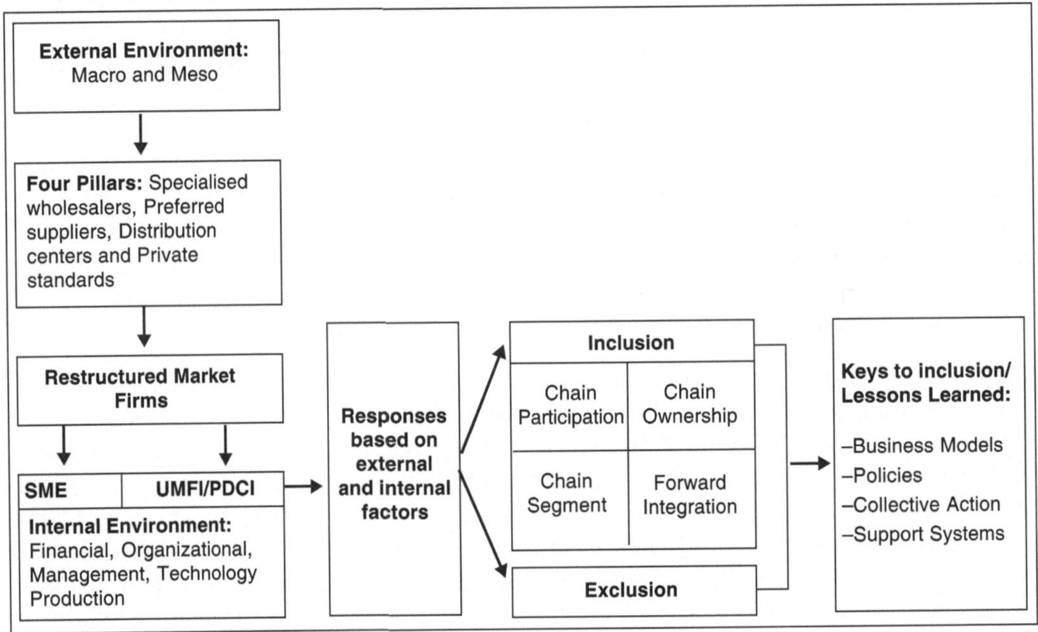

Fig. 7.1: Framework of Analysis

The objectives of this study are to:

- describe the key elements of the innovation and its context at the level of the supply chain and of the relevant meso and macro trends, policies, and institutions,
- explain how the innovation emerged over time and how it resulted in greater inclusion of small farmers and/or rural SMEs,
- map the critical stages and critical success factors in the evolution of the innovation,
- identify evidence of inclusion, costs and benefits of the innovation, and how are they distributed across different actors in the supply chain, particularly small farmers and/or rural SMEs, and whether results are sustainable,
- determine the drivers towards greater degree of inclusion particularly in terms of policy principles, business models, collective action, and support systems, and
- explore implications for potential upscaling and/or replication and its challenges.

Primary data were gathered through interviews conducted with UMFI and PDCI representatives, a focus group discussion with the officers and key members of PDCI, and a survey of eighteen PDCI farmers. Secondary data such as records, reports and presentations made about PDCI and UMFI were used to supplement primary data.

Philippine Rice Industry

In the period 1990–2005, population of the Philippines increased at an average of 2.34 per cent annually, while rice consumption increased by 2.84 per cent (see Figure 7.2). Increasing demand put pressure on production especially when prices of inputs were increasing while the price of *palay* (unmilled rice) remained roughly the same (Table 7.1). Production cost is placed at USD 191.00 per ton in 2003 with a recorded annual increase of 5.51 per cent. Nominal wage for *palay* production has also gained a significant increase with an average annual increase of 11.36 per cent in 1990–1999. Thus, producers do not have the incentives to meet demand especially when government allows imports of rice and dampens output prices. Competitiveness of the rice industry is constantly challenged.

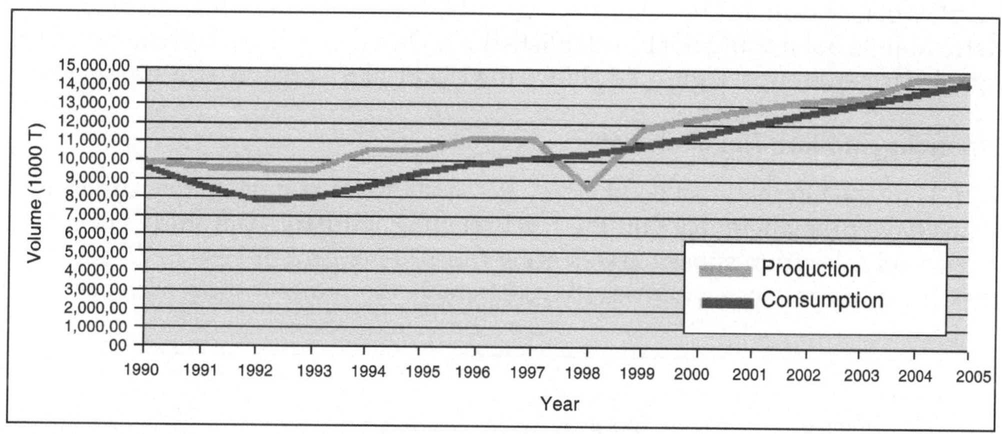

Fig. 7.2: Rice Production and Consumption

Source: FAOSTAT, 2006.

Table 7.1: Prices of Palay (Peso/kg)

Year	*1996*	*1997*	*1998*	*1999*	*2000*	*2001*
Special	8.74	8.48	8.95	8.61	No data	8.58
Fancy	10.26	9.90	10.68	11.07	No data	10.97
Ordinary	7.54	7.52	8.08	7.67	No data	7.90
Other Variety	8.19	8.03	No data	No data	No data	No data

Source: PIDS.

Philippine Organic Rice Industry

The organic rice industry is a very small subset of the Philippine rice industry. Out of an approximate area of 4 million hectares under rice in the country, area devoted to organic rice was estimated 11,754 hectares in 2001. In this year about 15,411 hectares were being planted with low chemical input applications.[1] Assuming that the number of low chemical inputs farms has already converted to full organic production, this will only account for 0.43 per cent of the four million hectares planted with rice. At present, there are only two producer groups that have been awarded certification by the Organic Certification Center of the Philippines (OCCP).[2]

The organic rice industry started in 1986 and the average yield for irrigated organic rice grew to 4 tons per hectare compared to 3.4 tons per hectare of conventionally grown rice. The net profit cost ratio of organic rice production is at 3.78 compared to 1.79 of high-yielding varieties of rice. This came with a production cost per hectare of 13,519.25 pesos (USD 281.65) for HYV and 7,148.00 pesos (USD 148.92) for organic rice. HYV produced 120 sacks (38 kg/sack) of rice while organically grown rice produced 105 sacks (44 kg/sack).[3]

Organic rice reaches consumers through efforts made by groups and individuals. The organizations that market organic rice are UMFI, the Bukidnon Organic Products Corporation (BOPC),[4] Gratia Plena, and Sunnywood Enterprises. BOPC has outlets in the cities of Cagayan de Oro, Dumaguete, and Iloilo. Other distributors are present in Metro Manila but it could not be established whether their products come direct from organic farmer groups. Figure 7.3 shows the UMFI-PDCI organic rice supply chain.

Expanding Modern Retail Industry

A study by the International Food Policy Research Institute showed that supermarket chains have dramatic impact on the food retailing industry. The study cites that in Brazil food sales from supermarkets grew from 30 per cent in 1990 to 75 per cent in 2000. In Latin American countries like Guatemala the share of supermarkets in food

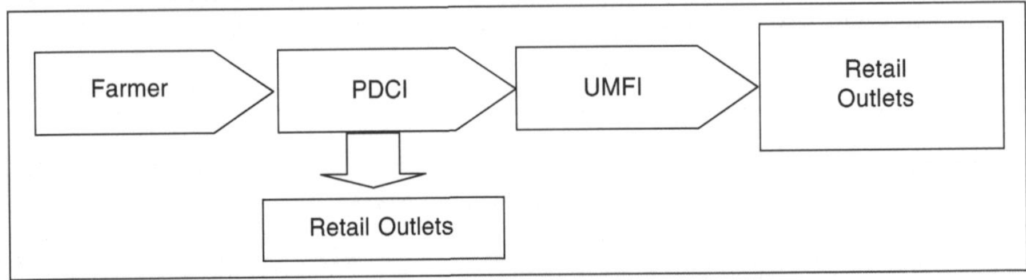

Fig. 7.3: UMFI-PDCI Organic Rice Supply Chain

1 Organic Rice Industry Orientation Paper commissioned by PDAP.

2 These groups are located in Bukidnon and Camarines Sur. Information was obtained through personal communication.

3 Xavier University, 1997.

4 http://www.organicrice.org/faqs4.htm

sale increased from 30 per cent in 1999 to 35 per cent in 2001. This shift is also true for Asian countries; in urban China and Thailand, food share sales of supermarkets have increased from 30 per cent to 48 per cent and 35 per cent to 43 per cent respectively for the period 1999 to 2001. This trend has driven many large multinational supermarket chains to set up operations in other countries.

In the Philippines, while only two (Makro and PriceSmart) foreign supermarkets/ hyper-markets have set up operations since the liberalization of the retail industry in 2001, sales performance of modern grocery distribution is bullish, increasing by 22 per cent from 2005 to 2006 (Table 7.2). From 1997 to 2001, the consumer patronage of supermarkets increased from 14 per cent to 22 per cent while the wet/public market patronage decreased from 85 per cent to 77 per cent.[5] Supporting these findings is a study conducted by AC Nielsen which showed that 49 per cent of manufactured products were sold through supermarkets and groceries. The same study also reported that supermarkets and groceries increased by 27 per cent and 35 per cent respectively from 2000 to 2001. Moreover, sales per capita of modern grocery distribution increased by 20 per cent from 2005 to 2006 (Table 7.2). This clearly shows that these channels play a significant part in the distribution and marketing of consumer products.

Table 7.2: Retail Market Indicators, 2004–2006

Retail market indicators	*Year*			*Growth rates (%)*	
	2004	2005	2006	2004–05	2005–06
Retail sales (USD mn)	38,319	43,718	50,103	14	15
Retail sales/capita (USD)	444	498	560	12	12
Grocery retial sales (USD mn)	24,172	27,284	30,948	13	13
Grocery retail sales/capita (USD)	280	311	346	11	11
Modern grocery distribution, total sales (USD mn)	8,946	9,813	11,520	10	17
Modern grocery distribution, total sales/capita (USD)	104	112	129	8	15
Modern grocery distribution, Grocery sales (USD mn)	7,552	8,382	10,198	11	22
Modern grocery distribution, Grocery sales/capita (USD)	88	95	114	8	20

Source: PlanetRetail, 2006.

In terms of trends and movements on consumer preferences, the market for products that were deemed healthy is increasing. Consumer surveys and market studies conducted by UMFI showed that while consumers do not know what organic products are with only 0.54 per cent of the Metro Manila population being familiar with the term, consumers do prefer products that are deemed "healthy". Their preference for "healthy" products is reflected on the premium price they are willing to give 50 per cent of the survey respondents stated willingness to pay 35 per cent higher than the commercial conventional counterpart. Supplementing these survey results, focused group discussion showed that healthy food products generally

[5] Asian Institute of Management, "Singapura Rice Case Study".

pertain to products that are fresh: vegetables, fruits, no preservatives-additives, no chemicals, all natural.

The structure of the modern retail industry in the Philippines is also changing. The concentration ratio in the retail sector (i.e., supermarkets) as measured by the National Statistics Office appears to be low at 1.1 per cent in 1994 since this is computed based on the sales of top four individual supermarkets divided by total sales supermarkets in the country. However, if supermarket chains are treated as one unit, the concentration ratio would be higher. Data from Planet Retail (2005) showed that the market share of 181 stores of the supermarket group account for 12 per cent of total supermarket retail sales (Table 7.3).

Table 7.3: Top Five Grocery Retailers in 2005

Company	*No. of Stores*	*Sales Area (sq.m)*	*Average Sales Area (sq. m)*	*Retail Banner Sales 2005 (USD mn)*	*Market Share (%)*
SM Group	181	438,250	2,421	1,63	11.9
Mercuty Drug	510	153,000	300	879	9
Robinsons	224	287,600	1,284	562	5.7
Rustan	183	214,348	1,171	449	4.6
SHV Makro	16	134,400	8,400	332	3.4
Sub Total	1,114	1,227,598	–	3,385	34.5
Other				6,428	65.5
Total				**9,813**	**100**

Source: Planet Retail, 2006.

The increasing population, concentration in urban areas and rapid increase of super markets present an opportunity to earn more income for small rice farmers. However, increasing production cost due to increasing input and labor costs negate the incentives offered by rice farming. On top of these, accessing the markets is also an issue. Supermarkets are more demanding in terms of product quality, volume and stability of supply. These are requirements that most small farmers are not able to comply due to their size and lack of financial resources for investing on technology.

With a lower cost of production, higher price, and a yield at par with conventionally grown rice, organic rice presents an opportunity for small farmers to increase their income and improve their welfare. However, even given these incentives for organic rice production, there are marketing challenges along the way.

Keys to Inclusion: Organizations

Upland Marketing Foundation, Inc. (UMFI) is a spin-off entity of the Upland Marketing Program of the Upland NGO Assistance Committee (UNAC) and the Philippine Business for Social Progress. Its board of trustees come from member organizations, which include the Philippine Business for Social Progress, Kalahan Educational Foundation, Philippine Partnership for the Development of Human

Resources in Rural Areas, Upland NGO Assistance Committee, and the Federation of People's Sustainable Development Cooperative.

Initial capitalization for the operations came from UNAC during the early years. UMFI received donor support for the salaries of some of its personnel, development of its business systems, training of personnel, and purchase of office equipment. However most of its working capital came from loans and the subsidies were smaller than the loans UMFI acquired to support its operations.

The vision of UMFI is to make "community-based enterprises as mechanisms for local economic development in marginalized communities through the generation of income and employment opportunities that are anchored on the processing/value addition and marketing of local raw materials into high value and marketable products to local and mainstream markets." Its mission, on the other hand, is to be a:

- "provider of affordable access to appropriate technology, financial resources, and growing markets to community based enterprises
- provider of high quality—healthy products to the consumers
- advocate of fair trade in the mainstream market."

UMFI's assistance to small scale organic rice growers to supply modern supermarket chains is a strategy that will contribute significantly to the realization of its vision and mission.

The Pecuaria Development Cooperative Inc. (PDCI) is an organization of agrarian reform beneficiaries composed of 426 members based in the municipality of Bula, Camarines Sur. As beneficiary of the Comprehensive Agrarian Reform Program, the group was awarded with 817 hectares of land for farming, housing, and educational facilities. Rice is planted on 130.87 hectares of irrigated and non-irrigated land. The cooperative was registered with the Cooperative Development Authority on September 31, 1991.

PDCI is the major supplier of UMFI with a total traded volume of 487 metric tons from 2002 to 2005, a volume that is worth approximately 12.9 million pesos (USD 302,390). The organization started with 14.2 metric tons in 2002 and reached a volume of 254 in 2005.

PDCI "envisions a progressive and united agrarian reform community with deep respect for ecology and gender equality and governed through a participatory and democratic process rooted in positive Bicolano and Filipino values, culture and with strong Christian Faith." Its mission is "as an autonomous rural organization is committed on building the capability of the organization and its member families towards a productive and sustainable community through a principled partnership and efficient and effective organization and farm resources management."

It can be gleaned that the vision and mission of both UMFI and PDCI are not incongruent. They want to pursue economic upliftment of their clients through sustainable or appropriate technology. Hence, strategic partnership makes sense and can be sustained.

History of the Innovation

Inclusion or exclusion of small producers happens through a series of events across time that changes the landscape of the market and economic structures. In the Philippines, most agricultural products are sold through a traditional supply chain where the producer sells the commodity to a buyer who in turn delivers to the wet market. The producer has very little involvement either in processing or in the analysis of the final market. Often, the buyer who takes the products off the producers' hands acts as the financier of the farmer in terms of the provision of inputs for the production of the commodity. In the emergence of new market structures and modern chains like supermarkets, small farmers are sometimes unable to respond to market changes because traditional structures prohibit them from engaging the market intermediaries in ways that allow them to learn how to respond to changes in market needs.

Government programmes on agrarian reform, forest stewardship, or ancestral domain brought about opportunities for farmers and their organizations to acquire land tenure. These efforts were then followed by programmes by both government and non-governmental development agencies on increasing farm productivity to increase farm incomes.

In the case of the UMFI partner communities, farmers and people's organizations were either given assistance on organic farming or value addition-technologies that utilized locally available resources. These interventions led to increase in farm productivity as farmers began to realize an increase in yield while communities engaged in food processing started producing finished products using local fruits and crops.

Despite these efforts, the income objectives of the communities were still not addressed. The farmers and people's organizations were having a hard time selling their organic rice and processed food products as a premium product. In both cases tapping the right market was the main problem and without access to proper markets, the efforts on increasing productivity did not lead to an increase in household income.

In the case of PDCI, organic rice was sold at the local market in Bicol but since the local market did not have a trade channel for organic rice, the product was classified as regular rice. Since organic rice did not come from certified seeds its maximum retail price was only 20.00 pesos (USD 0.42) per kg. While PDCI was able to sell organic rice at 25.00 pesos (USD 0.52), this was mostly through trade fairs in Metro Manila and to direct buyers also based in Manila and the volume was minimal. Most of the rice was sold between 18 and 20 pesos per kg (Table 7.4).

Table 7.4: Average Price of Rice

Rice Classification	*Physical Characteristics*	*Other Requirements*	*Prevailing Retail Price (per kg)*	
			PHP	*USD*
Premium	Purity, Whole/Long Grains	Certified Seeds	21–25	0.44–0.52
Well Milled	Purity, Whole Grains		19–20	0.40–0.42
Regular Milled	Broken Grains		16–18	0.33–0.38
Fancy/Aromatic/ Glutinous	Purity, Whole Grains		25–30	0.52–0.63

Source: NFA.

From a review of the business operations, the cost of producing organic rice was higher than the wholesale price. As a strategy to entice farmers to engage in organic rice production, the PDCI provided a premium fixed price for palay produced using organic farming practices. This was a common practice and strategy among communities engaged in organic farming. PDCI decided to peg palay prices at 10.00 pesos (USD 0.21) per kg. In the period 1997–1998, market price for palay ranged from 8.00 pesos (USD 0.17) to 9.00 pesos (USD 0.18) per kg. Although the strategy worked as farmers shifted to organic farming, the subsidy made their rice trading operations unprofitable. The data in Table 7.5 show the cost of organic rice based on a review of the cooperative's business operations. The review revealed the cost to be 19.35 pesos.

Entering Dynamic Markets

Wet markets failed to recognize the product differentiation offered by PDCI when organic rice was sold through the traditional chains. Lessons learned by other community based enterprises were that supermarkets provided an attractive option because the shoppers in supermarkets had a better appreciation of the premium product, although volume played an important role to cover costs.

Dealing with supermarkets also involved other costs. It is a common practice for supermarkets to ask for listing fees, a specific amount to be paid by a supplier before a product is accepted by the store. This would range from a low of 50.00 (USD 1.04) pesos per sku[6] to a high of 85,000 pesos (USD 1,770.83) per outlet. After the listing fees comes, the varied array of discounts on top of regular discounts. There is an introductory discount during the first three months, an anniversary discount, and special promo discount.

Finally, the suppliers also had to contend with the cost of promoting and advertising their products in the store. Product sampling, which is the most common and effective way to introduce new products to shoppers, would have a cost of 500 pesos (USD 10.42) per day to 3,500 pesos (USD 72.92) per weekend/store. Promotional

[6] stock keeping unit

Table 7.5: Organic Rice Production Cost

Activities	*PHP/kg*	*USD/kg*
Palay (14% MC, 65% Milling Recovery) Buying at P 10/kg	18.31	0.3815
Drying Cost per Kilogram	0.47	0.0098
Milling Cost per Kilogram	0.21	0.0044
Sack Cost per Kilogram	0.10	0.0021
Hauling Cost per Kilogram	0.18	0.0038
Delivery Cost per Kilogram	0.08	0.0017
Total Cost of Organic Rice	19.35	0.4031
Average Selling Price per Kilogram	19.00	0.3958
Net Loss/Kilogram	0.35	0.0073

Source: UMP-PDAP Study.

materials like flyers, posters, and brochures help increase consumer awareness but also entail additional costs.

The two situations are typical of most of the businesses or enterprise initiatives of the farmers and people's organization that UMFI worked with. The community could not tap better markets for their products; for those that were able to could not maintain the markets because of cost considerations. In the case of organic rice, to the local market in Bicol was not the right market for the product.

The main criterion of UMFI for choosing a supplier is that the supplier must be a community-based enterprise (CBE)—a business that is owned and managed by a poor community or people's organization. The supplier must be legally registered and has the capacity to maintain the quality of the product. The product must pass industry standards set by the government and should be deemed saleable by UMFI (based on market information). In cases where UMFI has to sell products from the private sector, the product must not compete with existing products coming from CBEs and would help pave the way for a new market for products that CBEs could produce in the future.

Hiring the Right People

Supermarkets were a demanding set of buyers that required a manner of approach that personnel of development agencies and NGOs do not usually have. Supermarkets required sales personnel who knew how to deal with them, dressed in business attire, were willing to wait long hours just to give a product demonstration, spoke the language of the supermarkets, and had knowledge of the consumer markets they were targeting. Initially, UMFI sale force was knowledgeable in dealing with producer groups but did not have the patience for the bureaucracy of supermarkets. They dressed in rugged and very casual garments, much like the clothes they would wear when dealing with the producer communities which the supermarkets thought looked unprofessional and unclean.

Hiring of people from the business sector was uncommon within the NGO community. Organizations would rather convert an organizer or a technician into a marketing-sales person than hire a real sales person. A combination of mistrust, cost, and attitude of doing everything on their own is among the causes of this practice. The organization says this because UMFI did the same initially and it got the organization totally nowhere.

Sales people from private companies have knowledge and understanding of the intricate policies and procedures that govern supermarkets. For an NGO to learn these from scratch would take a lot time without guaranteed access or efficient and effective operations. Industry sales people have the contacts with retail and supermarket chains, buyers or people managing these channels that remain in their positions or move only from store to store. They have good rapport would have wider access, and could facilitate easier entry of products to more stores.

UMFI decided to hire sales people with private company experience and assign them in Manila to manage the accounts and perform the task of booking orders, delivering the products, product merchandising, and sales collections. These activities also had to follow fixed schedules that varied from store to store.

UMFI does not provide higher compensation but the incentives (commissions) are comparable to those offered by big companies. UMFI also provides continuous training and skills upgrade for its personnel. For the top manager who came from a multinational company, the rate is lower than what was received previously but the pressure and load of work is less in UMFI. Finally the people have also developed a sense of mission to be of service for others.

Responding to Consumer Preference

Trends in the consumer market continue to reveal that there is increasing interest in safe and healthy products that promote a healthier lifestyle. At this stage of the development of the innovation used by UMFI, the attributes of products they marketed had to be redefined. For example, the packaging of one of the jams had to be redesigned because one of the supermarket buyers commented that the label should not say "made by indigenous people". This label gave the impression that the jam was made by indigenous people who may not know how to prepare food in a manner that complies with sanitary standards. Although this perception may be completely unsubstantiated, UMFI decided to delete the label which may give the false impression that the jam does not conform to sanitary standards.

UMFI therefore had to learn to satisfy the needs of supermarket buyers, whether real or perceptual. For organic rice, UMFI used the brand label "Pecuaria Healthy Rice" and not organic rice because it did not have organic certification[7] and the preferences of the consumer was for healthy products and not necessarily organic products.

---

[7] Organic certification was acquired from the OCCP last January 2007.

Using House Brands

Using house brands emerged as a response to the risks posed of relying on one supplier. In 2006, PDCI was beset by typhoons that affected organic rice production. UMFI had to constantly renegotiate and reschedule delivery dates because of delays in supply delivery. It needed to find other suppliers who could co-supply the market requirements to stabilize supply. UMFI however had already established contacts with other suppliers in the early years thus allowing the foundation to maintain the volume requirement. This averted the possibility of losing the foothold in the supermarket that UMFI had gained. If UMFI lost the market, PDCI and other CBEs will also lose access to supermarkets.

With the move to source from different producer organizations, UMFI was persuaded to use "Healthy Rice" rather than "Pecuaria's Healthy Rice". This gave UMFI the strategy of using a house brand rather than a producer's brand. This helped spread the cost and benefits derived from the brand. The supermarkets accepted the new label because trust with UMFI has already been established.

Tactical Partnership with Small and Medium Enterprises

The strategic or tactical partnership with small and medium enterprises (SMEs) was a critical stage of the innovation. During the initial years, there was very limited volume of products to be sold coming from the communities. Products from SMEs gave UMFI the volume of trade it needed to partly cover its costs of sales and distribution. Partnership with the private sector allowed the innovation to work and maintain its hold on the markets while the farmer groups improved their capacities and volume of production. In 2004, UMFI's volume of organic rice increased and in 2005 the foundation limited the marketing of products from private SMEs to provide focus on CBE products (Table 7.6 shows the percentage sales contribution of products between private SMEs and CBEs).

Table 7.6: Percentage Sales Contribution from SMEs and CBEs

Year	*2001*	*2002*	*2003*	*2004*	*2005*	*2006*
CBE Products	31%	37%	44%	85%	99%	99%
Private SMEs	69%	63%	56%	15%	1%	1%
Total	100%	100%	100%	100%	100%	100%

Source: UMFI Sales and Marketing.

The other critical stage was when expansion of operations grew faster than the capacity of UMFI to generate resources to support operations. Supermarkets paid UMFI from 30 to 120 days after delivery while UMFI paid the farmers anywhere from cash on delivery to 45 days. The gap of the receivables period meant that UMFI had to have reserve cash to support the orders of the supermarkets. In 2004, sales dipped because of cash-flow problems as the trade volume increased. Partner-producers found it hard to maintain the flow of supply if UMFI did not pay cash. Delay in the infusion of capital made partner-producers stop deliveries until payments were made. The arrival of loans saved the business operations from collapsing.

All loans were obtained from development organizations engaged in the business (Oikocredit, Federation of People's Sustainable Development Cooperative) of financing social enterprises. Interest rates are market rates and while some are collateralized, others get guarantee support from donor organizations like Interchurch Organization for Development Cooperation (ICCO). The grants and subsidies UMFI currently receives are not used for the business operations but for development work that UMFI also conducts like developing new products and assisting communities establish their enterprises.

Elements of Innovation

UMFI saw the need to access supermarkets outlets for the communities as a major hurdle. Learning from its previous efforts, UMFI saw that providing market information, conducting training and linking communities to buyers did not always result in tangible or sustainable trade. While UMFI saw the potential of mainstream supermarkets as markets for many of its partner communities, it also saw the limitations of the communities to directly access these markets. Experience and data show that communities cannot be linked directly to these markets. Communities from the provinces do not have the resources and expertise to tap and maintain these markets although their products need these markets in order to generate the income they need, and the markets need the products that the communities offer.

UMFI decided that instead of just providing information and training and trying to link these communities to the market, the foundation will engage in actual trading of community products to mainstream supermarkets. This decision was greatly supported by the farmers and people's organization as UMFI became their official marketing arm-distributor in Metro Manila markets.

As UMFI engaged the market, key changes were made within the structure and operations of UMFI and its partner suppliers. The first thing that UMFI did was to hire a new set of personnel who were from the retail trade as these people had the knowledge, experience, expertise, and contacts within the industry. This was followed by an upgrade on its logistic capacity by acquiring needed equipment, facilities and business-operational systems, including an increase in operational working capital.

As a marketing arm-distributor, UMFI is tasked to open and maintain outlets/ distribution channels like supermarkets. UMFI to a certain extent also conducts below-the-line promotional activities. In return for these services, UMFI gets a discount ranging from 15 to 20 per cent. For other costs like promotional activities, payment of special discounts, reproduction and distribution of marketing materials, UMFI charges the suppliers at cost plus cost of time spent by UMFI personnel. Since UMFI is also located in Manila, the supply requirements of its partner suppliers (like sacks, glass bottles, labels, boxes) are bought and sold by UMFI to its partner suppliers. These items carry a markup ranging from 10 to 15 per cent.

Niche Consolidator and Champion Rider Product Strategy

The niche consolidator strategy was to market a combination of champion and rider products. By marketing several CBE products, the combined volume of these groups was to contribute to the volume needed to sustain distribution operations in Metro Manila. However, UMFI saw that even with the combined volume of many CBEs, the amount of business generated was still small to make operations viable. This was then supported by the "champion vs. rider product" strategy employed by UMFI. With the champion-rider product approach, UMFI had to look for a champion product—a product that had good market potential and that can also be produced in bulk once the market picks up the product. Products such as rice and *Muscovado* sugar are considered champion products. These are the products that by their big volume of trade allow UMFI to generate the income to cover its costs. The champion products are thus the major source of UMFI income from marketing. The rider products are specialty products that have smaller market demand—low turnover products. These are products with niche or specialty markets that are produced or supplied in small volumes or quantities by a CBE. The innovation will move on to a stable position if the number of champion products is increased and would have a maximum sales contribution of not more than 20 per cent of total sales.

As a consolidator of service back to CBEs, UMFI was able to provide product development services like improvement on packaging and product quality to address the main concern of supermarket against CBE products. UMFI provided services that ensured that products are of the expected quality and appearance and always available.

Branding and Product Positioning

As against many organic products at the onset, UMFI was keen in determining how it would position its product in the market. Using market data and assessing trends and even products in the market, UMFI would choose what specific product features to highlight. With organic rice, marketing the "health" dimension of the product than the "organic" features seemed to have worked as other new products have copied this brand name (new competing products also call their rice Healthy Rice). UMFI registered the phrase "Healthy Rice" as a brand name and not as a claim; as such it was not covered by the regulations of the Bureau of Food and Drugs (BFAD).

With muscovado sugar, UMFI also did not choose the "organic" label as the positioning strategy. UMFI rather positioned the product as a perfect partner for coffee.

Keys to Inclusion: Lessons Learned

UMFI has been constantly monitoring changes in the market and in the industry to prepare itself or adjust its strategies to tap new and emerging opportunities. In the initial stage when organic rice was launched, UMFI opted to position it as premium rice and highlighted the term chemical and pesticide free as against the common strategy of others to highlight "organic" in packaging and promotion of the rice. Because of this, new entrants are also copying and using the term "healthy rice" on their products. The same was done for muscovado sugar.

The packaging of the healthy rice and launching of new product line of rice is the result of constant monitoring of the industry and market. The latest offshoot is the planned re-launching of "Healthy Rice" under a new label and the launching of High Fiber Rice as a result of observation of the market that many people purchase rice and other health food products because of their fibre content. This was also validated through interviews and encounters with key customers and informants.

Monitoring of the environment redounds to the benchmarking efforts of the organization where efforts to identify best practices and industry standards are done and incorporated in regular business operations. Among the changes within the organization are monitoring of the cost to sales ratios of major expenses like transportation (3 per cent) merchandising (3 per cent), product returns (1.5 per cent), outsourcing of non-core business functions like merchandising and trucking.

Transparency with Partner Communities

Transparency with partner communities is another important element. This allows UMFI to tailor-fit services, identify potential problem areas, and work out or maintain strategies to keep the business competitive in the market. The danger of non-transparency is the building of mistrust between supplier and consolidator-distributor. Lack of knowledge and understanding of the business operations could erode trust and confidence between the parties, which would lead to deadlock situations or no-win solutions.

Transparency will also anchor a more effective supply chain management initiative as decisions, strategies, or interventions that will impact on margins and costs could be easily or openly discussed. The communities' increased understanding of the total business chain would also allow them to rethink or abandon short-sighted or unrealistic views and demands on the business. This allows the farmers groups to mature in their perspective. UMFI discusses pricing with suppliers regularly. UMFI discloses to suppliers the cost, expenses, and even margins UMFI makes.

Benefits and Costs of Inclusion

With UMFI performing product consolidation, sales, and distribution of products and the farmer groups upgrading their capacities, many products were introduced to supermarket outlets. In 2001 when UMFI started its commercial operations as a product distributor-marketing arm of farmers, it could not reach 100 stores all located in Metro Manila. Sales for the year reached only 1.8 million pesos (USD 38,944). As of December 2006, UMFI serves 223 supermarket outlets in all over the country (not counting the convenience stores of 7–11 and Mini-stops). Sales for the year reached

25.7 million pesos (USD 535,416.67) or an average of 2.14 million pesos (USD 44,583.33) per month. Sales performance for the first quarter of 2007 was 9.2 million pesos (USD 191,666.67) or a monthly average of 3.06 million pesos per month (USD 63,750). For the first champion product, organic rice sales reached almost 13 million pesos (USD 270,833.33) in 2006 (Table 7.7).

Table 7.7: Traded Volumes of Organic Rice

Years	*Volume*		*Estimated Value (PHP in million)*	*Estimated Value (USD)*
2002	285 sacks	14.2 MT	PHP 0.35	7,291.67
2003	1,254 sacks	62.7 MT	PHP 1.60	33,333.33
2004	3,128 sacks	156.4 MT	PHP 4.20	87,500.00
2005	5,082 sacks	254.1 MT	PHP 6.80	141.666.67
2006	9,110 sacks	469.3 MT	PHP 12.99	270.625.00
Total	**9,749 sacks**	**956.7 MT**	**PHP 25.94**	**540,416.67**

Source: UMFI, 2006.

Benefits for PDCI and Farmers

Inclusion in the organic rice supply chain has led to significant increase in the income of the farmers. Because of reduction of production expenses and the higher buying price of the produce. Table 7.8 compares the performance of 36 farmers in 2000 and 2006. The figures were obtained from the records of PDCI, which documents the volume of palay sold to the cooperative and buying prices. Palay sold in 2000 was composed of high-yielding varieties, chemical free, or a combination of both. It was in this year that farmers underwent the transition from conventional to organic production. On an average, there was an increase from 3,065.18 to 5,014.18 kg (64 per cent) in the volume sold per farmer and an average increase from 8.83 pesos (USD 0.18) to 10.21 pesos (USD 0.21) (16 per cent) for the price paid per kg of rice. The percentages translate to an average gross sale from 27,069.75 pesos (USD 563.95) to 51,202.85 pesos (USD 1,066.73) or an 89 per cent increase.

Table 7.8: Volume and Sales Difference

	2000	*2006*	*Percent Increases*
Average Volume (Kg)	3,065.18	5,014.18	64
Average Gross Sales (PHP)	27,069.75	51,202.85	89
Average Price (PHP)	8.83	10.21	16

Source: PDCI records.

Benefits in terms of reduction of production costs were also obtained by the farmers when they shifted to organic rice production. A survey of 18 farmers showed that while yield declined under organic rice farming compared to conventional/inorganic farming and production costs have not changed significantly, net income of farmers increased by 119 per cent (Tables 7.9 and 7.10). This is mainly because of better prices with a difference of 46 per cent. The price premium can be attributed both to the quality attributes of the brand and the product as well as to the type of market outlet. Supermarkets generally provide higher prices compared to traditional markets.

Table 7.9: Average Costs of Production per Hectare

Production Activities	*Conventional*			*Organic*			*Difference*	
	PHP	*In USD*	*%*	*PHP*	*In USD*	*%*	*PHP*	*%*
Land Preparation	5,995.10	124.9	26.89	6,942.59	144.64	31.72	–947.49	–15.8
Planting	302.63	6.3	1.36	205.26	4.28	0.94	97.37	32.2
Seeds	1,262.18	26.30	5.68	1,609.79	33.54	7.35	–347.61	–27.5
Irrigation	10,047.89	209.33	45.21	10,713.16	223.19	48.94	–665.27	–6.6
Fertilizers	3,108.48	64.76	13.99	2,419.23	50.4	11.05	689.25	22.2
Herbicides	757.75	15.79	3.41	–	–	–	–	
Pesticides	750	15.63	3.37	–	–	–	–	
Total	**22,224.03**	**463**	**100**	**21,890.03**	**456.04**	**100**	**334**	**1.5**

Source: Survey of PDCI farmers, 2007.

Table 7.10: Comparative Sales, Income and Yield Performance: Conventional *vs.* Organic Rice

Item	*Conventional*	*Organic*	*Difference*	
			Value	*Percent*
Yield (bags/hectare)	83.06	73.78	–9.28	–11.17
Price per kilo (PHP)	7.26	10.63	3.37	46.42
Gross sales (PHP)	30,150.78	39,214.07	9,063.29	30.06
Net income (PHP)	7,926.75	17,324.04	9,397.29	118.55

Source: Survey of PDCI Farmers, 2007.

PDCI Adaptation to Innovations

The increasing demand for organic rice in the market is an opportunity presented to PDCI that must be acted upon. In order to meet with the increasing demand, PDCI is required to encourage more farmers to engage in organic rice farming to boost their production levels.

To encourage more farmers to convert to organic rice production, the initial strategy was to peg the buying price of palay at 1 peso higher than those given by traditional buyers. In order to maintain the farmers who were already into organic rice production, it provided input assistance for seeds and organic fertilizers that was payable after the harvest.

UMFI conducted studies in local rice trading dynamics, which identified the current players in the industry and their practices; business operations review, which focused on how cooperatives conduct their business operations; and consumer surveys to see how the market behaves.

Distribution of Benefits

There is a significant difference in the price of organic and non-organic rice or unbranded rice. But how are these distributed across players in the chain? One way to answer this question is to look at the share of each player in the chain to total margins (i.e. retail less farm price). Table 7.11 shows that PDCI accounts for more than 50 per cent of margins. This is followed by UMFI with 33 per cent and about 14 per cent for supermarkets. This does not mean however that PDCI gets most of the benefits since this indicator does not include costs incurred. PDCI does the milling, hauling, and trucking of rice to Manila (Table 7.12). UMFI provides the storage, packing, and transporting of rice from warehouse (Manila) to supermarket outlets. Supermarkets incur costs of selling the product to final consumers. Unless we get detailed costs of various players in the chain for performing marketing and other functions, we cannot ascertain exactly who benefits most in the chain. It is clear, however, that farmers can increase their income by selling to high value markets such as supermarkets through PDCI and UMFI.

Table 7.11: Distribution across Players in the Chain: Red *vs.* Brown Rice (2007)

Price	*Red*	*Brown*	*Margins*		*% Share to Total Margins*	
			Red	*Brown*	*Red*	*Brown*
Farm Price	12.50	12.50				
PDCI Selling Price (FOB Manila)	31.00	26.00	18.5	13.5	56.32	51.92
UMFI Selling Price Supermarket	40.82	34.65	9.82	8.65	29.89	33.27
Supermarket Suggested Retail Price	45.35	38.50	4.53	3.85	13.79	14.81
Total			32.85	26.00	100.00	100.00

Table 7.12: Price, Margins and Costs, Brown *vs.* Organic Rice

		Brown	Red			
Organic Rice	SRP	38.5	45.35			
Supermarket Margins	Discount	3.85	4.54			
Supermarket	**Margins %**	**10.00%**	**10.00%**			
	UMFI Selling	34.65	40.82			
UMFI Packaging/Return	Packaging	2.55	2.55			
Costs	5% Returns	1.3	1.5			
	UMFI Net	30.8	36.77			
FOB Manila	Buying	26	31			
UMFI	Margins	4.8	5.77			
UMFI	**Margins**	**15.58%**	**15.68%**			
PDCI	Selling	26	31			
PDCI	**Margins %**	**15.46%**	**29.09%**			
PDCI	Margins	4.02	9.02			
Total	Cost Rice	21.98	21.98			
Estimate	Trucking	1.25	1.25	Naga to	Manila	Transport
Direct Costs	Palay-Rice	1.5	1.5	Drying	Milling	Hauling
Estimate	Cost Rice	19.23	19.23	65%		
Buying	Palay	12.5	12.5	Recovery	14% MC	

Participation in Chain Management

Chain management is a shared role between UMFI and its suppliers. UMFI serves as the official marketing arm-distributor of the products of CBEs in Metro Manila and selected provinces in the Philippines, while CBEs, like PDCI, are responsible for the production side. The suppliers are not yet shareholders of UMFI although there are plans to increase their stakes in the business of UMFI. At present, they are being consulted on plans and directions of UMFI and will soon be formed into a committee that UMFI will consult and discuss with regarding the foundations plans and future direction. UMFI has always consulted the final price of the product with the partner suppliers.

To ensure that suppliers meet the quality standards set by and between UMFI and its partner supplier, any shipment that falls below the agreed standards is rejected by UMFI. UMFI has an internal quality control officer who inspects all shipments made to UMFI. If a community or supplier suffers shipment rejection, UMFI will assist the supplier determine the cause and assist the community address the problem. All transactions with the suppliers are sealed by a purchase order from UMFI.

Sustainability and Replicability

The keys to the success of the innovation are the strategies and competence of persons involved with the organization. With the existing system, they are able to maintain an operation that is profitable with funding support from donor agencies. It is important to note, however, that funding support played an important part during the initial years of the organization and in product and personnel development. At present, all the costs of operations are sourced from the business, while loans are the current sources of funds and financing for marketing operations.

Implementation of the strategies and continuous employment of innovations need to be maintained in order to achieve sustainability. The responsive characteristics that UMFI has, will play an important role in its keeping its foothold in the market. Likewise, support to producer organizations must be continuously extended in order to sustain supply.

The innovations that were introduced by UMFI are well documented and can be used as a model for other organizations who would want to engage into development of a similar venture. However, central to these strategies are the capabilities of individuals involved in the implementation of innovations. Commitment, dedication, and business acumen possessed by the personnel fuel the success of the strategies of the innovations.

The other value of the innovation is that its application is not limited to smallholder producers but can also be used to develop small and medium enterprises and other backyard industries.

Conclusion

The main lesson derived from this study is that smallholder producers can be successfully linked with dynamic markets but will require extensive knowledge of both market and production environment. This also requires significant amount of investment and efforts for business incubation. Strengthening of organizations is also highlighted in order for them to meet deliveries and quality requirements.

Collaborative management and involvement of producer organizations in the management of the chain is important. Through feedback mechanisms developed by UMFI, producer organizations are able to fine-tune production in order to meet market requirements.

References

Balisacan, A.M., Sebastian, L.S. and Associates (2006). "Securing Rice, Reducing Poverty: Challenges and Policy Directions Overview". Southeast Asian Regional Center for Graduate Studies and Research in Agriculture (SEARCA).

Berdegue, J.A. and Peppelenbos, L. (2005). "A method for the analysis of innovative practice in connecting smallholder producers with dynamic supply chains," *Resource Paper for Component* 2, Regoverning Markets Program.

Cua, C.Q., Guerrero, C.Y., Tang, S.C., Tiu, C.S., (2001). "Marketing Plan to Upland Marketing Foundation," Incorporated. *Unpublished thesis* (Bachelor of Science). De La Salle University, Manila.

Philippine Organic Rice: Industry Orientation Paper. PhilDHRRA. November 2004. Paper commissioned by the Philippine Development Assistance Programme.

Kelly, P. (1998). "The politics of urban-rural relations: land use conversion in the Philippines", *Environment and Urbanization,* Vol. 10, No. 1.

Singh, K. (1992). "Peoples Participation in Natural Resources Management," *Workshop Report* 8. Institute of Rural Management, Anand.

WRF Case Study of PDCI.

http://www.geocities.com/phildhrraweb/WRF_Case_Study_PDCI.doc

www.asiarice.org/sections/whatsnew/Malabanan.pdf

www.unescap.org/rural/doc/OA/Philippines.PDF. Date Accessed June 6, 2007

http://www.organicrice.org

http://www.planetretail.net

http://faostat.fao.org

http://pids.gov.phs

8

Linking Mango Farmers to Dynamic Markets in Indonesia

Ronnie S. Natawidjaja, Yosini Deliana, Wayan Rusastra, Tomy Perdana, Togar A. Napitupulu, Hanny Sulistyoningrum and Yovie M. Rahayu

Indonesia ranks fourth among mango producing countries, after India, China, and Thailand. One of the important production zones of mango in Indonesia is Pemalang, Central Java. In this area, mango can be harvested during off-season, May to August, while mango in other producing areas is generally harvested in the months of October to January. The specific harvesting period should be a considerable advantage to farmers in term of bargaining position with traders in determining mango's selling price. However, apparently local collectors (*tengkulak*) and wholesalers (*bandar*) are still those who benefit the most from off-season mango.

In Pemalang, since farmers are generally bounded by a loan received from a trader, farmers let traders decide on selling the harvest. Therefore, farmers do not know the accurate volume of mango production. This kind of exchange system creates vulnerability to farmers' bargaining position, so that they obtain relatively lower price compared to the market price. This lop-sided exchange system has also resulted in farmers' lack of motivation to improve productivity as well as quality of mango.

Through rapid development of modern retail and more competitive market, within the last 10 years, some suppliers to supermarkets have attempted to involve farmers directly in the supply chain. However, these efforts failed because of farmers breaching on the contract agreement. Contract breaching generally happens because supplier cannot always offer the highest price to farmers. One of the systems which has been operated since 2003 and successfully brings farmers into direct negotiation with the main modern retailer (such as *Carrefour*) is the partnership between *Bimandiri* (specialized supplier to modern market) and mango farmer's group of KUBM (Kelompok Usaha Bersama Mandiri/Self-help Collective Business Group) in Pemalang, Central Java.

Dynamic Changes of Mango Market

In the period 1994–2004, Indonesia's mango production increased about 7 per cent per year (Table 8.1). However, since new harvested area of mango had rapidly increased by about 40 per cent during the last decade, national productivity of mango decreased sharply. Mango productivity in 2004 was only about 7.7 tons/hectare. The Directorate General of Horticulture set a target for mango productivity to be 10.6 tons per hectare through a programme focused on intensification and replanting of mango farms (Ministry of Agriculture, 2006).

Table 8.1: Harvested Area and Mango Production Growth in Indonesia

Harvest and Production	*1994*	*2004*	*Growth (%/year)*
Harvested area (hectare)	36,981	185,773	40
Production (ton)	826,824	1,437,665	7

Source: Central Bureau of Statistics, Indonesian Statistics, 2005, Jakarta.

Java Island makes a large contribution to national mango production. In 2004, the share of Java was 78 per cent (Table 8.2). Other important central producing areas of mango are Bali and Nusa Tenggara (9.8 per cent), Sulawesi (5.6 per cent), and Sumatra (4.7 per cent). The central producing area of mango in Java Island is East Java with a contribution of about 38.5 per cent. West and Central Java have relatively balanced production with shares about 18.9 per cent and 17.2 per cent, respectively. The regencies of Pemalang, Tegal, Pekalongan (Central Java), Indramayu (West Java), and Probolinggo (East Java) are central producing areas in Java Island. Pemalang Regency, on which the study is focused, had a share of about 4 per cent in mango production of Central Java (247,292 tons).

Most of Indonesia's mango production fulfils domestic consumption, which is currently at 60.9 per cent of FAO recommendation, namely 65.75 kg per capita per year (National Seminar on Mango Agribusiness, 2006). Hence, there is still a large opportunity to increase mango production even just to satisfy domestic consumption in response to an increase and improvement of distribution in income. International trade in mango is relatively very small, 95.6 tons of net exports in 2005 (Tables 8.3 and 8.4). Import and export volumes of mango were 869 tons (0.06 per cent) and 964 tons (0.07 per cent) respectively, which are below 1 per cent of total production.

Table 8.2: Mango Production in Indonesia (2004)

Region	*Production (ton)*	*Proportion (%)*
Sumatra	68,325	4.8
Java	1,125,839	78.3
West Java	271,297	18.9
Central Java	247,292	17.2
East Java	553,086	38.5
Bali and Nusa Tenggara	141,159	9.8
Kalimantan	15,928	1.1
Sulawesi	81,215	5.6
Maluku and Papua	5,199	0.4
	1,437,665	100.0

Source: Central Bureau of Statistics (2004), Vegetable and Fruit Production.

Even though the export volume of mango is relatively small; mango is exported to several countries. Diversified exporting country destinations could indicate high potential for the future mango development. Four countries have a share of proportion of more than 10 per cent, Middle East Countries (Kuwait, Arab Emirate Union, and Qatar) with a share of 29.43 per cent, Saudi Arabia (21.34 per cent), Singapore (14.67 per cent), and Taiwan (10.17 per cent) (Table 8.3).

Table 8.3: Export Destinations of Indonesia's Mango (2005)

Country Destination	*Export Volume*		*Export Value*
	Quantity (kg)	*Proportion (%)*	*(USD)*
Hong Kong	50,825	5.27	43,589
Taiwan	98,025	10.17	23,745
China	43,734	4.54	36,614
Singapore	141,482	14.67	216,476
Malaysia	83,344	8.64	36,691
Saudi Arabia	205,772	21.34	184,738
Middle East Countries	283,744	29.43	372,058
Others	57,368	5.94	86,070
Total	964,294	100.00	999,981

Source : Central Bureau of Statistics (2005), Statistical Export of Indonesia.

Imports of mango indicates good prospect for high quality mango in the domestic market, as well as challenge for developing Indonesia's mango production. Imports came from Thailand (71.58 per cent) and South Africa (17.14 per cent) (Table 8.4). Indonesia's mangoes are harvested from October to January, and imported mango fulfills the domestic demand gap starting from February to September. One factor that leads to whole year provision of mango is supermarket demand development which utilizes a modern supply chain for fresh agricultural products. When domestic supply has a problem, supermarket procurement system could drive an increase in import volume because of supermarket's ability to access international market networks directly or through a regional hub.

Supermarket growth in Indonesia is consistent with cluster developments of urban residents which demands comfort and better service for food provision. This has become the main driver of retail revolution in fresh and processed food in developing countries (Reardon, 2005; Natawidjaja, 2006). In the period 1997–2003, supermarket turnover increased faster than that of traditional markets (15 per cent versus 5 per cent), while the share of the modern retail segment increased to 29.6 per cent in 2004, and is expected to become 35 per cent in 2007 (Rangkuti, 2004; Nielsen, 2004). For fresh fruit purchase (including mango) in particular, most urban consumers (85 per cent) prefer the traditional market because of lower price. However, survey carried out by A.C. Nielsen, 2004 shows fast shifting of consumers' purchase pattern from traditional markets to supermarkets at the rate of 1.5 per cent per year.

Even though current development of off-season mango is limited because of production constraints, there is considerable potential. This is revealed in the price of off-season mango which is relatively very high (Rp 15,000/kg *versus* Rp 3,000/kg during on-season). Demands of supermarkets on product continuity (volume and quality) and price stability will play an important role in off-season mango development as well as expanding the market impact.

Table 8.4: Import Origin of Mango to Indonesia (2005)

Country Origin	*Volume*		*Import Value (USD)*
	Quantity (kg)	*Proportion (%)*	
Thailand	621,831	71.58	322,282
Singapore	53,962	6.21	41,704
Malaysia	29,770	3.43	9,809
South Africa	148,853	17.14	52,917
Others	14,276	1.64	10,636
Total	868,692	100.00	437,348

Source: Central Bureau of Statistics (2005), Statistical Import of Indonesia.

Data show that even under mango can be expanded and potential for an increase of farmers' participation and intensity in off-season mango farming. Off-season mango farms have extended to neighboring villages and district of the village researched (Asem Doyong Village, Taman Sari District). It has even led to a development of another farmer group near Pemalang. In the research area, level of participation of farmers in applying off-season mango technology is increasing, as also the size of farm per household. In near future, mango production is predicted to spread all along the year. Supermarkets and traditional markets will play larger role in supporting off-season mango development through sustainable technological and capital investment on mango farms.

Innovation in the Mango Supply Chain

Institutional innovation in supply chain has changed traditional marketings which tend to be long and inefficient whereas modern marketing chain is shorter and more efficient. Besides, there is also a change on the selling system at farm level from selling mango using the *tebasan*[1] system to a wholesaler to become a harvest organized by farmer groups and selling to supermarkets after post-harvest handling. The new system has made a change to the farmer's role, from a price taker into a price decision maker.

Mango farmers in Pemalang use a traditional long marketing chain for off-season or on-season mango (Figure 8.1). In this chain, farmers can play only a passive role, especially at marketing level. Although farmers have employed technology to produce off-season mango which made possible for mangoes to be harvested at the time of strong demand (excess demand), they keep using the *tebasan* system in selling their product. Such a selling system benefits only the buyers, collector (*tengkulak*), or

[1] In this system farmer sells the green mango on the tree without harvesting.

wholesaler, who have better knowledge on market information; therefore, farmers find themselves as price takers in the chain. Farmers realize their weak bargaining position but they have no choice.

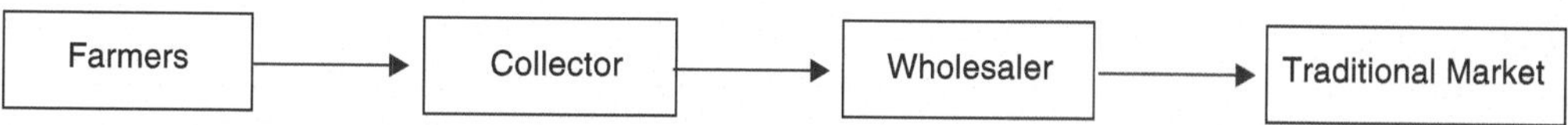

Fig. 8.1: Mango Marketing Channel in Pemalang before the Institutional Innovation

After the institutional innovation was developed which employs a transparent margin system, the marketing chains become shorter (Figure 8.2). This change is happening because of *Bimandiri* involvement which povides technical assistance and funds to farmers. *Bimandiri* as a dedicated wholesaler to supermarkets gives the farmer group direct access to the Hero supermarket chain. Through this system, farmers get assurance on marketing opportunity and the possibility to receive a higher price than that is given by the traditional market. However, in this system, farmers should be prepared to play an active role on various activities such as cultivation techniques, disease control, and post-harvest handling. In harvesting, farmers do not sell their mango; instead, they leave the fruit to harvest to the care of farmer groups of *Aspirasi Bina Usaha.*

Bimandiri develops a partnership with mango farmers based on transparent and mutual trust, by which mango marketing risk is not merely of farmers but of both sharing the same risk. All parties involved in this system know the margin they will earn. *Bimandiri* gets a fee of 5 per cent from the sale of mango for the services it renders to the farmer groups in assuring supermarkets for quality and quantity. Services given to farmers include introduction and test of new varieties, provision of agricultural inputs through soft loans, quality control, accounting, and contract negotiation with buyers. The term and services practiced in the partnership of *Bimandiri,* indirectly also affects other farmers in mango farming, such as an openness of information on technology, price, and marketing opportunities for farmers in rural areas.

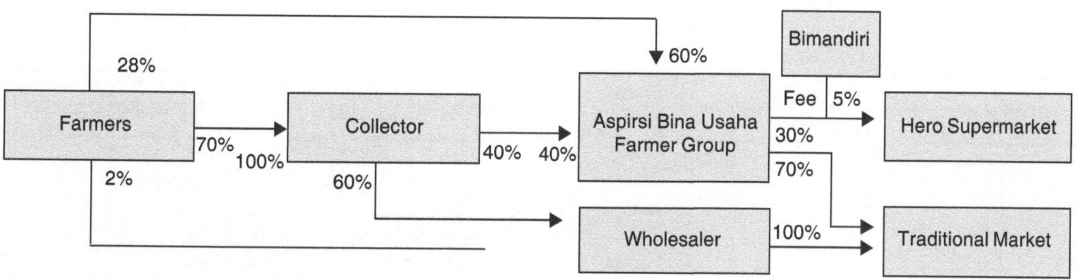

Fig. 8.2: Off-Season Mango Marketing Channel in Pemalang after the Institutional Innovation

Nevertheless, since Aspirasi Bina Usaha is a large farmer group with 46 members and diverse interests, some problems have cropped up in the group dynamic such as mixed incentives and conflict of interests. This has led to a group debt for production inputs loan of as much as Rps 300 million that has not been repaid to *Bimandiri*. Figure 8.2 shows that Aspirasi receives mango not only from members (60 per cent) but also from outside farmers through collectors (40 per cent) and sells to both supermarkets (30 per cent) and traditional markets (70 per cent). Since not all members have the same vision about the partnership with *Bimandiri*, some are just free riders. The institutional innovation created was very dynamic and capable of making self-correction and improvement. *Bimandiri* and the farmer group members who are genuinely interested in the innovation overcame the free riding problem by separating themselves (making exclusive) and creating a new farmer group named KUBM in order to make an improvement in the innovation.

Figure 8.3 shows how the marketing channel in Pemalang looks like after the KUBM farmer group was created. There are three channels in Pemalang; the first chain is the KUBM farmer group supplying to Carrefour and the traditional market. The second is a wholesaler, mainly supplying to the traditional market, but also some of them going to the supermarket (Carrefour) and to a specialty store network (Total Group). The third is the through Aspirasi supplying to the traditional market.

Innovation found in this case study consists of technology, product, strategy, and institution. The transparent margin system belongs to institutional innovation. Generally, innovation is defined as a process that can create value added and organization relationship between suppliers and consumers through new product development, solution, service, and new method of commercialization (Covin and Slevin, 1991; Knox, 2002; Lumpkin and Dess, 1996).

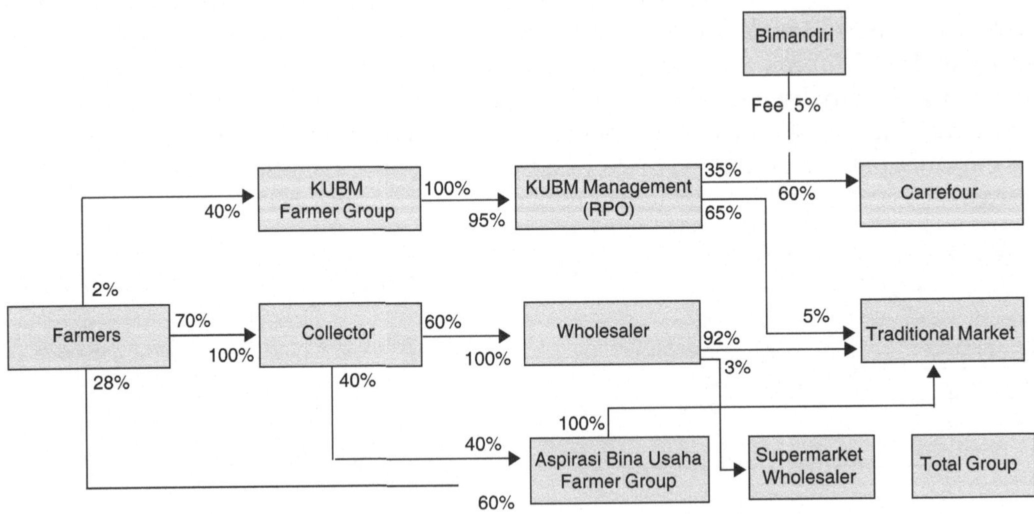

Fig. 8.3: Off-Season Mango Marketing Channels in Pemalang after the Institutional Innovation was Revised

Transparent margin refers to value system, net chain, relation, or partner (Holstede, 2002; Lamming *et al.*, 2001; Egger and Hamel, 1998; Hamel, 1991). Transparency is subjective and can be interpreted as a system referring to mutual understanding and accessibility among stakeholders and referring to individual perception. Transparency level can change over time and depends on objective change, capability, and willingness of the system to give information to those requiring it.

There are four dimensions of innovation in a food supply chain: economic, environment, technology, and social/legal (Trienekens and Willems, 2002). Economic dimension is related to cost and benefit. Environmental dimension is related to production method, distribution, and trade. Technological dimension is related to technological method (product, technological process, transport technology, information, and technological communication) in order to increase production quality and quantity, safe distribution, and safe product. Social dimension is related to social affairs which impedes products.

Therefore, the transparent margin partnership system can be defined as a new system that gives value added to farmers and other stakeholders by linking farmers directly to modern retailers. This partnership system can be identified as an innovation since it satisfies economic, environment, technology, and social dimension in the mango marketing system.

Innovation Development in Pemalang

Development of institutional innovation in Pemalang started with technological innovation, i.e. off-season mango cultivation technology, which was developed by a pioneer, namely H. Soewarno, in 1995. The market structure of mango in the production zone did not give good incentive to farmers, which meant that farmers could not enjoy benefits from the technological innovation. However, farmers using the technological innovation were increasing and information about off-season mango technology spread fast across the region although it was not always successfully applied since it required high technical skills.

The innovation resumed after an outsider come in, namely *Bimandiri,* which acts as a corporate entrepreneur by designing strategic innovation in order to win market competition in the supply chains to modern markets. *Bimandiri* collaborated with Aspirasi Bina Usaha and this resulted in co-innovation in the form of transparent margin system. Subsequently, the Aspirasi Bina Usaha farmer group broke up and six members of the group founded a new farmer group broke up called KUBM. *Bimandiri* resumed transparent margin system with KUBM. Aspirasi Bina Usaha farmers then returned to the old system, supplying to the traditional market. This development made the farmers belonging to Aspirasi excluded from innovation development. In the Aspirasi group, roles and responsibility of members involvement is not clear, which makes the board of Aspirasi end up as a trader (*bandar*) struggling for own interest rather than for members' interest.

As an institutional innovation, transparent margin system has succeeded in organizing the informal market system (open market based on negotiation) into a formal contract arrangement (contract based). Through the change of partnership system, KUBM has been able to expand its planting area from 36 hectares (4,680 trees) to 45 hectares (5,800 trees) within only one year. On the other hand, Aspirasi found its land area unchanged and remained at 72 hectares (10,028 trees) in the same period.

In generating an innovation, there are two processes at work, namely the main process (core process) and process that makes the innovation happen (enabling process). The concepts behind core process are generation concept, product innovation, processes of innovation, and acquisition technique, while enabling processes are leadership, system and tools, and resources (Chiesa *et al.*, 1996). The output of those processes is the achievement of competitiveness status. An example of process-based innovation approach is small industry development in China. Ren *et al.*, (2006) reveal that benchmarking (through an application of innovation technique) can be a management reference for further adoption and an appropriate innovation approach as the basis to create successful innovation. This was done by Bimandiri; in order to beat its competitors, *Bimandiri* carried out a benchmarking exercise with KUBM.

Hypothesis 1: Private companies tend to work with unorganized or loosely organized small-scale producers.

This study show that Bimandiri, a private company, is willing to work on long-term partnership with the KUBM farmer group, a well organized small-scale farmers which control a 45 hectares farm with 5,800 mango trees.

Factors Creating Inclusion and Exclusion during the Innovation Process

One factor that has encouraged farmers in the KUBM group to adopt innovation (inclusion) of transparent margin system is the capability and willingness to change in response to a demand of the modern market. Farmers' capability in responding to the change appears from the skill, competency, and capacity possessed by each farmer in the group. The change is required by the demand of the dynamic modern market which in turn always demands farmers' ability to adapt.

Bimandiri's motivation as a supply chain champion to collaborate with KUBM is mainly because of the group's capability to adopt innovation. Basic capability which the *Bimandiri* first looked for from farmers was the skill of producing off-season mango. Members of KUBM were pioneers in off-season mango technology. *Bimandiri* also likes to collaborate with farmers who are capable of expanding their volume. Members of KUBM are owner-operator farmers who also manage other mango farms and hence have capability of expanding their volume when needed. Another character that *Bimandiri* is looking for from farmers is having strong commitment and responsibility. KUBM which was founded by ex-members of the Aspirasi group was recommended by Syngenta, partner of Aspirasi, as a trustworthy group.

> **Hypothesis 2: Farmer organizations need to implement exclusionary arrangements with members (e.g. strict selection criteria) in order to consolidate their position in dynamic markets and remain competitive in the supply chain.**
>
> *The study show that in order to respond effectively to a change demanded by the dynamic market, eight members of the Aspirasi farmer group needed to create exclusionary arrangements by establishing a new group called KUBM to consolidate their position and remain competitive in the supply chain.*

Transparent margin system has been able to encourage farmers to establish cooperative formation through five management steps namely learning, steering, forming, implementing, and developing (Tuckman, 1965; Banet, 1976; Chamala, 1995). Farmers who are able to follow the need to change will survive, while those who are not will be eliminated and excluded. After the innovation process proceeds and makes some changes, inclusion and exclusion farmers will have different characteristics (Annex 8.9). The change process is described in Annex 8.5 and 8.6. The biggest changes in the process were in product, marketing, stakeholder, technology, management, organization, and finance.

In order to achieve success in the innovation, every stakeholder involved must be able to manage critical change points. Stakeholders involved in transparent margin partnership system are in three levels. They are: level 1, directly involved in the change process such as farmers, KUBM, management of KUBM, *Bimandiri*, and Carrefour; level 2, indirectly involved the change process such as the group of Aspirasi, local market actor, central market actor, and field extension agent; and level 3, not involved at all in the change process such local government, field extension officer, Sygenta, and other private parties. (See Figure 8.4). Every stakeholder has different characteristics and roles in the transparent margin system (Annex 8.10).

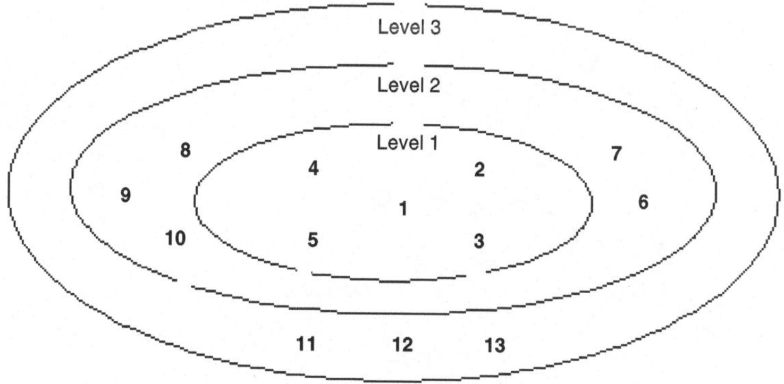

Fig. 8.4: Stakeholder Level in Transparent Margin Innovation

Notes:

Level 1:
1. Farmers
2. KUBM Farmer Group
3. KUBM RPO
4. *Bimandiri*
5. Carrefour

Level 2:

6. Aspirasi Farmer Group
7. Local market actors
8. Central market actors/agents
9. Local government
10. Extension agent

Level 3:

11. Extension agent
12. Sygenta
13. Private sectors

Actors at level 1, when the innovation process happened, mobilized, responded, and made necessary changes. So, the actors played active roles in the innovation, particularly farmers of the KUBM group, management of KUBM, and *Bimandiri*; while Carrefour in fact did not take any action. The KUBM group supports the management of KUBM by continuing innovation and supplying product continuously under prevailing rules. Responsibility and commitment from the management of KUBM enabled to overcome the financial problem encountered by the farmers.

However, actors at levels 2 and 3 did not give solution to the problem emerging in the innovation process. At level 2, there was only Aspirasi which made a change, although only in quality handling. Meanwhile, at level 3, stakeholders responded appropiately but did not make any change. In this case, local government did not play any role in both inclusion and exclusion processes.

In its development process, the innovation has been nurtured by two farmer groups, namely Aspirasi and KUBM. Annex 8.11 describes the change reactions and problems happening within the groups in the process. The problem faced by Aspirasi and KUBM was mainly financial management. Non-cash payment system and a financial problem have demonstrated that the Aspirasi group was not an appropriate organizational environment, which made the innovation transferred to a smaller group namely, KUBM. The stakeholder's role in assisting farmers solving the problem was an important factor that kept farmers continue adopting the innovation. Additionally, problem solving capabilities, financial management, and others may be factors that kept farmers continue adopting the innovation.

Fig. 8.5: Critical Factors for Innovation Success

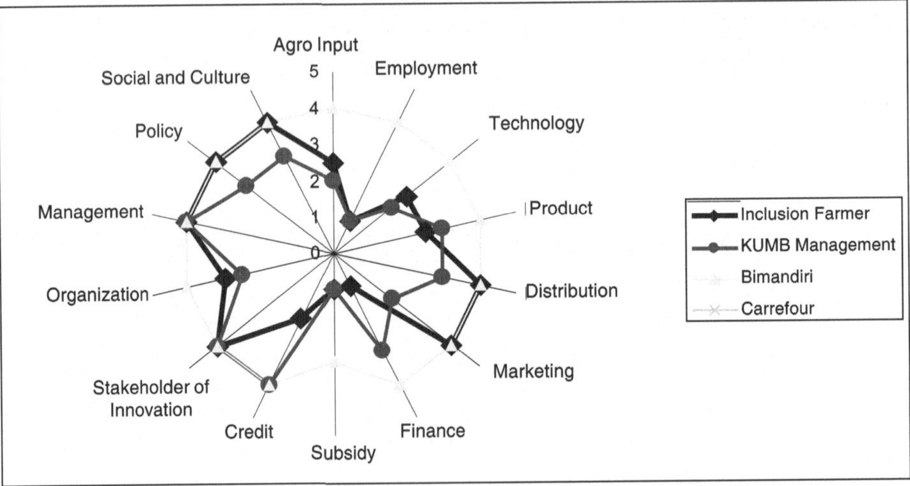

Based on interviews with the actors (Annexes 8.7 and 8.8), important factors for the success of the innovation are shown in the Radar Chart (Figure 8.5). The figure shows that most important factors for inclusive farmers, KUBM management, *Bimandiri*, and

Carrefour were involvement of stakeholders and management in innovation institutional development. Both factors can be considered as *critical stage factors* (CSFs) in assuring the success of innovation. Farm inputs, labour cost, technology, product specification, distribution, marketing, financial issue, subsidy, organization, and regulation/policy have been handled by the existence of *Bimandiri* as a dedicated supermarket wholesaler. The role of *Bimandiri* has been to enable farmers to carry out direct negotiations with Carrefour.

Interestingly, the analysis shows that inclusive farmers perceived subsidy as relatively not important; and neither for *Bimandiri*. This indicates that farmers never felt directly benefit from government subsidy. In fact, some farmers observed that subsidy and aid program disturbed the farmer's institutional system. Meanwhile, *Bimandiri* and Carrefour perceive that government's subsidy is not required as long as farmers are committed to the institutional agreement in the partnership as it will prevent a high transaction cost. Social and cultural factors are not considered as problems since among farmers, KUBM management, *Bimandiri*, and Carrefour comprehend each other is in facilitating the exchange.

Hypothesis 3: Small farmers' organizations that have accessed dynamic, restructured markets always require subsidies or grants to sustain their activities.

The study shows that farmer's organization did not require subsidy or grant for sustaining its activities. Through the partnership with Bimandiri-Carrefour, KUBM management was able to develop self-supporting business and gave incentive as well as compensation to all actors involved for their roles and functions.

From the inclusion farmer's point of view, the role of stakeholders (*Bimandiri* and Carrefour) was as an advisor as well as information and price provider. Basically, *Bimandiri* had assisted farmers in selling their product to the modern market. Its also indicates that strong trust had been developed in the partnership; farmers could deliver mangoes to Carrefour without hesitation and agree to the price determined by the retailer. Stakeholder's factor is very important for inclusive farmers because *Bimandiri* had provided advance funds (before the retailer paid), technical assistance, information, and market knowledge. Thus consistent with McFadzean, O' Loughlin, and Shaw (2005) who state that an entrepreneur not only requires and looks for financial gain but also other kinds of gains. *Bimandiri* and Carrefour are considered as pioneer for farmers to capture the good market opportunity. The relationship among stakeholders in the partnership has been growing since farmers have demonstrated higher commitment to deliver mangoes to Carrefour through KUBM. The management system implemented in the partnership was perceived as easy to understand and benefited all parties involved. That condition could be sustained if an open and transparent communication among actors involved existed.

Hypothesis 4: Private companies working with small-scale producers always make use of public subsidy arrangements.

The study shows that Bimandiri, as a private company, is willing to collaborate with smallholder farmers without making use of public subsidies from the government. In contrast, Bimandiri is keen on providing advance funds for KUBM farmers in order to help farmers purchase production inputs.

Figure 8.5 also identified the management factor as the second most important, because through good management, all planning, organizing, and monitoring can be implemented efficiently. In terms of marketing policy, *Bimandiri* provided and guaranteed farmers a production channel to the market. This situation has put farmers on the face of a competitive market and becoming a challenge to them. However, farmers must commit to produce best quality of mangoes. Farmers followed the norm of partnership because of high price incentives for quality and quick payment. The system is becoming very important to escape farmers from the capital loan trap of local traders. KUBM has been well-managed and provides salary to the management board based on position and responsibility. The memorandum of understanding (MoU) between KUBM farmers and *Bimandiri* is aimed to keep a commitment of all parties involved under the law. In terms of product policy, *Bimandiri* has a primary function on assurance of quality standard and quantity fulfillment.

Impact of the Innovation Development

Farmers involved in the transparent margin partnership felt that several factors have changed after their inclusion, among other things: increase in income, received market guarantee for the product, higher price from the traditional market, faster payment, and better access to market information. Impact of the transparent margin system can be analysed from four kinds of flow changes in the supply chain of mango: physical product, information, knowledge and capital flows.

Product Flow

A change in physical flow of product occurred after the introduction of the transparent margin system. Prior to the innovation, product flow was through the conventional marketing channels: from farmers to collectors, wholesaler, and to traditional wholesale markets (Figure 8.1). After the innovation the marketing chain has been shortened, and the volume delivered has also changed (Figure 8.2). At the time of partnership with Hero, amount delivered to the supermarket was only 30 per cent, while the remaining went to the traditional market. After the KUBM group entered into partnership with Carrefour, the figure increased to 35 per cent, with the remaining going to the traditional market (Figure 8.3). The illustration shows that a partnership with Carrefour is more profitable than one with Hero. This is also apparent from the decrease in management fee, from 15 per cent (5 per cent for Hero,

5 per cent for *Bimandiri*, and 5 per cent bridging fee) to only 5 per cent for *Bimandiri* as management fee.

Information Flow

A change in the information flow also occurred after the introduction of institutional innovation. Before the innovation, price information from traditional markets as passed on to farmers via dealers and collectors. Under such conditions farmers had no alternative choices and marketed their products only to traditional markets. Furthermore, they did not have information on the prevailing prices in the market, which left them to a passive role as price takers. After the innovation, when farmers first collaborated with Hero, one witnessed substantial change in information flow from not only price information but also to include quantity, quality, delivery schedule, and some kind of formal agreement between the group and Hero. Later this improved when a new collaboration was established with Carrefour and the collaboration with Hero was terminated. A significant improvement with the new arrangement is that information on market opportunity was introduced which was absent in the collaboration with Hero. Market opportunity provided by Carrefour was perhaps meant to adhere to the delivery schedule by the suppliers.

In the partnerships between farmers and Hero and later with Carrefour, farmers were still integrated into the traditional market through collectors and dealers as around 65 per cent of their produce were sold through this channel. Interestingly, the innovation brought some changes in information flow from the traditional market: where there was only price flow, now it includes quantity information flow. This condition reflects the propagation effect of the innovation on the surrounding marketing systems.

Knowledge Flow

After the innovation was introduced, there was additional flow of know-how, that is, quality supervision implemented by *Bimandiri* and Hero to guarantee quality, quantity, and continuity, which were absent in the traditional market system. After the partnership with Carrefour was established, flow of know-how from *Bimandiri* to the management of KUBM also occurred, which enabled farmers to have direct access to the Carrefour distribution centre. This was done to enable farmers to quickly follow changes in the market. For example, farmers were quickly responsive to the quality of mangoes with regard to freshness and shrinkage level required by the supermarket.

Capital Flow

Prior to the innovation, there was only capital flow from the dealer to the collector to aid the collectors in providing upfront money to farmers. During the partnership with Hero *Bimandiri* provided reserve funds to Aspirasi with a 5 per cent management fee. After the partnership with Carrefour began despite some obstruction in the payback process, the arrangement was continued. This proves that capital aid from the government was not the main factor for the success of such innovation. The most important thing the member's commitment to manage the funds, to be able to follow changes in a dynamic market.

The farmer who could follow the innovation adopted a contract system, and was thus able to obtain price and market guarantee. In the contract system there was agreement on quality, quantity, delivery schedule, and information on market opportunity. In this contract system, when related to the agency theory, KUBM plays the role as agent for Carrefour and also as agent for farmers, whereas Carrefour acted as principal. In the case of mangoes in Pemalang, the principal could not monitor the behaviour of its agents, and it was with the help of *Bimandiri* that the partnership could come about. *Bimandiri* indirectly brought forward change in know-how and capital. The networking increased the company's social capital through increase in access to information, assistance technique, and financial support (Coleman, 1990; Burt, 1997; 2007).

Through *Bimandiri* KUBM farmers were given access to the modern market. Farmers achieved higher bargaining position with the existence of price negotiation between farmers and Carrefour. Besides, there was improvement in organization and management of KUBM, resulting in trust from Carrefour. In network theory, collaboration is based not only on profit, but also on power and trust (Uzzi, 1997).

Impact on Governance of Supply Chain

Institutional analysis of governance of supply chain divides the actors into three roles: legislative governance, executive governance, and judicial governance (Kaplinsky, 2000). The innovation resulted in a change in supply chain governance. In spite of the absence of written regulations, every stakeholder has the right and obligation to play out his or her respective role.

Prior to the innovation, the functions of legislative governance, executive governance, and judicial governance were executed by the dealer in the traditional market. After the innovation, the three roles were not anymore centred on the dealer, but were spread and played, among others, by Hero, Aspirasi, and *Bimandiri*. There was a shift in the role of legislative governance from Hero to Carrefour, and a transfer in the role of executive governance from Aspirasi to the management of KUBM, whereas the role of judicial governance was still with *Bimandiri*.

The flow of governance legitimacy before the innovation is presented in Annex 8.1, Table A. It shows that the dealer played the role of legislative governance, executive governance, and judicial governance in the traditional market. It is this dealer who made the rules, implemented the rules, and monitored the rules, playing his role at will. This is shown by the poor relation of governance legitimacy flow among all the market actors in the traditional market.

After the innovation, there was a change in legitimacy governance flow (Annex 8.1, Table B). Hero played the role of legislative governance, Aspirasi the role as executive governance, and *Bimandiri* played the role of judicial governance. This is shown by the high relation of legitimacy governance flow among the three actors. Hero made a standard for suppliers, among others, punctual product delivery schedule, and delivery frequency and quantity, which were previously not implemented. *Aspirasi* implemented the rules by providing assistance to member farmers to meet always the stipulated standards. *Bimandiri*, on the other hand, monitored supplier implementation in meeting already stipulated quality standards.

When Carrefour replaced Hero, there was a change in governance legitimacy flow. Carrefour performs the role of legislative governance, KUBM management executive governance, and *Bimandiri* plays its role of judicial governance (Annex 8.1 Table C). This is shown by the high relation of governance legitimacy flow among the three actors. There was a difference in the role of executive governance as played by Aspirasi and KUBM management. Aspirasi in providing technical assistance to farmers referred to field extension specialists which adhered to the government programme, and followed less the changes taking place in modern dynamic markets, so as to result in the Aspirasi farmers being excluded from the innovation. KUBM management, on the other hand, provided technical assistance to farmers under its care by referring to the *Bimandiri* programme which suited the changes occurring in dynamic modern markets.

This indicates that only farmers included in the innovation were capable of following changes in dynamic modern markets, whereas the excluded farmers would return to their relationship with traditional market actors who had low relation of legitimacy flow. As a result, farmers who had their market opportunity eliminated, had no guarantee of product quality, and no price guarantee and market security, resulting in transaction being made only in the spot market.

The discussion shows governance legitimacy flow among stakeholders during transaction. Annex 8.3 shows that even though there were differences in roles in governance legitimacy, individual relationship among stakeholders was good, except with Carrefour, which shows poor relationship with a value range between 5 to 8. This is reasonable because Carrefour as principal in agency theory (Douma and Schreuder, 1991) did not observe the agent's behaviour, and the principal did not have information concerning the agent's behaviour either. The principal could not directly observe the agent's behaviour and got only signals related to the agent's work efforts.

Hypothesis 5: Farmer organizations that supply to dynamic markets have little or no influence over chain governance issues.

KUBM farmers' organization had effect on supply chain governance, especially in implementing rules (executive governance). This shows that KUBM management could make bargaining position to become better and control product quality.

Active Role of the Supply Chain Champion

Bimandiri is a model of the supply chain champion; priority in business operations is given not to short term gains, but to develop markets. Thus its business orientation is with an eye on long run profit.

Bimandiri has positioned itself as entrepreneur who advocates innovation, not as a trader (Amit *et al.*, 1993; Drucker, 1985; McGrath, 1996; Stevenson and Jarillo, 1990). An entrepreneur is a catalyst for the coming about of innovation (Schumpeter, 1961). Suppliers like *Bimandiri* are needed by Carrefour as reliable partners in following changes in very dynamic markets.

Corporate entrepreneurship links entrepreneurial behaviour to organization (Echola and Nec, 1998). This is a foundation for management to face governmental challenges and urge the coming about of innovation (Barringer and Bluedorn, 1999). This is also a form of responsibility to stimulate the coming about of innovation in organizations through testing of new potential opportunities, resource acquisition, implementation, exploitation, and commercialization of new products or services (Guth and Geinberg, 1990; Kurato, *et al.*, 1990; Sathe, 1989; Stopford and Baden-Fuller, 1994; Thornberry, 2003). Corporate entrepreneurship also includes various behaviours and acts which enhance the company's capability to take risks, the extent of opportunity, and innovation (Zahra, 1991, 1995).

Leibenstein (2005) says that entrepreneurs always engage in one or several activities, among others, organize and make use of the right resources as a condition to produce and market new products or services; coordinate contract arrangement between partner and his supplier; arrange the right organizational structure and culture to develop and manufacture new products or services; respond to market deficiency with resources additive in the absence of a market, and provide contact between buyer and seller at different locations. *Bimandiri* is seen to engage in almost all activities in corporate entrepreneurship.

From the analysis of stakeholders' rights, obligations, and benefits (Annex 2), KUBM farmers were categorized to avoid risk by surrendering mangoes to KUBM management due to the existence of market and price guarantee. KUBM management may be categorized as a self-insured type of risk, because it kept reserve funds when mango prices declined, but withdrew when mango prices were favourable. *Bimandiri* shared the risk, because it received 5 per cent management fee without going into production itself. On the other hand, Carrefour mitigated risk by expecting quality and punctual product continuity.

Hypothesis 6: Private sector (processors, retailers) is generally seen as having a passive role, buying product when available at the right quality, price, risk profile, and transaction cost.

Bimandiri as a private company played an active role in determining quality, price, risk, and control of transaction fees. Bimandiri provided technical assistance to KUBM management, starting from cultivating techniques, cutting techniques, post-harvest handling, grading, labelling, and packing, resulting in better quality.

Aspirasi may be said to be bold in risk taking, because it looked for its own market and transacted with traditional market actors at fluctuating prices. Beulens (2000) shows that there are five kinds of risks in transparency dilemma: namely, contamination risk, poaching risk, risk of stealing, asset specificity risk, and loss of resources control risk. With regard to transparency dilemma, in this case, there was the tendency for KUBM to engage in poaching risk, because the resources it acquired benefited only KUBM farmers or KUBM management.

Value Chain Mapping

The marketing chain of off-season mango from Pemalang, after the improved institutional innovation (by the establishment of KUBM) (Figure 8.3) has several value chain alternatives. In this part only six value chains will be mapped and analyzed, namely, the value chain through KUBM and through Aspirasi (Figure 8.6). Chains 1A and 2A are the farmers' marketing channels directly through KUBM, in particular with permanent members. As shown in Figure 8.3, 35 per cent of the off-season mangoes sold by KUBM were channelled to Carrefour (1A), whereas the rest were channelled through the traditional wholesale market. Value chains 3A and 4A are the marketing channels from independent farmers bought by KUBM through collector traders/middlemen by way of pre-harvest transaction. The ratios of mangoes channelled to Carrefour and the traditional market are also the same, namely 35 per cent and 65 per cent. Meanwhile, Chains 8A and 9A are the off-season mango marketing through Aspirasi, directly as well as through middlemen, bought by way of pre-harvest transaction.

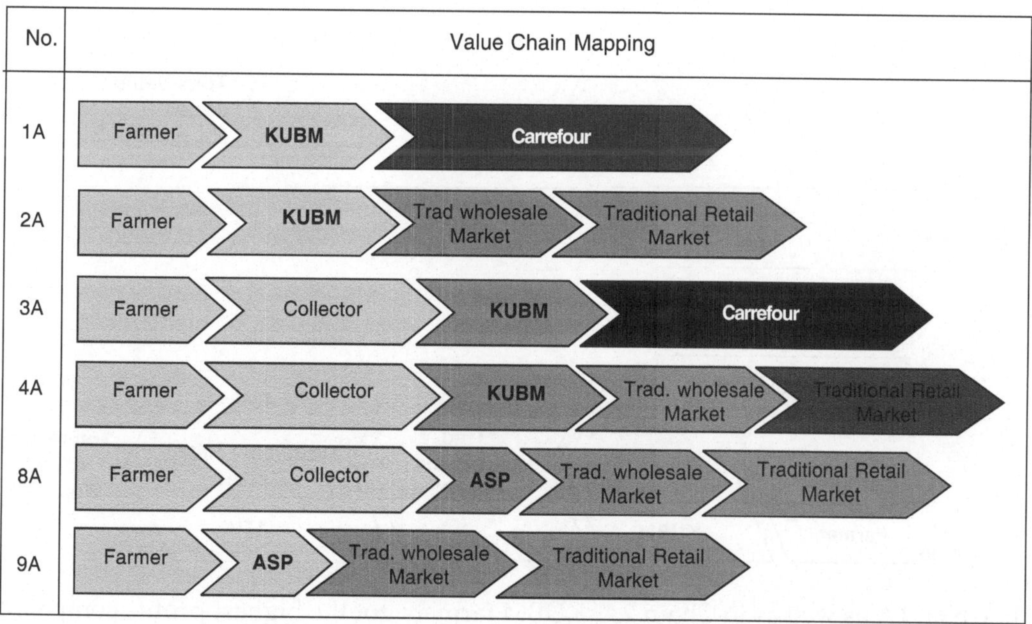

Fig. 8.6: Off-Season Mango Value Chain Mapping in Pemalang

In each chain, majority of the farmers got their highest profit share (value added) because of the high price for off-season mangoes. As shown in Annex 8.11, off-season mango selling prices on average ranged between Rp 4,000 – Rp 9,000, whereas prices of on-season mangos ranged between Rp 1,200 – Rp 1,500. Majority of farmers in Pemalang were independent farmers who were not committed to a group. They usually sold their produce to collectors on a pre-harvest basis. Indeed, in general when farmers sell their produce to collectors or dealers, they usually use the pre-harvest selling system. It was only KUBM and Aspirasi groups that were willing to buy on the basis of quality. It is to be regretted, however, that the mangoes the farmers produce had only low percentage of good quality (Grade A). Thus the remainder still had to be sold to the traditional market.

(a) Off-Season Mango Supply Chain through KUBM

Chain 1A is the chain which became the main objective of KUBM farmers, that is, to Carrefour modern retail market. This channel provided high added value for the farmers because of the highest quality and price. However, not all mangoes produced by KUBM farmers could be accepted by Carrefour, only about 35 per cent. The unaccepted mangoes were sent to the traditional retail market (Chain 2A).

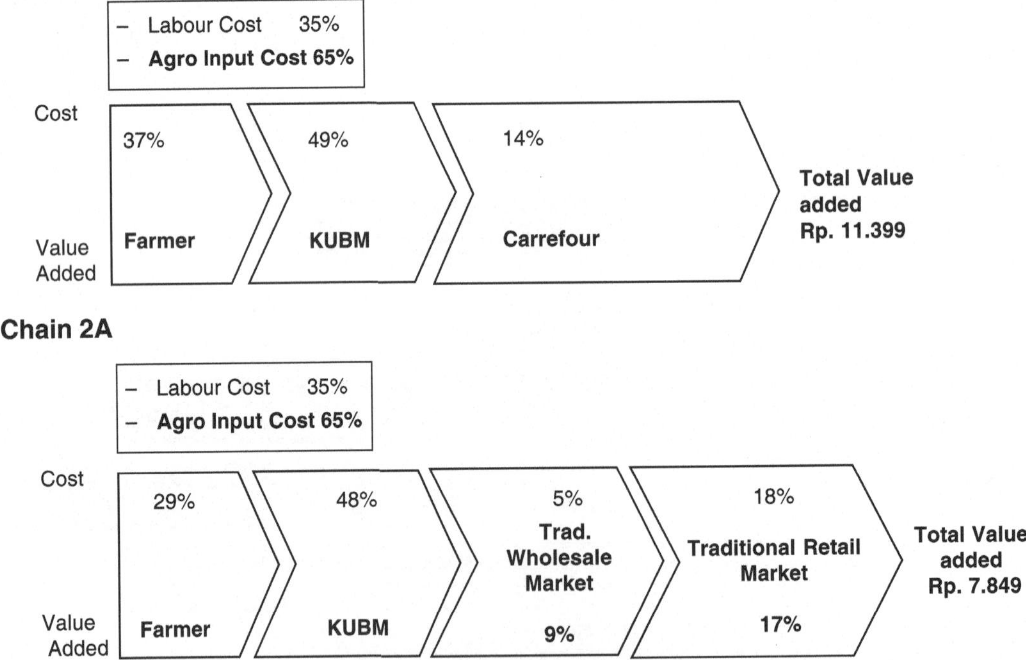

In Chain 1A as well as in Chain 2A, KUBM farmers got the highest profits compared to the whole of value added activities in the chains mentioned, that is, 67 per cent and

60 per cent. Thus this means that institutional innovation has caused an impact on increase in farmers' income. The total value added of Chain 1A was Rp 11.399 per kg of mango, higher than that of Chain 2A of Rp 7.849 per kg. This is, of course reasonable, because activities in Chain 1A produced mangoes of better quality. The total added values produced in both value chains were the highest.

To obtain such a high added value, farmers had to sacrifice an amount of Rp 1,326 per kg for agro input expenses (65 per cent). This is really what happened in the field, farmers increased the use of pesticides to obtain higher productivity in the course of pursuing the highest profits in off-season. Because of the small quantity of mangoes available in off-season, wherever KUBM farmers marketed their mangoes, the modern market (1A) or the traditional market (2A), profit was still highest.

(b) Off-Season Mango Supply Chain through KUBM Indirectly (Independent Farmers/ Non-Members)

Chains 3A and 4A are KUBM sale chains with additional buying source. To keep up with the modern market, KUBM was required to meet the demand continuously. To meet this demand, KUBM, besides obtaining mangoes from member farmers, had part of their products supplied by middlemen farmers (5 per cent). In Chain 3A, middlemen traders got large profits. In Chain 4A, however, farmers got the highest profit.

The total value added of Chain 3A was Rp 11,647 per kg of mango, and 42 per cent of this total value added went to middleman traders. The activities carried out were harvesting and providing goods. The activities needed a sacrifice of only Rp 128 per kg of mangoes, the greater part being used for provision of goods (66 per cent). In this chain the middleman farmer to KUBM offered the smallest sacrifice at the highest profit. The selling price was high, but the buying price from farmers using the pre-harvest system was low. In this value chain, independent farmers did not get the greatest part of profit even though they sold to KUBM through middlemen. The total value added in Chain 4A was Rp 8,098 per kg of mango. The activity carried out by independent farmers was worth a great part of the profit. The whole of the expenses spent for the activities in this supply chain was Rp 974 per kg, and the largest expense was for agro input cost, that is, 52 per cent.

Chain 3A

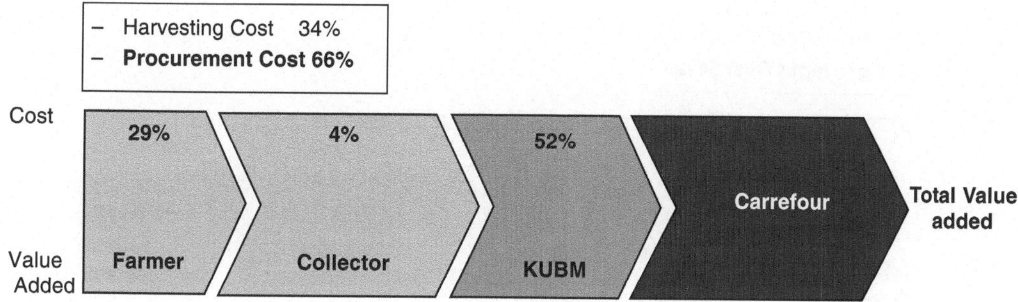

Chain 4A

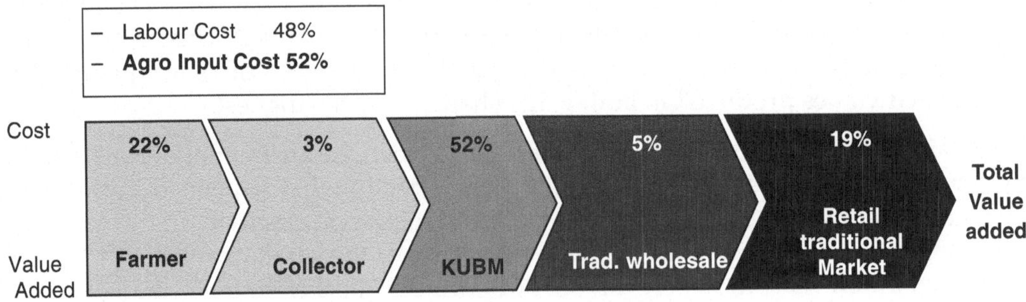

(c) Off-Season Mango Supply Chain through Aspirasi

Chains 8A and 9A are off-season mango marketing chains through Aspirasi with the objective of marketing aimed at the traditional wholesale market. The supply chain consisted of two parts of value chains, namely, without middleman traders and through middleman traders. The greater part of mangoes procured came from middleman traders (60 per cent), and the other 40 per cent originated from Aspirasi member farmers. In Chains 8A and 9A farmers had large profits, namely, 38 per cent and 52 per cent respectively in total value added.

Chain 8A

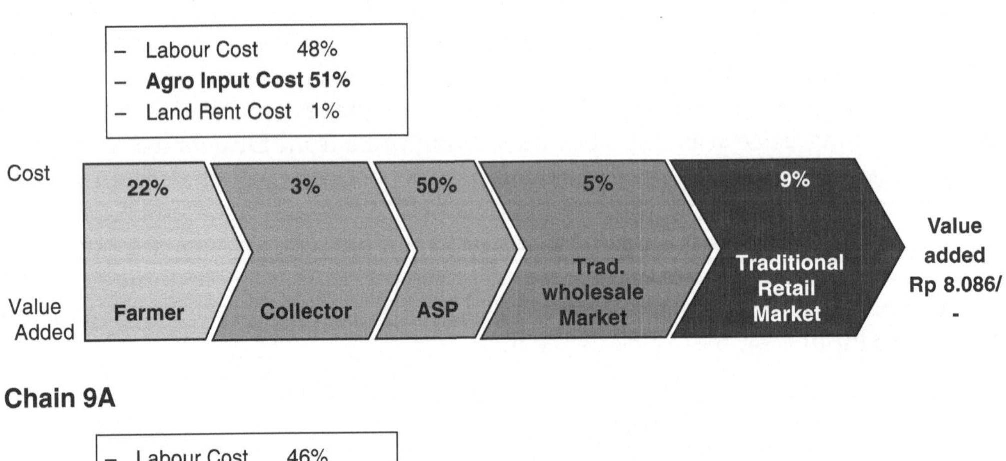

Chain 9A

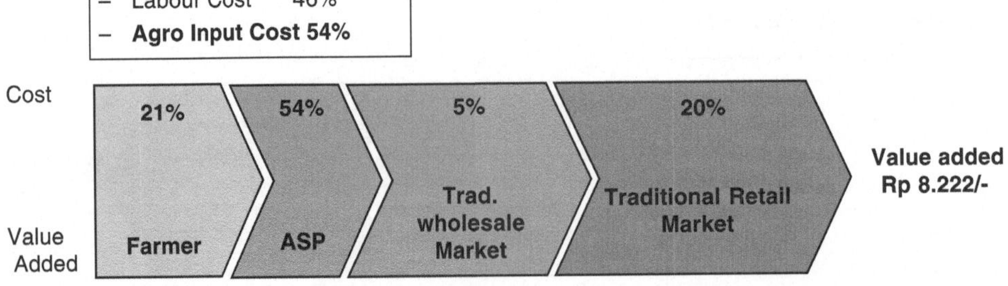

Total value added in Chains 8A and 9A does not differ very much, namely, Rp 8.086 and Rp 8.222 per kg of mango. The sacrifice by the farmer in Chains 8A and 9A was respectively Rp 974 and Rp 890 per kg of mango. The greatest sacrifice made by farmers in both chains was for agro input cost, 52 per cent and 54 per cent respectively. To keep with high prices, farmers increased the use of chemicals. The frequency of use of chemicals was not as high as that of use of pesticides by KUBM farmers. Both chains illustrate that the shorter the supply chains the higher the profit for farmers.

When comparing Chain 8A with Chains 3A and 4A (farmer's sale through a middleman), one cannot find difference in profit between the farmer who sold his product to KUBM and one who sold his product through Aspirasi. From the point of profit received by the farmer in each chain, sale through Aspirasi yielded higher profits for the farmer. Comparing Chain 9A with Chains 1A and 2A (farmer's direct sale), one can find a difference in profit. Farmers who sold his product directly to KUBM obtained higher profits compared to those who sold their products directly to Aspirasi. However, to effect sale through KUBM, the farmer had to offer 11 per cent greater sacrifice, in particular for agro input cost.

Benefit and Cost

Institutional innovation promotes increase in income and improvement in financial flow so as to become a motivator for stakeholders to continuously carry out innovation. In this case study, institutional innovation has changed benefit and cost at several levels.

Benefit and Cost at the Farmers' Level

Production expenses, production, product value, and profit at the farmers' level experienced changes because of the innovation. Productivity, quality standard, and product value, all of which were high, resulted in higher profits for included farmers compared to those of the farmers in general. This is apparent when one compares KUBM farmers, independent farmers who sold to KUBM through middlemen, and

Table 8.5: Differences in Production Cost, Production Level, Quality Standard, Product Value and Profit between KUBM Farmers, Aspirasi Farmers and Independent Farmers

Variable	*KUBM Farmers (1A)*	*Aspirasi Farmers (9A)*	*Independent Farmers (3A)*
Production Cost	Rp 1,326/kg	Rp 1,326/kg	Rp 973/kg
Off-Season Production	13.5 tons	12.0 tons	10.0 tons
Quality Standard and Share	30% A, 40% B, 30% C	12% A, 8% B, 20% C, 50% D	Without grading
Product Value per Grade	A = Rp 9,000; B = Rp 6,000; C = Rp3,000	A = Rp 9,250, B = Rp 6250, B = Rp 3,250, B = Rp 2,000	Rp 4,000
Profit	Rp 7,674/kg	Rp 4,297/kg	Rp 3,026/kg

Aspirasi (ASP) farmers (see Annex 8.11 for detail). The supply chain that provided the highest value added was the innovation supply chain in column 1A, that is KUBM farmers. Table 8.5 shows a comparison of profits received by KUBM farmers with that of other farmers. One can see from Table 8.5 that production costs and production level of included farmers were higher than that of excluded farmers.

The production cost of included farmers was greater than the production cost of farmers in general. Table 8.6 shows that the highest cost was for off-season spraying. To increase their production KUBM farmers resorted to increase in spraying, which came to more than 65 per cent of the total cost.

Table 8.6: Comparison of Production Cost of KUBM Farmers, Aspirasi Farmers and Independent Farmers

Production Cost	*KUBM farmers (1A)*	*Aspirasi farmers (9A)*	*Independent farmers (3A)*
Labour cost	35%	48%	46%
Agro Input cost	65%	51%	54%
Land rent	0.1%	1%	1%
Total cost (₹/kg)	1,326	890	974
Percentage of Total Cost in the Value Chain	37%	29%	21%

In relation to production cost, column 1B and column 2B in Annex 8.11 illustrate that if KUBM farmers had used only their agricultural activities and had only marketed their product to the traditional market, the profit they received would have been smaller than the agricultural activities of other farmers. This high production cost shows that innovation could not be tried for on-season commodities where the marketing objective was aimed at the traditional market. Meanwhile, the greater part of the farmers' product entered the traditional retail market. This was one the reasons why not all farmers were interested in becoming included farmers.

Sale of mangoes to KUBM yielded higher value because of grade quality requirements which was not too high but not bad either. The quality of mango produced by the KUBM farmers was: 30 per cent grade A, 40 per cent grade B, and 30 per cent grade C. This was not the case with Aspirasi as ex-innovation inclusion, its supply management was not controlled resulting in uncontrolled quality of the produce. Even though the farmers' productivity was not different and even though Aspirasi offered higher prices to farmers, low quality resulted in sharp decline of the value received by the farmers.

In Table 8.5 one can see that the price paid by KUBM to its members was lower than that of other market actors. When one compares the quality standard, majority of KUBM farmers (40 per cent) produced Grade B mangoes with a price of Rp 6,000. Meanwhile, for other farmers, most of their product (60 per cent) belonged to Grade D with a product value of Rp 2,000. This fact may answer the question as to why farmers preferred selling their product using the pre-harvest system to middlemen traders.

Table 8.7: Comparison of Profit Level of KUBM Farmers, Aspirasi Farmers and Independent Farmers

Cost	*KUBM farmers (1A)*	*Aspirasi farmers (9A)*	*Independent farmers (3A)*
Value Added (Rp/kg)	7,674	4,297	3,026
Total Cost (Rp/kg)	1,326	890	3,026
Benefit-Cost Ratio	5.79	4.83	3.11

Even though production cost was high, productivity, quality, and high prices yielded higher profits. Table 8.7 illustrates the profit level of each category of farmer; the profit level of KUBM farmers was high compared to other farmers. The net benefit cost ratio for each farmer, namely, 5.79, 4.83, and 3.11 respectively, proves that innovation was capable of spurring improvement in income at farmer's level.

Hypothesis 7: There is no clear evidence to support that inclusion and exclusion within dynamic markets define the difference between 'winners' and 'losers' (respectively)

The study show that inclusion farmers (members of KUBM) generally gain higher profit than exclusion farmers (members of Aspirasi) in both marketing channels, the marketing chain to the supermarket as well as the marketing chain to the traditional market.

Benefit and Cost at the Supply Chain Level

At the supply chain level, institutional innovation led to changes in distribution of profit in the whole of supply chain and led to changes in transaction value and volume in the supply chain. Change in profit level distribution is seen from the net benefit-cost ratio value of each actor (ratio of value added/kg and cost/kg). Change in transaction value and volume is seen from selling price and percentage of product flow in the chain. Table 8.8 illustrates the net benefit-cost ratio of each actor in every supply chain.

In the KUBM supply chain without middleman traders (Chains 1A, 2A, and 9A), farmers made the highest profit level in every chain. When mango marketing to KUBM was carried out through middleman traders (Chains 3A, 4A, and 8A), profit was the highest.

The highest net benefit-cost ratio was for the middleman trader in Chain 3A, that is 38.20. Middleman traders, for sale through KUBM and Aspirasi, still received higher profits for off-season commodities. The middleman trader was one of the market actors carrying out business on small sacrifices, but capable of making manifold income. However, the middleman trader faced sufficiently high risk level too because of the buying system from farmers which was the pre-harvest system.

The net benefit-cost ratio in Chain 2A to the traditional wholesale market as an outlet of low-quality mangoes was 0.52. KUBM was aware that sale to the traditional

Table 8.8: Net Benefit-Cost Ratio Masing-Masing Pelaku Dalam Setiap Rantai Pasokan

Actor	*Value Chain of KUBM*		*Value Chain of KUBM through Collectors*		*Value Chain of Aspirasi*	
	1A	*2A*	*3A*	*4A*	*8A*	*9A*
1. Farmers						
– KUBM Farmers	5.79	3.53	–	–	–	
– ASP Farmers	–	–	–	–	–	4.83
– Independent Farmers	–	–	3.11	3.11	3.11	–
2. Collector	–	–	38.20	14.68	8.31	–
3. KUBM	0.71	0.52	0.73	0.54	–	–
4. Aspirasi	–	–	–	–	0.90	0.84
5. Traditional Wholesale Market*	–	–	–	–	–	–
6. Traditional Retail Market	–	1.58	–	1.58	1.58	1.58
7. Carrefour	4.77	–	4.77	–	–	–

* Profit was obtained through marketing fee provided by the wholesaler.

wholesale market would not yield high value added because the mangoes were left overs of low quality.

Replication Potential

Increasingly stiff competition in modern retail markets will spur the application of more efficient procurement system. In the near future, large modern retail market actors (like Carrefour, Giant, Hypermart) will introduce centralized fresh and processed food products procurement systems through Distribution Centres (DC) and are expected to replace the prevailing store-to-store procurement system.

This change will have an implication on the readiness of the existing fresh and processed food product suppliers and processors. This readiness takes the form of ability to supply a large volume continuously, to face the increasingly strict application of product quality standards, and to improve production processing cost efficiency.

In anticipating this change, suppliers to modern retail markets should design a new procurement system. This system should be capable of guaranteeing product availability continuously in terms of large quantity, consistent quality, and competitive and differentiated prices. In realizing this, suppliers should take the initiative to have direct relationship with producers or organized farmers.

The business partnership model implemented by *Bimandiri* and KUBM is one alternative best practice in anticipating decentralization procurement policy currently envisaged by modern retail markets. The margin transparency system is a form of co-innovation formed as a result of KUBM and *Bimandiri* strategic alliance in the mango supply chain at the village of Asem Doyong, Pemalang. The continuity of this partnership is determined by strong commitment and trust of both parties, marketing institutional transformation, innovation learning, and risk management built-in the partnership, and the role of the village production organization which is based on the marketing value.

Policy intervention is needed to promote wide replication of this kind of partnership. Its realization needs creative attitude and process from decision makers and researchers to develop the determining factors of partnership systems like the one implemented by *Bimandiri* and KUBM.

To replicate the success of the margin transparency system, the government could take the following steps:

1. Search for champions from entrepreneurs in a chain of agricultural commodity supply to modern retail markets. Champion is an entrepreneur, like *Bimandiri,* who possesses corporate entrepreneurship to develop a co-innovation creation system with its partners. In this search process, the Government may collaborate with research institutions and universities.
2. Provide incentive to champion to carry out replication of marketing institutional transformation. The champion in question should be spurred to become a marketing agent of the village production organization. In this marketing institution there is no transfer of ownership from producer and/or village production organization to champion; what happens is only transfer of product control. Ownership transfer only occurs from producer to the final destination market. As agent, champion will get commission or share in output from the business process it carries out in an effort to provide added value for the producer-end market relationship. This value added business process creates a transparent information system, and provides fund for financial support and technical assistance. The incentive the government could provide to champion is access to modern financial market facilities such as factoring, investment fund, working capital fund, and partnership with state- and university-owned research institutions to accelerate the process of co-innovation creation and chain upgrading through exchange of experience and innovation learning.
3. Facilitate the establishment of multi-stakeholder organizations specifically aimed at monitoring and advocacy of partnership process in the modern retail market business. This organization acts as a trusted resolution agent in the event of conflict between actors involved in the modern supply chain.
4. Facilitate funding for research and development of an effective and efficient integrated agribusiness supply chain capable of competing in the global market (domestic and international).
5. Facilitate the development and certification of an integral chain care such as HACCP system, GAP, GPP, GHP, GMP, and traceability system.

Conclusions

The margin partnership system is a co-innovation of marketing institution which gives access to farmers, connects farmers directly to supermarkets with support from *Bimandiri,* the value chain champion, in the form of quality assurance, continuity of supply, technical assistance, and provide bridging capital service to farmers. There is no product ownership changes (no exchanges) within the marketing institution. Exchanges are only made between farmer group KUBM and Carrefour, the modern retailer, *Bimandiri* receives a commission of 5 per cent from sales made in the partnership.

The margin system has created dynamic changes in producer's level. The system has encouraged farmers to work in a group and has transformed the farmer's relation with the market, from spot market based to become contract based negotiation.

The motivation of specialized supermarket wholesaler to develop a partnership system comes from the need to respond to the demand of the dynamic market which is possible only by organized farming which guarantees product quality and continuity.

Factors that support farmer's inclusion are ability, willingness and trust in adapting to a change in the rule of the game created by the dynamic market and an incentive system that supports individual as well as group business development.

Farmers gain the most from the transparent margin system, shown by higher income than before the system was adopted and got higher prices than the traditional market. Additionally, the system give the farmer faster payment after harvest and provided access to market information.

Sustainability of the partnership system depends on strong commitment and trust of all agents involved, institutional transformation ability, innovation learning process, risk management function that built in the system, and the role of rural production organizations on the basis of marketing value added. The government can help in the replication process by giving incentives to the supply chain champion and other supporting agents according to the need of dynamic market development.

Looking at the success of *Bimandiri,* in providing market access to small mango producers without any subsidy or support from the government, it is suggested that the government should not interfere in the working partnership. However, the partnership system that potentially links farmers with dynamic markets and increases farmer's income like what *Bimandiri* and KUBM have developed should be systematically promoted and supported as follows:

1. Give incentives (tax deduction, technical support, etc.) to an agribusiness company, supermarket supplier or food industry who likes to take a leadership role to become *the supply chain champion* who creates a partnership with small farmers in a transparent system.

2. Provide capacity building training for rural production organizations on technical aspects such as GAP, GPP. GHP, food safety certificate (HACCP), managerial aspects, and farmer group dynamics.
3. Develop a financial system which supports actors in a dynamic market.
4. Support development of multi-stakeholders institutions which become truted mediation agents in conflict resolution in the modern market supply chain.
5. Provide incentives to facilitate development of a *public private partnership* in the area of research and development for agribusiness supply chain integration so as to enhance the competitive and comparative advantage of Indonesian products in the global market.

ANNEX

Annex 8.1: Physical Flow Changes in Distribution Supply Chains of "On-Season" Mango after the Innovation.

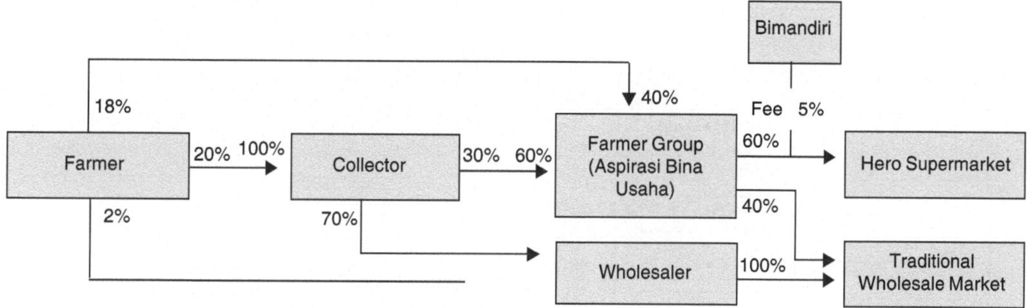

Annex Fig. 8.1A: Distribution Supply Chains of "On-Season" Mango after the Innovation

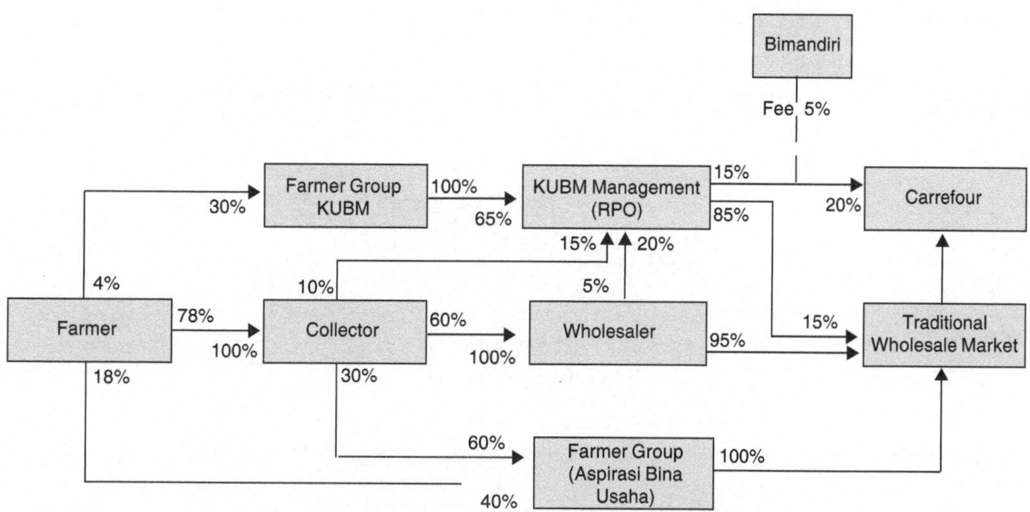

Annex Fig. 8.1B: Distribution Supply Chains of "On-Season" Mango after Improvement of Innovation

Annex 8.2: Information Flow Changes on Distribution Supply Chains of "Off-Season" Mango before and after Innovation

Farmers
inf. 1
Collector
inf. 2
Wholesaler
inf. 3
Traditional Wholesale Market

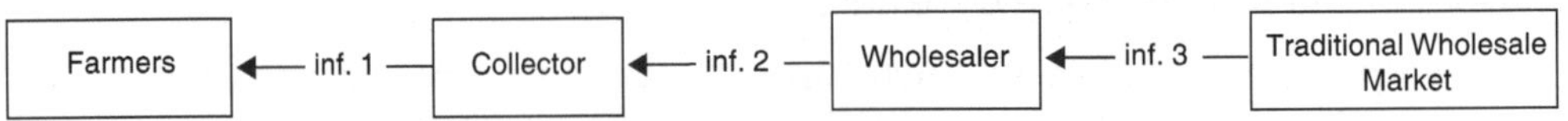

Annex Fig. 8.2A: Information Flow Chains before Innovation

Syngenta (input)
inf. 4
inf. 9
inf. 10
Bimandiri
inf. 14
Farmer
inf. 5
Collector
inf. 8
Farmer Group (Aspirasi Bina Usaha)
inf. 11
inf. 12
Hero Supermarket
inf. 7
inf. 6
Wholesaler
inf. 5
Traditional Market

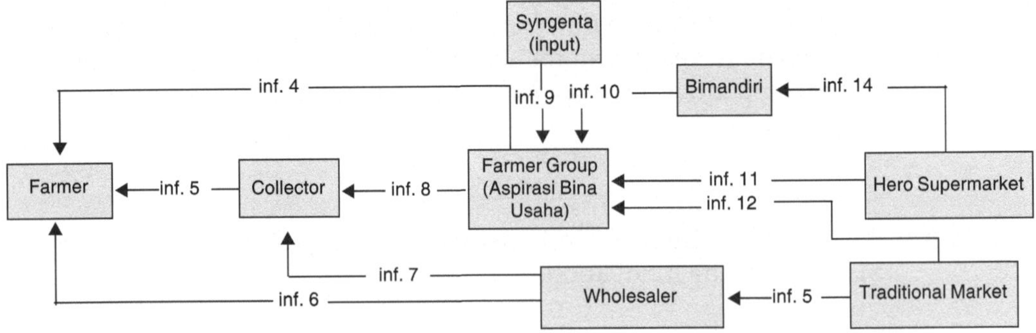

Annex Fig. 8.2B: Information Flow Chains after Innovation (*Aspirasi Bina Usaha* Group)

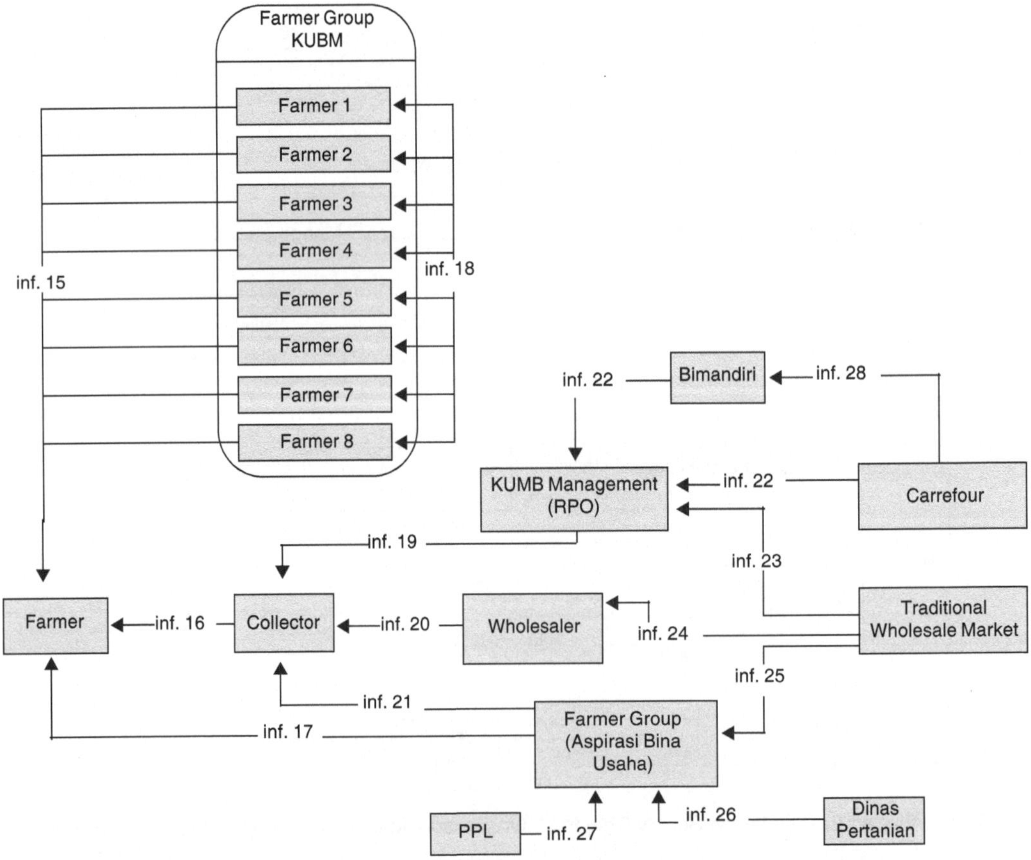

Farmer Group KUBM
Farmer 1
Farmer 2
Farmer 3
Farmer 4
Farmer 5
Farmer 6
Farmer 7
Farmer 8
inf. 15
inf. 18
inf. 22
Bimandiri
inf. 28
KUMB Management (RPO)
inf. 22
Carrefour
inf. 19
inf. 23
Farmer
inf. 16
Collector
inf. 20
Wholesaler
inf. 24
Traditional Wholesale Market
inf. 25
inf. 21
inf. 17
Farmer Group (Aspirasi Bina Usaha)
PPL
inf. 27
inf. 26
Dinas Pertanian

Annex Fig. 8.2C: Information Flow Chains after Improvement of Innovation (*KUBM* Group)

Annex 8.2 (continued)

Notes:

Inf 1 price information at farmer level
Inf 2 price information
inf 3 price and quantity information
inf 4 price information at farmer level
inf 5 price information at farmer level
inf 6 price information at farmer level
inf 7 price information
Inf 8 price information
Inf 9 market opportunity information
Inf 10 market opportunity information
Inf 11 information of price, quantity, quality and delivery schedule
Inf 12 information of price and quality
Inf 13 information of price and quality
Inf 14 information of price, quality, and trade agreement between group and Hero Supermarket
Inf 15 information of price at farmer level
Inf 16 information of price at farmer level
Inf 17 information of price at farmer level
Inf 18 information of price, quantity, quality, market condition, cost reduction per kg
Inf 19 price information
Inf 20 price information
Inf 21 price information
Inf 22 information of price, quantity, quality, market opportunity and delivery schedule
Inf 23 price and quantity information
Inf 24 price and quantity information
Inf 25 price and quantity information
Inf 26 information of market opportunity
Inf 27 information of another opportunity such as government bureaucracy and input
Inf 28 information of price, quantity, market opportunity and trade agreement between group and Carrefour.

Annex 8.3: Knowledge Flow Changes in Distribution Supply Chains of "Off-Season" Mango before and after Innovation

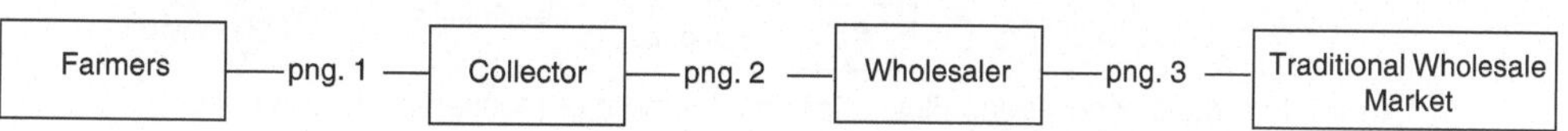

Annex Fig. 8.3A: Knowledge Flow before Innovation

PPL
Syngenta
Bimandiri
png. 15
png. 4
png. 9
png. 10
png. 11
Farmer
png. 5
Collector
png. 7
Farmer Group (Aspirasi Bina Usaha)
png. 12
png. 13
Hero Supermarket
png. 8
png. 6
Wholesaler
inf. 14
Traditional Wholesaler Market

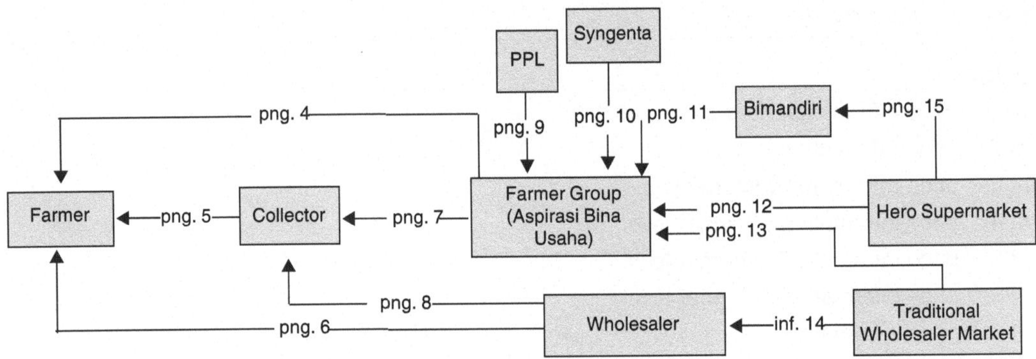

Annex Fig. 8.3B: Knowledge Flow after Innovation (*Aspirasi Bina Usaha* Group)

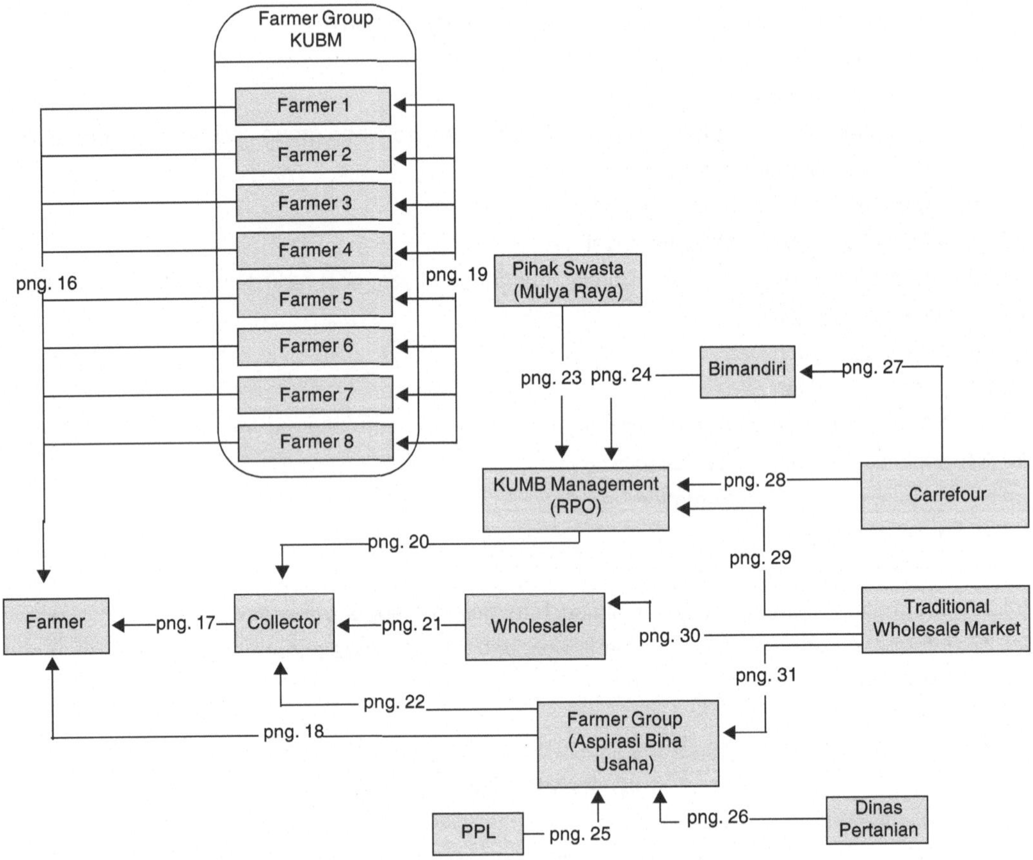

Farmer Group KUBM
Farmer 1
Farmer 2
Farmer 3
Farmer 4
Farmer 5
Farmer 6
Farmer 7
Farmer 8
png. 16
png. 19
Pihak Swasta (Mulya Raya)
png. 23
png. 24
Bimandiri
png. 27
KUMB Management (RPO)
png. 28
Carrefour
png. 20
png. 29
Farmer
png. 17
Collector
png. 21
Wholesaler
png. 30
Traditional Wholesale Market
png. 31
png. 22
png. 18
Farmer Group (Aspirasi Bina Usaha)
PPL
png. 25
png. 26
Dinas Pertanian

Annex Fig. 8.3C: Knowledge Flow after Improvement of Innovation (*KUBM* Group)

Annex 8.3 (continued)

Notes:

Png. 4 picking, quality, sorting knowledge
Png. 5 picking, quality knowledge
Png. 6 picking, quality, sorting knowledge
Png. 7 picking, quality, sorting knowledge
Png. 8 picking, quality knowledge
Png. 9 cultivation technique and group organization knowledge
Png. 10 cultivation technique knowledge
Png. 10 quality control knowledge
Png. 11 picking, quality, packing, sorting knowledge
Png. 12 picking, quality, packing, sorting knowledge
Png. 15 quality, quantity, continuity knowledge
Png. 18 picking, quality, sorting knowledge
Png. 19 picking, cultivation technique, sorting, organization and management knowledge
Png. 20 picking knowledge
Png. 21 picking and quality knowledge
Png. 22 picking, quality, sorting knowledge
Png. 23 waxing technique knowledge
Png. 24 quality, marketing, organization, management and knowledge negotiation
Png. 25 cultivation and group organization knowledge
Png. 27 quality knowledge
Png. 28 packing knowledge

Annex 8.4: Capital Flow Changes of Distribution Supply Chains of "Off-Season" Mango before and after Innovation

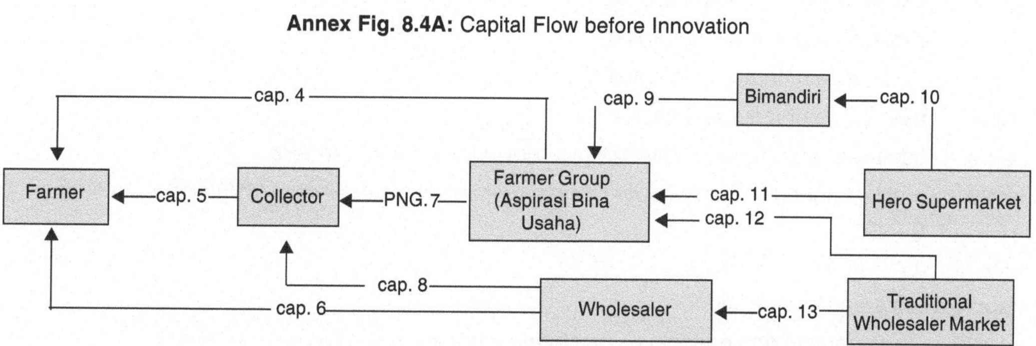

Annex Fig. 8.4A: Capital Flow before Innovation

Annex Fig. 8.4B: Capital Flow after Innovation (*Aspirasi Bina Usaha* Group)

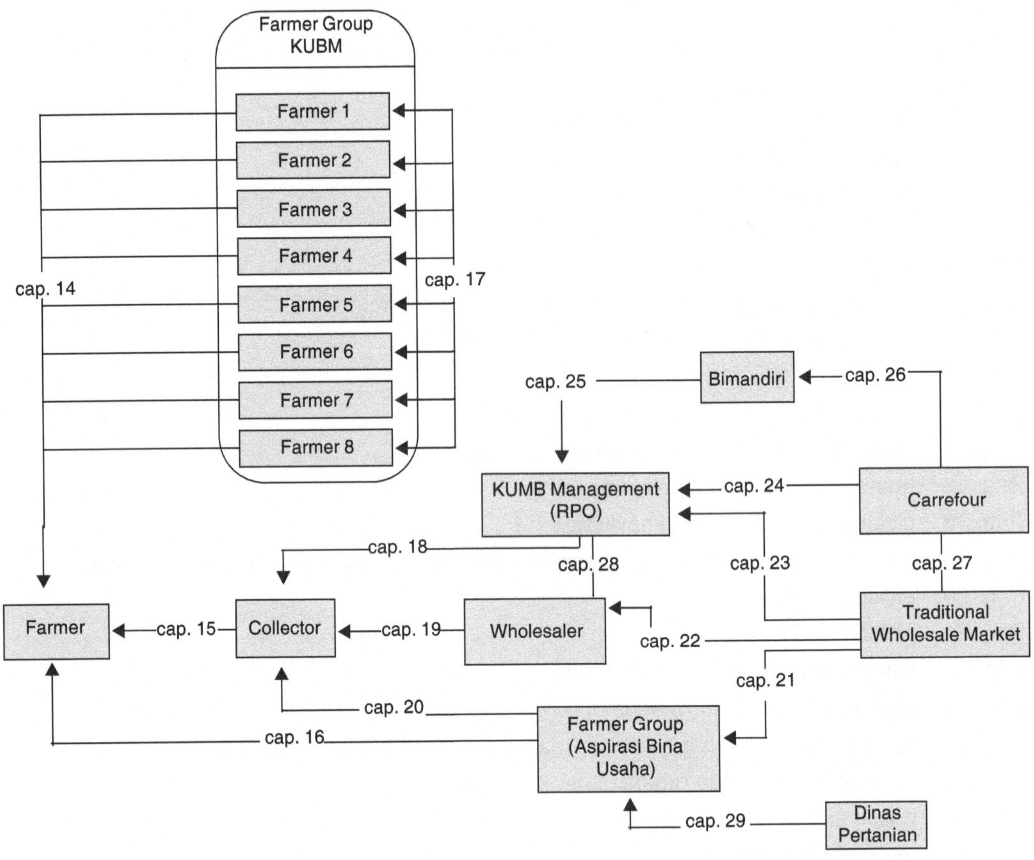

Annex Fig. 8.4C: Capital Flow after Improvement of Innovation (*KUBM* Group)

Annex 8.4 (continued)

Notes:

cap 2	capital support to help collector give down payment to farmers
cap 4	assistance of input and capital
cap 5	assistance of input and capital
cap 6	assistance of input and capital
cap 8	capital support to help collector give down payment to farmers
cap 9	capital support in term of advance payment from supermarket (5%) and input support to group
cap 14	input and capital support
cap 15	input and capital support
cap 16	input, capital, and agriculture mechanic support
cap 17	capital support from organization funds to pay off loan to *Bimandiri* and help cash payment to farmers

Annex 8.4 (continued)

cap 19	capital support to help collector give down payment to farmers
cap 23	capital support to KUBM to help cash payment to farmers (advance fund)
cap 24	capital support in the form of advance payment from supermarket (5%)
cap 25	agriculture mechanic, research field plot and soft loan support

Annex 8.5: Legitimacy Governance Flow before and after Innovation

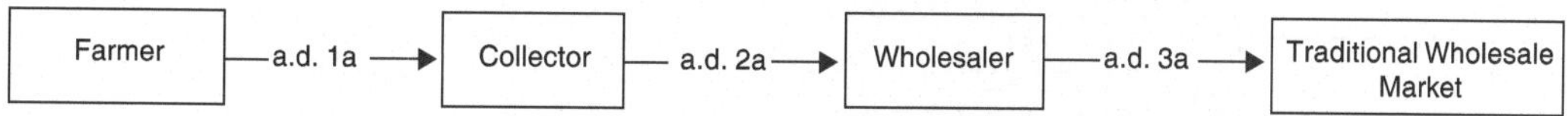

Annex Fig. 8.5A: Distribution Supply Chains before Innovation

Annex Table 8.5A: Relation of Legitimacy Governance Flow before Innovation

Legitimacy Governance	*Farmer*	*Collector/ Middleman*	*Local Trader*	*Traditional Market*
Farmer		Low		
Collector/Middleman	Low		Low	
Local Trader		Low		Low
Traditional Market			Low	

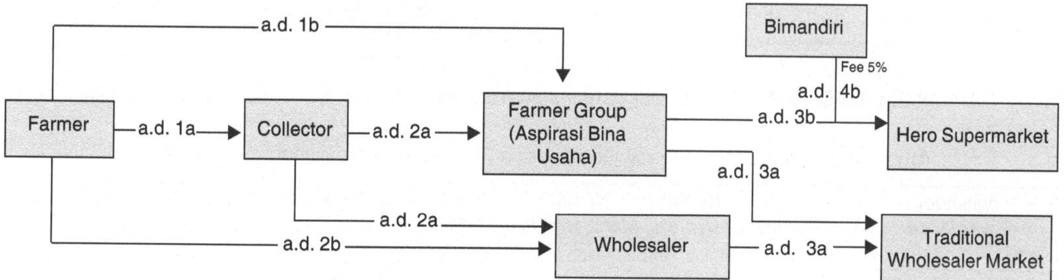

Annex. Fig. 8.5B: Distribution Supply Chains after Innovation (*Aspirasi* Group)

Annex. Table 8.5B: Relation of Legitimacy Governance Flow after Innovation

Legitimacy Governance	*Farmer*	*Collector/ Middleman*	*Trader*	*Aspirasi "BU"*	*Bimandiri*	*Hero Supermarket*	*Traditional Market*
Farmers		Low	Low	Low			
Collector/Middleman	Low		Low	Low			
Trader	Low	Low					Low
Aspirasi "BU"	Low	Low			High	High	Low
Bimandiri				High			
Hero Supermarket				High			
Traditional Market			Low	Low			

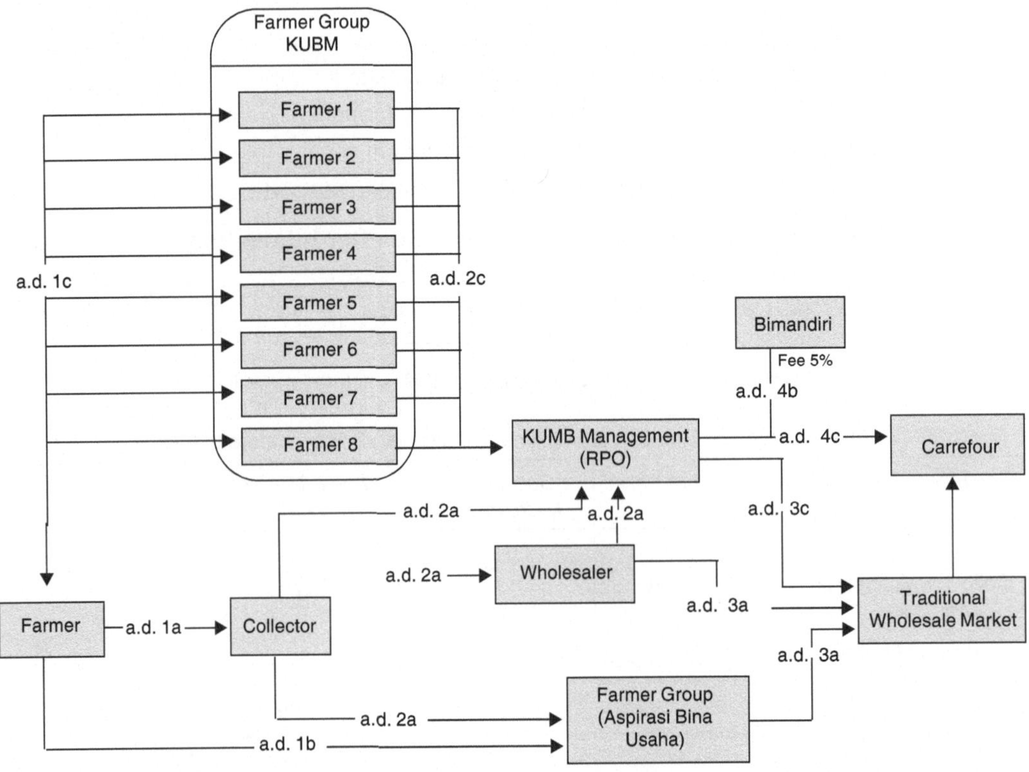

Annex Fig. 8.5C: Distribution Supply Chains after Improvement of Innovation (KUBM Group)

Annex 8.5 Table C: Legitimacy Governance Flow after Improvement of Innovation

Legitimacy Governance	*Farmer*	*KUBM Group*	*KUBM Management (RPO)*	*Collector/ Middleman*	*Trader*	*Aspirasi "BU"*	*Bimandiri*	*Carre-four*
Farmer		Low		Low		Low		
KUBM Group	Low		High					
RPO		High		Low	Low	High	High	Low
Collector/Middleman	Low		Low		Low	Low		
Trader			Low	Low			Low	
Aspirasi "BU"	Low			Low				Low
Bimandiri			High					
Carrefour			High					
Traditional Market			Low		Low	Low		

Notes:

a.d.1a: Low Trust Chain : (1) short time trading relation, (2) every middleman may get the price through negotiation, (3) Farmers produce in line with their ownership, (4) Field supervisions by middleman, (5) Farmers have many buyers (middleman trader) and middleman trader has many alternative of sources (farmers), (6) technical assistance only when needed, (7) no formal inter-actor relation and focused on purchase, (8) competitive price decision and hidden information, (9) having access to propose loan in the form of input, (10) periodical payment with some delays.

a.d. 2a: Low Trust Chain : (1) short time trading relation, (2) every middleman may get the price through negotiation, (3) contract relation follows written order from trader, (4) Field supervisions by middleman, (5) middleman has many buyer (trader) and trader has many alternatives of sources (middlemen), (6) absence of technical assistance, (7) no formal inter-actor relation and focused on purchase, (8) competitive price decision and hidden information, (9) some middleman traders have access to propose loan in the form of capital as advance fund, (10) periodical payment with some delays.

a.d. 3a: Low Trust Chain: (1) short time trading relation, (2) every middleman may get the price through negotiation, (3) trader is more flexible in delivery, (4) Field supervisions by middleman, (5) trader has many buyers (market) and market has many sources (traders), (6) no technical assistance, (7) no formal inter-actor relation and focused on purchase, (8) competitive price decision, (9) no credit aid is available, (10) periodical payment with some delays.

a.d. 1b: Low Trust Chain: (1) short time trading relation, (2) every middleman may get the price through negotiation, (3) Farmers produce in line with their ownership, (4) Field supervisions by middleman, (5) farmers have many buyers (traders) and group has many sources (farmers), (6) routine technical assistance, (7) have formal inter-actor relation but still focused on purchase, (8) competitive price decision and hidden information, (9) have access to propose loan in the form of input (10) periodical payment with some delays.

a.d. 2b: Low Trust Chain: (1) short time trading relation, (2) every middleman may get the price through negotiation, (3) Farmers produce in line with their ownership, (4) Field supervisions by middleman, (5) farmers have many buyers (traders) and trader has many alternative sources (farmers), (6) technical assistance is carried out when needed, (7) have formal inter-actor relation but still focused on purchase, (8) competitive price decision and hidden information, (9) have access to propose loan in the form of input (10) periodical payment with some delays.

a.d. 3b: High Trust Chain: (1) long time trading relation, (2) nobody get the price through negotiation, (3) group starts producing to follow written order, (4) checking at every delivery, (5) dependency level: some buyers for group and one or two seller sources to Hero supermarket, (6) technical assistance is carried every time, (7) communication through multi channel, (8) little competition, open information, (9) no credit aid (10) delayed payment

a.d. 4b: High Trust Chain: (1) long time trading relation, (2) nobody get the price through negotiation, (3) group starts producing to follow written order, (4) checking at every delivery, (5) dependency level: some buyers for group and one or two seller sources to Hero supermarket, (6) technical assistance is carried out every time, (7) communication through multi channel, (8) little competition and open information, (9) no credit aid (10) delayed payment with payment acceleration and bridging cost payment to Bimandiri

a.d. 1c: Low Trust Chain: (1) short time trading relation, (2) every middleman may get the price through negotiation, (3) contract relation: farmers produce in line with their ownership, (4) Field supervisions by middleman, (5) dependence level: farmers have many buyers and group has many alternative sources (farmers), (6) technical assistance is carried out when needed, (7) Seldom have formal inter-actor relation and focused on purchase, (8) competitive price decision and hidden information, (9) have access to propose loan in the form of input (10) good payment and no delay in payment (cash).

a.d. 2c: High Trust Chain: (1) long time trading relation (with submit process from group to RPO, (2) nobody get the price through negotiation, (3) contract relation: group is more flexible over instruction in production and submission, (4) no checking at every delivery,

(5) dependency level: some buyers to farmer and one source by RPO, (6) technical assistance is carried out every time, (7) communication is carried out through multi channel, (8) little competition and open information, (9) There is access to propose credit, long period payment with easy approval, (10) system employed is submission, payment is sometimes delayed.

a.d. 3c: Low Trust Chain: (1) short time trading relation, (2) every middleman may get the price through negotiation, (3) trader is more flexible over the instruction to produce (4) Field supervisions by middleman, (5) dependence level: trader has many buyers, and market

Annex 8.6: Right and Responsibility of Stakeholder Involved in Innovation

Stakeholder	*Right*	*Responsibility*	*Benefit*
Inclusion Farmers	– Acquiring technical assistance – Acquiring fund aid and/ or facility – All merchandise can be sold	– Submit all goods produced – Implementing technology given – Pay loan	– Production increase – Obtaining facilities in payment – Increasing income – Getting clearness product volume sold – Minimizing cheating by trader – Knowing market information
Management of KUBM	– Acquiring all yields produced by farmers – Obtaining payment agreed with shop – Attaining technical assistance from Bimandiri	– Providing technical assistance – Awarding facilities to farmers – Giving market information – Selling farmers' products – Ready to make promotion – Fulfilling all demands of shop – Completing quality requirements set up by shop	– Product is well-known among consumers – Producing quality product – All product is sold – Enjoying high price compared with in traditional market – Turnover generating – Understand
Bimandiri	– Obtaining 5% fee from total mango sale to Bimandiri's accessible market – Acquiring loan payment of advance fund at farmer level – Attaining information related to expectation and prediction of mango productivity before harvesting – Getting information of transaction between group and Carrefour	– Giving routine technical assistance to RPO (KUBM) – Granting aid in the form of advance fund – Providing aid and assurance of access to market	– Turnover increase – Minimized risk – Product continuity – Success of horizontal expansion – Product diversification in Bimandiri in mango commodity

Annex 8.7: Relation Inter-Stakeholder in Innovation

Stakeholder	*Inclusive Farmers*	*Management of KUBM*	*Bimandiri*	*Carrefour*
Inclusive Farmers		Meeting between KUBM and farmers: once a week (3) Method of problem solving (3) Method of price determination/price receive (1) Risk sharing (3) Level of dependency (3) Sum of value = 13	Meeting between Bimandiri and KUBM: once a month (3) Method of problem solving (3) Method of price determination(1) Risk sharing (3) Level of dependency (3) Sum of value = 13	Meeting between farmers and Carrefour: never (1) Method of problem solving (1) Method of price determination (1) Risk sharing (1) Level of dependency (1) Sum of value = 5
Management of KUBM	Meeting between KUBM and farmers: once a week (3) Method of problem solving (3) Method of price determination (3) Risk sharing (3) Level of dependency (3) Sum of value = 15		Meeting between KUBM and Bimandiri: once a month (3) Method of problem solving (3) Method of price determination (1) Risk sharing (3) Level of dependency (3) Sum of value = 13	Meeting between KUBM and Carrefour: every delivery of product (3) Method of problem solving (1) Method of price determination (1) Risk sharing (1) Risk sharing (1) Sum of value = 7
Bimandiri	Meeting between Bimandiri and farmers: once a month or per two months (3) Method of problem solving (3) Method of price determination (1) Risk sharing (3) Level of dependency (2) Sum of value = 12	Meeting between Bimandiri and KUBM: once a month (3) Method of problem solving (3) Method of price determination (1) Risk sharing (3) Level of dependency (2) Sum of value = 12		Meeting between Bimandiri and Carrefour: once a year (2) Method of problem solving (1) Method of price determination (3) Risk sharing (1) Level of dependency (1) Sum of value = 8
Carrefour	Meeting between Carrefour and farmers: never (1) Method of problem solving (1) Method of price determination (3) Risk sharing (1) Level of dependency (2) Sum of score = 8	Meeting between Carrefour and KUBM: every delivery of product (3) Method of problem solving (1) Method of price determination (3) Risk sharing (1) Level of dependency (1) Sum of score = 9	Meeting between Bimandiri and Carrefour: once a year (2) Method of problem solving (1) Method of price determination (3) Risk sharing (1) Besarnya Level of dependency (2) Sum of value = 9	

Score: 5–8 = Poor 9–12 = Fair 13–15 = Good

has many sources, (6) no technical assistance is carried out, (7) Seldom have formal communication relation and still focused on purchase, (8) competitive price decision and hidden information, (9) have access to propose credit with payment after product is sold, (10) delayed payment

a.d. 4c: High Trust Chain: (1) long time trading relation, (2) nobody get the price through negotiation, (3) group is more flexible over instruction of production, (4) minor checking at every part, (5) dependency level: some buyers to group and one or two sources by Carrefour, (6) technical assistance is carried out every time, (7) communication is carried out through multi channel, (8) price decision: no competition and open information, (9) no credit aid, (10) delayed payment

Annex 8.8: Performance Changes at Farmers Level before and after Innovation

Change	*Before*	*After*
Source of Input	Individual, input shop, middlemen	Individual, *Bimandiri*, central market
Input use	Should be	Should be
Labor Availability	Standard number	Standard number, only different in using
Cultivation Technology	Be required	Be required
Harvest Technology	No weighing and grading	Weighing and grading
Post harvest Technology	No picking method	Use of picking method
Processing Technology	No processing	No processing
Product Quality	No grading in which all quality is united	30 percent up to 50 percent include belongs to grade AB
Product Quantity	By potential of trees	By potential of trees
Product Distribution	Unorganized delivery product orientation	Delivery product based on market
Time Distribution	No conformity on delivery	Delivery is conformed to demand
Information and Knowledge Distribution	Guided by extension worker who sells pesticide as well	Guided by input supplier, while the role of extension worker was set aside
Market Destination	Central market	Clear market orientation (i.e., central market, modern market, and inter island market)
Extent of Marketing Volume	Depend on production	Targeted, and be able to receive product from non-members group
Marketing Process	Through middlemen, and initiate to carry out self-marketing	Direct access to market
Price, Product Value	One price, no sorting	By grade (off-season), no sorting (on-season)
Production Cost	Production cost only expend on technical cultivation practices, no post harvest treatment	Additional cost in marketing especially for label printing, packing, picking, and packaging

Contd...

Annex 8.8: Contd...

Organization Cost	No organization cost is applied as organization has not been established	There was allocation of money to pay labor in the management of *KUBM*. Some Rp 3,000 for every unit is allocated to finance harvesting, post harvest, and marketing
Innovation Cost	No innovation was applied	There is innovation cost due to many meetings between farmers and targeted market client and cost for promotion as a marketing strategy.
Investment Cost	No investment cost	There is incremental investment cost especially from exclusive farmers (even from outer village) to offer investment collaboration through KUBM
Explicit Subsidy	Not available	Not available
Explicit Subsidy	Not available	Not available
Credit	It can be from middlemen, relation, bank, and Jakarta central market	It can be from middlemen, relation, trader, and Jakarta central market
Number of Stakeholders	Farmers, farmer's group, Syngenta, collector, trader, and Jakarta central market	Farmers, farmer's group, Syngenta, input companies, trader, Jakarta central market, Lampung market, Carrefour, other modern markets, inter island trading market
Role of Stakeholders	Keep farmers being farmers	Encourage farmers to be both farmers and traders
Stakeholders' Rights	No stakeholders' rights	Obtaining all payment from sale of product produced by group after five percent fee for *Bimandiri*. Besides the products sold to *Carrefour*, group can sell the rest products and has the rights to get immediate payment
Stakeholders' Responsibility	No responsibility	Paying five percent to Bimandiri, having strong commitment to obey rules set up by supermarket in terms of quality, quantity, and continuity
Stakeholders' Profit	Limited on the products sold, profit is taken only the farmers are in their profession	More profitable in which profit orientation is based level of farmers, while trader's orientation is profit.
Relationship among Stakeholders	It is limited on transaction commitment with middlemen, without technical assistance provision	Less relationship with middlemen
Internal Organization/ Institution	There is no organization but only association	There is organizations

Contd...

Annex 8.8: Contd...

External Organization/ Institution	Good Relationship	More Competitive
Management	There is no organization management but only individual management	There is a regulation and clear delegation of authority based on the role and function of each component of organization
Product Regulation/Policy	There is no quality standard	There is quality standard
Marketing Regulation/Policy	There is no marketing regulation/policy (free)	There is particular regulation for outside farmers namely *Aspirasi.* It is implemented if both product of inclusive farmers and *aspirasi* enter one market, one should be give in to another one. Otherwise, both can enter but one should follow the regulation. This regulation aims to avoid conflict between parties from the same area.
Contract Regulation/Policy	There is no contract	There is contract in form of MoU between *Bimandiri* and *KUBM*
Organization Regulation/Policy	There is no regulation	Regulation is based on arranged management
Socio-Cultural	Bounded by middlemen (*tengkulak*) with *tebasan* system	More selective towards cash payment with higher price.

Annex 8.9: Historical Innovation

Year	*Event*
1980s	Conventional planting mangoes. On-season mangoes commodity. Certain people planted mangoes. Majority planted *melati.*
1980–1985	Conducted planting mangoes and oranges. Planting oranges were not prospective.
1985	Initiated to plant off-season mangoes.
1987	Government collaborated with one of political parties planting mango seed in Pemalang Regency.
	Planting off-season mangoes was primarily developed in Asem Doyong Village.
1995	Using *ZPT* (*zat perangsang tumbuh*/growth stimulate ingredient)
1997–1998	People recognized technical planting off-season mangoes.
2000–2001	Planting off-season mangoes had spread all over Pemalang Regency. Off-season mangoes had distributed along coastal area.
2002–2003	*Syngenta* was interesting to off-season mangoes in Asem Doyong Village.
	Establishment of spraying farmer's association promoted by input company (*Syngenta*), namely *Aspirasi* "*Bina Usaha*".
2003–2004	Farmer's group was introduced to *Bimandiri.*
2004	Aspirasi group gained loss due to *tebasan* implementation. The detriment becomes debt of group to farmers.
2005	Due to detriment, group was separated into two groups, namely *KUBM* and *Bina Usaha.* Number of inclusion had been changed from 38 persons to six persons.

Contd...

Annex 8.9: Contd...

	1. *KUBM* : *KUBM* was lead by Mr. Dauvi, with eight members. Currently, *KUBM* has 25 hectare of farmland. Bimandiri collaborated with *KUBM* marketing product to modern market. Partnership system "margin transparency" introduced by *Bimandiri* had been continued by *KUBM.* Bimandiri provided technical assistance and fund aid for the group. Market destination was Hero Supermarket and central market. *Bimandiri* and *KUBM* perceived Hero as bad supermarket; therefore, relationship with Hero was discontinued. 2. *Aspirasi* "*Bina Usaha*" Group : Aspirasi group runs continuously and carrying out leadership change with total members of 30 persons. It has 75 hectares of farmland separated in Pemalang, Tegal, and Comang. On December 9, 2005, *Aspirasi* group awarded as the first mango farmer's group champion in Pemalang Regency. After awarding championship, government gave more attention towards farmer's group. Subsequently, government provided farmers with physical and fund aids through the group. Conversely, after awarding championship, farmers perceived that the group became vulnerable.
2006	In the mid of 2006, Carrefour was initially interesting to *KUBM.* Afterward, *KUBM* was provided opportunity by Carrefour. The emergence of other groups : Farmers were dissatisfied with mango farmer's group "Aspirasi Bina Usaha". Consequently, another group was established, namely *Utama* (*Usaha Tani Maju*) group with 15 members.

Annex 8.10: Supply Chain Evolution

Year	*Supply Chain Event*	*Innovation Event*
1980–1985	Starting to plant mango	Changed from low economic plant to high economic plant
1985	Starting to plant off-season mango	Planting mango which previously flowering once a year to be flowering twice a year
1995	Starting to use *ZPT* (*zat perangsang tumbuh*/ growth stimulation hormone)	Using *ZPT* changed productivity particularly in off-season mango production.
2000–2001	Off-season mangoes were spread all over Pemalang, particularly at coastal areas.	Changed labor function, more cultivator farmers.
2003	Input company (*Syngenta*) established spraying farmer's association, namely *Aspirasi* "*Bina Usaha*"	Farmers established farmer's group. There was changed individual system to group system as the first group in the local village.
	Syngenta introduced farmer's group to Bimandiri supplier (*Bimandiri*).	Farmers began to recognize market. There was role change from pure farmers to farmer-trader.
2004	Aspirasi group was introduced to Hero Supermarket.	Farmers began to recognize quality standard of modern market.

Contd...

Annex 8.10: Contd...

	Farmer's group initially implemented quality standard. Hero Supermarket and Bimandiri conducted field observation.	Farmers implemented harvesting and post harvesting technologies (grading, sorting, and packaging).
2005	Aspirasi group was divided into two groups, namely *Aspirasi* (reshuffle output) and *KUBM.* Partnership system "margin transparency" was continued by *KUBM.* *KUBM* carried out reshuffle.	Changed in organization and management.
2006	KUBM was introduced to *Carrefour.* KUBM obtained the opportunity to deliver its product to Carrefour without via horticulture DC of Bimandiri.	Farmers expanded market orientation.

Annex 8.11: Critical Changes that should carry out by each Stakeholder in order to Achieve Succeeded Innovation

Change towards Succeeded Factor	*Inclusive Farmer*	*KUBM Management*	*Bimandiri*	*Carrefour*
Source of input	4	3	4	
Utilization of input	1	1	4	
Labor availability	1	1	4	
Cultivation technology	1	1	4	
Harvesting technology	4	3	4	
Post harvesting technology	4	3	4	
Processing technology	1	1	4	
Product quality	4	3	4	
Product quantity	1	3	4	
Product distribution	4	4	4	
Time distribution	4	3	4	
Information/knowledge distribution	4	3	4	
Marketing destination	4	2	4	
Percentage of marketing volume	4	2	4	
Marketing method	4	4	4	
Price, product value	4	2	4	
Production cost	1	3	4	
Organization cost	1	4	4	
Innovation cost	1	3	4	
Investment cost	2	4	4	
Explicit subsidy	1	1	3	
Implicit subsidy	1	1	3	
Credit	2	4	4	
Stakeholders' role	4	3	4	

Contd...

Annex 8.11: Contd...

Change towards Succeeded Factor	*Inclusive Farmer*	*KUBM Management*	*Bimandiri*	*Carrefour*
Stakeholders' rights	4	4	4	
Stakeholders' responsibility	4	4	4	
Stakeholders' profit	4	3	4	
Stakeholders' relationship	4	4	4	
Internal organization/institution	4	3	4	
External organization/institution	2	2	4	
Management	4	4	4	
Product regulation/policy	4	3	4	
Marketing regulation/policy	4	4	4	
Contract regulation/policy	4	2	4	
Organization regulation/policy	4	3	4	
Socio-cultural	4	3	4	

Annex 8.12: Median Value of Critical Change that should be conducted by each Stakeholder in order to Achieve Succeeded Innovation

Item	*Stakeholders*			
	Inclusive Farmer	*KUBM Management*	*Bimandiri*	*Carrefour*
Farm production input	2,5	2	4	
Labor availability	1	1	4	
Technology	2,5	2	4	
Product	2,5	3	4	
Distribution	4	3	4	
Marketing	4	2	4	
Financial	1	3	4	
Subsidy	1	1	3	
Credit	2	4	4	
Stakeholders	4	4	4	
Organization/institution	3	2,5	4	
Management	4	4	4	
Regulation/policy	4	3	4	
Socio-cultural	4	3	4	

Note: 4 = very important change
3 = important change
2 = moderate important change
1 = less important change

Annex 8.13: Skills, Competency and Capacity owned by Inclusive Farmers, and not owned by Exclusive Farmers so that they can be Eliminated from Innovation Process.

Ability	*Inclusion*	*Exclusion*	*Impact*
Skills	– Skills in technical cultivation on-season and off-season mangoes technical due to inclusion can be categorized as initiator in planting mangoes. – Searching alternative market. – Skills in obtaining information – Each farmer has different role, therefore, farmer's role should be based on farmer's skills.	– Only have skills in technical mangoes cultivation.	– Skills in technical cultivation is not sufficient in carrying out partnership system. – Who are not having skills except technical cultivation skills will not be able carrying out innovation.
Competency	– Deliver product on time and appropriately – Competency in expanding market. – Competency in expanding cultivation farmland (carrying out investment locally).	– Do not have guarantor in achieving certain market access that can helpful in all activities. – Individualistic, low capital, depending on trader and middlemen. – Accomplishing market demand timely based on the availability of production.	– With limited competency towards guarantor, market orientation become changeable, therefore, there is no certain and market orientation continuity. – Limited activity due to depending on capital of middlemen and trader. – Individualist characte-ristic can influence market capital, volume, selling capacity, and obtained selling price. – Inclusive farmers have privilege. – More expand market opportunity. – Anticipating market aspiration (consumers). – Production opportunity of inclusive farmers is higher than that of exclusive farmers.
Capacity	– Commitment – Responsible – Expert in technical cultivation – Experienced	– There is no commitment – There is no responsibility – Lack of optimal function and role of each member in organization	– In this innovation, commitent is important part that should be owned by group. – Less trust from buyers about quality, quantity, and continuity products.

Annex 8.14: Development Steps of Supply Chain Innovation and Evolution

Step-1: Identifying Stakeholders in Innovation Development

1. Farmers
2. *KUBM/KUBM* farmers
3. RPO management
4. *Bimandiri*
5. *Carrefour*
6. *Aspirasi* "*Bina Usaha*" group
7. Local market actors
8. Central market actors
9. Government
10. Agricultural extension workers
11. *Syngenta*
12. Other private sectors

Step-2. Identifying Characteristic of each Stakeholder

Stakeholders	*Basic*	*Location*	*Function*	*Time-generation*
Farmer	Men, rich/poor, young/old	Rural, near to the issue	Producer	Past, present, future generation
KUBM	Men, rich, young	Rural, near to the issue	Producer	Present, future generation
RPO management Bimandiri	men, rich, young men, rich, young	Rural, near to the issue Urban, near to the issue	Producer and trader Supplier	Present, future generation Present, future generation
Carrefour	Men, rich, young	Urban, near to the issue	Supermarket	Present, future generation
Aspirasi group	Men, rich, young	Rural, near to the issue	Producer	Past, present, future generation
Local market actor	Men, rich/poor, young/old	Rural, far away	Trader	Past, present, future generation
Central market actor Government	Men, rich, young/ old Men/women, rich/poor, young/old	Urban, far away Urban, far away	Trader Policy maker	Past, present, future generation Past, present, future generation
Extension worker	Men, rich/poor, young	Rural, far away	Governance	Past, present, future generation
Syngenta	Men, rich/poor, young	Urban, far away	Private sector	Past generation
Other private sectors	Men, rich, young	Urban, far away	Private sector	Present, future generation

Annex 8.14: (*continued*)

Step-3: Identifying Role of each Stakeholder in Innovation

Stakeholder's Role	*Farmer*	*KUBM Group*	*KUBM Management*	*Bimandiri*	*Carrefour*	*Aspirasi Actor*	*Local Group Market*	*Central Market Actor*	*Govern-ment*	*Extension Worker*	*Syngenta*	*Other Private Sectors*
Funding owner	✓	✓	✓	✓	✓	✓	✓	✓		✓	✓	
Funding receiver	✓	✓	✓	✓	✓	✓	✓	✓	✓	✓	✓	✓
Opposing	✓					✓				✓		
No comment	✓						✓	✓	✓			
Mobilizing		✓	✓	✓	✓	✓					✓	✓
Responding		✓	✓	✓	✓	✓					✓	✓
Conducting change		✓	✓	✓	✓	✓						

Annex 8.14: (*continued*)

Step-4: Carrying out occurrence problems mapping and observing role and position of stakeholders facing problems

Based on field data, there were two significant problems during innovation and evolution development. They were:

1. Problems on initial innovation :

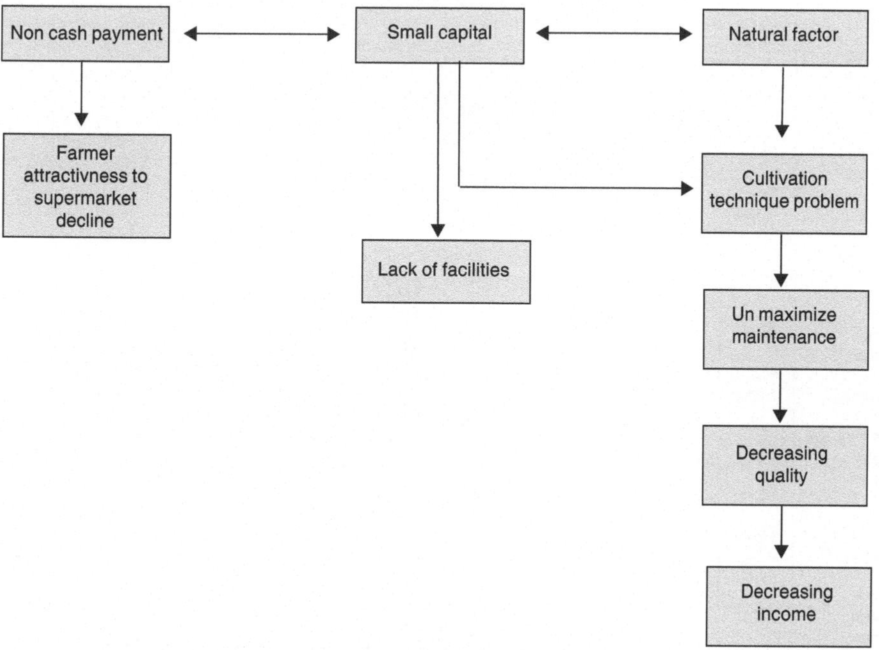

2. Problems on innovation development :

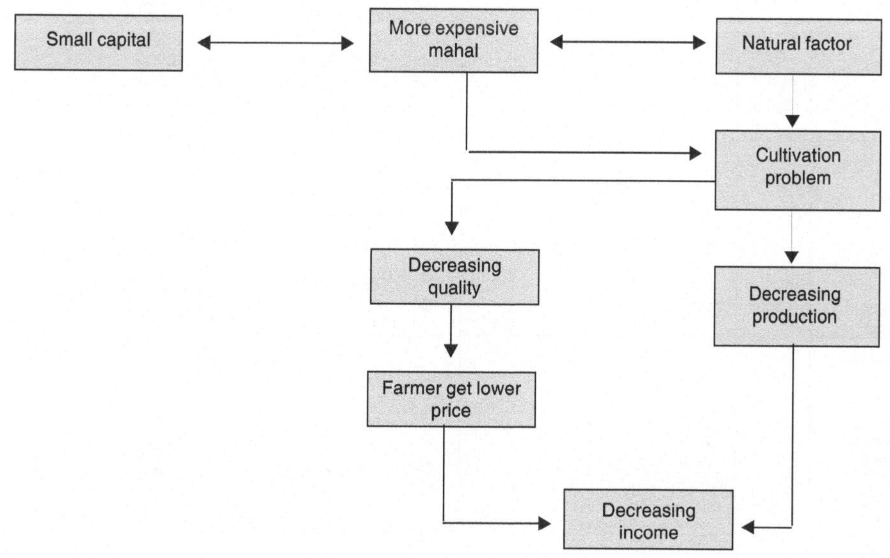

Annex 8.15: Mangoes Value Chain in Pemalang, Central Java, Indonesia

No.	*Chain Actor and Activity*	*Unit*	*Farmers-KUBM-Carrefour*		*Farmers-KUBM-Wholesale Traditional Market-Retail Traditional Market*		*Farmers-Collector-KUBM-Carrefour*		*Farmers-Collector-KUBM-Wholesale Traditional Market-Retail Traditional Market*		*Farmers-Collector-ASP-Wholesale Traditional Market-Retail Traditional Market*		*Farmers-ASP-Wholesale Traditional Market-Retail Traditional Market*	
		Season	*Off-Season*	*On-Season*	*Off-Season*	*On-Season*	*Off-Season*	*On-Season*	*Off-Season*	*On-Season*	*Off-Season*	*On-Season*	*Off-Season*	*On-Season*
		Chain	1A	1B	2A	2B	3A	3B	4A	4B	8A	8B	9A	9B
I	A. *KUBM* farmers													
	Total Cost	Rp/kg	1,326	1,308	1,326	1,308								
		%	(37)	(40)	(29)	(42)								
	Value Added	Rp/kg	7,674	192	4,674	192								
		%	(67)	(3)	(60)	(10)								
	Selling Price	Rp/kg	9,000	1,500	6,000	1,500								
	B. Free Farmer													
	Total Cost	Rp/kg					974	974	974	974	974	974		
		%					(29)	(32)	(22)	(34)	(22)	(34)		
	Value Added	Rp/kg					3,026	226	3,026	226	3,026	226		
		%					(26)	(4)	(37)	(10)	(37)	(10)		
	Selling Price	Rp/kg					4,000	1,200	4,000	1,200	4,000,00	1,200,00		
	C. ASP Farmer													
	Total Cost	Rp/kg											890	890
		%											(21)	(32)
	Value Added	Rp/kg											4,297	610
		%											(52)	(26)
	Selling Price	Rp/kg											5,188	1,500,00
II	Collector :													
	Total Cost	Rp/kg					128	128	128	128	128	128		
		%					(4)	(4)	(3)	(4)	(3)	(4)		
	Value Added	Rp/kg					4,872	172	1,872	172	1,060	172		
		%					(42)	(3)	(23)	(8)	(13)	(8)		
	Selling Price	Rp/kg					9,000	1,500	6,000	1,500,00	5,188	1,500,00		
III	*KUBM* :													
	Total Cost	Rp/kg	1,756	1,461	2,193	1,595	1,732	1,420	2,168	1,553				
		%	(49)	(44)	(48)	(51)	(52)	(47)	(50)	(54)				
	Value Added	Rp/kg	1,244	3,039	1,141	84	1,268	3,080	1,165	126				
		%	(11)	(53)	(15)	(4)	(11)	(52)	(14)	(6)				
	Selling Price	Rp/kg	12,000	6,000	9,333	3,179	12,000	6,000	9,333	3,179				
IV	*Aspirasi*													
	Total Cost	Rp/kg									2,180	1,565	2,255	1,639
		%									(50)	(54)	(54)	(59)
	Value Added	Rp/kg									1,965	114	1,891	39
		%									(24)	(5)	(23)	(2)
	Selling Price	Rp/kg									9,333	3,179	9,333	3,179

Contd...

Annex 8.15: Contd...

No.	*Chain Actor and Activity*	*Unit*	*Farmers-KUBM-Carrefour*		*Farmers-KUBM-Wholesale Traditional Market-Retail Traditional Market*		*Farmers-Collector-KUBM-Carrefour*		*Farmers-Collector-KUBM-Wholesale Traditional Market-Retail Traditional Market*		*Farmers-Collector-ASP-Wholesale Traditional Market-Retail Traditional Market*		*Farmers-ASP-Wholesale Traditional Market-Retail Traditional Market*	
		Season	*Off-Season*	*On-Season*	*Off-Season*	*On-Season*	*Off-Season*	*On-Season*	*Off-Season*	*On-Season*	*Off-Season*	*On-Season*	*Off-Season*	*On-Season*
		Chain	1A	1B	2A	2B	3A	3B	4A	4B	8A	8B	9A	9B
V	Wholesale Traditional Market													
	Total Cost	Rp/kg			228	32			228	32	228	32	228	32
		%			(5)	(1)			(5)	(1)	(5)	(1)	(5)	(1)
	Value Added	Rp/kg			706	286			706	286	706	286	706	286
		%			(9)	(15)			(9)	(13)	(9)	(13)	(9)	(12)
	Selling	Rp/kg Price			9,333	3,179			9,333	3,179	9,333	3,179	9,333	3,179
VI	Retail Trade Market :													
	Total Cost	Rp/kg			839	198			839	198	839	198	839	198
		%			(18)	(6)			(19)	(7)	(19)	(7)	(20)	(7)
	Value Added	Rp/kg			1,328	1,409			1,328	1,409	1,328	1,409	1,328	1,409
		%			(17)	(71)			(16)	(63)	(16)	(64)	(16)	(60)
	Selling Price	Rp/kg			11,500	4,786			11,500	4,786	11,500	4,786	11,500	4,786
VII	*Carrefur:*													
	Total Cost	Rp/kg	520,000	520,00			520,00	520,00						
		%	(14)	(16)			(16)	(17)						
	Value Added	Rp/kg		2,480,00		2,480,	2,480	2,480						
	%		(22)	(43)		(21)	(42)							
	Selling Price	Rp/kg	15,0000	9,000			15,000	9,000						
	TOTAL COST	Rp/kg	3,601	3,289	4,584	3,133	3,353	3,041	4,336	2,884	4,348	2,896	4,211	2,759
	TOTAL VALUE ADDED	9 Rp/kg	11,39	5,711	7,849	1,971	11,647	5,959	8,098	2,220	8,086	2,208	8,222	2,344

9

Keys to Inclusion of Small-Scale Producers in Dynamic Potato Market in Thailand: CMK Housewives' Group

Aree Wiboonpongse, Songsak Sriboonchitta and Puttawan Khuntonthong

Potato was introduced as a cash crop in Thailand about 45 years ago. Production concentrated mainly in northern Thailand. In Chiang Maia,[1] the first location of low land potato production has experienced major changes in production and marketing.

Table type potato is one of a few crops for which the Thai government implemented supply control policy. For this purpose, the Potato Growers Cooperative was formed to determine annual amount of tuber seed imports and to decide on seed quota for its members. As for processing type potato, the government allowed firms to import tuber seed for processing. Like other new industrial crops, potato was planted partly by firms and mostly by contracted growers. Contract farming in potato is one of the successful cases of this system for agricultural development of small and resource poor farmers. The integration of farm production with processing firms provided market access to farmers and reduced price risk.

Because of the rapid increase in demand for French fries and snack chips, area under potato has expanded in the past 10 years. Processing firms have extended their contracts to many provinces in the north and three provinces in the northeast. While the contract system of potato has spread to new areas, the original site of contract potato began to leave the system. However, these growers remain part of the supply chain. Does this withdrawal imply failure of the contract system and exclusion of growers from the supply chain? It is the purpose of this paper to find answer to this question. We define departure from contract farming as the main innovation. The second innovation is pertaining to management of a women's group processing defective produce.

Potato Sector in Thailand

Farmers in the lowlands in Thailand had experimented with potato cultivation in the cool season for many years. They found the crop most profitable and thus adopted it in their cropping system for over 45 years. Both government and non-government agencies began to realize potato's potentials and took steps to improve production and promote varietal trials. Consequently, a large number of cultivars were tried out in the farmers' fields and experimental stations.

[1] Chiang Mai is the second largest city of Thailand and is a tourist attraction. It is over 700 years old and is the capital city of the Northern region.

Because of the growth of tourism in the early 80s, demand for potato by hotels and restaurants increased considerably. In 1976, a factory was set up to produce potato chips to catch the early trend of snacks business. However, the firm faced unstable and limited supply of the raw material. To solve the problem, the firm started to make contracts with growers in 1987 for the first time in Chiang Mai. The selected variety was Kenebec (DOA, 2005).

Northern Thailand has been the major production centre for potatoes. In the 70s and 80s it accounted for as much as 80 per cent of production. In 2005, the area was 12,233 acres and about 95 per cent of planted area was in the north. Production reached 97,411 tons (in 2005). Presently, potato is ranked as a major crop of the north, especially in Chiang Mai, Tak, and Chiang Rai provinces. It also began to gain attention in the three provinces in the northeast (Table 9.1).

Processing type potatoes accounted for 90 per cent of total production. While land under table potato declined, the processing type has gained more land in the past three years. Certainty of market as well as absorption by the processing industry is the key reasons for the increase. Three years averages of yield were 2,380 kg/rai (8.33 ton/acre) and 2,227 kg/rai (the table type has 7 per cent higher yield) (Table 9.2).

Table 9.1: Potato Production by Provinces

		Area (rai)			*Total Production (ton)*			*Yield (kg/rai)*		
		2003	2004	2005	2003	2004	2005	2003	2004	2005
	Whole country	42,184	43,890	42,817	86,732	99,813	97,411	2,081	2,291	2,288
North	Chiang Rai	2,173	2,834	2,818	3,392	5,750	5,743	1,592	2,068	2,053
	Lampang	875	2,241	2,180	1,289	3,169	3,087	1,494	1,422	1,422
	Lamphun	1,299	1,723	1,688	1,786	2,843	2,802	1,703	1,738	1,695
	Chiang Mai	23,043	1,833	21,080	44,237	52,785	51,216	1,930	2,438	2,444
	Tak	12,279	13,192	13,042	30,054	29,613	29,211	2,461	2,245	2,247
Northeast	Loey	292	400	382	825	1,481	1,404	2,825	3,703	3,724
	Nongkai	1,301	700	695	3,099	1,960	1,888	2,382	2,800	2,744
	Sakhonakorn	922	967	932	2,050	2,212	2,060	2,223	2,287	2,222

Note: 2.5 rai = 1 acre.

Source: Office of Agricultural Economics, 2006.

Table 9.2: Production of Table and Processing Potato

Variety/Year	*Planted Area (rai)*			*Production (ton)*			*Yield (ton/rai)*		
	2003	2004	2005	2003	2004	2005	2003	2004	2005
Table	6256	5,527	4,427	11,880	14,338	11,759	1.90	2.59	2.66
Processing	35,928	38,363	43,067	74,852	85,475	102,122	2.08	2.23	2.37

Note: 2.5 rai = 1 acre.

Source: Office of Agricultural Economics, 2006.

Cultivation of Potato

Although the northern region generally has favourable environment for potato production, production is limited to certain areas. Potato requires sandy soil, good water condition throughout the growing season, and night temperature between 15 and 18 degree Celsius. The crop grown in the cool season (short day length) is harvested faster than the crop grown in the hot season. With these requirements, potato is found in the low lands and some of the highlands in various provinces in the north and northeast.

Potato supply comes mainly from the lowlands (300 meters above sea level) where most farmers grow potato after the main season rice crop starting from November-December (cool season) and harvest in February-March. Farmers may choose to grow Spunta (table type) and/or Atlantic (processing type which replaced Kenebec cultivar).

Farmers in San Sai (the original site of contract potato cultivation) and some other well irrigated districts grow three crops a year, i.e. potato after the rice crop (July-October) and then sweet corn/baby corn (April-June) on the same potato land. This cropping system appears to be most suitable and allows farmers to grow potato year after year without a need to change plots in order to avoid pests and diseases.

Most of highland potato comes from Tak province and some districts in Chiang Mai and the north-eastern provinces. At the altitude of 800–1,500 meters above sea level it is possible to grow potato in rain-fed areas. Growers in the up/highlands produce two potato crops on the same plots. The main season is also in the early cool season which is contracted with processing firms. Growers take risk to grow a second crop (in rainy season) when climatic condition is not favourable; this results in lower yield and poorer quality. As expected, more disease accumulation causes crop damage after two consecutive years of production. It should be noted that no firms made contract with growers for the rainy crop.

Table 9.3: Cropping Systems in Lowlands and Highlands

	Jan	*Feb*	*Mar*	*Apr*	*May*	*June*	*July*	*Aug*	*Sep*	*Oct*	*Nov*	*Dec*
Highland	Potato				Potato				Chinese cabbage or corn		Potato	
Lowland	Potato			Corn			Rice				Potato	

Potato Growers

Unlike most contract growers in general, potato growers in San Sai district, the original site of the crop, were not the resource least farmers. In the past 40 years they were among those with good irrigated land and apt to exploit economic opportunities relative to most farmers as the district is located within 20 km from Chiang Mai city. However, the average farm size in the upper north is smallest; particularity in Chiang

Mai province the average is approximately 4 acres (10 rai). In the lower north where agricultural land is less mountainous, the farm size, in general, averages more than threefold.

Table 9.4 highlights sampled potato growers' characteristics for both Chiang Mai and Tak provinces. Contract growers in Chiang Mai refer to growers in Mae Tang district while non-contract growers are sample growers in the original site, i.e. San Sai district. As for Tak, most of non-contract growers were contracted for the cool season crop.

Farmers hold too small a land to earn sufficient income. Thus 80 per cent potato growers in Chiang Mai rented land (totally or partially). Most of the growers in Tak cultivated their crop in the recently intruded public land. They usually hold only the "land-use right" which is eligible for land ownership.

Potato production in Tak is three to five times larger than that in Chiang Mai. Production experience ranges from 2 to 13 years indicating a mix of the first to third (the present) generation of growers (also indicated by ages of growers). Evidently, the oldest growers still continue potato production in San Sai. Average total income of four groups of growers varied in relation to production size.

Table 9.4: Potato Growers' Characteristics in Chiang Mai and Tak Provinces

	No. of Growers	*Potato Planted Land (Rai)*	*Potato Growing Experience (Year)*	*Age of Grower*	*Total Income from Potato (Baht/Year)*
CF in Chiang Mai	30	3.14	5.10	44.70	99,000
SD		1.88	3.72	15.64	54,350
NCF in Chiang Mai	34	4.74	8.50	46.15	133,400
SD		2.09	4.53	9.61	62,623
CF in Tak	16	13.67	8.69	35.60	155,500
SD		11.00	3.41	8.07	85,276
NCF in Tak	14	12.14	6.43	34.07	110,000
SD		9.69	3.54	8.93	61,644

Source: Survey, 2006

Note : Area is expressed in rai (2.5 rai = 1 acre); income is in baht/year (40 baht = 1 US $).

CF = Contract Farming, NCF = Non-Contract Farming

Demand for Potato

Life style of Thais has changed rapidly in the past 10–15 years and even faster than other countries in the region. This is seen in the expansion of modern retail stores and shopping habits (Wiboonpongse and Sriboonchitta, 2005) as well as widespread western fast food chains.

At the initial stage, potato production expanded slowly as production was absorbed by the fresh market and because of slow growth in demand for processed potato. Because of the change in consumption style, demand for potato snacks and western fast food has increased rapidly over the past decade. Growth of consumption of French fires and potato crisps is estimated at 30–50 per cent per year from 1992 to 1995. Further, demand for potato of the processing company increased from 118,000 tons in 1997/98 to 165,390 tons in 2005 (this includes all forms of potato materials, i.e. fresh chilled/frozen, flour/meal and powder, flakes, starch etc). The highest record was 171,500 tons in 2003 (Table 9.5).

Processing firms supply potato snacks to Thailand and neighbouring countries in Southeast Asia (USDA, 2004).

Thais consume potato products in two forms: snacks (chip, crackers etc.) and table potato cooked in soup and curry. From the surveys, it is estimated that demand (Thai and tourists) for table potato approximated 4,135 tons in 2005 (domestic production available for consumption was only 2,725 tons)

The first form shares 90 per cent of the total supply (domestic and import). Thailand is known as the largest market for snacks in Asia-Pacific. In 2003, value of snacks consumption reached US $ 280 million (USDA, 2004).

There are 2,000 brands of potato snacks on shelves. In 2002, snacks made of potato flour and granules gained the highest share (35 per cent) in the snacks market followed by crisp chips (30 per cent). Other main snacks including peas/nut, shrimp crackers, and fish snacks share 10 per cent each (Figure 9.1).

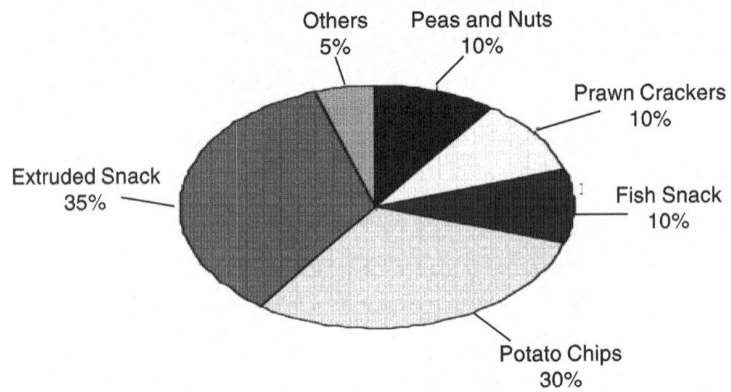

Fig. 9.1: Market Shares of Snacks in 2002

Source : USDA, 2004

For crisp chips alone, the value was as high as 308 billion baht in 2005. The processing firms forecast that the market for this particular product would increase by at least 10 per cent annually for 2006 and 2007. Despite the attractive figure of growth, consumption per head is only 1 kg a year which is less than 50 per cent of that in Korea or Japan (USDA, 2004: http: Siamturakij, 2006).

Because of high substitutability among snacks, product price receives top priority in consumers' decision of which brand to buy (USDA, 2004). Processing firms therefore attempt to keep their cost at competitive level.

Although snacks are consumed throughout the year, there appears to be distinct seasonality. The high rates of turnover coincided with festivals such as Christmas, New Year (both in December-January and April, the Thai New Year) as well as the period of super sports e.g. Football World Cup (interview with firms, 2006). With the exception when special events are telecast, demand for snacks declines during the high fruit season.

Market Share in the Potato Snacks Business

According to USDA (2004), four brands are well-known in Thailand: Frito-Lay and Barli held 65 per cent and 20 per cent share of the chip market in 2003. (Figure 9.2). The share of Frito-Lay might be underestimated; the Pepsi Company believed it had over 70 per cent share of chips in the Thai market.

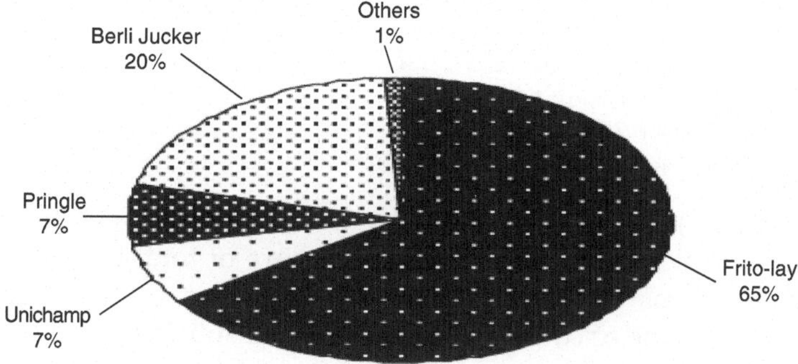

Fig. 9.2: Market Shares of Potato Chip in 2002

Source: USDA, 2004

Import Demand for Potato

In spite of the fact that potato snacks are not native to Thais, consumption of and demand for potato in Thailand is far beyond domestic production (USDA, 2004).

In 2005 the total output was about 97,410 tons, while demand totalled 1,65,000 tons (Office of Agricultural Economics, 2006: Department of Customs). Thus imports accounted for 41 per cent of total demand in 2005 (Table 9.5).

Thailand imports potato and various forms of products from 23 countries. The import value has gradually increased during the past five years from 1,250 to 1,438 million baht (40 baht = 1 US $). The value of fresh potato in the consumption figures in the past three years (starting 2003) shows a decline from 210 to 150 million baht. Value of imported seeds seems to remain rather stable. Potato starch is a notable item. Its value reached 561 million baht in 2005 (Appendix 9.1). Potato starch and inulin are important inputs for snacks industry. As the demand for snacks continues growing, it is expected that import of this item will tend to rise. Thailand depends only on two sources, Germany and Netherlands for imports of starch and inulin. Five top important sources of fresh potato are England (30 per cent), Australia (28 per cent),

Table 9.5 : Demand for Potato in Thailand and Imports (1000 tons)

Year	*Domestic Production*[1]	*Import*[2]	*Total Demand*	*Percentage of Domestic Production to Total Demand*	*Percentage of Import Potato to Total Demand*
1996	65.14	25.39	90.53	71.95	28.05
1997	89.55	28.45	118.00	75.89	24.11
1998	93.78	29.81	123.59	75.88	24.12
1999	90.38	35.40	125.78	71.86	28.14
2000	100.12	48.39	148.51	67.42	32.58
2001	90.94	43.13	134.07	67.83	32.17
2002	97.37	43.28	140.65	69.23	30.77
2003	86.73	84.77	171.50	50.57	49.43
2004	99.81	63.38	163.19	61.16	38.84
2005	97.41	67.98	165.39	58.90	41.10

Source: [1] Office of Agricultural Economics, 2006
[2] Department of Customs, Thailand : BAAC
Calculated by using quantity of fresh and processing potato.

Canada (16.2 per cent), China (9.8 per cent), and Germany (Appendix 9.2). Recently, import from Laos ranks sixth with 5.2 per cent share of total import. Laos growers are contracted by firms in Thailand as a consequence of the ACMECS policy (collaborative programme of countries in the Mekong Sub-region). Thailand imports seed for table potato mainly from the Netherlands and for processing from England, Australia, and the United States.

In 2003 because of the drop in domestic production, two largest firms decided to lay off some employees. The pressure stemmed from low supply during the rainy season. The government was requested to reduce the import tariff and increase quota for fresh potato. The tariff was reduced from 124 per cent to 27 per cent during July to December. (USDA, 2004 Department of Customs, 2006).

Government Policy on Contract Farming

A number of studies have reviewed the success and failure of the contract farming experience in Thailand. These include Manarangsan of Suwanjindar (1992), Laramee (1975), Gedgaew (1993), Glover (1992), Wiboonpongse and Sriboonchitta (1995), Bloomfield *et al.*, (1996) as well as several studies carried out by the Office of Agricultural Economics (OAE, 1989, 1991, 1993).

The private sector in Thailand had practiced contract farming long before it was formally defined. According to Golver, Thailand contract practices were far advanced in relative to the practices in other countries in the region. As far as public policy is concerned, contract farming was first implemented in the Sixth National Economic and Social Development Plan (1987–91). The agricultural development policy included guidelines for development of agro-industries, which had objectives to promote export and import substitute commodities through improving quality and management system, to assist agro-industrial plants in transferring appropriate technology to farmers, and to support farmers in production planning. In order to augment the guidelines, the Thai government formulated the so-called "Four-Sector Cooperation Plan to Develop Agriculture and Agro-industry" (four-sector plan). Agroindustrial firms, farmers, financial institutions (Bank for Agriculture and Agricultural Cooperatives, BAAC) and government agencies worked together. The plan aimed at improving the production system so as to reduce price risk, market uncertainty, and improve farmers' technical knowledge and in turn raise production efficiency.

Implementation of bilateral Free Trade Agreements (FTA) between Thailand and China (2004) and more recently the agreements made with Australia and New Zealand greatly affected the garlic and dairy sectors in the north. To alleviate the controversial FTA, the government set forth to compensate farmers who switched from garlic to other crops in a contract system. In May 2006, the MOAC announced contract farming as a strategy for agricultural restructuring (Manager Newspaper, 2006). Five commodities affected by were listed: bell pepper, asparagus, potato (to replace garlic and onion), garlic and cattle (dairy and meat) to be produced in contract with processing firms (rather than producing in the usually non-contract market).

Potato Supply Chain

Potato is one of the crops having short distribution channels. Ninety per cent of production (Atlantic cultivar) goes to processing firms located in the north and only 10 per cent (Spunta) goes to the fresh market.

Table Potato

Supply of table potato has been controlled since the crop became commercial. To limit supply and monitor the supply control, the government set up 12 province companies. Two potato cooperatives, one in San Sai (Chiang Mai Potato Growers Cooperative: CPGC) and the other in northern district (Fang Potato and Garlic Growers Cooperative: FPGGC) are responsible for management. The government permits import of 302 tons/year of Spunta seed with tariff exemption. Both cooperatives decide the amount of seed to be imported and the price basing on demand in the previous year. The purpose of supply control is to avoid undesirable farm price.

CPGC serves 3,544 members. From interviews with the CPGC leader and members, only 2,500 members have been actively contacting the coop. In 2005, about 1,500 members wanted potato seed. As for FPGGC, 50 per cent of its members (the total of 1500 members) wanted potato seed. Each member of both cooperatives was allocated 50 kg of Spunta seed in 2005 which is enough for only about 800 square meter of land (or 0.22 acre). Optimum land as indicated by members is 10 rais (4 acres) and this requires a minimum of 90 kg of seed/rai. This size is expected to be suitable for investment because of high production risk (in the case that farmers rely solely on the crop and because Spunta is less disease resistant). This issue arises every year between members and cooperatives. There is no solution to the problem. However, when a farmer member seriously decides to grow Spunta, other members in the family can also apply for membership to obtain their quotas. Also seed can be purchased from other coop members. Quite often the grantees resell their quotas to local middlemen who assemble for actual growers. Thus the price of resold Spunta seed goes up by 15–25 baht/kg on top of the cooperative price.

Imported seed from the Netherlands (c.i.f. price) costs 40–45 baht/kg. The cooperatives charged 55 baht/kg from their members. Seed arrive in Chiang Mai at the end of October and will be ready for planting in November.

The procedure for obtaining seed quota approval and import is long as depicted in the Appendix 9.3. The whole process requires six months. In practice, import quota would be approved, thus the cooperatives usually inform foreign seed exporters in advance (for seed production delivery in November). Beside, the imported seed, in recent years some growers have tried to keep their own seed. In 2005, it was estimated that 700 tons out of the total production of 3,425 tons were stored for seed. However, these seeds performed rather poorly. According to growers, the yield was reported to be only 25 per cent of that produced from imported seeds.

Wholesalers & Retailers and Marketing Channel

Local assemblers brought the quota seed from coop members (70 per cent of grantees do not grow Spunta) and sold it to growers in the up/highlands. After harvesting the same assemblers bought produce back and sold it to wholesalers in Bangkok.

Presently, several professional assemblers own cold storage facilities. This helps in stretching Spunta supply throughout the year. Prior to having cold storage, Spunta potatoes were stacked on the ground and could be stored for only two months. Imports of table potatoes from China normally enter the Thai market during June–August (rainy season). Cold storage technology allows farmers to grow Spunta in three different altitudes of land (up/high/low lands) and harvest in different months.

Total production of Spunta in the north was estimated at 3,425 tons from 137 tons of import seeds and 700 tons of farmers' collected seeds. Assemblers bought table potato from both seed sources in two methods. The first method is to pay a flat price for ungraded potato. The price is based on quality. The other method is to pay prices for grades A, B and C. Prices reported by the growers in 2006 were 14–16 baht/kg for A, 7 baht for grade B, and 9 baht for C respectively.

Potatoes purchased from growers are stocked in cold storage. Local assemblers supply Spunta to Bangkok wholesalers only when they receive orders. Local assemblers were not keen to know the size of demand by final buyers. Figure 9.3 shows the marketing distribution channels. Bangkok wholesalers absorb 80 per cent of table potato which subsequently goes to hotels/restaurants and retailers. Despite

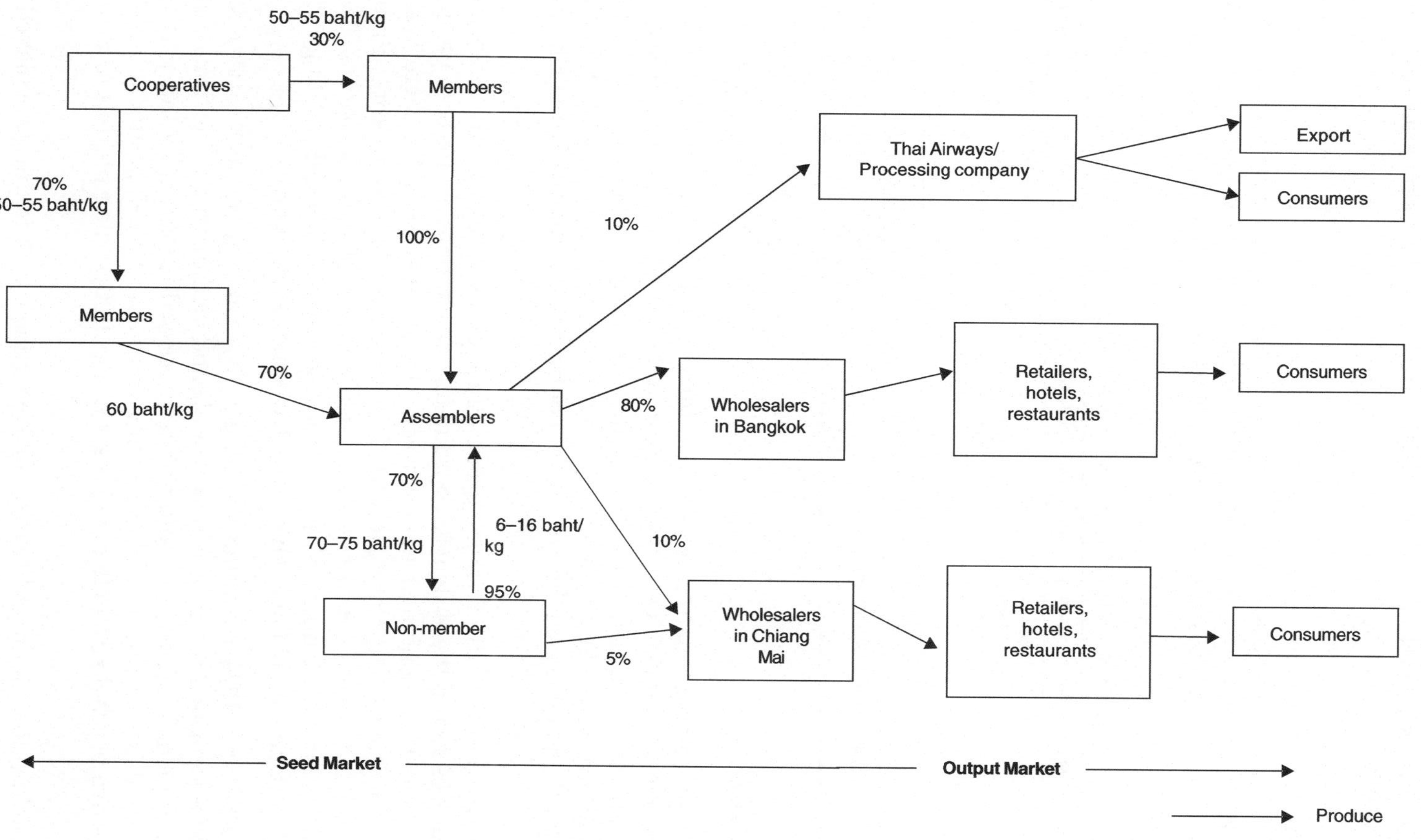

Fig. 9.3: Marketing Channel for Table Potato and Prices

supply control, prices of table potato fluctuated from year to year depending on tourist movements.

Spunta is available through domestic production and imports. The first cold storage facility was started in 1992 in San Sai and the number increased to 11 in 2006. This enables assemblers to keep Spunta produce from both up/highland and low land (as well as import from China) to meet demand throughout the year (Table 9.5). The other main task of the cold storage facilitators is to store the seed of the processing type (Atlantic variety).

Table 9.6: Seasonal Supply of Spunta (Table) Potato

	Feb	*Mar*	*Apr*	*May*	*Jun*	*Jul*	*Aug*	*Sep*	*Oct*	*Nov*	*Dec*	*Jan*
Planting period				Off season on high land						Low land and high land		
Harvesting period		Low land/high land					High land					
Import					Import from China							
Supply from storage		Supply from cool storage						Storage of import and cool storage				

Source : Interview, 2006.

Processing Potato

In 1987, when processing potato was first introduced in the San Sai area, farmers in the north became acquainted with the contract system. Like other contract crops, at the adoption stage farmers lacked sufficient technical know-how on potato cultivation and production inputs especially seed. The success of contract farming in the 80s was partly made known by the case of contract potato cultivation in Chiang Mai.

The firms made contracts with farmers' groups through local agricultural extension offices. The offices served the system as coordinators and supporters for both parties and ensured that they honoured the contracts (Figure 9.4). In 1995, there were altogether eight groups of potato growers working with three processing firms. However, in 2001, the contracts were terminated because of various reasons. The processing firms provided financial support for seminars, technical meetings for farmers, and visits to annual fairs, which directly benefited growers.

During 1993–94 and 1994–95 farmers received the same guaranteed prices for different grades from all firms, 5.50 baht/kg for big and medium sizes. The firms paid 1.70 baht/kg for small size which could not be processed for chips. By this pricing agreement and contract arrangement, processing firms absorbed all production. This carried a positive psychological effect to most farmers in that their produce was not left unsold.

Recently, Mae Jo University together with the Department of Agriculture achieved a major contribution on mechanical harvesting of potato which saves labour. As import of seed takes long and is expensive (30 baht/kg in 2005), an attempt to produce tuber seed domestically has been carried out by Chiang Mai University in collaboration with the Royal Project Foundation and a processing firm. Mini tuber seed of Atlantic cultivar has been successfully produced via tissue culture. However, as a substitute for import, it requires further efforts to bring the cost down to an effective level (interviews with firms and brokers, 2006).

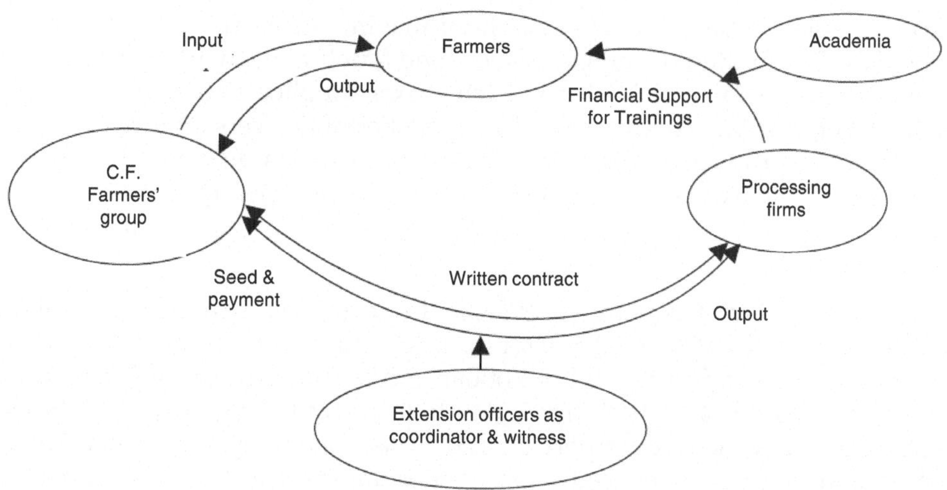

Fig. 9.4: Small Growers' Linkage in the Supply Chain of Processing Potato

Source: Wiboonpongse *et al.* (1998).

Case Study 1: Response of Small Growers to Dynamic Market Environment

Contracts appeared and continued in several sectors and in various parts of Thailand including processing potato in the north. However as observed by Sriboonchitta and Wiboonpongse (2005), marketing practices of potato growers in the case study area (San Sai, the original site of potato contract) had gradually changed. Most growers (in 2004) either bought the seed from firms via brokers or used their own seed. They no longer had contract selling but rather sold their potato to brokers at prevailing market prices.

The innovation at this point was seed storage which enabled small growers to have production and marketing alternatives. It is one of the major objectives of this paper to investigate the causes of this reverse relationship of growers and processors in the supply chain. As hypothesized, a crucial factor of success in the contract system is quasi-monopsonistic condition (Glover and Ghee, 1992). Other studies also indicate that the competitive environment and volatility of Thai markets were not conducive to the contract system. As for processing potato, the contract system has been expanding in most areas except in this particular location. This implies that all potato growers face the same environment at both macro and meso levels.

At the micro level (in San Sai district) where growers have expertise in potato production, they adopted the new contract crop, i.e. baby corn, in their rice-potato system. Contract corn was introduced by brokers of many processing firms in 1997. Corn had replaced existing chili and other vegetables it extended rapidly. The cropping system became intensive because of high demand for contract-land and contract growers, especially for experienced and reliable farmers (Sriboonchitta and Wiboonpongse, 2005).

As for processing potato, brokers have been playing a significant role in the local supply chain. The findings from the survey found four brokers working in 2005 in San Sai (for a production area of 5,560 rai). Each broker supplied to one or two firms via his sub-broker, a broker could reach a large number of growers (Figure 9.5). Eighty-nine per cent of production (large and medium sizes) was delivered to processing firms. Growers sold extra large (Grade O) potatoes as table potato to the fresh market (at 10–12 baht/kg). Unacceptable sizes (smaller than 4.5 cm) were kept in cold storage for seed (Figure 9.5).

The Potato Growers' Cooperative (PGC) also acted as a broker in collecting processing potato (from its members) for the largest firm. The survey revealed that 95 per cent of growers in San Sai did not obtain seeds from processing firms. Some of these growers possibly switched back and forth to grow under contract with firms via brokers when they needed imported seed. The remaining 5 per cent included switchers and growers who needed production inputs partially from firms. Thus most of the 5 per cent were working partly in contract.

In the past, potato processing firms employed their own personnel to supervise farmers and via some leading farmers who acted on the behalf of these firms. Presently, each (of 4) broker ran business to make profit. He estimated production

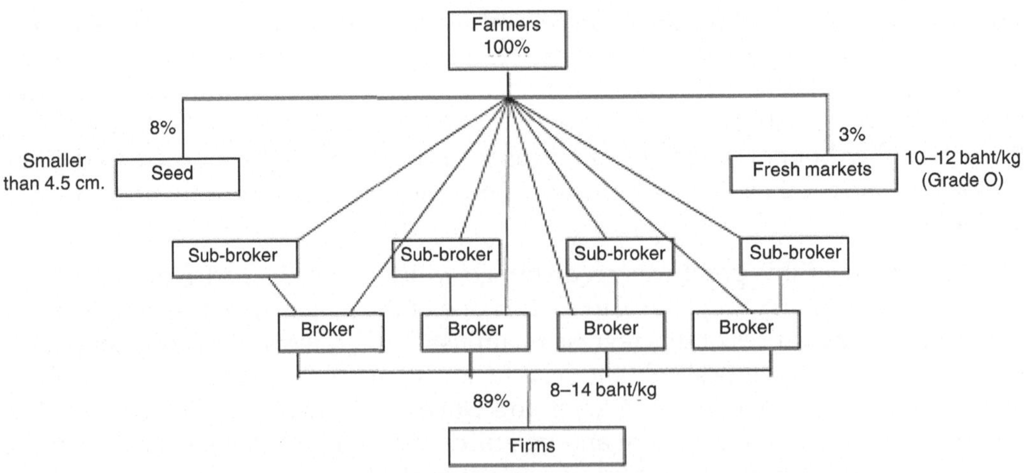

Fig. 9.5: Distribution Channel of Processing Potato in San Sai District

Source: Interview, 2006.

and sought for quota from each processing firm. The amount he proposed the firm was estimated on the basis of his relationship with growers and his selection criteria. For example, one broker who also owned an input store would choose his acquainted clients who had suitable soil and sufficient irrigation. He inspected the land for its suitability of land before accepting growers. (In general, all brokers in other crops would have agreed quotas to supply to processing firms before contacting growers.) The firms are responsible to provide imported seed to brokers and thus to growers as has been practiced since 1983.

In San Sai, almost all growers depended on their own seed to save cost. The imported seed cost 30 baht/kg (in 2005) while the cost of owned seed was 12 baht/kg. Since the imported seed was more expensive, growers planted only 150 kg/rai of imported seed. Besides cost saving (2,400–3,000 baht/rai instead of 4,500 baht), the imported seed is normally sectioned into 3–4 pieces which are susceptible to diseases while own small seed is planted without wound.

Since the imported seed is G1, growers normally change their own seed in the third year by buying unacceptable small size from brokers who also own cold storage (to keep Spunta for fresh market and small Atlantic for seeds). It should be noted that small seeds could come from other districts/provinces. Keeping own seed or buying domestic seed has become possible because of cold storage facilities (in 1988) in the district and from brokers and farmer's innovation (experiments on length of storage, temperature, and germination).

Cost saving on seed is not the only major incentive. The ultimate goal of farmers is to get high price in early season. While the imported seed is normally planted in November, with owned seed, farmers could plant earlier in order to enjoy the price at 14 baht/kg in December. The price declines as supply comes close to the main harvesting period in February (Figure 9.6).

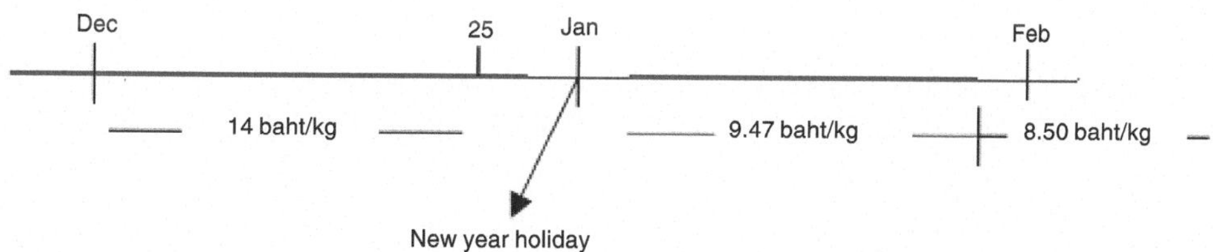

Fig. 9.6: Price of Processing Potato in San Sai, 2005

Source: Survey, 2006.

In growing the early season crop, San Sai growers faced high production risks (unexpected heavy rain and diseases). Therefore, some farmers harvested after January and accepted a moderate price. These growers decided to have free choice to supply to any brokers (in case they did not buy input supply on credit). They enjoyed the opportunity of being non-contractees as long as the price difference between contract and non-contract was over 0.10 baht/kg (interview, 2006).

Selling outside the contract, growers were able to choose planting and harvesting dates. Potato can be harvested between 70–100 days after planting. Therefore, growers can wait for desirable price. Despite that all brokers had agreed to pay same prices at specific times, they offered growers different services as incentives, e.g. free transportation or quick payment. The cooperative paid its clients one day after delivery while it took other brokers seven days. This practice implies relatively high competition among the limited number of brokers.

Comparison of Figures 9.5 and 9.6 illustrates the changes in the form of inclusion of small potato growers in the processing potato supply chain to decide and trade off between high price for low weight (e.g. 70 days with 20 per cent weight loss) or lower price for fully mature produce with full weight (e.g. 100 days maturity). In the non-contract system, as most growers aimed at the highest price in December, some growers contacted a few brokers and promised to deliver their crops. However, it had happened that all brokers also competed for potato to supply the specified daily quota.

Financial Analysis

It is common to find a cooperative member in San Sai cultivating both types of potato as well as find growers in Tak being in both contract and non-contract systems. In the past, growers in San Sai allocated their land partly to Spunta and partly to Atlantic cultivars under contract so as to earn high price from farmers and to stabilize income from the other. Presently, the combinations of two types of potato still prevail. Farmers choose the composition of crops that is suitable to available resources and risk preferences. Table 9.7 summarizes the characteristics of Spunta and Atlantic cultivars. Growers spent 2,000 baht/rai more for Spunta because of its expensive seed. Yield of Atlantic is lower than Spunta and Spunta is less disease resistant. Given price fluctuations and small demand, future role of potatoes in farm income is obviously limited.

Table 9.7: Comparative Costs of Table and Processing Types and Advantages to Growers

Type	*Production Cost (Baht/rai)*	*Source of Seed*	*Pest Resistance*	*Price Advantage*	*Grading*	*Quality*	*Market Absorption*
Processing (Atlantic)	16,000– 20,000–	Either imported or owned seed	Better	• Know in advance • Better	• Sell by 2 grades (accepted	95% acceptable not accepted • Sell ingraded	90%
Table Potato (Spunta)	20,000– 22,000	80% of production are from imported seed	Not resistance to plant diseases	• Do not know in advance (price fluctuate year by year)	Sell by 3 grades (A.B.C.)	Most of production are in grade B and C	10%

Source: Survey, 2006.

Comparison of costs, yields, and margins to growers of processing potato in San Sai and Tak for both contract and non-contract reveals that the non-contractees in San Sai (Chiang Mai) enjoyed the highest net margin, which was 7,866.15 per rai (Table 9.8). The average cost per rai of contractees in Chiang Mai was lower than the non-contractees in San Sai (because of amount of seed used); however the yield in each area was different. The contractees in Tak enjoyed the highest yield but the total cost was highest as well; this resulted in lower margin.

Table 9.8: Comparison of Processing Potato in Contract and Non-Contract in Tak and Chiang Mai Province

	No. of Growers	*Total Cost (baht/rai)*	*Yield/Rai (kg)*	*Seed Cost (% to Total Cost)*	*Price Received (baht/kg.)*	*Total Revenue (baht/rai)*	*Margin to Growers (baht/rai)*	*Average Cost (batn/kg)*
CF in Chiang Mai	30	16,133.39	2,407.23	33.25	8.22	19,779.43	3,646.04	6.70
NCF in Chiang Mai	34	18,596.47	2,745.59	14.93	9.64	26,462.63	7,866.15	6.77
CF in Tak	16	22,663.45	3,318.75	25.50	8.13	26,963.84	4,301.40	6.83
NCF in Tak	14	11,701.16	1,157.14	18.78	12.73	14,728.78	3,027.61	10.11

Source: Survey, 2006.
Note: area in rai, (2.5 rai = 1 acre) income is in baht/year (40 baht = 1 US $)
CF = Contract farming, NCF = Non-Contract Farming.

Case Study 2: Small Women's Potato Processing Group

Potato has not been an item in Thai traditional recipe; therefore most of defective produce was sold to feed cattle. Over 20 years ago, some of defected potatoes (Spunta variety) were transformed to dry potato slices so-called "Munkalya". The fried-dried potato chip was acceptable as snack. It gained popularity among tourists to take back home as products from Chiang Mai. Demand for this product had declined when potato chips processed from fresh (non-dry) slices entered the Thai market. Presently defective Spunta potato is processed as Munkalya and French fries to serve local markets, especially school children. As for processing type (Atlantic), the same product form as produced by large firms is processed into chips from unaccepted potato. A women's group in San Sai district was formed with support from local government agencies. The main objective of the group is to make the best use of substandard produce whose quantity has increased along with expansion in production. The women's potato processing group established in 1997 is most successful and thus is selected to illustrate a business model for community enterprise.

It should be noted that a policy to support local groups to create value added to farm produce has long been in existence. After the economic crisis in 1997, many policy measures were launched for accelerating local groups to create local employment and income. The so-called "Community Enterprise" has become a specific name for registered groups under the public law 2005.

Background

The Farmers' Wives Group of Chedi-Mae Krew (CMK) was formed in 1997 with support of the District Office of Agriculture (DOoA). DOoA has been carrying on this activity since the 80's nation wide. The main objective of San Sai DOoA was to encourage CMK to process defective potato purchased from the members' farms.

CMK has 40 (later 42) members; each member holds at least one share of 100 baht. The initial capital worth 71,100 baht enabled the group to invest on production equipment and raw materials (Wiboonpongse, *et al.* 2005).

CMK expanded its function to provide saving and credit activities. This in turn allowed CMK to absorb more defective potato.

As a registered group, CMK was required to have a clear organizational structure. The board of committee comprises the chairperson and committees as shown in Figure 9.7.

CMK has a well-structured organization. Each committee member is assigned to the right job and thus is able to achieve high performance.

Unlike most other housewives groups, CMK's committees handled each of its responsibilities rather well. This is an important strength that helps release heavy load from the group leader. The leader's particular responsibility to CMK has been overall planning and monitoring work plan, coordinating with government agencies, and attending local meetings.

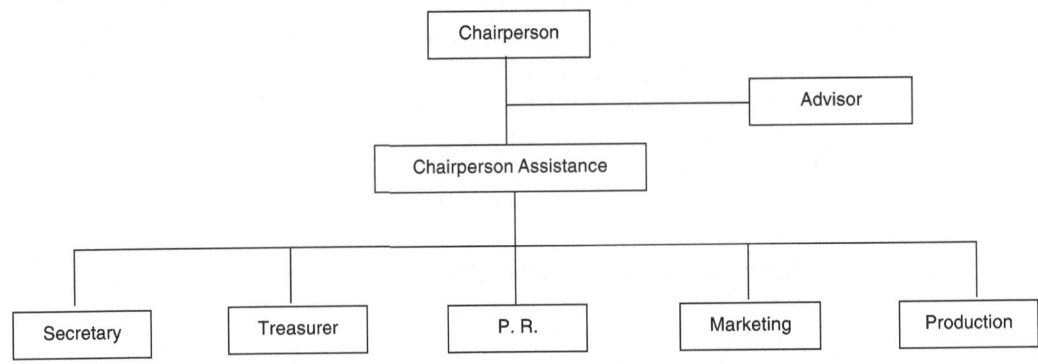

Fig. 9.7: Organizational Structure of the CMK Committee

Source: Wiboonpongse *et al.*, 2004.

The chair person Mrs. Boukham Wipasa has only four years of formal education. Her major occupation is farming.

Boukham has played several roles in the community she belongs to. Mr. Wipasa, the leader's husband, has played a significant role in advising the group. His background of cooperative management provided business orientation attitudes, concepts, and progressive approach to group management.

CMK has received continuous support from several government agencies mostly for production equipments and packaging machine (approximately 1.1 million baht on cash and loan). CMK has invested about 0.28 million baht of its own money which accounts for only 19 per cent of total investment. The main sources of support in equipment are the Department of Cooperative Promotion (DCP) Ministry of Agriculture and Cooperatives (MOAC). It should be noted that good access to DCP is because of the network of Mrs. Baukham's husband.

Production, Product and Marketing

In 1997, CMK began with only two products (dried potato and crackers). In the following year, with support from DOoA, the group expanded its production to crisp chips by using defective Atlantic variety rejected by large firms. (These rejects, because of abnormal shape or poor harvest handling, usually would be wounded and cannot be stored for seed).

CMK employs 13 members and committees to work on processing production. The group frequently seeks technical advice from the local universities and government agencies.

During the past five years, the group has improved its products and packaging substantially. Efforts put forward to packaging were recognized as being distinguished compared to the groups of the kind. Products and packages are diverse so as to serve different consumer targets. The original chip was followed by other various flavours (e.g. b-b-q flavour) to catch with change in consumers' preference as influenced by large firms. In the initial stage, the group sold chips in simple plastic bags in bulk (0.5 kg. per bag) without brand for local markets within the district. After joining the exhibitions and fairs (organized by government agencies) in Bangkok and other provinces, CMK realized its market potential as well as observed and learned from other advanced groups' products. CMK reduced packaging to serving sizes with sticker of the group's name as its brand name.

In 1999, the group decided to expand its market and adopt modern packaging resembling that of large firms. The foil package with color and design was employed which enabled to contain nitrogen to prolong the shelf life of the chip. The related equipment and foil packages were sponsored by the Department of Cooperative Promotion. The brand was "Chip Chip" but it was disapproved since it replicated an existing brand. The new brand of CMK became "Merry" chips and is in the same category as Frito-lay etc. and available on shelves in mini-marts and snack bars in local stores.

Presently (2006), CMK targets middle and local market segments. School children and teenagers are major consumers. Cooperative shops in universities and special shops for community cottage food serve as publicity outlets for CMK to widen the consumer base. Thus, the group sets prices slightly lower than famous brands. Besides, using its own brand, CMK also produces for other brands as ordered (Figure 9.8).

CMK plans to expand its production to meet the orders of a big discount chain named Makro for the national market. This will come after improvement of the processing plant to Good Manufacturing Practice Standards (GMP) as well as installing automatic processing equipment to ensure uniformity of product quality. CMK expects to receive these facilities from the Chiang Mai Provincial Office.

Along with production expansion, CMK plans to improve its marketing management by hiring marketing personnel and adopt more aggressive marketing strategies.

Is CMK Excluded from Supermarket Channel?

Product of CMK appears on the shelves of supermarkets in two different ways: on the special shelves arranged for OTOP[2] products and on the shelves organized by supermarket at BIG-C (7 days period and only 3 periods are allowed for each group per year). This spot allows the group to earn 4,000–7,000 baht per day. In general, once a group's products are accepted to be put on shelves, there is an open opportunity for continuation of supplying to this channel for that group.

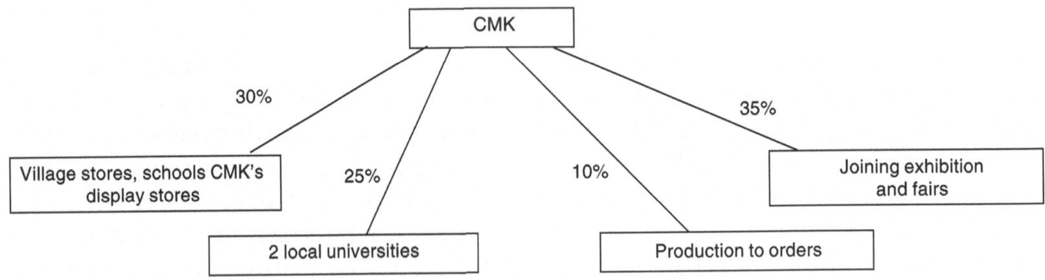

Fig. 9.8: Market Targets of CMK

Source: Interview 2006.

As being an OTOP product, CMK could make direct link with supermarkets or via collectors (or vendors). The stores will normally look for desirable products (by procurement unit) and arrange to contact the OTOP producers. To enter supermarkets, no entrance fee is charged but community groups need to follow standard agreements and procedures.

- Consignment systems
- Payment period is 45 days
- Commission is 20–30 per cent of sale value
- Products are replaced once a month.

---

[2] OTOP stands for "One Tambon One Product" (sub-district product representatives) which is under the national programme of the Thai government since 2001 to promote community groups' products and local wisdom to acceptance of national and global markets.

CMK also sold wholesale to vendors who placed CMK foil package chips in supermarkets in the northern regions. In the supermarket CMK has dealings in both foil as well as nice looking plastic packages. CMK does not find this channel preferable. The group found several problematic issues. Five major problems are as follows:

- The credit term of 45 days is too long, causing cash flow problems
- The commission rate is too high
- CMK products are not well known and not comparable to Frito-Lay®, Testo®, and other famous brands, thus low rate of turnover
- Expired products add to high unit marketing cost
- Being a small brand, CMK products are placed on non-attractive shelves.

Another special centre of OTOP products is located in a shopping mall of the North Village in Central Airport Shopping Mall, Chiang Mai City. The group uses this place to retail as well as publicize its brand.

Financial Analysis

Financial gains received by the members are two-fold, one from being able to sell damaged/defected and unacceptable potato (both Atlactic and Spunta varieties) at 5 baht/kg. In 2006, it is expected that total absorption of CMK alone is 200 tons, and the incremental income at least was 0.7 million baht. This is 9000 return to those who used to sell potato to feed cattle (and 1 million if none was assumed unsold). The second financial benefit is derived from employment of 13 members/committees who work on the processing plant and distribution. Other members earn 10 per cent from dividends and other welfare measures. In 2003, CMK earned 317,380 bahts and net profit of 95,040 bahts from processing the net return is expected to rise further in 2006 as raw material supply increased from 6,000 kg in 1998 to 200 tons in 2006. They expect to use 300 tons of raw materials in 2007.

Production cost and returns in 2005 show that net return to one kg of finished products varies substantially. The highest profit is from Mankalaya (88.84 baht/kg) but the market for this product is limited only to local/village level (Table 9.9). The crisp chip packed in 300 gram packs (plastic bag with brand) had the largest share at 47.00 baht/kg. The most modern packaging in foil containing 20 grams earned much lower profit (22.5 baht/kg). It is difficult for a small enterprise to expand its market at the high end. Despite having no advertising cost, the wholesale price of 3.75 baht/20 gram was considered to be too high to compete with large brand names. Economics of scale seems to dominate other advantages of small producers and even for CMK, the relatively advanced community group.

It is apparent that CMK chose the right market segments. The modern supply chain does not have room for small scale and thus it is not necessary for the group of this kind to aim at this segment for its prosperity. Niche marketing has proved to be an appropriate concept as long as the group enterprises could change consumers' taste and being able to catch up with trends influenced by large firms.

Table 9.9: Cost and Return to Chip Potato

Item	*Total Cost*	*Wholesale Price (baht/unit)*	*Net Return/Unit*	*Net Return Equivalent*
Crisp Chip	35.89	50	14.11	47.00
Crisp chip in foil package 20 gm	3.30	3.75	0.45	22.5
Mankalaya (non-fried 1000 gm)	31.16	120	88.84	88.84

Source : Wiboonpongse *et al.* 2005, interview 2006.

Adaptation of CMK to Dynamic Market

CMK has been responsive to market trends. While Mankalaya has declining in popularity, crisp chip has gained along with increasing quantities of defective Atlantic potato. CMK has demonstrated its abilities to adapt to market changes (as summarized in Table 9.10).

CMK has employed all together 13 members and committees to work on processing production. Each receives daily wages plus social welfare in the same way as provided by companies. CMK gives dividend once a year. It has allocated 10 per cent of the profit for machinery maintenance and the same proportion for local social activities.

CMK paid 4–5 baht/kg to its members for defective potato, which is a good price compared to 8 baht/kg of the contract price. In 2003, CMK made approximately 100,000 baht profit from processing and saving functions. The value added on defective potato of a total of 200 tons means a significant contribution to growers' income.

Potato products of the four local groups are in three forms, the Spunta variety is for Mankalaya, Atlantic is for chips and small odds and ends or broken slices are mixed with rice flour to make crackers. While other groups aimed at only local markets (within the district), CMK improved its packaging and extended its market boundary. Its target customers have remained the same i.e. students. Thus, CMK set its price lower than that for products from large corporations.

Beside government support in general, CMK's success is attributed by its leader's ability to have better access to support and expertise in management.

Impact of Innovation on the Supply Chain

In this study, innovation in management (technical know-how on local seed germination) and adoption of cold storage has led to changes in supply chain. Possible reasons for potato growers leaving the contract system include the followings.

Table 9.10: Implication of Changes in Supply Chain for Defective Potato at SME

Period	*Supply Chain Event*	*Product*	*Market*	*Problem*	*Solution*	*Innovation Events*
1990s	Most of the defective potatoes were purchased by dairy farms at 1–2 baht/kg. There was a need to make better use and increase the value of defective potatoes.					
1997	In 1997, forty potato growers' wives formed a group (CMK) to process their defective potatoes. The committee was formed with specific responsi-bilities assig-ned to appropriate persons.	• *Mankalaya* (dried potato) • Potato snacks packed in simple plastic bags	• San Sai sub-district	• Production length was limited to 3–4 months during hot season since *mankalaya* needs sun drying.	• Try to expand production	• Use Atlantic variety to process non dried chips.
1998	Started to process chips like those produced by large firms (using Atlantic variety)	• *Mankalaya* (dried potato) • Potato chips • Potato crackers • Packed in good branded plastic bags	• Expand market to local school children.	• Inappropriate processing technique led to short product shelf life.	• Need to install new frying equipment.	• Modify longan-drying oven for grease reduction in fried chips.
1999	CMK's crisp chips became popular at the district level. Natural-salted chip was the original flavour of the group's product.		• Expand market to Bangkok and other provinces by joining exhibitions/ fairs.	• Manual peeling and slicing are labour intensive and time consuming. • No raw material off-season.	• Requested peeling and slicing equipment. • Purchased substandard potatoes from other districts.	• To improve efficiency and product uni-formity, CMK sought support from the District Agricultural Office for cleaning and slicing machines.

Contd...

Table 9.10: Contd...

Period	*Supply Chain Event*	*Product*	*Market*	*Problem*	*Solution*	*Innovation Events*
2000	Product seasonings were available from a local company	• *Mankalaya* (dried potato) • Potato chips salt, chicken and b-b-q flavours • Potato crackers • Plastic branded packaging.		• Limited product choice to customers.	• Added two more flavours.	• Two more flavours: (chicken and b-b-q) were added to crisp chips.
2000	CMK planned to expand its retailing.			• Lack of know-how on storing raw material to keep good quality of chips.	• Stored potatoes at room temperature with 50 per cent storage loss.	• CMK decided to brand its products "Chip Chip" in the hope of maintaining and increasing share in local markets
2001	Gaining consumers' confidence in product quality is required for certain food categories.					• CMK improved its production practices to meet standards for certification.
2004	Increasing demand for chips/snacks leading to competition among international brands. Products of these firms were also available in local schools and local markets.		• Supply to shopping malls and stores in two universities in Chiang Mai Province.	• Short shelf life due to inappropriate packaging. • Chips were damaged during shipping.	• Used new foil packaging and added nitrogen to prolong shelf life.	• CMK implemented own brand. "Chip Chip" was designed with aluminium foil packages similar to international brands but targeted at teenagers. CMK obtained subsidy from the Department of Cooperatives Promotion to cover high costs of

Contd...

Table 9.10: Contd...

Period	Supply Chain Event	Product	Market	Problem	Solution	Innovation Events
						implementing new packaging. The subsidy (for 300,000 packages and related equipment) was worth 600,000 baht
2004	Strong competition between two large firms using product differentiation strategy led to a great variety of new flavours.	• *Mankalaya* (dried potato) • Potato chips salt, chicken and b-b-q flavours • Potato crackers • Plastic packaging with branded packaging.				• CMK adjusted to market trends by adding two new flavours. The group also changed its brand to "Merry" as "Chip Chip" was similar to another existing brand. • Improve quality and design of plastic bag with brand. • Use new foil packaging.
2004	CMK responded to the change in the chip market by using foil packaging and aiming to sell in the same segment as the large firms.			• Cost of packaging was high. • Unable to survive in modern stores.	• Modified packaging	• Focus on middle level market segment • Lower packaging cost and price at competitive level
2005	As a consequence of the expanding market, CMK hoped to extend its processing operations beyond three months					• CMK leader conducted simple storage experi-ment. It succeeded in storing raw material up to four months in an air-conditioned room at 20–25°C.

Contd...

Table 9.10: Contd...

Period	*Supply Chain Event*	*Product*	*Market*	*Problem*	*Solution*	*Innovation Events*
2005	CMK becomes a learning centre at provincial level owing to its success in value creation for potatoes, one of the main crops of northern Thailand					• CMK attempted to increase production size and keep costs at a level comparable with large firms. Thus, CMK absorbed more raw materials from non-members in the district. Inputs rose from 6 tons in 1997 to 200 tons in 2006.
2006	The group's income reached 1,080,000 baht and raw materials increased by 400 per cent within two years (from 50 tons in 2004 to 200 tons in 2006.)					
2006	CMK plans to expand its markets and is in the process of hiring marketing personnel.					• CMK will receive new equipment support from the Chiang Mai Provincial.

- **Price Incentive:** Farmers who can arrange their cropping schedule to grow process potato and harvest in November to December would receive the highest price because of shortage of supply. Since freshly harvested potatoes result in best quality chips, firms are willing to pay 14 baht/kg instead of over 27 baht for imported potato.[3] The firms reported that only 20 per cent of import (from Canada) met processing quality.
- **High Cost of Imported Seed:** The cost of imported seed was 4500 baht/rai (i.e. 30 baht/kg) while the local seed costs 2,400–3,000 baht/rai (12 baht/kg). The range depends on plant density. Besides, sectioning (or cut) of imported seed could lead to become rots.
- **Choices of Brokers:** Despite that four brokers supplied to the same few firms, growers felt they had alternatives. Freedom on broker choices was highly valued by most farmers reflecting traditional social value and culture especially in the northern region. As mentioned earlier, some brokers provided more incentives to growers, and often paid more than the agreed price.
- **Environmental Advantages:** Growers in San Sai appreciated the major advantages they have (in order of importance): potato production experience/expertise, soil suitability (sandy soil), good irrigation throughout the year, and proximity to processing firms.
- **Win-Win Situation:** Since growers aimed for high price, they were willing to take production risks. Because of high production risk, firms had no intention to have contracts with growers but had the advantage of buying fresh raw material as the price was much lower than less fresh[4] imports. This way, firms could concentrate and devote their investment in new areas where they could find more contractees.
- **Innovation:** Improvement management ability coupled with adequate supports enabled farm families to extend from farm production to processing of rejected farm outputs.
- **Direct Market Participation:** The local market is essential to ensure security while product development helps potato growers to be able to compete with large processors in local markets as well as to extend the boundary.

In the case of potato production in Thailand, all farmers purposively incorporated potato in their cropping system for the market. Since the crop was first introduced (45 year ago), potato growers had outlets for the produce. Presently, supply of table potato is controlled to meet expected demand so as to maintain favorable prices. Although imported seed of table potato (Spunta) is rationed to members of the Potato Growers Cooperative, members can trade their quotas and make profit. All table

---

[3] As revealed by the processing firms, only 40 per cent of the purchased raw materials could be processed to good quality chips. Therefore, the average (whole year and from all sources) price of potato the firms can bear is 17 baht at the maximum.

[4] Freshness of raw potato is the main determinant of chip quality, therefore "zero-day storage" results in the best golden chips.

potato is absorbed by local brokers before supplying to main markets in Bangkok. All brokers are local SMEs and in fact some of them are the second generation of potato growers themselves. The same brokers trade in both types of potato.

Our study finds three forms of inclusion of small growers (Figure 9.9).

1. The Potato Growers Cooperative is classified as chain-ownership as it is a collective action of members in determining annual imports of tuber seed for supply control. The cooperative manages the first part of the supply chain (input of seed).
2. For the processing potato in general, the supply chain works through contract system, which means there exists forward integration. Small growers are contractees who receive technical advice from processing firms' personnel and input suppliers. The second incidence is a real forward integration exemplified by local processing groups. The case of Chedi Mae Kraw highlights the usage of defected potato for value added.
3. The third form is classified as chain segment. This is illustrated by the case of San Sai pressing potato growers (as well as off-season potato growers in Tak). Although the potato market was not intentionally segmented by growers, they actually sold extra size to fresh markets, processable size to selected brokers, and undersized potatoes were stored for seed (or sold).

The fourth category of farmer's participation, "chain partnership", was not observed in our case study.

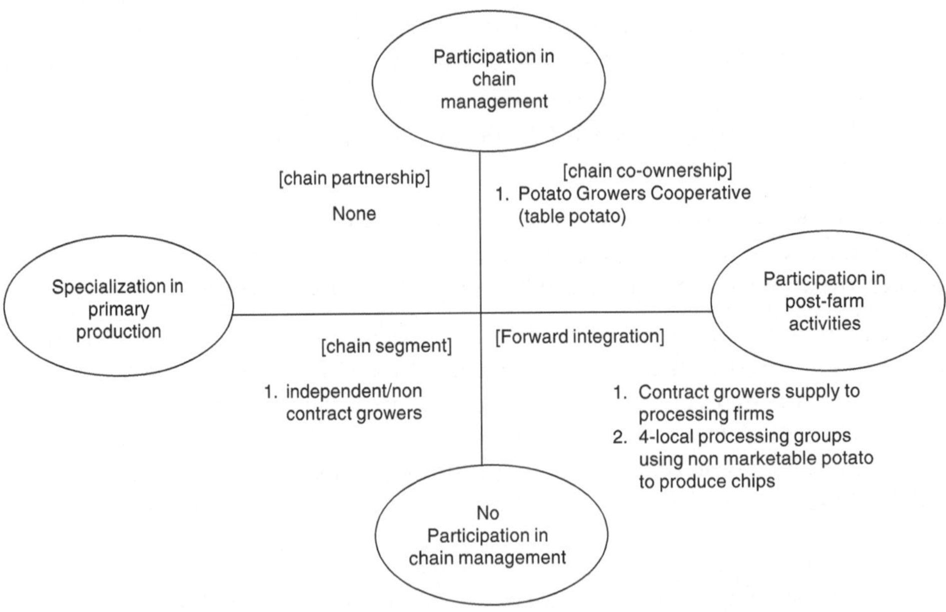

Fig. 9.9: Forms of Inclusion of Potato Growers in Thailand (2006)

Conclusion

The market of processing potato in the original site of potato production in Thailand has been restructured. The contracted growers in 1987 and second-generation growers presently manage to cultivate outside the contract via professional brokers (who used to be and still are growers), growers in San Sai district freely choose to contact one or more brokers and decide whom to sell based on the best non-price offers.

The macro environment indicates rapid increase in demand for both table type potato (because of growing tourism) and processing type potato (consumers' preference for snacks is rising). Thus production has increased from 18,000 tons (1990) to 97,411 tons (2005). Furthermore, large processing firms have moved to international procurement by imports and contract farming in neighbouring countries. The government policy opted for close integration between raw material production and value added agro-industry. For this purpose, the contract farming system was promoted in the 6th National Social Economic Development Plan (1987–1991). With efforts of local officers in coordinating contract arrangements, favorable biophysical and socio-economic environment, contract potato farming was one of the most successful cases in integrating small/resource poor growers into the supply chain.

At the meso level, the potato sector has received continuous technical support from local universities and government research agencies on varietal selection, cultivation practices, mechanical harvesting, and post-harvest management. Cold storage facilities have been improved.

At the micro level, a few leading potato growers became professional growers and brokers. Working in close relationship with processing firms, one of them had opportunity to visit and learn from a few potato producing countries. His (also others') experiments on stored local produce for seed have made a great impact on the growers' decision in growing early season potato. This was a significant innovation leading to a change in the supply chain and availability of supply for processing firms.

Grading of potato has contributed to changes in the supply chain. Over-size potato is sold in the fresh market at a good price and undersize ones are sold for cattle feed (1–2 baht/kg) or local fresh market became valuable domestic seed (12 baht/kg). Moreover, defective potatoes, which accounted for almost 5–10 per cent of total production, was absorbed by local women's processing groups. Value added to potato and increase in employment of women is outcomes of this innovation.

Like other producers in general, CMK had ambition to produce quality products for modern retail supermarkets. Efforts to improve product varieties and packaging similar to those of leading firms support this notion. However, the major impediment is economy of scale. The unit cost of modern (foil) packaging was too high relative to its price. The large firm is certainly the price leader in this potato chips market. To be able to sell in the same store, CMK products need to be cheaper.

Supermarkets did not appear to be the best destination for potato chips of small scale/community group producers to sell in their own brand names. CMK has been adaptive and able to identify its target segment: local market, schools and university students, and OTOP consumers. However, it can be involved in this channel by producing products under supermarkets' brand names.

The innovation leading to the success of this local small group of farmers' housewives is management. More specifically, it is the ability to learn and to adapt to market environment and ability to identify appropriate market segments.

Following are recommendations for small growers to participate in the dynamic market:

- Contract farming provides direct access for small growers to the supply chain. Initial efforts from the public sector have proven to be a key factor of success.
- Public-private partnership on technical improvement is required to drive development of the sector (suitable variety of seed is important).
- Confidence in production management as well as experience in supply chain can drive growers' innovation. Identifying driving forces and local leaders are important to accelerate development and changes in the innovation and supply chain. Growers can become professional SME (brokers).
- Given several advantages of contract farming for small farmers (access to technology, input and output markets, and price stability), it is also desirable to increase competition so that farmers have market alternatives. The win-win situation should be explored and encouraged by the public sector to further benefit growers and firms.
- The increasing trend in demand for contract growers and land under potato and other crops is a good driving force for further innovations and thus restructuring market opportunities.

Recommendation for Small Scale Producers

- Continuation of public sector's support up to optimal time/level is necessary to help build a strong foundation for a community group to proceed at its own pace.
- Capacity building on human resources in management is important both in business aspects as well as in organization (especially when there is lack of strong personal capability of leader).
- Small scale producers (farmers) should be trained on product development and make the best use of farm produce.
- Appropriately designed packaging for target segments is important and needs to be emphasized.
- Certain marketing events organized by the public sector are helpful for small producers to participate in the broadening market.

Appendix 9.1: Import Values of Potato and Products (Million baht)

	Potatoes, fresh or chilled	*Fresh potatoes*	*Seed*	*Flakes, granules and pellets*	*Flour, meal and powder*	*Other vegetables prepared or preserved otherwise than by vinegar or acetic acid, not frozen, potato*	*Other vegetables prepared or preserved otherwise than by vinegar or acetic acid, frozen, Potato*	*Uncooked or cooked by steaming or boiling in water, frozen.*	*Potato starch inulin.*	*Total*
2001	0.00	0.00	123.23	33.16	21.07	299.13	306.24	0.15	468.37	1,251.35
2002	0.00	0.00	116.32	36.13	39.02	278.23	315.83	0.01	384.81	1,170.36
2003	13.57	209.60	131.00	26.65	26.97	216.56	374.90	0.27	428.19	1,427.70
2004	15.71	194.64	135.74	36.94	31.94	198.72	441.39	0.32	471.36	1,526.77
2005	28.18	151.01	137.66	33.16	13.82	4.96	508.39	0.06	561.02	1,438.26

Source: Department of Customs, 2006.
Note: 40 baht = 1US $

Appendix 9.2: Sources and Import Values of Potato Seed *(Million baht)*

	2001	*2002*	*2003*	*2004*	*2005*
Australia	51.514	41.648	32.338	52.371	39.429
China	.065		0.173	.092	
United Kingdom	60.454	57.049	85.909	59.778	91.073
Netherlands	6.939	8.193	4.580	7.275	5.929
United States	4.260	3.973	5.018	8.555	
Laos		5.458	2.960	0.222	
New Zealand			.019		.019
Denmark				.032	
Georgia				7.405	
Namibia				.010	
Israel					1.209
Total	123.233	116.320	130.997	135.741	137.657

Source: Department of Customs, 2006.
Note: 40 baht = 1US

Appendix 9.3: Procedure for Obtaining Seed Quota Approval and Import

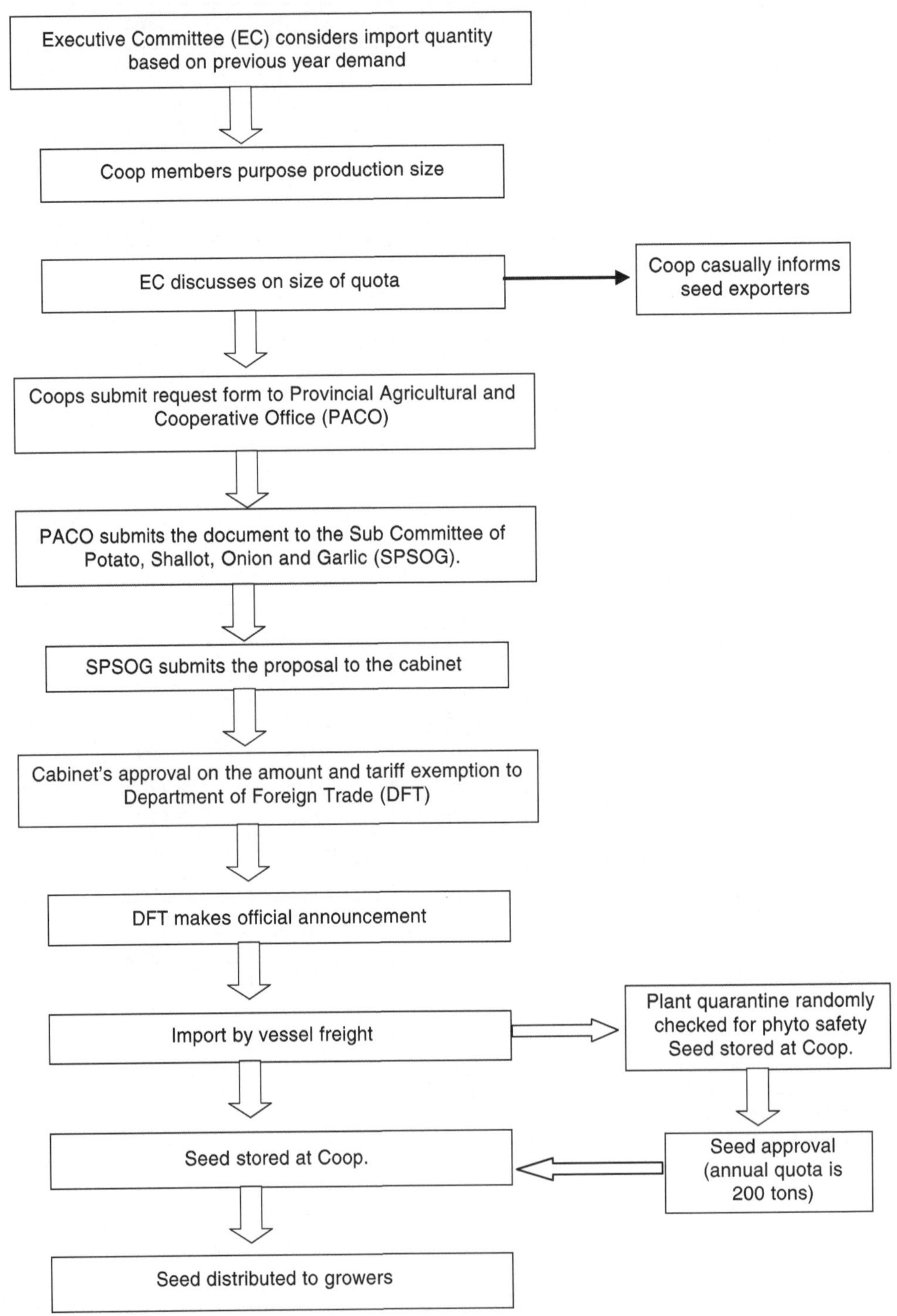

Source: Interview, 2006.

References

Asian Association of Agricultural Colleges and Universities (AAACU). 2002. "Global

Agribusiness: The Role of Asian Agricultural Academic Institutions". *Proceeding of the 14th Biennial Conference,* Chiang Mai University, Thailand. December 12–14. 2002.

Bloomfield, S., S. Sriboonchitta and A. Wiboonpongse. 1996.Chiangmai Frozen Foods, Ltd. : A case study. Chiang Mai University, Chiang Mai. 12 p.

Canadian Embassy Bangkok. 2000. The Market for Seed Potatoes in Thailand.

Cooperative Report. Cooperative Promotion Department. (Online]. Available: http://web2.cpd.go.th/tamneap_coop (May 10, 2006).

Department of Agriculture, Ministry of Agricultural and Cooperatives. 2005. Information on Potato in Thailand. [Online]. Available: http:www.doa.go.th (July 7, 2005).

Department of Customs, Ministry of Commerce. 2006. Import and Export Potato. [Online]. Available: http://www. customs.go.th (May,4, 2006).

Food and Agriculture Organization (FAO). (2006). Potato Production. [Online]. Available: http://www.fao.org\trade\FAOSTAT Database Results.htm (May 10, 2006).

Gedgaew, C. 1993. "Optimal farm plans under risk in Amphoe Sansai Chiang Mai province: contract *versus* non-contract farming." *Master thesis,* Faculty of Economics, Chiang Mai University, Chiang Mai.

Glover, D. 1992. Introduction, pp.1–9. In Glover D. and L.T. Ghee (eds.). Contract farming in Southeast Asia: three country studies. Institute Pengajian Tinggi/Institute for Advanced Studies, Kuala Lumpur.

Gnun, P. "Analysis Production and Marketing of Potato in Chiang Mai Province", *Research.*

Kaseamsomboon, P. 2000, "Health Impact Assessment of Agriculturalists on Contractual Arrangement". Health Systems Research Institute, Ministry of Public Health, Nonthaburi, Thailand. [Online]. Available http://library.hsri.or.th

Khumchompoo, W, C. Leesuwan, V. Vanich, and P. Thanchuang. "Rate of Adoption of Innovation among Farmers Concerning Contract Farming", Chiang Mai University, Chiang Mai, Thailand.

Laramee, P. 1975. Problem of small farmers under contract marketing with special reference to a case in Chiang Mai province, Thailand, *Economic Bulletin for Asia and the Pacific,* 26, 2/3 (Sep/Dec):43–57.

Linsay. F. (2002). "Agribussiness" *Proceedings of the 14th Biennial Conference on Global Agribusiness: The Role of Asian Agricultural Academic Institutions,* Chiang Mai University, Chiang Mai, Thailand.

Manager newspaper 2006 [Online]. Available: http:// www.manager.co.th (March 30, 2006).

Manarungsan S., and S. Suwanjindar. 1992. "Contract farming and outgrower schemes in Thailand, " pp.10–70. In Glover D. and L.T.Ghee (eds.). "Contract farming in Southeast Asia : three country studies." Institute Pengajian Tinggi/Institute for Advanced Studies. Kuala Lumpur.

OAE. 1993. "Study on contract between baby corn farmers and private firms," Ministry of Agriculture and Cooperatives, Bangkok. 73 p.

OAE. 1991a. "Study on contract between duck farmers and private firms in Cholburi and Chachengsao provinces," 1990/91, Ministry of Agriculture and Cooperatives, Bangkok. 39 p.

OAE. 1991b. Evaluation on asparagus extension project under the 4–sector cooperation plan for agricultural and agro-industrial development, 1987/88. Ministry of Agriculture and Cooperatives, Bangkok, 27 p.

OAE. 1989. Study on prawn marketing contract of land settlement cooperative, Suratthani province. Ministry of Agriculture and Cooperatives, Bangkok. 52 p.

Panusan, W. 1983. Report on Potato Production in Thailand. International Potato Course, IAC, Wageningen, Netherlands.

R.E. Rhoades, R.J. Hijmans and L. Huaccho (CIP). 2002. Potato in Thailand. [Online]. Available: http://www. cipotato.org/WPA/asia/Thailand.htm (May 15,2006)

Siamturakij newspaper. 2006 [Online]. Available: http://www.siamturakij.com/book/index.php (May 25, 2006)

USDA Foreign Agricultural Service. 2004. Thailand Product Brief Snack Foods Industry 2004 [Online]. Available: http://www.fas.usda.gov/gainfiles/200407/146107002.doc (May 12, 2006).

Wiboonpongse, A. and S. Sriboonchitta. 2004. "Contract Farming in Thailand: Lessons Learned." *A paper requested by ADBI for ADBI-UNESCAP Regional Workshop on Contract Farming and Poverty Reduction Issue and Research Methodology*, 9–12 August, 2004. United Nations Conference Center, Bangkok, Thailand.

Wiboonpongse, A., S. Sriboonchitta, *et al.* (2005). "The Roles of Contract Farming in Agricultural Transition in Thailand", *J. ISSAAS.*, 4, 4: 74–97.

Wiboonpongse, A., S. Sriboonchitta, P. Khuntonthong, and K. Moonla. Development of Local Researchers and Tripartite Research Exercise to Strengthen Community Enterprises: Phase I for the Upper North: The Farmers' Housewives Group of Chedi Mae Kreow, Sponsored by Thailand Research Fund (in Thai).

Yodchaisan, S. (2002). "Production and Marketing of Potato 2001/02".

10

Keys to Inclusion of Small-Scale Producers in Dynamic Markets: Carrefour's Quality Lines in China

Dinghuan Hu and Xia Dandan

The structural reform and the adoption of contracted responsibility system based on households in Chinese rural areas, implemented since the 1980s, have distributed the land that originally belonged to the people's communes and production brigades to farmer households according to the number of family members. The scale of production in China is very small. The land area per household is less than 0.4 ha. Corresponding to small-scale farmers in the agricultural production sector, a large number of small-scale dealers are concentrated in the agri-food sector (Dinghuan Hu, 2006). They are engaged in purchase of agri-food from small scale farmers, transportation, wholesale, retail, etc. In the traditional agri-food supply chain composed by a large number of small-scale farmers and small dealers, all the individuals are independent operating entities. There are no cooperative and long-term stable supply and demand relations among farmer households, among dealers, and between farmer households and dealers. The enthusiasm of the participants combined with the so-called "invisible hand" on the agri-food supplying chain has ensured stable and sustained supply of agri-food in China since the policy of reform was initiated. However, in the domain of production, owing to the shortage of funds and rarely technical assistance, small-scale farmers have not benefited from advanced planting and management technology (Niu Ruofeng, Xia Ying, 2000; Hu Dinghuan, 1998). Because there is no effective supervision system, overuse of pesticides and chemical fertilizers by small scale farmers always takes place. Moreover, some of the small-scale farmers even use highly poisonous and high residual pesticides in order to improve the yield and appearance of agricultural products. Indiscriminate use of pesticides not only causes serious damage to agri-food safety, but also environmental pollution (Zhang Lijian, Hu Dinghuan, and Yang Weimin, 2006). In the domain of agri-food circulation and processing, the supplying chain from field to dining table is divided into relatively independent stages and there is no relation among dealers at different stages except for temporary selling and purchasing relations. Agri-foods are sold and purchased several times before they reach consumers. As traceability cannot be realized in the supply chain, more chances emerge for speculators; some speculators for example, inject water into pig body, some use additives that impair consumers' health in food processing (Dinghuan Hu, 2004, 2005).

Since the mid-1990s, changes have taken place in consumers' demands. Citizens' income increased rapidly along with continuous rapid growth of GDP. Demand has switched from the previous quantity of food to quality, safety and diversity.

The first supermarket was set up in China in 1990. Since then supermarkets have developed rapidly. In large cities and many medium-sized cities, supermarkets have become the main places for purchasing household necessities and foods. According to CCFA, in 2004, average sales of supermarkets in 12 large cities in China accounted for 24.3 per cent of the total volume of retail sales (Table 10.1).

Table 10.1: Sales of Supermarkets in Total Retail Trade in 12 Large Cities in China (2004)

	Total Retail Sale (Billion US $)	*Total Sales of Supermarket (Billion US $)*	*Share of Supermarkets (%)*	*Stores of Supermarkets*
Shanghai	236.8	89.6	37.8	10220
Beijing	211.2	61.6	29.2	5000
Tianjin	101.6	24.0	23.6	0
Chongqing	92.0	20.0	21.7	3000
Qingdao	58.4	16.8	28.8	3785
Shenyang	77.6	20.8	26.8	4000
Wuhan	92.8	24.0	25.9	2350
Suzhou	60.0	9.6	16.0	1093
Ningbo	57.6	13.6	23.6	0
Taiyuan	21.6	4.8	22.2	0
Hongzhou	68.0	12.0	17.6	1222
Yantai	42.4	5.6	13.2	1400
Herbing	68.0	3.2	4.7	253
Average			24.3	

Source: China Chain Store and Franchise Association.

In 2006, Arief Goldman, *et al.* from Hebrew University investigated 1200 consumers in six large cities in China. Their survey showed that the proportions of agri-foods and food bought from supermarkets by consumers were as follows: vegetables 22 per cent, poultry 35 per cent, aquatic products 33 per cent, fruits 37 per cent, meat 46 per cent, bread 55 per cent, manufactured and packaged foods 79 per cent, and non-food goods 94 per cent.

China opened its retail market in 2004 and supermarket chains from abroad entered China's market one after another, aggravating the competition among supermarkets and between supermarkets and traditional retail stores. Chinese consumers have the habit of purchasing raw and fresh agri-food every day, therefore, raw and fresh agri-foods have become an important measurement of supermarkets' attractiveness to consumers. At present, owing to the imperfect agri-food circulation system and infrastructure, the cost of raw and fresh agri-foods sold in supermarkets is generally higher than that of vendors on wet markets (Hu Dinghuan, 2006). Therefore, from the view point of marketing strategies, many supermarkets position their sales of raw and fresh agri-food in medium and high level markets. Many supermarkets provide choices of organic and green agri-food in chain stores. In 2005, we investigated more than 20 supermarkets in Beijing. We found that there were on average 48 varieties of vegetables sold by these supermarkets, and 26 of them were organic or green vegetables, which accounted for 52 per cent of vegetables (Table 10.2).

It is said that few agri-food suppliers purchased ordinary agri-food from the wholesale markets, marked with the symbols of organic or green foods, and sold to supermarkets.

In what way do organic and green agri-foods enter China's supermarkets? What methods have been used to produce organic and green agri-foods? What kinds of organizations and systems can guarantee that these agri-foods reach organic and green food standards? These problems are closely related with consumers' health and supermarkets' reputation, but nobody has studied them seriously in China till now. To answer these questions, we conducted case studies of raw and fresh agri-food quality line of Carrefour supermarket.

Table 10.2: Proportions of Organic and Green Vegetables in Vegetables Sold by Supermarkets in Beijing

Name of Supermarket	*Varieties of Vegetable*	*Varieties of Organic and Green Food Vegetable*	*Share of Organic and Green Food Vegetables (%)*
Huarun	20	15	75
Hualian	32	17	53
Huapu	20	20	100
Hua'an	18	10	56
Zhuangsheng	42	15	36
Auchan	87	46	53
Huaguang	87	47	54
Carrefour	92	30	33
Chaoshifa	35	29	83
New World	68	68	100
Jinkelong	18	0	0
Lotus	68	50	74
Meilianmei	67	34	51
Huaguan Shopping Center	70	33	47
Taixingyuan	33	16	48
Yikelong	47	25	53
Wumart	20	9	45
Hengyuan	75	40	53
Lotus (Liuli ridge£©	30	14	47
Shuntianfu	72	30	42
Average	48	26	52

Source: Survey by author, 2005.

Development of Carrefour

The special trademark, Carrefour, has been disseminated widely in the world now. The French meaning of the trademark is crossroads. In the 1980s, the world's first department store emerged in France. The establishment of department store means that retail dealers can put all the goods in a large store for concentrated selling, thus meeting the requirements of consumers for purchasing goods at one place. After the second world war, people's desire for consumption had been kindled. Carrefour emerged to fulfill this requirement at that time. In 1959, two families with Macel Fournier and Lois Defrorey as their representatives set up Carrefour Company. In the beginning, Carrefour was not successful. In summer of 1960, the first store was in a basement with an area of 650 m^2 in Annixi of Haote Safuyi. After three years, a large department store with an area of 2500 m^2 in the market of Sainte-Genevieve-des-bois in suburbs of Paris was set up. There were 12 cashier counters and a parking lot for 450 cars. This was the hypermarket initiated by the Carrefour, a retail store combined concentrated selling goods practiced in department store and free collecting goods together. This kind of hypermarket with special characters was well received by French consumers and has become one of the marketing models in retail commerce. Consumers can buy every thing they need in one store. Compared with traditional retail stores, the retail price is 5–10 per cent lower in Carrefour. Just because of the low price, annual sales of Carrefour increased by 50 per cent from 1965 to 1971.

The development of hypermarket and supermarket brought an unprecedented shock to small retail shops in France and caused strong criticism and resentment among entrepreneurs of medium and small enterprises. In order to protect the medium and small retail enterprises and increase employment rate, the French government took steps to restrict domestic large supermarkets. In 1972, France begun to impose special duties on retail dealers in supermarkets through legislation and the tax was used as retirement pensions of small scale retail dealers who were put out of business. The amount of tax paid by Carrefour each year accounts for 1.5 per cent of its annual volume of sales. Carrefour began its expansion to foreign countries in 1969 and the first hypermarket established abroad was in Belgium (Chen Guang, 2004).

In the mid-1970s, Carrefour began its expansion in international markets outside of Europe. The first store was established in Brazil and the first supermarket was established in Argentina in 1982. Carrefour marched into Asia in 1989 and the first supermarket was established in Taiwan province of China. Carrefour established the first supermarket in Beijing, the capital of China, in 1995.

Till March 2006, Carrefour had established 6987 chain stores. Among the 6987 chain stores, 870 are hypermarkets, 191 of which are in France, 332 in Europe (excluding France), 103 in America, and 164 in Asia. Carrefour also has 1426 ordinary supermarkets, 207 convenience stores, and 122 "cash and carry" warehouses.

At the end of 2005, gross sales of Carrefour in the world were 74.5 billion euros, compared with 72.7 billion euros in 2004. In this, the gross sales of hypermarkets were 58.8 per cent, that of ordinary supermarkets was 17.8 per cent that of discount stores was 8.6 per cent and that of others 14.8 per cent. Seen from regional sales, gross sales in France were 47.8 per cent of total sales, that of Europe (France not included) 37.7 per cent, that of Asia 7.7 per cent and that of America 6.8%.

Although Carrefour did not enter China's mainland market until 1995, the speed of its development in China is much faster than that in any other country in the world. Till June 2006, Carrefour had established 78 chain stores in China. Carrefour established the first store in Beijing. It marched into Shanghai and Shenzhen in 1996 and into Tianjin in 1997. Carrefour established hypermarkets in Chongqing, Zhuhai, Wuhan, and Dongguan in 1998. It set up 35 hypermarkets in more than 20 cities in 2002 and set up the fortieth branch store in Hangzhou in 2003. Till July 2006, Carrefour has set up 79 chain stores in China. The reason why Carrefour has developed rapidly in China is that Carrefour has very good economic benefits on the one hand and on the other the development of Carrefour in China has realized scale-utility such as the establishment of distribution centres so as the reduce circulation and distribution cost.

Table 10.3: Sales and Number of Chain Stores of Carrefour in China

	Sales (Million US $)	*Number of Stores*
2002	1243	35
2003	1680	41
2004	2030	62
2005	2179	76

Source: CCFA.

Food Safety and Carrefour Quality Line

Food safety, especially that of raw and fresh agri-food in China, is a very serious issue in China. Pesticide residue in apples from apple-producing area of Shandong Province was tested by experts in 2000. Results of the test showed that among the 12 kinds of pesticides tested, pesticide residues of nine of them were found. Residues of DDT and alkron are 10.91 per cent and 3.33 per cent, higher than the standards. Experts had investigated the apple-producing environment and apples of 45 apple gardens in 8 cities (prefectures) in main apple-producing areas in Shandong Province in 2000. Results of the investigation showed that the test rate of cadmium, lead, mercury, chromium, and arsenic in soil and irrigation water was 100 per cent. The contents of cadmium and mercury in irrigation water were 4.4 per cent and 2.22 per cent higher than the standards and the highest contents were 24 per cent and 50 per cent higher than the standards. The test rates of chlorine and fluorine in irrigation water were 8 per cent and 4 per cent, respectively. The tested rate of lead, cadmium, and asentic was over 93 per cent, that of copper, zinc, fluorine, mercury, and chromium was 100 per cent, respectively, and the contents of them in irrigation water were respectively 1.47 per cent, 11.29 per cent, and 18.06 per cent higher than the standards. The highest rates were 25 per cent, 230 per cent, and 130 per cent respectively higher than standards.

Pesticide residue in vegetables is the main reason for unsafe vegetables. The results of the second fixed-site monitoring on pesticide residue in vegetables in 37 provinces (cities) of the whole country by agricultural departments in 2003 showed that there were 18 kinds of vegetables containing pesticide residue 15 per cent higher than standards and four of these vegetables contained pesticide residue 13 per cent higher than standards. Safety problems in animal and poultry products are clenbuterol, BSE (bovine spongiform encephalopathy), avian influenza, Newcastle disease, etc. Safety problems in aquatic products are the misuse or overuse of drugs, additives, and diluting or packing of goods and so on with the increasing environmental pollution in recent years. In monitoring drug residue in fish conducted by the State Aquatic Products Quality Test Center in 1999, it was found that the contents of sulphonamides were higher than the standards and residues of chloromycetin, furazodidone, and other antibiotic substances were also found. Stilboestrol residue was also found in a few aquatic products. Owing to the content of chloromycetin residue in frozen shelled fresh shrimps, trade embargo on animal source products was imposed by the European Community in 2002.

Unsafe factors of food run through the entire process of food supply. Microbial pollution, residues of pesticides, and animal drugs are higher than the standards, imperfect environment of producing area, the backward production methods, lower levels of food processing, the potential risks of new technology and new marketing models, the sham and shoddy commodities, and other factors directly restrict improvements in food safety in China.

The profiteering attitude of the producers is also one of the reasons for unsafe food. There are 40 Mu vegetable gardens in a village of Zhuhai, Guangzhou, and the vegetables were irrigated with seriously polluted industrial waste water. The appearance of the vegetables is good as the farmers had used growth regulator on them, so the vegetables were sold very well. These vegetables were sold to residents of two famous large and expensive house districts, and tens of thousands people nearby.

Carrefour's Quality Line

Generally speaking food accounts about 70 per cent of sales in supermarkets; and about 50 per cent of this are raw and fresh agri-food, i.e. the proportion of raw and fresh agri-food is 35 per cent of sales in supermarkets. Along with economic development and improvements in people's living standards, consumers attach more importance to the quality of raw and fresh agri-food, varieties of choice, and supply of quality and fresh agri-food. Raw and fresh agri-food counters in supermarkets have increased the number of consumers by 15–50 per cent. Among the supermarkets in China, Carrefour is characterized by marketing raw and fresh agri-food. Carrefour classifies raw and fresh agri-food into five categories: fish, meat, vegetables and fruits, salad plants, and breads.

With increase in the consciousness of consumers on food safety, the demand for high quality and safe agri-food has increased gradually. Therefore, Carrefour began to sell the green food supplying line under its own brand, and this is the Carrefour raw and fresh agri-food quality line in this case study.

There is a story behind the creation of the Carrefour quality line. In the early 1990s, a director of the Carrefour headquarters in France made a tour of Africa with his wife. His wife fell ill after she ate polluted food during the tour. Unfortunately she was died not very long after she came back to France. The director became aware of the importance of food safety. He believed that a guaranteed effective food quality line not only can increase profits for the enterprise, but also can create social benefits. Therefore, he created an internal quality line in Carrefour in 1990. The quality line of organic bread was created by Carrefour in cooperation with Boule Bio Company in 1993 and the quality line of salmon was created in cooperation with Norway in 1994. The quality line of Poitou Charente mutton was created in 1995. There were 12 quality lines created by Carrefour in 1996 and the number of quality lines increased to 60 in 1997. Carrefour created the first external quality line in 1998 and 456 quality lines were created in 2003.[1]

Carrefour created the first quality line, lichee quality line, in China in 1999. According to conventions, the creation of a quality line by Carrefour in a country needs at least 10 years of operation. However, Carrefour created a quality line in China only four years after operation, which shows that Carrefour has attached great importance to China's market. With the successful creation of the lichee quality line, Carrefour created pomelo and pomelo quality lines in Xiamen and Zhangzhou in 2002. In 2003, Carrefour signed a contract with French supplier for salmon quality line and that with Shanghai Agriculture, Industry, and Commerce Group for pork quality line. Carrefour signed a contract with Beijing Resource Meat Union Factory for meat quality line and signed a contract with fruit supplier from Weifang of Shandong Province for apple quality line in 2005. Carrefour signed a contract with XS of Beijing for vegetable quality line in 2006.[2]

Up to now, the proportion of raw and fresh agri-food with quality line is still very small. However, as special commodities with great development potentiality, Carrefour has paid great attention to them. Since the creation of quality lines, Carrefour has set up special counters for quality line goods. There are clear marks and description of quality line above or on the counters. The products of quality line are specially packaged not only with a label of quality line on packaged goods, but also a traceable code. Consumers can find the producer of products, the name of the greenhouse where the product was produced, farms where the fruits are produced, the pig where the pork comes from, and pesticides and fertilizers used in the process of production by using traceable barcode.

---

[1] Interview with Roland Vaxelaire, Quality, Responsibility and Risk Management Director of Carrefour Head Office.

[2] Interview with Wei Dai, Public Affaires Director, Carrefour, China.

Contents of Carrefour Quality Line

What is the Carrefour quality line? The quality line is the control and supervising line conducted by Carrefour on raw and fresh agri-food from planting, processing, and circulating in order to guarantee the quality and safety of products. Carrefour defines the products of quality line that sits between non-pollution and organic agri-foods and these agri-foods are equal to green food in safety and quality. Organic agri-food means that pesticides are not used during the process of planting. As for green food, not only is the safety guaranteed, great attention also has been paid to the protection of environment during the process of production and the use of pesticides and chemical fertilizers is limited. The focal point of non-polluted agri-food is environmental protection.

The definitions of agri-food of quality line are: (1) keep traceability of agri-food in the entire supply chain from planting to eating; (2) produce agri-food without pesticide residue; (3) quality of agri-food is stable; (4) environment-friendly production and processing technology; and (5) acceptable price by the great majority of consumers. The production cost and marketing price of agri-food of quality line should be lower than that of organic agri-food. The reason is that up to now only a small part of consumers is capable of buying organic agri-food even in developed countries.

Carrefour's quality line agri-foods possess five values:

(1) *Taste of the Products:* Carrefour supplies agri-food with taste better than that of ordinary products. Here taste means freshness and oral taste. For different agri-foods, quantitative indexes are stipulated, such as the contents of sugar and acid, grade of maturity, and freshness. These indexes are clearly defined in the quality line manual of different agri-foods.

(2) *Price of Agri-Food:* Besides high and stable quality, quality line agri-foods are moderately priced. At the same time, in order to guarantee quality, Carrefour pays for products at price higher than the market price and a part of the profits will be returned to farmers.

(3) *Food Safety:* The motto of the quality line is "making contributions for people and consumers' health". Therefore, raw and agri-food of the quality line must have traceability and are frozen in the entire process of transportation. The quality line requires that the soil, water, and air where agri-foods are grown must be in accordance with standards of green food. In the meantime, use of pesticides and fertilizers is strictly restricted.

(4) *Sustainability:* In order to protect the society, economy, and ecological environment, use of pesticides is strictly restricted. Waste materials and packing materials are strictly managed. Use of genetic improved varieties and raw materials are prohibited. Use of hormones and animal source protein in feed are not allowed either.

(5) *Reliability:* Looking for the best agri-food producing area and protection and develop traditional agriculture.[3]

Development of Quality Line[4]

The development of quality line products of Carrefour is carried out in a sequence. Firstly, the quality line department determines the products need to be developed. During this process, they do a great deal of studies. Then they look for suppliers. Usually, they look for suppliers through the purchasing department within Carrefour, or according to recommendations of agricultural universities and the academy of agricultural sciences. At first, Carrefour will select several candidate suppliers. Staff of the quality line department will inspect the candidates one by one. In the meantime, suppliers are asked to provide a test report on soil, water source, and air of farm. Staff of the quality line department will visit the suppliers several times and make investigations of the planting process, environment, and management. If necessary, Carrefour also invites experts from colleges and universities to give instructions to suppliers. In the period of getting familiar with each other when agri-foods of suppliers meet the requirements of quality line, suppliers are allowed by Carrefour to supply products for a period of time and a procurement contract for agri-food is signed.

A long period of time elapses Carrefour before suppliers are chosen. Some suppliers were eliminated owing to the reason that they could not adapt to the purchasing model of quality line. However, Carrefour does its best to assist the suppliers and gives favourable price.

Management of Quality Line

One of the characteristics of Carrefour is the adoption of the management system with its chain stores as the centre. The chain stores, the head of chain store, and the head of each sector have large powers in operation. The head of store and the head of sector have the rights to determine the combination of commodities, purchasing commodities, pricing, etc.

However, within Carrefour, the quality line and the agri-food of quality line are managed and controlled by a department directly under the headquarters. This department is in charge of the development plan of quality line, selection of agri-foods and suppliers, negotiation, training of suppliers, supervising on suppliers and suppliers' contracted farms, compilation of quality manual of the quality line, the quantity of ordered goods and pricing, etc. That is to say that the department of raw and fresh agri-food quality line has a special position within Carrefour. The managers of the quality line department have close relationship with suppliers. In the time of

---

[3] Information provided by Sylvia Wang, National Fresh Quality Line Developer, Carrefour, China, Merchandise Division.

[4] Information provided by Grelay Ye, National Fresh Quality Line Manager, China, Merchandise Division.

establishing a quality line, mangers inspect the suppliers' work at two-month intervals. After the establishment of quality line, inspections are conducted 2–3 times each year. The principle is that managers should be familiar with all the actions and works suppliers have done.

Supervision of the quality line of raw and fresh agri-food is carried out by a special committee from Carrefour headquarters. The members of the committee include the head of raw and fresh agri-food department of chain store, the head of chain store, the head of the regional area, and the managers of raw and fresh agri-food department of the headquarters. This committee examines and approves the programmes of quality line submitted by raw and fresh agri-food quality line, discusses the purchasing price with managers of quality line department, and participates in important negotiations.[5]

Relationship/Condition of Transaction

Carrefour has a variety of cooperative forms with agri-food suppliers in China. The most important of them are: outright purchase and joint operation. In outright purchase, Carrefour directly purchases agri-foods from suppliers and markets in Carrefour's stores. In joint operations Carrefour rents counters to suppliers and Carrefour collects 15–20 per cent management fee. The difference between the two modes and quality line is that Carrefour checks the quality and safety of agri-foods it directly purchases agri-foods, but does not interfere the production and distribution of these products.

However, Carrefour carries out general management of quality and safety of agri-foods produced by suppliers who participate in the quality line. In order to promote long-term and sustainable cooperation with suppliers, Carrefour gives preferential treatment to them. For instance, Carrefour invites suppliers to training programmes run by Carrefour and organizes them to go to France to study. It purchases agri-foods at higher price from suppliers of quality line. Carrefour also ensures early payment to quality line suppliers. The time for payment stipulated by Carrefour for common suppliers is 60 days while that for quality line suppliers is 30 days.

Cases of Construction of Quality Line

We now take up cases of construction of quality lines. These cases include: litchee, mandarin and pomelo, banana, pork, and vegetables.

Litchee quality line[6]

The first raw and fresh agri-food quality line constructed by Carrefour in China was for litchee. Litchee has a special position in China and is acclaimed as "the king of

[5] Information provided by Jean Anthoine, General Manager, China-Central & West, China, Executive Board.

[6] Interview with Mr. S, manager of Guangdong X Lichee Farm, June 2006.

fruits". The imperial concubine Yang (A.D. 719–756) was a favorite of Tang Xuanzong Li Longji, the emperor of the Tang dynasty, and relished litchee. In order to curry this beauty and meet her desire, Tangxuanzong ordered some postmen to transport fresh litchee by riding horses from more than 1000 km distant Guangdong Province to the capital Chang'an (now the Xi'an city) without rest. More than 1000 years ago, it was very difficult to keep litchee fresh. Su Shi (1037–1101), a great poet, history, was banished by the Song emperor to Nanhai of Guangdong which was a desolate and uninhibited area at that time. However, he was not depressed because this area produces the most delicious litchee. He wrote verses extolling the fruit. He wrote: "If I could eat three hundred litchee fruits every day, and I wanted to be a Lingnanese forever." These verses express the Chinese are fond of litchee.

Carrefour first opted to construct the quality line of litchee in 1999. Sanlinna was in change of the work of quality line at that time. Through the recommendation of a professor from South China Agricultural University, Sanlinna found Mr. S, a big litchee growing household in, Guangdong Province, in August 1999. Mr. S had more than 7 ha of litchee farm and the variety he grew is Feizixiao. Mr. S's litchee farm was well known in Guangdong Province and many people came to visit his farm and learn litchee growing technology from him. The governor and associate governor of Guangdong Province had visited his litchee farm. The government departments of Xinxing County bought some quantities of litchee from Mr. S' farm and gave to higher authorities as gift.

Salinna expressed satisfaction with the quality and planting technology of Mr. S's litchee. Since Carrefour had no standard materials on quality line of litchee (France does not grow litchee), Carrefour asked Mr. S to make an application for green food of litchee and asked him that his farm should reach the standards of green food within two years. Mr. S made an application and the green food certification cause in 2000. He also submitted the test report on soil, air, and water to Carrefour in that year. At that time, five litchee farms had signed letters of intent with Carrefour to supply litchee. Each farm had more than 2500 plants of litchee (40 plants per mu). Only Mr. S's farm could meet Carrefour's standards and accept Carrefour's payment conditions.

Owing to the cold current in Guangdong in 1999, output of litchee was seriously affected in 2000 and there was a great demand for litchee in market in that year. Carrefour's quality line purchased seven tons of litchee from Mr. S that year. Carrefour's quality line sold more than 30 tons of litchee in 2001. In 2002, owing to reduction of output of Mr. S' farm, Carrefour could buy only 20 tons. Owing to the extremely mugginess climate in Guangdong Province, all the litchee transported to Shanghai by Mr. S went bad and could not be sold. Both Carrefour and Mr. S suffered heavy losses. Carrefour's quality line found that it was difficult to guarantee sustainable supply of litchee for stores without good storage facilities. Carrefour found H. Fruit and Vegetable Fresh-keeping Co. Ltd which had litchee fresh keeping technology. Carrefour asked Mr. S to cooperate with H. Company and became a production base of the company. Mr. S supplies litchee to H. Company and the litchee is processed for fresh keeping by H. Company and then sent to Carrefour. Thus Carrefour has solved the problems of litchee processing and long distance transportation.

The quality standards of Carrefour's quality line are as follows: The diameter of litchee should be more than 30 mm, saccharine degree 15 degrees or more, and not injured by insects. The soil, air, and water in litchee producing area should be in accordance with the standards of green food (mainly according to the test report provided by the local agricultural department). Spray pesticides in litchee orchards are not allowed two months before harvest and samples should be submitted to the pesticide residue test department for testing and the test report should be faxed to Carrefour headquarters. Pesticides used in production should be those allowed for green food. Carrefour stipulates that the proportion of organic manure used in production should be 75 per cent of all fertilizers used, and hormones are not allowed. In year round production, farms should keep agricultural records and contents include irrigation, weeding, names, quantity, and time of fertilizers and pesticides used in production, harvesting period. To encourage litchee suppliers, the price offered by Carrefour is 30 per cent higher than the market price.

Carrefour's quality line discusses next year's litchee purchasing plan with suppliers in October of each year. Suppliers organize production according to this plan. Suppliers can produce litchee themselves or purchase litchee from cooperators whose products are approved by Carrefour's quality line. Carrefour sends the purchasing plan to suppliers again two weeks before delivery by suppliers. Since the output of agri-food is seriously influenced by natural conditions, suppliers can adjust the delivery time according to the conditions. Two days before delivery, Carrefour sends the order again and inform them the quantity to be delivered at each store. Carrefour has a distribution centre in Shanghai and litchee suppliers can transport goods to this centre. Carrefour has no distributing centre in north China and suppliers in parts of the country other than Beijing deliver their goods through fruit suppliers in Beijing area.

Carrefour quality line suppliers enjoy favourable terms such as no store-entering fee, sales promotion fee, etc. Carrefour published the standard manual of quality line of litchee in 2003.

Quality Line of Mandarin and Pomelo[7]

With the successful commissioning of the quality line of litchee, Carrefour began constructing the quality line of mandarin and pomelo in 2002. mandarin and pomelo are two kinds of special fruits produced in ZZ county, Fujian Province. Carrefour's chain stores in Shanghai begun marketing mandarin and pomelo in 1999 and they sold well. During the period of selecting next batch of quality line fruits by the quality

[7] Interview with Mr. Z, manager of Fujian ZZ Agri-development Company, in July 2006.

line, the manager of purchasing department in the east region (Jiangsu, Zhejiang, and other provinces with Shanghai as the centre) introduced ZZ Company to the staff of the quality line for mandarin and pomelo. Through discussion and verification, the quality line department decided to construct the quality line of mandarin and pomelo.

In 2001, Salinna and her assistants visited ZZ Agricultural Development Co. Ltd. in Fujian Province (hereafter call it Mr. Z for short). Salinna investigated Mr. Z's farms and processing workshops. ZZ Company is a fruit producing and processing enterprise with mandarin and pomelo farms of its own. Carrefour requested Mr. Z to provide test reports on soil, air, and water of mandarin and pomelo farms according to the stipulations of the technical manual of quality line. The quality line sent Ms. Y to do the authentication work of mandarin and pomelo. Ms. Y went to mandarin and pomelo farms six times in 2001 to understand the production aspects. The planting households were asked to fill production records and use of pesticides and fertilizers on different forms. The packing workshop should have a full-time recorder to take notes on sugar content and acidity of mandarin and pomelo.

ZZ Company supplied 300 tons of pomelo and 500 tons of pomelo for Carrefour in 2002. In 2003, owing to the increased demand of Carrefour's quality line for mandarin and pomelo, Carrefour proposed that Mr. Z farms cooperate with other farms and ZZ Company was asked to supervise and manage the process of production of other farms. Processing, packing, and transporting of fruits are still done by Mr. Z.

Managerial personnel of quality line investigate Mr. Z and their cooperating households regularly. In 2004, Carrefour invited a lecturer from Xianzhengda Fruits Company to give lectures on basic knowledge of pesticides to managerial and technical personnel. In 2005, Carrefour invited technician Mr. HZ to explain the pruning techniques of pomelo to farmer households.

ZZ Company supplied 500 tons of pomelos to Carrefour quality line annually from 2003 to 2005. ZZ Company exported pomelo to France with the assistance of Carrefour. Mr. Z supplied 1000 tons, 11 tons, and 4000 tons of pomelo in 2003, 2004, and 2005 respectively.

Quality Line of Pork[8]

At the end of 2002, Carrefour's quality line found that there were two standard pig slaughter houses, Shanghai AI Company and Shanghai Food. Carrefour did not invite Shanghai Food to participate in quality line because Carrefour found that, although this company had very good slaughtering equipment, it did not have commercial pig farms of its own. All the pork-type hogs are purchased from small scale households. Carrefour considered that the quality and safety of agri-food produced by small-scale farmer households could not be guaranteed. The quality line inspected pig farms and slaughter house at two-month intervals in that year.

[8] Interview with Mr. G, National Fresh Quality Line Management, in July 2006.

In June 2003, Carrefour approved AI Company as its cooperator of quality line of pork. The examining and approving meeting proposed that two Carrefour chain stores could be selected for test marketing quality line pork. The experiment lasted for one month. The person in charge of quality lines trained the heads of raw and fresh food department and section of Carrefour Jinqiao Store, and distributors from AI Company. The aim was to let them know the difference between quality line pork and ordinary pork sold by Carrefour, and the managerial principle of quality line pork in chain stores. A six-month experiment was conducted in these two stores by the staff of the quality line who would advise the company to improve once problems were discovered. The approval of pork quality line was completed in December 2003 and Carrefour signed a contract with AI Company.

Carrefour began to test and demonstrate the pork quality line in the eastern cities other than Shanghai in April 2004. Personnel from the stores in Hangzhou and Ningbo of Zhejiang Province, Nanjing, Wuxi, and Suzhou of Jiangsu Province were trained by Carrefour one by one. In October 2004, all Carrefour's stores in eastern cities began to sell pork of Carrefour's quality line.

The pig farm of AI Company is situated in F County and belongs to May 4th Farm. This farm was operated according to the requirements of the Shanghai Agricultural Committee and is a safe pork producing base area. Carrefour has a special requirement of safety for pork produced by the AI Company, so the purchasing price of quality line pork is 10 per cent higher than that of ordinary pork.

There were some disagreements between Carrefour and AI Company in the construction of quality. However, through a great deal of harmonious work, a mutually accepted programme was worked out. The first dispute pertained to traceability of pork. Carrefour's traceability means maintaining complete necessary records on ancestry, feed, and drugs used in the entire process from the birth of piglet to slaughter. Besides, each piece of packaged pork must be connected with the archives of pig so that the sources can be traced once a problem occurred. Carrefour had to do a great deal of explanation and finally the traceability line for each piece of pork was constructed by the two parties.

The second dispute pertained to the use of fish powder in pig feed. According to the standards of French quality line, supplementation of animal source protein and fish powder in pig feed is not allowed. AI Company claimed that fish powder should be used for the growth of pigs. The controversy between the two parties was submitted to a French expert in pork quality line. The expert proposed that if the problem of non-animal source protein cannot be resolved by Chinese pig keeping technology, the use of animal source protein can be restricted within a period of time. Finally, the two parties agreed to the use of fish powder feed before the piglets reached 15 kg.

The third dispute pertained to supplementation of streptomycin. AI Company added a little streptomycin in feed according to its practice to decrease the incidence of disease in pigs. Supplementation of antibiotic substances in feed is not allowed by Carrefour's quality line. After repeated discussions, the company agreed that streptomycin would not be supplemented in feed of the second, third, fourth, and fifth pig farms that were used for supplying quality line pork while the use of it in other pig farms (seven pig farms altogether) was not restricted.

The fourth argument related to the duration of drug prohibition. The quality line proposed that use of any drug is not allowed two months before the pigs are slaughtered, but the production manager of AI Company did not agree. Because of Carrefour's insistence, both parties agreed not to use any drug two months before the pigs were slaughtered. In case drugs have to be used, pigs treated with drugs would not be supplied to Carrefour's quality line.

The fifth dispute was about genetically modified (GM) feed. According to Carrefour's quality line, feeding animals with GM feed is not allowed. However, more than 95 per cent GM soybeans imported from North America were used in feed in China. This standard of the quality line cannot be accomplished in China. So Carrefour's quality line does not advertise GM feed.

The development of pork quality line in Beijing began in 2003. Carrefour in the north region recommended Beijing Zi Food to the quality line. Zi is the pork supplier to Carrefour in the north region. This company has a pig breeding farm and a commercial pig farm. Authentication of the quality line for pork was accomplished in 2004 and Carrefour signed an agreement with the company. Zi began supplying quality line pork for Carrefour's chain stores in October. In early 2005, quality line pork was extended to Tianjin and now all the Carrefour's chain stores in Beijing and Tianjin sell quality line pork. The quality line for pork in Shenzhen was developed in 2006.

Quality Line of Bananas[9]

Not all the developments of quality line of agri-food are successful. While Carrefour was successful in developing quality line for litchee, mandarin, pomelo, pork, and others, it could not develop a quality line for bananas although many efforts went into it.

Carrefour began constructing the quality line of bananas in April 2002. In order to look for cooperators, staff of the quality line from Carrefour in China and experts of vegetables and fruits from the Carrefour's headquarters in France visited Zhongshan City and Leizhou City of Guangdong Province, Fujian Province, Hainan Province, and Yunnan Province. They inspected the entire banana producing areas and the wholesale markets in Beijing and Shanghai and studied the difference between local bananas and imported bananas.

In April 2003, through the recommendation of the Leizhou City government, Carrefour found D Company, a supplier of bananas and tropical fruits. D. has banana growing base areas in Haikou City (200 ha) and Sanya city (150 ha) of Hainan

[9] Interview with Ms. Y, National Fresh Quality Line Management, in July 2006.

Province. During the period of construction of quality line of bananas by Carrefour and D, a strong typhoon hit Hainan in September 2003. D suffered heavy losses and output of bananas decreased by 40 per cent.

Since typhoon and cold current hit Hainan Province quite easily, banana cannot be supplied year round and cannot be used in Carrefour's quality line of bananas. D rented 200 ha of banana orchards in Jinping County of Yunnan Province. The person in charge of Carrefour's quality line made on-the-spot investigations of this orchard in May and July of 2004. The banana producing area also passed the test of soil, air, and water source. Trial sale of the quality line bananas was made in five Carrefour's chain stores in Beijing in September 2004. The trial sale lasted only one month and a half and Carrefour stopped selling the quality line bananas on November 10. The reason was that Datang adopted traditional banana ripening-accelerating techniques. The shelf life of banana was very short and the stores suffered great losses. Carrefour decided to abandon the banana programme. Carrefour discovered that products cannot enter the quality line of supermarkets without modern processing and fresh-keeping techniques even if the quality of products is good. At present, China is short of raw and agri-food fresh-keeping and processing techniques. Deficiency in investment on scientific research by the government has restricted many agri-foods of high quality entering the modern market.

Quality Line of Apples[10]

China is an important apple producing country in the world and is also a country with highest apple consumption. Carrefour decided to construct the quality line of apples in 2002. Before selecting suppliers, staff of the quality line visited many apple producing enterprises. In 2002, Carrefour selected a fruit company (P Company) as the supplier. P Company has apple producing base area in Weifang city 150 km from Qingdao city. This base area belongs to 10 contractual farmer households. The quality line monitored this base area for more than a year and inspected it at two-month intervals. When the indicators of various items in the base area reached the standards of the quality line, the two parties signed a contract of supplying 100 tons of apples in 2003. In November 2003, P Company began supplying apples for Carrefour. However, in a period of one month before December, P Company only supplied 10 tons of apples and this was only 10 per cent of the contractual amount. The reasons were that the contractual farmer households sold apples to other companies and P Company could not purchase apples. P Company asked Carrefour to give it one more chance. Carrefour signed a contract with P Company for supplying 500 tons of grade I apples in 2004. However, P Company only supplied 300 tons of apple that year and the quality of apple reached only grade II and grade III. The quality line signed a contract with P Company for supplying 800 tons of apples in 2005. However, when the apples needed to be transported before the spring festival in 2006, P Company

[10]Interview with Feng Xiaoyan, manager of Shangdong Sanfeng Fruits Storage Limited Company, July 2006.

suddenly informed Carrefour that apples could not be supplied because the roof of the cold frame had collapsed and the stored apples were affected. Carrefour was very disappointed with P Company's action and had to terminate the agreement.

At the end of 2004, the world-wide purchasing department recommended quality line department SS Company of L City of Shandong Province. SS exports apples to Europe through Carrefour's worldwide purchasing department. After reaching an agreement with SS, Carrefour checked and accepted the base area. (Carrefour's standards of apple production had been accomplished in 2004). The test report on soil, water, and air came out in April 2005 and reached the requirements of the quality line. Carrefour signed a contract with SS for purchasing 1000 tons of apples. In 2005, SS accomplished supplying 1000 tons of apples. From that time on, SS has become the only cooperative partner of Carrefour's quality line of apples.

Case Studies of Quality Line Suppliers

In this part of the paper, we study five cases of construction of Carrefour's quality line. This part concentrates on suppliers of quality line commodities. We investigated the process through which suppliers became Carrefour's contracting suppliers and the effects to these suppliers cooperating with Carrefour and production technology of these enterprise or individual suppliers. The suppliers per se are producers of agri-food. Studies on Carrefour's suppliers of the quality line are essential to understand the changes in the market, development of supermarket, and effects and roles on producers of agri-food in China.

W Litchee Farm of Xin County[11]

Xin County W Litchcee Farm, a private fruit farm, was established in 1993. The total area of the farm is 7 ha and the annual yield of litchee is about 35 tons. The farm started cooperating with Carrefour in 1999.

Mr. Su, the farmer of W Litchee Farm of Xin County, Guangdong Province, was born in 1955. He joined the army after he graduated from high school in 1972. He was demobilized from the army in 1978 and became a forest worker in the agri-forestry department of Xin County. He worked for a governmental department popularizing forestry technology in 1981 and was engaged in popularizing technical work of fruit trees. He resigned from the governmental department and started his own business of building materials.

Su quitted his building material business and began to operate fruit farms in 1990. He rented 2.5 ha land from Chegang town of Xin County and got a bank loan of RMB 170000 for planting citrus. As there was a soft citrus market at that time, Su had a deficiency of RMB 330000. Su planted 400 litchee plants when he was planting citrus trees and his aim was "to support the long-term litchee project by using a

[11]Interview with Mr. Su, manager of Guangdong XW Lichee Farm, June 2006.

fast-yielding citrus project". He found litchee sold well and made a profit of RMB 130000 from the 400 litchee plants in 1993.

Mr. Su contracted more than 7 ha hill land in the suburbs of Xin County for planting litchee and it is the W Litchee Farm now. This piece of land was covered with citrus and the original owner went bankrupt. So the original owner sold the land to Mr. Su. The annual contracting fees was RMB 5000 and the term of contract was for 22 years. According to the contract, the rental price per ha in the first 15 years is RMB 1500 and in the next seven years it will be increased to RMB 1800.

Mr. S deforested all the citrus trees and planted litchee trees. The variety of litchee is Feizixiao and is a mid-season good variety. He invested RMB 320000 in that year and planted 2100 plants. Mr. S hired farmers in the adjacent area to level soil and plant trees and these works were not finished before April 1994. These litchee plants were sowed in 1996 and achieved great sales in 1998. The output was 1.5 tons. The unit price was 3 US $/kg and the sales amount was 45000 US $.

Before cooperating with Carrefour, about one-third of the litchee produced by Mr. W's Litchee Farm was sold to local governmental departments and bosses of private enterprises. The remaining litchee was sold to a fruit wholesaler in the nearby Doumen shi fruit wholesale market who had cooperated with Su for a long period of time.

Through the recommendation of Mr. W and Mr. Ch, professors from the South China Agricultural University, Mr. Su got in touch with Carrefour in August 1999. As Mr. W Litchee Farm was declared "the national sustainable agricultural demonstration project base area", Mr. S met teachers from South China Agricultural University. Only seven farms were chosen as the national sustainable agricultural demonstration project base area in the whole country and Mr. S' farm was the only one chosen in Xin County. Mr. W Litchee Farm also became a research subject of South China Agricultural University. When the farm became a national sustainable agricultural demonstration project base area, it attracted many visitors. On December 5, 1999, 11 persons from Carrefour including the person in charge of world-wide quality line from France inspected We Litchee Farm. On the next day, Mr. S signed a letter of cooperative intention with Carrefour in South China Agricultural University. In the meantime, there were five litchee farms signed a letter of cooperative intention with Carrefour. These farms are large and each farm has more than 2500 litchee plants.

Carrefour did not have any standard manual for litchee production at that time, so it asked Su to make application for green food of litchee. It also stimulated that Mr. W Litchee Farm should meet standards of green food production within two years. Mr. S made application for green food at the end of 1999 and litchee are produced according to the operational procedures of green food.

During the period of maturing of litchee in Mr. W Litchee Farm, Carrefour's purchasing personnel went with US $ 10000. Thanks to the good quality of litchee in Mr. W farm, Carrefour signed a purchasing contract of quality line litchee with

Mr. S started delivering one ton of litchee to Shanghai each day. Mr. W Litchee Farm supplied 7 tons of litchee for Carrefour, which accounted for 44 per cent of the gross yield of 16 tons of that year.

Cooperating with Carrefour quality line, Mr. W Litchee Farm has a stable litchee market and the price offered by quality line is 30 per cent higher than the average price in the ordinary market.

An extremely high temperature was occurred in 2004 and the relative humidity of the air was very high. Litchee fruits turned soft soon after picked. The first batch of litchee was transported to Shanghai by air, but it took more than 3 hours transporting litchee to Carrefour distributing center in Shanghai due to traffic jams. So the litchee had gone bad and became wastes. The distributing center refused to receive the litchee. After discussion with Carrefour, the supermarkets deducted 18 percent of the costs of litchee for Mr. W (including air freight cost). Mr. W suffered a heavy losses and Carrefour also suffered some losses.

H Company possesses technology for fresh-keeping litchee. As a H Company's litchee production base area, litchee produced in Mr. We Farm is transported to H Company.It is processed with fresh-keeping techniques, packed, and transported by H Company. Mr. W Farm sold 34 tons of litchee to Carrefour through H Company in 2005 and 50 tons in 2006.

Ten days before sending litchee to Carrefour, 5 kg of samples are sent to Zhanjiang Agricultural Bureau for pesticide residue tests and the test report is delivered seven days later. The original report is sent to Carrefour and litchee delivery by We farm is allowed only when the test report is considered qualified.

One of the important indicators of Carrefour's quality line is traceability. The code number of orchard and plucking date is printed on each box of litchee transported by Mr. W farm to Carrefour's chain stores. In the meantime, the copy of field records is faxed to the quality line section so that if food safety problems occur, the source of problem and people who are responsible can be traced.

Since Mr. W Litchee Farm does not possess fresh-keeping technology, it has become the production base area of H Company. This indicates that market changes also propose new challenges for agri-food processing, storage, and transport technology.

H Fruit and Vegetable Fresh-Keeping Co., Ltd.[12]

Guangzhou Conghua H Fruits and Vegetables Fresh-keeping Co. Ltd. is a cooperative shares system enterprise. It is an undertaking for popularization of high and new technology in Guangdong Province and is a leading enterprise of agriculture in Guangzhou City. The company was established in 1998. It is situated in Conghuashi City, a main litchee producing area and has a fruit and vegetable producing base area,

[12]Interview with Mr. O, Guangzhou C.H. Fruits and Vegetable Storage Limited Company, June 2006.

fresh-keeping and processing plant, cold chain storage, and transportation equipments. Eighty per cent of the products are exported to Europe, US, Japan, and the Southeast Asia. At present, it is a supplier of quality line litchee to Carrefour.

Mr. O is the chairman of H Fruit. He loved studying from very young. He was admitted to the speciality of agri-food processing and storage of the horticulture department of South China Agricultural University in 1987. His graduation thesis was "Conditions influencing litchee storage at low temperature". He worked for a vegetable and fruit import and export company after graduating and participated in vegetable and fruit export operations.

The Guangdong Scientific and Technology Commission organized a public bidding on the development of litchee storage at low temperature in the country in 1997 and South China Agricultural University won the bid. This project began in 1998 and Mr. O participated in it. The project was completed at the end of 1999. In order to popularize the results of the project and extend the litchee fresh-keeping technology, the government provided loans for Conghua shi company and South China Agricultural University to establish a company, called H Fruit and Vegetable Fresh-keeping Company. Mr. O was general manager of the new company.

After one year of operation, the Guangdong provincial science commission and government department released a new policy that companies like H should have no state-owned assets. In that year, the employees purchased Huanlong Company for US $ 562,500. Mr. O spent more than US $ 100,000 accounting for 21 per cent of the share. He became the chairman of the board of the company.

H Company covers an area of 14000 M^2 and has a cold frame with a capacity of 800 tons and a drying and processing workshop with an area of 3000 m^2. The company has rented 20 ha of land in the suburbs of Conghua City; 15 ha of them are covered with vegetables and 5 ha are covered with litchee trees. The rent is 81.25 US $/mu. The company has hired 7–8 workers to work in orchards and more than 80 work in vegetable plots.

H's main operations works are export of vegetables and fruits. Vegetables and fruits are exported to England, Netherlands, and France. Since 2000, the company began exporting vegetables and fruits to Southeast Asian countries such as Malaysia and Singapore. Recently, the company has developed the American market and exports vegetables and fruits to Canada and USA. The value of exports in 2005 was US $3.3 million.

Huanlong and supplies tropical and subtropical vegetables and fruits to Shanghai, Hangzhou and other cities.

Mr W's spoilage litchee invited the attention of Carrefour. Through the recommendation of South China Agricultural University, Carrefour came to know that H Company possessed the technology for litchee fresh-keeping. Staff of Carrefour quality line negotiated with H Company for cooperation. The construction of

Carrefour litchee quality line base area had been completed already. The quality of litchee was very good, but the problem was that the litchees were not treated with fresh-keeping techniques after harvest and litchees were easily rotten in long distance transportation. H Fresh-keeping technology prolongs the shelf-life of the fruit for one week. Carrefour, H Company, and Mr. W Litchee Farm began cooperating from 2005. Mr. W Litchee Farm has become H Company's litchee production base area. Cultivation and management of litchee are according to the standards of Carrefour's quality line and litchee fresh-keeping treatment is done using H Company's techniques. We farm plucks litchee according to instructions from H Company. After preliminary processing in the orchard, litchees are transported to H's processing workshop for fresh-keeping treatment and then transported to Carrefour chain stores in Beijing and Shanghai.

In 2005, H Company transported 50 tons of litchee to Carrefour's quality line and the value was more than US $75000. In 2006, because of abundant rainfall, yield of litchee decreased, and H transported only 36 tons of litchee to Carrefour.

Thanks to the adoption of H Company's fresh-keeping technology, the losses of Carrefour's quality line have decreased remarkably. In 2005, a new cooperative litchee producing base area in Zhuhai was added to H Company. This was a state-owned grade A food base area, i.e. the orchard of Zhuhai Institute of Pomology. This orchard covers an area of more than 1000 mu (1 mu = 1/15 hekare) of litchee trees. H Company and Carrefour investigated ZH Companyhai base area together. First of all, they asked ZH Companyhai to provide test reports on soil, water, and air, records of farm management, and agricultural activities. This orchard is now H Company's litchee production base area.

H Company purchases litchee from production base areas and after processing sells to Carrefour at a price that is 50 per cent higher than the market price of that year. The purchasing price of the cooperative farm is determined by the farm, Carrefour, and H Company, and is about 30 per cent higher than the market price of that year. So Companysiasm for production of litchee according to the standards of Carrefour's quality line is sustained.

Demand for quality line litchee has increased continuously, so H Company and Carrefour are looking for new cooperative base areas. For the sake of convenience, only those large-scale litchee farms with productive capacity higher than 2.5 tons can be base area.

In August 2006, H Company got in touch with Guangdong Y County Litchee Association and the two signed an agreement on litchee quality line in 2007. The association will provide a part of litchee of Carrefour quality line for H Company. Y County Litchee Association has more than 200 members of households; 10 per cent of them have large-scale litchee farms with more than 2500 litchee trees, 30 per cent of them have medium-scale litchee farms with 1000–2500 litchee trees, and 60 per cent of them have small-scale litchee farms with less 1000 litchi trees. H Company manages the quality line of litchee and purchases litchee *via* Y County Litchee Association.

Mandarin of ZY Agricultural Development Co., Ltd.[13]

ZY Agricultural Development Co. Ltd., was established in 2000. It is a special fruit company engaged in planting, processing (fresh-keeping), and marketing. It is supplier of pomelo, mandarin, banana, and other high quality fruits for Carrefour, Wal-Mart, Maidelong, and other large supermarkets. The company was elected as provincial level leading enterprise in 2005. The annual quantum of sales of fruits is 10000 tons.

Mandarin belongs to the citrus family and is a special local product of Zhangzhou area of Fujian Province. The coat of mandarin is orange yellow. It is juicy and delicious. Its solids content is about 15 per cent.

Carrefour started constructing mandarin quality line in 2002 and the main supplier is Fujian ZY Agricultural Development Co., Ltd. The general manager of the corporation is Mr. Zh. ZY is a family-owned business. It was set up with an investment by Mr. Z and his brothers. The corporation is mainly managed by Mr. Zh. Mr. Zh. was born in 1973 in a rural area. His father is a teacher and his mother is a peasant. He quit studies after graduating from middle school. He planted mandarin in his 5 ha of hill land when he was 17 years old. In 1989, he rented 30 ha waste land from the Xiafeng village of Nanjing County. He employed local farmers to cut down the trees on the waste land and plant mandarin trees. In 1994, the fifth year of reclamation of the land, mandarins were harvested and Mr. Zh. sold all mandarins to small vendors.

In 1997, Mr. Zh once again rented mountain land from others and the area of increased to 86.6 ha. With large enough area for mandarin plantation, the problems that Mr. Zh needed to resolve were lack of stable market for mandarin and price fluctuation. In several years the market price of mandarin was too low to compensate for plucking labour cost, so the mandarins were left rotting on trees. Transportation of mandarins by Mr. Zh to the wholesale markets in Beijing and Shanghai also met with problems.

Mr. Zh got information in March 1999 that Carrefour was looking for mandarin suppliers. He went to Shanghai with his brother to negotiate with Carrefour. He began delivering mandarin to the eastern region Carrefour (including Carrefous's chain stores in Shanghai, Jiangsu and Zhejiang) in the autumn of 1999. A total of 300 tons of mandarins were sold to Carrefour in 1999.

Mr. Zh enjoys some preferential treatment while participating in participation in Carrefour's quality line. Store entering fees, promotion fees, and sampling fees are not charged. The price of mandarins purchased by quality line is 20–30 per cent higher than that of ordinary ones. However, in order to improve the quality of fruit, Mr. Zh's investment in production and management of mandarin increased. According to the requirements, agricultural activities such as spraying pesticides and

[13] Interview with Zhuang Zhanzhong, manager of Fujian ZZ. Agri-development Company, July 2006.

use of fertilizers should be recorded. Not only these works should be done carefully in Mr. Zh's own mandarin producing base area, but also in other cooperative base areas. The quality manual of the quality line clearly stipulates which pesticides cannot be used and when pesticides can be used. The quality manual also stipulates the contents of sugar and acid, individual fruit weight, and diameter.

Staff of Carrefour's quality line go to Mr. Zh and the cooperative base areas for inspections every year. They check use of pesticides and records of agricultural activities. Besides these routine inspections, Mr. Zh is also required to provide test report on each batch of product. Carrefour also invited SGS Company (a European company engaged in testing) for testing the quality and safety of Mr. Zh's products. SGS Company samples from mandarins in Carrefour's chain stores and submits the report after testing.

In the marketing plan, Carrefour negotiates the next year's mandarin purchasing plant with Mr. Zh every September. Carrefour will inform Mr. Zh of the quantity of mandarins needed and the locations two weeks before delivery. Small adjustments are allowed. Mr. Zh delivers goods to the delivery centre in Shanghai and each of other Carrefour chain stores. The methods used for delivering goods are: delivery by the third party logistics company; delivery by ZY company itself; and delivery by Carrefour's local fruit suppliers.

Mandarins produced by Mr. Zh entered into Carrefour's quality line in 2003 and 300 tons of mandarin were sold that year. Sales in 2004 and 2005 stayed at 500 tons each.

Mr. Zh has contracted land from adjacent small farmer households. The rent was US $ 18.75/ha in 1989 and increased to RMB 750/ha in 1995, RMB 1200/ha in 1997, and RMB 2400/ha at present. The term of contract between the company and households is for 30–50 years. Once the contract is signed by the parties, land rent will not be changed.

Farmers whose lands have been rented to company can be employed by the company. The wages of regular workers are RMB 1200/month, while that for temporary workers are RMB 35/day for male and RMB 30/day for female.

Sweet Pomelo of Mr. Z Agricultural Development Co., Ltd.[14]

Sweet pomelo is a good breed of pomelo. Its origin is P County of Fujian Province where it has a cultivation history of more than 500 years. Sweet pomelo is orange yellow and bright in colour. It has a thick fragrance and the palatable part reaches 60 per cent or more. Wu Gengmin, a famous pomologist in China and a professor of Zhejiang Agricultural University, says this about sweet pomelo: "Its fruit is large and its coat is thin. It has no seeds in flesh. Its flesh contains abundant juice and is soft, without residue, sweet, and a bit acidic in taste. Its taste lasts for a long time and ranks the first of pomelo."

[14] Interview with Zhuang Zhanzhong, manager of Fujian ZZ. Agri-development Company, July 2006.

Mr. Z has 50 ha of sweet pomelo base area in adjacent Nanjing County. Construction of this base area was started in 1995. The marketing price of sweet pomelo at that time was good, so Mr. Z rented 50 ha waste hill lands from several households. The rent was US $ 112.5/ha. Mr. Z hired local peasants to reclaim wastelands and plant more than 8000 sweet pomelo trees. At the initial stage, Mr. Z did not know how to plant sweet pomelo trees, so it invited experienced peasants and technicians from the county forestry bureau to give instructions. It purchased pomelo seedlings from Pinghe County agricultural Bureau, the original county of sweet pomelo, at a price of RMB 12/seedling.

The pomelo trees bloomed with a few fruits in 1998. Yield per plant increased to 50 kg in 2000.

Negotiations between Mr. Z and Carrefour carried out in 1999 included sweet pomelo and the company sold more than 200 tons of sweet pomelo to Carrefour in 2000. Sweet pomelos were transported to Qingpu Materials Circulation and Distribution Centre in Shanghai.

Table 10.4: Quality Line Pomelo Supplied by ZZ Company

	2002	*2003*	*2004*	*2005*
Quantities (ton)	500	1000	1100	4000

In order to increase the yield of sweet pomelo, Mr. Z started cooperating with other farms in 2002 and these farms were used as base area. The standards Mr. Z used in selecting base areas were: area of planted pomelo is not less than 15 ha; management of orchards conforms to standards; and accords with the standards of quality line and implemented seriously.

In 2002, 12 farms were selected as base area, and the largest one was ZZ Agricultural Development Company and has 1200 mu of land. Zhongrun is a state-owned farm and others are privately owned.

Some farms could not reach the requirements of technology and management of Mr. Z, so 7 farms were eliminated next year. In 2003 and 2004, four farms were added and there were 8 farms altogether. One farm was eliminated again and now Mr. Z has 7 cooperative farms.

Here is an example of an eliminated cooperative farm. Peasant Lu A'cheng's farm is situated in Pinghe County and is 15 km from ZY Company. Lu has 20 ha of pomelo orchard and he started cooperating with Mr. Z in 2002. Lu had some difficulties in farm management and funds and his products could not meet the standards of Carrefour's quality line. ZZ Company asked Lu to make improvements the next year. However, Lu did not produce pomelo according to Mr. Z's standards, so he was eliminated.

Mr. Z considers that the standards of Carrefour's quality line are advanced. For the implementation of standards, changing the farmers' traditional production mode and habit is vital. The key problem is that farmers will not change their mode of management and habit before they see obvious economic effects. In agricultural department, the input-output ratio is always negative in the short run. For instance, Carrefour advocates that organic manure should account for 70 per cent of fertilizer used. The planting cost will increase if the amount of organic manure is increased but the yield of products cannot be increased proportionally. Farmers think that since more benefits cannot be obtained from the application of organic manure, why not use convenience chemical fertilizers?

Mr. Z was approved as a "leading enterprise" of Fujian agricultural industrialization in 2005. It won the sweet pomelo processing and fresh-keeping project of the Fujian Province Science and Technology Bureau.

The estimated output of sweet pomelo of Mr. Z in 2006 is 13000 tons of which 2500 tons are planned to be sold through the quality line, 2000 tons to be exported to France, and the rest would be sold to Southeast countries, and domestic markets.

ZG Agricultural Development Co., Ltd.[15]

ZG Agricultural Development Co., Ltd. is situated in P. County, the original production place of China's famous sweet pomelo. Mr. HY is in charge of the farm and technology. Mr. HY was born in 1947 and graduated from Zhangzhou Agro-technical School in 1975. He later worked as a crop technician for 8 years. He was elected as a village leader and was in that position for 10 years.

In 1990, Xiazhai Township of P. County reclaimed a mountain and planted 120 ha of pomelo trees. The township government made an investment of more than US $ 125,000 in pomelo orchards. Output of sweet pomelo reached more than 400 tons in 1997. As the town government was deficient in funds for continuing investment, the government decided to sell the orchard at a price of more than US $ 1 million. A company in Beijing under the Ministry of Finance became a large shareholder. Now this orchard has become a joint venture and the four legal bodies partnering are the Beijing company, Zhangzhou City, Pinghe County, and Xiazhai Township governments. The share of the Beijing's company is 64 per cent. Other partners have a share of 12 per cent each.

The company was set up in 1997 as ZG Agricultural Development Co., Ltd. (hereafter ZG). At present, ZG has more than 80 ha of orchards and 40000 pomelo trees. Output of sweet pomelo in 1998 was 900 tons and increased to 4200 tons in 2005.

The farm has 30 regular employees (including managerial personnel and workers) and more than 100 temporary workers. Before cooperated with ZZ Company, sweet pomelo produced by ZG were mainly transported by chartered wagons to wholesale markets in Shanghai, Beijing, Wuhan, Guiyang, and other cities.

[15]Interview with Mr. HY, manager of Fujian Pinghe Agricultural Development Co., Ltd., July 2006.

In 2003, ZG began cooperating with ZZ Company of Carrefour's quality line and has become one of the sweet pomelo producing base areas of ZZ Company. In that year, Carrefour's quality line sent staff from Shanghai headquarters carried out quality line investigation of pomelo farms. At that time, ZG orchards had been approved as green food base area by Fujian Province. However Carrefour still required Zhongrun to submit test reports on soil, water, and air. All the tested results proved to be satisfactory. The quality line has strict stipulations on the use of pesticides and fertilizers in pomelo cultivation. Carrefour sends staff to inspect ZG 2–3 times every year. Technicians from ZZ Company visit ZG regularly to inspect the implementation of the standards of the quality line.

Mr. Z purchases sweet pomelo from ZG on behalf of Carrefour. Mr. Z signs a purchasing contract and purchasing plan with ZG in advance. During the period of harvest, ZG transports sweet pomelo to Mr. Z's fruit packing and processing plant according to the plan and then transported to Carrefour after processing. Nothing needs to be done by ZG after sweet pomelo are transported to Mr. Z. ZG sold 2000 tons of pomelo to ZZ Company in 2005. ZG considers that the cooperation with Mr. Z is much more convenient than marketing the fruits by the company itself. Market and price are stable and sales value has increased. However, as the standards of the quality line are very strict, the company faces some difficulties.

Beijing XS Special Vegetables Base Area[16]

The construction of quality line for vegetables has a special value for Carrefour. Consumers' demand for vegetables in China is very high. However, as vegetables suffer infections of pests easily, the growing period of leafy vegetables is short, and the technology in controlling of pesticide residue is sophisticated so the construction of quality line of vegetables was not done until 2006. The first cooperator of Carrefour's quality line of vegetables was Beijing XS special vegetables base area (XS for short).

XS vegetables base area was constructed in 1984 and was a state-owned farm under the Beijing Agricultural Bureau at that time. At the beginning of construction, more than 20 ha of land was rented from XS Town and for 70 years. Beijing Agricultural Bureau made an investment of US $ 125,000. The fixed assets of this farm are US $ 8.125 million now. The construction of a vegetables base area was proposed by Deng Xiaoping who pointed out that the implementation of the policy of reform and opening to the outside world would attract many foreigners to work in Beijing and they would be eating local vegetables. Vegetables grown here are supplied to Friendship Department Store and large hotels. XS was chosen as the special vegetables supply base area for the Beijing Municipal Party Committee and the municipal government in 1995 and became the special vegetables supply base area for the state council. The special supply base area is a designated farm used for supplying

[16]Interview with Mr. Lin, Vice General Manager of XS Vegetable Farm.

vegetables for government leaders at higher levels. In order to ensure the health of leaders, only reliable farms can be designated as special supply base areas.

In the mid-1990s, supermarkets in Beijing developed rapidly. XS grasped this opportunity and developed market for its vegetables by fully using its advantages. In 1999, XS began supplying vegetables to Xidan Wanfang supermarket, the first supermarket in Beijing. It began supplying vegetables to Xidan Department Store in the same year. In 2000, XS began supplying vegetables to Itoyakado, a Japanese capital supermarket company. XS had special vegetable-selling counters in more than 70 supermarkets before 2006. XS's first vegetable base area was constructed in SH Companynyi County where the company has is headquarters. The first out-reaching base area was constructed in 1998 in D. village of Shunyi County and then expended gradually to Miyun and other areas in Beijing suburbs. At present, the varieties of vegetables grown exceed 450.

Vegetables produced in the base area of XS headquarters are specially supplied to the State Council, Beijing Municipal Government, and some hotels in Beijing. Beijing out-reaching base areas are distributed in Shunyi, Pinggu, Miyun, and Yanqing, and the total area is 160 ha. The six base areas outside Beijing belong to about 1000 small scale farmers, and XS manages these with its own staff. XS is responsible for production, providing technical assistance, and supervising the use of pesticides and fertilizers. The company also invites experts to give technical instructions. Leading cadres of the company inspect the arrangements and progress of work every week. The company provides professional and technical trainings to personnel in base areas and more than 1000 personnel received training in 2005.

Negotiations between XS and Carrefour were started in April 2005. Staff in charge of Carrefour's quality line went to investigate the base area. Water source, soil, and air were tested to see if they met with the requirements. Carrefour gave XS the manuals of vegetable production and packing. In the process of negotiations, Carrefour proposed that XS's production and management must accord with the requirements of the manual.

On September 10, 2005, quality line vegetables produced by XS were formally sold in Beijing Carrefour's Shuangjing store in Beijing. Seven vegetables were produced under the quality line initially: cucumber, cherry tomato, large tomato, cabbage, sweet pepper, carrot, and potato. In January 2006, Chinese radish was also added to the quality line. With the success of trial operations, the quality line vegetables produced by XS started to be sold in six Carrefour chain stores.

Traceability is a key point in quality line of vegetables. Each greenhouse has a coding number and detailed records. Field production records include fertilizer application, spraying pesticides, irrigation, amount of harvest, raising seedlings, etc. The code number on the top right corner corresponds to the greenhouse code number.

All the vegetables produced in XS vegetable base area can be harvested only when indicators of pesticides and fertilizers have been tested. Samples of the harvested vegetables should be tested again. Records of tests for the latest three years are kept in the computer database of the company. Harvested products are packaged in boxes according to different varieties. Each box has a code number and the names of farmers are printed on some boxes.

There are also some problems in the cooperation between XS and Carrefour:

1. Utilization of hormones. Farmers use plastic film greenhouses to grow vegetables in China. The fluctuation of temperature inside plastic film greenhouses where the temperature is too low in winter and too high in summer cannot meet the requirements of pollination. Therefore, hormones must be used in winter and summer in plastic film greenhouses. According to Carrefour's requirements, the use of hormones is not allowed, so domestic growers cannot meet these requirements.
2. Carrefour demands each farmer household should have a fertilizer pond. This cannot be achieved in China because investment in a fertilizer pond is high and farmers cannot afford it.
3. Sometimes use of pesticides cannot be controlled.

The differences between Carrefour's quality line products and domestic green foods are as follows:

1. Carrefour's quality line products have traceability while domestic green foods do not have it;
2. The price of Carrefour's quality line products is lower than that of domestic green agri-foods;
3. The quality requirements on Carrefour's quality line products are higher than that of domestic green agri-foods;

   Transportation and storage of Carrefour's quality line products need cold storage while that of domestic green agri-foods do not need. The cost of Carrefour's quality line products is 20– 30 per cent higher than that of domestic green agri-foods, while the selling price of Carrefour's quality line products is 30 per cent lower. Carrefour's quality line products fetch 2.7 per cent lower profit than normal profit.
4. Carrefour's quality line products demand a unified and fixed mode of packing.

Contract Farm of XS

Let us have a look at the XS cooperative base area. A part of the XS quality line vegetables is produced by the cooperative base area. One of the cooperators is Mr. T. who lives in Pinggu County. Mr. T rented 5 ha of land from the village government in 2002 and invested RMB 0.86 million for constructing 17 plastic film greenhouses. He hired 10 farmers from adjacent villages to manage these plastic film greenhouses and grow vegetables. In 2006, when XS became a vegetable supplier of Carrefour's quality line, Mr. T's farm was used as a cooperative base area. After investigation of Mr. T's farm by Carrefour's quality line, XS sent technicians to give technical instructions. Tong's farm supplies 300 kg of tomatoes, 200 kg of cucumbers, 200 kg of autumn squash, and 50 kg of tonka beans for XS every day. A part of the pesticides used by the farm is supplied by XS while another part of pesticides is purchased from the market by the farm according to the list provided by XS. Mr. T's farm has constructed the traceability system of vegetables according to the requirements of Carrefour and XS.

Conclusion

The significance of Carrefour quality line is that the supermarket, which is situated at the end of downstream, carries out integrated management of the entire supplying line of agri-food. Before adoption of quality line by Carrefour, in the history of China, the supplying chain of agricultural products was divided into several sections. The independent sections were linked by governmental plans or the invisible hand of market.

Since the implementation of the policy of reform, opening to the outside world and system of contracting production to households in China in the 1980s, the upper stream of the supplying chain of agricultural products in China is occupied by 200 million small-scale farmer households and in the middle stream we find thousands of small retailers who are engaged in distribution of agricultural products. This kind of production and distribution mode of agricultural products based on small-scale and small retailers has a very high efficiency but has a negative and inhibitory effect on increase of planned production of agricultural products and quality and safety of agri-foods. In recent years, exports of agricultural products have been restricted because of pesticide or animal drug residue exceeding the standards. Reports of food poisoning owing to high content of pesticide residue in vegetables purchased from domestic market have appeared in newspapers. If proper management measures are not adopted on the supplying chain of agricultural products, the problems of quality and safety of agri-foods in China cannot be resolved.

From the above case studies we have seen the development of Carrefour's quality line in China. It is true that the aim of the construction of Carrefour's quality line is to serve Carrefour supermarket oneself and to raise Carrefour's competitive power with other supermarkets and wet markets in China. However, there is a far-reaching significance for Chinese farmers, agri-food processing enterprises and consumers beyond Carrefour's competitive advantage. The important significance of quality lines introduced by Carrefour is innovation.

Firstly, the quality line has led to the innovation of production mode of farmer households. The originally independent farmer households have become an organic component of the quality line. The quality line gives farmer households instructions, supervisions, and management in production. This is beneficial to them since they can adopt more advanced food safety technologies and learn management theories. Farmers show a great concern on the results of production such as yield and appearance. In order to achieve these goals, they adopt every method they can such as adoption of high poisonous pesticides, over-use of fertilizers, etc. The quality line makes farmer households attach importance to the entire process of production of agri-food. The establishment of traceability not only has made the process of production of agri-food thoroughly exposed, but also has made farmer households enter into information technology production stage from pure materials production stage.

Secondly, changes have come about in the traditional circulation mode of agri-food in China. The circulation mode is divided into different sections and each section involves participation of a large number of individual employees. The upper and lower streams of the supply chain are connected by simple "selling" and "buying" (the invisible hand) and this kind of circulation mode is short of supervision and management measures and functions. This kind of circulation mode is the warm bed for opportunism (Williamson, 1975), and agri-food safety cannot be guaranteed. The transformation of the traditional circulation mode Carrefour is through direct management of agri-food production and processing. The "visible hands" (Chandler, 1977) of the enterprise are extended directly to the initial stage of the supply chain. Productive standards and plans of enterprises can be implemented effectively in the entire process of production. The more important aspect is that it has laid a platform for the "traceability of agri-food". The form of supplying chain adopted by Carrefour is one of the best choices for guarantying quality and safety in the existing agricultural production system in China. Without supervision and management of the entire supplying chain, quality and safety of agri-food cannot be guaranteed.

Thirdly, innovation is made in the production system of safe agri-food. At present, the supply mode of green food and organic food commonly adopted in China is based on the relations between suppliers and supermarkets. Supermarkets only supply a goods-selling platform for suppliers, but do not investigate these suppliers how they produce or obtain these products. In the market with full of "opportunism", not only the safety of agri-food cannot be guaranteed absolutely, but also the faith of consumers on agri-food will be undermined. Through management and control of the supply chain, Carrefour's quality line has obtained green agri-food of its own brand, tH Companys making these agri-foods not only safe in quality, but also has strengthened the popularization of Carrefour.

Fourthly, farmers' income has been augmented. Along with the economic development in China and increase in consumers' income, consumption of agri-food has shifted gradually from quantity to quality, safety, and agri-foods with high value added. Carrefour's quality line provides reliable agri-food with high quality and safety. The added values of these agri-foods are higher than those of ordinary agri-foods. Carrefour purchases these agri-foods by paying higher price. This has increased the income of participating farmer households.

Fifthly, Carrefour's quality line was helpful in the extension and popularization of China's safe and high quality agri-foods. In the market with fierce competition, once an innovative point has brought economic benefits or competitive power for innovators, many imitators will be certainly produced. Carrefour is the first supermarket which sells safe agri-food with its own brand in China. More and more consumers are attracted to the Carrefour's quality line. Some large scale super-markets, and agricultural, industrial, and commerce enterprises, have also tried this mode of management and produce safe agri-foods with their own brands. This trend is helpful to the popularization and extension of safe and high quality agri-foods in China and tH Companys optimizing agricultural production technology and agri-food supply chain in China.

Sixthly, although the suppliers of Carrefour quality line are large-scale farmer households up to now, the ideas of food safety and production technology adopted by these large-scale farms will play a demonstration role for adjacent small-scale farmer households. Provided innovation produces economic benefits, it will be disseminated rapidly and many imitators will appear and this is a Chinese characteristic. What counts is the existence of a market that is able to differentiate safe and high quality agri-foods from common one and putting into effect of a policy of favourable price for good quality. The development of supermarkets has created a favourable condition for practicing the policy.

However, we should not ignore current existing problems. The safe agri-food line similar to Carrefour's quality line needs to be supported by advanced planting and processing technology as well as infrastructure. The case of the failure of Carrefour's quality line of bananas is good evidence. The innovation of advanced technology and construction of infrastructure cannot be accomplished by only one supermarket. Therefore, construction of safe food line needs participation of many scientific research units, scientists, and governmental departments. At present, the Chinese government attaches a great importance to food safety. However, in addition to increasing tests for agri-food safety, more inputs in scientific research and infrastructure related to food safety are needed.

The second problem is that up to now suppliers of Carrefour's quality line are large scale farmer households, and not small scale farmer households who account for more than 90 per cent of the agricultural population in China. The average land area per small scale farmer household is less than 0.4 ha. We understand that Carrefour cooperates with only large scale farmer households for convenience in management. How to help small scale farmer households enter a quality line which is similar to Carrefour quality line? We think that it is necessary introduce a farmer cooperation association. It is necessary to organize small-scale farmer households to enter Carrefour quality line if Carrefour plans to expand its retail market share in China continuously. As the small-scale farmer households are protected by the macroeconomic policy, they not only account for a great majority of farmer households, but will also be around for a long time. As the number of small-scale farmer households is large and the supply is small, the purchasing and management cost will increase for Carrefour if a more effective purchasing and management mode is not adopted by Carrefour. Carrefour has to face this challenge.

At present, the cooperative forms of organizations of Chinese farmers have appeared once again. With the support of the government, farmer associations have been set up one after another in different regions. The associations organize scattered farmer households together and conduct business. The associations, have, in a way, reduced the purchasing and management cost of Carrefour in dealing with many small-scale farmer households.

The case studies show that development of supermarkets is gradually changing the agri-food production mode and technology in China. Although sales of raw and fresh agri-foods in supermarkets have reached mammoth proportions their potentialities are great and their roles should not be ignored.

References

Alfred Chandler, "The Visible Hand", Cambridge, Mass: Harvard University Press, 1977.

Chen Guang, 2004, "Carrefour's Strategies", Nanfang News Paper Press.

Chen Guang, 2006, "The Standard Management of Carrefour", Economical Science Press.

Dinghuan Hu, 1997, "The Theory of Micro Agricultural Integration", *China Rural Survey,* Vol, 18, PP.21–27.

Dinghuan Hu, 1998, "The Comparative Analysis of World Poultry Integration", *China Rural Survey*, Vol., 158, p 76–80.

Dinghuan Hu, 2004, "Development of Supermarket and Impact on Smallholders & Food Safety in China" A *Study on Binary Structure of Agrifood.* World Bank Institute, "Investment Climate Program will be to capture current and emerging best Chinese practices in Small and Medium Enterprises (SME) development and to disseminate this knowledge to government, business and academia in the western provinces in China." December 1st, 2004. World bank Beijing office.

Dinghuan Hu, Thomas Reardon, Scott Rozelle, Peter Timmer, and Honglin Wang, 2004 "The Emergence of Supermarkets with Chinese Characteristics: Challenges and Opportunities for China's Agricultural Development", *Development Policy Review,* Vol. 22, no. September, 2004.

Dinghuan Hu, 2005. "On Binary Structure of Agrifood—Impact of Supermarket Development on Agricultural Sector and Agrifood Safety in China—", *Chinese Rural Economy,* No. 2, 2005 (Serial No.), pp. 12–17.

Dinghuan Hu, Kevin Z. Chen, Qingzhen Sun and Minoru Tada, 2006, "The Impact of Supermarket upon Small Scale Farmers in China", *Working paper for the conference of Agri-food supply chain and Agricultural integration,* in Ya'an city, Sichuan Provinces, China.

Dinghuan Hu, 2006, 'Supermarket+agrifood processing enterprises+farmers, to exploring a new agricultural integration model in China', *Farmers' Daily,* 2006 June 8th, pp. 3.

Dinghuan Hu, F. Fuller and T. Reardon, 2006, 'Impacts of the repid development of supermarkets on China's dairy industry', *International agri-food chains and networks,* edited by J. Bijman, S.W.F. Omta, J.H. Trienekens, J.H.M.Wijnands, E.F.M. Wubben, Wageningen Academic Publishers, 2006, pp. 373–386.

Dong Xiaoxia and Bi Xiang and Dinghuan Hu, 2006. 'The Changes of Chinese Urben Retail Markets and Impacet on Farmer Household', *"Rural Economy"*, Volume 2, 2006, pp 87–90.

Niu Ruofeng and Xia Ying, 2000, "The Organization of Agri-Industralization and Mechanism of Practise", Beijing University Press.

Williamson, Oliver E. 1977, "Markets and Hierarchies: Analysis and Anti-Trust Implications", New York: The Free Press.

Zhang Lijian, Hu Dinghuan and Yang Weimin, 2006, "Study on Internalitive Affiliation between Agri-Syntheisi Prevention and Agri-Food Enter Supermarket in China," Preparing to publish.

11

Market Chain Changes in Small Farm Dominated Economy: A Case Study on Mushroom in China

Jikun Huang, Zhurong Huang, Xianfang Niu, Huayong Zhi,
Suxia Wang and Dinghuan Hu

Recent studies have shown that both downstream and midstream segments of the marketing chain in China have changed dramatically in the past 20 years. China has moved from a country with a food system based on rationing in the cities to one that was based on wet markets and small shops to one in which supermarket and restaurant sectors are growing faster than anywhere else in the world (Bi *et al.*, 2004; Hu *et al.*, 2004; Goldman and Vanhonacker, 2006). In the midstream the wholesale sector also is evolving in some fundamental ways, although less rapidly than the retail sector (Huang *et al.*, 2006).

The experience internationally suggests that there could be serious distributional impacts of the rise of supermarkets in downstream of the market chain. For example, there are case studies in Latin America, Central and Eastern Europe, Mexico, Brazil, and Kenya that suggest that it is the rich, large farmers that benefit from the rise of demand for fruits and vegetables and the emergence of supermarkets (Reardon and Timmer, 2007; Berdegué *et al.*, 2005; Schwentesius et al, 2002). Because of the high transaction costs involved with purchasing from millions of small farmers and difficulties in monitoring quality and food safety, it is often assumed that supermarkets and their agents (for example, specialized wholesalers; preferred suppliers) will turn to large and better-off farmers. As a consequence, the rise of demand for horticultural and other high-valued commodities in the consumption basket of consumer and the concomitant rise in supermarkets have created concern among the international community about the possible adverse consequences on small and poor farmers (Reardon and Timmer, 2007). However, a recent global wide review shows that the impacts of rising supermarket on production and marketing at farm level are still mixed (World Bank, 2007).

The studies in China further complicate the debates on the implications of rapid changes in downstream of the marketing chain on farmers. Several studies based on supermarket or industrial surveys show that the emerging supermarket and special supplier could be engines of food product market expansion and have facilitated agricultural development (Hu. *et al.*, 2004; Hu. *et al.*, 2006). However, recent studies led by the Center for Chinese Agricultural Policy (CCAP) based on stratified randomly selected households have showed a somewhat different story. They show that although there have been significant changes in downstream of the market chain, these changes have rarely penetrated into upstream because of high transaction costs between modern retails and small farmers in China (Wang *et al.*, 2006; Huang *et al.*, 2006). Production is extremely small scale and marketing is dominated by the sales of farmers to small traders and small wholesalers in horticulture in general (Wang *et al.*, 2006; Dong *et al.*, 2006) and vegetable in particular (Huang *et al.*, 2007). There is no formal contracting in vegetable and fruit. Buyers play no role in providing technology, technical advice or credit in horticultural and diary production in Greater Beijing (Dong *et al.*, 2006; Wu *et al.*, 2007) and vegetable production in Shandong (Huang *et al.*, 2007a).

Some argue that while random sampling framework can generate a representative of overall samples, new, emerging, and innovated practices of marketing chains may often be ignored and therefore need a case study. For example, in our earlier studies based on large stratified randomly sampling households in Greater Beijing, we did not find any household that had contract arrangement with and input service received from either supermarket or special suppliers (Dong *et al.*, 2006; Wang *et al.*, 2006; Huang *et al.*, 2007a and 2007b). On the other hand, surveys based on interviewing supermarket managers find that there have been emerging modern supply systems by shifting procurements from traditional markets to either directly procuring from farmers or farm organizations through contract arrangement or special suppliers that can guarantee stable supply of quantity and quality of agri-food (Hu *et al.*, 2006; Tan and Zhu, 2004).

To have a better understanding of small but growing new marketing chains, a case study that tracks changes is necessary. Understanding institutions and incentives through which the small scale farm households sell their agri-foods to supermarkets via newly emerging special suppliers have important policy implications for China if these new marketing chains can provide benefits to small farmers or improve food safety for consumers.

In this project we selected Lanbo Agricultural Science and Technology Co. Ltd. (or Lanbo) as a case study. Lanbo is one of rising special food suppliers for supermarkets. We select Lanbo and mushroom as case study for several reasons: Lanbo is a specialized and rapid growing supermarket mushroom supplier in Beijing; China is the largest mushroom producer in the world, the output of mushrooms reached 13.3 million tons in 2005, accounting for 70 per cent of global production; most mushrooms in China are produced by small scale farmers; the traditional mushroom supply chain in China is dominated by small traders and wholesalers, retailers procure their mushrooms either from wholesale markets or small traders; and Lanbo use its agents to procure mushroom directly from mushroom producers.

Overall the goal of this study is to have a better understanding of Lanbo's mushroom marketing chain and its impact on small farmers. To achieve this overall goal, we conducted two surveys. One was a survey mainly through interviewing Lanbo's manager and Lanbo's designated agent. The other was a micro farm household survey in two villages where farmers sold their mushroom to the agent.

Lanbo and its Business in Mushrooms

Lanbo is a special mushroom supermarket supplier in Beijing and has experienced substantial expansion in recent years. The original company of Lanbo Garment Factory, which started its business in mushrooms in the second half of 2002. In 2002, Lanbo supplied mushrooms to three supermarket stores only, two of Ito Yokado supermarkets and one of Pricesmart. By 2007, Lanbo's mushrooms distributed to more than 30 supermarket stores in Beijing. The manager of Lanbo told us that the company now is the sole mushroom supplier for Carrefour, Ito Yokado, Wal-Mart and Lotus, its marketing values has increased from less than 0.3 million RMB in 2002 to 8.9 million RMB in 2006, and is likely reach 15 million RMB (about US $ 2 million) in 2007.

Lanbo has several sources of mushrooms and they have changed over time. They include those come from its own production base, wholesale markets, nearby local mushroom production households, other mushroom companies, and designated agents outside Beijing.

In the initial stage, Lanbo rented 100 mu (1 hectare = 15 mu) from a village in Beijing and invested more than 2 million yuan (about US $ 250 thousands) to set up greenhouses, which were contracted to 10 individual households who are from other provinces and experienced in mushroom production. Therefore these farmers are relatively richer than average farmers. The contracts are normally fixed for 3–5 years. All production, technology, and management are unified within production base. Quality and safety can be easily controlled under this production base. Lanbo procured all mushrooms from these households. The procurement prices are based on ongoing market prices. Because the size of its own production base is small, its production of mushrooms accounts for only small part of Lanbo's mushroom business. In fact, we also learned that Lanbo can hardly earn its profit from its own production base because of high investment. But Lanbo gains a lot indirectly from having its own production base as it can serve as a window for high quality and safety mushroom supply.

Mushrooms from Wholesale Markets

In the initial stages, since mushroom supply from Lanbo's own production base was limited, the company mainly sourced mushrooms from the Xinfadi wholesale market in Beijing, the largest wholesale market in Asia. The share of mushrooms traded by Lanbo accounted for more than 90 per cent of mushrooms sold by the company in 2002. To improve its competitiveness over other mushroom suppliers for the supermarket in Beijing, Lanbo is now seeking alternative sources of mushrooms to ensure that its products are cheaper, are of better quality and safe. The manager told us that the shares of mushroom from the wholesale market in total mushrooms procured by Lanbo have declined from 80 per cent in 2003 to 60 per cent in 2004 and 30 per cent only in 2006. When we asked him major reasons of shifting sourcing mushroom away from wholesale markets, he said that higher price in the wholesale market was the main reason. He also pointed out the difficulty of quality control over small traders in the wholesale markets and high transaction costs (e.g. the company has to send people and trucks to wholesale markets to buy mushrooms).

Mushrooms from Local Households near Lanbo in Beijing

With assistance from the vegetable association of Shangzhuang Township where Lanbo is located, Lanbo started procuring the mushrooms from local mushroom households; and the volume of procurement has gradually expanded. While there is no written contract, in many cases the arrangement works like an oral contract; by 2007, about 50 households regularly sold mushrooms to Lanbo. Lanbo procures from these 50 households all mushrooms that meet the company's quality requirements (mainly size, appearance, and degree of dry of mushrooms). There are two kinds of marketing arrangements: Lanbo directly sending trucks to procure mushrooms at farm-gate, and mushroom producers sending mushrooms to the Lanbo distribution centre. The manager of Lanbo told us that cooperation with these households is for mutual benefit. First, rapid expansion of Lanbo's business in mushrooms has led more small-scale rural households to sell mushrooms to the company, which helps in selling mushroom by households. Second, mushrooms produced by these households are one of the stable sources. The company is also close to these mushroom production households; it sometimes can send people to supervise mushroom cultivation process and provide technical support. Unfortunately, during the course of this study, we were not able to visit these mushroom households and did not examine to what extent farmers have received technical assistance from the company.

Mushrooms from Other Companies

Lanbo has established relations with several companies in Beijing for buying mushrooms. Here we present two examples of this business. From 2003 to 2005, it had established links with the agricultural service centre of Dasuanzhuang village in Shunyi County. Agricultural service centre, owned by the local government, was in charge of establishing mushroom plant and organizing local farmers' mushroom production; Lando procured all mushrooms that met its quality requirements. However, Lanbo's manager stated that the company started buying mushrooms from other companies because of quality problems with the agricultural service centre. In 2005, Lanbo cooperated with Dadi Fubang Edible Fungi Co. Ltd. in Beishiqiao Township in Shunyi County, and especially *Pleurotus eryngii*. The company has excellent facilities for producing *Pleurotus eryngii*, and the products meet Lanbo's quality requirements in terms of insecticide residue, moisture content, and shape.

Mushrooms from Designated Agents

Restricted by the number of mushroom varieties available in Beijing and limited supply, Lanbo started sourcing mushrooms from facilities outside Beijing. Lanbo calls these mushroom production areas outside Beijing as Lanbo's supporting bases. These include Zunhua County and Pingquan County in Hebei Province; Fuxin City in

Liaoning Province; Shenxian County in Shandong Province; Shanghai Finc Bio-tech Inc.; and Gutian County in Fujian Province. There are two kinds of procurement arrangements: one is through hiring part time agents who procure mushrooms from individual mushroom producers (households); the other is to purchase mushrooms from large-scale industrialized mushroom production farms. The arrangements between Lanbo and the agents will be discussed later. Small-scale rural households cultivate mushroom under room temperature, which is restricted by seasons. In hot summer mushrooms cannot be cultivated. In order to maintain year-round supply of mushrooms for the supermarket, Lanbo has entered into agreements with some large-scale industrialized mushroom cultivation farms. Some of these large-scale industrialized mushroom cultivation farms have adopted equipment imported from the Netherlands, and have implemented constant temperature mushroom production. The characteristics of industrialized production are to implement standardized production and stable quantity supply and reach the standards in mushroom quality and safety. However, the problem is that the costs and prices of industrialized mushroom production are high, which affect consumer's demand. Therefore, mushrooms produced by industrialized production serve mainly as a variety and quantity supplement.

Mushrooms Imported from Other Countries

For some specific varieties, Lanbo imports varieties of mushrooms from Japan, South Korea, and Taiwan, China. One of major imported varieties is *Flammulina velutipes*. However, as the prices of these mushrooms are much higher, they account for only very small share of Lanbo's mushrooms delivered to supermarkets.

Sampling Measures and Sources of Data

Lanbo procures mushrooms from various sources. Among these, procurement from wholesale markets dominated in the first few years. However, the share of mushroom from wholesale markets declined significantly. On the other hand, procurement from farmers through its agents increased rapidly over time. We are particularly interested in Lanbo's business with small farmers.

There are three sources of Lanbo's mushrooms from farmers in different locations. The first source is from the company's own production base near its headquarter in Beijing. Because production in base (6.7 hectares) accounts for only a very small amount of total mushrooms procured by Lanbo and the greenhouses are owned by the company, it is not much relevant for scale up for small farmers in China. Therefore, we did not conduct intensive household surveys for these households. However, we did briefly interview five households within Lanbo's production base. The results show that the quality and therefore prices of mushrooms were relatively higher than average quality and prices in the wholesale market. But we also find costs of mushroom production are relatively high.

The second source is nearby mushroom production households in Beijing. We were told that there are about 50 households who sold mushrooms to Lanbo under contract arrangements. However, when we planned to start our household survey in May 2007, we were told by local farmers that there was no contact. Mushroom producers in Beijing can sell their mushrooms to either Lanbo or others depending on prices offered to farmers. Moreover, most of these 50 mushroom producers are not local farmers and are distributed in many villages. They are migrants from other regions and rent land from local farmers. Interviewing and analysing data from these households are problematical for two reasons: some greenhouses are managed by several migrants working together, while other greenhouses are managed by a single person or a couple; and there is no way to examine the issues of inclusion or exclusion of small farmers, family characteristics, household income, or assets. Eventually we gave up the survey of these households.

The third source of Lanbo's mushrooms local brokers or agents who procure from farmers in other provinces (e.g., Hebei, Liaoning, Shandong, Shanghai, and Fujian). While we do not have information on the amount of mushrooms procured from this channel, it seems to be a major source in recent years.

Selection of Study Areas and Households

In order to understand the marketing arrangements of Lanbo, local agents, and farmers as well as the likely impact of these arrangements on local farmers, a team from the Center for Chinese Agricultural Policy and Institute of Agricultural Economics conducted an intensive household survey in two villages in Zunhua county of Hebei province, about 135 km from Beijing.

We selected two villages in Zunhua County for the following reasons. During our industrial interview, we were told that Lanbo has developed a model that effectively links farmers with mushroom producers through its procurement agent (or local broker) in Zunhua County. We were also told that a similar arrangement is used in mushroom procurement from farmers in other provinces. A local mushroom producer from Ximenzhuang village of Zunhua County, Zhang, who works as an agent for Lanbo, was introduced to us. Zhang told us that he has been procuring mushrooms from local farmers in two villages (Ximenzhuang and Dongmenzhuang, in Ping'ancheng township) since 2002 and started business with Lanbo after 2004.

The survey covered three groups of households. The first group included all mushroom producers who sold part of or all their mushrooms to Lanbo's agent, Zhang, in the 2006 production season. This sample has 30 households (15 households in Ximenzhuang village and 15 households in Dongmenzhuang village). All mushroom producers who sold mushrooms to Zhang are included in our survey. The second group consists of mushroom producers who did not sell mushrooms to Zhang. In Ximenzhuang, there are 17 mushroom producers, of which only two never sold mushrooms to Zhang and, therefore, are included in our sample. In Donmenzhuang village, we randomly selected 15 households from those who never sold mushrooms to Zhang. After we cleaned up the survey data, we found that one household did not complete the survey owing to difficulty in recalling his prices and other information. The last group included randomly selected 32 non-mushroom households (12 in Ximenzhuang village and 15 in Dongmenzhuang village).

Local Agent and Mushroom Procurement Arrangement

Local part-time brokers working as agents for large wholesalers or special suppliers play an important role in bringing horticultural products from farm-gate to various markets (Dong *et al.*, 2006). Similar findings are observed in our study. Zhang and his brother (agents thereafter), while working for their own mushroom production, also procure mushrooms from other farmers and sell in the Xinfadi wholesale market in Beijing. They also act as Lanbo's agents in our two studied villages. Although so far there is no formal written contract between Lanbo and the agent, they have been working together through inform oral contract and mutual trust.

Lanbo paid the agent a sort of commission fee after receiving mushrooms from the agent. It is not a pure commission fee because the payment received by the agent is not actual procurement price plus commission fee. The price offered by Lanbo to the agent is based on the prices observed in the Xinfadi market by Lanbo plus 0.2–0.4 yuan/kg (0.4 yuan/kg in most cases), which is about 5–10 per cent of average procurement prices (4 yuan/kg) of mushrooms in our study villages. If the agent could procure mushrooms from local farmers at much lower prices than those in the Xinfadi wholesale market, he would earn more profit. On the other hand, if the agent paid local farmers at prices higher than those sold in the Xinfadi wholesale market, he could lose money. Overall, because the agent has to take the marketing price risk, he might get higher profit than a regular agent whose income is purely based on commission fee. Payment is made through bank transfer immediately after each transaction. It is worth noting that the commission fee used here might not be an appropriate term. For example, when we asked the agent how much he could sell of the same quality of mushroom delivered to Lanbo in the Xinfadi market, he said, in most cases, he could get prices similar to that offered by Lanbo in the Xinfadi market. But he is happy and willing to sell to Lanbo because the business is stable and he does not need to spend more time sitting in the Xinfadi market and waiting for buyers. Lanbo is also willing to work with the agent because the agent can ensure quality and regular supply of mushrooms.

To procure mushroom from farmers, Zhang hires three local mushroom producers to collect mushroom in the two villages we studied. In most cases, the agent pays a commission fee of 0.2 yuan/kg to these mushroom "collectors". In some cases, when the agent can sell at higher prices in the market, he can pay a commission fee as high as 0.4 yuan/kg. During the harvest season, between September and the next June, they always start their work at 7:00 am to collect mushroom from farmers and end at late evening when they come back from Beijing. The agent owns a truck with 2.5 tons loading capacity. Normally, by noon time he leaves the village and drives the truck to both Lanbo and the Xinfadi wholesale market. On average, the agent sells about 50 per cent of mushrooms to Lanbo and the rest in the Xinfadi wholesale market. Every two or three days, the agent sends about 2500 kg of mushrooms to Lanbo.

While overall prices of mushrooms are market determined, appearance and moisture content are two major quality attributes that differentiate prices among various mushrooms sold by farmers. The agent told us that Lanbo normally demands better quality mushroom, neither too big nor too small nor too wet but with a moderate moisture content. Moisture is tested by weighting mushrooms in a particular size of basket.

It is interesting to note that when we asked farmers who sold their mushrooms to the agent whether Lanbo is the second buyer of their mushrooms, some farmers did know this, but most farmers responded that they did not know to whom the agent sold their mushrooms. Farmers are more interested in prices offered by the first buyer. The market is very competitive. Besides the agent whom we studied, there are local small brokers who also procure mushrooms from individual farmers and sell in local markets or markets in Beijing and other provinces.

Household Mushroom Production and Marketing

Compared with non-mushroom producers, mushroom farmers are relatively poor. On average, households with mushroom production had average per capita durable consumption assets of 13,477 yuan in 2006, which was nearly 20 per cent less than that of non-mushroom production households (Table 11.1). That is, on average the poor produces more mushroom than the rich. The relatively poor state of mushroom households may be largely explained by their lower income from off-farm

Table 11.1: Characteristics of Mushroom and Non-Mushroom Households (2006)

	Mushroom Households					
	Average	*Sold to the Agent*	*Never Sold to the Agent*	*T-test: Diff. between (2) and (3)*	*Non-Mushroom Households*	*T-test: Diff. between (1) and (5)*
	(1)	(2)	(3)	(4)	(5)	(6)
Household samples	46	30	16		32	
Per captain assets (yuan)	13477	13955	12581	0.568	16593	0.449
Off-farm employment (%)	34.3	38.9	25.8	0.197	41.7	0.322
Family size (persons)	3.9	4.1	3.6	0.207	4.1	0.608
Household head age (years)	41	41	40	0.870	49	0.001
Head education (Years)	6.9	7.0	6.7	0.668	6.7	0.660
Family labor (persons)	2.8	3.0	2.6	0.179	3.2	0.203
Per capita land (mu)	1.8	1.8	1.7	0.419	1.5	0.165

Note: 15 mu = 1 hectares; 7.8 yuan = 1 US $. The critical probability value of t-test is 0.05.

employment. For example, the survey shows that, off-farm employment of mushroom households was 34.3 per cent in 2006, while the corresponding figure was 41.7 per cent for non-mushroom households.

Except for ages of household head, there is no significant difference in household characteristics between mushroom producers and non-mushroom producers. The statistical test shows that, compared with non-mushroom households, mushroom producers have similar levels of family population, labour, education, off-farm employment, farm size, and wealth (Table 11.1, column 6). Mushroom producers are normally younger than non-mushroom producers, the average household head age of the former (41) is about 8 years lower than the latter (49) in 2006 (Table 11.1). This might be explained by relatively average lower rate of off-farm employment in mushroom households as the youth works more in off-farm than the older people (Zhang *et al.*, 2004).

Divided mushroom production households into two groups, those the selling to the agent and those never selling to the agent, the results presented in Table 11.1 show that there is no significant difference in household's characteristics. In other words, when the agent procures mushrooms for Lanbo or sells them in the Xinfadi market, he does not differentiate between farmers.

Mushroom Marketing

In general, supply to traditional channels has dominated the procurement at farm-gate. For those who never sold mushrooms to Zhang or the Lanbo's agent, selling to local small trader and small wholesaler accounted for nearly all of their mushrooms (Table 11.2). Even for the group of farmers selling to the agent, the traditional channels still dominated. In 2001, the traditional channels accounted for 90 per cent. The rest (10 per cent) was sold to special suppliers. In response to rising procurement by Zhang, the composition of sales has been changing. In 2006, mushrooms sold to the agent accounted for 40 per cent of the sample that sold mushrooms to the agent.

An interesting finding is that even for the sample that included only households selling mushrooms to the agent, there were still about 60 per cent sold to small traders and wholesale. However, if we consider the agent as a modern channel, we could conclude that there has been a significant change in 2006 over 2001. The share of modern marketing chain has increased substantially from 10 per cent in 2001 to 42 per cent in 2006 (Table 11.2).

Mushroom Marketing, Production and Income

One of major issues of this study is to examine the likely impact of the marketing channel through Lanbo's agent procurement. To do so, again we divide all mushroom producers into two groups, those who never sold to the agent and those who sold to the agent. Are there any differences in production, technology, income, or prices between these two groups? Tables 11.3 and 11.4 provide the answer.

Table 11.2: Shares of Mushroom by Marketing Channel (2001 and 2006 in %)

	Average		*Households Sold to the Agent*		*Households Never Sold to the Agent*	
	2001	2006	2001	2006	2001	2006
Small trader or small wholesaler	94	73	90	58	100	97
Special supplier	6	1	10	2	0	0
Processing firm	0	1	0	0	0	3
The agent	0	25	0	40	0	0

The most striking finding from this analysis is that there is no significant difference between these two groups in any aspect of the issues examined. For example, average mushroom production areas are both about 1 mu (Table 11.3). Compared with market channels without selling to the agent, mushroom yield per mu is about 4 per cent lower in the marketing channel associated with the agent, but the difference is not statistically significant (Table 11.3). Similarly, there is no significant difference in net income per stick or quantity weighted average prices between the marketing channels.

Table 11.3: Mushroom Production and Income by Two Groups of Households (2006)

	Average	*Households Sold to the Agent*	*Households Never sold to the agent*	*T-test: diff. between (2) and (3)*
	(1)	(2)	(3)	(4)
Production areas (mu)	1.02	0.96	1.12	0.157
Yield (kg/mu)	18976	18710	19475	0.605
Net income per mu (yuan)	41806	43130	39324	0.331
Net income per stick (yuan)	1.99	2.07	1.84	0.160
Weighted average price (yuan/kg)	3.80	3.76	3.84	0.370

Note: We also tested the differences of various inputs (e.g., labour, types and amount of fungus, and other inputs) between (2) and (3). The results show that non of them are statistically significant.

Mushroom Marketing and Prices

Because the composition of marketing channels differ between these two groups and the mushroom households do not always sell to the agent, in order to see to what extent Lanbo's agent offers higher prices to farmers, we present prices received by farmers (Tables 11.4 and 11.5).

At the first glance, the results seem to confirm that the agent does pay higher prices to farmers than other marketing channels, which also seems consistent with our findings based on the industrial survey. For example, Table 11.4 shows that farmers received an average price of 4.14 yuan/kg from the agent, which is about 3.5 per cent higher than those paid by other modern marketing channels such as processors and special suppliers and about 6 per cent and 13 per cent higher than those paid by small wholesalers and small traders respectively.

Table 11.4: Mushroom Procurement Prices by Marketing Channels for 46 Households (2006/07 production season)

	Average Price (yuan/kg)	*Monthly Prices (yuan/kg)*									
		9	10	11	12	1	2	3	4	5	6
Small traders	3.66	2.26	2.41	4.37	4.03	4.40	4.27	3.91	3.94	3.83	2.47
Small wholesalers	3.89	2.61	2.92	3.96	4.40	4.22	4.26	4.28	4.00	3.54	2.55
Special suppliers	4.00	2.20	2.64	3.39	4.48	5.40	4.00	3.88	3.84	3.76	NA
Processors	4.00	NA	3.28	3.41	4.32	4.28	4.14	4.09	3.99	3.80	NA
The agent	4.14	2.70	2.91	4.59	4.66	4.55	4.48	4.22	4.14	3.85	2.77

Table 11.5: Mushroom Procurement Prices by Marketing Channels for 30 Households that Sold to the Agent (2006/07 production season)

	Average Price (yuan/kg)	*Monthly Prices (yuan/kg)*									
		9	10	11	12	1	2	3	4	5	6
Small traders	3.86	2.50	2.80	4.48	4.07	4.46	4.41	3.97	3.93	3.64	2.47
Small wholesalers	4.01	3.12	3.07	3.97	4.40	4.30	4.33	4.30	4.14	3.70	2.93
Special suppliers	4.72	NA	1.60	3.20	5.00	5.60	4.00	3.80	3.80	3.60	NA
Processors	3.74	NA	4.00	3.47	4.80	4.40	4.40	4.20	3.80	3.80	NA
The agent	4.14	2.70	2.91	4.59	4.66	4.55	4.48	4.22	4.14	3.85	2.77

When examining only the households who have sold mushrooms to the agent, one still can find relatively higher prices paid by the agent though not the highest. For example, Table 11.5 shows the highest prices offered to farmers are by special suppliers (4.72 yuan/kg), followed by the agent (4.14 yuan/kg), wholesalers (4.01 yuan/kg), small traders (3.84 yuan/kg), and processors (3.74 yuan/kg).

However, when we asked farmers why they received different prices at any given time from different buyers, they told us that this was because of quality. Normally, they first sold mushroom with less moisture content and good looking mushroom at higher prices to the agent or other special suppliers, and then sold remaining mushrooms to small traders or wholesalers. Because all mushrooms are produced in the same greenhouse, while there is difference in quality, there is not any difference in mushroom safety.

In sum, our household survey shows that there is no statistically significant difference between prices offered by the Lanbo's agent and other marketing channels after controlling for mushroom quality. Higher quality fetched at higher prices for any marketing channel.

Conclusion

This study provides several interesting findings. First, there is rapid growth of special suppliers of mushrooms for modern retails. Lanbo, a new mushroom supplier, started its mushroom business in 2002 and has now become one of most important mushroom suppliers for the supermarket in Beijing. Its sources have expanded from local to nationwide through its own and unique procurement system.

Second, while previous studies show that rapid growth of modern retail markets, on average, has rarely penetrated upstream in a small farm dominated economy, the study provides ample evidence of initial and emerging vertical coordination system with a specialized mushroom supplier and dedicated or semi-dedicated small traders (agents) who directly procure mushrooms from small mushroom producers. In response to quality demand from modern retails and to improve its market competition, midstream, special mushroom supplier in this case, has adjusted its marketing practices by gradually shifting its sourcing from wholesale market to its dedicated agents.

Third, while one may argue that this vertical coordination system is still in infant stage, just a sort of semi-vertical coordination, no formal contracts, and may be found only in this special product, mushroom, the system provides a new idea of integrating small farmers into a modern retail system through local agents who are living in villages where mushrooms are produced. Currently, although there is neither formal contract between special supplier and the agents nor between the agents and farmers, the system seems to be adapting to local situation well. For example, quality demand can be met at lower cost than otherwise because quality grading is done at farm-gate when the agent procures mushrooms from each individual household. The agent delivers quality mushrooms to the specialized supplier or company and sells the rest in traditional wholesale markets. The agents, who are often also mushroom producers and living in the village, procure the products from neighbours, which not only reduces transaction (or procurement) cost, but also establishes informal relationships and trust with villagers. The importance of this procurement system has been growing in Lanbo's; we expect it will also be growing in other products in the near future.

Fourth, the findings show that small and poor farmers are not excluded from emerging mushroom production. In fact, we found that the poor produce more mushroom than the rich. This may be explained by fewer opportunities for the poor in off-farm employment (Zhang *et al.*, 2004) and therefore they are engaged in mushroom production. These findings are consistent with previous studies in China, which also show that the poor produced more horticultural products (Dong *et al.*, 2006; Huang *et al.*, 2006).

Fifth, poor and small farms are also not excluded from the modern channel. The results of the household survey show that there is nearly no difference in household characteristics between farmers selling mushrooms to the Lanbo's agent and other small traders. The reason may be the fact that China's agricultural production is dominated by small farmers and land is equally distributed among households within village. The same conclusions were reported in other studies (Wang *et al.*, 2006; Dong *et al.*, 2006; Huang *et al.*, 2007a and 2007b).

Last, but not least, on the impact of marketing choice, statistically there is no difference in production, yield, and income among farmers opting for different marketing channels. Prices received from various buyers are very competitive and there is no significant difference after we control for quality. Buyers play no role in providing technology, technical advice, or credit in mushroom production.

Several policy implications could be derived from this study. First, because vertical market coordination or integration that links supermarkets, large special suppliers, local small agents, and farmers can meet quality demand from modern retails or consumers at lower transaction costs, efforts might be needed for both industry and government to facilitate the scaling up of this model. Some of the key elements of this market chain are that the agents are local farmers, they sort products at procurement level, the traditional and modern chains co-exist and meet current small farm production and small trader system. Second, while small and poor farmers are not excluded from either food market expansion or emerging modern marketing chains, for an economy where marketing is dominated by sales of small farmers to small traders and small agents, meeting the rising demand for food safety as China's income grows is a challenge. Policy makers may need to address the most critical aspects of the small farm to provide not only quality food but more safety food under competitive markets. Enforcing a food track record system might be a solution, which can also facilitate the scaling up of Lanbo's model as the tracking cost of this system is not difficult. Farmer cooperatives may also help in some cases in overcoming high transaction costs in dealing with millions of small farmers.

References

Berdegué, J.A., F. Balsevich, L. Flores, and T. Reardon (2005). "Central American Supermarkets Private Standards of Quality and Safety in Procurement of Fresh Fruits and Vegetables", *Food Policy,* 30(3): 254–269.

Bi, X., Dong, X., Huang, J., Hu. D. and Rozelle, S. (2004). "Securing small producer participation in restructured national and regional agri-food systems," China country project report on *Regoverning Markets,* Center for Chinese Agricultural Policy, Chinese Academy of Sciences. Beijing.

Dong, X., H. Wang, X. Dong, J. Huang, S. Rozelle, and T. Rearton. (2006). "Producing and Procuring Horticultural Crops with Chinese Characteristics: Why Small Farmers are Thriving and Supermarkets are Absent in Rural China," *Contributed Paper presented in IAAE Conference* on 13–18 November 2006 in Gold Coast, Australia.

Goldman, A. and W. Vanhonacker (2006). "The food retail system in China: Strategic dilemmas and lessons for retail international/modernization," A paper presented in the *Global Retail Conference,* July 17–18, 2006, University of Surrey, UK.

Hu, D., M. Tada, K. Chen, and Q. Sun (2006). "The Impact of Contract Productive model up Food Safety and Income of Small Scale Farmers—The Case Study of Apple Industry in Shandong Province," *Chinese Rural Economy,* No. 11, 2006.

Hu, D. Reardon, T., Rozelle, S., Timmer, P., and Wang, H. (2004). "The emergence of supermarkets with Chinese characteristics: challenges and opportunities for China's agricultural development", *Development Policy Review,* 22 (2004): 557–586.

Huang, J., Dong, X., Wu, Y., Zhi, H., Niu, X., Huang, Z., and Rozelle, S. (2006). "Regoverning markets: the China meso-level study," IIED's *Regoverning Markets Projects Report,* Center for Chinese Agricultural Policy, Chinese Academy of Sciences, Beijing.

Huang, J.X. Niu, H. Zhi and X. Dong (2007a). "Determinants of Vegetable Production and Cropping Pattern Changes in China", *Issues in Agricultural Economy,* 2007(7): 4–10.

Huang, J.Z. Huang, H. Zhi, Y. Wu, X. Niu, and S. Rozelle. (2007b). "Production, Marketing and Impacts of Market Chain Changes on Farmers in China: Case Study of Cucumber and Tomato in Shandong Province." *A project report under IIED's Regoverning Market Program,* Center for Chinese Agricultural Policy, Chinese Academy of Sciences, Beijing.

Reardon, T. and C.P. Timmer (2007). "Transformation of Markets for Agricultural Output in Developing Countries Since 1950: How Has Thinking Changed?" Chapter 55 in R.E. Evenson, and P. Pingali. *Handbook of Agricultural Economics, 3: Agricultural Development: Farmers, Farm Production and Farm Markets,* Amsterdam: Elsevier Press: 2808–2855.

Schwentesius, R., and Manuel, A.G., (2002). "Supermarkets in Mexico: Impacts on Horticulture Systems", *Development Policy Review,* 20(4): 487–502.

Tan, T. and Y. Zhu. (2004). "The study of the organization mode of produce supply chain," *Modern Economy Discussion,* 2004(5): 24–27.

Wang, H., Dong, X., J. Huang, S. Rozelle,, and T. Rearton (2006). "Producing and Procuring Horticultural Crops with Chinese Characteristics: Why Small Farmers are Thriving and Supermarkets are Absent in Rural China", the 26th Conference Paper of the *International Association of Agricultural Economists,* August 14–19, 2006.

World Bank, 2007. *World Development Report 2008: Agricultural for Development,* Draft. World Bank, Washington DC.

Wu,Y., J. Huang, S. Rozelle and Z.,Yang (2007)."The rising of dairy processing firms and farmers participations in dairy production in China," *Issues in Agricultural Economy,* forthcoming.

Zhang, L., A. deBrauw and S. Rozelle. (2004). "China's rural labor market development and its gender implications." *China Economic Review,* Vol. 15 (2004): 230–247.

12

Collective Actions of Small Farm Households in Big Markets: Ruoheng Farmer Watermelon Cooperative in China

Huang Zuhui Liang Qiao and Song Yu

China is a country with a large population. According to the sixth census of China in 2005, the population was 13.06 billion, 42.99 per cent of which were living in towns and 57.01 per cent of which were live in villages. The proportion of the population living in town went up to 6.77 per cent. The gross rural product only accounted for 15.9 per cent of GDP. The characteristic of big agricultural population makes agriculture as a foundation of economic development, social stabilization, and country self-supporting. Nowadays economic development in China is in an important phase, and the problems in agriculture have been the most important. Development in agriculture lags behind the whole economy and farmers' income is increasing slowly, leading to enlarging the income gap between rural and urban areas.

The produce-supply chain is facing a dilemma. Farmers as producers are in an unfavourable position. Small farm households are facing various difficulties in markets. On the one hand, costs of circulation and transaction are high. On the other hand, small farm households are not able to protect their interests. Thus, the distribution mechanism of the supply chain is incomplete, and the distribution and share of the gain and risk are in disequilibrium. On the one hand, small farm households have to shoulder both natural and market risks; on the other hand, their gains are much less than their risks and efforts. Farmers in inferior position usually get a lower share of added value in production, and the great majority of value addition is cornered by other participants of the supply chain.

Characteristics of the Circulation System in China and Farmer Cooperatives

At present, the produce circulation system in China is diversified. It includes not only the traditional production-supply-marketing system consisting of small farm households, peddlers, processing enterprises, wholesalers, and retailers, which depends on the links between wholesale markets in producing areas and selling areas, but also the modern supply chain dependent on new marketing terminals. There are two main problems in the produce circulation domain: lack of a main body of produce market. Farmers should be the main body, but it is not so easy for farmers to take on the role. Small-scale production, lagged conception, and capital power are far from the required level of "mature market main body"; short of square deal system. Farmers' rights and interests cannot be ensured effectively because of disorderly market systems and farmers' inferior status. The rural market economy in China is not perfect and the produce circulation system is in a critical transitional period.

As an institutional innovation, farmer cooperatives have evolved when the produce supply chain system is in chaos and the rural market economy is in a transitional phase. It is a spontaneous institutional innovation. If the existing institution can not realize the potential income derived from scale economy, risk and transaction costs, institutional innovation will take place. Farmer cooperative is an institution, which appeared spontaneously to help small-scale farmers take part in dynamic markets. Now, they are developing like a raging fire, especially in east and littoral areas. And a majority of cooperatives are in the planting industry. Others are in industries of breeding, processing, transportation, etc. Both domestic and overseas scholars have positive comments on its effective solutions to farmers' participation in market. It organizes small farm households to enter the produce supply chain, which apparently improves the inferior status of small farm households. But farmer cooperatives in China still face various problems. Regional development is, farmer cooperatives develop relatively well in areas with a developed market economy and develop poorly in areas with lagged economy. Besides, farmer cooperatives in China generally have small scales. The third problem is that there are small proportion of cooperatives in the circulation domain.

Small Farm Households' Problems in Supply Chain

With economic and social development, there are great changes in people's consuming habits. The traditional consumption system is being replaced by the "agro-industrialized food" system. With the flourishing development of the supermarkets and the appearance of the logistic industry and middleman, farmers are losing direct contact with consumers (Gereffi, 1999). Farmers get a smaller share of food value because most of the value is distributed among other participants in the supply chain. Besides, trade liberalization further enlarges the income gap between domestic and overseas agricultural producers (Litchfield *et al.*, 2003).

Congjiu Liu (2004) thinks that "family is still the basic cell of the agro-food circulation organization" and "it is not good for the improvement of the food qualities" if small farm households participate in the agro-food circulation dispersedly. On the one hand, the dispersal of circulation organizations will probably restrict the emergence of large industrial organizations, and it will be hard to realize scale economy of produce. On the other hand, producers and consumers are segregated, and market information can not play its role of coordinating production and consumption, which restricts improvements in produce quality.

It is very difficult for small farm households in many developing countries to enter markets. Tao Tan and Yihua Zhu (2004) say that there are three main barriers for small farm households to enter markets: the first one is the high transaction costs when small households enter markets alone; the second is lack of sufficient and accurate information because of poor education, and the third is the disadvantages of small farm households such as small production scale, shortage of capital, low competing ability and so on.

Necessity for Farmers' Collective Participation in Market

Jim Bingen (2003) suggests three ways to improve farmers' ability in participating in the supply chain: contract/business programmes, project/technology programmes, and process/human capacity investments. Human capacity investment is preferred and emphasized especially, with development of foundation skills and social capital as the initial focus, including assistance for collective self-help, literacy programmes, marketing activities and decentralized development planning. Furthermore, it can also facilitate technology adoption and extension.

It is thought that the key goal and function of economic institutions is to save transaction cost. That is to say, where there is possibility of saving transaction cost, there is likelihood of institutional innovation. In the produce circulation system, the possibility of saving the transaction cost comes from (Zuhui Huang, Dongying Liu, 2005):

- changing farmers' organizing conformation when they enter the circulation system;
- improving the investment prompting of the special technique and logistic circulation system;
- enriching the symbiosis between segments of the supply chain;
- keeping the quantity equilibrium of the logistic chain and the validity of the logistic.

Though there were constant arguments about farmer cooperatives, they are still protected by laws in most countries. This is because farmer cooperatives are thought to enable farmers to participate in markets.

Weatherspoon (2003) says that producers organized in large scale are capable of providing large volumes of produce regularly and ensuring food safety and quality more easily. Apparently farmer cooperative is one of the best forms of organization for organized producers.

Through farmer cooperatives, small farm households can build up mechanisms of credit and safety with other participators of the supply chain to realize mutual benefit and investment (Stochbridge, 2003).

Experience indicates that pure market mechanism and pure government mechanism are not enough. The former one is likely to lead to high transaction cost and market failure, whole the latter usually results in exorbitant organizing and controlling costs. Seen from the point of transaction cost and institutional arrangement, farmer cooperative is an institutional arrangement between market and government mechanism (Zuhui Huang, 2002). The more developed the market is, the more the farmer cooperative is needed to make up for the deficiency of the market mechanism and incomplete function of the government mechanism.

If farmers want to take the initiative in markets or gain most profit in produce circulation, they have to change their concept and identify the potential profit in production and marketing. The real actors have to be farmers; and with the socialization of production and development of the market economy, farmers have to be organized into farmer cooperatives (Dongmin Liu, 2001).

Methodology

There are many studies on various aspects of farmer cooperatives. However, many researches focus theoretically on farmers' benefits from farmer cooperative, institutional innovation and transaction cost, and the developing difficulties of farmer cooperative. Studies on demonstration are limited to brief description and simple analysis of cases. There are hardly cases penetrating into collective actions and institution innovation of small farm households in dynamic markets—farmer cooperative from the angle of farmers' participation in the supply chain and/or markets. This study of the Ruoheng farmer watermelon cooperative describes the course of the institution innovation and evolvement, and finds out the mechanism of the cooperative from organizing, marketing, and distribution.

We did this study through both literature review and field survey. First, we reviewed literature about produce supply chain, participation of small farm households in dynamic markets, farmers' innovations and farmer cooperatives. Then we collected some basic information on the Ruoheng watermelon cooperative and designed a questionnaire according to the study aim and content. Second, we conducted a field survey at Changshan village where the cooperative was located. We obtained the required data through questionnaire and interview. We interviewed head, members of cooperative as well as small farm households not joining in the cooperative. To ensure reliability of data we interviewed 5 members and 5 small farmers in terms of benefits and costs.

Watermelons in Zhejiang and Wenlin

Watermelon is a cosmopolitan fruit and ranks fifth in size among fruits. China has the largest growing area and gross output of watermelon in the world, and it can rightly be called the first country of watermelon.

Zhejiang is one of the biggest provinces growing watermelon. Area under watermelon in Zhejiang was 1.27 million mu in 2004. Gross output was 2.66 billion kg, with a gross production value of 2.6 billion yuan in 2004.

In order to enhance the output and develop quality, many farmers grow watermelon in greenhouses. Wenlin, which is in Zhejiang province, is named the hometown of greenhouse watermelon in China. Wenlin has a long history in growing watermelon.

In the natural and soil condition of southeast littoral, farmers in Wenlin have succeeded in planting watermelons of high grade with advanced producing techniques.

Ruoheng is a town in the southeast of Wenlin city, Zhejiang province, with an area of 115 sq. km, 111 villages and a population of 145,000. The town has many water courses. Agriculture is the root of the town. Both agriculture and township enterprises are well developed.

Changshan is a small village of Ruoheng. More than 40 families migrated into the village in 1989. They lived a poor life by growing rice. But now the village is famous for watermelon, which enables villagers to lead a rich life.

Innovation of Farmer Watermelon Cooperative

Youda Peng, who now is head of the cooperative, had some experience in growing watermelon in his hometown. He got some fine seeds from the Xinjiang Academy of Agriculture and grew watermelon in his 3–mu (0.2 hectare) farmland in 1992. Fortunately he got a net profit of more than 5000 yuan. The next year, he began to grow watermelon in greenhouse. Because of careful cultivation and favourable soil, watermelon grown in greenhouse not only riped earlier but also had a better taste. The watermelons sold well, and Peng had a net income of more than 10,000 yuan that year. As soon as Peng succeeded in growing watermelon, he extended the technique to the villagers. Now there are many major producers of watermelon in Changshan village. The annual per capita income is nearly 20,000 yuan.

Because of low temperature here, watermelons cannot be grown in winter. Villagers had an idea of growing it in Guangdong province, which has a relatively higher temperature. In 1998, Peng and other 35 farmers went to Guangdong and contracted more than 180 mu (12 hectare) glebe to grow watermelon, and they succeeded. The next year, the base in Guangdong was expanded to 600 mu (40 hectare).

In 1999, Peng registered the brand "Yulin" for the fine watermelon, and implemented "four unifications", i.e. production, quality inspection, packaging, and sale. The same year, the villagers established a growing base in Hai'nan province. With these two bases, "Yulin" watermelon could be grown the whole year. In summer, the watermelons were produced mainly in the Ruoheng base and in winter, in the Guangdong and Hainan bases to serve the national markets.

In July 2001, Peng and other 29 villagers established the farmer watermelon cooperative and set down local technique and quality standards for "Yulin" brand. The bases of the cooperative were extended to other provinces such as Guangxi, Jiangxi, Anhui, and Yunnan. At the end of 2005, the cooperative had 152 formal members. All the members were offered training on melon growing technique. A marketing group was organized. The cooperative established a marketing network in more than 50 fruit wholesale markets in more than 20 cities. These cities directly promote the development of a watermelon industrial belt of 80,000 mu (5333.33 hectare) in coastal southeast China.

In 2003, "Yulin" was recognized as a notable brand and the watermelon as a famous brand produce. Then the watermelon was approved as green food in 2005. Besides, Peng gained the titles of "outstanding leader of farmer cooperative", "competent purchaser and seller of excellent agro-produce and byproduct", and so on.

Establishment and Operation of the Cooperative

In July 2001, with the sanction of the Wenling Bureau of Agriculture and Forestry, the Ruoheng farmer watermelon cooperative was set up. In 2002, it was registered as an enterprise with a registration capital of RMB 522,000. The farming area and share of each member is decided by his production and management ability as well as contributions. The money paid for each share was RMB 1,000. Each member was not allowed to have more than 10 per cent of the total share. And as head of the cooperative, Peng had only 5 per cent share.

Farmers with over three-year experience in growing watermelon, and who have mastered the production technique of "Yulin-melon" and having some organizing and managing ability can become members. Like common enterprises, there is an internship and tryout time before a member becomes formal, and one who fails will be refused membership. Because of Peng's introduction, 130 farmers were admitted as quasi-members in 2006 and they will become formal members or rejected membership after one year.

Supply Chain and its Participators

The participators and their relationship within the supply chain of watermelon is shown in Figure 12.1.

Input Suppliers

Inputs for the cooperative are offered by fixed suppliers with long-term cooperation. They are usually relatively big factories. Since the "Yulin" brand watermelon has

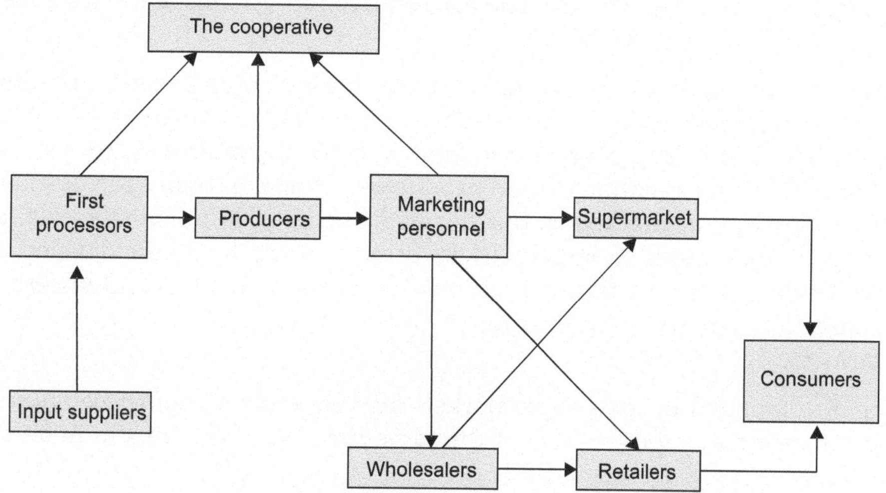

Fig. 12.1: Participators of Supply Chain and their Relations

strict requirements of production and technique, the variety and usage of fertilizers and pesticides are strictly controlled and all the seeds are supplied by the local academy of agriculture.

Purchasers, Producers, First-Stage Processors and Marketing Personnel

As farmers, they are cooperative members or labour force employed by the cooperative. There are four identities in the cooperative: core members, common members, quasi-members, and non-member work force.

The core members not only take part in the production or processing of the watermelon but also take responsibility for the daily management of the cooperative, including solving technical and marketing problems, taking charge of accounts, capital and personnel, and other issues.

The common members know well of the production technique, and are capable of organizing and managing the non-member labour force in production as well. They are the main force of production.

The quasi-members shoulder the same responsibilities as formal members. The difference is that they are still in the assessing period. And if they can not reach the requirement of the cooperative, they will be refused membership.

The labour force is employed by the cooperative to carry out some works which need less technique. They are not so familiar with the whole course of production of the "Yulin" watermelon. The cooperative usually employed them in bases located in other provinces.

Wholesalers, Supermarkets and Retailers

Watermelon is usually not grown according to contract. The cooperative sells watermelon by direct negotiation with wholesalers, supermarkets and retailers. The approximate proportions of selling volumes of these segments are 40 per cent, 25 per cent and 35 per cent respectively. The cooperative has established marketing net in many cities to facilitate marketing.

The rise of food supermarkets is transforming the marketing scene. Supermarkets ease up the conflict between small-scale farmers and dynamic markets. They find out the demand for produce by their information network and management system. Then they feedback this information to food producers. Thus, the connection of small-scale farmers with dynamic markets is transformed to connection of small-scale farmers with supermarkets. Besides, supermarkets bring and accelerate the development of contract farming. Contract farming not only removes chanciness and uncertainty in spot transaction, but also ensures comparatively steady-going sale income for small-scale farmers.

But the development of food supermarkets also engenders conflict between small-scale producers and supermarkets at the same time. Farmers are still in an inferior status when negotiating with supermarkets, and find it difficult to forge relationship with supermarkets. So it is important that farmers are organized through farmer cooperative for strengthening farmers' bargaining. Supermarkets also throw new challenges to cooperatives in the form of standardization and safety. The cooperative not only has to think about consumer demands when participating in the traditional circulation system, but also has to answer for the requests of supermarkets, i.e. consumer demand as understood by supermarkets. Thus the cooperative sells watermelons with normal package and normalized shape largely through supermarkets or special retailers, and sell other watermelons through traditional circulation channel.

Consumers

Consumers are at the end of the supply chain. With improving living conditions, people's consuming habits have changed a lot. They pay more attention to safety, taste and appearance of the product. And they have more diversified and specific demands. These demands of consumers make it necessary to improve production and processing.

Description of the Organizational System

Management is one of the key factors in the operation and development of the cooperative, which includes legislative governance, judicial governance, and executive governance. On June 1, 2005, Zhejiang province began to enforce "the regulation of farmer special cooperative organization in Zhejiang province", which is the first local regulation on farmer cooperatives in China. And the national regulation is coming. The "regulation" identifies the special legal person of a farmer cooperative, which is different from both corporation and enterprise.

The cooperative carries out economic activities as a legal person. Its management and operation is very unique, different from both enterprise and social organization. The decision-making mechanism of the cooperative is democratic management of the associator congress. It practices "one person, more than one vote" mechanism to embody the principle of efficiency (principle of maximizing farmers' income). But the cooperatives are usually established by able persons in the village, and the proprietor exerts key function in actual decision-making generally. Common associates, i.e. farmers, deliver themselves by giving advice or ideas by and large. Besides, they established a unified local standard of technique and quality, according to which they practice production, first-stage processing, and package. Farmers in the cooperative are committed to growing plans and technique standards set by the assembly.

As to personnel management, the cooperative offers fixed wages and bonus to its members and employs labour force every month. As to distribution of profit, it takes the form of double returns according to the transaction volume and share as well. After paying all costs, reserve fund and risk fund will firstly be deducted from the net profit. The left profit will be distributed among the members according to their shares and contributions. The "contribution" above refers to the watermelon output of each member or the internal transaction volume between the cooperative and its members. The reserve fund is used to expand new bases, and the risk fund is to pay for natural disasters and accidental costs such as typhoon.

Macro and Micro Context

Small farm households in China usually have to sell their produce themselves, which not only leads to high costs of production and transaction but also difficulties in marketing. The produce circulation system is diversified; there are both traditional production-supply-marketing systems and new circulation parts like supermarkets. In the following context, we will analyse the environment factors from perspectives of economy, policy, and culture.

Economic Environment

Although farmer's organizations, which developed from the 50s in China as mutual-help teams. Farmer cooperatives are of recent origin. We identified the key factors for the emergence of farmer cooperatives. Since China's reform and open-up in the 80s, new farmer cooperatives have come into being.

With the weakening of rural reforms and the change of the structure of the market economy, farm produce goes from scarcity to surplus. Farmers do not get more income from their increasing production and the rural economy develops slowly. With globalization and China's entrance into WTO, small farm households have more difficulties in dealing with dynamic markets. Farmers, managing separately in small scale, are powerless and are in inferior position. It is hard for them to enter the dynamic markets and protect their interests. So organizing of farmers is very necessary.

On the other hand, small per-capita farmland (less than 0.1 ha.) in China and the special property and economic system determine that small-scale production will exist for a long time. We can imitate neither American way nor Japanese way. China can only make innovations on industrial and operating organizations on the basis of household responsibility system. Farmer cooperatives not only hold and exert the advantage of family management but also make up for the deficiency of diseconomy of small-scale management and the inferior position in markets.

Politic Environment

The system of household responsibility carried out in 1979 is the basic condition for the rise of new-style farmer cooperatives.

In recent years, the Chinese government has promulgated several favorable policies to encourage the development of farmer cooperatives. For example, the report of the sixteenth people's congress pointed out that China must improve the organization of farmers in dynamic markets; and another national report pointed out that farmers should develop various special cooperative organizations with principles of free will and equality. No. 1 document of the central government brought forward some policies for encouraging the development of various farmer special cooperative organizations. All the policies have created a favourable institutional environment for farmer cooperatives and drive the cooperatives into a new developing stage.

Cultural Environment

The appearance and development of farmer cooperatives is influenced by the context of society, history, and culture. The innovation comes from traditional Chinese culture. The rural community is the soil for the growth and development of the cooperative. Different from western countries, the villages in East Asia are stable and villagers have closed consanguinity and geographical relations. Thus, it is relatively easy for villagers to cooperate with low transaction cost.

Table 12.1: Innovations Caused in the Supply Chain

	Supply Chain	*Innovation Event*
1995	Peng found that large scale watermelon growing could not only bring down the production cost but also attract wholesalers.	Peng and other six experienced farmers began to contract relatively large glebe to grow watermelons jointly. And their watermelons began to get some name in the markets.
1998	To meet year-round demand for watermelon, they have to grow in some other provinces with high temperatures.	Peng and other 35 villagers went to Guangdong province and established a base there. Thus they ensured all-year supply of watermelon.
1999	With the development of market economy and produce markets, as well as the continual increasing production, there was a need to grow watermelon with standard requirements. A brand was necessary to boost the marketing of the watermelon.	Supported and encouraged by local government, Peng and the villagers registered the brand "Yulin" for the watermelon, and carried out standard production in the form of "four unifications", i.e. unified growing, quality inspection, package, and sale.
2001	After registration of the "Yulin" brand, there were some fake "Yulin" watermelons. To promote circulation of watermelon and further expand the marketing net, villagers thought that a formal farmer cooperative was needed to ensure the proprietary technique and influence.	The Ruoheng farmer cooperative was founded by 29 members. They established local standards of quality and technique for "Yulin" watermelon. After this, four bases in other provinces were built.
2001	The first special sale shop was opened in Hangzhou.	The cooperative established marketing net and special sale shops in many cities continuously and appointed marketing personnel. Thus the marketing area and market share were expanded.
2005	With consumers' increasing concern and demand for quality and safety, green food became popular.	"Yulin" watermelon was recognized as green food, which again affirmed the quality standard and safety on the basis of taste.

Farmers' Participation in and Exclusion from the Cooperative and Supply Chain

In the supply chain, cooperative members participate in market activities and the produce circulation through the cooperative. But there are large quantities of small-scale farmers who do not belong to the cooperative because they do not think it profitable to join the cooperative; the subsidies from the government are possessed by the cooperative head or core members, as well as restrictions on entrance qualifications and the size of the cooperative.

Apparently, small-scale farmers and the cooperative are indispensable participators in the circulation of watermelon. They take part in production and sale of watermelons with different modes. And the cooperative participates in marketing and economic activities as a legal person, but small-scale farmers have to take on the responsibilities from production to sale on the basis of family.

Farmers' Inclusion or Participation in the Farmer Cooperative

In the beginning of Peng Youda's growing watermelon, most villagers did not trust him completely. From the first year of success in planting experimentally to the later scaling-up, villagers in and even around Changshan village began to have the idea of joining in watermelon cultivation. Then Peng Youda established the farmer cooperative and took farmers as member growers. All the members were local villagers. And the only qualification for entering the cooperative was enough capital to buy a share.

When the size the cooperative reaches a certain size, i.e. scaling-up with a steady step, its capacity of absorbing associators will be limited. And not all farmers who are willing to join the cooperative will be accepted. Putting some restrictions on the new members not only ensures incomes of existing members but also drives farmers to increase income group by group. Then the cooperative began to practice a quasi-members system in 2004. All farmers have to go through one-year probation before becoming full members. Three conditions are imposed for taking in new members:

- Necessary (three or more than three years) technique and experience in growing watermelon.
- Some ability in organizing production and management. Besides growing watermelon, all former members have to organize and manage some quasi-members and labourers.
- Capitals to buy a share of the cooperative.

Qualifications to Participate in Watermelon Circulation for Small-Scale Farmers and their Predominance

In order to be included in the circulation of watermelon, small-scale farmers who do not join the cooperative have to be provided with requirements different from that of farmers in the cooperative. The following are necessary qualifications: investing power; techniques for the production of watermelon; some marketing capabilities; and managing ability to take natural risks such as typhoon.

The most notable advantages of small-scale farmers over the cooperative are low price and the "seamless" sale channel. Small-scale farmers have diversified sale outlets. Besides selling their products to wholesalers, small-scale farmers can increase the sale volume through traditional produce markets or transporting the watermelon directly to selling areas.

Besides, small-scale farmers can grow different varieties of watermelons by different inputs. They do not have to be restricted by standard production and quality, so they can resort to diversification. Thus small-scale farmers can satisfy demands of other consumers.

Exclusion of Small-Scale Farmers from the Produce Circulation

1. *Capital:* The cooperative runs on shareholding system. Share capital and accumulated capital not only ensure various costs of cooperative operation but also build up the power of resisting risks. Furthermore, subsidies from the government and loans provided by banks guarantee good operation and resisting power of the cooperative. But small-scale farmers have to carry on their production on the basis of their limited capital, which restricts the production scale and brings high risk as well, especially in cities like Wenlin where typhoons are common.
2. *Technique:* Through innovative production technique and packaging "Yulin" watermelon has a relatively higher sale price than other local watermelons, which is the cooperative's main source of high profits. But small-scale farmers can only afford common materials. In addition, they lack the power of improving the quality and taste of watermelon, and they improve their technique by long-time experience.
3. *Sale:* First, most wholesalers are attracted by the cooperative. Only very few wholesalers preferring to low price will deal with small farm households. Second, all supermarkets are inclined to do business with the cooperatives which has a large production scale. Besides, the cooperative can deliver large volumes on a regular and timely basis and can more easily ensure food safety and quality standards. Also, the bases of the cooperative dispersed in several provinces make it possible to supply the product all-year round. The cooperative has established marketing network in more than 20 provinces.
4. *Subsidies from Government:* Nowadays, the development of farmer cooperatives is vigorously encouraged and sustained by the government. Although small-scale farmers are entitled to exemption, they hardly get subsidies from government. For instance, according to Peng, the cooperative received a subsidy of RMB 650,000 for the typhoon.

Forms and Cost/Benefit of Participation

In the supply chain of watermelon, the cooperative and small-scale farmers participate with different identities and modes, and have different burdens and obligations on their shoulders. The cost and benefit of the cooperative and small-scale farmers are described below. A comparison between them is made to show if the innovation of the cooperative brings up some benefits.

1. The approximate production course of watermelon. Seeds are sown in November; ripe watermelon is harvested in next May; the selling lasts until the next November. That is to say, the period of watermelon from seeding to sale is year round on the whole.
2. The wage of the members in the cooperative is 1000 yuan a month. Both members and small-scale farmers spend all their time and effort on the production of watermelon. They do not have other income besides the sale of watermelon.
3. Male farmers with over three-year experience in growing watermelons are interviewed because male farmers are usually responsible for the purchase of production materials and know better about costs and benefits. Data on the costs and benefits obtained from interviews with five farmers are almost the same, which shows the data are representative and credible.

Cost/Benefit of the Cooperative

The costs of the cooperative are described in Table 12.2.

Table 12.2: Costs of the Cooperative *(yuan/mu)*

	Cost
Seeds	45
Fertilizer and pesticide	1100
Plastic films	1100
Bamboo slices	800
Package materials	1500
Machine costs	250
Cost of land rent	850

Summing up the costs in the table, we get the cost per mu in 2005, i.e. RMB 5,645. But the labour costs of the cooperative are not included in the calculation. Because labour costs are offered to members in the form of wages, and they are incomes of members, labor costs are considered as benefits of members.

Each member's income from his or her labour in 2005 was RMB 2400 per mu. The average output per mu is 2,600 kg. Peng considered it normal compared to former years. Although there was a big typhoon in 2005, it did not have big influence on the yield of watermelon.

The sale volume of the cooperative in 2005 reached 26,000 tons and the average price was 3.00 yuan/kg. So the total sale income was RMB 78,200,000. Assuming the average output was 2600kg/mu, the cooperative gained RMB 7,800/mu.

Cost/Benefit of Small-Scale Farmers

Through interviews with five small-scale farmers, we have obtained their average costs in 2005. These costs are described in Table 12.3.

Table 12.3: Costs of Small-Scale Farmers *(yuan/mu)*

	Cost
Seeds	27
Fertilizer and pesticide	1100
Plastic films	1100
Bamboo slices	432
Machine costs	110
Burettes	80
Costs of wage labour	45
Costs of land rent	850

Summing up; we find that the average cost per mu of five small-scale farmers is RMB 3,744. The cost of non-wage labour, i.e. the labour cost of farmers themselves, is 2400 yuan according to the wage level of the cooperative. Besides, the cost of wage labour comes from the following facts: small-scale farmers have to employ one or two labourers when putting up plastic canopies or in midseason, and 0.9 labour per mu is needed on average, and the cost of the wage labour is 50 yuan per day, so the average cost of wage labours is RMB 45/mu in 2005.

The average output of five small-scale farmers is 2,500 kg. But unlike the cooperative, the five small-scale farmers all thought the watermelon yield was much lower than the average yield in former years as a result of the big typhoon in 2005.

The average price of the watermelon of small-scale farmers is 1.2 yuan/kg. The small-scale farmers get a profit of RMB 3,000/mu.

Comparison of Costs between the Cooperative and Small-Scale Farmers

After the description of the costs and benefits of the cooperative and small-scale farmers, it is easy to see the differences between them. Table 12.4 provides data for comparison.

In the column of "net profit per mu", the data are absent, for which there are some reasons. In the costs of the cooperative and small-scale farmers, some items such as plastic films, bamboo slices and burettes are not be contained fully because these items of inputs are used repeatedly and the costs should be shared in several years. But usage of them in each year is not fixed and known. On the other hand, all items of

Table 12.4: Comparison of Costs and Benefit between the Cooperative and Five Small-Scale Farmers

	Cooperative	*Small-Scale Farmers*	*Difference (yuan)*
Cost per mu (yuan)	5645	3744	1901
Yield per mu (kg)	2600	2500	100
Produce price (yuan/kg)	3.0	1.2	1.8
Profit per mu (yuan)	7800	3000	4800
Net profit per mu (yuan)			2699

costs are used for the comparison between the cooperative and the small-scale farmers, so the costs are presumed to be assumed as the costs of 2005, as long as the data of the two bodies are in accordance. And the assumption leads to higher costs than actual costs. So the net benefits of the two bodies are not known, and only a comparison is given.

The costs of the cooperative and the small-scale farmers are RMB 5,645 and RMB 3,744 per mu. Apparently the cooperative has a higher cost. The main disparity comes from the cost of first-process, labels, net bags and paper boxes for package, which lead to difference of 1500 yuan. Some input items like bamboo and machine expenses are the source of difference too. But the expenses on seeds, fertilizers and pesticides, and plastic films are almost same.

But the extra expense of RMB 1901 is valuable. It leads to different prices of the watermelon between the cooperative and small-scale farmers, which are 3.0 yuan/kg and 1.2 yuan/kg. Such a big gap depends not only on the marketing network but also on fine taste, standard package, good quality, safety, and brand effect of the watermelon.

Watermelon yields of the cooperative and small-scale farmers are not different either. While the head of the cooperative thought the yield in 2005 was at a normal level, the five small-scale farmers considered it was lower over the former years. This indicates that the cooperative has a higher capacity of risk taking than small-scale farmers.

Because of the joint effect of yield and price, there is notable difference in profits between them. Their profits are RMB 7,800 and RMB 3,000 respectively.

In the last row, we can see a disparity of RMB 2,699 in the net profit per mu. So farmers in the cooperative can gain an extra of RMB 2,699 yuan per mu, if overhead expenses are not considered.

Distribution Mechanism of the Cooperative

The cooperative has its financial accounting on the basis of bases. After paying all the costs, the net profit will firstly be deducted by 10 per cent for reserves and commonweal fund for expansion and welfare; then 5 per cent of the net profit will be set aside as risk fund to pay for natural disasters and accidental costs such as typhoons. Risk fund will be mobilized among the bases if needed; at last, profit will be distributed to members according to their shares and contributions. Such distribution mechanism can enhance members' enthusiasm in investment and production.

There are three kinds of members in the cooperative: core members, common members, and quasi-members. Whether the benefit distribution mechanism can reflect the contributions of the three kinds of members properly is a good way to measure the innovation of the cooperative. All the members have to carry on production as a full-time job, and they can get a wage of RMB 1,000 and an additional bonus every month. Core members and common members enjoy profit return. Quasi-members are not entitled to profits until they become formal members. All members have to comply with the same power and obligation. Besides, formal members should guide quasi-members to produce and help them solve technical problems in production. Core members are also responsible for the management of the cooperative. Core members get a reward for management, which is offered in the form of wage or bonus. The distribution mode of the cooperative makes each gain his proper reward by returning the benefit to members, which is an important behaviour of the tenet serving the farmers.

To explain the different gains of the cooperative and small-scale farmers, a simple function of cost/benefit is established, that is : $r = (R - C)(1 - I)$.

- r net profit per mu of members;
- R profit per mu of the cooperative;
- C cost per mu of the cooperative;
- I profit subsistent ratio of the cooperative (the ratio of reserve fund and risk fund).

The corresponding notations for small-scale farmers are r1, R1, and C1. The group of equations can be formed as:

$$r1 = R1 - C1$$

$$r = (R - C - 1 - I)$$

To prove the fact that the members have higher incomes than small-scale farmers, it is necessary to show that r > r1, i.e. $(R - C)(1 - I) > R1 - C1$. Putting the data we can:

$$(r1 + 2699) \times (1 - 15\%) > r1,$$

$$r1 < 15294.3$$

According to the interviewed data, R1 = 3000£¬and r1 = R1£ – C1£¬so r1 < 3000.

Thus it is certain that r1 < 15294.3. That is to say, after drawing out of the reserve and risk fund, cooperative members have apparently higher incomes than small-scale farmers. And it shows the distinct and substantial benefit brought by the cooperative.

Potential for Expansion and Extension

From 3–mu farmland in 1998 to thirteen bases and an area of thousands mu, from a registration capital of RMB 500,000 in 2002 to a total stock capital of RMB 21,000,000 in 2005, from 29 members to 152 formal members and 100 quasi-members, from a common farmer to a well-known "king of watermelon", the cooperative is developing very fast. According to Peng's plan, the cooperative will go on increasing the bases and expanding the area at the rate of 20 per cent. Besides, the cooperative has the idea of growing watermelon in foreign countries, and the most possible destinations are Vietnam and Burma.

Discussion

Institution innovation takes place when the interest bodies realize that they can gain more or their existed interests are intimidated with the development of the economy.

The interest bodies will carry out a reflection of action and appeal to a more advantageous institutional arrangement. The cooperative is a collective action of small-scale farmers to get more benefits when they are intimidated and driven by various environmental factors. The development of the cooperative is certainly not incidental, but influenced and restricted by economy, policy and culture.

The cooperative not only improves the efficiency of the market mechanism but also makes up for the incomplete function of the governmental system. With the continual development of the market economy and liberalization of global produce trade, farmers in the inferior status have to be organized so that they can enter markets through collective action to improve their status and power. It is a spontaneous institutional innovation.

Vigorous support from local government has helped in the development of the cooperative. The local law of the farmer cooperative provides it the identity of a legal person. The local government popularizes the cooperative in different ways, which enhances the status of the cooperative greatly. Besides, it government offers subsidies for natural disasters every year and encourages the rural credit cooperative to provide a loan to the cooperative. All these have created conditions for prosperous development and expansion of the cooperative.

The achievement of the cooperative has close relations with the institutional structure and operational mode. Various innovations on the cooperative principles and development mode go along on the basis of the tenets of "serving the farmers" and "returning profit to the farmers". These innovations can be generalized as follows:

Aspect One: Innovations on the Tenets of the Cooperative

The traditional tenets of farmer cooperative include free accession, free quit, democratic management, one person one vote, fair deal, profit returning, and so on. Farmer cooperatives of the new generation do not rigidly comply with the traditional tenets any more. They have established tenets which are more favourable. They put into practice particular innovational tenets, which is one of the shining points of the cooperative.

1. *System of Quasi-Members.* The cooperative participates in the market and various activities as a legal person. And there are some elements of company system such as quasi-members and internship. This system does not change the tenet of serving farmers, but it absorbs farmers reasonably. If all the farmers can enter the cooperative freely, technique and quality will not be guaranteed. And if the cooperative admits more members than it needs, the cooperative will be inefficient. With the system of quasi-members, the cooperative can absorb homologous members with the expansion of the cooperative. Cooperative's gradual admission of members not only enhances the training effect but also protects the interests of the old members.
2. *System of "One Member, More than One Votes".* When there are important decisions, all the shareholders usually vote. But they do not take the system of "one member, one vote". They vote according to their shares, but the number of certain member's votes cannot exceed ten. This system of voting avoids the over large influence of core members. Core members and common members have the same rights, and the cooperative head has a share of 5 per cent. So this system of voting can avoid the conflict between core members and common members. Besides, it realizes the tenet of democratic management and boosts the enthusiasm of investment.
3. *System of Double Return According to Shares and Transaction Volume.* The system of double return according to share and transaction volume is an important guarantee of the fine operation and development of the cooperative. It encourages members' investment, and more important, it boosts the producing enthusiasm of members. Besides, it avoids low efficiency of free riders, and saves costs of prompting and supervising members. And members will be committed to improvement of quality and yield of watermelon.

Aspect Two: A Leader with Strategic Courage and Insight

In the rural areas of China, there are few inputs in education and cultivation of human resources, which leads to scarcity of human resources with knowledge of corporation management, law, farmer cooperative, etc. An entrepreneur with team spirit is a necessary condition for the birth and development of farmer cooperative.

With the establishment and development of the watermelon farmer cooperative, Peng became a famous man. He studies the production technique of watermelons. Besides, he makes great effort in improving his stuff as an entrepreneur. He is responsible for all the things of the cooperative, from decision-making to benefit distribution of each member. Because most farmers have little education and weak communication skills, management of the cooperative is very difficult. And with the expansion of the cooperative, Peng is facing more difficulties and pressures.

Aspect Three: Continuously Improved Production Technique and Fine Brand Image

One of the benefits brought by the cooperative is "spill-over effect of information". In the cooperative, members contact others freely and information is highly shared.

Innovations or useful information will be popularized and communicated rapidly at very low cost. This is to say, the usage efficiency of information or knowledge is very high, and the extension of new techniques or information is especially rapid.

The cooperative was established and developed on the basis of "one village (town), one product". It is an economic movement which originated from Japan. Farmers in some village take advantage of local resources and adjust measures to local conditions. The concept of "one village, one produce" is being extended and developed fast. It is an effective mode of improving the regional economy and increasing income. It enhances ability to compete in markets by improving produce quality and extending production size.

Taking the soil condition and benefit into account, villagers chose watermelon as the product, and specialized in its production step by step. Compared with complete production in the past, "one village (town), one product" is more propitious to form a distinct and famous brand. And the brand "Yulin" enormously improves the sale price of the watermelon, and makes it well-known. This brand is not only a brand image of the cooperative, but is also a regional brand. Regional brand has more extensive and more sustaining brand effect, compared with the brand of certain corporations. It is an intangible asset shared by all farmers in the community. Not only the cooperative, but also small-scale farmers benefit from the brand. Besides, "Yulin" brand attracts many wholesalers, which also increases sale for small-scale farmers.

Why is the Cooperative Effective by Joining up Small-Scale Farmers?

The watermelon cooperative has brought about substantial benefits to its members. Farmers having participated in the cooperative think they are not far from the market any more.

Farmers participate in markets through the farmer cooperative and gain a bigger share of benefits, the reasons for which are negotiation ability, reduction of transaction costs, and benefits brought by brand effect. Besides, the cooperative often attends some governmental meetings and various science seminars, which brings farmers useful information on technical improvement, improved management, market information, and trends in and out of China. But small-scale farmers have no opportunities of accessing this information.

Increased Income Caused by Reduction of Transaction Costs

Farmers' income has improved a lot after they joined the cooperative. On the one hand, the standard production and brand effect bring high price for watermelon, and on the other hand, the reduction of transaction costs brings more benefits.

Transaction costs are made up of cost of finding transaction objects and pricing, cost of bargain, cost of signing contracts, cost of executing the transaction, cost of supervising, and cost of maintain transaction order. The transaction costs of farmers include cost of production, supply and sale through the market mechanism.

Production and circulation of agro-food are based on family management. On the one hand, cost of stimulation is very low because of the credit mechanism based on consanguinity and kindred. On the other hand, because of abundant labour resources, farmers' opportunity cost of production is very low. Thus family management has a relative low production cost, but a high transaction cost in the environment of increasingly developed and complicated market economy.

1. In the modern markets, there is serious information and power asymmetry in farmers' purchasing of producing, selling, and consuming. So the costs of information, negotiation, preventing fake products, and maintenance of their own rights and interests are very high.
2. Agricultural assets are highly specialized. Because of the high degree of asset specificity, it is hard to change their use, and time and room for using. Great economic loss will happen if they are used improperly, which will lead to higher transaction costs.
3. Separate purchase and sale of small-scale farmer results in diseconomy of transaction scale. And if separate farmers can be organized together, it will bring on reduction in transaction frequency and friction, and thus reduce transaction costs.
4. Small-scale farmers have to bargain with the government if they want to protect their own interests and rights, and ask for more public goods and services. Individual farmers cannot afford such transaction cost.

In order to improve negotiating ability and reduce transaction costs, it is a good for small-scale farmers to join up and negotiate and deal with markets and government.

Sustainable Benefit of Increased Incomes Brought by the Cooperative

There is another form of innovation prevailing in China, i.e. "company + farmers". But decades of practice have proved that it is not a good institutional form for raising the income of farmers. The aim of company is maximizing profit. When there are excess gains, it may give average social profit to farmers. And when the company gets average social profit, it will assign a small portion to farmers just enough to cover the costs. But when there is little profit or even minus profit, probably most losses will be passed on to farmers.

Different from company, farmer cooperatives are organizations of farmers, i.e. they are established, managed, and processed by farmers. The aim of farmer cooperative is to realize farmers' common affluence. The gains of farmer cooperatives are returned to farmers, after taking out a small proportion for accumulation fund and risk fund. We can believe that cooperative will bring farmers substantial benefits if it sticks to the tenet of returning profits to farmers, the scale of the cooperative is not expanded excessively, and the brand effect exists.

Opportunities and Challenges of Expansion and Extension

Growing at the rate of 20 per cent every year, the cooperative is developing very rapidly. Its increasing bases and expanding scale leads to not only its widening marketing network and increasing market shares but also to decreasing transaction cost. Because the intangible assets (such as producing technique, marketing network, and management experience) owned by the cooperative are fixed costs, the bigger the scale, the lower will be the using cost per unit. The scale of the cooperative depends on its decreased transaction and increased innovation cost. Only when the costs of institution innovation and maintenance are smaller than the reduced transaction costs, the expansion of the cooperative will be effective and advisable.

The biggest barrier to the expansion of the cooperative is not lack of capital but shortage of technical talents, poor management, and scarcity of farmland.

Advanced technique is a key to the production of watermelon. But when the cooperative is expanded to a certain scale, it will be difficult to attract able persons specialized in growing watermelon. Thus the cooperative has developed the system of quasi-members. All those who want to enter the cooperative have to pass a period of internship. In the internship period, quasi-members will receive training until they are qualified. The system of informal members not only promotes the development of farmers but also maintains the producing efficiency of the cooperative.

With the expansion of the cooperative, there are more and more non-local members, which bring a challenge to the management of the cooperative. The original cooperative of community did not call for much special management. Management was ensured by the prestige of the leader and local customs. Besides, local members with similar culture, skill and expectations facilitated negotiation and transaction. That is to say, previously management was based on community, and functioned on traditional routines and systems of authority. But management after expansion is more complex and difficult. It is a challenge for the managers of the cooperative.

Scarcity of farmland is a barrier to the further development of the cooperative. Watermelon can not be grown on the same field continuously. The farmland where the watermelon is grown has to be planted with other crops for more than three years before it can be used to grow watermelon again. So the cooperative has to develop new bases to carry on production. There are some requirements about the soil, temperature, humidity, and so on for the growth of watermelon, all of which should be considered for the expansion and sustainable development of the cooperative.

Opportunities and Challenges of Developing Cooperative in Other Provinces or Foreign Countries

After the establishment of the marketing network in most provinces or cities in China, it is natural to have the idea of selling watermelons outside China and even growing it in foreign countries. Grow watermelon in foreign countries will not only broaden the marketing network of watermelons and gain a position in overseas markets, but also reduce costs of marketing and transport.

Besides the difficulties in technique, human resources, and management, multinational production is faced with differences in language, communication, and culture. And more important, can native seeds be seasoned with the soil there? The cooperative will have to carry out trials on overseas bases and make some improvements if necessary. And the costs of trials as well as improvements are high. And capital, which is not a problem in domestic expansion, will also be a barrier to multinational production.

As to human resources, not only persons specialized in technique but also common labour force is insufficient. It's infeasible to take farmers with low education abroad because they cannot adapt to the different environment. So the cooperative will have to employ local labourers abroad. It is impractical to build bases in developed countries because of their high labor cost. Therefore, transnational bases have to be restricted to developing countries with relatively cheap labour force.

Farmer entrepreneurs usually lack in strategic management skills. Development of farmer cooperatives depends on the culture of community and traditional routines to some extent, which is an important challenge for the multinational development of farmer cooperatives.

Key to Extension of the Cooperative

Farmer cooperatives, which rose in the 80s and developed in the 90s, are flourishing now in China. It is quite necessary to guide their development with successful cases. The watermelon cooperative is a typical cooperative of the new generation. It is a relatively successful cooperative in terms of benefits it brings to farmers and contributions it brings to local economy. Such a development model is worth extending. In southeast China where there is a relatively developed and perfect market economy, similar farmer cooperative can be found.

Developed market economy, system of produce supply chain, and circulation channel are preconditions for the birth of farmer cooperative. If farmer cooperatives are established or extended compulsively, they will be a failure. If there is environment for the development of farmer cooperatives and government support and inspiration, development of farmer cooperatives will take place. Cooperatives established spontaneously are the most vigorous.

Besides the environmental factors, a leader with strategic foresight is also important. Such leaders are usually village cadres with high prestige or able persons who have mastered the technique of certain products.

Conclusions

Looking at the farmer cooperatives in China or in developing countries with similar modes of development, there are some implications from this study. We can draw the following conclusions from our analysis:

Farmer cooperatives play such a core role in providing information and technique channels for small-scale farmers, participating in markets and supply chain, and negotiating with government on behalf of small-scale farmers. Farmer cooperatives not only enhance farmers' sense of security and competition but also improve their negotiating ability.

Effective farmer cooperatives have not only large scale production and marketing network but also effective agricultural production and diversified opportunities.

Farmer cooperatives not only reduce the high transaction costs but also increase farmers' share in the supply chain through strengthening negotiation power, guarantee of produce quality, and brand effect. Farmer cooperatives play an important part in increasing income and development of agriculture.

While farmer cooperatives participate in market and pursue maximum profits, they stick to cooperative tenets. Members can claim the surplus profit, which inspires farmers' enthusiasm.

Farmer cooperatives not only reduce transaction costs but also keep the economy residuals coming from the saving of transaction costs within agriculture to build self-accumulating ability and developing power of agriculture.

As an institutional innovation, there is necessarily innovation cost. Only when the income of institutional innovation is more than the cost, the institutional arrangement will be achieved. But now, the market economy in China is immature, and the conception, knowledge accumulation, and behavior of both government and farmers are far from satisfactory. Because of various factors, innovation cost of new-style farmer cooperatives is high. It is the high cost that leads to distorted development (small scale work, weak service function, and nonstandard running) of farmer cooperative. It is the best path of seeking minimum cost. Distorted development reduces transforming and running costs of farmer cooperatives, but it results in low power in the market competing and resisting market risk.

References

Bo Jin and Hailin Guan. "Analysis of the formation mechanism of industry centralization [J]." Social science transaction of Shanxi altitude school, 2005(3): 53–55.

Congjiu Liu. "The reconstruction of agro-food circulation based on supply chain [J]." *Chinese Cooperative Economy*, 2004(5): 53–56

Dongmin Liu. "Industrialization of agriculture and produce circulation [M]." Audit publishing company of China, Mar. 2001.

Gereffi G. "International trade and industrial upgrading in the apparel commodity chain [J]." *Journal of International Economics*, 1999(48): 37–70.

Jim bingen, Alex Serrani and Julie Howard. "Linking farmer to market: different approaches to human capital development [J]." *Food Policy*, 2003(28): 405–419.

Litch *et al.* "Agricultural trade labialisation and proved dynamics in three developing countries [J]." *American Journal of Agricultural Economics*, 2003(12): 1285–1291.

Stockbridge M. "Farmer organization for market access: learning from success [J]." *Literature Review*, London: Wye College, 2003.

Tao tan and Yihua Zhu. "The study of the organization mode of produce supply chain [J]." *Modern Economy Discussion*, 2004(5): 24–27.

Weatherspoon D.D and T. Reardon. "The rise of supermarkets in Africa: Implications for agrifood system and the rural poor [J]." *Development Policy Review*, 2003(2): 333–335.

Zuhui Huang and Dongying Liu. "The construction and institution analysis of the produce logistic system in China [J]." *Agricultural Economic Problem*, 2005(4): 49–53.

Zuhui Huang and Wunhua Jiang. "The institutional perspective of agricultural and rural development theory discussion and appliance analysis [M]." Chinese Agriculture Publishing Company, Oct. 2002.

13

Supermarkets Penetrating Chinese Countryside: The Suguo Model and its Impact on Smallholders and SMEs

Naiquan Sang

Nearly three decades of market-oriented reforms and endogenous development of the economy has led China enter into a new stage of industrialization and urbanization, causing such changes as huge scale of rural-urban migration, growing middle-class, changing lifestyle, improved transportation system, and maturing agribusiness market. All of these changes are altering food consumption, production, and distribution patterns. Supermarkets have emerged and quickly spread from metropolitan cities to secondary cities and even to towns since the mid-1990s (Hu, *et al.*, 2004). This quick spread of supermarkets is reshaping the way the agri-food system is governed, and supermarkets are playing an increasingly important role in the Chinese agri-food system.

The mainstream literature on supermarket has claimed that the rapid rise of supermarkets may bring significant challenges and potential opportunities for smallholders and SMEs (Reardon *et al.*, 2003; Boselie *et al.*, 2003). The most critical challenge may come from the shift of supermarket procurement system away from traditional wholesalers toward specialized wholesalers, preferred suppliers, distribution centres, and even private grades and standards. Large scale commercial farmers are preferred and contracted as outgrowers while small farmers may be marginalized because small farmers may be not able to meet the requirements of supermarkets. This accepted theory has been challenged by other researchers based on field survey data from Greater Beijing (Rozelle, *et al.*, 2005). They claim that big changes occured in the retail industry, big changes occurred between retailors and wholesalers, but nothing changed at farm gate procurement: the supermarket revolution has little impact on small farmers.

In contrast with these two extreme points of view, this study proposes that the supermarket revolution may bring significant impact on smallholders and SMEs in China if the criteria of impacts are relaxed to include both production and consumption effects. We admit that the procurement is a critical linkage between farmers and supermarkets. However, even if without direct contact of supermarkets with farmers, farm production could be influenced by supermarkets through their agents or small traders. The consumption effects are particularly important under current situation, as domestic consumption has been found to be a new growth pole when foreign trade conflicts are getting increasingly intensive. Based on a case study of the Suguo supermarket, this paper demonstrates that smallholders and SMEs may benefit significantly from the supermarket revolution, especially when the supermarket penetrates into countryside.

Growth of Suguo Supermarket

The Suguo supermarket is a Nanjing based local supermarket under CRE Vanguard. The characteristic of this supermarket is its successful penetration into the rural countries of nearby six provinces around the headquarters (Jiangsu, Anhui, Shandong, Henan, Hebei, and Hubei). It has been ranked among top 10 supermarkets in China since 1996. Annual sales amounted to 22.8 billions RMB by its totally 1612 chain stores with 50,000 employees in 2006; about 50 per cent of total sales were contributed by those chain stores in rural countries. Based on the rural-oriented business strategy, Suguo supermarket has successfully expanded its market share within the region. It has 50 per cent market share in Nanjing, mainly contributed by over 400 self-owned chain stores in this city. In 2004, the 400 self-owned chain stores in Nanjing sold RMB 1 billion of food products as meat, milk, eggs, vegetables, fruits, aquatic products, rice, and other grains. Suguo plans to open a hundred self-owned chain stores in a hundred counties around Nanjing while the franchising chain stores have retreated to towns and villages in next five years.

Regionally Intensive Development Strategy

Suguo offers multi-dimentional services or a combination of various services in a specific region. This region-intensive development strategy achieved great success in Nanjing to compete with FDI supermarkets. Then the strategy was copied in other middle cities such as Yang-zhou, He-fei, Ma-anshan, Huai-nan, Gao-chun, Li-shui, Jiang-yan, and Bao-yin.

Convenience Shops: Suguo opened convenience shops first on February 14, 1999. So far, more than 200 convenience shops have been opened, each of them with area of 100 square meters. They are all open around the clock, supply free services of over 20 kinds. These have made Suguo popular with consumers.

Large Comprehensive Supermarket: In 2000, Suguo opened large comprehensive supermarkets with Chinese characteristics. The first warehouse supermarket opened on September 3, 2000, the shopping mall of 10,000 square meters with more than 3000 commodities. On January 10, 2001, Suguo opened warehouse supermarkets at North Zhongshan Road and Xinglong. The three warehouse supermarkets are located in the east, west, and north of the city respectively.

Community Stores: In 2002, Suguo opened its community shop, whose function nearly includes as traditional food market, agricultural products market, non-staple food shop, grocery and small stores, and so on. The Yingyuan Community shop, as an example, is spread over 5,000 sq.m and sells more than 20,000 commodities.

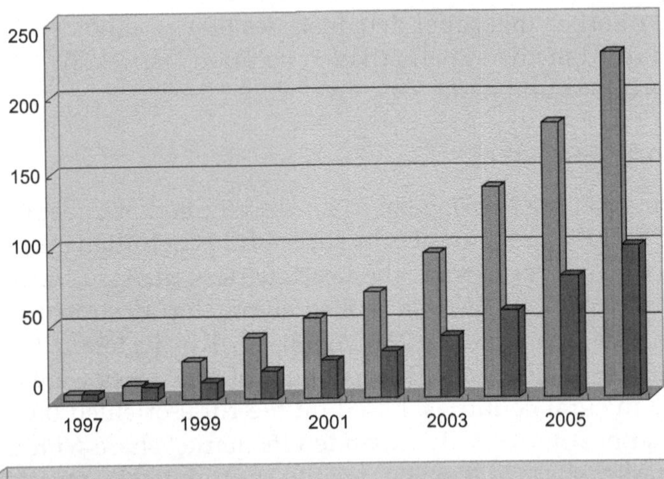

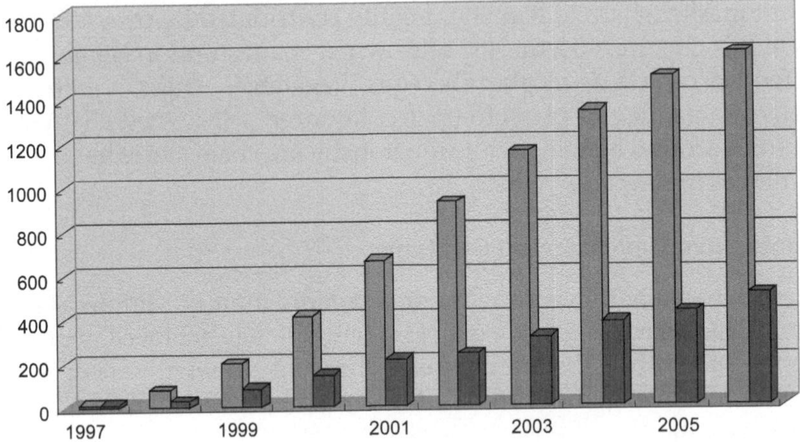

Fig. 13.1: Suguo Total Sale and Self-owned Sale

Home Kitchen Project: In October 1999, Suguo provided the services of fresh food cooking, bread and food processing, and food cleaning. "Home Kitchen Project" moved the kitchen into the supermarket, which has changed people's customs and method of consumption. Meanwhile, in accordance with improvement in people's living standards and changing demand for supermarket commodities, Suguo modifies its commodity combination constantly, and brings in hundreds and thousands of essential commodities such as food, washing products, costumes and electric appliances step by step.

Penetrating into Countryside

Two years after the company was founded, Suguo decided to penetrate the rural markets by franchising supply and selling cooperatives. Why did Suguo supermarket adopt the rural-oriented business strategy? Four factors led Suguo to make such decision.

Firstly, rural markets were believed to have greater potential than urban markets. This is particularly true in economically advanced Yangtze river delta region. However, the demand of farmers for capital and consumer goods was not appropriately satisfied. Hence, there was a business chance.

Secondly, Suguo originally evolved from supply and marketing cooperatives. As a result, Suguo can take advantage of the existing networks of supply and selling cooperatives. By franchising, little investment was required and little risk was taken in doing this business. On the other hand, the networks of supply and selling cooperatives nearly collapsed during the market-oriented reforms. The fundmental issues lay in institutional and management capabilities. By contracting with the cooperatives, Suguo requires them to conduct complete institutional and management reforms. This led to the revival of cooperatives, originally state-owned firm.

Thirdly, Suguo supermarket did not enough financial capabilities. In order to expand in other markets Suguo needed a less costly approach. Franchising cost little to Suguo supermarket, and it could also enter the rural market very quickly.

Fourthly, competition in the retail industry in metropolitan and large cities is very intense particularly in the scenario of post-WTO. FDI supermarkets rushed into China. They firstly emerged in metropolitan cities, then quickly moved to secondary and tertiary cities. Suguo was not competitive in terms of funds, talents, and management capabilities. It needed time to learn from FDI and other excellent domestic supermarkets. Suguo believed that rural markets were less competitive, and may have first-move advantage in countryside.

In April 1998, Suguo opened the first rural chain store in Lieshui County by franchising the supply and selling cooperative of Lieshui county. On December 1998, Suguo supermarket opened the second chain store by franchising in Hefei, the provincial capital city of Anhui province. Since 1998, successful the supply and selling cooperatives quickly spread to six provinces around Nanjing, including Jiangsu, Anhui, Shandong, Henan, Hebei, and Hubei. More than 1200 chain stores were opened through the franchising mode in these regions. Since 2002, Suguo has started exploiting the rural market by opening both self-owned chain stores and franchisee chain stores. Self-owned chain stores are target the county markets while franchisee chain stores are in towns and villages.

Supermarkets penetrating into countryside have improved farmers' shopping environment and promoted rural consumption. Fifty per cent of total sales of Suguo came from these chain stores in rural countries and 70 per cent of commodities sold are agri-food or related products.

Reforms on Supply and Selling Cooperatives

Before franchising the supply and selling cooperatives as chain stores of Suguo, the cooperatives have to carry out institutional and management reforms. The supply and selling cooperatives were formerly state-run firms. Their property rights are not clear. Therefore, the institutional reforms on property rights are necessary to turn state-run enterprises into joint-ventures or private firms. Through instituional reforms, almost all of the cooperatives became private or partnership enterprises.

Management reforms are also crucial for the efficiency and competitiveness of the firms. These reforms include recruitment of employees, obligation of positions, incentives, and punishment. The new mechanism has shown remarkable performance, the competitiveness of chain stores has significantly improved, and the external image of shop was totally changed after introducing the brand of Suguo supermarket.

All the franchisees of Suguo have to observe seven unified principles of chain store operation, including unified procurement, distribution, accounting, pricing, layout, management, and image of the stores. When Suguo franchises the cooperatives, it provides supervision on management and operation of chain stores. The chain stores have to set up POS system. Suguo also provide professional training to chain store managers to help them resolve practical issues. Suguo paid special attention to monitoring and evaluating franchisees of the cooperatives at the end of the year.

Plans to Further Exploit Rural Market

The basic idea behind "open a hundred stores in a hundred counties around Nanjing" is to promote Suguo's regionally intensive development strategy. There should be 1–2 large shops, preferential price shops and shopping squares, facilities with some standard supermarkets, and convenience shops in order to acquire more than 40 per cent market. Inspired by the Suguo model, the Ministry of Commerce of China conducted a project called "market project for a thousand of towns and 10 thousands of villages". This project aims to open 250,000 chain stores at village level in next three years. Encouraged by the above market project, Suguo accelerated the speed of "open a hundred stores in a hundred counties". "Suguo convenience shops" have been opened in small towns and central villages, enabling the chain network to cover all the rural markets. In the next step, Suguo plans to establish its own chain stores in 100 county seats within three years, with direct-marketing shops strengthening the material circulation distribution and management of the rural chain shops. Based on the county where self-owned chain stores are already opened, some direct-marketing shops have spread to large towns, developed allied shops in small towns and central villages, pushing forward gradually.

Macro and Meso Context of Suguo Model

Since the beginning of the market-oriented reforms by the end of the 70s, the annual growth rate of GDP has been over 10 per cent in China. Such fast economic growth was pushed mainly by investments, foreign trade, and FDI. As a result, China was turned into a country highly dependent on the world market, particularly after joining WTO. However, the large amount of trade surplus resulted in the increasingly intensified trade frictions of China with major trade partners. Under such circumstances, consumption, especially rural consumption, was suggested as a new driver of economic growth. It is argued that there are 1.3 billion population in China with 80 per cent of them living in rural areas. The rural market is getting larger and larger because of the rising incomes of farmers, improved public goods, and social security in rural China. The movement pushed by the government to construct so-called new socialist countryside will significantly increase the rural demand for both capital and consumer goods.

Pilot Project of Chain Store Operation at Village Level

In contrast with the increasing rural demand, the rural retail industry is quite back ward cannot meet the requirements of farmers. The supply and selling cooperatives were the legacy of the command economy. During the transition to the market economy, these supply and selling cooperatives nearly collapsed. The dominant retailers in rural countries are very tiny private family shops. The prices of goods sold by these private shops are high but the quality is low, and food safety cannot be guaranteed. Demand for capital and consumer goods could not be satisfied properly in rural China. Low quality seeds and chemicals seriously affected farm production, while low quality and unsafe foods harmed farmers. To address these issues, the government encouraged the development of the modern retail industry in rural countries, and particularly welcomed supermarkets penetrating the countryside. Suguo's practice demonstrated that supermarkets penetrating the countryside could provide farmers with cheaper goods. Inspired by the successful experience of Suguo, the ministry of commerce of China conducted a "market project for one thousand towns and ten thousand villages" in 2005. The project aimed to improve the consumption environment of rural residents by establishing 250,000 chain stores at village level in the pilot regions during the three years. The supermarkets are encouraged to extend their operation to countryside by means of financial subsidies and low interest loans.

Government Support for Agro-Industrialization

Since the mid-90s, the government addressed the issues of agro-industrialization by encouraging large-scale food processors and retailers to function as channel captains of food supply chains. During the transformation, Chinese agriculture has increasingly turned into commercialized and specialized agriculture. However, the average of farmland is 0.5 hectare with several pieces of fields. Linking these small farmers to the market is very difficult because the transaction costs are very high. Several forms of vertical coordination emerged in this context. Contract farming and outgrowers were encouraged by the government. The channel captains of food supply chains are critical of vertical coordination of food production and marketing. Therefore, the government cultivated some large scale food processors, wholesalers, and retailers through policy support. Suguo was listed as one of 15 large marketing enterprises supported by the Ministry of Commerce of China, and also listed as one of 40 chain store operation enterprises appointed by the Ministry of Agriculture.

Competition from Foreign and Domestic Supermarkets

The current competitors of Suguo are foreign and domestic supermarkets. Walmart, Carrefour, and Metro are top three supermarkets in the world. Shanghai Hualian is the largest domestic supermarket. These supermarkets are financially and managerially strong. Metro and Carrefour in Yuhua and Xiaguang districts of Nanjing have monthly sales of over 100 million yuan. Shanghai Lianhua supermarket opened more than 20 chain stores and has now become the second largest super- market in Nanjing. Huacheng supermarket expanded from 19 chain stores to 40 chain stores. Jinrunfa supermarket and Beijing Hualian also opened chain stores here. In addition, some middle and small supermarkets such as Jiahui also got some market share in Nanjing. Competition facing Suguo is very intense. However, Suguo also has its competitive advantages. Suguo aims to bring consumers with convenience and benefits. Community stores were opened for that purpose. Suguo also has the advantages of location, low cost expansion and scale economy.

Both foreign and domestic supermarkets have some advantages and hence could pose threats to Suguo. There are two ways of turning potential competitors to current competitors. One is that potential competitors actively expand in the area occupied by current competitors. The other is for Suguo to expand in the area which will be occupied by potential competitors. Based on Suguo's current capacity, its competitiveness is not as strong as that of big retailers. In addition, other commercial firms such as small shops, franchised shops, and grocery stores also pose threat to Suguo.

Facing severe competition from more than 10 foreign supermarkets, Suguo has neither retreated nor directly confronted them. Instead, Suguo adopted a different business strategy. Foreign supermarkets operate on large scale, as a result, they could not make the dense networks to meet the demand of different consumers. On the contrary, Suguo could open small chain stores to satisfy such needs.

The strategy adopted by Suguo is to consolidate its headquarters in Nanjing, and then transfer its focus to the countryside.

Impacts of Suguo Model on Smallholders and SMEs

The mainstream supermarket literature suggests that small farmers and SMEs may be challenged or even marginalized owing to the shift of supermarket procurement system from traditional wholesale markets to preferred suppliers and distribution centres. Supermarkets respond to consumer demands on food safety and quality by increasingly procuring from large commercial farmers. However, there is also evidence that small producers can benefit from the rise of supermarkets in developing countries. Suguo supermarket has extended its chain store operation to rural areas which actually provides a platform for SMEs. Following is a case of "a dish of pickled vegetables", which shows how agribusinesses have benefited from the penetration of Suguo into countryside.

"A dish of pickled vegetables" is the wholesaler brand name of Yunlu Pickled Vegetables Company, established in 1998. The original purpose to establish this company was to create a brand from which both producers and retailers could benefit; however, both of them cannot get rid of the wholesaler. The founder of this company, Hu Xiaoping, suffered losses because of the collusion by the producers and related retailers. The mechanism of this wholesaler brand name is to bind three sides of producers, wholesalers and retailers together to share the benefits of increasingly popular brand name and growing market. The crucial element of this mechanism is to keep the market growing. Therefore, Hu found Suguo supermarket as the platform for his business. Fortunately, it is a successful story. With the quick expansion of Suguo in urban and rural markets, the demand for pickled vegetables is growing very quickly, which provides the opportunity for Hu to organize more and more producers. Infant cucumbers have been cultivated in Hu's hometown for many years. However, because of little demand for it, small farmers can benefit very little from this production. When there is good harvest, small farmers lose from excess production. Hu believed that processed infant cumcubers could be very popular among urban and rural consumers. He suggested to set up a factory to process the cucumbers and encourage small farmers to produce more infant cumcubers. The plan was successful and the factory sold RMB 1.8 million of infant cucumbers in the first year. Currently, the value of processed cumcubers has gone upto RMB 80 million. The planting area of infant cucumbers has reached 10,000 mu (1 mu = 1/15 hectare). Local small farmers can stably depend on this cucumber production. After a successful beginning, Hu began to widen the range of pickled vegetables to include more than 200 products, including preserved szechuan pickle, Sauerkraut, etc. Hu organized more than 60 production bases nationwide, which cover over 100,000 small farmers to produce fresh vegetables for processing. Sale volumes reached RMB 80 million, and the company sold RMB 30 million RMB alone of processed vegetables through chain stores of Suguo.

The case of pickled vegetables is just one successful story for Suguo to provide a platform for SMEs. Suguo has helped many SMEs become successful businesses; for example Jiangsu Meat Company sold RMB 35 million of meat through Suguo, accounting for two-thirds of total sale volume. Nearly 1000 SMEs found their way to sell in Suguo supermarket, many native and special local products were turned into successful businesses, promoted by Suguo supermarket in a manner according to consumers. The quality and standards of these products were upgraded, which promoted market demand.

Improving Rural Consumption Environment

The original strategy of Suguo supermarket penetrating into countryside was to expand market with less investment. However, standardization of chain store operation could really improve the rural consumption environment. In fact, there were lots of counterfeit consumer goods and capital goods in rural markets, especially unsafe foods. The countryside not only produces unsafe foods but also consumes unsafe foods, which harmed the health of rural residents. In order to provide cheap and genuine consumer and capital goods for small farmers, the rural commercial system should be regulated and modernized. Encouragement of merchant firms to extend their chain store operation into countryside could effectively prevent the prevalence of fake products in rural areas, because the supermarket has its own standards of safety and quality. Based on this consideration, the ministry of commerce designed a "market project for a thousand townships and ten thousand villages". This project aims to encourage merchant firms to extend their chain store operation into rural countries. The project was inspired by the experience of Suguo supermarket and vows to open 250,000 rural chain stores in three years since 2005. The success of the project will significantly improve farmers' shopping environment.

Taking Advantage of Small Traders

Suguo supermarket procure fresh and processed foods through its procurement system. However, small traders dominate the channel of procurement. Suguo supermarket set up a small scale Distribution Centre (DCs) in the suburb of Nanjing in Feburary 2004 to support fresh and processed food supply to 100 self-owned chain stores in Nanjing city. A modern distribution centre in Maqun has been launched while the fresh and processing section is still under construction. Nevertheless, even if the chain stores supported by DCs, small traders are still dominant agents of transaction connecting small farmers with DCs. The food supply chains of Suguo supermarket are not directly controlled by the channel captain through contracts or vertical integration. In contrast, the supply chains are somewhat loose, which reflects the huge transaction costs and enforcement costs. By taking advantage of a large number of small traders, Suguo can save transaction costs. There is very little of beureaucratic cost which is highly incentive for such kind of supply chains.

The small traders are usually farmers, who collect vegetables and fruits. Suguo supermarket has signed contracts with these small traders with requirements of food safety and quality checked by third parties and spot-checks. The small traders collect vegetables in certain areas, which provide stable channels for small farmers.

Establishing Own Production Bases

According to our field work forty per cent of fresh foods are procured through the channel of preferred suppliers, majority of whom are small traders, 40 per cent of fresh foods are procured through the channel of production bases, 10 per cent procured from wholesale markets, and 10 per cent procured from spot markets. Although Suguo has loose supply chains, has also set up some production bases in suburban areas. These production bases, of course, could be beneficial for the participant farmers.

Comparative Study of Suguo Procurement System

In 2004, Suguo established a small Distribution Centre (DC) to serve the self-owned chain stores in Nanjing. The centre employs 300 workers, and procures fresh food from a variety of sources. The first channel is wholesale markets, such as Bai Yun Ting and Tian Yin Shan. This channel accounts for less than 10 per cent of total procurement, mainly for off-season vegetables and fruits from Hainan and Shandong provinces. The second channel is the preferred suppliers or small traders with whom Suguo has signed contracts. The price is determinated on daily wholesale market price. These small traders collect vegetables and fruits mainly based on trust. This channel accounts for 40 per cent of total procurement. The third channel is so-called production bases, where many small farmers produce same products. This apparently improves the scale economies of marketing and saves transaction costs. Suguo established several production bases around Nanjing, such as Jiangpu, Luhe, Jiangning, Lieshui, and Gaochun. This channel accounts for about 40 per cent of total procurement. The fourth channel is spot markets; although declining, it still accounts for less than 10 per cent of total procurement.

In 2005, a modern distribution centre was built in Maqun. This centre occupies an area of nearly 17 hectares. The service radius is 300 km. Within Maqun DC, a fresh food distribution centre is under construction with an investment of RMB 50 millions. The construction area is 10,000 sq.m with 1000 tons of cold storage space. According to the startegic plan of Suguo supermarket, distribution centres may be built in Nanjing, Xuzhou, and Hefei in order to support the large scale networks of chain stores in rural areas.

Procurement System of Export-Oriented Agribusinesses

The procurement system for food supply chains in export-oriented areas, such as in Shandong province, could be quite different from the channels for domestic retailing. Because of very strict requirements by foreign buyers, food processors and marketing enterprises took strict measures to ensure food safety and quality standards. Food processors send their inspectors to check if the production code is properly followed. In order to save transaction costs and monitor costs, food processors prefer large and commercial farmers. Usually they set a minimium scale while selecting farmers. They also rent large land to let farmers to plant on it and employ people to monitor farmer's work.

In contrast, food supply chains mainly for domestic selling have lower requirements for food safety and quality. The reasons include high transaction costs and low willingness to pay. Therefore, any expensive step to ensure food safety and quality could not be the priority of supermarkets. However, Suguo also invested a lot on a feasible plan for food safety and collaborated with the ministry of science of China.

Based on these differences, channel captains of food supply chains in export-oriented areas may marginalize small farmers while they may not signicantly marginalize small farmers in domestic operations.

Conclusions

The basic concept of inclusion or exclusion of small farmer due to the rise of supermarkets should be carefully defined. It should not be narrowlly defined within production area. Providing small farmers a better consumption environment for both consumer and capital goods is also crucial for countries such as China. Suguo supermarket penetrated into the countryside and opened up opportunities for smallholders to consume better, genuine, and safe food. Any measure stimulating rural consumption is quite important.

Contrary to popular beliefs, closer vertical coordination or even vertical integration may be not an appropriate choice in the case of China, where land is equally distributed to every smallholder. Only in this particular case, there is some degree of choice of producers' scale; usually majority of smallholders are small, which means the procurement system cannot discriminate them. Even if DCs are adopted by supermarkets, small traders are still welcome and will prevail in the future. These small traders can efficiently deal with smallholders with some degree of food safety and quality consideration.

Middlemen or SMEs can also stimulate the production of smallholders, which is evidenced by the case of "a dish of pickled vagetables".

Suguo model was successful in procuring from small holders and provided a platform for SMEs. It also provide farmers a better consumption environment. This model has been highly praised by many national leaders. The Ministry of Commerce of China inspired by the model lauched the "market project for one thousand townships and ten thousand villages". However, to what degree this model could be replicated depends on several factors.

The first is rural market potential. We admit that the rural market is huge as the Chinese economy grows; however, in the current stage, the gap between urban and rural areas still quite large. Rural consumption is cash increasing but still slowly. Considering that supermarkets can absorb only part of purchases, therefore, are opportunities to open chain stores in rural areas. Otherwise, over-competition will result.

Secondly, it also depends on reasonable logistics support. The advantage of chain store operation lies on scale economy. The key element is logistics support. Without appropriate logistics, the separate chain store could not compete with other shops. Although highway construction is proceeding at a fast pace, logistics support are far behind. This is a restrictive factor.

The last factor is government support. Based on the market project promoted by the ministry of commerce of China, the government has promised RMB 10 billion subsidized loan and financial supports of 0.5 billion yuan to those merchant enterprises which open chain stores in rural areas. Suguo supermarket bears little risk of business operation because it only takes franchising and receives fees from the supply and marketing cooperatives. Actually, the rural chain stores are not so profitable. Therefore, funds are needed to encourage the spread of chain stores into countryside.

References

Boselie, D., Henson, S., and Weatherspoon, D. (2003), "Supermarket Procurement Practices in Developing Countries: Redefining the Roles of the Public and Private Sctors." *American Journal of Agricultural Economics*, 85(5):1155–1161.

Dong, X. Bi, X. and Hu, D. (2006), "The Changes in Urban Retail Market of Agriculrural Products and Its Impacts on Rural Households." *Chinese Rural Economy*, Issue 2.

Gale, F., Tang, P., Bai, X., and Xu, X. "Commercialization of Food Consumption in Rural China." *Economic Research Report*, No. 8, USDA.

Hu, D., Reardon, T., Rozelle, S. Timmer, P., and Wang, H. (2004), "The Emergence of Supermarkets with Chinses Characteristics: Challenges and Opportunities for China's Agricultural Development." *Development Policy Review*, 22(5): 557–586.

Li, Q. (2003), "Fully Explore Rural Market to Promote Jiangsu Urban-Rural Coordinated Development." *Jiangsu Business Review*, Issue 3.

Reardon, T., Timmer, C.P., Barrett, C.B., and Berdegue, J. (2003), "The Rise of Supermarkets in Africa, Asia, and Latin America." *American Journal of Agriculrural Economics*, 85(5): 1140–1146.

Rozelle, S., Huang, J., Dong, X., Wang, H., and Reardon, T. (2005), "Marketing Supply Chains with Chinese Characteristics: Petty Traders, Supermarket Giants and Poor, Small Horticulture Producers." *Working Paper*, EAAE Meeting, Copenhagen.

14

Looking Ahead

Vijay Paul Sharma, Bill Vorley, Jikun Huang, Abid Qaiyum Suleri
Larry Digal and Thomas A. Reardon

Agri-food markets in developing countries are undergoing significant changes. These changes can be rapid once they take off, challenging the response capacity of the public sector, businesses, farmers, and other stakeholders. Restructuring in agri-food markets is driven by a demand-pull and supply-push factors such as population growth, rising incomes, increasing urbanization, market liberalization, business opportunities, rising importance of food standards, changes in consumer preferences including increased concerns for food safety and quality, etc. One of the significant features of this restructuring is the proliferation of modern retail food outlets. In South and South-East Asia, the modern retail sector is expanding rapidly as economies improve and as population increases. Public policies are important catalysts of change as agriculture is still an important sector in many developing countries. These changes in agri-food markets lead to changes in supply chains in terms of new technologies, better management, procure systems, role of food safety standards, and industry structure. Many of the market changes offer increased opportunities as well as challenges to producers, consumers, businesses, and other players in the food chain. However, participation of smallholder producers in changing markets depends on their skills and asset base.

The literature on the impact of smallholder participation in dynamic agri-food markets is diverse. Some studies show that many small producers are unable to tap these opportunities as they lack the resources to compete. Meeting quality and volume requirements of high-value markets for them becomes difficult because transaction and consolidation costs are high. Moreover, small-scale producers do not have adequate financial resources to invest in technology for meeting the quality standards of high value markets.

Some cases that have demonstrated unique and successful stories of consolidation and integration of food marketing chain have been presented in this book. Experiences and lessons from these case studies are important not only for enabling farmers to participate in modern market chains, but also for modernizing agriculture and ensuring better supply of safe foods. Twelve case studies (four each from South and South-East Asia and China) highlight these issues and have generated important conclusions and policy implications.

South Asia

Agriculture is and will remain the mainstay for a large proportion of India's rural population, many of whom are poor. Promoting more rapid and broad based agricultural growth will be extremely important for alleviating poverty in rural areas. The current crisis in Indian agriculture will only exacerbate the situation unless prompt remedial action is initiated by the government. One way to boost agricultural growth and increase farm income is to shift from a traditional cereal-based cropping system to high value agriculture, and link producers to markets. High value agriculture gives higher returns but is also risky. Majority of farmers are small and marginal, and have poor links with markets and low risk-bearing capacity. This restricts their participation in fast changing markets. Corporate agriculture, especially through contract farming, is being promoted by central and state governments to solve some of these problems. Contract farming is expected to increase farmers' access to better quality inputs including credit. It also has the potential to eliminate and/or reduce the market and price risks that farmers face. However, success is dependent on the nature of contracts, legislation for regulation of contract farming, enforcement, dispute resolution mechanisms, etc.

The present models of contract farming are not completely integrated, since companies provide only seeds and sometimes extension services. None supply other vital inputs such as pesticides, fertilizers, and, more importantly, credit. For credit, farmers are still dependent on informal sources. One finding from the case study of contract farming in Punjab is the exclusion of small farmers from contract farming since contracting companies have preference for medium and large farmers to reduce their transaction costs and ensure quality standards. Success of contract farming will largely depend on integrating small and marginal farmers in the contract farming system.

The lessons from this study also have wider significance in connection with the question of how successful approaches to contract farming can be developed. Firstly, it is important to provide an integrated set of services, including credit, and not just extension services and seed. Secondly, partnerships between public and private sector companies or organizations are needed in order to provide integrated services. Thirdly, there is need to improve the bargaining power of smallholder producers while reducing the transaction costs for companies through promotion of producers' groups, associations, or cooperatives. Small farmers will be able effectively to participate in the changing markets and establish links with new market chains (supermarkets, agribusiness companies, processors, exporters, etc.) only if they have access to basic infrastructure, inputs, and services, and are organized.

As an institutional innovation, the HOPCOMS example combining horizontal and vertical coordination holds great promise in providing a platform for small farmers to connect with dynamic markets. In practice, it does well in some aspects and not at all in others. Its main strength is in vertical coordination. Through low cost, HOPCOMS is able to procure produce from farmers and get it to consumers through a network of decentralized procurement centres and scattered retail outlets. However, HOPCOMS needs to expand its role and provide crop advisory services, inputs, and market intelligence to farmers. Though this objective did figure early in the history of HOPCOMS, it has got diluted over time. HOPCOMS procurement centres could be used as a platform to provide agricultural inputs and extension services by other agencies. Improvements in vertical linkages such as provision for credit, inputs, crop planning advisories, and inclusion of bottom-up approach in its operations combined with horizontal coordination would unleash a new potential for HOPCOMS to be the innovation it truly ought to be. For this, however, professional management with long term vision for the organization is required. HOPCOMS is run like an extension of any government department. It does not function as a dynamic change agent. If it continues at this rate, it could well be assigned into oblivion by the currently aggressive marketing practices of retailers. And the losers would be small farmers.

On the other hand, the Mother Dairy Fruits and Vegetables study provides interesting lessons on how farmers' links with an NGO could be the most important driver of inclusion of smallholder producers in modern supply chains. The case studies show that farmers' ability to form groups can be an important attraction for a company considering building direct links with them. This could significantly reduce the cost of linking them with dynamic markets and thus reduce the need for public funds. Also, strong farmers' organizations can take control of the supply chain, giving farmers a greater say in the functioning of the chain.

High prices offered by modern chains have had an important influence on the behaviour of traditional channel players like private commission agents and dealers from wholesale markets. Farmers' ability to respond to changing market demands has increased. For example, many farmers are diversifying into cultivating exotic and off-season (high value) vegetables, crops, and fruits. The supply chain can be replicated in other areas if large retailers are prepared to work with organized farmers and farmers are successful in forming efficient organizations. These organizations may require financial support from governments and donor agencies in their formative years but should aim at becoming self-sufficient through providing income generating services.

Rapid and continuous changes are taking place in the domestic and export procurement systems in Sri Lanka and impact of these changes is significant on small scale spice producers who are unable to stay on. However, the study of MA's Tropical Food Company in Sri Lanka shows that the company can successfully combine business performance with corporate social responsibility, thereby bringing sustainable benefits to the rural poor in Matale district. One key conclusion is the need for small scale producers to organize. Besides organizing and strengthening farmer organizations to enhance collective action, subsidizing transport and harvesting costs in some cases, and educating farmers about the importance of maintaining quality standards also can ensure greater inclusion in modern supply chains. At macro level, the government has to act as a facilitator by improving private sector participation in the agri-business sector through various incentives (tax holidays, export promotion, trade agreements, legislative governance, etc.).

China

China's food market has gone for fundamental restructuring. The downstream segment of the marketing chain has evolved dramatically in the past 20 years. China has moved from a country of wet markets and small shops to one in which supermarkets and restaurant sectors are growing faster than anywhere else in the world. Exports of horticultural commodities have shot up. It should be noted, however, the retail sector is very competitive.

The mid-stream (e.g. wholesale, processing and small traders) is also evolving in some fundamental ways. There is a phenomenal increase in the number of wholesale markets, processing firms, and special suppliers and their size is also increasing, especially of key players. In other words, there is evidence of consolidation and specialization and the emergence of markets that are focused on providing more high quality products. From a market that is made up of mostly small traders to one, the change is towards a set of more permanent small and moderate wholesalers. Some of the large wholesalers and processors have formal and informal ties with supermarket chains. However, even large wholesalers are relatively small and there are literally thousands of actors and markets are very competitive. On the buying side there has been much less change and most buying is still done directly from farmers by employees of the small trading firms and wholesalers, by their agents or from farmers who bring their commodities to the market.

While the downstream markets are shifting, the nature of markets has shielded farmers or upstream of the market chain from the shifts. Wholesalers, small traders, and procurement agents of processing firms and retailers purchase most of food products from farmers directly without contracts. The rapid restructuring of the downstream retail market and the midstream food processing industry has hardly penetrated into farm production and procurement. Overall, while there are some cases of farmers selling their products to modern retails, farmers have been isolated from rapid marketing chain changes in downstream.

The main drivers of this transformation are raising incomes, urbanization, domestic market liberalization, and international trade liberalization. Indeed, China's markets are being driven by rapidly rising demand in an unregulated environment that allows for easy entry at all levels of the marketing chain.

While China's food and agricultural products will continue to be produced by millions of small farmers, there are great challenges ahead. Although markets at all level are competitive and food is being provided to the cities in an efficient and inexpensive way, with about 240 million small farms with average farm size of only 0.5 hectares participating, there will be great challenges for Chinese farmers to be modernized, organized, and integrated into a dynamic and modern market system, and to meet the nation's increasing demand for food safety in the coming years.

While the overall picture presented above dominates China's current food system, there are some unique and successful stories of consolidation and integration of the food marketing chain. Gaining experiences and lessons from these special cases are important not only for enabling farmers to participate better in the modern market chain, but also for modernizing China's agriculture and ensuring better supply of safety foods. Four case studies highlight these issues and generate several important conclusions and policy implications.

First, farmers' cooperative may be one way of largely integrating millions of farmers, including some small farms and poor farmers, into the emerging market chains. The Watermelon Cooperative study shows that an effective farmers' cooperative can help farmers reduce marketing risks, enable farmers to benefit from market chain changes and market expansion, besides other benefits. However, it is interesting to note that not all farmers can participate in this kind of farmer cooperatives. In many cases, including the Watermelon Cooperative case, pre-conditions for membership may often exclude small farms and poor farmers. These poor farmers' marketing situations might be worse because of coexistence of farmers' cooperatives and small individual farms. How to help those who are excluded from farmers' cooperatives is an issue that needs further study.

Second, for a successful farm cooperative, human capital, technology, innovated management, and financial support are critical. Farmers' cooperatives are still new in China. In 2006, only about 5 per cent of farmers were members of different kinds of farmers' cooperatives and associations. Moreover, more than half of the cooperatives and associations are not functioning well. The Watermelon Cooperative study demonstrates that human capital, particular farmer's leaders, advanced technology, innovated management (e.g., brand development), financial support from local community and government are key to the success of a cooperative. With these pre-conditions, the cooperatives can modify industry structure, unify produce standards, improve product quality, and increase farmers' income. In this regard, government public services in terms of farmers' capacity building, training, technology extension, and fiscal and financial supports are essentials.

Third, while the food market is competitive and efficient, ensuring supply of safe food to consumers requires substantial efforts by both public and private sectors. With most of the transactions being characterized as pure spot market for most agricultural products, it is very difficult and costly to have traceability in the system. Farmers are not accountable once their products are passed on to traders in exchange for cash. There is also a great challenge in meeting the demand by consumers for food safety, provided that the competitive market is dominated by small traders. In this regard, China recently has initiated several policies to facilitate agricultural product safety. These include enacting and implementing the Agricultural Product Safety Law enacted in 2006, establishing agricultural product safety inspection and monitoring system under the Ministry of Agriculture, improving safety awareness of producers, and promoting national standard development. While these movements in the public sector are in the right direction, how they can be effectively implemented is an issue that needs further study. On the other hand, the study of Carrefour's Quality Lines in China provides interesting clues to how the private sector manages quality and safety issues in China. Supervision and management of the entire supply chain and brand development are key factors to ensure quality and safety of agri-food supply. Advanced crop planting and product processing technologies as well as better production and marketing infrastructure are pre-conditions to lower the supervision cost and increase the efficiency and competitiveness of the system. These pre-conditions imply that suppliers of Carrefour's quality line can only be large scale farm households. Small scale farm households are often excluded from the supply. In this regard, innovative farmer's cooperatives with inclusion of small farmers by policy interventions (tax concessions, credit, and financial support to those farmers' cooperatives that intend to include small farmers) might be a solution to include them in modern supply chains.

Fourth, because the modern marketing chain through innovative farmers' cooperatives (e.g., Watermelon Cooperative) and quality control measures (e.g., government inspection system and Carrefour's quality line) accounts for only a small share of the market and often excludes small farms, China may need to put more effort to improve current market intermediates that are small in size but very efficient in operation. These intermediates include a large number of local brokers, small wholesalers, processors, and special suppliers. The study of mushroom in China provides an interesting example of how special suppliers of mushrooms for modern retails developed and how they are able to include small farmers with very low transaction costs. In response to quality demand from modern retails and to improve its market competitiveness, marketing practices have gradually shifted from sourcing from wholesale markets to sourcing from dedicated agents. The most innovative and cost effective arrangement of this mushroom supply chain is that procurement is through local agents who live in villages where mushrooms are produced. Although there is no formal contract among special suppliers, agents, and farmers, the system seems to be adapting to the local situation well and quality demand can be met at lower cost than otherwise because quality grading is done at farm gate. More importantly, small farms are not excluded from mushroom production and modern marketing chain. However, while small farms are not excluded from either food market expansion or emerging modern markets and quality demand can be met in this mushroom market chain, there is no evidence of ensuing food safety. Policy makers may need to address the most critical aspects of small farms to provide not only quality food but more safe food. Enforcing a food track record system might be a solution.

Last but not least, while there is little penetration of supermarkets into farm production, there is emergence of supermarkets penetrating into Chinese countryside and improving consumer's environment. The study of Suguo Model examines supermarket penetration and impact from a completely different angle. This study argues that providing small farmers a better consumption environment for both consumer and capital goods is also crucial. The supermarket penetrated into the countryside and opened up opportunities for smallholders to consumer better, genuine, and safe food. The study also argues that vertical coordination or even vertical integration may not be an appropriate choice in the case of China, where land is equally distributed to every smallholder. This finding, indeed, is consistent with the results presented in the mushroom study. In the current production system, middlemen or SMEs can stimulate the production of smallholders, which is strongly evidenced in the studies of pickled vegetables and mushrooms study.

In sum, there is no one solution or model that can facilitate small farmer's inclusion in the new or emerging market system. Farmers' cooperatives may help many farmers to benefit from food market expansion and market chain changes. However, without policy intervention, small farms and poor farmers are often excluded from the benefits provided by farmer's cooperatives. An inclusive kind of farmer cooperation requires strong support from the government and private sector in terms of human capacity, innovative technology, and fiscal and financial support for all farmers, particularly for small farms and poor farmers. Ensuring safe food supply is a challenge. More efforts are needed in developing infrastructure and capacity to implement the current food safety laws. In this regard, the private sector can also play an important role by establishing their food brands. In the near future, moving to a complete vertical coordination or integration seems not possible for all or major food products and their markets. More efforts are required for improving current market intermediates that have been key in linking hundreds of millions of small farmers with national and international markets. Because they are so efficient, they will continue to play a major role in China's food market.

South-East Asia

The South-East Asian studies show the way to enable small scale producers take advantage of the opportunities in restructuring agri-food markets. One key conclusion is the need for small scale producers to organize. Farms in the region, like those in many developing countries in Asia and Africa, are small and fragmented. Supermarkets and fast-food outlets require volumes at right quality and timing. The four studies on best practices in the Philippines, Indonesia, and Thailand underscore the need to organize farmers into groups. This is further supported by the survey of 500 potato growers in Indonesia. Marketing supplying to supermarkets through farmer's groups created the highest value added and farmers received the highest portion of value added since the farmers performed post-harvest handling and sold graded potatoes. There are apparent advantages in organizing small farmers to meet market requirements but the timing or frequency of delivery on a consistent manner is a challenge for many small scale farmers. The Philippine case on vegetables adopts a cluster approach to address this. By following production protocols on schedules, volume, and variety of vegetables, farmers become reliable suppliers that meet buyers' requirements. In the case of Indonesia, the producer organization is not limited to sourcing mangoes from its own members but also from other non-member mango producers. This is also the case of Philippine organic rice and vegetables except that the buyer sources not only organic rice and vegetables from the main producer organization but also from other sources outside the producer organization.

There are clearly advantages in organizing small scale producers not only in meeting volume requirements owing to economies of scale in production but also in achieving economies of scale in marketing as well as in facilitating development assistance. However, many issues are faced by producer organizations which explain why many of them fail. This includes lack of capability in managing organizations, weak entrepreneurial skills, diverting produce of member farmers to other buyers in cases where the organization undertakes collective marketing, and issues that threaten the sustainability of the organization.

Another key conclusion is the role of a marketing intermediary or consolidator in linking small scale producers with modern markets. In the study of mango in Indonesia, a specialized wholesaler for supermarkets (Birmandiri) acts as the marketing intermediary. In the case of Philippines vegetables, this role is assumed by Normincorp which sells to different markets such as supermarkets, fast-food outlets and wholesalers. For Philippines organic rice, it is Upland Marketing Inc. that acts as the marketing consolidator for supermarkets. These marketing consolidators are knowledgeable about market requirements and are run by professionals who deal directly with market outlets. In addition, the study also shows that the presence of commission agents supports inclusion of small scale producers in modern markets. Marketing agents or intermediaries are important in helping small scale producers' link with modern markets.

Another key conclusion is the critical role of effective supply chain or marketing management. While this is mainly assumed by the marketing intermediary, this should be well understood or practiced by other actors in the chain that includes small scale producers. The Thailand case shows that small scale producers' penetration in modern markets requires understanding the requirements of various market segments or options. While marketing is not the main role of organic rice and vegetable farmers in the Philippines and the mango producers in Indonesia, communicating and understanding the importance of meeting market requirements in terms of quality, timing and variety is essential.

Finally, the key conclusion is the need to assist small scale producers in production and marketing. Meeting requirements of modern markets means improving quality of products, processes, and operations of small scale producers. To be able to compete and achieve sustainability in the long run, development assistance is necessary. All cases have stressed the role of some form of assistance not only from the government but also from non-government and private sectors. Linking small scale producers with high value markets entails development cost which can come from private and public sources.

Policy Implications

The following policy implications emerge:

Identify producer organizations that are currently supplying to modern markets or those that have the potential to succeed in this type of business. Linking to high value markets is not for everybody and requires development cost. Choosing the target group to be assisted is a critical step towards helping small scale producers. After identifying target organizations, an integrated package of assistance to these target producer organizations should be provided. This includes capacity building, access to credit, and technical assistance. Capacity building is required to improve skills in managing organizations, entrepreneurship, and in understanding the requirements of the market and how to meet them. Assistance given to these organizations should be evaluated and documented to understand key success factors for replicating and showcasing best practices.

Identify marketing intermediaries that have extensive linkages to small scale producers. A package of assistance linked to expansion or strengthening of linkages with small scale producers should be provided to these target intermediaries. This can include access to credit for suppliers and expansion, organizational development, and others. They can also be tapped including their buyers to train producer organizations in meeting market requirements. Programmes developed for marketing intermediaries that link small scale producers with high value markets should be assessed for possible replication.